Origins of Objectivity

Origins of Objectivity

TYLER BURGE

CLARENDON PRESS · OXFORD

OXFORD
UNIVERSITY PRESS

Great Clarendon Street, Oxford OX2 6DP

Oxford University Press is a department of the University of Oxford.
It furthers the University's objective of excellence in research, scholarship,
and education by publishing worldwide in

Oxford New York

Auckland Cape Town Dar es Salaam Hong Kong Karachi
Kuala Lumpur Madrid Melbourne Mexico City Nairobi
New Delhi Shanghai Taipei Toronto

With offices in

Argentina Austria Brazil Chile Czech Republic France Greece
Guatemala Hungary Italy Japan Poland Portugal Singapore
South Korea Switzerland Thailand Turkey Ukraine Vietnam

Oxford is a registered trade mark of Oxford University Press
in the UK and in certain other countries

Published in the United States
by Oxford University Press Inc., New York

British Library Cataloguing in Publication Data

Data available

Library of Congress Cataloging in Publication Data

Library of Congress Control Number 2009942576

Typeset by SPI Publisher Services, Pondicherry, India
Printed in Great Britain
on acid-free paper by Clays Ltd, St Ives plc

ISBN 978–0–19–958140–5 (Hbk.)
     978–0–19–958139–9 (Pbk.)

2

Dedicated with Love and Appreciation
to
DORLI

Contents

Preface   xi

PART I

1. Introduction   3

   Individual Representationalism   12
   A Different Standpoint   22

2. Terminology: What the Questions Mean   30

   Representation   30
   Representation-as and Representational Content   34
   Representation Failure and Representation As Of   42
   Objectivity   46
   Particulars, Attributes, Properties, Relations, Kinds   54
   Resources and Conditions   56
   Constitutive Conditions and Natures   57
   Summary   59

3. Anti-Individualism   61

   Anti-Individualism: What It Is   61
   General Grounds for Anti-Individualism   73
   Anti-Individualism Regarding Perception   82
   The Shape of Perceptual Psychology   87
   Perceptual Psychology Presupposes Anti-Individualism   98
   Perceptual Capacities Shared Across Species   101
   Individual Representationalism and Perceptual Psychology   103
   Perception and Concepts   104
   Anti-Individualism and Individual Representationalism   105

PART II

4. Individual Representationalism in the Twentieth Century's
   First Half   111
   Individual Representationalism in Psychology   112

viii *Contents*

Individual Representationalism in Mainstream Philosophy
    Before the Mid-Twentieth Century   115
Individual Representationalism in "Continental" Philosophy
    Before the Mid-Twentieth Century   129

5. Individual Representationalism after Mid-Century: Preliminaries   137

The Demise of Logical Positivism, Behaviorism, and Descriptivism   140
Descriptivism and the Causal Picture of Reference   143
Individual Representationalism and Anti-Individualism: Again   149

6. Neo-Kantian Individual Representationalism: Strawson and Evans   154

Kant   154
Strawson—Two Projects   156
Strawson on Kant   160
Strawson on Solipsism   162
Strawson on Feature Placing   163
Strawson on Particular-Identification in Thought   171
Strawson on Criteria for Representation   176
Postlude: Strawson on Criteria in Identificational Reference   180
Evans on Strawson   181
Evans on Constraints on Objective Reference in Perception   184
Evans on Demonstrative, Perceptual Thought   191
Evans on Conditions for Representing Kinds and Particular Objects   194
Evans on Spatial Representation in Thought   199
Neo-Kantian Individual Representationalism: Summary   208

7. Language Interpretation and Individual Representationalism:
    Quine and Davidson   211

Quine's Starting Point: The Argument from Default Neutrality   212
Interlude: Evans's Critique of Quine on Referential Indeterminacy   216
Communication and Evidence: Quine's Notion of the Empirical   223
Before Objective Reference: The Pre-Individuative Stage   227
Truth Conditions and Structure   230
The Pre-Individuative Stage: Proximal Stimulation
    and the Physical Environment   232
Divided Reference: The Supplemental Linguistic Apparatus   235
Quantification   238
Further Elements in Quine's Individuative Apparatus   250
The Basic Assumption   254
Identity and Resemblance   260
Davidson on Conditions for Objective Empirical Representation   264
Davidson's Two Arguments   267
Davidson on Belief   276

Language-Centered Individual Representationalism: Summary   281
A Retrospective on Individual Representationalism   283

PART III

8. Biological and Methodological Backgrounds   291

   Deflationary Conceptions of Representation; Biological
       Function and Representational Function   292
   Representational Function and Natural Norms   308
   The Lower Border of Perception: Sensory Information
       Registration and Perception   315
   Perception and the Environment: The 'Disjunction Problem'   319
   Primitive Agency   326
   Perceptual Psychology and the Distinction between
       Sensory Information Registration and Perception   342
       Convergence   347
       Lightness Constancy   351
       Planar Slant from Planar Surface Texture   355
       Depth from Convexity of Image Regions   359

9. Origins   367

   Perception as the Individual's   369
   Perception as Sensory   376
   Perception as Representation   379
   Perception as Objectification   396
   Perception as Objectification as Opposed to Perception
       as Extraction of Form   416
   Phylogenetic Distribution of Perceptual Systems   419
   Examples of the Sensory-Registration/Perception Distinction   421
   Perception, Representation, Propositional Knowledge   430

10. Origins of Some Representational Categories   437

   Perception and Body   437
       Body Representation as Originating in Perception   438
       Singular Applications in Perception of Bodies   450
       General Elements in Perception of Bodies: Conditions for
           Body Attribution   454
       Perception of Body and Attribution of Solidity
           and Generic Shape   465
   Perception and Origins of Mathematical Capacities   471
       Estimating Numerosity and Ratios of Aggregates   472
       Mathematical Tracking of Indexed Particulars   483
       The Two Mathematical Capacities   490
   Perception and Origins of Spatial Representation   492

Beaconing   498
Path Integration   499
Landmark Use   507
Map Use   509
Spatial Representation in Navigation by Jumping
    Spiders and Other Arthropods   514
Perception and Origins of Temporal Representation   518
Association, Computation, Representation   529

11. Glimpses Forward   532

The Epistemic Status of Constitutive Principles
    Governing Perception   532
The Upper Border of the Perceptual: Perception and
    Propositional Attitudes   537
Propositional Attitudes, Individual Representationalism, and
    Conceptualization of Perception   544
Origins, Levels, and Types of Objectivity   547

Bibliography   552
Author Index   583
Subject Index   591

Preface

My primary aim in this book is to understand and explain origins of representational aspects of mind, particularly in representation of the physical world. Under what conditions does accurate—objective—representation of the physical world begin? Since the inquiry centers on *what it is* to represent the physical world in this initial way, and since objective representation of the physical world is the most elementary type of representation, the aim is to understand the nature of representational mind at its lower border. A corollary of this primary aim is to explain the extreme primitiveness of conditions necessary and sufficient for this elementary type of representation—perception. A secondary aim is to show that nearly all prominent philosophical work on this topic over the previous century over-intellectualized these conditions. That is, philosophers claimed that meeting the conditions requires psychological capacities that are much more intellectual than the capacities in fact are.

In pursuing the primary aim, I show that perception differs from other sensory capacities. Using a conception of representation as a distinctive psychological phenomenon that is embedded in scientific use, I argue that non-perceptual sensory states are not instances of representation. Calling them 'subjective representation' is mistaken, or at best misleading. Perceptual representation that objectively represents the physical world is phylogenetically and developmentally the most primitive type of representation. I argue that human beings share representational mind, exercised in perception, with a breathtakingly wide range of animals. Representation of the physical world begins early in the phylogenetic elaboration of life.

In Part I, I explain the problem of understanding relevant conditions on objective representation of the physical world. In Part II, I sketch the breadth of the tendency in philosophy and the broader culture to over-intellectualize these conditions. I criticize, in some depth, prominent examples of the tendency.

In Part III, I develop conceptions of representation and perception. I explain that *representation* and *perception* are psychological "species" or kinds, isolated at least implicitly by science. They are to be distinguished from other sorts of functional information registration—and, in the case of perception, other sorts of functional *sensory* information registration. An example of non-perceptual, functional sensory information registration is the sensing of light and dark by molluscs. Another example is the visual-vestibular system in many animals that coordinates gravitational sensory information with movements of the head to accommodate vision. 'Representation' is often used, in science and philosophy, to apply to such systems. I argue, on scientific grounds, for a narrower application. The point is to show that representational mind is to be distinguished from other functional information systems. It constitutes a distinctive "species" or kind—a "cut" in nature. Perception is situated just above the lower border of that "cut". As noted, this border—which demarcates origins not only of perception, but also of representation and objectivity—begins at more primitive levels than philosophy has traditionally recognized. These are the origins of representational mind.

I have tried to make philosophical abstractions accessible to readers who are not, and are not bent on becoming, professional philosophers. The book has no glossary. But the index is constructed so that references to pages that contain basic explications of quasi-technical terms are italicized among entries for those terms.

Part II deals with recent history of philosophy. The last two chapters of Part II contain detailed criticisms of prominent philosophical views. But the rest of the book, even in its detail, should be accessible, with effort, to individuals with philosophical interests, regardless of their relation to professional philosophy. In Part III, I connect philosophical abstractions to some of the concrete richness of the animal world.

So the book is written on different levels. It is written for professional philosophers: I try to explain the deepest, most detailed understanding that I can. It is written also for others interested in an issue that should engage any reflective person—origins of representational mind—a capacity that eventually blooms into science and other high expressions of human culture.

The book is best understood, obviously, by reading all of it carefully. But different readers may be inclined to read different parts differently. Professional philosophers may find some of the initial explanations in Part I broadly familiar. They may be inclined to press on. Readers who are not concerned to work through philosophical views that I reject may be inclined to skip some of the detailed criticism in the latter chapters of Part II (Chapters 6 and 7). I do not recommend such inclinations. I simply predict them.

Whatever the reader's background and interests, however, I offer this counsel, firmly and insistently: *patience*. Patience is a primary virtue in philosophy. Genuine understanding is a rare and valuable commodity, not to be obtained on the cheap. One cannot reap philosophy's rewards breathlessly, or by looking for the intellectual equivalents of sound bites. Very large claims are at issue here, claims that bear on understanding some of the matters most important to being human. Understanding requires investing time, close reading, and reflection.

I have found repeatedly that professional philosophers, who think that they know something about the subject, mistake what is being claimed or what terms mean, often mistakenly assimilating a view to a familiar *ism*—when patient reflection on starting points (here, in Part I) would yield better understanding.

Similarly, readers who do not think of themselves as caring much about the variety of philosophical viewpoints may gain a deeper feel for their own inclinations and culture if they reflect (in Part II) on how and why so many philosophers over-intellectualized thought and perception about the physical world. Of course, the positive account, in Parts I and III, will be better understood by understanding positions that it opposes.

The account of perception in Part III, particularly Chapter 9, is the heart of the book. I draw not only on philosophy but on perceptual psychology (mainly vision science), physiological sensory psychology, developmental psychology, animal psychology, ethology, and zoology to provide an account of how human sense perception of the physical world is related to sensory capacities of many other organisms—from amoebae, paramecia, ticks, and molluscs, whose sensory capacities are non-perceptual, to spiders, bees, reptiles, fish, birds, and non-human mammals, some of whose sensory capacities are genuinely perceptual. I try to get at what is constitutive, or essential, to perception, and at how perception differs from other sensory capacities that enable organisms to obtain information from their environments and use this information to adapt to their niches. Understanding this difference is the key matter. I believe that it marks the beginning of objective representation of a mind-independent world. It also marks the beginning of *mind* as a representational capacity that forms a distinctive topic for psychology.[1]

Much current work on sensory systems focuses largely on brains. The excitement caused by pictures of brains, and the implications for financial support, have seduced many areas of psychology away from the behavioral, functional, and representational issues that form the natural framework even for neural studies. The monthly claims of insight into psychological phenomena—pain, perception, fear, love, attention, and so on—that center on the location of neural activity without any good sense of the psychological significance of the activity at that location will, I think, come to seem as shallow as they are. A better balance, even in popular culture, between the psychological and the neural will be established. The pendulum will right itself.

---

[1] Sensory states are not a topic *distinctive* of psychology. Such states are also studied in biology—for example, the biology of single-celled organisms. As I argue in Chapters 8 and 9, such states are not in themselves representational, in the sense of 'representational' that I shall develop. I shall argue that this sense corresponds to a significant kind, or "cut" in the world. The consciousness of *conscious* sensory states is potentially a distinctively psychological topic. I believe that the most primitive types of consciousness are, however, also not in themselves representational. So far, there is no science of consciousness—no psychology of consciousness. Maybe, one day this situation will change. There are promising signs here and there. By contrast, there is a large, relatively mature science of representational states—most impressively, perceptual states. It is an open question whether or not consciousness starts, phylogenetically, before perception does. I explain in Chapters 8 and 9 that perception's approximate phylogenetic beginnings are known. We know when perceptual *reference* begins. I think that no one knows, nearly so well, where consciousness begins—where, for example, phenomenally conscious pain begins, or where phenomenally conscious perceptual states begin. My primary focus in this book is on representational aspects of mind. These aspects are more ubiquitous aspects of mind than conscious aspects. I think that the depth of their philosophical importance is at least equal—indeed currently greater.

Almost all neural research of any broad interest must be guided by detailed ethological, functional, or representational theorizing. Perceptual psychology, the most impressive and highly developed part of psychology, is, I think, a model for psychological science. The real breakthroughs in understanding *mind* that are already implicit in psychology have not been widely recognized. I hope to contribute to this recognition.

I emphasize *mind* not because I think that minds float free of brains, or other aspects of physical reality. I think quite the contrary. I emphasize it because I think that explanations and descriptions in mentalistic or psychological terms provide deep, scientifically indispensable insight into the way things are.

The last eighty or ninety years have seen recurrent tendencies, in science, philosophy, and general intellectual culture, to be uneasy about, patronizing toward, or even hostile to, invoking mentalistic notions (psychological notions) in science. Behaviorists in psychology were so convinced that mentalistic notions are unsuited to science that they banned them altogether. Behaviorism collapsed because this ban issued in barren science. Only a few decades after this collapse, the enthusiasm for neural research, mentioned above, led many—both in science and in popular culture—to mix brain talk with psychological talk in confused ways, with the more-or-less explicit suggestion that the latter is second class and dispensable. Many philosophers—even some who take psychological explanations to have scientific value—maintain that psychological talk needs *philosophical* vindication, some philosophical explanation of its respectability. The vindication usually involves an attempted reduction to non-psychological terms—behavioral, functional, informational, or neural terms.

I explain in Chapter 8 why I believe that all such views are mistaken, indeed out of touch with science. Science itself—most impressively vision science, but more broadly perceptual psychology and developmental psychology—has vindicated psychological, mentalistic notions. The explanatory power of the sciences vindicates these notions' viability for scientific purposes. The emergence of mathematically and explanatorily rigorous explanations in perceptual psychology, and the use of results from perceptual psychology by sciences like animal psychology and developmental child psychology, place scepticism, hostility, patronization, and unease about the scientific value of psychological notions at odds with science itself. The basics of the relevant sciences are entrenched. Some are mature enterprises. Philosophical claims that there is an *antecedent* need to show psychological notions to be respectable are, I think, quixotic. There remain, of course, scientific and philosophical questions about relations between psychological explanations and other sorts of explanations. But philosophy is not needed to show that psychological notions are scientifically respectable. Science has already done that.

Although the book draws on various sciences, it is firmly a work in philosophy. The questions of the book concern conditions necessary or sufficient for empirical representation of physical reality. Certain versions of these questions are scientific ones. What species do it? At what stage in their development do individuals do it? How do the various perceptual systems work? What relations hold between perception and belief? In this book, the primary versions of the questions about conditions for empirical representation of physical reality are *constitutive questions*. A constitutive question concerns conditions on something's being what it is, in the most basic way. Something cannot fail to be what it is, in this way, and be that something. *Constitutive conditions* are necessary or sufficient conditions for something's being what it is in this basic way. To be constitutive, the conditions must be capable of grounding ideal explanations of something's *nature*, or basic way of being.

Science tends not to reflect much on *what representation or perception is*. It treats only cursorily, if at all, the *natures* of representation and perception. It tends to remark only "by the way" on what conditions have to be in place, in any possible situation (not just in actual fact), for something to count as representation or perception. Science is more interested in finding explanations of how and why things happen than in asking about natures. Occasionally, I criticize answers to constitutive questions by scientists. I do so by reference to scientific considerations. Often good scientific work can proceed without answering constitutive questions correctly. Still, obtaining clarity about key concepts, and delimiting boundaries of fundamental kinds indicated by such concepts, can strengthen and point scientific theory. It can help deepen understanding of frameworks within which scientific explanations operate.

In its attempt to answer constitutive questions, philosophy sometimes gets in the way, or stumbles. Philosophy certainly has no claim to infallibility. In many famous cases, answers to constitutive questions have been shown to be very wrong by developments in the sciences (both mathematical and empirical sciences). These events do not show philosophy to be useless. They show that its subject matter is hard. Often, in addition, philosophy is done poorly. When done well, philosophy has made some impressive contributions toward clarifying basic concepts and reflecting on basic kinds invoked in the sciences. Such contributions are less infrequent, and tend to be more fundamental, with new and maturing sciences. I believe that philosophy is well positioned to contribute to understanding constitutive matters in sciences that concern representation, perception, and the phylogenetic and developmental emergence of thought.

The main task of this book is to ask and answer constitutive questions about empirical, primarily perceptual, representation of physical reality. Chapters 8 and 9 offer answers to such questions. Many other, more specific constitutive questions figure in the book. For example, Chapter 10 deals with constitutive questions about conditions on having specific perceptual capacities—capacities to perceptually represent temporal or spatial relations, the capacity to perceive something as a body, and various proto-mathematical perceptual capacities. Earlier chapters (especially Chapters 4–7) criticize certain answers to constitutive questions.

Constitutive questions are sometimes assimilated, in popular thinking, to questions about the definitions of terms. Construing such questions in this way risks many misunderstandings. There are importantly different types of definition. Only very specific types of *scientific* definition have much chance of answering constitutive questions. Most types of definition have only a tenuous relation to such questions. Constitutive issues are certainly not merely linguistic issues over meaning or usage, though they have implications for best usage *for scientific or other descriptive/explanatory purposes*. Attempts to answer constitutive questions are attempts to understand the deepest, most necessary, facts about basic kinds, or "cuts" in the world, that can ground explanation. Insofar as these attempts involve questions about how to use terms or concepts, they are attempts to determine how best to think or speak *in the service of* obtaining a deep, descriptive, and explanatory hold on reality. I discuss the notions of constitutive question and nature, and issues of philosophical method, in greater depth in Chapters 1 and 3. Constitutive issues dominate the book.

This book springs, of course, from a particular historical context. I alluded to the spectacular maturation of perceptual psychology since the 1970s, and the ways other sciences have drawn on this science. Philosophy has undergone an important independent development, beginning slightly earlier. A major revolution in understanding reference began in the 1960s. The revolution began in philosophy of language. The gist of this beginning is that linguistic reference by way of various simple expressions—proper names, demonstratives, certain common nouns for natural kinds—depends much more on individuals' causal relations to the environment (sometimes mediated through a community of speakers) than on individuals' capacities to describe or know something about the referent. My work in the late 1970s and the 1980s served to extend this point beyond language to mind, from linguistic reference to the nature of psychological states, and from a few types of representational devices to a huge range.[2] The effect of this whole revolution on understanding language and mind was to show that not only reference but the natures of individuals' psychological states tend to depend more on relations to specific types of entity in the world than on an individual's knowledge, descriptive powers, or definitions. I explain these matters in Chapters 1 and 3. Most of the work in this tradition centers either on language or on relatively sophisticated psychological states—states that only human beings are likely to have.

I began publishing on perception in the mid-1980s. This work was not, at first, central to my contributions. Few others in the tradition just discussed reflected in any serious way on perception. In retrospect, this situation seems anomalous. Perception grounds most of the phenomena that were discussed in the effort to understand the causal underpinnings of reference. So the revolution in philosophy centered on the tail of the elephant rather than its trunk and head. An objective of this book is to correct this perspective on a huge, deep phenomenon. It is to show how both perceptual reference and the specific *ways* individuals perceive the

---

[2] I provide an overview of these issues in Chapter 3 and in the Introduction to my *Foundations of Mind: Philosophical Essays, Volume 2* (Oxford: Clarendon Press, 2007).

world (their perceptual groupings and categorizations) depend more on ways individuals are physically and functionally related to specific types of entities in the environment than on individuals' ability to describe or know something about what they perceive.

The failure to focus on perception in the revolution in understanding linguistic and psychological representation reflects a larger irony that governed thinking about empirical representation *throughout the twentieth century*. A persistent theme in the book is that philosophers repeatedly made claims about empirical representation without knowing much about perception—more particularly, without reflecting on scientific work on perception.

Until mid-century, perception was a central topic in philosophy, in fact at the center of the most prominent work. Ignorance during that period was more excusable because, although the basic approach of modern perceptual psychology had been established in the nineteenth century, scientific results were scattered and not associated with extensive mathematicization until after the mid-twentieth century. Even so, accepted philosophical wisdom about perception in the first half of the century now looks woefully out of touch, not only with common sense, but with what was scientifically available then. In the second half of the century, perception receded to a background issue for most of the most prominent philosophers. However, some of these philosophers made strong commitments about perception and empirical belief (usually in the service of discussing other topics more central to their work), without paying the slightest attention to the emerging science. Even now, when perception has re-emerged as an important topic in philosophy, quite a lot of philosophical work on the topic is insular and irrelevant because of lack of genuine understanding of relevant science. Not a few present-day philosophical claims are flatly incompatible with what is scientifically known. And many philosophers who write on perception make only cursory references to perceptual psychology—usually the first chapter of David Marr's *Vision*. Such references often show, almost immediately, no real understanding of the methods and results of the science.

Although scientific work can be conceptually confused, and although philosophical issues are often legitimately different from scientific issues, good philosophical work on topics where there is scientific knowledge must take the science into account. Philosophy has done considerably better in some areas—philosophy of language, philosophy of logic, and various other sub-areas of philosophy of science and mathematics. But very little work on perception has caught up with relevant science. I hope that this book will stimulate change.

Perception is not the only area in which philosophy has failed to use relevant science. Some recent discussions in the metaphysics of time, causation, the nature of physical bodies, and so on feed on intuitive puzzles and propose points of view that lack the slightest touch with what sciences say about these matters. If philosophy is not to slide toward irrelevance and become a puzzle-game-playing discipline, good mainly for teaching the young to think clearly, some central parts of philosophy must broaden their horizons. Of course, there are deeply committed, knowledgeable individuals in all areas of philosophy. And much of the difficulty is the sheer complexity of the world's knowledge base. Even so, philosophy is markedly better at connecting with knowledge bases in some areas than in others.

I believe that philosophy has a tradition and a set of methodological and conceptual tools that position it uniquely to make important contributions to understanding the world. I believe that these contributions can and should be appreciated by non-philosophers. My complaints are intended as motivation, not as one more piece of philosophy bashing. Philosophy's contributions can have intellectual depth equal to that of any other discipline. Many of its topics remain of broadest human concern. Where, constitutively, representational mind begins is such a topic.

My interest in this subject began in 1982 when I taught as a visitor in the Philosophy Department at MIT and took classes on vision in the Psychology Department from colleagues of the then recently deceased David Marr. I believe that I was the first to introduce discussion of Marr's work into philosophy, in the mid-1980s. I have remained interested in the psycho-physics of perceptual systems, eventually gaining a further window into the subject through my older son, Johannes Burge, who obtained a recent Ph.D. in vision science at Berkeley. I am grateful to him for many discussions of vision and touch. Since the ideas in this book developed over many years, I have incurred too many unremembered debts to hope to acknowledge even very many debts individually. I do appreciate the contributions of many interlocutors. During that visit to MIT, Jerry Fodor initiated me into the world of practicing psychologists; and I had several long discussions about psychology with Noam Chomsky. Later, I learned of the work of Randy Gallistel on representational capacities of animals. We were colleagues at UCLA for some years and continued to correspond after he left. Disagreements expressed in this book are vastly outweighed by ways in which I have learned from him. Kathleen Aikens wrote an article on sensory capacities and later gave me suggestions that, together, got me reading the large literature on sensory systems—initially articles in the vast (misleadingly titled) *Handbook for Physiological Psychology*. This reading expanded into a lifelong project. The richness of the animal world came to awe and amaze me. I owe a debt of gratitude to Susan Carey for vigorous discussions of developmental psychology, and for guidance through relevant literature. I am grateful to Christopher Peacocke for many discerning critical suggestions and for long-standing, if intermittent, dialog on some of the central topics of the book. I thank Ned Block for extensive philosophical stimulation, for valuable discussions of relevant science, for advice on both philosophical and diplomatic matters, and for steady friendship. I owe anonymous referees for several helpful criticisms and suggestions. Members of my seminar at UCLA in Spring 2008 provided a valuable forum for discussing parts of the typescript. Members of earlier seminars on perception at UCLA sharpened my thinking. I thank Peter Graham for saving me from a significant error in the 2008 seminar and for other useful remarks. I am indebted to Tony

Brueckner for a valuable comment on Strawson, to Alex Radalescu and Andrea Bianchi for separate ones on Evans, and to Ingrid Steinberg for a significant suggestion about presentation.

Earlier versions of parts of this work were presented over the last fifteen or so years in the following lecture series: the Hempel Lectures at Princeton University; the Seybert Lectures at the University of Pennsylvania; the Thalberg Lecture at the University Illinois, at Chicago; the Townsend Lectures at University of California, Berkeley; the Carus Lectures at the American Philosophical Association in San Francisco; the Kant Lectures at Stanford University; and a series of unnamed lectures at the University of Bologna. I have given swatches of the material in individual lectures or conferences at the following institutions: University of Alabama; University of Arizona; Arizona State University; Australian National University; University of British Columbia; Brown University; University of California, Irvine; University of California, Riverside; University of California, Los Angeles; University of California, Santa Barbara; Cornell University; Deutsche Konferenz für Philosophie, Berlin; Georgetown University; University of Göttingen; University of Kansas; University of Miami; University of Munich; New York University; Syracuse University; and University of Washington. I have benefited from discussion on these occasions. I want to acknowledge debts for especially valuable comments from Michael Bratman, Dagfinn Föllesdal, Krista Lawlor, Colin McGinn, and Gavin Lawrence.

An abstract of a paper that provides an overview of some main themes in the book is published: 'Abstract: "Perceptual Objectivity"', in G. Apel (ed.), *Kreativität XX Deutsche Kongress für Philosophie* (September 26–30, 2005) (Hamburg, Felix Meiner Verlag, 2006). Significant sections of the book are extracted and presented in two articles: 'Perceptual Objectivity', *The Philosophical Review* 118 (2009), 285–324, and 'Primitive Agency and Natural Norms', *Philosophy and Phenomenological Research* 74 (2009), 251–278.

I am especially indebted to my family—including my two sons, Daniel and Johannes—but centrally my wife, Dorli, for patience, love, and support. I am also grateful to my father, Dan Burge, now deceased, for his example of Aristotelian intellectual voracity in trying to assimilate, understand, and *feel appreciatively* some of the immense complexity and variety of our world.

PART I

The answer may be after all ... that general considerations fail or mislead, and that even the fondest of artists need ask no wider range than the logic of the particular case. The particular case, or in other words his relation to a given subject, once the relation is established, forms in itself a little world of exercise and agitation. Let him hold himself perhaps supremely fortunate if he can meet half the questions with which that air alone may swarm.

Henry James, Preface to *The Spoils of Poynton*

Wenn euer Lied das Schweigen bricht
Bin ich nicht ganz allein.

Schubert/Lappe, *Der Einsame*

1 *Introduction*

What does it take for an individual to represent the physical world objectively? More specifically, what are minimum constitutive conditions necessary for an individual to represent the physical environment in such a way as to attribute, sometimes accurately, specific physical attributes to physical particulars? What conditions must be met if an individual is to represent particulars in the physical environment as having such attributes as sizes, shapes, locations, distances, motions, colors, textures, and kinds like being a body? What psychological and environmental resources are necessary if such representation is to be possible?

In effect, these questions ask what it takes to represent a mind-independent world in a way that attributes some of the primary attributes that that world in fact has. They ask about minimum conditions for obtaining the simplest, most primitive form of objectivity.

Psychologically speaking, the most basic type of representation of the physical environment is *empirical* representation. I shall be primarily concerned with empirical representation.

'Empirical' has two related uses. One concerns the nature of warrant or justification for belief or decision. An *empirical warrant* is one whose warranting force depends partly on perceptual belief, perception, or other sensory states. The other use concerns the nature of representation. *Empirical representation* is a type of representational state, occurrence, or activity. From here on, I often shorten 'state, occurrence, or activity' to 'state'. An empirical representation either *is* a perception, or is a representational state that constitutively depends on perception for being the kind of representational state that it is, or is a representational state that constitutively depends on the exercise of other *sensory* capacities besides perception for being the kind of representational state that it is. Both uses of 'empirical' figure in the discussion. The second dominates.

An example of empirical representation that is itself perception is a perception of, and as of, a moving silver sphere.

An example of a representational state that depends on perception for being the kind of representational state that it is is a belief that *that* silver sphere is moving. I assume here that the belief depends for its representational nature on a perception as of some particular silver sphere and its movement. Depending for its representational nature on a perception might reside in the belief's taking over some aspect of its own way of presenting its subject matter (the sphere, the color, the movement) from the way the specific perception presents the same subject matter.

An example of a representational state that depends, for being the representational state it is, on exercise of non-perceptual sensory capacities is a belief <u>I am feeling a tickle</u> or <u>I am in pain</u>. I will later maintain that *in themselves* pains and tickles are not instances of perception, or any other sort of representation, as I use 'perception' and 'representation'. These beliefs are, however, products of sensory capacities. I assume that they are the beliefs that they are because of their relations to actual sensory feelings.

All three of these types of example are species of empirical representation.

Empirical representation, indeed perceptual representation, is psychologically and developmentally central to all representation. Representing specific aspects of the physical environment is surely psychologically impossible without it.

Some philosophers go further. They regard empirical representation as conceptually necessary for representation of all other things. I do not accept this view. I think that certain types of representation of mathematical, ethical, and psychological subject matters are conceptually and epistemically independent of empirical representation. But perception and empirical thought about the physical environment are certainly primary in three respects: developmentally, psychologically, and phylogenetically.

Empirical representation of the physical environment is thus a central instance of representation. Understanding such representation is a way of deepening understanding of all representation. Representation—intentionality—is, along with consciousness, the most striking feature of mind. So understanding empirical representation deepens understanding of mind.

Commonsensical and natural-scientific knowledge have their roots in empirical representation of the physical environment. So understanding such representation forms an essential background for understanding developmental and phylogenetic origins of knowledge. This point extends to the main norms closely associated with knowledge—truth and epistemic warrant. By understanding conditions on elementary sorts of representation of the physical environment, we deepen our understanding of these matters as well.

Elementary types of empirical representation of the physical environment constitute central instances of objectivity. Objectivity is a value for mental representation. How is this value realized? What is its place in the development of mind and of knowledge? Understanding minimal conditions on objective representation of the physical environment yields insight into the basis of many of the more sophisticated types of objectivity.

Representation, perception, objectivity, mind, veridicality, knowledge, warrant are closely interconnected. My primary focus will be representation, perception, and objectivity. It is well to remember, however, that reflection on minimal constitutive conditions on empirical representation of the physical environment affects a wider circle of ideas.

The questions with which I began have phylogenetic and developmental corollaries. We can ask what species attain objective representation. We can ask at what stage in their individual development do humans and other animals attain objective representation. These questions hinge on what sorts of psychological equipment an individual must have to engage in objective representation. They also hinge on what sorts of relations an individual must bear to the environment to effect such representation.

The original questions are about *constitutive conditions*. At a very rough approximation, these are "conceptual" questions. There is a conceptual dimension in the very understanding of the key *terms* of the questions. What, more precisely, do they mean? How are we to understand such terms as 'representation', 'perception', and 'objective'? I discuss the terms in more detail later. It should be clear, however, that, on big questions like these, there is room for misunderstanding. Smoke represents fire in a certain sense. That is not what I mean by 'represents' in my questions. What understanding of the term motivates interest in the questions and admits of interesting answers?

There is another "conceptual" dimension that bears on answers to the questions, even once an understanding of the terms of the questions is provisionally stable. Suppose that we substitute 'perceive' for 'represent' for the moment. Perception is a type of representation. We know that the number three cannot perceive a body. We know that a rock floating in another galaxy outside the light cone of the explosions of the World Trade Towers cannot perceive those explosions. We know these things without having to engage in special investigations. We know them by knowing something about conditions under which perception is possible—conditions under which perception can be what it is: *perception*.

By associating such knowledge with a "conceptual" dimension, I do not mean that the knowledge follows from the nature of the concepts alone. I did not merely consult and analyze my concepts of perception, numbers, moving bodies, rocks, light cones, and buildings to arrive at answers. That is why I have used the term 'conceptual' in scare quotes. Some of the relevant knowledge and understanding is empirically warranted, but very general and secure. Some of it is apriori, but not a matter of analysis of concepts. Little if any of it derives from analysis of concepts into component parts. In saying that our knowledge has a conceptual dimension, I mean merely that our background knowledge and our understanding of specific types of representation can yield insight into general conditions that bear on what makes objective representation possible.

A certain type of "conceptual" question is a constitutive question—a question about what are called *constitutive conditions*. I explain these notions in more detail in Chapters 2 and 11. The intuitive idea is that a constitutive question concerns conditions on something's being what it is. Constitutive conditions ground explanations of something's *nature*, the aspect of what it is that could not possibly be different if it is to be and remain what it is. Thus a simple constitutive condition on accurate perception of a particular of a certain kind is that it be caused by what it is a perception of. Part of the explanation of what it is to be an accurate perception of such an entity is that it be caused by what it is a perception of. Something could not be an accurate perception of a particular of a certain kind if it did not meet that condition.

The cases of the number and the rock were meant to suggest relatively trivial constitutive conditions on perception. They bring to mind that a perceiver must have certain psychological equipment that neither numbers nor rocks have. They bring to mind that even individuals with the right psychological equipment must be in the right causal relation with what they perceive in order to perceive it. Neither numbers nor that rock can be causally affected by the body or the explosion. We know these things through briefest reflection. The cases illustrate the kind of knowledge of constitutive conditions that I have in mind.

Sometimes knowledge of such conditions is less trivial. Relevant conditions can be matters of serious controversy. I think that sometimes even difficult issues can be settled in a knowledgeable way.

One task for philosophy is to deepen knowledge and understanding of constitutive conditions. Our questions concern what psychological abilities an individual must have and what relations to the environment an individual must enter into if objective empirical representation is to be possible—indeed, if it is to be what it is. The questions ask for explanations that enable us to understand constitutive conditions on the natures of perception, representation, and objectivity. Answering the evolutionary and developmental versions of our initial questions is largely a task for the empirical sciences. These sciences tend not to use such notions as objectivity at all. Their uses of notions like representation and perception may or may not coincide with uses that figure in the general questions that interest philosophers and that appeal to common-sense reflection. So there is a natural interplay between clarifying terms and reflecting on general conditions that are tasks for philosophy, on one hand, and empirical knowledge about organisms offered by sciences like psychology, ethology, and zoology, on the other.

I am interested in developmental and phylogenetic origins of objectivity. In fact, reflection on what is known empirically about these origins will help guide and clarify answers to the questions regarding minimal constitutive conditions on empirical objectivity that are my primary interest. These minimal constitutive conditions are *constitutive* origins of empirical objectivity. These origins are not in themselves temporal. They are the first grounds in the order of constitutive explanation.

Answers to questions about all three types of origins of empirical objectivity—developmental, phylogenetic, and constitutive—are closely interwoven. In a sense, answers to questions about constitutive origins are the most basic. One cannot fully and deeply understand empirical results about the temporal emergence of kinds of psychological state unless one understands the notions (about the kinds) that one uses in understanding those results. On the other hand, empirical work on the developmental or phylogenetic order in which kinds of psychological state emerge can affect understanding the kinds themselves, and the conditions that are constitutively necessary for the kinds to be what they are.

In the past century philosophy has had a lot to say in answer to the questions that I began with. In fact, answering these questions has been one of its main preoccupations.

Like mathematics, physics, biology, history, law, and other rich disciplines, philosophy is not subject to simple characterizations. It confronts a wide variety of problems. No one problem drives it. But a credible case can be made for holding that our initial questions regarding minimal conditions for objective empirical representation constitute a defining problem of twentieth-century theoretical (as distinct from practical) philosophy. By that I mean that most major twentieth-century theoretical philosophers place the problem near the center of their work, and that the problem brings together many of the primary concerns that are most characteristic of twentieth-century philosophizing.

In the twentieth century a definite bias marked nearly all philosophical answers to our questions. The main thrust of the answers was that, to represent aspects of the physical environment, an individual must have psychological resources that can represent *preconditions* under which such representation is possible. The individual was supposed at least to be *capable* of representing such conditions internally, thereby doing the objectifying him- or herself.

This required objectifying representation took one of two forms. Either the individual was required to have psychological resources that are explanatorily more primitive and from which objective representation of the physical environment could be constructed. Or the individual was required to embed representation of the environment in a broader array of supplementary representations that in effect specified some necessary preconditions for objectivity. Some resources to *explain* objective representation were required to be present among the individual's psychological resources. Unless the individual could, in some way, represent such conditions internally, attribution of basic properties, relations, and kinds of the physical environment was held to be impossible, even unintelligible.

This requirement was never stated at the level of generality that I just employed. But instances were repeatedly articulated. The requirement in one form or another was so widely agreed upon, and presented with such seeming authority, that it came to inform popular intellectual culture, even though it had implications that were surprising to common sense.

The requirement is very restrictive. Given relatively uncontroversial empirical assumptions, it implies that non-human animals cannot represent, through perception or perceptual belief for example, the physical environment as having specific macro-physical attributes. It implies that children must grow into any ability to represent the world.

It was commonly maintained that a fish, bird, ape, or human infant has visual stimulations, but that these cause either mere awareness of sensations or merely reflexive sensitivities that connect with the environment in ways that satisfy the individual's needs. Especially after mid-century, it was often held that unless language or some other relatively sophisticated conceptual structure is present, there is no sense to asking whether human children have states that are, in any literal way, accurate or inaccurate in representing physical reality.

The constraints were supposed to rest on "conceptual" grounds, in the broad sense discussed earlier. The conceptual grounds were understood to have a priority that would show any view that flouted the constraints to be naive or confused.

Claims of priority in philosophy are not always a bad thing. Sometimes a philosophical framework can guide a science, particularly in its early stages. Philosophy has repeatedly played a salutary role in the early development of sciences. Philosophy can make contributions that are neither simply generalizations of what sciences already tell us, nor guesses about what sciences will come to tell us.

When philosophy tries to lead, however, it must take care that its lead be good. Where its accounts are surprising to science and common sense, its arguments had better be strong. I believe that the arguments for answers given to our initial questions were not strong.

The scientific issues associated with our questions were *not* parts of mature sciences during much of the twentieth century. While the relevant psychological sciences were immature, the idea that philosophy could instruct science was not to be rejected out of hand.

Moreover, for much of the century, large movements in psychology seemed to reinforce philosophical viewpoints. This reinforcement was no accident. The beginnings of experimental psychology were just as influenced by traditional British empiricism as were the philosophers who dominated early responses to our questions. Thus Wundt and William James were just as steeped in empiricist conceptions of perception as Russell and Moore were. Further along in the century, Piaget's work in psychology was just as influenced by Kantian ideas as was the work of Strawson. Philosophical accounts of objectivity seemed to dovetail with psychological accounts.

Of course, a large movement in psychology ignored our questions altogether. Behaviorism rejected theoretical appeal to representation. When, however, Quine tried to combine behaviorism with some acknowledgment of the representational character of language, he appealed to generic constraints already prevalent in philosophy. Philosophy was not at odds with large parts of psychology through much of the century.

Late in the century, a divide did develop. A significant stream in psychology turned against this syndrome of views. This stream matured into serious, well-grounded science, particularly the science of visual psychology. Yet philosophy continued on its own path. By the last third of the century, restrictive accounts of minimal empirical objectivity were taken by many philosophers to have a force that made input from science unnecessary or irrelevant. Even now, it is common to regard objective representation of the physical world as the special achievement of human beings, once they have acquired enough conceptual sophistication or language.

At present, only a few philosophers have squarely opposed the syndrome of views that I shall criticize. Among those who oppose the syndrome, most are driven by reductionist projects that, I believe, lack independent plausibility or appeal. Some of these projects seem not so much to reject the earlier views as to change the subject by employing new notions of representation.

The reductionist projects do invoke a broad but recognizable use of the term 'representation'. Roughly, on this use, one set of phenomena represents another set if there is a systematic correlation between the sets. One can add that the representing set is the causal product of the represented set, or is reliably associated with the represented set. And one can go further, maintaining that the representing set functions to enable an individual to cope with the represented set.

These ways of using the term 'representation' occur in psychology as well as philosophy. They are so broad that they apply to the states of furnaces, plants, and bacteria. Moreover, the use is easily dispensable in favor of the terms in which I just explained the usage. Information, correlation, causation, function, and so on are not distinctively psychological terms. There is nothing in itself wrong with this use of the term 'representation'. But it is dispensable, redundant, and misleading. More importantly, the usage tends to obscure a more narrowly circumscribed kind that *is* distinctive to psychology.

I believe that there is a kind, *representation*, that is distinctively instantiated in perception, language, and thought. This kind is a fundamental and distinctive feature of mind. It lies at the origins of primitive forms of objectivity and of perspective or point of view. It is a kind distinctively associated with explanations in terms of states, occurrences, or symbols with *veridicality conditions*—conditions for being accurate, or for being true or false. It is a kind that involves attribution and reference to the world.

This kind, *representation*, has been obscured in philosophy and psychology. The kind has been seriously and systematically mischaracterized by the large current in philosophy that I alluded to—the current that required, as a condition on representation, that it be accompanied by a capacity to represent preconditions on representation. The kind is largely ignored in the more recent currents in psychology and philosophy that employ the term 'representation' in such a broad way that it has no distinctive psychological application. I believe that, without being fully aware of its own accomplishment, the science of perceptual psychology has discovered a kind, distinctive of psychology, that the term naturally applies to.

My objective in this book is to go some way toward answering the questions with which it opened. Answering the questions requires developing an understanding of representation as a distinctively psychological kind, associated with distinctive types of explanation in terms of states with veridicality or accuracy conditions.

The most primitive type of representation is perception. I take perception itself to be a distinctive kind, clearly distinguished from mere sensory registration or sensory discrimination. So I shall explicate the notion of perception so as to clarify this distinction. The account of perception will be closely associated with the science of perceptual psychology. Both kinds, *representation* and *perception*, are best understood through their constitutive association with a primitive sort of *objectivity*.

Three primary themes of the book are that objective representation is the basic sort of representation, that objectivity and representation begin in perception, and that perception is a very widespread and primitive capacity, present in numerous animals other than human beings.

After setting background in Part I of the book, I lay out and criticize, in Part II, the philosophical tradition sketched earlier—the tradition that mischaracterizes representation by claiming that it must be accompanied by representation of some preconditions for representation. In Part III, I isolate *representation* as a distinctive psychological kind—I think *the most important psychological kind*—from broader types of "representation". And I distinguish perception from non-representational types of sensory discrimination.

I show that the narrower conception of representation has a significant explanatory role in science and philosophy. I do so partly by developing a distinction between perception and sensory discrimination. This distinction hinges on a distinctive sort of objectification present in perception, an objectification that provides substance to the role of veridicality conditions—hence representational states—in explanation. I touch on some of what is known about the perceptual systems of various animals.

The beginnings of perception in the evolution of various animals are simultaneously the beginnings of a primitive sort of objectivity. Those beginnings are also beginnings of a primitive sort of mind. Representation, perception, and objectivity are where mind begins.

Much of the discussion—essentially all of Part II—is historical and critical. Let me comment on these two orientations.

The historical orientation is necessary to convey the breadth and depth of the syndrome of views that I will be discussing. The syndrome appears in philosophies of many types and orientations, and even in popular intellectual culture. I try to give some sense for the breadth and depth of the syndrome in Chapters 4–7.

Criticism of some of the views that I reject is no longer needed. The views that dominated the twentieth century's first half have long been widely, and rightly, rejected. I discuss them in a summary way in Chapter 4. It is illuminating, however, to see that the positions that replaced these older views carry much of the same baggage. The constraints that the newer views place on objective representation are hardly better grounded than those that they replaced. But the newer proposals, roughly from the middle of the century onward, cannot be rejected so summarily, since they retain many adherents. So I cannot discuss effectively very many of the latter-day proposals. I shall, however, criticize, in detail, some prominent representatives of these views in Chapters 6 and 7.

My perspective stems, of course, from a positive philosophical standpoint. The standpoint is an outgrowth of a thesis that I first argued for in 1979. This thesis is known as *anti-individualism*. Anti-individualism is the claim that many mental kinds constitutively depend on relations between individuals and a wider environment or subject matter. Being in specific mental states constitutively depends, not just on psychological capacities, but on relations to specific aspects of a broader environment. In the case of empirically based psychological states, the states are what they are partly by virtue of non-psychological, causal relations between individuals and a wider environment. I explain these matters further in Chapter 3. Here I sketch the position in broad strokes.

Crudely, the effect of the position on our questions is to render unnecessary many of the ways that individuals were thought to have to build up an internal representation that mirrors preconditions for objective representation. The individual's being embedded in an environment and bearing non-representational relations to it do much of the work that was supposed to be done by supplementary representational capacities under the individual's control.

This description oversimplifies enormously. Anti-individualism in its most general form is compatible with some forms of the view that I want to criticize. What lies behind my criticism is reflection on the specific nature of perception and on scientific work on perception. This reflection informs elaboration of anti-individualist principles regarding perception. Anti-individualism regarding perception is thus informed by reflection on empirical knowledge in perceptual psychology, physiological psychology, and ethology.

Elaborating perceptual anti-individualism and explaining how science is at odds with prominent philosophical approaches to explaining objective empirical representation constitute the beginning of a different philosophical understanding of empirical representation. The different approach takes objective empirical representation to be an evolutionarily primitive capacity, present in a wide variety of animals.

Objective empirical representation is not an achievement special to human kind. This capacity lies at the phylogenetic, developmental, and constitutive beginnings of representation. Veridical representation of the physical environment does not depend on a psychological development that breaks through subjective types of representation. Nor does it need supplementary representational capacities that represent other matters. It does not need language, generalization, or an appreciation of an appearance/reality distinction. Objective empirical representation is the starting point.

In fact, it constitutes three starting points. Perception, representation, and objectivity begin together. The point is constitutive as well as phylogenetic. Explaining this claim and making it plausible require elaborating all three notions, especially the first two. Perception is distinct from other sorts of sensory registration. A sensation/perception distinction is often alluded to in psychology, but rarely well explained. I hope to do better. A better conception of perception distinguishes perception not only from sensation but also from propositional thought.

I believe that such a conception of perception sharpens our conception of representation. I will explicate a distinctively psychological notion of representation.

The mistake about representation that marked most of twentieth-century philosophy was to require too much—a superstructure that represents preconditions for representation. A correlative mistake, now common in psychology, is to require too little. It is common to rest with a use of 'representation' that does not distinguish perception from sensation, or even from the sensitivity to stimulation involved in plants. I criticize resting with this use in Part III, especially Chapter 8.

These more specific notions of representation and perception are supported, not only by common sense, but by scientific practice. They are not sharply articulated in science. Articulating them is a task for philosophy. I hope to make clearer that representation and perception are significant psychological kinds that already ground scientific explanation. The kind *representation* is to be sharply distinguished from the kind *information registration* and from various other types of correlation. The kind *sensory-perceptual system* is to be sharply distinguished from the more generic kind *sensory system*.

The kind *representation* constitutively involves capacities to represent veridically, and to have accuracy or veridicality conditions with non-trivial explanatory potential. The kind *perception* constitutively involves capacities to represent objectively—to represent some of the basic mind-independent features of the environment veridically, as they are. Since representation of the mind-independent physical environment is phylogenetically primary, objectivity and representational mind begin together, in elementary perceptual capacities. My main interest, however, lies in the fact that objective perceptual representation is a beginning that delineates the lower border of representational mind. These phenomena provide a basis for understanding *what mind is*, in its most basic form.[1]

I sketch only a part of what is a very complex story—both historical and substantive. I hope that, nevertheless, something of interest will come through.

In the remainder of this chapter, I go over, in more detail, some of the same ground just traversed. I say more about the syndrome that dominated twentieth-century philosophizing regarding constitutive conditions for empirical representation of the physical environment. Then I say more about my standpoint. That standpoint is grounded in anti-individualism. This view provides a starting point for distinguishing representation from broader correlational phenomena, and perception from more generic sensory capacities.

INDIVIDUAL REPRESENTATIONALISM

A certain syndrome of answers to the questions that I have raised dominated thinking in the twentieth century. I call this syndrome *Compensatory Individual*

---

[1] This phenomenon is *representational* mind at its most primitive. The relation of this phenomenon to consciousness is complex and unobvious. The relation will come up now and again. As noted in the Preface, note 1, what conscious aspects of mind are at *their* most primitive is a subject for another day—perhaps era.

Representationalism—Individual Representationalism, for short. There are many positions within this syndrome. Most fall into one of two families. The two families are deeply opposed to one another on some matters. However, they share a general assumption about objective empirical representation. It is this assumption in all its forms that I reject.

The core assumption of the syndrome is that an individual cannot empirically and objectively represent an ordinary macro-physical subject matter unless the individual has resources that can represent some constitutive conditions for such representation. *Objective* representation of a macro-physical subject matter is attribution of some of the specific macro-features that the physical environment in fact has.

Thus, on this view, objective empirical representation of physical, environmental particulars cannot stand on its own, among an individual's representations. It must be derived from, supplemented by, or embedded in other sorts of representations available in the individual's psychology. These other sorts must represent some constitutive conditions for veridical representation of environmental particulars.

These modal claims ('cannot stand', 'must') are usually regarded as conceptual, in a fairly strong sense of 'conceptual'. They are often supposed to mark the very intelligibility of attributing representation of physical particulars as having specific physical properties.

To put the point in a way that suggests its motivations: Individuals qualify as engaging in objective empirical representation by having resources for explaining what they are doing. The individual's own representations incorporate within themselves conditions that can be used constitutively to *explain* objective representation of the environment.

All forms of the syndrome constitute hyper-intellectualization of constitutive requirements on perception, although some forms, especially continental forms, themselves inveigh against hyper-intellectualization.

The name that I have chosen for this syndrome of views, 'Compensatory Individual Representationalism', does not trip off the tongue. It is meant to provoke caution and reflection. Each of the three terms in the name indicates something important about the syndrome.

The syndrome maintains that there is an inherent insufficiency in empirical representation of ordinary particulars in the environment as having ordinary specific physical attributes. The insufficiency is *compensated for* by the individual's having *further* representational capacities that provide an explanatory basis for the idea that the individual can represent particulars in the environment objectively, more or less as they are. The further representational capacities make this capacity intelligible by representing constitutive explanatory preconditions.

The syndrome is counted a *representationalism* because it holds that some constitutive preconditions for objective representation of the physical environment must be mirrored *representationally*, or in capacities to represent those conditions.[2] It is a mark of the syndrome to hold that constitutive conditions must be internalized and representable.

The syndrome is counted Compensatory *Individual* Representationalism because the relevant representations are required to be available in principle to individuals' consciousness or use. The *individual* makes objectivity possible by being able to represent preconditions for it.

Contrary to the syndrome, I believe that objective empirical representation of the environment is possible even though *no* constitutive preconditions for such representation are representable in the individual's psychology. Empirical representation of physical particulars as having specific physical attributes is *representationally* sufficient in itself.

I mentioned two families of views included in Individual Representationalism. These families divide with respect to how the individual's own representations represent preconditions of objective representation. One family maintains that the individual builds representation of the physical environment from *more primitive* representational material, which represents elements, including *particulars*, that are preconditions for objective representation. The particulars are claimed to be subjective or proto-objective. They are not ordinary particulars in the physical environment. The other family maintains that the individual makes representation of the physical environment possible by employing supplementary representation of *general constitutive preconditions* or principles of objective representation. In either case, objective representation of the environment depends on the individual's having a representational capacity to meet fundamental conditions on objectivity *by representing them*.

The first family denies that objective representation of physical environmental particulars is constitutively *primitive*. Such representation is derived from more primitive representation of particulars. Usually the derivation amounts to a kind of definition or description that is supposed to constitute the representational content of ordinary representation of physical particulars. Sometimes the derivation is more analogical than logical or definitional. In all cases, representation of ordinary physical particulars is conceptually posterior to another sort of representation that is not in itself about the physical environment. The primitive representations of other particulars, together with more general representational capacities, are supposed to figure essentially in forming representations of ordinary physical particulars.

The more primitive *representata* (referents or indicants) were commonly said to be sensations, sense data, or appearances. Sense data and appearances were not always regarded as mental. In fact, they were more often regarded as non-mental,

---

[2] Compensatory Individual Representationalism is to be sharply distinguished from another view in philosophy called 'representationalism'. Representationalism holds that all "qualitative" mental states, like pain, are to be fully explained as representational states. I do not accept representationalism, but it plays almost no role in this book. The notion of representation that I develop will, however, recast the terms of debate over representationalism.

though mind-dependent.[3] Even where they were taken to be mind-independent and "objective", they were commonly taken to be apprehended in an infallible or authoritative way. The apprehension was modeled on introspection of phenomenal aspects of perceptual experience—on introspection of appearances or seemings. Apprehension of the purported relevant subject matter corresponds point by point with phenomenal aspects of sensory experience.

An example of a complex representation constructed from more primitive representation of particulars is a description like: the cause of these sense data or the constant law-determined element in this series of sensations. Representation of a physical subject matter is achieved when the individual can form such complex representations out of the simpler material. On such views, the capacity to represent causation, constancy, or law enables the individual to transcend representation of the primitive particulars, which are in effect only subjectively available. Proponents of these views maintain that unless such generic features of the world are represented, perception cannot represent physical particulars as having physical properties.

On some views, the representation need not represent law as such, as long as it represents law-determined patterns of sense data. The fact that the sense data are in a law-determined pattern grounds explanation of representation of physical reality. Sense data that fall in the pattern are still part of a precondition for objective representation. Thus again, representation of physical entities is supposed to be conceptually posterior to representation of other sorts of particulars that enter into preconditions of objective representation.

First-family views tended to take a first-person phenomenological perspective as the natural starting point for philosophy. They motivated their starting point, in awareness of sense data, by arguing from a conception of what is fundamental for consciousness or what is a basis for knowledge or certainty.

These lines of thought owed much to traditional British empiricism. Although not all first-family philosophers were empiricists—notably, Russell was not—

---

[3] Russell and others took different positions on this matter during their careers. Sense data were often counted "objective appearances". C. D. Broad, for example, whom I discuss in Chapter 4, maintained that there are non-physical, "neutral" objective appearances or *sensa* that perception represents. Some philosophers nowadays maintain that there are "objective appearances" that are relational properties but part of the physical optical world. They too are counted 'objective appearances'. They are, like Broad's sense data, explained as relational, phenomenologically accessible properties. I believe that perceptual representation of, and as of, ordinary bodies, events, and their properties is explanatorily and developmentally more basic than representation of any such objective appearances. I believe that postulating these appearances as the first objects of perception is a variant on the mistake of sensa-data theorists—confusing mode of representation with object of perception. Given appropriate conceptual abilities and given appropriate attention, we can perhaps attend to and take as objects such phenomena. But in primitive perception, such phenomena are not commonly primitive objects of perception. Moreover, inasmuch as such appearances are objective, psychology must explain veridical perception of them, how particular properties (size versus shape or color) are extracted in perception of them, under what conditions we have illusions of them, and so on. For more on this matter, see my 'Disjunctivism and Perceptual Psychology', *Philosophical Topics* 33 (2005), 1–78, especially 69 note 19.

most were. For some traditional empiricists, such as Hume or Berkeley, objective empirical representation is merely a complex concatenation or sequence of references to mental items. These items might be ideas, sensations, or sense data. For philosophers influenced by Russell, objective empirical representation is a logically complex description that connects objective matters to sense data. For early Carnap, influenced both by Russell and by Kant, objectivity lies in constant, individual-independent, law-like patterns extractable from the stream of sense data.

These forms of Individual Representationalism dominated philosophy in the first half of the twentieth century. Although this sketch is over-simple, I hope that it marks a recognizable trend. Representatives of the view are Russell, Moore, Broad, Price, Ayer, Schlick, early Carnap, Husserl, Merleau Ponty, William James, C. I. Lewis. I discuss this family of views in Chapter 4.

In mid-century, first-family views gave way to a second family of individual representationalist positions. Second-family views specifically criticized first-family views for taking the root of objective empirical representation to lie in types of apprehension modeled on introspection. The newer views avoided taking the phenomenality of experience as the starting point for accounts of objectivity, and for philosophical reflection generally. These views concentrated on use, function, and inferential connection. They tended to take the *basic, first* subject matter of empirical representation to be physical particulars and their attributes.

Second-family versions of Individual Representationalism do not maintain that prior representation of non-physical particulars is essential to forming representations of particulars in the physical environment. They maintain that representation of physical particulars must be backed by capacities to represent *general* conditions that are constitutively basic to objective representation of physical particulars. In this way, aspects of the nature or structure of objectivity are represented within the subject's own perspective. Whereas first-family views deny that empirical representation of physical particulars is representationally *primitive*, second-family views merely deny that such representation is *autonomous*.

In effect, the second family requires individuals' representations to contain *general* materials to *make sense* of objective representation. Again, ostensibly simple, direct empirical representation of the physical environment is held to be impossible without help from further representational resources of the individual. The individual must have the representational resources to make empirical representation objective—in effect to do the objectifying himself. The further representational resources are general.

For example, perception or perceptual belief about bodies as having shapes and locations might be held to be impossible unless it is supplemented by higher-level cognitive capacities. Examples of supplementary capacities are a capacity to represent a distinction between appearance and reality, or a capacity to represent laws or causal generalizations, or a capacity to represent criteria for identity or individuation. The distinction between appearance and reality, the existence of laws or law-like patterns, and conditions for identification and individuation are constitutive conditions on objectivity. Second-family views maintained that individuals must represent such conditions—have conceptual-izations for them—in order to represent the physical environment empirically.[4]

In rejecting the phenomenological starting point for philosophy, second-family views took a more third-person perspective on empirical representation. They tended to motivate their views by asking what differentiates objective repre-sentation from mere sensation or mere response to stimulation. They asked, what in the individual's psychology certifies that representation is to a reality beyond sensations and proximal stimulations? They maintained that, if their requirements were not met, nothing in the individual could differentiate objective representation from a stimulus response mechanism, or a thermometer. Thus an important motiva-tion lay in safeguarding attribution of empirical representation to individuals from the threat of replacing representation with something altogether different. Objectiv-ity of perceptual representation was supposed to depend on internal validation of objectivity through the individual's own collateral representational resources.

Whereas first-family Individual Representationalism, at least in mainstream philosophy, has its roots in British empiricism, the historical antecedents of second-family Individual Representationalism lie primarily in rationalist ideas.

Recall that Plato's cave metaphor indicates that, unless an individual masters general principles or has insight into essences, he or she will be looking at shadows that are misleading distortions of reality. Such an individual would be trapped in a provincial cave. Descartes holds a similar view. He maintains that one will be confined to a representation of misleadingly shallow, not-fully-objective aspects of the world unless one grasps fundamental mathematical and physical ideas or principles. Kant is perhaps the most significant historical inspiration for the tradition.

I do not claim that the rationalist antecedents are individual representational-ist. Some are, but not all are. The rationalist antecedents are usually embedded in theories of *knowledge*—in fact, often theories of *scientific knowledge*—not theories of elementary forms of representation.

Individual Representationalism radicalizes this rationalist tradition in a certain respect. The claim is that, not just to know, but to *represent*, physical entities, one must supplement perception and perceptual belief with cognitive capacities that apply to general *conditions* for objectivity. Often it was required that such conditions be not only representable, but *known*.

---

[4] Sometimes I write of an individual representationalist requirement of *representing a principle*. Unless the context shows otherwise, I will mean by this phrase 'representing the conditions that the principle describes and explains'. The idea is not that Individual Representationalism requires that a principle be *referred to*. Rather, it requires that some state or capacity of the individual have the representational content of a principle that describes and explains constitutive conditions. *Principles* are explanatory propositions consisting of representational content. So the idea is that a relevant principle must be the representational content of a perception, thought, or capacity, within the individual's psychological repertoire. I usually write around the shorthand 'representing a principle', but sometimes I allow convenience to trump explicitness.

Second-family Individual Representationalists were mostly *not* rationalists. Most did not believe in non-trivial apriori knowledge.[5] Empiricism dominated mainstream philosophy after Frege and Russell. Second-family Individual Representationalism had a further source of inspiration, independent of rationalism: reflection on language. Many proponents of the position viewed perceptual belief through the lens of requirements on linguistic use or communication. Still, second-family versions of Individual Representationalism are inspired by intellectualist emphases in traditional rationalism.

Representatives of second-family Individual Representationalism are Frege, Cassirer, Kripke's Wittgenstein, Sellars and Sellarsians, Dummett, Strawson, Evans, other Strawsonians, Quine and Quineans, and Davidson.

To recapitulate, the most important difference between the two families concerns whether empirical representation of the physical environment is derivative or primitive. Representatives of the first family maintained that perception and perceptual belief about physical particulars are to be defined, constructed, or otherwise accounted for, in terms of representations of other particulars. Members of the second family held that empirical representations of ordinary macrophysical entities are primitive, not derivative. Proponents of second-family views maintained a type of *holism*—that representation of ordinary physical particulars must be embedded in a supplementary network of representation of general conditions on objectivity.

The mid-century shift from first- to second-family views constituted a major turn in philosophy. The turn was toward understanding representation as being more fundamentally objective from the start. The move highlighted the role of patterns of activity and interconnections among psychological states in making representation possible. Focus on such patterns, rooted in Kant and Frege, was much more fruitful in leading to richer understanding of mature representation than was focus on phenomenological appearances.

From the point of view of our project, however, this shift was not fundamental. The second family is more similar to the first than its members realized. Like first-family philosophers, they required an internal mirroring of conditions of objective representation as a condition on such representation. Both families maintain that empirical representation of physical particulars is in itself representationally deficient. Both require that the deficiency be compensated for by the individual's representation of preconditions of objective representation.

First-family views take this compensation to lie in representation of particulars that are representationally more basic than ordinary physical particulars. The more basic particulars are then connected to elements in the physical environment by descriptions of the relation between the basic particulars and the

---

[5] *Apriori knowledge* is knowledge that is warranted, but not warranted through sensory material or perception. Apriori knowledge is typically warranted purely through understanding or reason. It is important *not* to assimilate apriority to certainty, unrevisability, or dogmatism. It is a status that concerns purely the nature of epistemic support.

elements in the environment, or through falling into patterns that signified or constituted patterns in the physical environment. First-family views might require any of the following capacities to connect the allegedly more basic particulars with entities in the physical environment:

(*a*) a capacity to use a descriptive or quantificational apparatus that describes a relation between sense data and an environmental cause of the sense data;

(*b*) a capacity to use counterfactual concepts or principles that define bodies as would-be possibilities of patterns of sense data;

(*c*) a capacity to represent, or at least be sensitive to, invariant patterns or laws in representation of sense data or phenomenal entities;

(*d*) a capacity for phenomenological recognition of mental acts or events that bestow objective meaning on otherwise neutral phenomenological material.

Second-family views also take perceptual representation of the physical environment to be deficient unless it is compensated for by the individual's objectifying representation. They do not postulate non-physical particulars as initial *representata*. They take the needed compensation to reside in representation of general conditions on the representation of physical particulars. Second-family positions might require any of the following:

(*e*) a capacity to use the notion of objectivity itself;

(*f*) a capacity to represent a seems/is or an appearance/reality distinction;

(*g*) a capacity to use concepts of truth or falsity, as applied to beliefs or sentences;

(*h*) a capacity to track, in one's beliefs, bodies, including one's own, through a comprehensive spatial order;

(*i*) a capacity to represent general constitutive conditions of individuation or reidentification;

(*j*) a capacity to represent causal relations or causal laws;

(*k*) a capacity to be conscious of oneself as a representing being;

(*l*) a capacity to unify representations into a coherent theory, represented as one's own;

(*m*) a capacity to use such linguistic devices as quantification, identity, sortal predicates;

(*n*) a capacity to represent linguistic standards that make public discourse possible.

Both first- and second-family views hold that objectivity is possible only through the individual's capacity to produce objectivity internally—by representing some of its conditions. The simplest-seeming empirical representation depends on *the individual's* capacity to represent *further* matters.

A picturesque and common version of Individual Representationalism, in both philosophy and psychology, takes *developmental* form. The idea is that individuals begin by being able to represent only subjectively, or in a parochial way. A child or animal is taken to begin in a pre-individuative, subjectively limited, or even solipsistic stage. Perhaps the individual begins with a capacity only to represent its own sensations, or appearances. Or the individual represents an unarticulated physical smear. Or the individual is stuck with chaos or simple stimulus-response mechanisms. Then the individual is passed through stages that lead to mature representation of the physical world.

Maturation was supposed to depend on acquiring further capacities that either build objective representations out of subjective ones, or enable the individual to represent *general* constitutive conditions determining objectivity. For example, maturation might involve grasping a principle for determining when entities are the same or different, or having a conception of the difference between true and false belief, or having a notion of mind-independent existence. These further representations enable the individual to transcend an initial subjectivity or parochialness, and to represent the objective physical world.

Members of the second family sometimes took up a halfway house. They maintained against the first family that the initial representations are of physical subject matters. Yet they claimed that the subject matters are very different from what mature human beings represent. For example, the subject matters might be undifferentiated masses, or features unconnected to stable physical bodies.[6] Such representation was treated as inchoate with respect to macro-attributes in the physical environment.

Some philosophers denied that there is an empirical or conceptual stage prior to objective representation of physical bodies.[7] These philosophers invoked holism about representation. According to such a holism, objective light 'dawns only over the whole representational system',[8] and is in no way built up or analyzable piecemeal from subjective stages or components. On such views, genuine objective representation is not preceded by a prior stage (developmental or conceptual) that could ever stand alone. Such views were *still* commonly forms of Individual Representationalism.

Although developmental pictures figured in individual representationalist views, the main philosophical issue does not concern development. Whether there is a *stage* of representation that precedes representation of physical particulars is not the primary issue. The initial stage may be the final stage. The key issues are constitutive, not developmental.

In barest summary, Individual Representationalism is marked by a negative view and a positive view about objective representation of ordinary macrophysical entities. The negative view is that ostensibly ordinary perception and perceptual belief regarding such entities is in itself constitutively deficient. It needs further *representational* help to be what it is. The positive view is that the representational help must be the individual's capacity to represent some preconditions for the relevant representation. The individual must validate

[6] Strawson postulates a primitive representation of features. Quine postulates a primitive representation of masses. See Chapters 6–7.
[7] Davidson, for example, avoids postulating a proto-objective stage, both developmentally and conceptually.
[8] The dawning metaphor comes, I think, from Ludwig Wittgenstein, *On Certainty* (London: Blackwell, 1969).

objectivity by being the source of objectification through resources for further types of representation, which provide resources for explaining or making intelligible the individual's representation of physical reality.

I want to note some variants of these core ideas that still come within our purview. Some philosophers asserted that the very notion of thinking of specific entities, or representing something in a certain way, is deficient. Behaviorists rejected mentalistic and semantical concepts altogether. On some interpretations, Wittgenstein holds that there is no fact of the matter regarding what rule an individual follows. Quine holds that there is a fundamental indeterminacy in attributions of representation.

Some qualification is needed if one is to take such views to be versions of Individual Representationalism. I think the qualifications less significant than the association. Quine's view and the views attributed to Wittgenstein are motivated by the core negative idea of Individual Representationalism. Although they take talk of representation to be misleading or second class, they propose compensatory supplements that parallel the proposals of Individual Representationalists who are less sceptical or more realist about representational states.

A striking feature of the history of this issue is that most Individual Representationalists, at each stage, accused their predecessors of being overly subjectivistic in their explanations. The initial sense data theorists—Russell, Moore, Broad, and others—took themselves to be freeing philosophy from the vagaries of idealism. Second-family individual representationalists—Sellars, Strawson, Quine, Davidson, and others—took themselves to be freeing philosophy from the subjectivistic methods of the sense-data theorists.

First-family members tried to resist this charge. Several insisted that apprehending appearances is an objective matter and that appearances are themselves objective, not mental.

I believe that first-family Individual Representationalists did model their accounts of objective representation too much on subjective forms of apprehension. If appearances are objective, one needs to ask what perspective one has on them, how one comes to represent them, how one makes mistakes about them. Such questions were not pursued. First-family members took up a first-person point of view on appearances.

Even second-family Individual Representationalism can be counted subjectivist in an extended sense. In requiring objectivity to involve individuals' representing its preconditions, the approach gives *perspectives* too large a role in explaining objectivity.[9]

---

[9] It would be misleading, however, to call second-family versions of Individual Representationalism subjectivistic, except in the extended sense just indicated. It would be a more serious mistake to think of either family as essentially *idealist*—as holding that all reality, including the physical environment itself, is to be explained in mentalistic terms. Some first-family individual representationalists were idealists. But the position does not entail idealism.

It is hard to identify a single underlying mistake that leads to Individual Representationalism. As we shall see, certain philosophical ideologies abetted different versions of the view—verificationism, vestiges of idealism, descriptivism, the quest for epistemic certainty. I conjecture that a tendency to overrate the role of individuals in determining the nature of their representational powers might be close to the common root. I leave this question open.

The Individual Representationalist standpoint dominated serious philosophical reflection about empirical objectivity throughout the twentieth century. The standpoint's claims, especially second-family claims, seemed to many to be a paradigm of philosophy. They seemed to provide a framework for understanding common sense and science. The claims had an air of excitement and depth. I think that all of them are mistaken.

Usually Individual Representationalism is supposed to be supported by general reasons that do not rely on any *specialized* empirical knowledge. Not one of the claims of Individual Representationalism is supported by argument, or other considerations, with any real force. All lean on a *Zeitgeist* that bred confidence that the core idea of the syndrome is sound.

The claims of individual representationalists are not self-evident. They run against common sense. They are incompatible with a sound philosophical understanding of empirical representation, and with empirical work in developmental, perceptual, and animal psychology.

I shall discuss and criticize a wide range of individual representationalist claims. I will try to expose their lack of cognitive substance. First-family views that held that there is a more primitive representation of particulars were driven by philosophical commitments that turned out to be dead ends. There is wide agreement on this point in philosophy today. I will not criticize first-family views, except cursorily. My task is to bring out the Individual Representationalism common to such views, and to connect this common feature to second-family views.

Second-family views contain, I think, more insight. They nonetheless rest on misdirected dogma about what is necessary to make objective representation possible or intelligible. They rest on mistaken theories of perception. I believe that both philosophical and empirical considerations undermine all forms of these views.[10]

A DIFFERENT STANDPOINT

Individual Representationalism has things backwards. Objective representation in perception is more basic than both representation of appearances and general representations of conditions on objective representation.

---

[10] A condensed overview that overlaps key passages in Chapters 1, 3, 6, and 7 is my article 'Perceptual Objectivity', *The Philosophical Review* 118 (2009), 285–324.

Contrary to first-family views, representation of ordinary macro-physical particulars in the physical environment precedes and does not depend on individuals' being able to represent other subject matters. Representation of elements of the physical environment, including bodies, precedes, both constitutively and developmentally, representation of sense data, appearances, or phenomenological features, even ones that are counted objective or non-mental. Perception and perceptual belief take as their first *representata* the physical particulars and properties that make up the physical environment.

Contrary to first-family views, objective empirical representation of the physical environment is *primitive* in that no other empirical representation is more basic—either developmentally or in the order of constitutive explanation or intelligibility. Objective perceptual representation of ordinary environmental particulars and their attributes is not constructed from perceptual representation of anything else. Such representation operates under principles that mark it as perceptual, and meets conditions of objectivity. It is fallible and does not rest on some more authoritative form of representation.

Contrary to second-family views, objective empirical representation of the physical environment is not contingent on any capacity to represent general preconditions on objectivity. Objective perceptual representation of the physical environment precedes and does not depend on an individual's ability to represent such general conditions. It precedes and does not depend on having thought, let alone language.

Both forms of Individual Representationalism rule out perceptual representation of physical particulars by animals and very young children. These rulings cannot be sustained apriori. In fact, they are empirically refuted. In many animals, objective perceptual representation occurs without the presence of higher cognitive abilities. Even in humans and apes, perception does not depend for its objectivity on relations to such higher abilities. In fact, many of those higher abilities—perceptual belief, for example—obtain their objectivity from perceptual capacities that operate under principles governing objectification.

An account of *objectification* in perceptual systems will be central in Chapter 9. The rough idea is that certain processes in perceptual systems systematically distinguish effects of stimulation that are special to the individual and the context from perspective-independent attributes of the wider environment. Explanation of the formation of perception keys on processes in perceptual systems that make this distinction. Such processes constitute the ground of perception, representation, and objectivity. They are unconscious. They are not imputable to the individual perceiver. They occur within perceptual systems. The principles governing processes in which idiosyncratic individual states are distinguished from effects (perceptions) of objective environment conditions are not themselves represented within the system. The system simply operates according to law-like patterns described and explained by scientific principles. This minimal objectivity in an individual's perception and perceptual belief is completely independent of abilities of the individual to represent the sorts of general conditions on objectivity required by second-family Individual Representationalists.

Objective representation need not be derived, rationalized, validated by the individual. The most elementary forms of empirical objectivity are the products of conditions that the individual has no perspective on. They are the products of *subindividual* conditions and *environmental* conditions. Subindividual conditions are unconscious, automatic, relatively modular aspects of perceptual systems and belief forming systems. Environmental conditions are twofold. They are the actual properties and relations in the environment that the individual interacts with and discriminates. And they are patterns of causal relations between the environment and the individual's perceptual and cognitive capacities, relations that ground individuals' sensory discriminations (including pre-perceptual discriminations) and that fulfill individuals' biological and practical functions.

The elementary forms of empirical objectivity are not products of the individual's doing any objectifying, or the individual's representing preconditions of objectivity. Objective empirical representation must conform to conditions of objectivity, including both environmental and psychological conditions. It does not depend on any of these conditions' being *represented* by or within individuals.

Philosophy can make objective representation intelligible without requiring that it be built from some more primitive form of representation, or embedded in a set of supplementary, higher-level representational abilities. The most elementary type of objective representation is fully present in perception, unaided by any higher cognitive capacities. Perception makes reference to particulars in the physical environment. Perception attributes physical properties, kinds, and relations to those particulars—categorizes or groups them. It is from a perspective. But it does not represent appearances or perspectives. It does not represent generalizations of any kind.[11]

Perception and perceptual grouping of entities in the physical environment is a primitive, autonomous capacity. A wide range of animals have objective representation through perception. Probably all mammals, perhaps all birds, many fish and reptiles, and some insects perceive physical particulars in the environment as having specific physical attributes. Their perceptions attribute spatial position and spatial relations, shape, motion, texture, color. These animals represent objectively in the sense that they represent mind-independent or constitutively non-perspectival physical particulars as having ordinary physical attributes that these particulars in fact instantiate. The perceptual states of these animals can be veridical or non-veridical about such a subject matter. Such capacities in perception do not depend on supplementation by other representational capacities.

---

[11] Of course, the attributions attribute kinds, properties, and relations that can be instantiated by various particulars. Attribution is general in this sense. But, at least in primitive occurrences, attributions always modify and guide representations of particulars. They do not constitute generalizations. General principles are not among the representational contents of any perceptual system, although perceptual systems operate under and are explained by general principles.

The simpler forms of perceptual belief inherit the objectivity of perception. Perceptual *belief* no more depends on the individual's capacity to produce objectification than perception does. Like perception, perceptual belief that attributes specific physical properties to bodies (as such) does not depend on the individual's being able to represent general conditions of objectivity. Perceptual belief conceptualizes attributions of perception and embeds its own attributions in capacities for propositional inference. Propositional inference does not require representation of principles of propositional inference. The objectivity of perceptual beliefs regarding the physical environment is not any more correctly explained by Individual Representationalism than is perception.

My view has three main sources.

The first is philosophical. An old view in philosophy that I have developed and provided with grounding is *anti-individualism*. I explain this view in Chapter 3. The key idea is that the natures of many mental states, including perceptual states, depend constitutively on relations to specific aspects of the physical environment. Some of these relations are non-representational. For empirical representation, the key non-representational relation is causation. Relevant relations need not be describable in the individual's psychology. The individual need not be able to produce supplementary descriptions of what he or she represents. For example, the individual need not have correct individuating descriptions of bodies to perceive or think of them as bodies.

Although anti-individualism, especially anti-individualism regarding perception, figures in my rejection of Individual Representationalism, the relations between the doctrines are complex. I want to stress very emphatically that *Individual Representationalism is not to be identified with individualism*—the contrary of anti-individualism. Individualism maintains that all or most genuine mental states do not depend for being the states that they are on any relations to entities beyond the body of the individual. Individualism says nothing about an individual's having to represent preconditions for empirical representation of the physical environment. Many individual representationalists, especially second-family ones, are not individualists at all. Many are anti-individualists. Reflection on anti-individualism about *perception* helps undermine Individual Representationalism. But even anti-individualism about perception is not logically incompatible with Individual Representationalism.

Anti-individualism, *properly elaborated*, provides a foil for Individual Representationalism. It elicits oversights that underlie claims of the syndrome. It indicates sources of individuation for representational states overlooked by Individual Representationalism. The dialectical effect of elaborating anti-individualism is to show that there are other resources for explaining constitutive conditions on objective empirical representation—besides those insisted upon by Individual Representationalism. Anti-individualism indicates ways in which perception and perceptual belief represent the environment—without requiring that the individual be capable of representing conditions for objective representation.

These issues are delicate. In Chapter 3, I explain in more detail why generalized anti-individualism is not incompatible with Individual Representationalism. By reflecting on the specific nature of perception and perceptual belief, however, anti-individualism can be elaborated so as to undermine Individual Representationalism's claims to plausibility. It provides a context in which the failure of Individual Representationalism seems natural.

Anti-individualism also provides a framework for understanding the empirical psychology of perception. It gives philosophical point to the empirical science.

A second source of my positive view is empirical science, primarily perceptual psychology. Ethology, physiological psychology, and developmental psychology are also relevant. Results in perceptual psychology, particularly the psychology of vision, since the 1970s undermine Individual Representationalism. They indicate that perception of physical particulars in the environment, and perceptual grouping of them as instances of specific physical attributes, do not depend on resources that Individual Representationalism requires.

Perceptual psychology is a large subject. I convey some sense for how science supports my positive view in Chapters 3, 8–10.

I believe that perceptual psychology implicitly assumes—indeed, requires—anti-individualism, and makes use of its general principles in framing its own methods and theories. Anti-individualism is embedded in the method and theoretical framework of the science.

Fertilization can work reciprocally between philosophy and science. Philosophical articulation of anti-individualism can yield for science insight into its basic presuppositions. Philosophy can help sharpen distinctions (such as that between perception and sensory discrimination, or between different conceptions of representation) that in scientific work are not as sharp as they might be. Science, in turn, provides applications, empirical content, and cases that enrich philosophical understanding and places limits on tenable philosophical positions. The first and second sources of my positive view are intertwined.

A third source, common sense, is intertwined with the first two. It is natural and commonsensical to hold that many animals and normal human babies perceptually categorize bodies and simple physical properties, without either building up this capacity from subjective representations or having a supplemental apparatus for representing general conditions of objective representation. Empirical representation of the environment does not seem to depend on the individual's ability to represent anything else.

Philosophy often insists that common sense is naive. On this topic, I think that the insistence needs re-evaluation. Argumentation against common sense on this matter has been deficient. In fact, it usually has devolved into dogmatic pronouncement. Philosophy was carried along by the momentum of initial mistakes by intellectually powerful thinkers. Its brief against common sense, in this case, can be shown by philosophy to be empty.

All these issues are complicated by a truly bewildering array of views on representation itself. There have been attempts to eliminate representational notions (such as belief and perception) from descriptive or theoretical contexts. Such efforts are, I think, driven by unscientific ideology. They lack support in the actual practices or theories of science. An impressively maturing science—perceptual psychology—makes fundamental use of representational notions.

A few philosophers and scientists have stretched or deflated representational notions so far as to claim that everything represents something or other. Tree rings represent age, smoke represents fire; the earth's orbit represents the gravitational powers of the sun; and so on.

A more common view is to assimilate representation to some form of *functioning* information registration and processing. *Information* is simply some sort of systematic statistical or law-like correlation between one system and another. Some correlations have a function—for example, the biological function of contributing to fitness for survival and replication. Thus tree rings do not function to correlate with age; smoke does not function to correlate with fire. So, on this slightly less broad notion of representation, tree rings and smoke do not "represent" what they correlate with.

The effect of using either of these broad conceptions of representation is to miss fundamental distinctions among scientifically relevant kinds. Even users of the latter notion, which I will be discussing in some detail, tend to take differences between plant sensitivity to light and visual perception by lower mammals to be mere differences in complexity, not in kind.

More specifically, these conceptions tend to miss a distinctively psychological kind that constitutively and non-trivially involves perspective and conditions of accuracy. And they tend to miss origins of objectivity.

My aims are to avoid the hyper-intellectualized theories of representation that dominated twentieth-century philosophical thinking and to improve on a leveling or deflationary conception of representation that reduces the notion of representation that are not at all distinctive of mind or psychology. Usage and understanding in psychology are no more uniform than they are in philosophy. I think order can be found only by reflecting on explanation. I return to these matters in Chapter 3 and Part III.

I assume that talk of perception, belief, desire, and intention has a place in scientific as well as in common-sense descriptions of the world. I assume that these types of psychological states are representational in the sense they are about something, indicate a subject matter as being a certain way, and (constitutively and non-trivially) have veridicality conditions—conditions on being accurate or true. These assumptions have been richly supported in empirical psychology and philosophical work. I believe that they are sufficiently well entrenched, not only in common sense but in serious scientific theory, not to require extensive support. What they need is explication, sharpening, delineation.

I think that explanation in terms of distinctively psychological representational notions is, as far as we now know, basic and ineliminable. That is, we have no reason to believe that psychological explanation in terms of representation can be reduced to some other type of explanation. I will not rely on this anti-reductionist assumption in most of this work, though I shall defend it a little in Chapter 8.

I use a robust notion of representation, not any of the leveling notions alluded to six and seven paragraphs back. This point is of some dialectical import. In disputing the views of individual representationalists, I do not simply change the subject. I do not invoke a conception of intentionality, or representation, that makes it trivially true that "representation" of physical entities precedes the supplementary resources invoked by individual representationalists. *Of course*, the amoeba's functional sensitivity to light and response to it in moving to congenial environments does not require a capacity to track its own position through a comprehensively represented space, or to represent an appearance/reality distinction, or to have a language. One does not need philosophy to understand that point.

Unlike generalized notions of information registration *cum* function, my notion of representation has specifically psychological import. I will not elaborate it further at this point. So far I have associated the notion with perception, belief, and intention—and with veridicality conditions. Chapters 8–10 will delineate my conceptions of perception and representation.

Let me map my route from here.

Part I sets the stage for more specific discussion. In Chapter 2, I refine the terms in my initial questions. In Chapter 3, I discuss philosophical background for opposition to Individual Representationalism—specifically anti-individualism. I also sketch some general points about the science of perceptual psychology.

Part II characterizes and criticizes purported support for various versions of Individual Representationalism. Chapter 4 centers primarily on first-family versions in the first half of the twentieth century. Chapter 5 offers an overview of some issues in the second half of the twentieth century. Chapters 6 and 7 center on Individual Representationalism in two prominent second-family versions. Specifically, in Chapter 6 I discuss the neo-Kantian tradition articulated by Strawson and Evans. In Chapter 7, I discuss the tradition of linguistic interpretation articulated by Quine and Davidson.

Part III develops a point of view meant to replace Individual Representationalism regarding origins of objective representation of the physical world. It elaborates conceptions of the key explanatory kinds: *representation* and *perception*. Chapter 8 sets the stage for distinguishing the distinctively psychological kind *representation* from broader kinds (often also called 'representation') shared by psychology with biology. It introduces a distinction between sensory registration and perceptual representation, sketches an account of primitive agency, and illustrates, in greater depth than I do in Chapter 3, types of explanation that are characteristic of perceptual psychology. Chapter 9 is the key chapter in the book. It attempts to isolate the psychological kind, *perceptual representation*, and further develops the distinction between sensory registration and perception.

Chapter 10 centers on perceptual origins of four representational categories that figure prominently in the perceptual systems of a wide variety of animals: body, certain elementary mathematical representation, space, and time. It also discusses which if any of them is constitutively necessary to having perceptual representation itself. Chapter 11 points forward to further issues suggested by main themes of the book.

2 *Terminology: What the Questions Mean*

Let us return to our original questions:

> What does it take for an individual to represent the physical world objectively? What are minimum constitutive conditions necessary for an individual to represent the physical environment in such a way as to attribute, sometimes accurately, specific physical attributes to physical particulars?

Before confronting the questions, I want to explicate key terms in them. Explication in this chapter is preliminary. It serves to set background assumptions and guard against confusion. Development, especially of the term 'represent', will come later.

The terminological discussion may seem overly analytical to some readers. But offhand use of some terms in the questions, particularly 'representation' and 'objectivity', have made a remarkable amount of mischief. Confused use of the former term has held back philosophy in major ways over almost its whole history, largely because aspects of ordinary usage encourage confusion. I want to avoid mischief and confusion right from the start. Those with little patience for terminology might skip this chapter. They can perhaps catch on to the terminology as it is used. If difficulty arises, the impatient reader can return to these sections, I hope chastened. The more patient reader will understand that ostensibly terminological and taxonomic issues set the framework for an investigation in ways that are not sharply separable from development of theory. The theoretical development in this book depends on careful use and understanding of basic terms and concepts. Patience regarding the terminological/conceptual underpinnings of the project will, I think, be rewarded.

REPRESENTATION

Some readers coming to this work from the history of philosophy may be inclined to associate the term 'representation' or even 'representational content' (which I introduce later), with traditional views according to which representations are the immediate objects of perceptual reference. On such views, representations are perceived. Or they are *objects* of perceptual awareness, or of some other awareness. Representations, on such views, are themselves represented: they are *representata*. Such views are often termed 'representationalist'.

I have absolutely no sympathy for such views. To understand what I am up to, the reader must take my term 'representation' and its variants as I use them, and not import historical doctrines into the discussion, unless I import them.

I begin by discussing my use of the term 'reference'. Reference is a central type of representation. *Reference* is both a certain *relation* to an entity in a subject matter, and a *function* (or exercise of the function) of a state, event, or activity to establish a reference relation. Exercises of the function may or may not fulfill the function.

In the first use, we may say 'Bill refers to Fido with his phrase "that dog"'. A reference relation holds between Bill, or between Bill's use of his phrase, and Fido. In the second use, we may say 'Bill engaged in reference by using his phrase "that pink elephant"', even though no reference relation is established between Bill, or his use of his phrase, and any entity.

The *reference relation* holds between a psychological state or event, or a piece or use of language, on one hand, and a subject matter, on the other. When I say 'x refers to y', I intend the reference relation. The relational use entails some state or activity with a *referential function*. But not all states or activities with referential functions establish a reference relation. When a reference relation is established by a person or animal—when the person or animal *refers to* something, some entity—the relation is always established *by way of* some thought, cognition, perception, or other psychological state or event, or by way of some piece or use of language, or other symbolism.[1]

States or events that *function* to refer have the constitutive representational function of connecting to a subject matter. Such connection is what the relation *reference*, as a successful fulfillment of the function, is.

Reference contrasts with *indication* (to be explicated shortly). Indication is also dually a relation and a function (or exercise of a function) to establish a relation, between psychological states or events, or pieces of language, and entities in a subject matter. The function of referring differs from the function of indicating in that the former does not have the further constitutive representational function of *attribution* or *functional application*.[2] Most reference—whether it

---

[1] Thus, when I speak of reference by an individual, there is at least a three-place relation, involving individual, subject matter, and psychological or linguistic mode. Equally, I think, if a thought, perception, or piece of language refers, it is always the thought, perception, or linguistic item employed by an individual or by individuals—or at least an abstraction from the perceptions, thoughts, or linguistic uses of individuals. We can think of the relation of reference between an English word and a subject matter. But we are idealizing or abstracting from uses by English speakers. So ultimately, reference involves mode, subject matter, and individual or individuals.

[2] Usually, reference depends on attribution or functional attribution, perhaps together with further operations. In referring to something, an occurrence of 'that body' involves attribution (through 'body'). Here reference is not possible apart from *some* attribution. But even in cases in which reference depends on attribution, attribution is not one of its functions.

be relation or function—does not occur apart from attribution or functional application. But, when a representational device (like a name or a perceptual demonstrative) functions to refer, it does not constitutively have the further function of engaging in attribution or functional application. In this respect, reference is the simplest type of representational relation and function.

Reference can be singular or plural. I concentrate on singular reference. When reference is singular, it is so in two respects. First, in singular reference, if *A* refers to *b*, then *A* refers only to *b*. *A* cannot singularly refer to two things. Second, in singular reference, if *A* refers to *b*, the reference occurs in a singular way. Examples of singular ways are 'the only chimp in the room', 'this worm', 'Aristotle' (intending the philosopher), '3', a perception as of a particular object.

Examples of singular reference are these: Al's occurrent thought that *that* chair is red refers to a particular chair (imagine Al looking at a chair). More particularly, the occurrent thought component that chair also refers to the chair.[3] Bert's visual perception refers to a bone—it singles out the bone. Al and Bert also refer to their respective objects.

Reference need not be to *objects*. It can be to events, to instances of properties or relations, to abstractions. Reference can be to anything real or existent. '2' refers to the number 2. A thought may refer to an abstract property or relation. The thought redness is a color property refers, specifically through its singular element (redness), to redness. A perception may refer to an instance of redness or an instance of a spatial relation, or an event, or a body.

I turn now from reference to *indication*. Recall that functioning to refer does not constitutively carry with it a function to engage in attribution or functional application. Since attribution is a constitutive representational function of the predicate 'is red' and the concept is red, they do not refer to anything. They *indicate* the property of being red. A primary representational function of predicates in language and predicative concepts in thought is *attribution*. So predicates and concepts indicate entities—bear relations to aspects of a subject matter. Their doing so is fundamentally in the service of attribution, attributing such aspects to further entities (often entities that are referred to). In occurrences in which no logical operations, such as negation, are involved, the predicate and the concept function to *attribute* what they indicate. For example, in That apple is red, is red functions to attribute what it indicates—the property redness, or the property of being red—to what That apple refers to. In attributing a property, they represent something *as* having that property. Similar points apply to relational predicates and relational concepts.

When such attribution is to something that is referred to, it characterizes or groups that something as such and such, or as being such and such. In a thought the barn is red (which I will suppose to be true), the thought attributes (through its component is red) the property of being red to a barn. The thought also attributes

---

[3] I refer to representational contents by underlining. Italics indicates either emphasis or attributes, which representational contents might represent.

(through <u>barn</u>) the kind, being a barn. Both these attributes are attributed to a barn, assuming that the thought, through its component <u>the barn</u>, succeeds in referring to a barn. The thought, through the singular subject description <u>the barn</u>, refers to a barn, and attributes being red, as well as being a barn, to the barn, through the attributive elements <u>is red</u> and <u>barn</u>.[4] The thought also indicates the kind *being a barn* and the property *being red*. It does so through the attributive concepts <u>is red</u> and <u>barn</u>.

Of course, attribution can occur in a thought or sentence that contains no singular elements, as in the thought <u>some barns are red</u>.

Like reference, indication and attribution occur in perception as well as in thought and language. A perception of an object as red (or as square) indicates the property of being red (or square) and attributes it to the object. The attribution depends on the perception's grouping instances of red (or squareness) together. The perception attributes an indicated property to a perceptually referred-to particular.[5] Perceptual attribution is the freely re-applicable element of grouping in perception.

In nearly every case in which an individual, perception, thought, thought component, or piece of language refers to something, it does so partly through some attribution.[6] The attributive element indicates a property, relation, or kind, assuming there *is* a relevant property, relation, or kind. And it attributes what it indicates to the referent. The attributive characterizes or groups what is referred to as having (or as being an instance of) the property, as entering into (or as being an instance of) the relation, or as being of the kind. The attributive <u>barn</u> plays these roles in the singular form <u>that barn</u>.

An attribution might not be veridical. Dalton might think: <u>that piece of gold is the same element as the metal in my mother's ring</u>. The metal in his mother's ring might be a cheap alloy. Then he would have referred to some gold and veridically attributed being gold to it, but misattributed a further property. Dalton might perceive something as yellow that is green. Then his perception mistakenly attributes the property of being yellow to what he perceives.

Dalton might think, looking at a lump of copper, <u>that gold there is valuable</u>. Then even the attribution that is part of his *primary way of referring* would fail to be veridical of what he refers to (the copper). In such cases of thought and

---

[4] For further elaboration of this account of attribution, of which predication is a specific case, see my 'Predication and Truth: Review of Donald Davidson, *Truth and Predication*', *The Journal of Philosophy* 104 (2007), 580–608. Some philosophers and linguists take definite descriptions not to be referring expressions, because of a purportedly deeper grammatical analysis. Bracketing substantive disagreements, I follow surface grammar as signaling singularity. Since 'the oldest barn in the world' has the surface grammar of singularity, I count it a referring expression. Nothing in what follows depends on the point.

[5] I think that a perception perceptually represents (refers to) *instances* of properties that it indicates. In effect, perception attributes indicated properties to property instances, as well as to entities that *have* the properties. In veridically seeing an object as green, one sees not only the object as green; one also sees an instance of greenness and sees that instance as being green.

[6] The few exceptions involve individual constant concepts: <u>3</u>, <u>God</u>, <u>that someone is tall</u>. I think that even <u>I</u>, <u>we</u>, <u>you</u>, <u>now</u>, <u>here</u>, involve implicit attributive restriction.

perception, I believe that there is always a further primary attribution, somewhere in the individual's psychology, that *is* veridical.[7] Dalton can think of some copper as gold only because he thinks of the copper, or perceives it, in some veridical way—for example, as a lump. Such an attribution is part of a singular mode of reference that figures in a further thought or perception that Dalton has.

Representation includes reference and indication as subtypes. It is a generic notion. Thus, in indicating the property of yellow and attributing it to various lumps of metal, Dalton represents the property of being yellow. In the veridical thought, that lump is gold, Dalton represents the kinds *gold* and *lump*, as well as the particular lump of gold.

Representation also includes whatever relation obtains between functional notions and functions, and between operators (say, logical operators) and operations. 'Representation' stands for any sort of intentionality in perception, cognition, or language.

As I explain below, representation can transpire even if there is nothing represented. But, when 'represents' takes a specific direct object, representation is said to be successful in representing something—to have a *representatum*. I use '*represents* ___' (with direct object in the blank) to apply both to successful reference to any entity (*representatum*) and to successful indication of kinds, properties, or relations (all *representata*) in a subject matter.

REPRESENTATION-AS AND REPRESENTATIONAL CONTENT

The term 'represents', of itself, does not signify any *specific* way in which representation is effected. Let us again focus first on 'refers'. If Dalton referred to gold, he referred to gold in some way. But the locution 'Dalton referred to gold' does not say how Dalton referred to gold. The quoted locution does not indicate that Dalton referred to gold as gold, or as the most widely valued precious metal, or as the metal in his mother's ring. It does not say whether Dalton used language, thought, perception, or what not.

The 'refers to —— as ___' locution does provide partial specification of *how* the referent —— is referred to. Suppose that Dalton thinks a thought that gold there is heavy, referring in thought to a particular lump of gold. Then Dalton, and his thought, referred to the lump partly by attributing to it the kind, gold. He refers to it as gold. He could have referred to it instead as a rock (that yellowish rock), or as a lump, or as a shiny thing on the laboratory table. He would still be referring to the lump of gold in these ways, but not referring to it *as* gold.

In his thought, that gold there is heavy, Dalton also attributes to the lump the property of being heavy, and thinks of the lump as being heavy, though this

---

[7] In some cases, perhaps the veridical attribution lies in the psychology of someone on whom the individual is relying through communication.

attribution of heaviness is not part of the way he effected the reference. Strictly, it is not part of the way he refers to it. Strictly, he referred to it as gold and as being in a certain position. He attributed to the lump being gold, being in a certain position, and being heavy.

We can allow such attributions as 'ways he referred to it', in a secondary sense. If Dalton thinks that lump of gold is valuable, referring to a lump, he refers to the lump as a lump and as being of gold in the primary sense and as valuable in the secondary sense.

Other types of representation besides reference invite the *as* terminology. There is, for example, indication of gold as gold.

An individual—or an individual's perception, thought, other type of psychological state, representational content, or piece of language—*represents* something *as such and such* if and only if it represents something by way of a such-and-such type of representation (or representational content). Thus a perception represents something as square if and only if it does so by way of a square-type of representation. The sense of 'square-type' is, of course, not that the representation is square. Rather the relevant representational kind is individuated in terms of the representational kind (representational content) square.

The explication holds even if there is no successful representational relation to a subject matter. Suppose that there is no such kind-attribute as *phlogiston*. A thought represents something as phlogiston if the thought is a phlogiston-type of thought. Most such thoughts, other than conditionals and negative existentials, will be mistaken.

Most but not all representation-as involves attribution. Representation-as can occur through individual constant concepts (see note 6). The first concept in the thought $3+5=8$ represents 3 as 3, because it is a 3-type of representation, or representational content. Similarly, that brown hair (as applied in a context) represents something not only as brown, as hair, and as brown hair, but also as that brown hair—as long as one compensates for the context appropriately.

I understand 'represents as ____' in a specific sense. Just having a ____-type representation as an element in a representation or representational content is not sufficient to represent as ____. If I think that is blue or yellow or that is not red (successfully perceiving something), I do not represent something as blue, or as yellow, or as red. I represent something only as blue or yellow, or as not red. Not red is a red-type of representation (as well as a not-red-type of representation). To use a red-type presentation to represent something as red, the use must be representationally committal—whether it is an attribution, functional application, referential application, or use of an individual constant. Thus, in the thought that choreographer is intelligent and not arrogant, the individual is represented as a choreographer, as that choreographer, as intelligent and not arrogant, as intelligent, and as not arrogant. The individual is not represented as arrogant. Arrogance is indicated but not attributed. In the thought there is no such thing as phlogiston, there is an attributive occurrence of phlogiston, but there is no committal attribution. Nothing is attributed or indicated. Nothing is represented *as* phlogiston, though the thought involves a phlogiston-type of representation, a representation as (of) phlogiston.

I said that the 'as ____' locution provides *partial* specification of how something is referred to in a primary or secondary sense. How much specification? That Dalton referred to the gold as gold entails that Dalton used a gold-type representation or representational content. Since as a lump, as spherical, as the metal in a given ring, and as an element with atomic number 79 are not in themselves gold-types of representation, or representational content, referring to something as gold is not the same as referring to something in any of these ways.[8] So the locution 'as gold' provides some information about how something is referred to.

On the other hand, there are many ways of referring to something as gold. One can use language or thought. One can use the singular term the gold in my pocket, or the attributive gold and yellow, or the attributive piece of gold, or simply the attributive gold. If something is a gold-and-yellow-type of representation, it is a gold-type of representation.[9]

Reference-to —— as ____ occurs in perception. One can perceptually refer to something as cubic in perceiving it as cubic. It is crucial that one not *assume* that *perceiving* something *as* such and such entails anything about *conceiving* or *thinking* of it *as* such and such. Perception-as (equally, as we shall see later, perception-as-of) is simply perceptual attribution. I will be discussing conditions under which perception, including perceptual attribution, is possible. One of the issues is whether perceptual representation requires thought.

The primary *concepts* (equivalently, conceptual ways of representing or conceptual representational contents) are attributives in *propositional* structures. I use 'thought' to apply only to propositional attitudes, or representational contents with propositional structure. I believe that perception is not propositional and hence is not thought. Perception lacks propositional structure. So perceptual attributives are not concepts, and perceptions are not thoughts.

Many perceptual attributives represent entities as square. Different *visual* perspectives can represent something as square in different ways (for example, corresponding to different visual angles on a square something). Thus there are many square-types of perceptual attributives. I discuss this point in more detail in subsequent chapters.

Reference to —— as ____ is a form of representation of —— as ____. Indication-as and attribution-as are further forms of representation-as.[10]

---

[8] Element with atomic number 79 applies to exactly the same thing(s) that gold does. The equivalence is even, in a strong sense, necessary. And certainly gold *is* the element with atomic number 79. But element with atomic number 79 does not count as a gold-type representation. It was a discovery that gold is the element with atomic number 79. Gold was represented as gold before it was represented as an element with atomic number 79.

[9] On the other hand, I think that an elm-type of representation is not *ipso facto* a tree-type of representation.

[10] I have used the locutions 'represents [or refers to, or indicates] —— as such'. These locutions are shorthand for 'represents [refers to, indicates] —— as ——', with the understanding that the same

A certain type of *representation as* will be prominent in later discussion. I call this type '*specification*'. A representational state (or representational content) *specifies* an attribute *A* if and only if the state or content represents *A* as *A* and does so in any context of use and with respect to all possible situations (worlds). For example, if a representational state (or representational content) specifies aluminum, it represents aluminum as aluminum and represents aluminum in any context of use and with respect to any possible situation (or world).

I have written of *ways* in which entities are represented. I shall discuss ways of representing that are more specific than the representation-as terminology suggests. There are always different ways of representing such and such, for any given such and such. There are different ways of representing *as* such and such, for any given such and such. There can even be different ways of *specifying* exactly such and such, for any given such and such.

When I write of a *way* of representing, I mean 'way' in a special sense. I have in mind not causal mechanisms, but *modes* of referring, indicating, attributing, functionally applying. Such modes have roles in psychological as well as semantical (representational) explanation. Such modes *mark* or *help type-individuate* psychological states. That is, they are aspects of representational psychological kinds. A particular way of representing something as a body helps type-individuate a *kind* of psychological state. The way of representing is an aspect of the kind of state.[11]

Such modes of representation constitute the *perspective* of an animal or person. They mark how the world is, representationally, for an individual.

Thus 'way of representing' or 'mode of representation' indicates both the way that the act, state, event is typed representationally and the way that the act, state, event functions to represent. In cases of representation failure, to be discussed in the next section, there remain *ways of representing* that type-individuate acts, states, events, or pieces of language.[12]

Expositional convenience supports nominalization. I have written of modes of representation as *representational contents*. Representational content is an abstraction that has three explanatory functions. It is a way of representing, or a

expression substitutes in both blanks. Thus 'Dalton represents gold as such' means 'Dalton represents gold as gold'.

For 'Dalton *refers* to —— as ——', I allow extraction of the largest attributive expression in the expression filling the first blank to occur in the second blank, without repeating the whole first-blank expression. Thus 'Dalton refers to the gold as gold' is admissible as a paraphrase of 'Dalton refers to the gold as such'. 'Dalton refers to the gold as the gold' is also admissible.

[11] Marking and type-individuation are fundamentally not things we do. They are constitutive conditions or aspects of natures. They are factors in entities' being what they are.

[12] Modes of representing in the sense that I am developing (representational contents) can be associated with pieces of language or linguistic acts. I do *not* assume that representational contents are to be identified with meanings, on just any legitimate conception of meaning. I am developing a specifically psychological notion. I believe that language sometimes expresses representational contents. Representational contents may be one type of meaning. But I do not assume, or believe, that an account of all types of linguistic meaning can rest with invoking representational contents.

perspective. It is a fundamental aspect of psychological and linguistic kinds, at their finest explanatory grain. And it constitutes the veridicality conditions—accuracy conditions or truth conditions—of psychological and linguistic kinds.

A fundamental attribute of most psychological and linguistic phenomena is that they are representational in specific ways. Representational contents constitute, or help constitute, modes in which an individual thinks about, intends, or perceives a subject matter. One function of representational content is to constitute a mode of representation, or perspective. This first function is closely related to the second. Representational content helps constitutively mark, or type-individuate, psychological or linguistic states, capacities, acts, events. They are structured, perspectival, representational kinds. What kind of belief an individual has is determined by *what* the individual believes. What kind of perception an individual has is determined by how the individual perceives the world to be. These 'what's' and 'how's' are rough colloquial versions of representational content. The representational content of a belief is a *kind* of belief. The representational content of a perception is a kind of perception. Similarly, for other psychological and linguistic phenomena.[13]

Just as different instances of perception (or belief, or intention) can be of the same kind, so a representational content can be common among different perceptual states (or belief states, or intentional states). Some representational contents are shareable thoughts (thought contents); some are shareable concepts (elements in thought contents); some are shareable perceptions; some are shareable perceptual attributives (elements in perception contents). This potential for sharing is one basis for calling representational contents abstractions. The sharing is no more unfamiliar than the commonality of kind among different instances of a kind.

The third, and equally fundamental, function of representational content is to constitute, or help to constitute, a veridicality condition. Elements of representational contents *help constitute* a veridicality condition. The concept <u>green</u> helps constitute the veridicality condition the <u>forest is green</u>. The full representational content of a perception, belief, or intention *constitutes* a veridicality condition. Representational content is a perspectival way of representing at the finest explanatory grain relevant both to determining psychological or linguistic kind and to determining veridicality conditions. When a veridicality condition is fulfilled, there is a veridical representational content.

Representational contents of beliefs and declarative sentences can be evaluated for truth or falsity—just as beliefs and assertions can be. Beliefs and assertions are true (or false) if and only if their representational contents are. Similarly, the representational contents of intentions and imperatives can be evaluated for whether their veridicality conditions are fulfilled. The veridicality condition (representational content) of an intention comes to be fulfilled, or is

---

[13] As will emerge, these kinds occur at various levels of abstraction, even for a given belief or perception.

made veridical, if the intention is carried out in relevant action. The veridicality condition of an imperative comes to be fulfilled if the imperative is obeyed. The representational content of questions is to be understood analogously. The representational content of a perception can be evaluated for accuracy or inaccuracy—just as perceptions can be. Perceptions are accurate (their way of being veridical) if and only if their representational contents are. Since I am primarily interested in the representational contents of beliefs and perceptions, I will be primarily concerned with propositional truth and perceptual accuracy, when veridicality is at issue.

A *veridical* perception is a *correct* or *accurate* perception. A *veridical* thought is a *true* thought. Truth and accuracy (correctness) are subcases of veridicality. For example, the representational content of a belief that cats need their mothers is the thought content <u>cats need their mothers</u>.

All representational contents have or serve representational functions.[14] All representational contents either function to represent—as do singular referring contents, attributives, functional representation (<u>the successor of</u>)—or operate on representational contents—as do logical connectives and quantifiers—or are composites of representing representational contents—as are whole thoughts.[15] Thus a cat is not a representational content. A concept of a sphere, or a perceptual grouping of spheres, is a representational content.

A further constitutive role of representational contents was mentioned earlier—that of *marking*, or helping to type-individuate, psychological states or representational aspects of psychological states. This function is often overlooked. I emphasize it. Representational contents are aspects of psychological kinds. They help type-individuate a perceptual state, or a thought event, or a belief, as being an instance of a certain psychological kind of perceptual state, thought event, belief, or capacity. A perceptual or conceptual representational content

---

[14] Here the notion of representational function can be taken to be intuitive. I give it a more technical meaning in Chapter 8.

[15] I do not assume that logical connectives do not represent; I simply allow the possibility. I also leave open whether whole representational contents of thoughts have their own form of representation, as opposed to relying on their non-propositional components to represent. Full representational contents of perceptual states are always composites of representational contents, and always function to represent.

The plural of 'representation' can apply to particulars that instantiate representational content, or to vehicles that *express* representational content. Some philosophers, notably Jerry A. Fodor, in *The Language of Thought* (1975; Cambridge, MA; Harvard University Press, 1979), think that such vehicles in a psychology can be individuated *independently* of the representational content that they express. I doubt this view, at least as a general position about psychological states and events. I certainly believe that current psychological explanation does not imply or depend on the view. What I say in this book is largely independent of these matters. I believe that the notion of representation, like that of representational content, in scientific explanation, functions mainly as an abstraction that helps demarcate kinds of psychological states. Representational content, and instances of states with such content, also serve as structured entities on which computational explanations and other explanations of psychological transitions center. It is simply a mistake to think that computational explanations must assume the existence of psychological kinds that are individuated independently of their representational content.

that represents something as a body helps type-individuate a different psychological state (occurrence, capacity) than does a content that represents something as an event, or as being spherical.

Because of this aspect or role of representational contents in type-individuating psychological states, the question of whether there *are* representational contents (including propositional representational contents) is as outlandish as the question whether there are kinds of representational states (including propositional attitudes).

Representational contents are finer grained than the representation-as locution captures. Thus the contents lump of gold, gold, gold statue, and yellow and gold (assuming committal occurrences) are all gold-types of representation. All of these representational contents can be used to represent something as gold. 'Representational content' will be a basic explanatory term. 'Representation-as' is less basic. I took pains to introduce it because it will be useful in a lot of exposition that does not depend on the finest grain of explanation.

It must always be remembered, however, that the kind-discrimination provided by the representation-as locution is too crude to identify basic explanatory psychological kinds. It is representational content that marks psychological kinds. The 'as' and 'as such' expressions (and, later, the 'as of' expression) do not fully individuate a particular mode of representation, or representational content. They only indicate *genera* of representational contents. There are many representational contents for any given kind, property, relation, or particular that is represented in these 'as' expressions. The representational content is always more fine-grained than the *as* locution suggests.

There are, for example, many ways of representing bodies as such. One can represent bodies as such in language, thought, or perception. Each medium is associated with different ways. There are different perceptual modalities in which one can perceive a body as a body. The representational content of a visual perception of something as a body is inevitably different from that of a touch perception of something as a body.

There are intermodal non-conceptual contents. There is a scientific story about how the different modes of perceptual representation in the different perceptual modalities are related to one another, and how the overall psychology manipulates the different ways of attributing the kind *body* to perceived entities. Any perceptual attributive in a touch system that indicates the kind *body* is different from any visual perceptual attributive that indicates the same kind. Any intermodal system that mediates between different perceptual modalities, or between perception and action, represents the kind *body* differently than any of the perceptual modalities (vision, touch, and so on) do. The explanations in perceptual psychology as well as common sense require different representational typings of the different psychological states—different representational contents.

There are different ways of *visually* perceiving something as a spherical body—different visual representational contents that represent as (or as of) a spherical body. One can see a body as a spherical body and have different perceptual representational contents. One can, for example, see a body as a spherical body from different perceptual perspectives, deriving from different angles or distances. These perspectives commonly correspond to different types of visual perceptual states—all perceiving something as a spherical body. Visual perceptual systems will be in significantly different perceptual states, marked by different representational contents, when they form perceptual representations from the different angles or distances from an entity perceived as a spherical body. Introspectively, in conscious perception, there will be different ways the spherical body "looks" to be a spherical body. The different kinds of perceptual states and looks are type-individuated by different visual-perceptual representational contents.

The reason for this fine-grained typing of visual states is that a major objective of the science of vision is to explain how vision can attribute the same attribute by way of importantly different kinds of perceptual state—by way of different perceptual representational contents. There are detailed empirical explanations of how visual perceptual systems form visual states with representational contents so as to function to be of, and as of, a single property in the physical environment—for example, *spherical-bodihood*.

One can *conceptually* represent mercury—even exactly as mercury—in different ways. One can conceive of mercury *exactly* as mercury using the conceptual representational contents mercury, mercury and an element, mercury or a round square.[16] Representational content is more fine-grained than what is signified in the representation-as locution.

As is intimated in the foregoing, differences in ways of representing a given property or kind as such can derive from different levels of abstraction. Perceptual as well as conceptual attribution occurs at various levels of abstraction. A perception can represent a body as a body or as a cylindrical body. In both cases, the perception represents the body as a body. Representing something as a cylindrical body and representing something as a body are different ways of representing. But they are both representation of something as a body.

There are other reasons why representational contents are more fine-grained than what the representation-as locution suggests. But the foregoing considerations should suffice to get the main point across.

At bottom, representational contents are just kinds, or aspects of kinds, of psychological states. The structure of representational contents marks structural aspects of the capacities embodied in the psychological states.

For example, the state of believing that the frog has visual perception involves having certain inferential capacities. The belief involves a capacity to infer that something has visual perception, that the frog has perception, that the frog has

---

[16] Mercury and quicksilver are different concepts, different representational contents, even though they *represent* exactly mercury. I am assuming that quicksilver is not a mercury-type of representation. Representing something as mercury and representing it as quicksilver are different, even though the two expressions are (near) synonyms.

vision, and so on. These capacities are systematically related to inferential capacities associated with a belief that the frog has auditory perception. These capacities (and the beliefs themselves) have structural aspects inasmuch as they are systematically related to one another and to a more general capacity to carry out deductive inferences. The structural aspects of the representational content of the belief mark structural aspects of the relevant belief, and of inferential capacities constitutively associated with it. Both the representational contents and the psychological entities (states, occurrences, capacities) that they type-identify have structural aspects. Structure and representation are integral to the nature of the psychological kinds. These kinds partly *are* representational contents. Psychological explanation makes use of these structural aspects of psychological states, as well as their representational aspects.

I think that representational contents are abstract entities. But ontological issues will not be primary. I believe that the nominalization 'representational content' is theoretically secure. But the main *critical* line of argument in this book could dispense with it in favor of talk of kinds of psychological states or events. The theoretical vocabulary is, however, useful expositionally; and it allows deeper development of positive theory.

REPRESENTATION FAILURE AND REPRESENTATION AS OF

Representational contents and states can fail to represent anything. A person, perception, thought, or piece of language can fail to refer to anything. A perceptual content or perceptual state can be pure referential illusion. A singular thought—through failure of description or failure in demonstrative-marked application—can fail to refer to anything. An attributive element in a perception, thought, or piece of language can fail to indicate a real property, relation, or kind.

As I use the terms, failures to refer to, or indicate, anything real are failures to refer to, or indicate, *anything*. The perception, thought, concept, or piece of language has the function of representing (referring, indicating)—it still has a representational role. In such cases, I shall say that the perception, thought, concept, or piece of language *represents there being ____, or represents as of ____*. Then representation (referring, indication) is instantiated, but nothing need be represented (referred to, indicated).

In fact, even in successful cases of representation, there is representation-as-of. Representation-as-of occurs whether representation is successful or not. In the broadest sense, representation is representation-as-of. The point of the locution is to emphasize that representational states need not be successfully representational—need not represent anything. There need be no *representatum*.

For example, as I use the terms 'indicates' and 'represents', a thought or piece of language about phlogiston indicates and represents nothing, in the sense that it has no *representatum*. But there are entities or states that function to refer or indicate—that engage in (unsuccessful) reference or indication. Unsuccessful reference or indication is reference or indication without referring to or indicating anything—reference or indication without a *representatum*. A mistaken scientific theory tried to explain combustion with the term 'phlogiston' and the representational content phlogiston. Phlogiston is not a real kind and never existed. No thought or piece of language represents, refers to, or indicates phlogiston.

A thought or piece of language about Ossian refers to nothing. Since there is no real subject matter, there is no *representatum*, hence no representational relation to anything. In the famous literary hoax, some people pretended that Ossian existed, and many others believed that Ossian existed. But Ossian never existed. Nothing represents Ossian, ever. Ossian-type representation fails to represent anything.

Of course, the relevant sentences and terms that fail to refer, represent, or indicate are not meaningless. Similarly, there are genuine thoughts and concepts "about" Ossian and phlogiston. Thinkings about Ossian and phlogiston have representational contents typed as Ossian- or phlogiston-contents. There are Ossian- or phlogiston-representations, or representational contents. The thoughts have specific entailment relations to other thoughts. The language and thought just lack *representata*. As I use the terms, one can refer or indicate (in the sense of engage in an act of referring or indication), even though the representational content and the instances of reference or indication have no *representata*—no *objects* of representation. One can think, have perceptual states, or use language—each of which involves acts or psychological occurrences of reference—without succeeding in connecting to *representata* in a real subject matter. In such cases one does not represent, refer *to*, or indicate any entity. If there is nothing real or existent to refer to, indicate, or represent, no *representatum* is represented. I deplore introducing unreal or non-existent subject matters to be "objects" of reference or representation, when nothing but superficial grammar recommends doing so.[17]

Again, there *is* an Ossian-*way* of representing or referring. There *is* a phlogiston-*way* (or *ways*) of representing, indicating, or referring. There is *representation of there being* Ossian (phlogiston) and *representation as of* Ossian (phlogiston). In a certain sense, there is representation "about" Ossian (phlogiston).[18] The representational content is about Ossian (phlogiston) in the sense that

---

[17] Frege's work provided the keys to avoiding such introductions. Russell also showed ways to avoid the unwelcome result, with his theory of descriptions. In my view, Russell succumbed to the key error, however: that of thinking that all representation must be successful, must have an entity that is the object of representation. This view distorts his theory of perception and thought. I discuss some consequences of this error about perception in Chapter 4.

[18] In such cases, 'about ____' suggests a mode of representation, or representational content. It does not signify a relation (an 'about' relation) between an event, state, vehicle of representation, or representational content, on one hand, and a represented entity, a *representatum* (or referent, or indicant), on the other. Confused use of the term 'about' is one of the most common bases for confusion regarding representation. Confusion resides in postulating a *representatum* (or "object" of representation, or "intentional object") wherever talk of representation is meaningful. Grammatical

it is an Ossian- (phlogiston-) way of representing, or a type of representation with Ossian- (phlogiston-) significance or meaning. But there is no object, or *relatum*, or *representatum* of the representational content. The event, state, or vehicle of representation is typed in terms of its mode of representation—in terms of how it functions to represent—not its *representatum*. This mode of representation is the representational content of the representation. The representational content remains, even though it lacks a successful object of representation, a *representatum*, in the world, or in a real subject matter.

It is certainly colloquial to say that the name 'Ossian' represents, or refers to, Ossian. Such uses are colloquial even in full knowledge that Ossian did not and never will exist. It is colloquial to say that a thought about phlogiston represents phlogiston, even knowing that there never was such a thing as phlogiston. In avoiding such usage, I am not criticizing English. Colloquial usage is acceptable for colloquial purposes. But such usage can mislead and has misled in philosophy, and even in science. Surface grammar blurs a distinction that is important for understanding language and thought.

Similar points apply to perception. A perception can fail to represent a particular. It can be a perceptual referential illusion. Then the individual perceives nothing. Perceptual failure can go further. A perceptual content can fail to indicate or attribute any real property, relation, or kind. Then it might fail to represent *anything*—particular or attribute. I mean not just that no instance of the attribute is perceived. I mean that there is no attribute at all that the content indicates or attributes. Perceptual attributives can in principle be like the concept phlogiston. I think it likely, and certainly possible, that there have been perceptual attributions as of certain specific textures that do not indicate any texture that has ever existed or ever will exist.[19]

Thus a perceptual state can be an illusion in any of three ways. It can be an illusion by constituting a perception of something (perceptually representing or referring to a particular), but failing to attribute certain attributes to it veridically. An individual could perceive a hologram and mistakenly perceive it as a body. Or a perceptual state can be a singular referential illusion in which no particular is perceived. For example, an individual could have a perception as of there being a particular moving sphere, where the perceptual state arises from artificial stimulation of the retina. There would be referential illusion: no object or event is

object and subject-matter object are then frequently confused. Representation that involves representation failure, lack of *representata*, is a function of a state, event, or representational content—not a relation to a subject matter.

[19] I assume, in these cases, that if there never was or will be any physical instance of a (would-be) physical property, there is no such physical property. I do not intend, however, to lean on any particular ontology of properties. I want the reader to understand how I am thinking about the distinction between *representatum* and mode of representing. I intend a sharp distinction both with regard to representation of particulars and with regard to representation of properties, kinds, and relations. In cases of indication failure, I believe that the individual must associate the attributives that fail to indicate anything with other attributives that do indicate something. Thus phlogiston can fail to indicate only because further attributives, perhaps stuff or body, succeed.

perceived at all, not even the relevant stimulation. Or, thirdly, there can be perceptual illusion that extends to indication. Certain types of perceptual states can fail to indicate or attribute genuine properties or kinds. One could perceive some particular as of having Escher-like figurations that are impossible, or as of being of some texture that does not exist. The second and third types of representational failure could combine.

Even perceptual states that involve reference or indication failure are representational. They represent there being a particular, or they represent as of a specific attribute. The perceptual state, marked by a representational content— the mode of perceiving associated with the perceptual state—remains even as it fails to connect to *representata*, even if nothing is perceived, and even if nothing is indicated or attributed. I have been characterizing failures of reference in terms of conditions for veridicality associated with the perceptual states. Kinds of perceptual state are individuated in terms of their ways of referring, indicating, attributing. These *ways* are the representational content. Representational content incorporates conditions under which a perception is veridical or non-veridical. Similar points apply to thought.

All representation is representation-*as*. In itself, representation-*as* is representation-*as-of*.[20] My term 'representation-as-of' is intended explicitly to allow for representation failure; but, as noted, it also comprises representational success. 'Representation-as' allows for such failure as well, except where it takes the form 'represents —— as ___'. Then the direct-object expression before 'as' has a *representatum*. In representing the lump on the table *as* gold, Al engages in representation *as of* gold. Here, representation-as and representation-as-of are successful: gold is indicated and attributed. But no one can represent phlogiston, since phlogiston does not exist. The colloquial 'Al represents phlogiston as involved in combustion' is to be rephrased as "Al represents combustion as involving phlogiston" or 'Al represents *there being* phlogiston in combustion'. Then, Al engages in representation *as of* phlogiston. No phlogiston attribute is indicated, attributed, referred to, or represented—since there is no phlogiston (no *representatum*) to represent. Thus talk "about" phlogiston is to be rephrased—with less tendency to mislead—into *as* and *as of* talk—or into talk of phlogiston-type representation, or of representational content containing the attributive phlogiston. Representation-as and representation-as-of locutions are to be construed in these ways.

Representation is rather like shooting. Some shots do not hit anything, but they remain shootings. A way of representing, or mode of representation, constitutes a kind of representation (as of), and helps type-individuate kinds of psychological states and events. It has been a peculiar philosophical disease to warp theory so as

---

[20] I believe that all perceptual representation contains both applied-singular-demonstrative and attributive elements. There is no *purely* demonstrative representation. I think, however, that even demonstrative singular elements are perspectival. A given perceptual occurrence (application) of a demonstrative capacity (or this type) must be distinguished from other occurrent uses (applications) of the same capacity (or type). I understand my 'as' locutions to cover these distinct occurrences, even though in these cases the 'as' locution does not signal attribution as of a kind, property, or relation.

to exclude the possibility of representational failure, in language, thought, and perception. We will come upon some epidemics in what follows. My intent is to explain terminology so as to make it easier to avoid the disease.

OBJECTIVITY

I asked initially, 'What does it take for an individual to represent the physical world objectively?' 'Objectively' here means (approximately) <u>veridically</u> or <u>accurately</u>. But the answers to the question that I give will bear on a wide range of types of objectivity. In this section I reflect on some of these types.

I begin with conceptions of objectivity that apply to *subject matters*. We sometimes think of the objective world, or of an objective subject matter. We normally think of the physical world as an objective subject matter.

An element in some subject-matter conceptions of objectivity is *mind independence*: an objective subject matter is a subject matter that is constitutively mind-independent.[21]

On a narrow conception, an objective subject matter has no dependence whatever on mind or the mental for its nature, constitution, essence, or individuation. The simpler elements in the natural physical environment are objective in this sense. Planets, oceans, mud, water, space-time, atoms, trees, bacteria, and the simplest animals such as cnidaria are uncontroversially objective in this sense, philosophical idealisms aside.[22] Minds play some role in bringing *some instances* of these things into being. A person can intentionally plant a seed or breed maggots. But what it is to be a tree or a maggot has nothing constitutively to do with minds.

By contrast, minds, beliefs, feelings, organizations, nations, languages, and theories are not constitutively mind-independent, and hence not objective, in this sense.

As I noted three paragraphs back, there are strange philosophical views— idealist views—according to which the physical environment is, in one or another sense, a projection of mind. Such views nearly always reject any application for the conception of objectivity as mind-independence that I just set out, since they hold that although not all reality is non-objective, all reality is mental. I reject idealist views, and do not want to engage them. Idealisms tend to concede that untutored common sense regards much of the physical world as mind-independent. They rely on other conceptions of objectivity, including ones that distinguish between

[21] Some materialists regard mental states as identical with physical states. Identity is not a form of independence. So, in the absence of sharpening, no physical states that underlie mental states would count as objective. The relevant notion of independence surely needs sharpening. I waive this issue. These issues are deep, but my purposes in expounding subject-matter conceptions of objectivity do not require depth in this direction.

[22] I believe that certain abstract subject matters, such as the numbers and various mathematical structures, also do not depend on mind for their natures.

the (objective) physical world and fallible mental perspectives on it. Although I do not reject other conceptions of objectivity, I stand with common sense in maintaining that much of the physical world is constitutively independent of mind.[23] I will largely ignore idealisms.

I characterized the initial conception of objectivity as narrow. The narrowness is evident from the fact that the conception counts hammers, buildings, and other artifacts as non-objective, since, constitutively, they are made or used with some intention or other, and hence are not mind-independent. Counting such physical artifacts non-objective is certainly odd. The oddity points to further conceptions of objectivity, which I shall discuss shortly.

Narrowness emerges also in the fact that normal animals of some complexity, like normal birds and mammals including humans, probably must have minds, on any reasonable understanding of 'minds'. It seems impossible for the bodies that such animals have (always and normally) to lack consciousness or representational capacities. Perhaps this necessity is constitutive. Yet it is odd to think of such animals and their bodies as non-objective, because they bear constitutive relations to mind. So, again, this initial conception of objectivity as constitutive mind-independence is a narrow and crude one. It does correspond to one conception of objectivity. Since I will often be concerned with the simpler elements of the natural physical environment, it will often be sufficient to construe an "objective" subject matter in this narrow sense. But there are more liberal notions.

A central idea behind the mind-independence conception of objectivity is a contrast between elements of reality that are perspectival and those that are not. Perspectives or points of view are representational elements. They can be veridical or non-veridical. Or they can present some goal as to-be-pursued. The relevant central idea suggests a second conception of subject-matter objectivity: an objective subject matter is one that is *constitutively non-perspectival*. To be constitutively non-perspectival is constitutively not to have, employ, or be representational content. Thus representational contents, minds, belief states, some feelings, organizations, nations, languages, theories, and people are constitutively perspectival—whereas planets, oceans, mud, water, space-time, atoms, trees, bacteria, and cnidaria are constitutively non-perspectival.

Objectivity as being constitutively non-perspectival is a somewhat broader conception than objectivity as mind-independence. Thus hammers, buildings, and other artifacts that do not literally 'make a statement'—that are not about something further—are constitutively non-perspectival. They were made by beings with perspectives, but they are not perspectives and do not constitutively have or employ perspectives. So they count as objective on this conception.

---

[23] It is customary to bracket issues about God in reflecting on idealism. So mind-independence here means independence of any finite non-divine mind.

Moreover, the bodies of animals that have minds, as distinct, I think, from the animals themselves, do not constitutively have perspectives or employ perspectives.[24] They do not represent anything; they lack veridicality conditions. So this second subject-matter conception of objectivity is broader than the first.

A further subject matter exerts possible pressure on conceptions of objectivity that center on mind-independence. There are large, persistent disputes among philosophers about the nature of color. Some regard color as a fully mind-independent property, something like surface reflectance. Others regard it as partly mind-dependent. For example, some regard color as a 'secondary quality'—as constitutively a power in physical entities to cause a certain type of phenomenological experience. A few philosophers think of color as a representational illusion of a property in the physical world. The first view is, of course, compatible with taking color to be objective on the complete mind-independence conception of objectivity. The second view is incompatible with taking color to be objective on that conception. But it is plausibly compatible with taking color to be objective on the constitutively non-perspectival conception. On most versions of the secondary-quality view, color is not, and does not have, representational content. On such versions, color is a dispositional aspect of physical entities; it is represented by experiences that have certain qualitative aspects. Most versions of the third view of color, as an illusory mental projection on reality, are incompatible with taking color to be objective on either of the views of objectivity so far set out. I reject this third view. I find the grounds for not taking color to be a property of physical entities to be unconvincing. I have some sympathy for the first view of color, although both the first and second views have some plausibility.[25] Nothing that I say hinges on choosing between the first and second views of color. I will, however, assume that color is a property of physical entities, including some physical entities whose natures are in themselves often mind-independent in the strongest sense.

Subject-matter conceptions of objectivity that center on mind-independence, or even on being non-perspectival, cannot stand alone. They are too narrow to capture all that is meant by an objective subject matter. They must be supplemented.

A broader notion of an objective subject matter is *all that is real*. An objective subject matter, in this sense, is one that exists or that is real—that is

---

[24] I am assuming a distinction between necessary relations to minds, which some bodies may have, and actually having or employing representational content. Animal bodies do not represent anything, though animals do. But, as I noted, it is nevertheless arguable that such bodies bear necessary relations to minds (and to animals) that do employ or have representational content.

[25] Thus the second, secondary-quality view of color maintains that color is not a mind-independent property of physical entities. Its nature depends partly on relations to minds. I think that untutored common sense probably sides with the first view—the view that holds that color is a constitutively mind-independent property of physical entities. I believe that Locke and others were consciously opposing common sense when they first proposed the second, secondary-quality view, which takes color to be partly dependent on mind. As I say, I incline toward the common-sense view. But the issues are complex, and nothing in this work hinges on them.

not illusory.[26] On such a conception, minds and manners are as objective as stars and stalagmites. Ultimately, I believe that this conception is the most useful one.

I turn now to a related family of notions of objectivity—ones that center on *objective mode of representation* rather than *objective subject matter*.[27] These notions hinge both on the nature of the subject matter and on how the subject matter is represented. One obtains different notions by varying the conception of an objective subject matter and, equally, by varying the conception of how it is represented.

For example, one could take the very narrow, mind-independence notion of an objective subject matter that we began with; and one could add to it a relatively narrow conception of objective mode of representation. The relevant notion of an objective mode of representation might be a veridical representation of properties, kinds, relations that are mind-independent. For example, the veridical thought pure water is translucent would count as an objective representation in this sense. It attributes only unproblematically mind-independent kinds and properties. It does so without representing any mind-dependent matters. By contrast, translucence is Uncle Harry's favorite attribute would not be an objective representation in this sense (even if Uncle Harry's favorite attribute is translucence) because it represents mind-independent matters by representing mind-dependent matters. Thus the representational content represents translucence by way of representing preferences, which are mental.

Alternatively, one could combine the broad notion of an objective subject matter (all that is real) with a correspondingly broad conception of an objective mode of representation. An example of a broad notion of an objective mode of representation is the notion of a true or veridical representation.[28] This combination would allow veridical judgments about one's own "subjective" mental states to count as objective. The judgments I am in pain and I am hallucinating would be objective on this conception, assuming them to be true in a context.

Another family of notions of objectivity concern *law* or *law-likeness*. This family is in one respect narrower than the notions just sketched. Not all subject matters (specifically attributes) enter into laws; and not all truths concern law. On the other hand, this set includes cases that the narrow notions of complete mind-independence exclude. A pattern of laws or law-like patterns might hold among some mental kinds or properties. But laws seem not to hold among such properties as being the first property Uncle Harry attended to on his seventieth birthday.

---

[26] One must be careful here. Strictly, no illusory subject matter is real. So, although we talk of illusory subject matters, 'illusory' does not indicate a property of a subject matter. No such subject matters exist or are real, and thus no such subject matters can have properties. 'Illusory' indicates a property of representational contents or mental states that purport to represent subject matters that, in fact, do not exist, are not real. The illusions, the non-veridical representational contents or non-veridical beliefs, themselves are real. So they are part of 'objective reality'.

[27] Here it is the mode of representation, whether the representation represents objectively, rather than the status of the representation itself as a subject matter, that is at issue.

[28] I take truth to be propositional. It is one sort of veridicality. The *accuracy* of photographs, representational paintings, and perceptions are other sorts of veridicality.

Particular individuals' happen-so attendings are not, or need not be, the topics of psychological laws. Similarly, although we can give law-like explanations of the behavior of particular instances of mud, by focusing on their components, *mud* is not a property that enters into laws.

This family of conceptions of objectivity have both subject-matter versions and mode-of-representation versions. A subject matter is objective, in this sense, inasmuch as it consists of properties, kinds, relations, and particulars realizing them, that enter into laws or law-like patterns. A representation of the subject matter represents objectively, on this type of conception, insofar as it veridically formulates laws or law-like patterns, or instantiates such formulations—or does so in a way conducive for explanatory formulations of laws.

A further family of conceptions of objectivity centers on representationally associated *procedures* or *systems*. A procedure or system of representations represents objectively insofar as it meets methodological norms that are independent of the whims of a *particular* mind. At its broadest, a notion of this type might include procedures for determining illusory astrological predictions, as long as the procedures are not dependent on a particular whim or decree. Narrower conceptions of procedural objectivity are more to the point in most philosophical discussions. Rational procedures in logic or mathematics or empirical experimental procedures in natural science are often taken as prime examples. More broadly, any rational or reasonable procedures can be objective in this sense.

Another family of notions centers on *impersonality*. This family is blood related to notions centering on law. Impersonality conceptions are usually motivated by law-related conceptions, inasmuch as laws are widely regarded as appropriately formulated in impersonal terms, terms that are as far removed as possible from particular contexts or personal points of view. Objective representation in this sense is representation in impersonal form—form that eschews as much as possible personal pronouns, or perhaps even demonstratives and indexicals. One can add further restrictions—veridicality, procedural rationality, and so on.[29]

One further set of notions of objectivity center on *intersubjectivity*. A subject matter is objective in this sense if it can elicit agreement, or, more narrowly, rational agreement. Objective representation in this more narrow sense is representation that is rationally shared or shareable by appropriately equipped individuals.

An idea behind the procedural, impersonality, and intersubjectivity conceptions of objectivity is *relative independence of particular perspective*. In Thomas Nagel's words: 'A view or form of thought is more objective than another if it

---

[29] I think that all representation presupposes representation that involves analogs of indexicals and demonstratives. So this notion must be qualified. See my 'Belief *De Re*', *The Journal of Philosophy* 74 (1977), 338–362; reprinted in *Foundations of Mind: Philosophical Essays, Volume 2* (Oxford: Clarendon Press, 2007).

relies less on the specifics of the individual's makeup and position in the world, or on the character of the particular type of creature he is.'[30]

All representation is necessarily from some perspective or standpoint. Every representational content is one of many possible representational ways, standpoints, or perspectives for representing any given particular, property, relation, or kind. Some types of representation, those generated in scientific theories, are relatively more common or shareable for a wider range of thinkers. They are relatively less open to contextual, historical, perceptual, or species-dependent parochial limitations. According to a traditional ideal, representations that are least limited in such ways are available to any rational being.

There is a rough generic division among all these conceptions of objectivity. Some center explicitly on subject matter, or on representational relation to subject matter. All of the subject-matter notions, the notion of veridicality of representation, and the notions involving lawfulness are examples of this type. By contrast, some conceptions of objectivity center, at least in explicit formulation, on relations among representations. The conceptions that feature procedure, impersonality, and intersubjectivity are examples of this type. Call the first group *vertical notions*. Call the second group *horizontal notions*. All these notions have some legitimacy and use. They are not in themselves in competition with one another.

I believe that the root notions are the vertical ones. The narrow conceptions of objectivity as mind-independence and the broader conceptions of objectivity as any real subject matter, or as veridicality, are, I think, more basic than the ones that center on procedure, impersonality, or intersubjectivity. Where we are concerned with the objectivity of representational activities that bear on correctly representing the world, these latter conceptions borrow their force, I think, from the presumption that relevant "horizontal" patterns are conducive to representing a subject matter well.[31] Attempts to explain vertical conceptions in terms of horizontal conceptions are idealist.

A second important division among conceptions of objectivity lies within the vertical conceptions. Some vertical conceptions concern subject matter. Others concern relations of representations to subject matter. The latter require that a representation veridically, or rationally, or lawfully represent a subject matter. For example, a perceptual representation might successfully represent a body as a body and thereby count as objective. Here the subject-matter vertical conceptions

---

[30] Thomas Nagel, *The View from Nowhere* (Oxford: Oxford University Press, 1986), 5.

[31] I have not discussed conceptions of objectivity that appeal to epistemic warrant. A representation can count as objective if it is warranted or, more narrowly, warranted and true. Depending on the account of warrant, such conceptions can count as either (partly) vertical or purely horizontal. I think that any legitimate conception of warrant must partly depend on vertical conceptions explained in terms of veridicality (truth or correctness). Warrant is, I think, objective partly but constitutively because it entails conduciveness to truth, even though not every warranted representation is true. Similar points apply to the particular type of warrant involved in rationality. See my 'Perceptual Entitlement', *Philosophy and Phenomenological Research* 67 (2003), 503–548.

are explanatorily more basic than the relation-to-subject-matter vertical conceptions. The latter are constitutively explained in terms of the former, and not vice versa.

As I have indicated, the requirement of veridicality can be supplemented by some requirement that the representation reflect a standpoint or a method that is not necessarily special to a particular mind.[32] Most of the more interesting conceptions along this line are again explained in terms of some relation to veridicality.

I asked,

What does it take for an individual to represent the physical world objectively? What are minimum constitutive conditions necessary for an individual to represent the physical environment in such a way as to attribute, sometimes accurately, specific physical attributes to physical particulars?[33]

I take the physical world itself to be an objective subject matter. As noted, I assume that idealism is mistaken and that some aspects of the physical world are constitutively mind-independent. As a subject matter for empirical representation, these are the aspects that will be most prominent. But colors and bodies of animals with minds are elements in the physical world that are relevant physical *representata*. I assume that they are an objective subject matter at least on the second, constitutively non-perspectival conception of objectivity. The exact nature of various elements in the physical world will not be of great importance. For the most part, the reader can take 'physical world' in an entirely intuitive, common-sense way.

I believe that the constitutively non-perspectival aspects of the world (whether physical or abstract-mathematical) are not any *more* real than artworks that *are* constitutively perspectival, or than constitutively perspectival thoughts, intentions, conscious sensations, emotions, and perceptions. So I regard the most liberal conception of subject-matter objectivity (*all that is real*) as the most useful conception in broad attempts to understand the "world". These issues

---

[32] I believe that this requirement is additional, and applies primarily to the broad conceptions. Thus, given that pain is a real subject matter, a first-person attribution like I am in pain might count as an objective representation without the requirement, but fail to count as objective with the requirement. For the first-person attribution I am in pain is necessarily from a standpoint on a particular pain that is available only to the individual who has the pain. In the case of the narrow conceptions, the requirement that the mode of representation reflect a standpoint or a method that is not necessarily special to particular minds is often implicit in the requirement that the representation attribute properties (as such) that are mind-independent. Thus a perception of and as of a physical body to the left involves a general standpoint that another perceiver could in principle have on the same subject matter, if another perceiver were in the same position with respect to the subject matter.

[33] I do not say 'represent physical bodies as physical bodies', because I think that at primitive levels of perceptual representation, there is representation of physical bodies as bodies, even though the perceptual system lacks the representational content physical. Bodies *are* physical, but the perceiver lacks anything as general as the attributive physical and lacks any attributive for a contrast class (for example, mental or abstract).

will not, however, be central here. I am primarily interested in primitive empirical veridical representation of *physical* entities in the environment.

The occurrence of 'represent the physical world objectively' in my question must be understood very specifically. One condition packed into this phrase is that the representation be objective in the broad sense that it be a veridical, or approximately veridical, representation (of the physical world).[34]

So representing objectively is, for our purposes, representing veridically. One of the points at issue will be whether objective representation in this sense *must* represent the physical environment by representing mental matters. My view is, firmly, negative. Since the representational content of elementary representation of the physical environment will be in question, I want to pose the question without prejudging the issue. So any representation that veridically refers to, indicates, or attributes physical entities counts as veridical representation of the physical world.

A second condition is packed into the phrase 'represent the physical world objectively' in the questions that opened Chapter 1. The representations, or representational contents, that I am concerned with meet two conditions: (1) they succeed in representing actual physical entities, and (2) they represent physical entities in such a way that, given that the representational content is successfully representational, the content *entails* that the attributes are in fact physical.

Condition (2) does not require that the representation have the very content is physical or represent anything as physical. I am interested in representation of the physical environment by beings that may lack the abstraction capabilities implicit in the representational content is physical. Such beings might have a representational content like is a body. Is a body successfully represents a physical kind, and, since being a body entails being physical, its content entails that it indicates something physical if it indicates anything. (At any rate, I understand 'body' in that way.) Similarly, a veridical specification of a physical property in the form the space-occupying cause of these sense data entails an indication of a physical attribute (*space-occupying cause*) and a reference to a physical particular (the particular cause). The indication would, if it were assumed to be veridical, entail that a physical entity is represented. For being a space-occupying cause entails being physical. In each case—is a body and the space-occupying cause of these sense data—use of the representational content *represents the physical world objectively* in the way required by the questions that opened Chapter 1.

---

[34] In the philosophical traditions that I will discuss, it is sometimes held that individuals have physical-object representation, but that such representation bears little systematic relation to the physical attributes in the world. Such representation is not objective representation. Other traditions maintain that we "represent" the physical world only in the sense that we represent a structurally analogous array of entities that are entirely mind-dependent. Such representation is not objective representation of the physical world, because it is not even approximately veridical.

By contrast, a specification like <u>Cousin Bette's favorite property</u> does not *entail* that the relevant property, if any, is physical—even if Cousin Bette's favorite property were in fact physical. The representational content does not entail that the relevant property is physical. Similarly, condition (2) rules out representational contents like <u>the cause of this representation</u>. Even if all causes and all representational states were physical, this content would not *entail* this fact, as a matter of its meaning or content.

The point is that all parties to the discussion are interested in giving an account of elementary forms of physical-property- (physical-kind-, physical-relation-) attributions.

In summary, my initial question can be paraphrased:

> What does it take for an individual to engage in empirical representation that veridically (accurately) represents a physical subject matter and that has a representational content that entails that the attributed properties, relations, or kinds are physical if they exist at all?

I assume that the physical world is an objective subject matter on one or both of the first two conceptions of subject-matter objectivity. It is mind-independent or constitutively non-perspectival.

Again, I am *not* asking what it takes to have a representation with the very content <u>objective subject matter</u>, or <u>physical subject matter</u>, or <u>mind-independent subject matter</u>. Many of the beings that I am interested in lack any representational contents remotely so sophisticated. I am interested in representations with contents like <u>spherical body</u>, <u>red</u>, or <u>to the left of that body</u>.

PARTICULARS, ATTRIBUTES, PROPERTIES, RELATIONS, KINDS

Let us return to some of our questions:

> More specifically, what are minimum constitutive conditions necessary for an individual to represent the physical environment in such a way as to attribute specific physical attributes to physical particulars? What conditions must be met if an individual is to represent particulars in the physical environment as having such attributes as sizes, shapes, locations, distances, motions, colors, textures, and kinds like being a body? What psychological and environmental resources are needed if such representation is to be possible?

What are particulars, attributes, characteristics, properties, relations, kinds?

Particulars are non-shareable, non-repeatable, non-multi-realizable entities. Fido and a given spherical body are particulars. Redness, being-to-the-left-of, being spherical, and moving are not particulars—since they can be shared or realized by different particulars. I will be primarily concerned with *concrete particulars*, particulars in time. The number 3 and the null set can be considered abstract particulars, but I will not make use of such considerations.

Particulars may be individuals like Fido or events like the explosion of a bomb at a given time. They may also be *tropes* or *instantiations* (*instances*) of properties or relations. Thus the instance of redness on the surface of a wall, or the instance of sphericity in the moving body, counts as a particular. Particulars may also be instances of relations. Thus the instance of the relation *larger-than* that holds between two particular bodies can count as a particular.

Some philosophers maintain that the only particulars, or more liberally the only concrete particulars, are bodies, masses, and events. They reject the existence of property- and relation instances. I think that in the theory of perception, allowance of instances of such attributes is theoretically fruitful. I do not, however, care to fight this battle. Those who reject such entities can translate my locutions into their favored idioms.

I use '*attribute*' (the noun) as a generic term to cover properties, relations, and kinds, including elements and substance-kinds.

I use '*property*' and '*characteristic*' interchangeably. Properties are shareable aspects of particulars, or—at a higher level—of properties, relations, or kinds. Properties are aspects of single entities. *Relations* hold or fail to hold between, or among, more than one entity. Thus, intuitively, sphericity is a property; and being-bigger-than is a relation.[35]

The distinction often depends on one's level of analytical or ontological rigor. Tallness is intuitively a property, but, on closer reflection, tallness is seen to be relative to a comparison class. Speaking intuitively, tallness is a property of Shaquille O'Neal. But, speaking more analytically, Shaquille O'Neal is tall for a human being but not tall for an upright physical body on earth. I sometimes use 'property' to cover what are, at some levels of analysis, relations as well as properties. Mostly, I make the distinction in an intuitive way, without resting any great ontological weight on the distinction.

Properties and relations come in levels of generality. The property *scarlet* is a subspecies of the property *red*, and the property *red* is a subspecies of the property *colored*. The relation *being-a-cousin-of* is a subspecies of the relation *being-kin-to*.

Kinds are intuitively basic demarcations of entities. Thus being a dog is the kind of individual that Fido instantiates. Being brown is a property of Fido.

Like properties and relations, kinds can group or categorize at different levels of generality or abstraction. Thus being a mammal and being a living creature are also kinds that Fido instantiates. Being a perception as of a spherical body, being a perception as of a body, and being a perception are kinds of psychological state at different levels of generality or abstraction.

A kind is a demarcation that cannot change easily, or cannot change at all, while the entity that is an instance of the kind remains the same. Thus Fido could turn grey or gain weight, but he could not—at least could not easily—remain Fido and not be a dog or mammal. Moreover, what it is to be Fido is to be explicated in

---

[35] I take identity to be a property, although there are *representations* of identity that have relational form. '*Feature*' is a non-technical term that is often approximately equivalent with 'attribute'.

terms of his being a dog and being a mammal. Sometimes kinds are counted as basic or fundamental properties. Again, rigorous ontological issues will not be foremost in my account. So I use the term 'kind' in a relaxed, intuitive way, without insisting on deep metaphysical consequences. Certain kinds play a relatively central role in explanation. Such kinds will be of special interest.

'*Entity*' is a catch-all ontological term. It applies to particulars (concrete or abstract), attributes, and whatever else there is.

RESOURCES AND CONDITIONS

My initial questions 'what does it take?', 'what resources are needed?', 'what conditions must be met?' are intentionally vague at this stage.

I am interested in two kinds of resources or conditions as answers to these questions. The most obvious kind concerns psychological resources or psychological conditions. I ask what sorts of psychological, particularly representational, resources an individual constitutively must have in order to represent the physical environment as having specific physical properties. Must an individual know certain things in order to represent the physical environment? Must an individual represent something else in order to represent the physical environment? What sorts of psychological abilities must attend, or be integral to, perception and perceptual belief?

More specific questions are as follows. To perceive particular bodies as bodies, must an individual have beliefs about bodies? What sort of capacity to represent spatial relations is necessary? Does perception of the physical environment depend on perception of a more basic kind—perception of appearances, for example? Must an individual be able to represent mistakes about the physical environment to represent it successfully? Is language necessary for perceptual representation of bodies or spatial relations as such?

The other kind of resource or condition has to do with relations between the individual and the individual's environment. By understanding something about the role of environmental conditions, one is in a better position to understand what psychological conditions must also be met. As intimated in Chapter 1, fuller understanding of the role of individual–environment relations in objective representation might lead one to recognize that fewer or different psychological abilities are necessary for objectification.

For example, if the specific properties in the environment play a role in determining the representational contents of an individual's perception or perceptual belief, there may be less pressure to require that the individual be able to describe or know about the distinguishing features of what the individual represents in order to represent it. Suppose that an individual's having the concept body constitutively depends on the individual's systematic interaction with bodies, including perceptual discrimination of bodies from other relevant types of entities in the environment. Then it may appear less exigent to require, as a condition on representing bodies as such, that an individual have a criterion for when bodies, in general, are the same or different.

I am interested in knowing at what stages of psychological development particular types of animals have or fail to have primitive sorts of objective representation. And I am interested in knowing what species are capable of objectivity and what species are not.

These empirical questions figure in the discussion. My primary questions are, however, more general. When I ask what sorts of conditions must be met, or what resources are needed, I am asking a *constitutive* question—a question about constitutive conditions and about natures.

CONSTITUTIVE CONDITIONS AND NATURES

Constitutive questions are a subset of what in common parlance are known as 'conceptual' questions. Some philosophers whom I discuss take the questions as conceptual in a narrower sense. They ask, what psychological resources must an individual have if it is to be *intelligible* that the individual empirically represents an objective subject matter objectively? I am sceptical of such approaches, and of correlative claims of inconsistency or unintelligibility.

Even so, the questions that I am asking have a certain priority. They underlie and are more basic than the questions about development and species. Investigating these latter questions can shift one's understanding of the former. Empirical investigation often shows that putative answers to conceptual questions (even questions purportedly conceptual in the stricter senses) are mistaken. Still, whether a child represents the physical environment in an objective way depends on what it is to represent the environment in an objective way. This 'what it is' question is a constitutive question.

A constitutive question concerns necessary (or sufficient, or necessary and sufficient) conditions under which something is what it is. Such a question concerns conditions under which something has the *nature* that it has. As I conceive them, natures are approximately essences. I want, however, to push to the background many of the traditional metaphysical questions about essence.

Natures are associated with fundamental, or relatively fundamental, kinds or properties that have the potential to figure in systematic explanations. What counts as a relatively fundamental explanatory kind must be determined in the rough and tumble of explanation. Gerrymandered kinds, such as *being green or being divisible by 13*, are not relatively fundamental. Kinds that are adventitious, such as *being the nearest tree to Uncle Harry when he sang 'Die Fiorelle'*, are not relatively fundamental. Kinds like *mess* or *list* are not relatively fundamental. The natures I discuss are of obvious explanatory interest.

A constitutive question asks for necessary or sufficient conditions for something's being what it is or having the nature that it has. The relevant conditions are, however, a subset of all such necessary and sufficient conditions. To be an answer to a constitutive question, the answer must help *explain* something's having the nature that it has. Citing a relevant condition must aid in understanding something's nature.

The conditions cited in such answers need not be *parts* of the nature. The explanation that the cited conditions serve may be quite different from the explanation that the nature, or the explanatory kind, might serve.

The nature of a tree is being a tree, being a plant, being a living thing, and so on. The nature of a perception as of something's being spherical is being a perception as of something's being spherical, being a perceptual state, and so on. These answers as to what it is to be something are relatively straightforward. But the answers can grow more interesting. Natures can include conditions that constitute the kind, constitute what the kind "really is". For example, some type of DNA sequences, with allowances for certain variations, might help constitute what it is to be a tree. Being a physical object, developed to a certain stage, with such a DNA profile, might be what being a tree "really is".

Reductive explanations of this sort are, I think, fairly rare in science. Even in science, controversy attends most attempted reductive explanations. The just-sketched explanation regarding the nature of a tree is a case in point.

We have no reductive explanation for what it is to be a perception as of something's being spherical, or for what it is to represent something in an objective way. I do not expect such explanations. I will initially assume and later argue that, as far as we can now tell, psychological kinds are explanatorily primitive, in the sense that specifications of them are not exhaustively reducible in scientific or other explanatory enterprises to specifications that are not distinctive of psychology. In such cases, explanation makes reference to the natures—employs reference to natures in its law-like principles. There need not always be a further scientific explanation of the natures themselves.

Constitutive questions about psychological states can nevertheless remain interesting, even though the answers are not likely to provide illuminating reductive substitutes for ordinary specifications of the natures being asked about. To be an instance of a kind or to have a nature, something must meet certain collateral *constitutive conditions*. These are conditions that are necessary, sufficient, or necessary and sufficient to be something of that kind or with that nature, and that are in principle potentially relevant to explaining, understanding, illuminating the kind or nature. Of course, the kind or nature, and the associated constitutive conditions, are what they are independently of any actual explanations or understanding. The point is that constitutive conditions bear sufficiently directly on the natures being what they are that such conditions can ground explanation and understanding.

What it is to explain or illuminate in this context must be left somewhat open. I assume that for an animal's objective representation to be possible, the atmosphere in which the animal lives must be within a certain range of temperatures; there must be certain types of protein synthesis and transfer in the animal's body; and so on. These conditions do not count as constitutive. They are causally relevant. They may even be metaphysically necessary conditions. But they do not illuminate the nature of objective representation in the right way. Saying something about the difference between an animal's perception and a plant's sensitivity to light, on the other hand, might help illumine what perceptual representation is, and therefore what objective empirical representation is. Or saying something about whether perception must be accompanied by a capacity for belief, or by a capacity to represent laws, might illuminate the nature of perception or objectivity. Or showing that something could not possibly be a psychological state that represents sphericality, unless instances of the psychological system in which the state occurs had entered into causal relations with three-dimensional bodies, might illumine the nature of representation of shape.

The 'could not possibly' is not a point about biological necessity or evolution. The point concerns a stronger type of necessity, one that bears on our very understanding of the relevant nature or kind. The claim about necessity tends not to be a matter of analysis of concepts or of definitions. In this respect, it is rarely if ever 'conceptual' in a narrow sense, much less definitional. Sometimes such a claim is apriori warranted. That is, sometimes its epistemic warrant does not make reference to empirical sources. The warrant may be grounded in reflection or understanding alone—even though the reflection is not just a matter of analysis of internal conceptual structure. On the other hand, answers to constitutive questions, even those that are "philosophical" and "armchair", often have empirical warrants.

Constitutive questions often have the generality, elusiveness, and difficulty of philosophical questions. They are commonly different from scientific questions. But I know of no sharp, general distinction between constitutive questions and questions asked by empirical science. Fortunately, progress does not depend on explaining the nature of constitutive questions in advance. Whether an answer is constitutive and illuminating must be determined in philosophical back and forth. I think that readers can recognize constitutive, illuminating answers when presented with them. I hope that what follows will elicit such recognition.

SUMMARY

When I ask, 'what does it take for an individual to represent the physical world objectively?', I am asking what conditions must be in place if an individual is to engage in accurate, empirical representation of an ordinary macro-physical subject matter. The accuracy must involve indicating and attributing some of the central physical attributes that the subject matter in fact has, and doing so in such a way as to entail the physicality of those attributes. The objectivity of such representation lies not only in its accuracy and its specifying relevant attributes in a way that entails their physicality. It also lies in the physical subject matter's being mind-independent, or at least constitutively non-perspectival. The *conditions* that I am primarily concerned with are psychological and environmental conditions that are constitutive. They are conditions that must be in place if the relevant representation is to be possible, and that help make the relevant representation what it is.

Before discussing Individual Representationalism in detail, I next sketch basic outlines of anti-individualism.

3 *Anti-Individualism*

The philosophical standpoint that underlies my rejection of Individual Representationalism is *anti-individualism*. In general form, this standpoint is compatible with some types of Individual Representationalism. In the specific form that it takes through reflecting on *perception*, anti-individualism is incompatible with all types.

Anti-individualism is a view about constitutive conditions for individuals to be in certain representational states. It is not specifically about conditions for objective representation. Many mental states whose constitutive conditions it is concerned with, however, do represent an objective (mind-independent or constitutively non-perspectival) subject matter objectively (veridically). By reflecting on anti-individualism in both general and specific forms, one better understands origins of objectivity.

ANTI-INDIVIDUALISM: WHAT IT IS

In its general form, anti-individualism is the claim that

(A) the natures of many mental states constitutively depend on relations between a subject matter beyond the individual and the individual that has the mental states, where relevant relations help determine specific natures of those states.

It follows from (A) that *being in* many mental states constitutively depends on relations between an individual and a subject matter beyond the individual.

I am primarily interested here in mental states that represent the physical environment empirically. Adapted to these cases, anti-individualism claims that

(A′) The natures of mental states that empirically represent the physical environment depend constitutively on relations between specific aspects of the environment and the individual, including causal relations, which are not in themselves representational; the relevant environment–individual relations help determine specific natures of the states.

Unless context indicates otherwise, 'mental state' is a catch-all term for mental states (properly so-called), mental events, mental acts, and mental capacities, abilities, competencies. The view that I am discussing specifically concerns *representational* mental states, those that function to "be about" something—those that have veridicality conditions.[1]

There are disputes over whether all mental states are representational. The disputes hinge partly on what is meant by 'representational'. It is *un*disputed that the states that I discuss—beliefs, perceptions, and so on—are representational. They are naturally regarded as *constitutively* representational. By their natures, they function to represent-as.

(A′) notes that causation is a *non-representational relation*. I mean merely that causal relations are not representational simply by virtue of being causal, although causation is a constitutive aspect of some representational relations, like perceptual reference. Examples of *representational relations* between a mental state and a subject matter are *reference, indication, being veridical of*.[2]

Recall our notion <u>nature</u>. Natures are kinds that potentially ground fundamental, or relatively fundamental, explanation. An example of a mental-state nature is a belief that aluminum makes foil—a different kind of mental state from a belief that water is translucent. I write 'kinds that potentially ground relatively *fundamental* explanation' because I am interested in kinds that are relevant to non-trivial explanations. A belief held by men weighing more than 200 pounds is perhaps a kind of mental state. It does *not* ground relatively fundamental explanation.

I rest little weight on 'fundamental'. There are different dimensions of interest, different explanatory purposes. I allow natures to be *relatively* fundamental because I do not want to wrangle over whether natures are absolutely basic

---

[1] In framing these principles, I do not count among *mental states* factive states like knowing, or other states like (veridical) seeing or (veridical) remembering whose specifications necessitate in each instance representational success. The standard specification of such states *entails*—as a matter of the most elementary and superficial understanding—truth, veridicality, or some relation, such as perceptual reference, to the environment. Knowing something entails that it is true. Seeing something entails perceptually referring to it and being causally related to it. Anti-individualism is *trivially* true of such states. For truth entails relations to the environment; seeing and reference *are* relations to the environment. There are reasons to count as mental states in the strictest sense only states whose standard specifications do not entail representational success in each instance. These are states like belief and having a memory or perception *as of*. By contrast, states like knowing and (veridical) seeing are partly mental or psychological (knowledge involves belief, seeing entails having a perceptual state as of). But they have other aspects as well. One reason for not grouping them with ordinary mental states, or thinking of them as analytically prior to ordinary mental states, is that explanations in psychology center on kinds of psychological states that do not entail veridicality. The point is very clear in perceptual psychology, the most developed psychological science. The factive-type states are explanatorily less fundamental in psychology (though they are motivationally central for epistemology). See my 'Disjunctivism and Perceptual Psychology', especially note 28. The present discussion does not hinge on whether one includes factives and similar states among the mental states. Including the factives and factive-like states under the thesis is harmless, as long as it is understood that the thesis does not apply only or primarily to them.

[2] Some causal relations that are constitutively necessary to specific kinds of representational states have a representational state as one of their relata. Others are causal relations between relata neither of which is a representational state or event—for example, causal relations between an entity in the environment and a surface sensory receptor, or between a non-representational act of an individual and some entity in the environment. Causal relations *in themselves* are not representational: they are not relational by virtue of being causal.

according to some strict canon. I do think of natures as being as basic as kinds get. I am interested in kinds that ground serious explanatory enterprises. I believe that these kinds are objectively fundamental, explanatorily primitive.[3]

I think that representational psychological states are explanatory kinds that cannot be reduced to any others. For present purposes, it is enough to assume that they are not *obviously* reducible, or dispensable.

Anti-individualism contributes to understanding *what it is* to be a given kind (or instance of a kind) of mental state and what it is to be *in* a mental state.

As indicated in Chapter 2, natures can be taken to be essences. I use the less fraught term 'natures', because I think it unnecessary to take a strong position on the metaphysics of natures or kinds. One might think of the 'what it is' enterprise as the most fundamental philosophical account of mental states, whatever the metaphysical status that that account has. I intend the notion of a nature of a mental state to be compatible with common-sense ideas about when kinds of mental states are the same or different, and about what kinds are central in explanatory and descriptive enterprises.

Anti-individualism claims that the natures of many mental states are *constitutively dependent* on relations to the environment. I will not try to define the notions of nature and constitutive dependence. I will elicit understanding through explication and example.

It is not to be assumed that constitutive dependence is one-way. Frequently, dependence is reciprocal. For example, being an individual with representational mental states is constitutively dependent on having a memory that can re-employ some of those mental states.[4] There are circularities here. They are not vicious. For the explications of constitutive dependencies are not intended as definitions or reductions of the natures whose dependencies are being elucidated.

---

[3] When I say, here or elsewhere, that certain terms or concepts are *explanatorily primitive*, I mean that they have genuine explanatory uses and that the explanations that they serve cannot be reduced, without remainder, to other explanations that lack the terms or concepts. Some reductions in science do succeed in showing that certain theories, terms, or concepts are convenient but explanatorily reducible. Their explanatory and descriptive work can, in principle, be *completely* taken over by theories in other terms. Explanations in terms of heat seem to be thus reducible. They were reduced, seemingly without remainder, to explanations that appeal to motion of particles. If so, 'heat' is not explanatorily primitive. Being explanatorily primitive in this sense does not mean that the term or theory can provide full explanatory understanding without supplement. For example, most biological terms and theories are not explanatorily reducible without remainder to terms and theories in chemistry or physics, though perhaps a few biological concepts have been. (The fact that biological entities are all made up of physical entities does not show that biology is reducible to physics.) On the other hand, a full understanding of biology depends on supplementary explanations in chemistry or physics. I believe that representational elements in psychology are not reducible, without remainder, to other terms or concepts—and that theories that cite representational states are not reducible without remainder to theories that do not. Obviously, this point does not imply that psychology can operate in a vacuum, without supplement from other sciences. The notion of explanatory primitiveness hinges on a technical, if generic, conception of reduction. Constitutive explications or explanations of psychological kinds are rarely, if ever, types of reduction.

[4] For more on this matter, see my 'Memory and Persons', *The Philosophical Review* 112 (2003), 289–337.

Constitutive dependence is to be distinguished from causal dependence. It is trivial that many mental states causally depend on relations between environment and individual. Acquiring such states depends on being caused to have them. Constitutive dependence is dependence that figures in determining a nature. It is dependence that bears on the natures or constitution of mental states, on what it is to be, or be in, such states. Constitutive dependence is indicated in explanations, or explications, of the natures of mental states.

There is a modal claim here. If the nature of a mental state constitutively depends on certain relations to the environment, it is impossible to be in that mental state, if the relevant relations are not in place. The impossibility is stronger than causal impossibility. It goes more deeply into our understanding of how mental states and representation must, to be what they are, be connected to other things. Even construed non-causally, the modal claim is not all there is to constitutive dependence.

Constitutive dependence is stronger than causal dependence, nomically necessary dependence, and metaphysically necessary dependence. Constitutive dependence implies metaphysically necessary dependence, but is a yet stronger relation.

Constitutive dependence figures in explanations of the nature, essence, or "whatness" of the relevant mental states. Some necessities do not. It is necessary of every mental state that either the state is in a world in which $2+2=4$ or it is made of sheep's cheese (since necessarily every mental state is in a world in which $2+2=4$). It is necessary of every mental state that it is not a number or a mountain. These necessities are not referred to in explanation of the nature of any mental state. They are not constitutive necessities or constitutive dependencies.

A more delicate point applies to constitutive dependence. To say that the nature of a mental state constitutively depends on relations to an environment is not to say that the mental state *is* or 'contains' a relation to the environment. The relations need not be *part* of the structure or nature of the mental state. It is enough that they be cited in a correct explanation of conditions necessary for the state to be what it is.

Anti-individualism *per se* does *not* claim that mental states *are* relations to the environment, or that mental states are not in the head, or that entities in the environment are part of the mental state or of the state's representational content.[5] I reject these claims. Mental-state kinds ground psychological

---

[5] Hilary Putnam popularized the slogan 'Meaning ain't in the head' in 'The Meaning of "Meaning"', in K. Gunderson (ed.) *Language, Mind and Knowledge*, Minnesota Studies in the Philosophy of Science VII (Minneapolis: University of Minnesota Press, 1975); reprinted in *Philosophical Papers*, ii (Cambridge: Cambridge University Press, 1975). Although the slogan is colorful, I think it deeply misleading, and in fact based on confusion and error. Representational content is abstract, and thus not anywhere. Moreover, nothing in anti-individualism—or in what Putnam himself successfully argued—implies that states or events marked by representational content cannot be in the head. See the discussion of hearts and tectonic plates immediately below in the text. I criticize some of the confusions and errors in 'Other Bodies', in A. Woodfield (ed.), *Thought and Object* (London: Oxford University Press, 1982), reprinted in *Foundations of Mind*. For further

explanations. Most constitutive relations between the individual and the environment are not kinds that are cited in psychological or other scientific explanations. Still, they are relevant to a constitutive explanation of an individual's being in specific psychological states.

Individuals' mental states and events themselves do not have a location that would be surprising to common sense. They are not themselves outside the individual. Nor are they relations to things outside the individual. *Versions* of anti-individualism claim that mental states are not in the head, or are just relations to the environment. I regard these versions as incorrect. The thesis does not depend on any such claims.

In large measure, explaining constitutive conditions of natures or kinds is a philosophical enterprise. Philosophers have a special and persistent stake in it. But the enterprise is not exclusively for philosophers. Most intellectuals, including scientists, have a sense for what the enterprise is; and many make claims within it.

Let me give some examples of constitutive conditions. What it is to be a physical being is partly to occupy space, and also perhaps to have such properties as force or mass. What it is to be water is partly to be made up of hydrogen and oxygen. The kind oxygen is constitutively associated with having a certain number of electrons, protons, and neutrons. Life is constitutively associated with a capacity for reproduction and for carrying on certain functions. Being a heart constitutively involves functioning to pump blood in a circulatory system. Being an ape constitutively involves having certain DNA. Being a tool has something to do with being meant or used for some purpose. Being a prime number is being a natural number and not being divisible without remainder by other natural numbers except 1. Having knowledge constitutively requires having true belief. Being a moral person bears some constitutive relation to having good motives and acting well with respect to living beings, especially persons—and constitutively depends on a world in which change is possible. To be in a representational mental state is partly to be in a state that can be veridical or non-veridical.

Some of these constitutive points have been discovered by a science. They are certainly not all "philosophical" points. Philosophy does have a special interest in constitutive explanations—explanations of what it is to be a certain kind, or of constitutive conditions for being a certain kind. Some kinds, or classes of kinds, are of special interest to philosophy. In this work, the relevant kinds are representational mental states, especially perceptual states.

Anti-individualism about mental states that represent, or that represent as of, entities in the physical environment claims that what it is to be such states

---

criticisms, see Robert Stalnaker, 'On What is in the Head', in J. E. Tomberlin (ed.), *Philosophical Perspectives, 3: Philosophy of Mind and Action Theory* (Atascadero, CA: Ridgeview, 1989), 187–216. Putnam's mistake may also derive from a misinformed view of perception. See note 23 in Chapter 5 below.

constitutively depends partly on causal relations between specific aspects of the environment and the individual that is in those states. I want now to remark on the role of *relations*, particularly causal relations, in the constitutive account of the natures of mental states. I lead up to the case of mental states by discussing other examples.

Constitutive accounts are often thought of as centering on the *intrinsic* constitution of a kind of thing. We think of the nature of oxygen as depending purely on the atomic structure of the oxygen atom. It is easy to have the intuition that this structure can be fully understood without invoking relations between the atom and anything beyond it.

I think that this intuition is nearly always mistaken. One must reflect on what is required for this "intrinsic" structure. Even in the oxygen case, the component parts of the structure, the protons, neutrons, and electrons, constitutively depend on properties like force and mass. These properties have constitutive relational implications. The constitutive structure of the atom also depends on spatial relations. What it is to be a spatial relation depends partly on relational structure that goes beyond the atom's interior.

Not all constitutive accounts of natures or kinds seem, even initially, to be as "intrinsic" as those involving chemical structure. What is it to be a heart? It is constitutively necessary that to be a heart, an organ must have the function of pumping blood through a circulatory system. Pumping blood functions to nourish the organism's body. Anything that lacked these functions could not be a heart. Having these functions entails bearing relations—in normal conditions—to blood, blood vessels, and the rest of the organism's body, outside the heart's boundaries. The relations figure in explanation of what it is to be a heart.

Note that the relations to these other entities are not part of the internal structure of the heart. Nor is the heart itself a relation. Thus the nature of the heart is constitutively dependent for being what it is on relations to things beyond it. But the heart itself has a structure that is not made up of those relations. I think that representational mind is like that.

Let us take another example. Tectonic plates are what they are only by virtue of bearing relations to a wider geological environment.[6] If the plates were not in causal relations to other plates and to forces within the earth, they would not be plates. If the plates were never spatially related to other geological masses, or masses over which they slide and into which they bump, they would not be plates. What it is to be a tectonic plate is constitutively dependent partly on bearing relations to other things.

The plates are not themselves these relations. They have an internal structure. Each plate must be a relatively rigid, coherent mass, if it is to be a tectonic plate.

---

[6] The example comes from my 'Individuation and Causation in Psychology', *Pacific Philosophical Quarterly* 70 (1989), 303–322, reprinted in *Foundations of Mind*. Similar examples can be given for planets, electron orbits in an atom, cell nuclei, and so on. The points about location that follow apply to all these examples.

Still, being a tectonic plate is constitutively dependent on a plate's bearing relations to things beyond its boundaries.

Anti-individualism claims that the natures of many mental states depend constitutively on relations between the individual in those states and other things. The natures of many mental states can be constitutively explained only by reference to a wider environment or subject matter. As with hearts and plates, mental states constitutively bear *relations* to things beyond them.

As with the heart and tectonic plates, no part of the structure of the mental states themselves is outside the individual in the wider environment. Mental states are not themselves relations to the environment.[7] The structures of mental states include the structures of their representational contents.[8] *These* structural features are not only constitutive. They are aspects, 'parts', of the states' natures.[9] The representational content of a belief and its structural elements are aspects of the nature of the belief (in addition to the belief's being a belief, as opposed to a hope or supposition). They are part of what it is to be that mental state. Psychological explanation makes explanatory use of these structures.

Anti-individualism is compatible with several positions on the mind–body problem. Certainly, mental states do not float free of underlying physical states. They are located where the individual who has the mental states is. Their *loci* in causal transactions are where common sense and empirical psychology take them to be. Analogies to hearts and tectonic plates are again worth bearing in mind. The fact that these kinds constitutively depend on relations to entities beyond their boundaries is fully compatible with hearts' and tectonic plates' being localized in space. They are not located where the relations, or the other entities to which they are constitutively related, are.

Anti-individualism as applied to empirical mental states that are as of physical entities claims that such states constitutively could not be the kinds they are if specific causal relations did not hold between the environment and the individual that is in those kinds of states.

As prelude to elaborating anti-individualism further, I will discuss the following principle, which I accept:

---

[7] We do speak of believing *of* a particular that it is such and such. Such talk suggests hybrids. The hybrids consist of the particular believed of and a mental state, usually only partially specified, that refers to the particular. These hybrids play some role in common-sense explanations. But they are less prominent in scientific explanations that seek laws or law-like patterns. The mental state is fundamentally a belief not a believing of. Similarly, genuine mental states are veridical or non-veridical, not merely veridical-of or non-veridical-of.

[8] In some cases, it may include qualitative aspects of mind. Some hold that it includes a neural or other physical basis for the mental states.

[9] In my view, these structural aspects or "parts" of the mental states' natures, such as the propositional contents and propositional structures, are themselves dependent for being what they are on there being relations to a subject matter beyond the individual, and on relations to other representational states. Thus not all, and perhaps in the end not any, of these structural features are 'intrinsic' in the strongest sense. Here too, I think it important to distinguish the natures that constitutively depend on relations from the relations themselves. They differ in the explanatory enterprises that they ground.

(B) For an individual to have any representational state (such as a belief or perception) as of a subject matter, that state must be associated with some *veridical* representational states that bear referential, indicational, and attributional representational relations to a suitably related subject matter.

The key claim of (B) is that having *any* representational states requires bearing certain "associational" relations to some *veridical* representational states. The idea behind (B) is an analog of the common idea that *successful* realization of a function forms a basis for understanding the function, and for understanding failures in realizing the function. To understand a hammer's function of pounding nails, one focuses on poundings, not on misses or on uses of hammers to decorate walls.

(B) is a very abstract thesis. Possible types of association are various. Although a 'suitably related subject matter' can be particulars or attributes that the initial representational state represents, it need not be. I begin with the latter point.

In the thought phlogiston figures in burning, the concept phlogiston lacks a *representatum* altogether.[10] To have the thought, an individual must bear certain relations to other thoughts or perceptions that are veridical and that bear representational relations to the physical environment. Since the environment includes neither the kind *phlogiston* nor instances of the kind, the "associated" veridical states (distinct from the thought phlogiston figures in burning) represent a different subject matter. The subject matter includes entities like physical bodies, events of burning, properties of mass or weight, and so on. A thought phlogiston figures in burning can have its phlogiston content only through relation to veridical representation in other mental states—veridical representation of physical subject matters suitably relevant to attributions as of phlogiston. In this case, there are veridical perceptions and beliefs from which the mistaken theory was inferred and in terms of which the theory was partly explained. Veridical representation involving indication of other attributes (*body*, *burning*, *mass*) forms the constitutive basis for theory involving the concept phlogiston. Psychological states with phlogiston-content are constitutively related, through inference and theory, to veridical representational states regarding relevantly related subject matter. These veridical representational states help ground the representational content phlogiston, even though there is no attribute that is the *representatum* of the concept phlogiston. They do so partly through their representational relations to real entities in the physical environment.

The representational contents of most representational states do have *representata*. In such cases, *veridical* representational states that indicate those *representata* play a constitutive role in enabling those representational states (both veridical and non-veridical ones) to be what they are.

---

[10] Phlogiston theory was a failed seventeenth- and eighteenth-century account of what we now regard as oxidization. It postulated a fire-like substance that was supposed to be released during combustion.

I turn to the notion of *association* in (B). The relations to veridical representation need not be in the psychology of the individual that has the representational states. A novice just learning phlogiston theory from an expert might not know any of the true observations that were used to support the theory, or any other truths relevant to giving the concept of phlogiston a use. The novice has the relevant representational states through communication with others. In such a case, the association with veridical representation that (B) requires consists in relations to the veridical representation in others.

Dependence by one individual on another's veridical representation can be more radical. A perceptual attributive may partly depend for its being the type of attributive that it is on employment in a perceptual system in the system's evolutionary history, before the individual was born. An individual frog might have been given only illusory, non-veridical perceptions as of moving bodies of such and such a size. The frog can have such illusions with such representational content because its perceptual system had evolved from ancestors in which relevant *veridical* perceptions occurred. In this case, it is plausible to think that the ancestral veridical perceptions were of, and as of, moving objects of the relevant size.

The idea of (B) is that representation *as of* is impossible apart from psychological relations, perhaps through a chain of inheritance or communication, to veridical representation of some generically related subject matter.[11]

I believe that principle (B) is necessary and apriori. Constitutive explanation of any representational states depends on their relations to veridical representational states. The principle leaves open which specific types of associational relations to veridical representational states occur, and what suitably related subject matters are.

(B) is closely related to anti-individualism. It is not strictly part of anti-individualism. Anti-individualism is about the role of individual–environmental relations in determining the specific natures, or kinds, of representational states. (B) does not make a claim about natures. It does not require that *specific* relations to the environment help determine the specific natures of representational states. In the cases of empirical mental states that represent as of the physical environment, anti-individualism claims that the environment–individual relations must include some that are not themselves representational relations.

Let us return to principle (A′). I believe that (A′) is necessary and apriori. The principle requires that *empirical* representational states as of the environment constitutively depend partly on entering into environment–individual causal relations. Such relations are constitutively necessary to the type-determination of empirical representational states.

Causal relations are not, by virtue of being causal (or in themselves), representational relations. The relevant constitutive causal relations include specific

---

[11] (B) is closely related to various versions of the principle of charity. See W. V. Quine, *Word and Object* (Cambridge, MA: MIT Press, 1960), ch. 2.

causal relations in which *no factor* in the causal relation is a representational state. In actual perception there are constitutive causal relations between the environment and pre-representational bodily sensors. For example, in vision, light causally affects retinal receptors. Registration of light on those receptors does not itself involve representation. Such causal relations are among the constitutive causal relations that help determine the natures of perceptual states.

I do not claim that it is *apriori* that the causal relations that are constitutively necessary to empirical representational states include causal relations that are fully non-representational. Perhaps we know only empirically that perception is never a relation purely between a subject matter—even a *physical* subject matter—and a disembodied perceiving spirit. I think that if it is empirical, the point is at least obvious. Among the constitutive causal relations in perception are relations between environmental entities, on one hand, and organisms' bodies and pre-perceptual sensory states, on the other. Some of these causal relations figured in the early phylogenetic stages of the formation of perception.

Causal relations that are constitutive to determining empirical representational states can take many forms. They can occur in the life history of the individual or in the evolutionary developmental prehistory of the individual's perceptual system. They can be involved in perception, veridical or not. They can connect the environment to non-veridical perceptual states through other representational (usually other perceptual) states. They can hold together chains of communication among people. They include both the causal impress of the environment on sensory systems and the practical causal actions by individuals on the environment.[12]

I emphasize that causal relations can enter into the constitutive condition for a mental state with a given representational content in quite indirect ways. For example, it is possible to be in a mental state that visually and mistakenly represents a body as having a particular concrete shape (like the jagged ridge of a mountain range), even though nothing even approximating the represented shape ever existed. No instance of that mental-state type ever bore causal relations to instances of that shape type. The mental-state type is what it is because it is systematically related (by psychological law-like patterns embedded in visual shape representation) to other mental states that do bear causal connections to (at least approximate) instances of other shapes.

The phlogiston example discussed earlier is again relevant here.

---

[12] For more on the variety of forms of causal relations, see my 'Perceptual Entitlement'. I emphasize the stimulus effect of the environment on perceptual systems, because this is the type of causation that is most central to empirical explanations of perceptual representation. Perceivers' functional *responses* to the environment are also a constitutive factor in determining perceptual content. Arguments that *action* plays no constitutive role in perception are given by Galen Strawson, *Mental Reality* (Cambridge, MA: MIT Press, 1994), ch. 9. I am not persuaded by these arguments. But I leave open here whether *action* or some broader category of functional response is required. I do think that perceptual content depends partly on use, in a broad sense of 'use'. See Chapter 8 and Chapter 10, the sections PERCEPTION AND ORIGINS OF SPATIAL REPRESENTATION and PERCEPTION AND ORIGINS OF TEMPORAL REPRESENTATION.

As with the *association* with veridical representational states required by (B), the causal relations required by (A') need not occur in an individual's history. An individual can perceptually represent there being a property even if the individual never interacts with any instance of the property, or even any instance within a range of properties that includes the property. Again, a frog could be given illusions as of moving objects by artificial retinal stimulation. It might never visually interact with moving bodies or with any shapes in its physical environment. It can still visually represent there being a moving body. The individual frog's perceptual system yields specific representational contents in response to specific patterns of retinal stimulation because its nature was formed through prior causal relations to the environment in the evolutionary development of the type of visual system that the individual frog has. Antecedent interactions between moving bodies and operations of perceptual mechanisms are central to the explanation of the kinds (primarily the representational content) of perceptual states that the frog has.

Anti-individualism regarding *perception* is an abstract thesis. It claims that a range of non-representational relations, including causal relations, between environment and individual must constitutively be in place, if there are to be perceptual states. Causal interactions with specific elements in the environment must underlie and help in the constitutive explanation of specific perceptual representational states. Anti-individualism allows a wide range of causal relations. It is the task partly of philosophy, but largely of empirical science, to determine their specific characters for specific cases.[13]

In this work, I focus on empirically based mental states. But general anti-individualism (principle (A)) and principle (B) both apply to mathematical beliefs and beliefs in logic. To hold beliefs in pure mathematics, one must have capabilities to form true beliefs about at least some simple aspects of mathematical subject matters, and perhaps other subject matters to which the mathematics applies. The true beliefs depend on relations, primarily semantical relations like reference and being true of. Such subject matters are not in general internal to the individual. I believe that such relations are partly constitutive of the relevant mental states. The *subject matter* is part of the determination of what the mental state is.

---

[13] Principles (A), (A'), and (B) are very general and abstract. They are not intended to be informative about what specific sorts of relations help determine the representational content of specific mental states. The ways in which theory and perception determine representational content (for example, in phlogiston theory) without relying on perceptual or other causal-based relations to *representata* are enormously varied, and probably impossible to codify. An individual can have concepts that *do* have *representata* without the individual's bearing causal relations to the *representata*. Some elements in the periodic table were specified before they were discovered. Even common-sense, kind-concepts such as water or aluminum could in principle be associated, perhaps by aliens, with imaginings and theoretical knowledge that would suffice to fix their content, without any veridical representations of, or causal relations to, *particulars* of which the concept is true. In such cases, representation depends on association with other representational states that are veridical and that bear causal relations to a suitably related subject matter. See the last pages of 'Other Bodies'.

Pure (unapplied) logic and mathematics do not involve *causal* relations to their subject matters. I conjecture that the representational relations themselves are the sole constitutive relations. To think mathematical thoughts, one must get things right about mathematical structures, functions, and objects. There is, however, an asymmetry in the constitutive determination of content: getting things right must be explained in terms of the subject matter—the things gotten right. Some claim that there must be *perceptual* applications of mathematical notions to non-mathematical objects. Perception is certainly necessary for learning mathematics. I do not see that a relation to perception is *constitutively* necessary, much less epistemically necessary, for attitudes in pure mathematics or logic. I do think that thought about mathematical subject matters requires *de re* applications to non-mathematical subject matters. But the entities could be thought events that are not perceived.[14]

A consequence of the claim that being in many mental states constitutively requires that there be relations between those mental states and a subject matter is that, for many mental states, being in them constitutively requires that there *be* a subject matter. This point bears on scepticism. Representational mental states cannot *all* be illusory.

I believe that generalized scepticism about the existence of the physical world postulates a metaphysically impossible situation. The issue about any scepticism is not, however, its modal status. It is not about constitutive conditions. It is about reasons and warrant. Can our warrant to reject scepticism be shown not to beg a reasonable question? This is a complex matter.[15] Grounds for believing anti-individualism are multiform. Some begin with particular cases that rely on empirical assumptions. These assumptions seem to beg the question against a sceptic. Negotiating this territory is a task for another occasion.

Another set of difficulties stands in the way of quickly mobilizing anti-individualism to answer scepticism. Earlier I noted the variety of causal relations that support a type of representational content. The example of phlogiston carries a cautionary tale. Whether a thought with any given representational content is supported by a causal relation to instances of the very sorts that it represents there being, or whether on the contrary it is supported by indirect causal relations that are infected by theory (explicit or implicit), is a question that scepticism can exploit. One must know which type of causal relation a given representational state is supported by, if one is to use anti-individualism to answer the sceptic regarding most specific beliefs. This point certainly applies to empirical beliefs

---

[14] See my 'Five Theses on *De Re* States and Attitudes', in J. Almog and P. Leonardi (eds.), *The Philosophy of David Kaplan* (Oxford: Oxford University Press, 2009), 246–316; and 'Postscript to "Belief *De Re*"', in *Foundations of Mind: Philosophical Essays, Volume 2* (Oxford: Clarendon Press, 2007). Of course, the *de re* applications that figure in the emergence of applied mathematical notions in *de facto* human development are empirical and do concern perceived entities in the environment.

[15] See my 'Some Reflections on Scepticism: Reply to Stroud', in M. Hahn and B. Ramberg (eds.), *Reflections and Replies: Essays on the Philosophy of Tyler Burge* (Cambridge, MA: MIT Press, 2003).

about environmental kinds, as I pointed out many years ago.[16] And one must know which type of causal relation is relevant without begging any reasonable or dialectically open question that a sceptic asks. Not all cases of reference failure, even of kind terms, derive from theory that we are introspectively aware of having constructed.[17]

Thus, although anti-individualism opens new ways to think about the mind–body problem and about scepticism, it does not *by itself* purport to resolve either issue. I say 'just as well', for present purposes. There is enough to do without taking on more.

I have briefly expounded the main notions in anti-individualism. Even more briefly, I have related it to some large philosophical issues. I want now to sketch grounds for believing it to be true.

GENERAL GROUNDS FOR ANTI-INDIVIDUALISM

Representational states are type-individuated partly in terms of their representational contents.[18] That is to say, such states are what they are partly by virtue of their representational contents. A visual perception as of a cylindrical solid is type-individuated as a visual perceptual state, of course. It is also type-individuated in terms of a specific perceptual way of representing cylindrical solidity. A belief that New Orleans is under water is type-individuated in terms of being a belief, and a particular way of thinking of the city New Orleans, a concept for water, and one for the relation *being-under*—all put together into a propositional thought content.

I said *a way* of perceptually representing cylindrical solidity, *a way* of thinking of the city New Orleans, *a concept* of water, and *a concept* of being-under. Ways of representing are representational contents.

As noted in Chapter 2, a perceptual representational content that represents as of a cylindrical solid is more specific than is conveyed in the phrase 'perception as of a cylindrical solid'. For any attribute (or attribute instance) such as solidity or cylindricality, there are many ways to perceive it—many perceptual perspectives on it, even *visual* perspectives on it. Further, for any attribute (kind, property, relation) *A* and for any way of perceiving something as *A*, there are many perceptual perspectives all of which are ways of perceiving something as *A*. For example, one can visually perceive something as being a certain size in numerous ways, depending on whether the size is closer or farther away. One can visually perceive there being a cylindrical shape in numerous ways, depending on the angle from which the shape is viewed.

---

[16] See my 'Other Bodies'.
[17] Descartes was sensitive to this point in *Meditation I*.
[18] See Chapter 2, note 11.

So the phrases 'perception as of being cylindrical' and 'perception of there being cylindricality' do not fully specify, or type-individuate, a representational content. They signify some content that indicates the property cylindricality, and that does so in a way that entails that it (the content) indicates the property of cylindricality if it indicates anything. Indicating that property is necessary but not sufficient for the identity of the content. Further, indicating that property as cylindricality is necessary but not sufficient for the identity of the content. The precise content depends on the precise way that, or on the precise perspective from which, cylindricality is indicated and attributed. The same point holds for concepts (as) of New Orleans, water, and being-under.

In common sense and empirical psychology these fine-grained ways of type-individuating mental states are the ones that enter into psychological explanation. These fine-grained ways help mark the natures of the representational mental states. The state could not be the same mental state and have a different representational content.[19] Representational contents help mark the natures of, and figure in the most serious explanations of, representational states.

A key fact about these ways of type-individuating representational states is that the representational contents can be veridical or non-veridical. Perceptions and imaginings (or their representational contents) can be accurate or inaccurate. Beliefs and suppositions can be true or false. Intentions, wants, wishes can be fulfilled or not. Then they *become* veridical or *are made* veridical, or they fail to become or to be made veridical.

Perceptions, beliefs, and intentions—the states themselves as distinct from their representational contents—undergo a type of representational failure if they (or their representational contents) are not veridical or fulfilled. A supposition can be non-veridical without failing as a supposition. Perceptions, beliefs, and intentions are not like that. It is part of their natures that they themselves undergo *a certain* failure, if they are not veridical (or, for actional states like intentions, if their veridicality conditions are not fulfilled). A belief undergoes a type of failure if it is false. A perceptual state undergoes a failure if it is inaccurate. An intention undergoes a type of failure if its representational content is not acted upon and made veridical. Perceptions, beliefs, and intentions are *committal* representational states. These points are apriori knowable.

Non-committal states, like perceptual imagination or propositional supposition, can have the same representational content as committal counterparts. The non-committal states have their representational contents only by bearing relations to committal states, those that have the representational function of being or becoming veridical. Thus I think that perception, actional goal representation,

---

[19] A few philosophers maintain that such specifications are non-essential. I think that this view serves only ideology, and is patently false. There is no basis in intuition or empirical explanation for it. On the other hand, as Arnauld insisted against Descartes, there is nothing either in common sense or in empirical explanation to show that the representational aspects of mental states constitute the states' *full* natures. I leave open whether some physical properties are essential as well. Physical properties certainly appear to be at least necessary conditions for mental states.

and belief have a constitutive priority over states like imaginings, storytellings, and suppositions. And representational successes of these committal states have a constitutive priority over their representational failures. Those states' natures constitutively depend on relations to conditions for success of their instances. That is to say, committal states are type-individuated in terms of a *function* to be representationally successful—to be veridical or to have their veridicality conditions fulfilled.

Type-individuation of states that attributes to some basic types of states (such as perception and belief) a representational function to be veridical—and to others (such as intentions and actional states) a function of inducing fulfillment of their veridicality conditions—associates a *specific sort of teleology* with the natures of those mental states. It is part of the nature of perceptions and beliefs that they have the representational function of representing veridically. These states succeed or fail, *in one respect*, depending on whether their representational contents are veridical. It is part of the nature of intentions, willings, and non-propositional representational actional states that they have the representational function to help induce fulfillment of their representational contents.[20] These actional states succeed, in one respect, if they induce action that fulfills their representational contents. Otherwise they fail, in the same respect. Success and failure are marks of teleology.

A type of state's having the representational function of being veridical (a type like perception or belief) is the fact that underlies that state's being committal with respect to its representational content's being veridical. Such states' being committal does not vary with context. Part of their natures is their having the representational function that they have. Talk of states' aiming at veridicality, or even presenting their representational contents as veridical, is metaphorical.

Of course, beliefs, perceptual states, and actional representational states can have other functions besides their representational functions. Some have practical or biological functions. Fulfilling these functions marks other sorts of teleology, distinct from the teleology involved in representational function.[21]

Many mental states have representational contents regarding the physical environment. How are we to understand constitutive conditions for these mental states? What makes representational connection to the environment possible?

A fundamental reason to believe anti-individualism derives from answering these questions. There are accounts of the natures of mental states that fail badly as answers to these questions. Generalized anti-individualism is, of course, a very abstract and limited account. It is filled in through more specific accounts of specific types of mental states. I believe, however, that any account, specific or general, that does not accord with it will fail.

---

[20] I assume as terminological matter that intentions and willings are conceptual, hence propositional.

[21] These points are developed in Chapter 8. See also my 'Perceptual Entitlement', *Philosophy and Phenomenological Research* 67 (2003), 502–548, especially section I.

For example, a behaviorist or functionalist reductionist account that tries to explain the natures of representational states by holding that they consist in a network of causal or dispositional relations (specified independently of representational contents) that is limited to connecting registrations of proximal stimulation with movements of the body completely fails to explain how representational states are even relevant to environmental entities beyond the surfaces of the body. Distal causes of proximal stimulation can vary wildly while proximal stimulation remains the same. So an account of the natures of mental states that centers on registrations of proximal stimulation leaves those natures constitutively irrelevant to the environment. Such accounts either ignore the representational natures of mental states or expect a representational relation to consist in something that bears no intelligible relation to it.

A similar point applies to accounts that try to explain the natures of states that represent the physical environment purely in terms of neural or physiological occurrences in the body. Since the same types of occurrences can be induced through artificial stimulation that bears no relation to elements in the distal physical environment that are represented by the states, the account again fails to explain the representational connection to the environment. The account is irrelevant to the fundamental thing to be explained.

A more traditional approach that fails in similar ways holds that the natures of representational states consist entirely in their subjective phenomenological features. Unless such features are invested with representational characteristics to begin with—in which case they cannot illuminate representationality—this approach has the same empty pretensions. Qualitative or phenomenological features of perceptual states do not *in themselves* bear any explanatory relation to the environmental properties that perceptual states represent.

Phenomenal features *are* systematically integrated into the representational competencies realized in many perceptual systems, including human perceptual systems. Phenomenal features are commonly aspects of perceptual representational content. They are often aspects of the *way* perceptual *representata* are presented in perception. Perceptual states that are phenomenally different are normally different kinds of perceptual states, with different representational contents, even if the perceptual states are of, even as of, the same entities. But phenomenal features cannot in themselves suffice to fix the environmental *representata* of the perceptual states in which they figure. Since phenomenal features cannot in themselves suffice to fix *representata*, they cannot in themselves suffice to fix the representational content, or natures, of perceptual states in which they figure.

The reason is that perceptual representational contents "semantically" determine their *representata*, if any. In particular, perceptual attributives semantically determine, or *specify*, the attributes that they attribute. They are not only *as of* the attributes; they are as of the same attribute in every context of use and with regard to any possible situation. (See Chapter 2, the section REPRESENTATION-AS and REPRESENTATIONAL CONTENT.) The aspect of a perception that groups something as a body, or as cyclindrical, indicates the kind *body* or the shape *cylindricality*, if it indicates anything—and does so in every context of use and regardless of what possible situation is under consideration. So, if a phenomenal feature is insufficient to determine the *representata* of perceptual states, it is insufficient to determine their representational content.[22]

A recurrent error in this area is to believe that anti-individualism is true of how referents are established, but that some entirely different account is true of how referents are perceived or thought about. For example, it has been thought that perceptual reference is determined causally, but perceptual mode of presentation is a purely phenomenological, "internal" matter—that is, a matter that anti-individualism does not apply to. Or it has been thought that a kind concept like water applies to whatever stuff is causally responsible for descriptive conceptions of water (colorless, odorless liquid in oceans, lakes, and rivers), but that *the way we think of or know things of* water is entirely captured by such descriptions. It is often added that in other possible environments our word 'water'—given what it means in English—or our concept water, would refer to whatever would be the prevalent colorless, odorless liquid in prevalent bodies of liquid, even if that liquid were not water.

These views are mistaken at every turn. The *ways* things are perceptually presented (their representational contents), *not just perceptual representata*, are determined to be what they are partly through systematic patterns of relations to the environment. This point will be developed throughout the book. Similarly, the *ways* things are thought of (particularly, what concepts occur in thoughts) in nearly all empirical states, *not just the referents of thoughts*, are determined to be what they are partly through patterns of relations to the physical environment. This point applies not only to the kind concepts, but to the descriptive conceptions associated with kind concepts (colorless, liquid, ocean, and so on) themselves.

The descriptive conceptions associated with concepts like water do not capture the semantical, epistemic, or psychological behavior of the concept water. Specifying something in thought *as water* is quite different—semantically, epistemically, and psychologically—from thinking of something as the colorless, odorless liquid in oceans, lakes, and rivers. One could think of something, and specify it, as water and wonder whether (doubt that) such descriptive ways of thinking apply to water.[23] So the associated descriptive ways of thinking,

---

[22] I believe that the whole argument—and the arguments soon to follow—can be given with the representation 'as of' terminology. It does not require the stronger terminology of specification. But most ordinary representation (indication) of environmental attributes, in perception and thought, is both specification of the attributes and representation as of the attributes.

[23] Hilary Putnam in 'Is Semantics Possible?' (1970), in *Philosophical Papers*, ii, made the important point that one could use a natural kind term and *not believe that the standard stereotypical description associated with the term applies to the term's referent.* He concluded that the referent of the term was not determined by the stereotypical description, and he conjectured that the meaning of the term could be captured by pairing its referent (or extension) with a stereotypical description associated with the term. (I criticize this idea in 'Other Bodies'.) Putnam should have made a further observation. He should have noted that one can *specify the natural kind in thought* (for example, one can think of a lemon *as a lemon*) and not believe the stereotypical description to be true

however closely associated with a kind concept they may be, are not to be identified with the ways of thinking that contain the kind concept—that indicate kinds like *water* as such.

Here is a further argument that one cannot assimilate a way of thinking associated with a specification of an attribute (a specifying, 'as-such' representational content) to stereotypical descriptions, whether or not one supposes that the referents of the stereotypical descriptions vary with environment. Suppose that one individual thinks of one metal, aluminum, and a second individual thinks of a type of metal that is *not* aluminum. Each individual *refers in thought* to a different metal. One refers to aluminum; the other refers to some other metal. Neither individual ever refers to the other individual's metal. We can suppose that neither individual ever heard of the other's metal, and never encountered any instance of it. Suppose, in fact, that the second individual lives on a distant planet. Suppose that the individuals share stereotypical descriptions of the respective metals. Each thinks of his metal as a light metal, of such and such an appearance, that is commonly used to make pots and pans. Neither individual knows enough science to think his metal's chemical formula. And neither would recognize a difference if he were presented with the other metal (but neither one is ever presented with the other metal).

Now suppose that the first individual thinks in such a way as to *specify* aluminum *as* aluminum (or simply thinks of aluminum *as* aluminum—see note 22), even though he knows nothing of its atomic formula. He learns English in a normal way. He is taught that aluminum (specified as aluminum) is a particular type of metal. He interacts with aluminum, thinking of it *as aluminum* in his daily life. I claim that the preceding scenario is a possible situation, not even a very outlandish one.

I think that the following is a logical truth:

> In specifying (or simply thinking of) something as aluminum in thought, one's thought refers to or indicates aluminum (through the <u>as aluminum</u> aspect of the thought), if to anything.

No way of thinking can specify (or simply represent) something as aluminum unless it refers to or indicates aluminum. To put the point another way, if someone's thought does not refer to or indicate aluminum, that individual cannot specify anything as aluminum—and cannot think of anything as aluminum. One can think of only aluminum as aluminum. Since the second individual does not think of (refer to) aluminum, he does not specify anything as aluminum in

---

of the kind (not believe that lemons are as the stereotypical description describes them). Moreover, even if an individual believes the stereotypical description to apply to the natural kind, that description could in fact fail to apply to the kind that one thinks of through a standard specification. The stereotype for lemon could fail to apply to lemons, thought of as lemons. These observations show that thinking of something as a lemon is not the same as thinking of something through the stereotypical description. They are different ways of thinking. I elaborate this point below.

thought—and does not think of anything as aluminum. Since the second individual does think of his metal as a light metal with such and such an appearance commonly used to make pots and pans, that stereotypical-descriptive way of thinking is not the same as thinking of his metal as aluminum. *The two individuals' ways of thinking, not just their referents, are different.* Their psychological states are different. Since anti-individualism concerns ways of thinking *as*—and often specifications in thought—its points cannot be captured by claiming that it concerns only reference, while ways of thinking are captured by stereotypical descriptions.[24]

Again, most non-compound concepts and perceptual attributives *specify* the properties, relations, kinds that they indicate. (Certainly, if they indicate attribute *A*, they are as of *A*.) Specifying something in thought as water is a generic type of thinking that is absolutely not to be identified with thinking of water as the colorless, odorless liquid that fills lakes, oceans, and rivers. That generic type of thinking is not to be identified with any ways of thinking that do not specify water as such.

These points generalize to all empirical thought that specifies attributes, all perceptual specifications of attributes, and all specifications in mathematical thought. That is, the point is applicable to virtually every non-compound attributive way of thinking. These generalizations are not important for present purposes. It is enough if one understands the basic point about the focus of anti-individualism.

All theories that try to confine anti-individualism to points about reference fail to match its relevance to specification, and even thinking *as of*. Ways of thinking and perceiving, not just their *representata*, are constitutively determined by patterns of interaction with the environment beyond the individual.[25] Anti-individualism helps explain not only reference and indication, but ways of representing referents and indicants in thought, perception, and other representational states. It applies to the natures of individuals' perceptual and conceptual attributives.

There is a non-reductionist individualist view. It maintains that nothing can be said about constitutive conditions for being in representational mental states that represent aspects of the physical environment. It holds that there are thoughts as of aluminum and perceptual states as of body, but adds that nothing whatever can be said about constitutive conditions for being in such states. The states simply are what they are.

---

[24] I made substantially this argument, in somewhat different form, in 'Other Bodies'.

[25] Thus the first and second individuals above differ in their ways of thinking because of differences in their relations to their respective environments. See my 'Other Bodies'. Even now, much two-dimensionalist thinking (roughly, thinking that associates *ways* of representing with stereotypical descriptions) simply transcribes errors that Putnam made (in thinking that meaning is to be understood exhaustively as a combination of descriptive stereotype and extension) into a slightly different technical vocabulary. This is, in effect, the mistake criticized in 'Other Bodies'. See also my 'Introduction', in *Foundations of Mind*, 11–13.

This view is not easily vulnerable to attack, inasmuch as it advances no positive thesis. But it is unacceptable. A thought as of aluminum is one thing. Aluminum is another. That type of thought has something essential to do with aluminum. It is as of aluminum. The idea that nothing whatever can be said about what constitutive conditions make it possible for it to be as of aluminum seems to me quite incredible, even obscurantist.[26]

The most general grounds for believing anti-individualism are independent of thought experiment. The celebrated twin-earth thought experiments are just illustrative. No one such experiment provides general grounds for anti-individualism. General grounds are twofold, and simple. They reside in two features of representational states already discussed in this chapter.

Here is one ground. Part of what makes representational states what they are—indeed, an aspect of their natures—is that they set veridicality conditions, which when fulfilled are true or accurate. Take a thought that aluminum is a light metal, where aluminum is thought of as aluminum, being a metal is thought of as such, and lightness is thought of as such. The thought is true if and only if aluminum is a light metal. This setting of veridicality conditions is an aspect of the nature of the thought. This aspect of the nature of the thought bears a non-accidental relation to aluminum, to lightness, and to metal. More generally, in setting veridicality conditions, which can be fulfilled by conditions in the physical environment, representational states bear systematic, non-accidental representational relations to the environment. It is not an accident that a thought as of aluminum bears a non-accidental relation to aluminum. And this sort of non-accidental relation is massively systematic. There is no other possible reasonable explanation of the systematicity and non-accidentality of the relevant representational relations than to hold that the representational kinds are grounded in specific causal interaction between environmental entities that are represented and competencies associated with the mental states. Such interaction is both afferent (the environment's forming and triggering the competencies) and efferent (the individual's responding to the environment). The explanation is not reductive. It appeals simply to background conditions that help constitute systematic connection between environmental attributes and states that representationally specify them.

Again, the representational contents of mental states that are *as of* specific types of environmental entities must be explained in such a way that the relation between the natures of representational states and the environmental attributes is shown to be systematic and non-accidental. A thought that aluminum is a metal (where the thought is as of aluminum and as of metal) has something to do with

---

[26] Of course, Descartes postulated a situation in *Meditations I*, in which an individual thinks as of there being a physical environment, but there is no physical environment, ever. See *Meditations on First Philosophy* (1641), in *The Philosophical Writings of Descartes*, volume ii, ed. and trans. J. Cottingham, R. Stoothoff, and D. Murdoch (Cambridge: Cambridge University Press, 1985). Descartes argued that this situation is impossible. His reasons were broadly anti-individualistic. See my 'Descartes on Anti-Individualism', in *Foundations of Mind*.

aluminum and metal; and analogous points apply to one after another representational state. This system of non-accidental connections between the natures of psychological states and non-psychological environmental attributes can be in place only if there are specific systematic, non-representational, typically causal, relations between environmental entities and the psychological states. These relations ground constitutive explication of both the representational relation and psychological states' representations of environmental entities *as being* ways that they are.

Again, it is not true that each representational content is constitutively dependent on causal inter-relations with instances of the particular type of entity that it represents there being. Sometimes a representational content fails to represent anything. Sometimes the causal relation between environment and mental capacities is indirect. The basic idea is still the natural one. The relevance of mental states' empirically based representational content to environmental entities is secured through systematic patterns of causal connection.

Here is the second consideration. An aspect of the nature of committal psychological states, like belief, perception, and intention, is to function to be veridical or to make their representational contents veridical. These states undergo a kind of failure if they are not, or are not made, veridical. Anti-individualism provides a framework for explaining this teleology. The representational function of committal psychological states must be constitutively associated with causal patterns that forged relations between functioning state and environmental satisfiers of the function. The fact that an intention to eat the banana succeeds or fails depending on whether a banana gets eaten must be constitutively associated with causal patterns that forged relations between such intentions and actual eatings of bananas, or at least some related type of eating. Again, the nature of the representational actional state is grounded in perceptual systematic relations between teleological notions (success or failure in representation) and non-representational causal notions. No other account fits the teleology of the fundamental representational states, the committal ones, into a broader causal framework.[27] Generalized anti-individualism is a modest thesis. But it has a certain epistemic inevitability.

I think that explanations in representational terms do not reduce to explanations in other terms: psychological states described in such terms are explanatorily indispensable.[28] Some of the most rigorous, powerful parts of psychology use

---

[27] Again, the systematic, non-accidental relation between the nature of the state and the physical world must allow for reference- and indication-failure, and so on. The natural anti-individualistic framework incorporates these complications.

[28] Some reductionistic accounts are compatible with anti-individualism. I believe, however, that all reductionist accounts of representational states, even anti-individualistic reductions, fail. Certainly, all extant reductions have been obviously inadequate. For example, all functionalist accounts require removal of representational terms in favor of terms like 'causes' and specifications of behavior and response. Such reductions are patently inadequate. One cannot remove the theoretical terms from *any* scientific explanation and expect to have comparable theoretical explanation—much less the same meaning. Depending on whether they are analyses of meaning or scientific reductions, reductionist

representational terms. Explanation of perceptual accuracy and illusion, and explanation of the formation of perceptual states, are ineliminably in representational terms. Such terms are a secure part of science. See note 3.

Anti-individualism does not explain particular representational successes or failures. Such explanation is the task of perceptual and cognitive psychology. Anti-individualism provides a framework for explanations by empirical sciences insofar as they are relevant to understanding veridicality and failure of veridicality. The framework explains how the law-like patterns found by such explanations illuminate constitutive relations between representational kinds and environmental *representata*.

No philosophical account of the natures of representational mental states that is incompatible with anti-individualism can explain why representational mental states, through their representational content, bear the representational as-of relations that they bear to entities in the environment, or have the teleological natures that they have. These considerations form the most basic and powerful grounds for anti-individualism.

ANTI-INDIVIDUALISM REGARDING PERCEPTION[29]

Grounds for believing anti-individualism regarding *perceptual states* are instances of the grounds just sketched.[30, 31] To solidify a sense for the key application of

---

functionalist accounts are wildly out of touch, with the meaning of mentalistic terms or with actual scientific explanation. See my 'Postscript: Mind–Body Causation and Explanatory Practice', in *Foundations of Mind*, note 25.

[29] Although I focus on anti-individualism regarding perception in this work, anti-individualism is much broader. In addition to the general considerations advanced in the previous section, I have produced three arguments for anti-individualism that center on phenomena other than perception—schematic appreciation of what a natural kind is, linguistic communication, and questioning received wisdom. Each argument hinges on objectivity in representation. Each highlights a different aspect of anti-individualism. Each centers on psychological capacities that are relatively sophisticated in comparison to perception. Since my focus here is on origins of objectivity, I do not discuss these arguments. Here is a compact bibliography: The arguments use the twin-earth methodology introduced by Hilary Putnam in 'The Meaning of "Meaning"', in *Philosophical Papers*, ii. I discuss the relation between Putnam's thought experiments and mine in the Introduction to *Foundations of Mind*; in the 'Postscript to "Individualism and the Mental"' in *Foundations of Mind*; in 'Individualism and the Mental', *Midwest Studies in Philosophy* 4 (1979), 73–121, note 2; and in 'Other Bodies'. The three arguments occur respectively in 'Other Bodies'; 'Individualism and the Mental'; and 'Intellectual Norms and Foundations of Mind', *The Journal of Philosophy* 83 (1986), 697–720. Relevant to the second argument is my 'Wherein is Language Social?' in A. George (ed.), *Reflections on Chomsky* (London: Basil Blackwell, 1989). All my papers cited here are reprinted in *Foundations of Mind*. For an overview, see the Introduction to *Foundations of Mind*.

[30] In the mid-1980s I produced a thought experiment designed to show that the natures of perceptual states are constitutively dependent on relations between perceptual systems and the environment. See 'Cartesian Error and the Objectivity of Perception', in J. McDowell and P. Pettit (eds.), *Subject, Thought, and Context* (New York: Oxford University Press, 1986); and 'Individualism and Psychology', *The Philosophical Review* 95 (1986), 3–45, both reprinted in *Foundations of Mind*. I believe that this thought experiment works as far as it goes. But it depends on very special conditions.

(Note 30 continued, and note 31 begun, next page.)

anti-individualism in this book, I beg the reader's indulgence and go over some of the same ground in more detail.

Perceptual states are the kinds that they are partly by virtue of the representational contents that they have. Perceptual representational contents constitute accuracy conditions. Take a visual perceptual state as of a cylindrical solid. There are two aspects of perceptual representational content of the state—general and singular. The *singular* aspect functions fallibly to single out (refer to) perceived particulars. When successful, the perceptual state refers to a particular cylindrical solid, and perhaps particular instances of cylindricality and solidity. The *general* aspect in the representational content functions fallibly to group or categorize particulars by attributing some indicated kind, property, or relation to them. When successful, the perceptual state attributes cylindrical solidity to a particular cylindrical solid.

Since the singular aspects depend on context to refer to particulars, they are individuated in terms of occurrences. That is, the singular aspects of the representational content are the representational content parts that they are partly through being associated with particular occurrences in time. Such singular aspects are called '*singular applications*'. Singular aspects of perceptual representational content depend for successful *referential* representation on being caused by particulars (that are appropriately singled out in vision). The singular aspects do not have referents, nor do they have the specific referents that they have, through context-free characterization of referents. Perceptual reference cannot succeed unless general elements guide singular elements. The point is that the general elements cannot do all the referential work. Some of the work is done by the perceptions' being caused by particulars that are referred to.

Context-bound perceptual singular applications can be retained in memory. A perceptual memory can share a singular aspect with the perception that it

---

I believe that it was a strategic mistake to center defense of anti-individualism about perception on cases involving special conditions. For this reason, I do not rehearse the thought experiment.

Ironically, reflection on why it is so hard to get perceptual cases in which two individuals are behavioral and physical duplicates while differing in their perceptual states provides strong ground for believing anti-individualism about perception. Bodies and behavior are so finely tuned to perceptible environmental attributes that we are almost forced to conceive of a world with different physical laws, connecting environment and individual, in order to elicit cases in which an individual is behaviorally and physically the same as an actual individual (as far as is relevant to psychological explanation), but differs in perceptual states. Given the point of thought experiments, imagination of different physical laws is legitimate. But the thought experiments that imagine such cases are not the real point. The very pressure to appeal to different physical laws elicits the centrality of physical laws' connecting environment and individual in the individuation of perceptual states. This centrality is what anti-individualism regarding perception insists upon. See Introduction to *Foundations of Mind*, 16–22. For fuller developments of remarks that follow, see 'Perceptual Entitlement'; and 'Disjunctivism and Perceptual Psychology'.

[31] I will focus on elaborating the argument from veridicality conditions broached in the previous section. I leave to the reader elaboration of the argument from the teleology of committal representational states.

preserves. So, although singular elements are ultimately individuated in terms of particular context-bound occurrences, an occurrent singular element in a memory can be bound to a token singular element in a perception, as tokens of the same type. Thus singular elements can hold together temporally separate psychological states as instances of a fine-grained singular application type.

The kind of individuation that is primary for psychological explanation centers on the *general* attributional aspects of perceptual representational content. I focus on these aspects.[32]

The representational content of perceptual states partly determines perceptual state kinds. It also sets veridicality conditions—conditions for veridical, accurate, perception. The veridicality conditions of perceptual states are constitutive to their natures.

Consider what these veridicality conditions are. Not only is perception inevitably as of particulars. It also inevitably groups particulars as being of certain types. It attributes these types—properties, relations, or kinds—to particulars. The particulars can be individuals, events, or instances of properties or relations. A perceptual state is accurate inasmuch as it both refers to particulars and attributes to them attributes that it indicates, and that the particulars have.

A visual state might be a perception as of a smooth cylindrical solid on a rough-textured surface. An auditory state might be as of a sound of a certain pitch whose source is at such and such a distance directly to the right (where 'certain' and 'such and such' stand for particular perceptual ways of indicating a specific pitch and distance). The perceptual state is the mental kind that it is partly by virtue of its ways of representing properties, relations, and kinds. The representational content constitutes a fallible perspective on such attributes (and particulars), and sets conditions for being veridical, accurate, regarding these environmental entities.[33]

It cannot be accidental that the perceptual state is type-individuated in ways—by their accuracy conditions—that bear on specific physical properties, relations, and kinds. In cases of successful indication, a perceptual state as of *A* is non-accidentally related to the attribute *A*. That is, the conditions for representational success that partly *constitute* kinds of perceptual state bear a systematic, non-accidental relation to the physical attributes that they not only indicate, but represent *as such*. The natures of perceptual states are non-accidentally related to specified physical attributes.

It is not credible to think that the perceptual states are just what they are, without there being any more to be said about conditions under which they have

---

[32] For more on particular and general elements in perception, see my 'Five Theses on *De Re* States and Attitudes', and 'Disjunctivism and Perceptual Psychology'.

[33] In given cases, attributives may fail to indicate. The key point is that the representational content, which is a fallible perspective as of an attribute, must be distinguished from any of its *representata*. See 'Disjunctivism and Perceptual Psychology'.

the representational natures that they have. There must be some account of the connection between the perceptual states, with their representational contents, entailing veridicality conditions *as of*, and physical environmental entities that satisfy the conditions. What conditions must be in place if a perceptual state is to indicate some environmental attributes, and represent them in such a way as to specify them? What network of relations grounds explanation of the non-accidentality of the systematic connection between a perceptual state's being the kind it is by virtue of being *as of* specific environmental entities, on one hand, and the environmental entities, on the other?

The only remotely credible answer is, I think, a necessary truth: the natures of the perceptual states are what they are through a systematic network of causal relations between instances of the environmental attributes and processes that entered into the formation of the specific kinds of perceptual states that an individual is capable of being in and that are as of (and even specify) those environmental attributes.

Again, even though perceptual states depend on underlying physical states, a reduction of one vocabulary or theory to another is not to be expected. Both explanatory vocabularies are probably scientifically ineliminable. Of course, the physical cannot be reduced to the representational. The idealist stratagem of explaining perceived physical properties in terms of perceptual states is unacceptable. Our deepest understanding of the world takes much of the world to have no mental attributes at all.

So both the physical properties that are perceived (perceptually attributed) and the representational perceptual states that represent them are what they are, and are not to be unmasked as something further. Both are explanatorily irreducible, ineliminable. A representational state's being fundamental in this sense is consistent with being dependent on other kinds—physical kinds, biological kinds, environmental kinds, neural kinds, for example. Moreover, psychological explanations must be integrated with other types of explanations.

What I claim is that it is not acceptable to leave things with this anti-reductionist point. There must be systematic specific constitutive connections involving causal patterns between the specified (or simply indicated) physical conditions and representational perceptual states. The constitutive explication of these connections must not leave what is obviously a close, non-accidental connection between the two seeming brute, surd, or coincidental. See note 3.

Constitutive explications that appeal purely to neural, behavioral, or functional features that stop at an individual's surfaces cannot account for the relation between the representational content's having specific veridicality conditions— being as of environmental entities—on one hand, and the environmental entities, on the other. There is nothing *per se* within the limits of an individual's body from which one could recover anything relevant to specific properties in the environment that perception is as of.

To explicate the background of systematic connections between the veridicality conditions of perceptual states and physical attributes in the environment that the states are *as of*, one must recognize that the nature of the perceptual states constitutively depends on systematic patterns of causal interaction with attributes in the environment. This conclusion entails perceptual anti-individualism.

The constitutive explication takes the direction of the constitution relation to be asymmetric. The standards for being veridical that are parts of the natures of perceptual states are constitutively dependent on attributes in the environment. The attributes in the environment are not constitutively dependent on those veridicality conditions.

Any view that acknowledges error in perception must recognize that the subject matter of perception has constitutive priority over the standards of veridicality, the conditions for getting the subject matter right. Standards of veridicality must be explained in terms of veridicality. Even non-veridical perceptual states are type-individuated in terms of standards of accuracy—in terms of conditions under which they would be veridical. Veridicality must be *semantically*, as well as *constitutively*, explained in terms of something further—that which renders the states veridical. This "something further" is the subject matter of the perception—including the types of entities that successful, veridical perceptions are perceptions of, and as of. Since a veridical perceptual state is contingently veridical, both veridical and non-veridical perceptual states are explicated partly in terms of the nature of the subject matter. The nature of the subject matter is not similarly explained in terms of veridicality, or contingently veridical perceptual states.[34] Traditional views that maintained that the *esse* of a perceptual object is its being perceived collapse the constitutive asymmetry. I reject such views. The existence and representational nature of perceptual states are asymmetrically dependent on the existence and physical nature of environmental entities.

I re-emphasize that asymmetrical dependence of the natures of perceptual states on a perceived subject matter holds at a very abstract level. Perceptual states can represent there being properties (kinds, relations) that never existed. Such perceptual states are constitutively dependent on systematic relations to other representational states (primarily perceptual states) that *are* successful. The success is not just referential or indicational success. It is also success in representation (usually specifications) *as of*. Thus every perceptual state is constitutively dependent for its representational nature partly on relations to some

---

[34] I believe that this point holds even for secondary-quality views of color. See Chapter 2, the section OBJECTIVITY. On such views, colors are taken to be physical dispositions to cause certain phenomenological experiences. Not only do colors lack veridicality conditions; the phenomenological experiences are specified not in terms of *their* veridicality conditions (otherwise the account would be circular), but in terms of their phenomenological qualities. I am not committed to any secondary-quality view, but I believe that such views should be able to recover a version of the asymmetry that I am discussing.

environmental attributes, at least indirectly through other states.[35] This constitutive asymmetry lies at the heart of anti-individualism.[36]

Perceptual anti-individualism is an abstract thesis. It indicates that mental states cannot be what they are in isolation from a surrounding environment. The main considerations that support it do not require specialized background knowledge.

THE SHAPE OF PERCEPTUAL PSYCHOLOGY

The considerations just advanced to support perceptual anti-individualism are supplemented by reflection on method and theory in perceptual psychology. I shall sketch some points about the science that will help elaborate perceptual anti-individualism and help undermine Individual Representationalism.[37]

I believe that the science of perceptual psychology presupposes anti-individualism about perception. It presupposes that perceptual-state kinds are constitutively dependent for being the kinds that they are on patterns of relations to attributes, laws, and other regularities in the physical environment. The science determines specific ways in which kinds and operations in perceptual systems reflect environmental attributes, laws, and other regularities. Perceptual psychology makes anti-individualism about perception empirically specific.

Perceptual psychology has become serious and mature science since the 1970s. It has empirically well-grounded mathematicized results. In this section I present some elementary facts about the science to serve two purposes. The facts indicate how the science embeds anti-individualism, and they form background for criticisms of Individual Representationalism in Chapters 4–7. In Chapter 8, I provide more detailed sketches of explanations in the science. These sketches illustrate connections to anti-individualism in more depth. They provide a framework for my positive accounts of perception, representation, and objectivity.

The science of perceptual psychology is motivated by the goal of contributing to an explanation of how individuals perceive. More particularly, vision science assumes that individuals have approximately accurate visual perception some of

---

[35] Some hold that properties like color are purely in the mind. I do not accept such accounts. But even if colors were in the mind, they would be mistakenly attributed to environmental entities. This attribution must be accounted for anti-individualistically, inasmuch as it contains some representation as of a physical environment. Secondary quality views hold that colors are dispositions in physical entities to cause certain qualitative experiences. Even if the qualitative experiences have their natures independently of relations to the physical environment (as I believe some qualitative experiences do), the perceptual attribution of color to physical dispositions must, again, be explained anti-individualistically.

[36] Idealist views can accept anti-individualism in a certain sense. They can accept an asymmetry at a certain level of explanation. But they cannot accept that anti-individualism and this asymmetry are part of the final story about perceptual state individuation. They must take the non-representational environmental entities to be non-representational only from a limited point of view. (Kant's transcendental idealism would make such a claim.) They cannot take them to be non-representational from the fundamental explanatory point of view, as I do.

[37] What follows in this section condenses and refines discussion in DISJUNCTIVISM AND PERCEPTUAL PSYCHOLOGY, especially section III.

the time. And it tries to contribute to an explanation of how such perception comes about to the extent that it does. The formation of non-veridical perceptual states—various sorts of perceptual illusions—is a further target of explanation. For reasons that will emerge, this second target is a natural corollary of the primary goal—to help explain how accurate perceptual states are formed.

These points about the goals of the science, and associated points about the anti-individualism that describes a framework in which the science is embedded, should not be cartoonized. The science is clearly motivated by the goal of helping to explain veridical and non-veridical perception. But the idea that there are neatly and easily discernible types in the world that match neat categories in perception is an oversimplified idealization at best. Not only is a lot of perception inaccurate. Most accurate perception is only approximately accurate. A large part of the science is devoted to explaining the range of accuracy of the "estimative" perceptual states. For example, distances are attributed to within some degree of accuracy. In some domains, notably color perception, the precise physical property that is being matched is in dispute and may vary from context to context. The nature and extent of representational matches between the contents of perceptual states and the particulars and attributes in the environment are matters of empirical investigation. A corollary is that both the attributes in the environment that are perceptually attributed and the natures of the representational contents of the states are matters of empirical investigation.

Both the science and anti-individualism are motivated by a very *general assumption*: that individuals' perceptions are *approximately* accurate with respect to *some* environmental particulars and attributes *enough* of the time to ground a form of explanation that takes states with veridicality conditions to be the product and participants in the law-like formation patterns being explained. This general assumption is, of course, in accord with common sense. The assumption has been richly supported through the explanatory success of the science. So *wholesale* error theories about perception and theories that maintain that representational vocabulary cannot enter into an explanatory science are at odds with empirical explanation. Of course, the empirical explanation and its guiding assumption are not meant to address generalized scepticism about perception. That is a further philosophical issue. The science assumes that veridical perception occurs, and tries to explain it. The fact that explanations have become richer, more rigorous, more refined, and in their broadest outlines stable, provides grounds for confidence in the science and in its general assumption.

The primary contribution of the science of perceptual psychology in explaining how individuals perceive, and how their perceptual systems form veridical visual perceptions, to the extent that they do, is to explain, by appeal to law-like generalizations, the processes by which perceptual states with specific veridicality conditions are formed from specific types of proximal stimulation, stimulation of individuals' sensory receptors. The science also explains conditions under which a given type of proximal stimulation can give rise to illusions as well as veridical perceptions. The difference between veridical perception and illusion often depends on differences in the actual, occurrent distal antecedents of a given type of proximal stimulation. As we shall see, explanations of the formation of perceptual states from proximal stimulation provide insight not only into veridical perception but into conditions under which illusions occur. The full explanation of veridical perception depends, of course, not only on the account of the law-like operations by which perceptual states are formed from proximal stimulation. The relation between proximal stimulation and perceptual state is only one part of the full causal relation between environmental *representata* and perceptual states. The full explanation also depends on explaining the other main part of the causal relation between environmental *representata* and perceptual states. The other main part consists of causal relations between the *representata* and stimulation of individuals' sensory receptors. Such relations are not specifically psychological. Perceptual psychology here appeals to what is known in other sciences to fill out the explanation of how veridical (as well as illusory) perceptual states are formed. For example, vision science appeals to explanations from optics to fill out the explanatory story of seeing. A lot is known about how types of entities project light frequencies onto the retinas of perceivers. In relying on the natural sciences to help with this part of the explanation of veridical perception, psychology must take care to make reference to attributes that are plausible candidates for *representata*, at least as elements in the relevant causal chains. *Swarm of micro-particles* is a less relevant attribute than *macro-physical body*, for example.

The contribution of perceptual psychology centers primarily on the parts of the causal chains that lie within the psychologies of individuals. Perceptual psychology focuses mainly on explaining how specific types of representational perceptual states with veridicality conditions are formed from specific types of proximal stimulation. I shall return to this overall scheme for explaining veridical and illusory perception in Chapter 8, the section REPRESENTATIONAL FUNCTION AND NATURAL NORMS, and Chapter 9, the section PERCEPTION AS REPRESENTATION.

I want to focus now on the distinctively psychological part of this overall scheme for explaining veridical perception and perceptual illusion. Since *vision* is the best understood type of perception, I center on it in what follows.

The *primary problem for the psychology of visual perception* is to explain how perceptual states that are of and as of the environment are formed from the immediate effects of proximal stimulation—principally from registration of patterns and spectral properties of light striking the eyes. Such registration itself corresponds to a spatially and temporally organized pattern of firings by retinal detectors. Perceptual states that veridically represent the distal environment are formed from a series of transformations that begin with this sort of registration.

There are other sources of input into the visual system—proprioceptive input, including extra-retinal registration of eye position, and top-down higher-level input. For many basic explanations of fundamental visual processes, the retinal stimulations are primary. For simplicity, I focus on retinal registration of light arrays as input into the system.

A key to the interest and difficulty of solving the primary problem is a fact about the relation between registrations of proximal stimulation and representation of the distal environment. The information available in registrations of patterns and spectral properties of the light striking the retina—and the registrations of such light arrays—significantly *underdetermine* the distal causes of those registrations, hence the objects and properties that are represented in perception, hence representational content as of those objects and properties. The same firings of retinal sensors are compatible with numerous possible (even physically possible) causes. So any given pattern of sensory registrations underdetermines the types of entities in the environment that are perceived by humans and other animals.

The initial sensory registration of proximal stimulation in itself also underdetermines what perceptual representations the perceptual system will form. Apart from further factors, the sensory registration does not and cannot determine what perceptual states are formed. So it underdetermines how the individual perceives the environment *as being*. That is, the registrations of proximal stimulations on the retina—both more or less immediate ones and more temporally extended ones—are compatible with a variety of types of distal causes. And the registrations of proximal stimulations do not in themselves entail the formation of the perceptual representations that are in fact formed. The same points apply to the results of augmenting retinal registrations with sensory registration of all other proximal input, such as proprioceptive input, into the visual system.

The same (or indiscernible) types of light array could be produced by a distant large object or a closer smaller object, if certain further conditions are met. The registrations of proximal stimulation could have been caused artificially, with no natural environmental antecedents. Or they could have been caused by natural but non-standard antecedents in the environment. In either case, the individual and the perceptual system undergo illusions. Whereas the perceptual system can only respond to proximal stimulations, it forms perceptual states that are as of specific types of distal antecedents. Often these perceptual states are veridical.

Perception is *as of* particulars, properties, relations, and kinds that occur distally, in the environment. The initial states of the perceptual system, the initial sensory registrations of proximal stimulation, are not perceptual. The registrations of arrays of light intensity carry information, but are not perceptual representations. The light intensities registered on the retina are not perceived. Ordinarily, there is no perceptual state, conscious or unconscious, that represents them or is *as of* them. Objects of perception are entities in the environment. How are perceptions that are as of environmental entities formed, given that the proximal stimulations that the system has immediate causal access to are not fully determined by the distal properties that the perceptions represent as being there? This question is the central question of vision science. Answering it is solving what is commonly called '*the underdetermination problem*'.[38]

---

[38] The framework in which the underdetermination problem is stated is a cousin of Noam Chomsky's argument for the psychological reality of a grammar from poverty-of-stimulus

The fact that the same registrations of proximal stimulations are the possible, and sometimes actual, products of different environmental antecedents motivates the primary problem of visual psychology, the undetermination problem. That problem, to repeat, is to explain how information contained in the registration of light arrays is converted into perceptions of, and as of, entities in the distal environment.

A major part of this problem is to explain the transformation of the registrations of light intensities on retinal receptors—a two-dimensional array—into perceptual representations of, and as of, entities in three-dimensional space. Again, all retinal registrations, together with all further input from proximal stimulation, underdetermines the physically possible distal causes.

Underdetermination takes a great variety of forms. Intuitive considerations, however, suffice to illustrate the basic fact of underdetermination.

Underdetermination is exhibited in visual illusions. The Ames room is a trapezoidal room with a sharply receding back wall. From certain positions, it is misperceived as rectangular. The sizes of familiar objects in it are also misperceived because distance relations are misperceived. The same sensory registration of proximal stimulation could have been produced by a rectangular room with objects rescaled appropriately. Then the same registration of proximal stimulation would have produced a veridical perception of, and as of, a different distal cause. The same registration of proximal stimulation is compatible with either of these two possible distal causes, yet we perceive the situation as being one way rather than the other.[39]

A suggestive intuitive consideration that illustrates underdetermination lies in reflection on the geometrical considerations raised earlier. The light intensities that constitute the primary proximal stimulation are registered on the retina in a two-dimensional array. The registration is on an array of receptors—each corresponding to a surface area of stimulation. The registered information can be constructed as a two-dimensional array giving information correlated with light intensities. There is a determinate solution to how light from a three-dimensional scene projects onto a two-dimensional surface. The visual system must, however, use the two-dimensional array of information—the registration of light intensity on the bank of retinal receptors—to perceptually represent a three-dimensional scene. This 'inverse problem' has infinitely many mathematically possible solutions. Some of these solutions are not physically possible. There remain many physically possible solutions in most cases. What principles

considerations. See *Aspects of Syntax* (Cambridge, MA: MIT Press, 1965). The underdetermination problem is the older cousin. It was stated by Helmholtz.

[39] Most textbooks on perceptual psychology discuss the Ames room. See Stephen E. Palmer, *Vision Science* (Cambridge, MA: MIT Press, 2002), 247–248. Gibson and others noted that the Ames illusion depends on the observer's not moving. See J. J. Gibson, *The Ecological Approach to Visual Perception* (Boston: Houghton Mifflin, 1979). The point does not affect the example. Psychology must explain why the illusion occurs in the absence of motion. Of course, there are illusions that persist through bodily motion.

lead to perceptual representation as of just one of these cases, representation that is often accurate?

I oversimplify the problem. The problem has a dynamic dimension. There are feedback loops at various stages of visual processing. There is input from other sensory modalities. For all that, the form of the primary problem that I have outlined has guided a lot of research and yielded a considerable amount of scientific knowledge.

The primary problem is to explain how the visual system overcomes under-determination. Despite the fact that individuals fall into perceptual illusion, they and their visual systems overcome this problem in the overwhelming majority of cases. Often, they do so with proximal stimulation limited by short time exposure and lack of auxiliary information.

The dominant scheme in the psychology of vision for explaining how these problems are overcome goes back to Helmholtz.[40] The idea is to explain a series of unconscious, largely automatic transformational processes that lead from registration of the array and spectral properties of light striking the retina to the formation of perceptions as of specific aspects of the distal environment.

The transformations operate under certain principles that describe psycholog-ical laws or law-like patterns. These laws or law-like processes serve to *privilege* certain among the possible environmental causes over others. The net effect of the privileging is to make the underdetermining proximal stimulation trigger a perceptual state that represents the distal cause to be, in most cases, exactly one of the many possible distal causes that are compatible with (but not determined by) the given proximal stimulation. I call psychological principles that describe, in an explanatory way, these laws or law-like patterns *formation principles*.[41]

Formation principles describe processes that begin with selective filtering of the initial sensory registration. Such processes eventually yield perceptual states whose representational contents are underdetermined by the information registered by the initial proximal stimulation. So they are subject to perceptual error. The formation principles have the force of inductive principles, although they can be formulated as deductive or computational principles ('If the registra-tion of proximal stimulation is of type P, then perception as of an F is formed').[42]

[40] H. von Helmholtz, *Treatise on Physiological Optics* (trans. of 3rd German edn.), iii (New York: Dover Publications, 1867/1925).

[41] In 'Disjunctivism and Perceptual Psychology', I called these principles 'biasing principles', to emphasize the fact that they were biased toward certain possible environmental causes (or possible *representata*) over others. I came to think that uses of 'bias' in perceptual psychology might conspire to make this term mislead some into thinking that the principles somehow distort reality. In fact, the principles usually track the most likely environmental cause. But nothing in the proximal stimulation itself explains this tracking. Thus the laws yield states that represent, in a pre-set way, one among many equi-possible environmental antecedents of given proximal stimulation. The pre-set way derives from prior causal patterns explained by anti-individualism. *This* bias tends to be beneficial to accurate representation.

[42] Most points made here occur in any mainstream text in visual psychology. See Palmer, *Vision Science*, 9–11, 18–24, 55–59; and Vicki Bruce and Patrick Green, *Visual Perception: Physiology, Psychology, and Ecology* (1985; 4th edn., Hillsdale, NJ: Lawrence Erlbaum, 2001).

Although the basic problem and basic explanatory scheme are stated by Helmholtz, the approach began to yield mathematically rigorous and empirically plausible solutions with the advent of the computer model and computer simulations, in the 1970s. Work by David Marr and colleagues consolidated a methodology and offered solutions to a variety of problems in visual perception, in a way that signaled the arrival of visual psychology as a maturing science.[43] The solutions they proposed have been improved upon. Their methods have become entrenched.

Explanations postulate principles that govern the visual system's forming perceptions, in effect, to solve numerous particular problems. There are principles governing representation of an edge, given certain types of luminance

---

[43] David Marr, *Vision* (San Francisco: W. H. Freeman and Company, 1982). As noted in the Preface, philosophers often refer to Marr's work in superficial ways. Some even suggest that this work—and mainstream visual psychology in general—does not apply to human *sight*. (See note 57; Chapter 8, note 97; and Chapter 9, note 3.) They suggest that the science applies *purely* to enabling, subindividual processes—either to processes in the brain, or to information processing that is not concerned with mental, person-level representation of particulars in the environment, and is not concerned with visual attribution of properties, locations, kinds, and relations to those particulars. Such suggestions are out of touch with the science. The science explains how individual vision, including human vision, connects representationally to the world. Some of the states and nearly all the processes that it describes are unconscious subindividual and modular; some states are imputable to the perceiver, but unconscious. But most of the perceptual states that are final products of the formation processes that it describes and explains are imputable to the perceiver, and in human beings are usually quite conscious. This orientation to explaining the sight of humans and other animals is explicit in the experimental method, as well as in the science's theories. Although the theories focus on the referential, or more broadly representational, aspects of the conscious states—and are not about consciousness—they provide a very systematic and full account of the representational aspects of perceptual states, conscious and unconscious. And this account explains perceptual relations to the environment (as well as illusions), whether the perceptions be conscious or unconscious. Part III of this book develops these distinctions in some detail. Marr himself was not ideally clear about the distinction between sensory registration and perception that I elaborate. But see his *Vision*, 343–344, where he reflects on at least a related distinction.

Marr's three levels of explanation are often misunderstood. I will say a few words about them. The three levels are: (*a*) Computational, (*b*) Representational and Algorithmic, and (*c*) Hardware Implementational (see *Vision*, 24 ff.). Despite Marr's title for it, level (*b*) is often thought to be a purely syntactic level. But level (*b*) invokes specific representational contents, as well as specific relatively deterministic rules for processing them. (Although labeled 'algorithmic', such routes always allow for interference, including noise, and for malfunction.) The mainstream work in vision science that I discuss is primarily at levels (*a*) and (*b*). Marr's extreme idealization in specifying the levels is commonly underestimated. In actual scientific work, these two levels are not segregated; they are mixed. Few explanations leave the nature of the representational contents or the nature of the causal process unconstrained—beyond *whatever* processes and representational contents would solve an abstract computational problem. There are, for example, constraints on causal order, referential and other constraints on the representational content of states, and so on. Few explanations are purely at level (*a*). Similarly, few explanations are absolutely specific and complete as to either algorithm or *exact* representational content. Often the specifications of content go only a little beyond 'as of' specifications. Thus few explanations are purely at level (*b*). Understanding computational solutions to visual-representational problems—which Marr highlights as the point of explanations at level (*a*)—is certainly central to scientific work on vision. But most theories that center on explaining how problems are solved constrain the nature of the representational contents and the temporal order and main elements in the causal process. Thus most theories go some way toward realizing level (*b*) explanations.

contrasts in the registration of proximal stimulation. There are principles governing representation of lightness or color of a surface as distinct and separate from illumination of the surface. There are principles governing representation of depth from binocularity, texture, shading. There are principles for representing whole objects, even though parts of them are occluded. A lot is known about how the visual system works in a wide variety of animals, including humans.

To summarize what I have said so far. The visual system's primary receptors register dynamic patterns and spectral properties of light. These arrays are consistent with many types of distal stimuli that could (and sometimes do) cause a given type of registration of proximal stimulation. No processing of the arrays could infallibly correlate with the environmental conditions that cause them. Perceptual representation is consequently sometimes mistaken, even in cases where its internal workings are optimal. The psychology of vision tries to explain how the perceptual system normally gets things approximately right, to the extent that it does, on the basis of registration of light arrays and other types of input.

To solve its paradigmatic problem, perceptual psychology tries to discover formation principles *governing* (describing and explaining) the laws (*formation laws*) by which perceptual systems form perceptual states. The states are type-individuated by perceptual representations that are veridical in the cases where things are as the outputs of the formation principles indicate. Perceptual errors are also explained: registration of a given type of proximal stimulation is caused by conditions other than those that the formation laws treat as normal by yielding default representations of them.

The formation principles tend to serve the representational function of the perceptual system in providing veridical perception of entities in the environment. The relevant entities are the explanatorily relevant environmental antecedents of the proximal light arrays. The theory assumes that perception represents elements in the distal environment. This intuitive assumption is grounded in a larger explanatory point of view. What count as potential perceptual objects—as *relevant* distal antecedents—are roughly those that can be discriminated under certain conditions, that the internal processes are best explained as bearing perceptual constancies with respect to,[44] and that are ecologically relevant to the individual's basic functions—functions such as eating, navigating, mating, fleeing danger.

None of the transformations that occur in the visual system are attributable as acts to the perceiver. They are operations within the perceiver's visual system, determined by laws describable in terms of computational formation principles. They are inaccessible to consciousness and not under the perceiver's control. I believe that there is no sense in which the principles are "accessible" to the perceiver or the perceiver's perceptual system. The content and form of the

---

[44] I discuss perceptual constancies in Chapter 9. This condition can sound empty in the abstract. In concrete explanation, it eliminates alternatives.

principles are not the content or form of any states in the perceptual system. The principles describe laws or law-like patterns of transformation according to mathematicized principles. Most or all of the *perceptions* that result from these patterns of transformation *are* attributable to the perceiver. Humans and animals have the perceptions (perceptual states with representational content) whose formation the theory explains. The point of the theory is to explain human and animal perception.

The transformations that lead from registrations of light intensities to perceptions are in effect automatic. The transformations are, with allowances for interferences and special cases, effective procedures, procedures that follow an algorithm. The principles governing them (describing and explaining their transformations) are *computable*. The states, with their content, and the principles governing the states can be modeled on a computer. I count both the transformations, or transformational operations, and the principles *computational*.

For many philosophers, the notion of computational states or explanations is theory-laden in a way that I do not intend. When I call states or explanations 'computational', I do not mean that there are transformations on syntactical items, whose syntactical or formal natures are independent of representational content. I also do not mean that the principles governing transformation are instantiated in the psychology, or "looked up", even implicitly, in the system.

A common philosophical picture of propositional-attitude psychology maintains both of these points. On this picture, psychological systems "access" both *primitively* syntactical items (vehicles of representation that are what they are independently of any content) and rules for manipulating the syntactical items. Transformations in the psychology are regarded as changes in a syntactically formulated proof-system, with syntactical structures and look-up rules both formulated in the system.[45]

---

[45] The common picture derives from Fodor, *The Language of Thought*. Fodor is primarily concerned with the psychology of thought (belief) and speech perception. But he envisions applying his account to all perception. See pp. 42–51, 116 ff. Some philosophers take a "computational" theory to imply such a picture. This view is not standard in psychology. Vision theory is computational in the sense discussed in the text. It does not involve the commitments that Fodor's account does. The problem is not just that perceptual states lack a *sentential* syntax. The main problem is that there is no formal or syntactical structure of any kind that is individuated independently of the laws instantiated by perceptual—contentful—states. Here there is perhaps a disanalogy to psycho-linguistics. Chapters 8–10 below return to issues regarding principles governing perceptual transformations. Such principles are certainly not implicitly "looked up". They are not the representational content of any states in the system, however unconscious. Fodor sometimes writes as if the principles are present in the system in the way inference rules are *formulated* in a logical system—only not in natural language, and not consciously.

It is important not to assume that psychological theories of syntax carry over to psychological theories of vision. I am sceptical over whether Fodor's account applies even to all instances of ordinary thought, though it is a useful idealization. One should be cautious about common metaphorical slogans like 'the visual system is a syntactical engine' or 'the brain is a syntactical engine'. I criticize confusion engendered by such metaphors in 'Disjunctivism and Perceptual Psychology', 75 note 54.

Two things are wrong with applying this picture to visual systems. One is that there is no explanatory level in the actual science at which any states are described as purely or primitively syntactical, or purely or primitively formal. One will search textbooks and articles in perceptual psychology in vain to find mention of purely syntactical structures. No explanatory work is given to them. No laws are formulated by reference to them. Invoking them derives from ideology that provides no ground for insisting that the science has overlooked or failed to distinguish purely syntactic kinds as important elements in perceptual systems. The picture mislocates the point and force of the science's explanations. The explanations center on law-like patterns of transformation among contentful perceptual states. The representational content of perceptual states has form and structure. But any purely syntactical descriptions of such states are abstractions from the states' representational content. Such abstractions depart from the nature of the patterns and the focus of the theory. In the science there are no purely formal structures that provide an independent underpinning for the representational, contentful, perceptual states. The principles of the science center on instances of representational kinds individuated by representational content (and their relations to registered information).

The following point is of great importance: the formulations of principles in terms of representational content are *primitive*, not a further commentary on a primitive non-representational structure. The vehicles of representational content are states in the perceptual system. But these vehicles are not individuated separately, as a word shape might be individuated independently of its meaning. Although there is certainly a supplementary theory to be discovered about the physical underpinnings of perceptual states, there is currently no empirical reason to think that underlying physical states will have a syntactic form that can be specified independently of the structures of representational contents of perceptual states.

The representational content of the perceptual states are constitutively determined by relations to environmental entities. This point, entailed by anti-individualism, is evident in the characterizations of perceptual states in the science. The science characterizes such states as perceptions (as) of shape, color, motion, body, and so on. No syntactical state is characterized in such ways. Explanations in the science specify states with representational content. The transformations that explanations specify depend essentially, according to the science, on the representational contents of the states involved.

The other thing wrong with the picture as applied to visual systems is that there is no evidence that the principles of transformation are themselves in the psychology, in the sense of being the content (or form) of any state or event.[46] Such principles are not "consulted", "looked up", "accessed" in the system. Psychological states change as a result of proximal stimulation, according to

---

[46] As intimated in note 43, not all expositions of the language-of-thought hypothesis maintain that rules of transformation are accessible within the system.

patterns described and explained by the mathematicized formation principles. But those principles are not in any further sense accessible or embedded in the perceptual system.

The formation principles describe and explain laws instantiated in transformations in the system. They are not *applied* in reasoning or cognition, even "implicit" reasoning or cognition, within the system. Thinking of them as applied by the system hyper-intellectualizes the system, and invokes the ideas of accessibility and implicit look up. Such views are residues of Individual Representationalism. They take the system to contain representations of the laws determining its operation. Thinking of visual systems this way would be almost as bad a mistake as thinking of the planetary system as applying principles governing its motion.[47]

The states (both representational states and non-representational states) of the visual system change according to laws or law-like patterns described and explained by the formation principles. The principles include mathematics and references to perceptual states that are not representationally available to perceptual systems, much less most perceivers. There is no evidence for postulating implicit lookings-up of the relevant principles. The principles are not formulated or represented in the system, much less by the perceiver. Perceivers need not have any state, however unconscious or "implicit", that has the content of the principles. There must be some psychological patterns in the system that make the principles true. But the principles are not the content of any state or capacity in the system.

By contrast, the registrational and representational states whose transformations are explained by the principles *are* states of the perceptual system. Most of the representational states are states of the perceiver as well as the perceptual system. That is, not only does the perceptual system produce a perception as of a cylindrical solid. The perceiver perceives something as being a cylindrical solid by having that perception. The representational states have representational content. This content helps determine the representational natures of the main entities, the psychological states and events, described and explained by the theory.

The idea that the visual system is analogous to a purely formal, content-free proof theory does not square with the science. What is correct about counting the theories computational is that they attribute (approximately) algorithmic laws of transformation among states in the perceptual system. The laws can be modeled on a computer. The laws, however, *cannot be described in purely syntactical or purely formal terms*. The principles that describe the transformations among states in the visual system concern specific kinds of perceptual—representational—states. Nor are the laws formulated *in* the perceptual system. The theory containing the principles is computable. But the principles are not the content of any state or states in perceptual systems, nor are the forms of the principles embedded in the systems.[48]

---

[47] Only 'almost' as bad, because the planetary system does not contain representational states.

[48] Although the theory makes no use of a representationally neutral formal structure, the theory can be expected to connect with theories of neural structure and process. How neural theory relates to

The science of perceptual psychology is in its early maturity. It is clear, however, that its methods yield rich returns. The methods of visual psychology apply to other perceptual systems besides vision—principally hearing and some aspects of proprioception and touch.

PERCEPTUAL PSYCHOLOGY PRESUPPOSES ANTI-INDIVIDUALISM

Empirical psychology does not theorize much about constitutive conditions. It explains processes not natures. It operates at a lower level of abstraction than anti-individualism. Nevertheless, its basic methodology and the general character of the psychological laws that it postulates involve commitment to anti-individualism.

How is the empirical psychology of vision committed to perceptual anti-individualism? In a nutshell, its kinds are partly determined by representational contents. Representational contents of states are fixed by laws that explain how approximately veridical perceptual states are formed. These laws and the kinds that they embed, in turn, are typed by relations to attributes, regularities, and laws in the environment. Let me open the nutshell a bit.

As I have indicated, the central methodology of the science is driven by the same consideration that drives anti-individualism—the explanation of representational success. The psychology explains perception—an ability of individuals veridically to represent elements in the environment as being certain ways. It explains the representational success of perceptual states whose representational contents provide numerous perspectives on any given attribute A, where all of these perspectives are perceptions of *A as A*. Failures of approximate veridicality—illusions—are explained primarily in terms of abnormal environmental conditions' producing proximal stimulations that would yield veridical representations under more normal conditions. Of course, the specific abnormal conditions are spelled out.

In every case, formation principles—and the states and transformations that they describe—mirror basic facts in the broader physical environment. These are facts regarding spatial relations, natural forms of motion, the way light patterns tend to correlate with shadows and edges, the way surfaces tend to have unseen backsides, and so on.[49] They mirror either environmental laws or deep environmental regularities that hold for the most part.

---

vision theory will play out empirically. I think that there is no armchair argument that the physical underpinnings must constitute a syntax that matches that of the perceptual states, or that the psychological forms can be applied directly to neural states. However, in the very early stages of vision, connections between psychological theory and neural theory are fairly close.

[49] For illuminating discussion of ways formation principles reflect the environment, see Elizabeth Spelke, 'Principles of Object Perception', *Cognitive Science* 14 (1990), 29–56; Roger N. Shepard, 'Ecological Constraints on Internal Representation: Resonant Kinematics of Perceiving, Imagining, Thinking, and Dreaming', *Psychological Review* 91 (1984), 417–447; P. J. Kellman, 'Kinematic Foundations of Infant Visual Perception', in C. E. Granrud (ed.), *Carnegie-Mellon Symposia on*

The natures of perceptual states—the perceptual-state kinds—are constitutively interdependent with psychological laws or law-like processes that embed them. These psychological kinds and laws reflect and are partly constitutively determined by attributes, laws, and deep regularities in the environment. The psychological kinds, marked by their representational contents, are constitutively interdependent with the general character of the psychological laws determining their formation and causal potential. These laws, in turn, depend on and reflect attributes, laws, and patterns in the distal environment. The psychological laws and operations are what they are because they were causally determined as counterparts of attributes, laws, and patterns in the distal environment. So the natures of specific perceptual states are constitutively associated, via causal relations, with specific attributes, laws, and patterns in the environment.[50]

There is no getting around the fact that the laws determining the formation of perceptual states are laws that determine formation of states *with representational content*. The basic kinds, both *explananda* and *explanans*, in perceptual psychology are representational. Perceptual-state kinds are what they are by virtue of their representational content, together with the perceptual modality.[51] Commitment to representational contents as type-individuating perceptual states and abilities is central to the science's objectives, methods, and explanations. The representational contents of the states are fixed by the general character of transactions into which they enter and by the normal causal and discriminative relations that perceptual states and their associated transformations bear to the physical environment.

The reliance in visual psychology on postulating representational states derives partly from the fact that the primary problem of the theory of vision is to account for how individuals come to perceive accurately or inaccurately. The postulation of representational content also derives from the role of representational content in marking ability. The abilities that representational content marks have turned out to be very complex. The processes that lead from registration of light arrays to perception are layered, interdependent, and sensitive to a large number of conditions. Attempts to account for perceptual ability without

---

Cognition, vol. 23, *Visual Perception and Cognition in Infancy* (Hillsdale, NJ: Erlbaum, 1993); E. S. Spelke, P. Vishton, and C. Von Hofsten, 'Object Perception, Object-Directed Action, and Physical Knowledge in Infancy', in M. S. Gazzaniga (ed.), *The Cognitive Neurosciences* (Cambridge, MA: MIT Press, 1995).

[50] Although the term 'anti-individualism' is not used among psychologists, there are many instances of awareness of these points. See Marr, *Vision*, chapter 1; Shepard, 'Ecological Constraints on Internal Representation', especially 422; Spelke, 'Principles of Object Perception'; Roger N. Shepard, 'Perceptual–Cognitive Universals as Reflections of the World', *Behavioral and Brain Sciences* 24 (2001), 581–601; W. S. Geisler, 'Visual Perception and the Statistical Properties of Natural Scenes', *Annual Review of Psychology* 59 (2008), 10.1–10.26. See also my 'Individualism and Psychology' and 'Disjunctivism and Perceptual Psychology'.

[51] Thus neither states characterized entirely in neural terms nor states characterized in "syntactical" terms that abstract from representational content play any significant role in the explanatory principles of the theory.

postulating representational content have failed in systematic ways, on empirical grounds.[52]

The methods of perceptual psychology take it that part of what it is to be a perceptual state of a given kind is to enter into the psychological formation laws and processes. These laws and processes are described by the formation principles. Exactly what the laws are is, of course, empirically discovered. The theory is, however, committed to a general view of what the laws are like. They parallel and reflect environmental laws or deep regularities commonly associated with proximal stimulations. The laws are explicable only by reference to the way in which patterns in the perceptual system's natural environment have molded the nature of the perceptual system and its perceptual states. The science is thus committed to perceptual anti-individualism.

Thus, in solving its primary problem, visual psychology presupposes anti-individualist principles, and fills them in with empirically supported laws. The methods and results of visual psychology presuppose and make use of perceptual anti-individualism.

It is independently plausible that the natures of perceptual states depend on patterns of relations between them and attributes of the physical environment. The relation between a perception as of a moving sphere and moving spheres is clearly not accidental. The nature of the perception is partly specified in terms of environmental attributes. Some attributional states are molded by the attributes that they represent through systematic patterns of causation.

The idea that such states have a representational nature that is completely independent of the environment that they represent is not only implausible. It constitutes explanatory wand waving. Either the idea postulates a nature that already implicitly includes representational content, in which case no explanation is given. Or it postulates a representational power on the basis of a feature that does not explain the power.

For example, attempts to individuate perceptual states *purely* or *primarily* in phenomenological or neural terms cannot provide anything like satisfying insight into the representational nature of perceptual states. Reflection on the role of formation laws or law-like processes in determining perceptual kinds yields an empirical elaboration of anti-individualism. Such reflection shows how perceptual anti-individualism both informs and is made specific through empirical explanation.

---

[52] A prominent psychologist who rejected visual representational content was J. J. Gibson (see *The Ecological Approach to Visual Perception*). I discuss empirical failures of Gibson's program in 'Disjunctivism and Perceptual Psychology', especially note 21. See also Shepard, 'Ecological Constraints on Internal Representation'; Bruce and Green, *Visual Perception, Physiology, Psychology, and Ecology, passim*; Palmer, *Vision Science*, 10, 53–56, 74, 82–84, 318–319, 409–413. There are other attempts to avoid appealing to representational content in the psychology of perception. I cannot discuss all of these. I think it fair to say that they are not mainstream and that the prospects for dispensing with representational content in perceptual psychology are remote.

The primary grounds for holding that there are perceptual systems are empirical.[53] The explanations provided by psychology are, of course, warranted and constrained by specific empirical evidence. But the psychological kinds indicated by these explanations can be understood only in an anti-individualistic framework. In both its basic explanatory kinds and its basic methods, perceptual psychology is committed to anti-individualism.

PERCEPTUAL CAPACITIES SHARED ACROSS SPECIES

All these perceptual systems involve *objective* representation—representational states that make veridical attributions to aspects of physical reality. Three general features of explanations in perceptual psychology are relevant to our theme of the conditions on objective representation.

One is that perceptual systems are domain specific. Purely perceptual representational contents represent only attributes that an animal can discriminate as a result of processes that begin with sensory states that are sensitive to a specific causal medium—light, sound, contact, and so on. Most visual perceptual systems form representations as of a small number of types of environmental attributes— integrated body, shape, spatial relations, motion, texture, brightness, color, and perhaps functional properties like food, danger, shelter. Representation *as such* of kinds like elementary particles, teacups, pianos, and recessions depends on capacities that go beyond the perceptual system proper.

I know of no apriori principle of separation. Separation derives from empirical theory.[54] The science focuses on discriminative abilities that have access only to proximal stimulation in a given medium. It focuses on discovering formation principles that concern perceptual states that attribute attributes that are ecologically important to the basic biological needs and activities of animals. Empirical science indicates that perceptual systems (and actional systems that are guided only by perceptual systems) have representational primitives that are confined to a relatively limited set of attributes.

A second feature of perceptual systems is that transformations in them are relatively independent of specific input from other systems—particularly from higher-level cognitive systems such as belief and language. This feature is called *encapsulation.*[55] The point requires qualification. It has been overstated. Input into one perceptual system often affects perceptual representations of another. If touch is given input that would normally yield representation as of one width for a

---

[53] I leave open here whether there may be additional grounds that are non-empirical.

[54] These issues are well discussed by Zenon Pylyshyn in 'Is Vision Continuous with Cognition? The Case for Cognitive Impenetrability of Visual Perception', *Behavioral and Brain Sciences* 22 (1999), 341–365.

[55] See Jerry A. Fodor, *The Modularity of Mind* (Cambridge, MA: MIT Press, 1983); Zenon Pylyshyn, 'Is Vision Continuous with Cognition?'

body, and vision is given input that would normally yield representation as of a very different width, the perceptual representations in each system are affected. Similarly, there is feedback between primitive action systems and perceptual systems.[56] In humans and other higher animals, beliefs can affect what is attended to; and attention affects perceptual operations. In humans and higher animals perception interfaces with conception and belief in complex ways. Nevertheless, the processes of perceptual systems, even in humans, are *relatively* independent of higher-level cognitive states. (Language perception is a special case and requires further qualification.) Many of the primary operations in perceptual systems have been successfully studied while provisionally abstracting from crosstalk among sensory and cognitive systems.

Third, many perceptual capacities are shared across species. The first two features of perceptual systems help explain this sharing. Take domain specificity. Since the range of attributes that visual systems deal with is relatively limited and of importance to the survival of many species, it is not surprising that similar solutions to perceptually representing those attributes evolved.

This point requires qualification. Some senses are explained better in informational than in representational terms. There are specializations among representational perceptual systems that produce failures of overlap. Fish use sensitivity to the motion of fluids by touch. Rays are sensitive to electrical fields. Spiders are sensitive to vibrations in their webs. There are differences in degrees of acuity and in dominance of different senses in different animals. The same perceptual problem often admits of various solutions.

Still, the perceptual systems of a wide variety of species often embody similar solutions to perceptual problems. Nearly all mammals have visual systems that are in their basic formation principles broadly similar to human visual systems. Some principles governing visual perception apply to a much wider array of animals than mammals. Many of the ways that visual systems achieve depth perception are common to mammals, birds, fish, and certain insects like bees, locusts, and a few types of spiders. For example, localization of the distance of an object is partly explainable in many species by principles of convergence that describe transformations that depend on the distance between the two eyes and the angles of sight established by the eyes.

Relative encapsulation also helps make sharing across species possible. Since, empirically, the nature of perceptual representations and the principles governing their formation are relatively independent of background information, different species can share at least some types of representation and formation processes.

I discuss perceptual psychology in more detail in Chapters 8–10. Here, I hope to have signaled the importance of the science and something of its basic shape. I hope also to have indicated how perceptual anti-individualism forms a background for the science. What I have said so far should suggest how the science

---

[56] See A. Gemma, C. S. Calvert, and B. E. Stein (eds.), *The Handbook of Multisensory Processes* (Cambridge, MA: MIT Press, 2004).

might indicate that a wide range of animals have accurate perceptions as of many macro-attributes of the physical environment.

INDIVIDUAL REPRESENTATIONALISM AND PERCEPTUAL PSYCHOLOGY

The approaches to perception characteristic of Individual Representationalism are very different from the approach just outlined. First-family individual representationalists hold that a layer of perception is prior to perception of the environment. Representation of the environment is built up from representation of appearances or sense data or of perceptual states. Second-family individual representationalists have little detailed to say about perception. They do hold, however, that perceptually to represent the physical environment as having specific attributes, an individual must have further cognitive abilities. These include abilities to represent general conditions that make objective representation of the physical environment possible.

I will evaluate Individual Representationalism from the standpoint of both anti-individualism, especially perceptual anti-individualism, and mainstream empirical perceptual psychology. Almost no discussion of perception by Individual Representationalists is informed by what is known about the topic. Nevertheless, we can ask whether there are resources in the doctrine to deal with the considerations just sketched.

Proponents of Individual Representationalism could reject the psychology. Or they could hold that the psychology may be right about non-human animals but must be at best incomplete in its account of human perception. Or they could maintain that philosophical accounts of individuals' perception have a different subject matter from that of empirical psychology, so Individual Representationalism and perceptual psychology are not in competition.[57]

In Part II, I think that it will become clear that Individual Representationalism lacks resources to defend such lines. The doctrine rests largely on unargued assumptions that are not in themselves plausible. The doctrine commonly rests on the bare claim that objective representation would be 'unintelligible' if it did not meet proposed requirements. Often it is enough simply to reflect on the intelligibility of an alternative to realize that a version of Individual Representationalism should be rejected. I cannot discuss all versions of the doctrine. I confront a significant sampling. The reader will have to extrapolate.

---

[57] I discuss this last line briefly in Chapter 6, the section EVANS ON CONSTRAINTS ON OBJECTIVE REFERENCE IN PERCEPTION, and in more detail in 'Disjunctivism and Perceptual Psychology'. See note 43 above; Chapter 8, note 97; and Chapter 9, note 3. The position is untenable. Psychology clearly assumes, and makes systematic methodological use of the assumption, that humans and animals— whole individuals—have the perceptual states that are attributed in the theory. I believe that the position rests on remarkable ignorance of the science. The other lines mentioned in the text are discussed more fully in the following chapters.

PERCEPTION AND CONCEPTS

In what follows I distinguish between perceptual and conceptual representational contents. As explained in Chapter 2, on my usage, *concepts* are certain elements of the representational contents of *propositional thought*. I believe that in principle, both particular thoughts and particular perceptual states *can* sometimes occur only at subindividual levels—that is, only in modular subsystems. In such cases, the representational natures of the states are still determined by causal patterns indicated by anti-individualism. But, paradigmatically, both perception and propositional thought are imputable to individuals. Unlike perception, propositional thought essentially involves an ability by individuals to engage in inference that depends on propositional form or structure.

I think that perception is not propositional, hence not conceptual. Although both perception and propositional belief categorize, group, and attribute, they do so in different ways. I believe that the perceptual capacities of perceivers and perceptual systems are not organized propositionally. *Explanations* are, of course, carried out propositionally. The perceptual content is referred to in a propositional theory. But I believe that the representational content on which computational operations in perceptual systems operate is not itself propositional. Such content is not structured or organized propositionally. Explanation tends to operate on categorizational (perceptual-attributive) capacities whose structure is that of various magnitudes. The most prominent magnitude structures in perceptual representational content map onto structures of spatial magnitudes in nature.

Computational propositional *explanations* explain and describe these sorts of non-propositional perceptual content. But the computations within perceptual systems operate on the magnitude structures themselves, not on the propositional structures of explanations in psychology. Although perception contains both singular and attributive elements, and although the attributive elements categorize at various levels of abstraction, the singular and attributive elements are not combined in true propositional structures.[58]

Pre-theoretically, it seems unnecessary in accounting for the perceptual capacities of various lower animals—say, amphibians, insects, pigeons—to take them to engage in propositional inferences. This view accords with the mainstream of perceptual psychology. The science has shown no need to attribute propositional capacities to these animals. However, quite extensive scientific work on the sensory systems of many of these animals shows them to perceive, to have perceptual memories, and to act on representational content that derives from perception. Thus there is empirical reason to distinguish between conception and propositional thought, on one hand, and perceptual attribution and perceptual states, on the other.

The distinction between perceptual attribution and conception will arise periodically. But *the main argument that I make against Individual Representationalism*

---

[58] I discuss this abstract notion of organization somewhat further in Chapter 11, the section THE UPPER BORDER OF THE PERCEPTUAL: PERCEPTION AND PROPOSITIONAL ATTITUDES.

does not depend on the distinction. Even if perception *did* involve conception and propositional structure, perception would not, of itself, supply the representational *apparati* required by the views that I will criticize. Such views hold that to perceive the physical world, a perceiver must have certain *specific* capacities. Whether or not perception is conceptual, I believe that it will become clear that perception itself does not involve or require any of the relevant capacities.[59]

ANTI-INDIVIDUALISM AND INDIVIDUAL REPRESENTATIONALISM

An overview of relations between anti-individualism and Individual Representationalism may help orientation for what follows.

I believe that the intuitive and theoretical considerations that support anti-individualism, both about perception and about thought, are so basic that they leave no reasonable alternative. Failure to accept the view, once presented with it, tends to derive either from being distracted from the central considerations or from misunderstanding what is being claimed.

Anti-individualism reapportions the contributions of individual and environment in determining the natures of individuals' mental states. An individual's resources to represent-as are not determined by the individual's ability to represent constitutive conditions, or by anything else that is located within the boundaries of the individual. Non-representational relations to specific attributes of the environment play an ineliminable role in constitutively determining what perceptual representations or empirical thoughts the individual has, and can have.

The thrust of this reasoning is uncongenial with Individual Representationalism. Individual Representationalism holds that an individual cannot represent an objective subject matter unless the individual can represent preconditions of objectivity. The individual is required to be able either to build up representation of objective particulars partly from subjective representations, or to represent fundamental general features of objectivity.

Anti-individualism can be used to show, against first-family views, that representation of objective matters are not, and cannot be, built up from subjective representation. Descriptive and constructional resources together with appeal to apprehension of appearances do not suffice to fix representations of the physical environment. This point had been made, independently, by numerous critics of sense-data theories. Anti-individualism enriches the negative point with an account of why sense-data theories fail.

The requirement of second-family versions of Individual Representationalism— the requirement that the individual be able to represent fundamental, general features of objectivity—is the hardier one.

---

[59] For example, perception does not provide a capacity to represent a seems/is distinction (required by certain neo-Kantians), or the apparatus of quantification (required by Russell and Quine), or linguistic capacities (required by Quine and Davidson).

Anti-individualism shows that an ability to represent objective subject matters does not require the individual to have representational control over them. Anti-individualism, in its most general form, shows that causal relations between empirical representational mental states and some environmental entities must play a constitutive role in determining specific representational identities of some of these states. Thus it shows that the individual cannot do all the work in determining the identities of empirical representational mental states.

Anti-individualism also shows that having particular perceptions and thoughts does not require being able to provide explications that determine what types of entities they refer to or indicate. Having a perceptual attributive or a concept does not depend on the individual's being able to represent, *separately*, specific conditions for its application. Having particular perceptual attributives and particular concepts depends ineliminably on psychology–environmental relations.

These points do not, however, show that individuals need not have the competence to represent general features of objectivity in order to apply percepts and concepts to an objective subject matter. Generalized anti-individualism does not entail that the *only* factors that constitutively determine the nature of mental states are specific causal relations to the environment.[60] In fact, all representational states can be what they are only by being associated with other psychological competencies, including specific representational competencies. Thus both psychology–environment relations and intra-psychological relations are constitutively necessary to representational states' being what they are.

Individual Representationalism, particularly in its second-family form, is compatible with anti-individualism in its most general form. Individual Representationalism can accept anti-individualism, but insist that some intra-psychological relations that help determine the nature of mental states include relations to capacities to represent general conditions on objectivity.

Thus Individual Representationalism can hold, compatibly with generalized anti-individualism, that to apply specific perceptual attributives and concepts, say, to physical bodies or spatial relations, the individual must be able to represent general conditions for objective representation. For example, it might require that the individual be able to represent a distinction between appearance and reality. Or it might require that individuals be able to represent general causal principles or general criteria for reidentification. P. F. Strawson, Evans, and Davidson, whose work is anti-individualist in letter or spirit, maintained Individual Representationalism.

---

[60] Some philosophers hold that no more is needed to have a perception or concept *as of* a property than to be differentially responsive to that property. On such views, representational capacities do not constitutively require relations among psychological states. They require only capacities to respond to environmental circumstances. Such views are commonly anti-individualistic, but are not entailed by anti-individualism. I reject them. See Chapter 8.

Nevertheless, I believe that all forms of Individual Representationalism are mistaken. Specific elaboration of anti-individualism undermines Individual Representationalism, and places origins of objectivity in a very different light.

Origins of empirical objectivity lie in perception. Perceptual anti-individualism and scientific accounts of perception show that there is no need for compensatory capacities that individual representationalists insist upon. Proponents of Individual Representationalism must maintain that perceptual anti-individualism and mainstream perceptual psychology are incomplete or mistaken as accounts of individuals' perception.[61]

The issue is whether the philosophical views underlying Individual Representationalism can support such contentions. I believe that the views are strikingly ungrounded. First-family Individual Representationalism is untenable on numerous grounds. Second-family proponents have undeveloped, indeed unsophisticated, accounts of perception. Their views grew and flourished in an intellectual milieu that uncritically backed their general lines of thought. They hyper-intellectualized objective representation without good reason. I trace sources of Individual Representationalism in the next four chapters.

Part of understanding the failure of Individual Representationalism lies in appreciating the weakness of the considerations given to support it. Often the doctrine was so basic to philosophical (and at times, psychological) work that it received no argument at all. Where there was argument, it tended to be cursory, overconfident, and conclusion driven.

Deeper understanding of the failure of Individual Representationalism derives from reflecting on science—particularly perceptual psychology, developmental psychology, and ethology. Some of this science matured only since the 1970s. But the basic modern way of explaining perception has nevertheless been a significant current in psychology since the late nineteenth century. During the first half of the twentieth century, when perception was a focal point of philosophical discussion, proponents of first-family Individual Representationalism failed to engage with this current. From mid-twentieth century to the last years of the century, perception was not a central concern for mainstream philosophy. When perceptual psychology matured into a science in the 1970s, second-family proponents of Individual Representationalism paid little attention. Throughout the century, empirical work on perception had astonishingly little impact on philosophical reflection on perception.

---

[61] These moves are sometimes made to seem less vulnerable by two supplementations. One is to claim that the required capacities are tacit or implicit. I criticize this claim in Chapter 9, the section PERCEPTION AS OBJECTIFICATION. The other is to maintain that although in non-human animals, perhaps, a kind of perception occurs, in humans the relevant perception must be supplemented by a capacity to represent constitutive conditions of objectivity. I criticize this move in Chapter 5, the section INDIVIDUAL REPRESENTATIONALISM AND ANTI-INDIVIDUALISM: AGAIN. There is overwhelming empirical evidence that human perceptual systems operate in broadly the same way as those of non-linguistic animals, and even animals that clearly lack propositional thought. The same empirical evidence shows that perceptual representation of the physical environment does not, in *any* perceivers, depend on capacities required by individual representationalists.

A better account of origins of objective representation must center on better understanding of perception. Elaboration of anti-individualism about perception and appreciation of the science of perception not only help undermine Individual Representationalism. They point toward a different understanding of origins of objectivity.

In Part II, I discuss Individual Representationalism critically. In Part III, I develop a more systematic account of perception. That account shows how the objectifying jobs that Individual Representationalism attributes to individual representation are filled by specific environmental–individual relations and by subindividual psychological capacities. Origins of objectivity are more primitive than individual representationalists recognized.

PART II

I have heard it said
There is an art, which in their piedness shares
With great creating Nature. Say there be;
Yet Nature is made better by no mean
But Nature makes that mean; so over that art,
Which you say adds to Nature, is an art,
That Nature makes.
  Shakespeare, *The Winter's Tale*, 4.4.87–92

4 *Individual Representationalism in the Twentieth Century's First Half*

In this chapter I begin to evoke a sense of the immense presence that Individual Representationalism has maintained in philosophy. In Chapter 1, I described two families of Individual Representationalism. Both hold that objective representation of entities in the physical environment constitutively depends on the individual's representation of preconditions for objectivity. First-family views maintain that representation of particulars in the physical environment depends on prior representation of other sorts of *particulars*. Second-family views maintain that representing *general* preconditions for objectivity are necessary for the possibility, indeed often intelligibility, of representation of environmental entities.

I concentrate mainly on first-family views in this chapter. They dominate the first half of the twentieth century. My historical sketch is cursory. It is meant to be evocative, not probing. I center on description, with only occasional critical remarks.

Although the sketch concerns the first half of the previous century, there are, as intimated in Chapter 1, historical antecedents to Individual Representationalism. Empiricists, Locke, Berkeley, Hume, and Mill take the primary objects of awareness to be ideas. Ideas either represent themselves or are represented by further ideas; or individuals are otherwise immediately and directly aware of them in perception. Ideas are supposed to be apprehended, "perceived". Representation of the physical environment is explained in terms of representation or awareness of ideas. Berkeley and Mill went further. They took not only representations of physical entities, but physical entities themselves to be products of such constructions. Crudely put, they held that physical entities are "made out of" ideas.

Although this *phenomenalist* version of empiricism reappears in the twentieth century (in Russell, Ayer, Carnap, C. I. Lewis, Goodman, and others), it is, fortunately, never dominant. The claim that *representation* of physical entities is to be explained in terms of representation or apprehension of sense data is, however, widely maintained in the first half of the century. *Sense data* are phenomenological appearances or phenomenological perspectives. They are close analogs of the *ideas* invoked by traditional empiricists.

In twentieth-century philosophy, sense data were not always regarded as mental. More often they were taken to be neither mental nor physical.

Nevertheless, apprehension of sense data was taken to have the phenomenological, authoritative, quasi-infallible features that subjective forms of representation are commonly taken to have.

INDIVIDUAL REPRESENTATIONALISM IN PSYCHOLOGY

I begin with instances of Individual Representationalism in empirical psychology, early in the twentieth century. Some of these instances influenced philosophy. Some were influenced by philosophy, particularly by British empiricism. All nourished an intellectual atmosphere permeated by Individual Representationalism.

Wilhelm Wundt introduces the position at the very beginning of scientific psychology. Wundt maintained a simple empiricist picture, inspired by Berkeley, Hume, and Mill, according to which perceptions of the physical world are complexes of simple sensations of heat, cold, light. Spatio-temporal representations are supposed to be concatenations of units of consciousness accessible to introspection.[1] Objective representation is constructed from simple, conscious, subjective representations that are fundamentally *felt* sensations. The view that the objective is built from the subjective through some sort of construction is the simplest form of Individual Representationalism.

William James wrote: 'The baby is assailed by eyes, ears, nose, skin, and entrails at once ... feels it all one great blooming buzzing confusion'.[2] James thought that a world had to be constructed out of chaos by representing patterns among the sensations. Both patterns and the sensations themselves are preconditions of objective representation.

James takes the initial sensations of an infant to be undifferentiated:

The first sensation which an infant gets is for him the Universe. .... In his dumb awakening to the consciousness of *something there*, a mere *this* as yet (or something for which even the term *this* would perhaps be too discriminative, and the intellectual acknowledgment of which would be better expressed by the bare interjection 'lo!'), the infant encounters an object in which (though it be given in a pure sensation) all the 'categories of the understanding' are contained.[3]

---

[1] Wilhelm Wundt, *Outlines of Psychology*, trans. C. H. Judd (Leipzig: Englemann, 1907), 31–32.

[2] William James, *The Principles of Psychology* (New York: Henry Holt and Company, 1890), i, chapter xiii, p. 488. See also 'Percept and Concept: The Import of Concepts', in *Some Problems of Philosophy* (New York: Longman's, Green, and Co., 1911), 50.

[3] James, *The Principles of Psychology*, ii, chapter xvii, pp. 1–8. The quote is from p. 7; the italics is James's. The obvious relation of this passage to Quine's subsequent conception of development through differentiation (and even to Quine's use of the word 'lo'—'lo a rabbit'—in expressing early predifferentiated responses to the world) is surely not accidental. James characterizes the new-born mind as 'entirely blank' with no resources for distinguishing mind-dependent reality from environmental reality. See ibid. 287–300. Interestingly, again by comparison with Quine, James regards the savage's mind as 'chaotic', and as a 'jungle'.

James was influenced by Wundt. More basically he was influenced by their common source, British empiricism. James takes sensations of heat, pain, and other "simples" to be the first representational resources of an infant. James thought that such sensations are not localized in space and do not represent any other items in space. Parceling such simples into objective representations occurs in development. James's idea that the objective is constructed out of the subjective through such parceling is another simple version of Individual Representationalism.

Like many other Individual Representationalists, James does not regard the initial condition as solipsistic. He regards it as an undifferentiated, poorly articulated registration of objective reality.[4] James's Individual Representationalism resides in the claim that an individual's representation of objective reality is to be explained in terms of a prior stage of representation of particulars that is limited by the individual's inability to differentiate ordinary properties and things in the physical environment. Objectivity is constructed from representational materials available at this prior stage, or from acquisition of general principles that transcend the stage. The prior stage of representation fits the environment poorly. Subsequent development of objectivity requires levers of construction or generalization within the individual's representational capacities.

Behaviorism in psychology dominated American psychology from the 1920s into the 1950s. Behaviorism was hostile to representation. But its concentration on surface stimulation, both as the causal source of psychologically relevant disposition and as the main touchstone in the analysis of psychological states, abetted Individual Representationalism. I shall reflect on this connection in discussing Quine (Chapter 7). Concentrating on proximal stimulation inevitably led psychology to center on individuals' local resources. An account of representation of environmental reality was doubly problematic for the behaviorist. It was problematic in being representational at all. It was further problematic in connecting the fundamental unit of psychological theory, proximal stimulation, with an environmental reality that could vary in many ways while proximal stimulation remained constant.

A primary source of resistance to behaviorism, Piaget's developmental psychology, was also a source of Individual Representationalism. In contrast to James, Piaget held that the initial developmental stage is solipsist-phenomenalist. He maintained that the child must pass through stages whereby practical manipulation of objects allows construction of a representation of a mind-independent world.[5] The stages involve mastery by the individual of principles governing causation, the mind-independence of bodies, and so on.

---

[4] Ibid. ii, *passim*, for example, 2, 319.

[5] Jean Piaget, *The Construction of Reality in the Child* (New York: Basic Books, 1954). Piaget had a huge influence on American psychology, particularly as it first emerged from the long domination by behaviorism. See George A. Miller and Robert Buckhout, *Psychology: The Science of Mental Life* (2nd edn, New York: Harper & Row, 1973), chapter 21.

Piaget's claim that practical manipulation (an analog of verification procedure) is necessary to acquire objective representation has been empirically refuted. Since the late 1970s, psychology has taken another route. Still, Piaget's picture dominated developmental psychology during much of the twentieth century. Note the direction of explanation—from a subjectivistic starting point to supplementary representational abilities that allow objective representation.

Many were attracted to Piaget's conception, because child development seemed to be analogous to the broadening of horizons that occur in education and in the development of science. Child development, adult education, and human history all seemed to be emancipations from the idiosyncratic and subjective to the shared and objective. When developmental psychology emerged from the stranglehold of behaviorism, it fed on Piaget's line of thought.

Psychology was not monolithic, of course. Even early in the century, there were currents contrary to those just highlighted. In opposing Wundt's atomistic conception of the starting point of psychology, Gestalt psychologists highlighted perceptual constancies and the fact that such constancies occur not only in young children but in chickens and apes. Perceptual constancies, to which I shall return in Chapter 9, are capacities to represent environmental attributes, or environmental particulars, as the same, despite radically different proximal stimulations.[6] The recognition that perceptual capacities appear in a variety of animals does not sit well with Individual Representationalism.

While focusing on his enemy, psychological atomism, Köhler articulates the connection between "gestalt" forms of psychological organization and a wider physical environment:

Since the rules governing this organization conform to the structure of objective units, to objective divisions, to objective 'belonging together', in very many cases the result of their operation is a kind of reconstruction of those aspects of the objective physical situation which are temporarily lost on the way between the objects and the sense organ...
Considering the situation impartially, we may come to the conclusion that organization of the field, as an original sensory fact, is much more important biologically than the properties of local stimulation are.[7]

This point remained important in the Gestalt conception. However, it was not systematically developed through experiment. The heavy reliance in Gestalt psychology on phenomenological introspection seemed to many, not just

---

[6] Wolfgang Köhler, 'Optische Untersuchungen am Schimpansen und am Haushuhn', *Berliner Abhandlungen* phys.-math. Kl. Nr 3 (1915); 'Die Farben der Sehdinge beim Schimpansen und beim Haushuhn', *Zeitschrift für Psychologie* 77 (1917), 248–255. Köhler's original experiments centered on brightness constancy. Later, many other perceptual constancies were highlighted in similar ways. For fuller accounts, see Wolfgang Köhler, *Gestalt Psychology* (New York: Horace Liveright, 1929), chapter III; and K. Koffka, *Principles of Gestalt Psychology* (1935; New York: Harcourt, Brace & World, 1963), 87–90; see also pp. 211–264.

[7] Köhler, *Gestalt Psychology*, 177–178.

behaviorists, to be insufficiently grounded in scientific experimentation.[8] In post-behaviorist cognitive and perceptual psychology, many of the specific claims made by Gestalt psychologists were experimentally refuted. Nevertheless, the more general claims and emphases of the movement, including the one just quoted, were on the right track.

Not until the 1970s did a psychology re-emerge that experimentally tied basic organizational principles to environmental patterns. At this point, psychology—particularly perceptual psychology and developmental psychology—turned decisively away from Individual Representationalism.

INDIVIDUAL REPRESENTATIONALISM IN MAINSTREAM PHILOSOPHY BEFORE THE MID-TWENTIETH CENTURY

The strands of Individual Representationalism that most concern me grow from the work of Frege and Russell. These strands are embedded in what is commonly called 'analytic philosophy'. I believe that this term is no longer appropriate. It has long failed to describe the tradition. Its connotations are now at best misleading. I prefer not to use it.[9] I use the term 'mainstream twentieth-century philosophy' for this tradition. Its broad international character and its continuity and intellectual power seem to me to have earned this description.

Mainstream twentieth-century philosophy originates in two aspects of Frege's work. One is Frege's discovery of symbolic logic and his application of it to problems in the theory of mathematical knowledge. The other is his use of logic as a means of understanding linguistic structures and linguistic meaning, broadly conceived.

These origins mark the tradition in a significant way. By centering on logical-linguistic structures and on problems in mathematics, and in later phases, problems in natural science, the mainstream tradition took on a distinctly intellectualistic bias. Its problems tended to center on the more sophisticated areas of human endeavor.

Frege and Russell were rationalists. That is, they believed that important types of human knowledge do not depend on sense experience for their warrant or justification. This belief oriented their work toward more intellectual aspects of cognitive life. Despite Russell's rationalism, much of Russell's epistemology, especially his theory of perception, is deeply indebted to British empiricism. Through most of the twentieth century, the mainstream turned away from the rationalism of Russell and Frege and embraced empiricism. Nevertheless, both

---

[8] For detailed exposition of these currents and many more, see Edwin G. Boring's classic *A History of Experimental Psychology* (1929; New York: Appleton-Century-Crofts, Inc., 1950).

[9] I discuss this terminology and various meanings and misconstruals of the term 'analytic philosophy' in *Truth, Thought, Reason: Essays on Frege: Philophical Essays, Volume 1* (Oxford: Clarendon Press, 2005), 1–10.

Russell's account of empirical knowledge and the subsequent dominant empiricism of the mainstream were strongly marked by the intellectualist origins of the tradition.

Thus the sense-data theories that grew out of Russell's work helped themselves to Russell's theory of descriptions. As we shall see, this theory postulates quite sophisticated representational abilities. The logical constructions championed by the early Russell went beyond his theory of descriptions, of course. The methods that he pioneered and championed hugely influenced subsequent philosophers. Carnap embedded his empiricism in abstract constructions of counterfactuals and laws. Quine tied his empiricism to mastery of complex logical-linguistic structures. And so on.

The anti-intellectualism of Hume, who appealed only to association among sensory "ideas" as a way of building up mental complexity, influenced early psychologists, such as Wundt and James. Hume emphasized all-purpose, associationist ways of connecting ideas. His anti-intellectualism influenced several currents in psychology and philosophy. In the larger scheme of things, however, his associationism played only a secondary role in twentieth-century philosophy. The insights deriving from the logical-linguistic tools of Frege and Russell were so substantial that even natural empiricist allies of Hume tended to transcend the oversimplifications of associationism. This development constituted genuine progress.

A less salutary side of the appreciation of propositional structure in language and psychology was a tendency to frame accounts of even the most primitive types of representation and cognition in excessively intellectualistic ways. I call such ways instances of *hyper-intellectualization*. For example, accounts of perception in the first half of the century betrayed a truly odd combination of traditional British sense-data theory and intellectualistic methods of logical construction. Accounts of perception through much of the century constitutively connected perception with rational, propositional capacities. These accounts are hyper-intellectualized. In the century's second half, perception—hence the origins of objective empirical representation—was given little sustained attention, even in accounts of empirical representation.

In this philosophical climate, Individual Representationalism thrived. Its requirement that the individual be able to represent preconditions of objectivity invited use of tools of logical construction to spell out the particular preconditions that a given philosopher thought necessary to objectivity. Having a capacity to use these tools came to be postulated as a necessary condition on objective representation, even in perception. The primary and distinctive forms of Individual Representationalism in the twentieth century have a markedly intellectualist cast.

As Hume, Mill, Wundt, James, and the behaviorists illustrate, Individual Representationalism does not have to derive from hyper-intellectualist assumptions. Moreover, the continental phenomenological tradition, which I shall discuss later in this chapter, is relatively non-intellectualist. It emphasizes the elements in perception that are independent from conception and thought.

Hyper-intellectualization is nonetheless prominent in Individual Representationalism during the previous century. Hyper-intellectualized forms are the most distinctive and original forms of the syndrome during the period.

I want now to sketch various kinds of Individual Representationalism.

Frege, the fountainhead of mainstream twentieth-century philosophy, was primarily focused on mathematics. He does, however, remark on empirical representation. In arguing for the centrality of propositional attitudes, and their abstract thought contents, in understanding science and mathematics, Frege articulates a key idea of Individual Representationalism: sensory capacities cannot in themselves represent aspects of the physical world. They need supplement:

If man could not think and could not take as the object of his thought something of which he was not the owner, he would have an inner world but no environment.... By the step with which I win an environment for myself I expose myself to the risk of error....

Having visual impressions is certainly necessary for seeing things, but not sufficient. What must still be added [a capacity to grasp abstract, structured, propositional thoughts] is not anything sensible. And yet this is just what opens up the external world for us; for without this non-sensible something everyone would remain shut up in his inner world.[10]

Here Frege sounds a theme that dominated mainstream philosophy in subsequent decades. Representation of the objective physical environment is, he claims, attainable only through grasp of propositional structures. It is attainable only through a capacity for judgment. Perception apart from thought would not suffice. Frege offers absolutely no argument for this large idea.

The remarks just quoted may not have been very influential. They are tangential to Frege's main work. A deeply influential passage occurs, however, in the earlier *The Foundations of Arithmetic*.[11] There Frege holds that internal geometrical intuitions and images are subjective, and even intersubjectively unknowable. He holds that what is objective lies in 'what is subject to laws, what can be conceived and judged, what is expressible in words'. He claims that what is purely intuitable is not communicable. Frege appears to mean that aspects of perceptual experience that are unaided by judgment—even judgment of laws— are, or would be, purely subjective. The passage that I quoted from his later work certainly suggests this position.[12]

---

[10] Gottlob Frege, 'The Thought' (1918–1919), in *Collected Papers*, ed. Brian McGuinness (Oxford: Basil Blackwell, 1984), 367, 369 (in the original, pp. 73, 75).

[11] Gottlob Frege, *The Foundations of Arithmetic* (1884), trans. J. L. Austin (1950; Evanston, IL: Northwestern University Press, 1968), section 26.

[12] As should be evident, Frege's view is more congenial to second-family forms of Individual Representationalism than to first-family forms. In this and many other respects, he was ahead of his time.

Only through judgment or belief, and perhaps even language, can an individual represent universal, law-like principles. On Frege's view, a capacity to think such principles is needed to make objective perceptual reference to a spatial world. Frege further claims that language is necessary for thought. Again, he presents these views without argument.

Frege's work contributed to a focus on objective, shareable representation. It is very far from Russell's subjectivistic epistemology, which I shall discuss shortly. Still, Frege's sharp division of the 'intuitable' from the objective, and his association of reference to a common world with mastery of laws and language, exerted a large influence on Russell and Carnap, first-family Individual Representationalists. Through his influence on these two philosophers, together with his influence on Wittgenstein, Frege had a huge effect on philosophy in the second half of the twentieth century.

Quite apart from what Frege thought about perception, his example in reflecting on objective representation in language, logic, and mathematics led subsequent philosophers to frame accounts of objective representation in relatively intellectualistic terms. Like Frege, many took perception to need supplement from propositional judgment, if it is to aid in representation of an objective world.

Russell came to Individual Representationalism through his theory of knowledge. He is an early and influential twentieth-century advocate of sense-data theory. This theory developed traditional British empiricism—the empiricism of Berkeley, Hume, and Mill. Russell is concerned with certainty. He holds that, among empirical elements of knowledge, only knowledge by "acquaintance" with sense data is certain.

The term 'sense data' (later also 'sensibles' and '*sensa*') garnered a wide variety of construals, by Russell and his successors. Sense data were, however, always conceived as items of which the perceiver has immediate and infallible sensory awareness. They were regarded as the first *objects* of perception. Paradigmatically they were regarded as objects of perceptual *awareness*. Sense data were always distinguished from physical objects and properties. This distinction was motivated by consideration of error and illusion. According to the theory, we lack infallible awareness of physical entities, since we are subject to perceptual illusion with regard to them; but we have infallible awareness of sense data. Even if we are mistaken about whether a physical object is before us, we cannot be mistaken about whether sense data are before us, or about what their features are. So went the theory.

Russell maintained that representation and knowledge of the physical environment are derivative. Such representation and knowledge go through definite descriptions constructed, through sophisticated logical devices, from acquaintance with sense data and with descriptive universals.[13] Relevant definite

---

[13] Acquaintance with empirical universals is supposed to depend on abstraction from acquaintance with sense data.

descriptions are those like 'the physical object that causes such-and-such sense data'. In his theory of descriptions, Russell analyzed sentences containing descriptions into quantified sentences. So, 'the physical object that causes such and such sense data is brown' is analyzed as 'there is a physical object that causes such and such sense data, and every physical object that causes such and such sense data is that one, and it is brown'.

Thus Russell holds that not only knowledge but the very representation of the physical world is derivative. Both depend on descriptions embedded in complex propositional thought.[14] The descriptions require representing a causal relation between physical objects and one's sense data. The descriptions also require quantification and an associated logical apparatus. The starting point for representation of the physical environment is acquaintance with sense data. Representation of the physical environment, and knowledge of it, are indirect and derivative.

Russell's theory of the nature of sense data shifted over time. He did not always conceive sense data as items in individuals' minds.[15] In fact, during most of his career Russell took a sense datum to be open to acquaintance by more than one mind. Many philosophers followed him in this view. Still, sense data were not regarded as physical entities.

Russell and his followers maintained that knowledge-by-acquaintance of sense data is certain and infallible, and that sense data are objects of perceptual reference. Acquaintance with sense data, not perception of physical objects and properties, was supposed to form the justificational foundation of empirical knowledge. The basis for representation of the physical environment is, on these views, more primitive than representation of physical entities. The basis is subjective, at least in the sense that it is accessible infallibly through phenomenological experience, and in the sense that no other person can correct an individual's acquaintance-experience. Although many philosophers held that the objects of acquaintance can be shared with others, they maintained that the epistemic route to these objects is a matter of subjective sensory feel. Sense data are alleged objects of acquaintance that co-vary perfectly with the subjective sensational states of individuals.

In some phases of his career, Russell goes further. At times he proposed that physical objects just *are* 'permanent possibilities of sensation'.[16] That is, physical objects themselves, not merely representations of them, are constructs from actual or possible congeries of sensa. They are patterns of actual or possible sensory items. This position is called *phenomenalism*.

---

[14] Bertrand Russell, 'On Denoting', *Mind* 14 (1905), 479–493; *The Problems of Philosophy* (1912; Oxford: Oxford University Press, 1982), chapter V; 'Knowledge by Acquaintance and Knowledge by Description'.

[15] Bertrand Russell, 'The Nature of Acquaintance' (1914), in *Logic and Knowledge*, ed. Robert Charles Marsh (London: Unwin Hyman, 1989).

[16] Bertrand Russell, *Our Knowledge of the External World* (London: George Allen & Unwin Ltd., 1914), chapter IV. Russell's phenomenalism seems to be motivated not only by his epistemic concerns, but by his desire to show the power of logical methods in producing constructions.

Phenomenalism is an extreme view. It takes not just representation of physical objects, but physical objects themselves, to be constructed from mental items, or at any rate from non-physical items that individuals sense infallibly. The view derives from Mill and ultimately Berkeley. It resurfaces in Carnap, Ayer, C. I. Lewis, and others, later in the century.

Russell never gave a satisfactory explanation of how mastery of a causal relation between physical objects and sense data is attained or justified. He never gave an adequate account of the justification of knowledge of the physical environment. Neither his phenomenalist view nor the less reductionistic view that physical objects are real and mind-independent, but known only through description, was given credible justification.[17] The problem of explaining the metaphysical, representational, and epistemic relations between sense data and physical entities concerned nearly all Russell's successors.

At the root of Russell's theory is the claim that in perception we are directly acquainted with perceptual objects that are not physical objects or properties. Russell maintained that these objects of acquaintance are the first objects of reference and the primary data or evidence for all knowledge, including empirical knowledge. They are the only particulars with which we are acquainted. Russell needed this point to preserve his strategy for answering scepticism. That strategy involved postulating a base of *certain* empirical knowledge and representation. Russell never gave a plausible independent argument for taking sense data (or indeed anything other than physical particulars and properties) to be the primary objects of perceptual representation.

I believe that Russell's view systematically conflates objects of reference and ways that those objects are referred to or represented. In the case of perception, the view conflates objects of perception or of perceptual representation with modes of perceptual representation.[18] In fact, the modes, representational

---

[17] Usually the constructional principle used to build objective representation from building blocks of subjective representation was required to be under the individual's control. Thus Russell took a representation of a physical body to be of the form the bodily cause of these sense data, where the individual was acquainted not only with sense data but also with the propositional functions cause and bodily, and the logical apparatus needed to construct the quantificational analysis of the definite description. Not all individual representationalists maintained that the individual must represent the relevant constructional principles, even though most did. Some phenomenalists, for example, maintained that it was enough for the individual to represent the sense data, by being acquainted with them. The counterfactual principles that describe which would-be collections of sense data constitute representations of physical bodies might be left to the scientist or philosopher. I think that this stand was probably Carnap's; see below. The phenomenalist could have maintained that it was enough for the individual to be sensitive to, or disposed to take as salient, the would-be collections that in fact constitute representation of physical bodies (and, for the phenomenalist, even constituted the bodies). Nevertheless, many phenomenalists did maintain that the underlying constructional principles are accessible to reflection. They held that the individual has to be able to represent them.

[18] Because of this conflation, it is slightly misleading to talk of acquaintance with sense data as a form of representation. Such acquaintance is, however, the basic sort of reference in perception. Russell counts sense data as objects of acquaintance, which is a sort of knowledge. He treats them as data, as the basic objects of perception. Such acquaintance lies for him at the root of representation, even though it is more presentation that representation.

contents, are not themselves perceived. They are perceptual perspectives on perceived entities. They mark types of perceptual state.

A consequence of this conflation is a further conflation. Russell systematically conflates evidence with phenomenal consciousness. At least in many cases, perceptual states are conscious for the individual perceiver. The representational function of perception is, however, not aimed at the consciousness itself. Rather the consciousness is part of how the perceptual capacity presents its objects—entities in the physical environment. The qualitative elements in consciousness are not objects of reference in perception. They are aspects of ways of referring; they are part of the perspectival framework of perceptual reference. In some cases, even among humans, perception lacks any phenomenal consciousness at all.[19] What functions as primary empirical evidence is what is referentially represented in perceptual belief. When perceptual belief is conscious, the evidence is what conscious perception and conscious belief make us aware of. These are entities in the physical environment, not aspects of our own consciousness. The science of perceptual psychology takes this same position. In the absence of serious argument to the contrary, which Russell never provides, the idea that perceptual reference and empirical evidence are, at bottom, apprehension of types of consciousness can be reasonably rejected.

Russell's approach to reference in terms of a sensory *given* had large repercussions for philosophy in the first half of the twentieth century. Although Russell's theory of acquaintance with sense data is now widely and rightly rejected, it is hard to overstate its influence during the first half of the century.

Two key elements in his conception are relevant to our themes. One is that in the most basic sort of sensory experience, there is a reference relation between observer and referent that is immune to error regarding the existence and attributes of what is experienced. The other is that in sensory experience, the basic objects of reference (the particular objects of acquaintance) are not particulars or attributes in the physical environment. Although the conception of sense data varies, these two elements remain largely constant.

It is important to remember that these doctrines bear not only on theory of knowledge. They also form the basis for an account of empirical reference or representation.

A powerful successor of Russell and Frege emerged in the positivist movement. Carnap offered a logical construction of scientific knowledge in *Die logische Aufbau der Welt*.[20] Carnap takes the 'autopsychological' as the basis

---

[19] See Chapter 9, the section PERCEPTION AS THE INDIVIDUAL'S.

[20] Rudolf Carnap, *The Logical Construction of the World: PseudoProblems in Philosophy* (1928), trans. Rolf A. George (Berkeley and Los Angeles: University of California Press, 1969). The following discussion centers on sections 54, 63–68. All quotations are from these sections. See also sections 16, 100, 103. In his choice and construal of the subjectivist constructional–epistemic basis of his system, Carnap was influenced by Husserl, earlier positivists, and Russell. See section 64. For excellent discussion of Carnap's intellectual roots, and especially his relations to neo-Kantians, see Michael Friedman, *A Parting of the Ways* (Chicago: Open Court, 2000). Friedman points out that in 1928 Carnap was not (quite) an empiricist. Carnap joined the positivist empiricists—for example, Neurath—shortly thereafter. (Note continued p. 122.)

for his construction. The autopsychological basis is 'restricted to those psychological objects which belong to only one subject'. He motivates this choice by holding that the constructional system 'should reflect not only the logical-constructional order of objects, but also their epistemic order'. Autopsychological objects are, he holds, epistemically primary in that 'recognition' of other objects 'presupposes, for its recognition, recognition [of autopsychological objects]'.

The elementary autopsychological objects are holistic momentary stages of the stream of consciousness. They are related to one another through memory of similarities among parts of such stages. Particular sense qualities and modalities are differentiated by groupings of these momentary stages via the memory relations. Particular sensory fields are then defined in formal ways, and visual objects are defined in terms of structures on these visual fields. Carnap uses Russell's logical techniques to carry out these constructions.

Carnap acknowledges that the solipsistic basis for his construction raises a problem. If the system rests on objects in an individual's psychology, the 'danger of subjectivism seems to arise'. The sort of objectivity that Carnap is concerned to account for is

independence from the judging subject, validity which holds also for other subjects. It is precisely this intersubjectivity which is an essential feature of 'reality'; it serves to distinguish reality from dream and deception.

Carnap outlines his strategy for meeting the threat of subjectivism:

The solution to this problem lies in the fact that, even though the *material* of the individual streams of experience is completely different, or rather altogether incomparable, since a comparison of two sensations or two feelings of different subjects, as far as their immediately given qualities are concerned, is absurd, certain *structural properties* are analogous for all streams of experience. Now, if science is to be objective, then it must restrict itself to statements about such structural properties, and . . . it can restrict itself to statements about structures, since all objects of knowledge are not content, but form, and since they can be represented as structural entities.

Objectivity is supposed to emerge from a subjective starting point through formulation of structural invariances that overlay and supplement a fundamentally subjective stratum of representation. Objectivity lies in the invariances. This view clearly develops Frege's view, mentioned earlier, that what is intuited in geometry is subjective and incommunicable; and what is objective in geometry is what is subject to law. Carnap regards the objective structures as relatively

---

Nelson Goodman's *The Structure of Appearance* (Cambridge, MA: Harvard University Press, 1951) was strongly influenced by Carnap's book. Goodman's work develops Carnap's constructional system. Goodman's exposition of the subjectivistic starting point of his system occurs on pp. 106–107.

abstract and accessible to reflection.[21] His position implies that objective representation is to be attained through sophisticated theoretical development.

Carnap's approach typifies positivist positions in the first two decades of the positivist movement. The logical positivists wanted to reconstruct philosophy in the image of science. They intended to provide scientifically acceptable constructions of scientific language and method. They hoped, in the process, to undermine traditional philosophical problems—showing them to be meaningless or pointless.

Positivism adapted Russell's theories of knowledge and representation for its own purposes. The movement supplemented Russell's focus on certainty with an attempt to account for natural scientific knowledge in a rigorous way that would exclude flights of metaphysical fancy. Positivism nevertheless accepted Russell's subjectivist starting point for its accounts of knowledge and representation.

A parallel, non-positivist development of Russell's ideas played out in British theories of knowledge. This tradition centered on the relation of perception to physical reality. In the background lay Russell's concern with certainty and with answering scepticism. This British tradition saw itself as dealing with functional, metaphysical, and epistemic questions about perception and perceptual knowledge. Although this tradition differed from positivism in seeing itself as a continuation of traditional philosophy, it shared with positivism the Russellian subjectivist conception of perceptual experience.

G. E. Moore was impressed by Russell's acquaintance/description distinction. He pursued his theory of perception under the guidance of Russell's notion of acquaintance, which he sometimes called 'direct apprehension'. He maintains with Russell that all empirical knowledge is based on experiences consisting in direct apprehension of sensibles. Moore argues that if two people look at the same coin from different angles, the visual sensible that each sees or directly apprehends is different. Since they are different, they cannot both be identical with either the surface of the coin or the coin itself. There seems no reason to prefer one person's sensible to another's in identifying it with the coin or its surface. So

---

[21] Wittgenstein's *Tractatus Logico-Philosophicus* (1921; London: Routledge & Kegan Paul, 1961) was probably an influence on Carnap and more generally on positivism. The book develops broadly Russellian constructivist methods that build complex thought from simples. Wittgenstein seemed to regard the simples as objects of acquaintance, but he did not elaborate the point. Wittgenstein goes beyond Russell in claiming that purported propositions that are not constructible using such methods are nonsense or meaningless. The positivists added that the primitive propositions must be expressed by observation statements and that the proposition expressed by a complex statement must be a method of empirical verification. The early Wittgenstein was uninterested in epistemology and agnostic about the nature of objects of acquaintance. So, although his construction seems empiricist and positivist in spirit, it is not so in letter. Moreover, his abstention from pronouncements on the nature of objects of acquaintance prevents his view from being strictly individual representationalist, as far as I can see. Nevertheless what little he does say about acquaintance appears largely compatible with Russell's Individual Representationalism. For his remarks on acquaintance (*kennen*), see 2.0123, 2.01231, 3.263, 4.021, 4.243, 6.2322. For the qualification 'largely', see 6.3751.

he concludes that visual sensibles (sense data) are to be distinguished from surfaces and physical bodies.[22]

I believe that this reasoning perfectly illustrates the basic conflation in Russell's account of perception, and reference generally. This is the conflation of mode of presentation or representational content (or phenomenal aspect of mode of presentation or representational content), on one hand, and object of representation or *representatum*, on the other. This partly intentional, but largely unargued, conflation drove the conviction of the post-Russellian British tradition that sense data—which were for them fundamentally perceptual perspectives—are *objects* of perception. Philosopher after philosopher held this conviction without argument. The conviction was for a half-century the foundation of reasoning about perception, representation, and knowledge in the British tradition.

Moore was also impressed with Russell's temporary phenomenalism, although he seems never to have accepted it. He plays up its virtues against unsatisfactory objections, raised worries about it, pits it against the view that sense data are object surfaces (a view he was attracted to despite arguing against it), and favors the line that sense data are neither mental nor physical. He professes himself confused about how we can know that sense data have their 'source' in physical objects.[23]

The idea that the first objects of perception are sense data—objects of infallible, direct apprehension—remained the foundation of Moore's thinking. Moore insists that in a perceptual judgment of the form that is an inkstand, it is 'quite certain' that the object judged about is not the inkstand. He rests this claim on the further claim that the 'presented object about which the judgment plainly is' is not the whole inkstand. He writes that 'any child can see' the truth of this further claim. The presented object is supposed to be the sense datum. Here we see a man striving to maintain touch with common sense, but driven to genuine oddity by being in the grip of a philosophical error.

In a secondary sense, Moore concedes, the judgment is about the inkstand. He holds that any such judgment must primarily be about the sense datum, which 'mediates' perception of the inkstand. He holds that, 'if there is anything which is this inkstand, then, in perceiving that thing, I am knowing it *only* as *the* thing which stands in a certain relation to this sense-datum'. He goes on to claim that any such inkstand is 'quite certainly only known to me by description, in the sense in which Mr. Russell uses that phrase'. Moore insists that these points are so clear that he wonders how anyone could deny them, and he muses that perhaps no one ever had.[24]

Moore struggles with the question of the nature of sense data and their relation to physical objects. His discussion is ingenious and open-ended. However, he

[22] G. E. Moore, 'The Status of Sense-Data' (1913–1914), in *Philosophical Studies* (London: Kegan, Paul, Trench,Trubner & Co. Ltd, 1922), 187.
[23] Ibid. 187–196.
[24] G. E. Moore, 'Some Judgments of Perception' (1918–1919), in *Philosophical Studies*, 229–237.

never questions the ideas that perceptual judgments are *not* primarily judgments about physical objects, and that both perception and perceptual judgment make primary reference to sense data. Physical objects are represented only through a derivative relation to sense data.

C. D. Broad produced an exceptionally detailed account of the relation between sensory experience, sense data, and physical entities. He distinguishes sensation events from the entities, *sensa*, that they are sensations of. Such *sensa* 'lead us to judge that a physical object exists and is present to our senses'. Broad regards *sensa* neither as surfaces (or other parts) of physical bodies nor as contents of the mind. He holds that they depend on both mind and body for their natures and properties. He believes that *sensa* have an intermediate, 'peculiar' existential status. Broad takes *sensa* to have geometrical properties and to be colored. In fact, he argues himself into the strange view that only *sensa* and not physical objects have spatial properties and enter into spatial relations in the 'strictest sense'. He claims that physical objects enter into only an analog of spatial relations.[25]

On Broad's view, sensings of *sensa* are private, authoritative events. Such sensings are immune to error. In this respect, they are like Russell's acquaintance. Broad holds that getting beyond *sensa* to physical objects is a step that requires judgment. Broad's Individual Representationalism is not solipsistic. Still, he maintains that in perception itself the individual has a merely private relation to perceptual objects. He holds that achieving objective representation of the physical environment is a task of considerable intellectual complexity.

Broad recognizes that his theory is far from common sense. He writes defiantly: '*Any* theory that can possibly fit the facts is *certain* to shock common-sense somewhere; and in face of the facts we can only advise common-sense to follow the example of Judas Iscariot, and "go out and hang itself".'[26]

H. H. Price takes Broad's reflections on *sensa* a step further. Price holds, with Broad and Russell, that 'the material thing whose existence we take for granted differs radically from any datum that we sense'.[27] Price asserts that sense data are transitory, spatially incomplete, and lacking in causal properties. Material bodies have the contraries of these various characteristics. Price goes further than Broad

---

[25] C. D. Broad, *Scientific Thought* (London: Routledge & Kegan Paul Ltd, 1923), chapter VIII; *The Mind and its Place in Nature* (London: Routledge & Kegan Paul Ltd, 1925), chapter IV. Does the representational relation to the 'neutral' entities as occurring in spatial relations, which Broad postulates, count as an *objective* representational relation? Since the entities are supposed to be perspective-independent, the natural answer is 'yes'. Broad's 'neutral' entities are nonetheless sense data that are the correlates of subjective sensory awareness. He thought that we are infallible both about their existence and about the attributes we apprehend them to have. Such claims of infallibility for immediate, phenomenological acquaintance can be reasonably regarded as subjectivistic. They are not open to check or criticism from different perceivers on the same subject matter. So, although they are officially non-mental and 'objective', the relevant *sensa* can be commonsensically regarded as bearing an incestuous relation to mind.

[26] Broad, *The Mind and its Place in Nature*, 186.

[27] H. H. Price, *Perception* (London: Methuen Co. Ltd, 1932), 145.

in maintaining that the main, knowable characteristics of physical bodies are 'constructs' out of sense data.

Price stops short of phenomenalism. He stops short only by holding that physical occupation of space cannot be constructed out of sense data. Nevertheless, the main empirical characteristics of physical bodies are, for him, congeries—or counterfactual possibilities—of sense data. Sense data themselves are, according to Price, neither mental nor physical. Price's view is a large step toward phenomenalism. With his predecessors, Price claims that such neutral 'phenomena' are accessible only privately, to individual minds.[28]

Following in the tradition of Russell, Moore, Broad, and Price, A. J. Ayer tries to simplify Price's ontological view by returning to Carnap's phenomenalism.[29] Physical bodies themselves are to be regarded, according to Ayer, as constructs from actual and possible sense data. He maintains, 'any proposition that refers to a material thing must somehow be expressible in terms of sense data, if it is to be empirically significant'. Physical bodies are to be regarded as 'permanent possibilities of sensation'.[30] Thus, for Ayer, not only is representation of physical bodies conceptually and epistemically posterior to representation of sense data. Physical bodies are themselves mere constructs from actual and counterfactual encounters with sense data.

The phenomenalist point of view—whether or not it was accepted, as it was by Ayer and (during certain periods) Carnap and Russell—had a surprising respectability among eminent philosophers in the first half of the twentieth century. The role of sense data in philosophy was so central that the ontological status of physical bodies was constantly in question. Even where philosophers clung to more straightforward views about the nature of physical objects, there remained a consensus that accessing physical bodies—epistemically or just representationally— is problematic. Access was said to run through sense data. Sense data were taken to be internal to an individual mind, or at least accessible only privately and infallibly by each individual.

C. I. Lewis was the primary American epistemologist who carried on the British appeal to sense data. Lewis's work centers on justification more than ontology or representation. Like Ayer, however, he falls into a phenomenalist account of the ontological status of physical bodies.

Lewis calls sense data, or *sensa*, the sensory *given*. He takes the sensory *given* to be the base of representation and justification. He holds that the given is a 'presentation-content' whose non-inferential givenness is its own justification.

---

[28] H. H. Price, *Perception* (London: Methuen Co. Ltd, 1932), 316–321.

[29] A. J. Ayer, *The Foundations of Empirical Knowledge* (1940; London: MacMillan & Co. Ltd, 1962); see especially pp. 220–274. Ayer criticizes Carnap's conventionalism. He maintains that although there is scope for choice of language, and although many issues are 'merely linguistic', the phenomenalistic order of explanation is objectively superior to alternatives (see pp. 78–135).

[30] Ibid. The quotes come from pp. 231, 244, respectively. See also Ayer's 'Phenomenalism' (1947–1948) in *Philosophical Essays* (London: MacMillan & Co. Ltd, 1954). See also H. H. Price's 'Review of *The Foundations of Empirical Knowledge*', *Mind* NS 50 (1941), 280–293.

With his British predecessors, Lewis claims that error regarding the given is impossible.[31] A physical object is 'never a momentarily given as such, but is some temporally-extended pattern of actual and possible experience'.

According to Lewis, both the representation of such objects and the justification of belief in them lie in predictable and verifiable relations among the given elements in experience.[32] Lewis stands firmly in the tradition that takes representation of sense data to be prior to representation of physical bodies. More specifically, perceptual belief about environmental objects derives both content and justification from hypothetical, broadly probabilistic predictive forms of verification that ultimately lead back to sensory experiences. Such experiences are not experiences of objective, physical objects or properties in the environment.

Lewis writes of the hypothetical predictive relation as

an inductively established correlation by virtue of which one observable item in experience is a probability-index of another. Without such real connections no belief in, or statement of, any matter of objective fact could have any content of meaning whatever.[33]

Again, according to Lewis, sensory experience does not make reference to physical objects in the environment. Objectivity results from constructions that involve predictive propositional beliefs.

In this review, I have made no detailed reference to Wittgenstein. His work is hard to pin down. His early writing in *Tractatus Logicus-Philosophicus* is certainly in the spirit of constructivist, first-family forms of Individual Representationalism (see note 21). He is, however, non-committal both on the nature of the atoms or building blocks of the construction, and on the nature of representation of those building blocks.

Wittgenstein's later work is evasive about *theses* on most topics. It is unclear whether Wittgenstein was committed to Individual Representationalism. Wittgenstein does attack subjectivistic elements in philosophy. He attacks the idea that there can be private languages and the idea that mental items or mental states can be accessed only privately. This attack is at least implicitly directed at sense-data theories. He criticizes construals of meaning that give great weight to phenomenological feeling or sensation. There is a constant emphasis on understanding linguistic meaning through public criteria as applied to observable behavior and observable linguistic use. Moreover, there is a broad anti-individualist

---

[31] C. I. Lewis, *An Analysis of Knowledge and Valuation* (1946; La Salle, IL: Open Court Publishing Company, 1950), 26; see pp. 182–183. The translation of 'datum' as 'given', and the idea that sense data were at least to be initially explained as the sensory given goes back at least to Moore. See his 'The Status of Sense-Data', 171. Moore appears to be trading on well-established usage.

[32] The quote is from C. I. Lewis, *Mind and the World Order* (New York: Charles Scribner's Sons, 1929), 37. Lewis's fuller development of the representational and justificational relations between the sensory given and empirical belief occurs in *An Analysis of Knowledge and Valuation*, p. 178 and chapter VIII.

[33] Lewis, *An Analysis of Knowledge and Valuation*, 250.

element in his work. Wittgenstein is usually thought of as a defender of objective methods and the objectivity of representation. In many respects, this assessment is correct.

Nevertheless, Wittgenstein's work directly encouraged Individual Representationalism. His emphasis on having *criteria* for the applications of words and his focus on language and on the complex background to any linguistic reference led others to seek in linguistic usage a basis for understanding the representational aspects of experience, indeed of all objectivity. We shall see more specific embodiments of this idea in Chapters 6 and 7.[34]

Saul Kripke's prominent interpretation of Wittgenstein's work takes it to entail the fundamental tenet of Individual Representationalism.[35] Kripke's Wittgenstein offers only a surrogate for objective representation. In a sense, Kripke's Wittgenstein does not believe in representation as having definite content. Here, Kripke's Wittgenstein is like Quine. In a sense, neither believes in objective representation at all. The attribution of representation or thought about definite mind-independent entities is taken to be a misleading gloss on patterns of behavior (in Quine's case) or usage and phenomenal experience (in the case of Kripke's Wittgenstein). Wittgenstein's view is supposed to give a 'sceptical' solution to a sceptical problem.

For Kripke's Wittgenstein, however, the formulation of the sceptical problem uses a core idea in Individual Representationalism: if objective representation were to be possible, there would have to be an association of perceptual representation with a further representation of fundamental conditions of objectivity. This idea constitutes an analog of a more specific idea in second-family Individual Representationalism: objective representation is possible only if relatively simple sorts of empirical representation are supplemented by other sorts that represent *general* conditions for the application of the simple sorts—criteria for application.

Kripke's Wittgenstein claims that if an individual cannot represent or otherwise reproduce the conditions of objectivity, or associate them with a criterion for applying terms to possible cases, the individual cannot represent objective matters. Kripke's Wittgenstein denies not the primitivity of (would-be) objective representation of the physical environment, but its autonomy. To represent definite properties and objects in the environment by ostensibly elementary empirical means, an individual's perceptual capacities must be associated with further, higher-level representational capacities. These capacities are capacities to represent *general* preconditions of objectivity. In this respect, the view is in line with the second-family forms of Individual Representationalism, which dominated the twentieth century's second half.

---

[34] See, for example, Ludwig Wittgenstein, *Philosophical Investigations* (1953; New York: MacMillan Publishing Co., 1968), 193–214, especially 209.
[35] Kripke does not isolate Individual Representationalism. He attributes to Wittgenstein views that are in fact constitutive of at least the negative theses of Individual Representationalism.

For Kripke's Wittgenstein, the further, higher-level capacities are the correcting capacities of others in the individual's linguistic community.[36] Kripke's Wittgenstein does not require that the correctional capacities be the individual's. So a key claim of Individual Representationalism is absent in Kripke's Wittgenstein. The sceptical solution does not require that the individual have higher-level correcting capacities, if he or she is to have (the sceptical analog of) objective representation. Still, the view is motivated by individual representationalist ideas. Those ideas are simply given a social cast, a cast later taken up by Davidson.

According to Kripke, Wittgenstein holds that to be counted as having psychological states with definite representational content regarding a physical world, or regarding anything else, an individual must be in communication with other language users. Or, at least, the individual must be 'taken into the community' of language users. Their dispositions to respond linguistically provide a check on the individual's own dispositions and yield a surrogate objectivity.

The whole line of thought depends on claiming that *since the individual cannot articulate or justify his own reactions—cannot himself represent conditions for objective application—further representational activity is required to make possible (a surrogate for) objectivity.* Autonomous, primitive objective representation is impossible. Further representational activity is needed to indicate preconditions for objectivity—activity marked by criteria of application. The conditions are mirrored in socio-linguistic correctional patterns, if not in individual psychologies.

INDIVIDUAL REPRESENTATIONALISM IN "CONTINENTAL" PHILOSOPHY BEFORE THE MID-TWENTIETH CENTURY

I turn from this sketch of Individual Representationalism in mainstream philosophy in the first half of the twentieth century to a yet briefer sketch of related ideas in the "continental tradition" during the same period. This tradition propounds ideas parallel to those in mainstream twentieth-century philosophy.

---

[36] Saul Kripke, *Wittgenstein on Rules and Private Language* (Cambridge, MA: Harvard University Press, 1982), see especially 49–54, 87–95, 98–102, 107–109. We shall see this negative point in the Individual Representationalism of the work of Quine and Davidson. Davidson explicitly connects his views to those of Wittgenstein, indeed Kripke's interpretation of Wittgenstein. See Donald Davidson, *Subjective, Intersubjective, Objective* (Oxford: Clarendon Press, 2001), 116, 121, 129, 143.

Kripke centers mostly on following a rule in mathematics. His points are, however, clearly intended (as interpretations of Wittgenstein) to apply to any representational activity. Kripke calls the sceptical paradox that he attributes to Wittgenstein 'the most radical and original sceptical problem that philosophy has seen to date' (*Wittgenstein on Rules and Private Language*, 60). I believe, to the contrary, that the problem is toothless. I think that Kripke's attempt to show that the problem is a major one, particularly in response to the view that representational states are 'primitive' states, not to be assimilated to or explained in terms of non-representational dispositions or sensations, is extremely cursory and uncharacteristically weak. See ibid. 51–54.

The "continental" tradition is less overtly intellectualistic than the mainstream. It engages in recurrent criticism of mainstream intellectualistic approaches, especially approaches to perceptual experience. It is less concerned with logic and language, and more centered on phenomenological reflection.

I believe that implicit in the method of phenomenological reflection is, however, a form of intellectual hubris. The idea is that the conditions determining objective representation are ultimately sufficiently under the control of the individual to be retrievable through reflection. I believe that this approach is misguided in two ways. First, it overrates how available to reflection basic preconditions of objectivity are. Second, it overrates the importance and clarity of phenomenology as a route to understanding perceptual (or other) representational content. It overrates the degree to which the nature and categories of perceptual experience are, or need to be, open to phenomenological reflection.

Husserl takes 'primordial' phenomenological elements of experiences to underlie reference to the physical world. These elements are neutral about the existence and nature of environmental reality. Husserl initially 'brackets' the representational relevance of these elements to the physical environment. He understands objectivity as a construction out of them. An objectively referring perceptual experience is a product of a 'transcendental construction' out of these neutral 'noetic' elements. The key idea is that this construction derives from acts of the individual that can be reconstructed through phenomenological reflection. Philosophy's job is to find the bases for the construction and to reconstruct.[37]

Here we have an analog of the constructivist projects of Carnap and the British sense-data theorists. One begins with ur-elements that are either mental or 'neutral' (neither mental nor physical). One then builds up a representation of physical reality through rules of construction. The difference lies in the methods of construction.

Husserl rejects proto-typical empiricist and intellectualist versions of construction. According to the proto-typical *empiricist* view, patterns of association of sensory qualia, or certain inferences regarding those patterns, provide what objective meaning there is. Husserl criticizes the reductionism of this view. A proto-typical *intellectualist* approach holds that some intellectual capacity, typically a capacity for judgment or propositional inference, confers objectivity on otherwise non-objective sensory material. Husserl believes in various levels of objectivity-bestowing acts. Some are subpropositional and 'immanent' within perception. Thus Husserl distinguishes between perception and propositional

---

[37] Edmund Husserl, *Ideas—General Introduction to Pure Phenomenology* (1913), trans. W. R. Boyce Gibson (London: George Allen & Unwin Ltd, 1952). The points made here are derived from sections 33, 41, 55, 85–90, 94–97, 101, 131, 150–151. See also *Experience and Judgment* (1938), trans. James S. Churchill and Karl Ameriks (Evanston, IL: Northwestern University Press, 1973), especially Introduction and Part I.

attitudes and, correspondingly, between noematic acts that underlie perception and those that underlie judgment.[38]

There are insights in Husserl's separation of perception from judgment. From the present perspective, however, differences between Husserl and these two proto-typical mainstream approaches (British sense-data theory and Carnapian constructivism) are less impressive than similarities. With both traditions, Husserl holds that objectivity derives from idealized events (which he counts as 'transcendental' acts) that are accessible to the individual through reflection. The acts operate on a base that is either subjective or non-committal regarding the physicality of the objects of experience. Such reflection is called 'phenomenological'.

Like most of the sense-data theorists, Husserl regards his method as not looking into the contents of an individual mind. Reflection is supposed to yield knowledge not of psychological transactions but of essences or objective structures, and of idealized acts. Nevertheless, the method assumes that one can reconstruct the nature of objectivity by reflecting on pre-objective elements that are accessible to armchair individual reflection.

Significantly, Husserl assumes, in his 'bracketing' method of phenomenological reflection, that it is possible to understand the nature and content of perception from an antecedent and independent perspective—without any consideration of perceptual reference to the physical environment. The content of perception, on his view, can be fully understood while remaining agnostic about elements in the physical environment. The point here is not just that Husserl takes up a first-person point of view on perceptual contents. It is that he construes those contents as not already implicating reference and attribution to the physical environment. In this respect, Husserl's conception of perception is very like that of the phenomenalist/sense-data-theorists inspired by Russell.

Heidegger took up Husserl's methodology. In *Being and Time*, he championed reflection on phenomena that 'showed themselves' to reflection. As with Husserl, the relevant reflection is supposed not to presuppose science, common sense, or ordinary perception. The fundamental category for Heidegger's investigations, *Dasein*, applies to entities that are '*in each case mine*'. Such categories are to be understood by entering a 'peculiar phenomenological domain' and abstracting from the 'merely present-at-hand within the world'. The main ontological categories for Heidegger are found through a phenomenological reflection that is available to the individual and that purports to reveal a primitive order *prior to spatial order*.[39]

Heidegger's idea of reflection is partly inspired by Kantian transcendental reflection. Yet Heidegger pursues the idea very differently from Kant. In contrast

---

[38] Husserl, *Ideas*, Author's Preface to the English edition, sections 19–20, 100–101, and *Experience and Judgment*, part I.

[39] Martin Heidegger, *Being and Time* (1927), trans. John Macquarrie and Edward Robinson (New York: Harper & Row, Publishers, 1962), 60–63, 67–71, 78–90; H: 35–40, 41–46, 54–62.

to Kant, Heidegger holds that the categories obtained by such reflection will reorient those of science and common sense rather than be found to be embedded within them. Thus philosophy is supposed to employ a phenomenological reflection that abstracts from entities that seem 'ready to hand' and even from ordinary perception and perceptual judgment. The reflection is supposed to get at more basic existences (having to do with a sense of *practical capacity*) independently. These existences are bound up with the subject's point of view and constitute the makings of what is fundamentally real or objective. Consciousness of objects in the world is derived from consciousness of a more basic practical capacity.

I do not believe that Heidegger thought of these existences as mental or as simple objects of introspection. I do not believe that he held that outer representation is a construct from a prior inner representation. But there is a formal analogy between Heidegger's procedure and tenets of first-family Individual Representationalism. For Heidegger objectivity does not derive from perceptual interaction with the physical environment. It consists in individual practical activity or capacities for such activity that are *accessible* to the reflecting individual.[40]

Although Heidegger emphasizes differences from Husserl, he shares with Husserl the view that reflection provides full access to the fundamental character of something prior to objectivity, and from which objectivity—or consciousness of objects—in common sense or in science is to be derived. Objectivity, including any representation of a spatial order, derives from reflection on and construction from prior elements *accessible to reflection*.

Merleau-Ponty follows Husserl in rejecting the view, which we encountered in Frege, that judgment is 'what sensation lacks to make perception possible'. He emphasizes differences between perception and judgment. These emphases seem salutary. He takes the meaning-giving element on which objective reference to the physical world depends to be less intellectual than Frege does. But with Husserl, he holds that 'the act of perception' should be grasped from within by 'authentic introspection'. What is grasped in 'authentic introspection' is an 'act which creates at a stroke, along with the cluster of data, the meaning which unites them—indeed which not only discovers the meaning *which they have*, but moreover *causes them to have a meaning*'.[41] Despite the 'at a stroke' rhetoric, Merleau-Ponty takes perception to require a concatenation of perspectives over time. All these perspectives are introspectible.

---

[40] See especially Heidegger, *Being and Time*, sections 12–13, 37, 44.

[41] Maurice Merleau-Ponty, *Phenomenology of Perception* (1945), trans. Colin Smith (London: Routledge & Kegan Paul, 1966), 32–36. Merleau-Ponty is more empiricist than Husserl. I believe that his interpretation of Descartes's wax passage of the second *Meditation* as placing Descartes in the proto-typical intellectualist tradition described in the text above is less fair to Descartes's own conception of perception and less sensitive to the generic quality of Descartes's conception of 'thinking' than is Husserl's discussion. See Husserl, *Ideas*, section 34. Merleau-Ponty does provide a vivid criticism of the weaknesses of proto-typical empiricist and intellectualist views.

The 'at a stroke' rhetoric replicates Husserl's idea that meaning is 'bestowed' by phenomenological mental activity that is attributable to the individual and that is accessible to the individual through reflection. It is not clear how this activity makes even purported representational connection to the physical environment. I believe that this idea, shared by many in the phenomenological tradition, provides no clear answer to the question it poses.

Merleau-Ponty maintains that meaning-constitution is something special to mature humans.[42] He holds that the world is 'marginal to the child's first perception as a presence as yet unrecognized . . . which knowledge will subsequently make determinate and complete'. He follows Husserl in holding that the nature of meaning-constitution is open to phenomenological reflection. He differs from Husserl in not holding that meaning-constitution is an act. It is supposed to be 'beyond' the active/passive distinction. But with Husserl, he holds that there is an 'order of meaning that does not result from the application of spiritual activity to an external matter'.[43] And with the whole phenomenological tradition, he maintains that objective representation is a construction from prior representational, experiential material,[44] and that the material and construction are recoverable by the individual through phenomenological reflection.

As with Husserl and Heidegger, Merleau-Ponty's philosophical method takes an introspective, phenomenological starting point. This starting point appears to be individualist. He maintains that one can understand perception or language independently of consideration of actual referents in the physical environment. He believes that the *conditions for objectivity* are introspectable because they are phenomenological products of acts or events in individual minds.

I conclude this section by discussing Cassirer. I place Cassirer last, even though his main work stems from the 1920s, before both Heidegger's and Merleau-Ponty's. Cassirer's thinking is more modern in two respects.

First, it makes fuller use of science and other human activities in attempting to understand their underlying presuppositions. It seeks to understand presuppositions of these activities not primarily through phenomenological reflection but by reflection on the activities themselves.

Second, his view of the conditions of objectivity anticipate the views of Strawson and Quine. He sees the origin of objectivity not so much in a construction from proto-objective material, or in a phenomenologically recoverable, meaning-bestowing act on such material. Rather he sees the origin in the individual's representation of *general conditions* of objectivity. He is thus, like Frege, a relatively rare second-family individual representationalist in the first half of the

---

[42] Merleau-Ponty emphasizes the role of the body in meaning constitution. He largely avoids the idealism that marks much of Husserl's work. Though not entirely: see Maurice Merleau-Ponty, 'The Primacy of Perception and Its Philosophical Consequences' (1947), in *The Primacy of Perception and Other Essays*, ed. James M. Edie (Evanston, IL: Northwestern University Press, 1971), 16.

[43] Merleau-Ponty, *Phenomenology of Perception*, 326–334. The last quote is from 'Phenomenology and the Sciences of Man' (1961), in *The Primacy of Perception and Other Essays*, 77.

[44] Ibid. 80.

twentieth century. His neo-Kantian background led him to enunciate themes that anticipate the kind of Individual Representationalism that dominated the latter half of the twentieth century. Moreover, he is like Quine and Davidson in regarding mastery of language as the only means by which the needed representation of general conditions becomes possible.

In accord with the times, Cassirer postulates a pre-individuative, pre-objective representational state. His Individual Representationalism resides in his thinking that to achieve objectivity, an individual must have capacities to represent general conditions of objectivity—roughly, criteria.

Cassirer's account of the emergence of objectivity is distinctive. He postulates an 'expressive', animistic level of perceptual meaning, which he takes myth to articulate:

The farther back we trace perception, the greater becomes the preeminence of the 'thou' form over the 'it' form, and the more plainly the purely expressive character takes precedence over the matter or thing-character. The understanding of expression is essentially earlier than the knowledge of things.[45]

Cassirer tells his version of the story of the emergence of objective representation from a prior pre-objective stage. The prior stage for animals is a type of perception

that does not yet yield stable things with determinate attributes which may change in the thing itself but also possess an intrinsic property of permanence. From the complex whole of a perceptive experience the animal does not detach particular characteristics by which it recognizes a content and which identify it as the same content regardless of how often and under what different conditions it appears. This sameness is not at all a factor that is contained in the immediate experience—on the plane of sensory experience itself there is no 'recurrence of the same'. Every sense impression, taken purely as such, possesses a peculiar, never recurring tonality or coloration.[46]

Cassirer believes that animals never emerge from this non-objective stage.

The prior stage for humans is one of myth and animism. Cassirer invests the expressivist-animistic stage with a romantic liveliness and dynamism. He associates it with instability and 'Heraclitean flux'. Language makes possible representation of stable attributes of the physical environment. Cassirer speculates that there is 'an elementary stratum of linguistic utterance in which the tendency toward representation is present only in its germinal beginnings, if at all. Here language moves almost exclusively in purely expressive elements and characters.' He continues: 'in the child the function of designation stands only at the end

---

[45] Ernst Cassirer, *The Philosophy of Symbolic Forms*, iii. *The Phenomenology of Knowledge*, trans. Ralph Manheim (1929; New Haven: Yale University Press, 1957), 63. Volume iii was first published in 1929. Volumes i and ii were published in 1923 and 1925 respectively.

[46] Ibid. iii. 120. The claim of a lack of mastery of a principle of identity is obviously similar to points made by Strawson and Quine. I remark further on broader similarities among these thinkers below.

of linguistic development; here, too, the words of the objective language which he acquires by learning have for a long time not the specific, objectivizing meaning which highly developed language connects with them.'[47]

The key element in language mastery that allows emergence from express-ivist-animistic forms of experience is supposed to be the mastery of names. But even the initial uses of names are pre-objective:

in the development of the child there is no doubt that the intuition of the world of things does not exist from the beginning but must in a sense be wrested from the world of language. The first "names" which the child masters and uses with understanding seem to designate no fixed and permanent objects but only more or less fluid and vague general impressions.[48]

Language is supposed to provide a stability and equilibrium which pre-linguistic experience lacks. From flux and instability, the child gains objectivity through the mastery of names—and implicitly through the tools for reidentification that language provides.

The investigation of language has shown us the general direction in which this positing of characteristics moves. From the passing dream of images, language first singles out certain factors, certain stable particularities and attributes. . . .

When the representative function of names has thus dawned on a child, his whole inner attitude toward reality has changed—a fundamentally new relation between subject and object has come into being. Only now do the objects which hitherto acted directly on the emotions and will begin in a sense to recede into the distance: into a distance where they can be "looked at," "intuited," in which they can be actualized in their spatial outlines and independent qualitative determinations.[49]

These lines of thought anticipate lines in Strawson and Quine.

Although the emphases in the phenomenological tradition are less intellectu-alistic than the mainstream tradition—with less emphasis on logical or linguistic methods of construction—the tradition remains individual representationalist. Basic experience is of non-environmental, introspectible particulars. Objectivity derives from mentation by the individual that bestows objectivity on this ante-cedent material. The meaning-bestowing events are recoverable in phenomeno-logical reflection. Such meaning-bestowing events in effect form the base of a construction that yields objectivity.

Like early Carnap, Cassirer respected this phenomenological tradition, but stood apart from it. Both thought that perception needed more formal structures if it is to provide objective reference to the environment. Both saw modern mathe-matics as the source of structure that ultimately provides objectivity. Cassirer

---

[47] Ibid. iii. 109.

[48] Ibid. iii. 121.

[49] Ibid. iii. 115, 113. I find Cassirer attractive in his development of a plurality of *levels* and *types* of objectivity, and in his sensitivity to the fact that some of these types are grounded in non-scientific aspects of human culture. All of these types are, however, well beyond what are *in fact* the primitive origins of objectivity.

differed from Carnap in postulating intermediate forms—expressivist forms associated with animism and myths—prior to elementary linguistic and mathematical forms. Neither gave reflection on phenomenal experience the role it had in the phenomenological tradition. Cassirer was nearer to the approaches of the latter half of the century in that he did not assume that objectivity is constructed from antecedent sensory material, as early Carnap did.[50] He saw objectification as embedding sensory experience in structures that represent general conditions on objectivity.

I will not follow these reflections on early twentieth-century "continental" philosophy into the work of continental successors during the century's second half. The hermeneutical tradition concentrates on language and human history as sources of what objectivity it acknowledges. Where it does not give up on objectivity altogether, I believe that it continues and radicalizes the individual (or social) representationalist themes that I have been outlining. I leave it to others to check or develop this conjecture.

[50] Later Carnap is a complex figure whom I do not discuss here.

5 *Individual Representationalism after Mid-Century: Preliminaries*

I will not survey second-family versions of Individual Representationalism. Since they are more alive philosophically, discussing them requires more detail. I discuss only a few positions. In this chapter I focus on relations between second-family Individual Representationalism and other standpoints that either reinforced it or began to undermine it. In Chapters 6 and 7, I discuss some second-family views in depth.

Sense-data theory was the prevailing form of Individual Representationalism in mainstream philosophy during the twentieth century's first half. By the early 1950s, the influence of sense-data theory was fast evaporating. In the positivist tradition, in the 1930s, a shift from taking sense-data language as basic to taking physical-object language as basic had already begun. This shift stemmed from reflection on natural science. The British sense-data tradition later fell of its own weight. It had strayed too far from science and common sense.[1]

Sense-data theories did not influence subsequent philosophizing except negatively. They left little residue. They died unmourned. Philosophical attention shifted away from perception. The main charges against sense-data theories are, however, worth highlighting, since *they* mark subsequent philosophizing very deeply.

Apart from their departures from common sense, sense-data approaches were rejected on two main grounds. First, they were cricized as *subjectivistic*. By basing accounts of representation on experiential episodes that are private and uncorrectable, such approaches were said to miss the objectivity and intersubjectivity in language and science. Second, sense-data approaches were criticized for

---

[1] J. L. Austin's attack on Ayer in *Sense and Sensibilia* (Oxford: Clarendeon Press, 1962) epitomizes the shift. The ordinary language philosophy that supplanted sense-data theories in England was relatively short lived. Austin's attack was a late expression of a broad shift. See also Wilfrid Sellars, 'Phenomenalism', in *Science, Perception, and Reality* (London: Routlege & Kegan Paul, 1963). I believe that much had been done to overthrow sense-data theories before Austin wrote. Wittgenstein's *Philosophical Investigations* and Strawson's work in the early 1950s helped bury sense-data theory. As noted, the positivist tradition had begun to shift away from sense-data theories in the 1930s, though one can find traces of it in W. V. Quine's 'On What There Is' (1948), in *From a Logical Point of View* (New York: Harper and Row, 1953). See his claim, late in the essay, that phenomenalistic schemes are epistemically more basic than physicalistic ones.

being *atomistic*. Opponents maintained that they provided representation with simplistic starting points. Opponents held that representation depends on contextual stage-setting or on supplementary psychological capacities.

Wittgenstein pressed such criticisms in his later work. His attack on the notion of a private language, and his illustration, at the beginning of *Philosophical Investigations*, of stage-setting capacities that go into the simplest sorts of linguistic reference were extremely influential. They seemed to limit how subjective or atomistic any linguistic capacity could reasonably be taken to be. They suggested that publicly accessible *use* determines meaning.

An equally important impetus against subjectivistic and atomistic starting points in theories of representation was the rediscovery of Frege.[2] Frege's emphasis on the publicity and intersubjectivity of language, and his claim that there is a common objective subject matter in scientific thought and in the use of language, ran diametrically opposed to subjectivistic and phenomenological starting points. His view that propositional content must be understood by considering *patterns of inference* seemed to undermine atomistic accounts of representation.

Attacks on subjectivistic and atomistic starting points—hence on logical constructions out of sense data—were pressed in the early work of P. F. Strawson and W. V. Quine, as we shall see.

These trends took on more force because language had become the dominant focus in mainstream philosophy.[3] When interest shifted from perception to sophisticated linguistic abilities, subjectivistic and atomistic approaches became vulnerable. The roles of intersubjectivity and a common objective world in making communication possible became obvious. The roles of contextual stage-setting and interdependence of cognitive capacities in making higher-level thought possible were almost equally evident. Focus on these matters elicited weaknesses in the theories of representation that dominated the first half of the century.

Sellars's work exemplifies these trends. More than most other prominent philosophers after mid-century, he retained interest in perception. He criticized

[2] This rediscovery consisted in several events. One was Carnap's exposition of Frege in *Meaning and Necessity* (1947; Chicago: Chicago University Press, 1956; reprinted 1967). Another was Church's exposition of Fregean theory in 'The Need for Abstract Entities in Semantic Analysis', in *Proceedings of the American Academy of Arts and Sciences* 80 (1951), 100–112; and in the introductory chapter of his *Introduction to Mathematical Logic* (Princeton: Princeton University Press, 1956). Church had been advocating the importance of Frege's work for years. But his systematic presentation of a general Fregean point of view occurred only in the early 1950s. A third factor was the translation by J. L. Austin of Frege's main philosophical work in *The Foundations of Arithmetic*, and the translation of the great papers in the philosophy of language, *Translations from the Philosophical Writings of Gottlob Frege*, ed. P. Geach and M. Black (1952; Oxford: Blackwell, 1966).

[3] Language had occupied this position for the positivists all along. They were, however, primarily concerned with an idealized language for science. They focused on objectivity in scientific procedures. Language was a less prominent topic for British sense-data theorists, with the exceptions of Russell and Ayer.

sense-data theories as subjectivistic. He opposed the atomism of his predecessors. He insisted on a role for language in critically understanding "direct perception" of the physical world. He wrote:

For while one does not have the concept of red until one has directly perceived something *as* red, *to be* red, the coming to see something as red is the culmination of a complicated process which is the slow building up of a multi-dimensional pattern of linguistic responses (by verbal expressions to things, by verbal expressions to verbal expressions, by meta-linguistic expressions to object-language expressions, etc.) the fruition of which as conceptual occurs when all these dimensions come into play in such direct perceptions as that this physical object (not that one) over there (not over there) is (rather than was) red (not orange, yellow, etc.).[4]

So philosophical work at mid-century took on a more realist, more objectivist flavor. It emphasized dependence on context, public availability of expression, and interlocking psychological capacities that make cognition and language use possible. Many philosophers insisted on a role for language even in perception and the simplest perception-based thought, as Sellars's remarks illustrate.

Underlying these changes in philosophical outlook, Individual Representationalism retained a hold on nearly all philosophical work that discussed conditions for objective representation. Objective representations were no longer seen as products of construction. Representation of non-physical particulars, available only through subjective phenomenological routes, was no longer taken as prior to objective representation. But the individual was still required to have psychological resources to represent preconditions of objectivity.

Many philosophers claimed that initial human forms of representation are limited by a child's inability to represent such conditions. Some postulated a proto-objective stage, overcome by mastering capacities to generalize. Some claimed that objective reference derived from supplementing feature-placing representation with capacities to represent criteria of identity. Even those who did not postulate proto-objective stages maintained that a network of conceptual or linguistic resources capable of representing criteria or rules was necessary for

---

[4] Sellars, 'Phenomenalism', 90. No serious science of perception agrees with Sellars in taking seeing something to be red as the 'culmination' of the sophisticated linguistic practices that he describes. Sellars leaves no room between (*a*) 'S has a sensation of x', in the sense of 'S is in that state brought about in normal circumstances by the influence of x on the relevant sense organs', and (*b*) 'S has a [linguistically informed] thought of x'. See ibid. 92–93. That is, he allows for no perception of entities as having physical properties that is not backed by *linguistically informed thought* that attributes such properties to such entities. He moves quickly from a non-representational notion of sensing to a propositional sensing-that—again backed by linguistically informed thought— with no room for any type of perception in between. A type of perception in between has been the primary topic of successful scientific study, as I have indicated in Chapter 3; see also Chapters 8–10. A similar attitude informs Sellars's 'Empiricism and the Philosophy of Mind' (1956), also in *Science Perception and Reality*. See pp. 129–134, 147–156. Sellars assumes that propositional, linguistically informed thought is the only source of objective representation. Objective representation is epistemic representation. Epistemic representation requires a linguistically grounded propositional ability to represent conditions under which objectivity and knowledge are realized. See p. 169.

representing the physical environment.[5] These claims rested on a basic assumption: the individual must represent preconditions of objectivity if objective representation of the environment is to occur. The form of Individual Representationalism shifted. Its core idea remained.

THE DEMISE OF LOGICAL POSITIVISM, BEHAVIORISM,
AND DESCRIPTIVISM

So far I have discussed the fall of sense-data theories, the work of the later Wittgenstein, and the rediscovery of Frege as factors in shifting the focus of theories of representation. Three further events figured significantly in shaping the direction of mainstream philosophy in the second half of the twentieth century.

The primary event was the fall of *logical positivism* at mid-century. As a central tenet, logical positivism claimed that the cognitive, empirical meaning of a statement, or the content of a thought, consists in a method for confirming or disconfirming it.[6] This claim was known as *Verificationism*.

Quine agreed with the logical positivists that cognitive meaning is, if anything, method of confirmation or disconfirmation. He claimed against them that there is no such thing as a method of confirming or disconfirming a single statement: all confirmation is of theories. He concluded that there is no such thing as the cognitive meaning of a statement. Hempel recounted positivism's failures to account for cognitive meaning in science, concluding that the program was hopeless.[7]

A second large event was the fall of behaviorism. *Behaviorism* tried to reduce mentalistic discourse to, or replace it with, discourse about dispositions to behave in response to proximal stimuli. Behaviorism had dominated large reaches of psychology since the 1920s. It was embraced by the positivists, and significantly influenced philosophy of mind in England and the United States. In the late 1950s behaviorism was widely rejected as an empirical theory, as a definitional enterprise, and as a framework for theorizing.[8]

---

[5] Quine and Strawson exemplify the first two types of views. Sellars and Davidson exemplify this latter type.

[6] The discussion that follows is drawn partly from my 'Philosophy of Language and Mind: 1950–1990', *The Philosophical Review* 101 (1992), 3–51; an expanded version of the part of the article that is on the philosophy of mind is reprinted as 'Philosophy of Mind: 1950–2000' in *Foundations of Mind*.

[7] W. V. Quine, 'Two Dogmas of Empiricism' (1951), in *From a Logical Point of View*, reprinted in *Quintessence: Basic Readings from the Philosophy of W. V. Quine*, ed. Roger F. Gibson (Cambridge, MA: Harvard University Press, 2004); *Word and Object* (Cambridge, MA: MIT Press, 1960), chapter 1; Carl Hempel, 'Empiricist Criteria of Cognitive Significance: Problems and Changes' (1950), reprinted in *Aspects of Scientific Explanation* (New York: Free Press, 1965).

[8] See George Miller, 'The Magic Number 7 Plus or Minus Two: Some Limits on our Capacity for Processing Information', *Psychological Review* 63 (1956), 81–97; J. Bruner, J. Goodnow, and G. Austin, *A Study of Thinking* (New York: John Wiley, 1956); G. Miller, E. Galanter,

The third event was the fall of descriptivist accounts of reference and meaning, and the development of alternative accounts. *Descriptivism* is a loose syndrome of views that maintain that the meaning and reference of many terms—natural-kind terms and proper names, especially—are uniquely determined by descriptions that are supposed to be more or less tacitly connected with the relevant terms. Descriptivism was rooted in Russell's use of the theory of descriptions to try to account for the meaning and reference of ordinary names. The syndrome was developed by the later Wittgenstein, by Strawson, and by Searle in the 1950s.[9] In the late 1960s and early 1970s it collapsed.

The reaction against descriptivism emphasized the roles of context, dependence on others, and dependence on causal relations to the environment in determining the meaning and reference of relevant terms. This reaction began with work on demonstrative reference by Strawson and flowered in work by Kripke, Donnellan, and Putnam. These three showed that the referents of proper names, demonstratives, referentially used descriptions, and natural-kind terms are not normally fixed by descriptions employed by, or even available to, language users.[10] A new picture of linguistic reference, as grounded in causal relations, replaced Descriptivism. In my development of anti-individualism, application of this point spread from language to mind, from reference to representational content, and from a few types of representations to nearly the whole range.[11]

Logical positivism, behaviorism, and descriptivism encouraged Individual Representationalism in fairly evident ways.

Logical positivism and descriptivism appeal to resources available to individuals. A commonly held corollary of these views is that objective reference depends on an individual's capacity to understand methods or descriptions that are partly constitutive of objectivity. Behaviorism cites dispositions to respond to proximal stimuli. All these views offered constitutive accounts (or deflations) of

---

and K. Pribram, *Plans and the Structure of Behavior* (New York: Holt, Rinehart & Winston, 1960); G. Sperling, 'The Information Available in Brief Visual Presentations', *Psychological Monographs* 24 (1960); Noam Chomsky, *Syntactic Structures* (The Hague: Mouton, 1957); A. Newell, J. C. Shaw, and H. A. Simon, 'Elements of a Theory of Human Problem Solving', *Psychological Review* 65 (1958), 151–166.

[9] Wittgenstein, *Philosophical Investigations*, sections 79, 87; P. F. Strawson, *Individuals* (1959; Garden City, NY: Anchor Books, 1963; reprinted London: Routledge, 2002), chapter 6; John Searle, 'Proper Names', *Mind* 67 (1958), 166–173.

[10] Strawson, *Individuals*, chapter 1 and the opening of chapter 4; Saul Kripke, *Naming and Necessity* (Cambridge, MA: Harvard University Press, 1972); Keith Donnellan, 'Reference and Definite Descriptions', *The Philosophical Review* 75 (1966), 281–304; 'Proper Names and Identifying Descriptions', *Synthese* 21 (1970), 335–358; Putnam, 'The Meaning of "Meaning"'.

[11] Burge, 'Individualism and the Mental'; 'Other Bodies'; 'Intellectual Norms and Foundations of Mind'; 'Cartesian Error and the Objectivity of Perception'; 'Individualism and Psychology'; 'Perceptual Entitlement'. In the Introduction to *Foundations of Mind*, I discuss the relation between anti-individualism and the criticisms by Donnellan, Kripke, and Putnam of descriptivist theories of reference. See also the 'Postscript to "Individualism and the Mental"', same volume.

representational phenomena in terms of resources *local to individuals*. All are vulnerable to anti-individualism.

Verificationism's impact in encouraging Individual Representationalism was by far the greatest of the three. Its influence survived its fall. Verificationism held that objective meaning constitutively depends entirely on an individual's confirmational abilities: lacking such abilities, an individual's linguistic meaning or thought content could not progress beyond expressivist meaning, or some other subjective, non-cognitive meaning. It could not be objectively representational.

Anti-individualism undermines verificationism as an explanation of representational content.[12] Confirmation procedures are intelligible only as the application of such content. Such application presupposes non-representational, world-individual causal relations. Many of these relations are causal relations that help form perceptual meaning independently of procedures—of anything the individual *does*. Non-representational, causal relations partly fix the representational content of confirmation procedures. Representational content is not grounded purely in confirmation procedures.

Behaviorism encouraged Individual Representationalism indirectly. Behaviorism is not committed to any view about representation. But behaviorism is a de-intellectualized analog of Individual Representationalism. Once put in the service of a theory of representational capacities, behaviorism explains representational content in terms of dispositions to respond to proximal stimuli. It grounds such content in matters local to the individual. There is thus a problem in understanding how content can project beyond the individual to kinds in the physical environment. The problem lies in the parochial nature of the dispositions and their irrelevance in themselves to specific distal conditions.

It is natural for behaviorism to try to explain objectivity of language and science in terms of the individual's reproducing from his or her own local resources conditions for objectivity. It is natural to require that the individual be capable of registering in dispositions (perhaps verbal dispositions) something that makes behavior relevant to objective attributes of the world. Thus behaviorism encourages Individual Representationalism. In Chapter 7, we shall see this point take shape in Quine's work.

Behavioral dispositions to respond to proximal stimuli cannot replace mental states, partly because they cannot account for differences between veridical and non-veridical states. Distinguishing perception and misperception cannot be grounded purely in response to proximal stimuli—quite apart from other difficulties with behaviorist explanations. Behaviorism restricts itself to conditions that are too local to yield such an account. Moreover, the appeal to dispositions

---

[12] Few philosophers were verificationists by the time anti-individualism was articulated. I am discussing substantive relations among principles here, not historical description of the fall of logical positivism. Since opponents of the movement (for example, Quine and Strawson) maintained aspects of verificationism even after its demise, it is important to understand considerations that count against the view, beyond the historically effective refutations. A similar point applies to my expositions of behaviorism and descriptivism.

does not capture the normative element in veridicality and non-veridicality. Since part of what is explained by appeals to representational states is how we get things right or wrong, behaviorism cannot replace mentalistic explanations. This is a basic point of anti-individualism. Only by considering causal and functional relations to a wider environment, and by allowing some scope for teleology, can one understand veridicality and error.

Descriptivism claims that to determine a referent, an individual must have descriptions that represent attributes that distinguish it from everything else. Unlike logical positivism, the view does not require the individual to be able to test for such attributes. Although the view is compatible with rejecting Individual Representationalism, it was almost always conjoined with it.

The descriptions required by descriptivists to explain how individuals represent particulars and kinds are frequently not available to individuals whose thoughts and language succeed in representing those particulars and kinds. The descriptions that *are* available commonly do not suffice to determine the referents or contents of mental states. Indeed, as anti-individualism emphasizes, having the descriptions depends on a range of causal relations that need not be representable by the individual. The nature of mental states, as well as linguistic meaning and reference, depends on more than is available to the individual, even on reflection.

By centering explanation in individuals' procedures, dispositions, or representational powers, all three doctrines encourage Individual Representationalism. Individual Representationalism takes objectivity of reference, meaning, and representational content to be explained in terms of individuals' resources. It claims that to project outward to an environmental reality, representational content must be built up or supplemented by individuals' representation of conditions that make objective representation possible.

Since the fall of descriptivism figures most directly in the development of anti-individualism and my opposition to Individual Representationalism, I will discuss this event further.

DESCRIPTIVISM AND THE CAUSAL PICTURE OF REFERENCE

The developments in late-twentieth-century philosophy most relevant to undermining Individual Representationalism are the change in conceptions of linguistic reference and the development of anti-individualism about the nature of mental states.

In the causal picture of linguistic reference, the individual plays a more modest part in fixing reference than descriptivist views require. Similarly, anti-individualism about mind assigns the individual less representational control over the content of his or her mental states than descriptivist theories require.

These developments are at odds with the spirit of Individual Representationalism. They were not, however, immediately accompanied by its rejection. As noted in Chapter 3, anti-individualism is strictly compatible with the view. The causal picture of linguistic reference is as well. Many who embraced these developments continued to maintain Individual Representationalism.

I shall sketch the historical background for this dialectical situation.

In the late 1950s, Strawson persuaded many that all reference to objects in space ultimately rests on contextual demonstrative reference. Strawson used the following duplication argument. To identify a particular, one must know which particular it is. To know which particular it is, one must be in a position to differentiate that particular from possible lookalikes. Any scene containing objects could in principle have a descriptively and qualitatively indistinguishable duplicate somewhere else in space. So, to distinguish the object one identifies, one cannot rely on description or on qualitative aspects of experience alone. One must rely on actual perceptual relations to the object (perhaps through memory or other supplements) and use a demonstrative relation to the object in perceptual belief (again perhaps with supplements).[13]

Strawson takes demonstrative reference to be irreducible to descriptions that lack demonstratives or indexicals.[14] Russell held this position as well. He claimed that all reference ultimately depends on acquaintance, and acquaintance is not description. Acquaintance is the vehicle of demonstrative reference for Russell. So demonstrative reference is not reducible to description for Russell. Russell held, however, that reference to elements in the physical environment depends on and is fixed by description. The descriptions are anchored in infallible acquaintance with sense data. Unlike Russell, Strawson took perceptual demonstrative reference to apply to physical objects, not sense data. He took demonstrative reference to be based on perception of physical objects.

In Chapter 6 I criticize Strawson's (Russell-inspired) appeal to a 'knowing which' stricture on demonstrative (hence 'identifying') reference—the first premise in the argument above. The stricture led to a great deal of philosophical error.

There is another difficulty with Strawson's argument. The mere possibility of a duplicate scene does not seem to threaten one's knowing which object one is referring to, even if 'knowing which' *were* a condition on reference. Why should insensitivity to differences with remote lookalike scenes threaten knowledge? The inability to distinguish lookalikes is the human condition. Explaining to sceptics *why* possible lookalikes do not threaten knowledge is difficult. But there is no intuitive force in the idea that in themselves distant lookalike scenes undermine knowledge.

What made Strawson's observations forceful was not, I think, his argument. What gave them force was recognition that we need not have sufficiently complete, demonstrative-free descriptions in order to differentiate a physical

---

[13] P. F. Strawson, *Individuals*, chapter 1, sections 1–2.

[14] I do not know whether anyone except perhaps Leibniz ever thought that *all* demonstrative reference is reducible to description. What Strawson did was to emphasize this non-reducibility, and develop its consequences. He was influenced by Kant's appeal to intuition, a not-purely-descriptive representational capacity.

particular from all others. We rely on contextual, demonstrative relations to physical particulars in ways that cannot be reduced to complete definite descriptions or qualitative "look".

Strawson offered a second consideration that highlights the non-descriptive character, and centrality, of demonstrative reference. He claimed that a language can be learned only through formation of beliefs based on experience, and that expression of experience is partly but irreducibly demonstrative.[15] This plausible observation elicits a central role for demonstrative reference in the early stages of language-learning. I re-emphasize that Strawson took the initial objects of demonstrative reference to be publicly accessible physical entities. In this respect, he broke decisively with the sense-data tradition.

Two aspects of Strawson's work obscured the depth of these contributions. One is that Strawson elaborated a qualified descriptivist account of the reference of *proper names*. This account became a target of criticism by Donnellan and Kripke. The other obscuring aspect was Strawson's insistence that all non-degenerate reference to the physical environment be associated by the individual with general criteria for application. In this section I focus on the first of these two features of Strawson's work. In Chapter 6, I discuss the second.

Let us back up a bit. Russell had maintained that the logical form of a proper name is, under analysis, that of a definite description. He held that most such definite descriptions have singular elements in them. These are elements that correspond to episodes of acquaintance—primarily acquaintance with sense data. The description itself, hence the meaning of a proper name, is not singular at all. In fact, the description, hence name, does not correspond to any natural unit of meaning. It is to be understood only through understanding complex, *general*, quantified propositions in which the descriptive predicative element is embedded.[16]

Russell's claim that a single definite description is at least tacitly associated with each ordinary proper name was influential. But by mid-century few accepted it. Behind this shift lay an increasing focus on natural language as a communal phenomenon. It was assumed that this communal phenomenon could be reflected upon in isolation from individual psychology. Russell's one-name one-description picture was attractive as long as one focused on *individual* speakers and their *thoughts* on occasions of use. The picture was much less attractive in a climate

[15] P. F. Strawson, 'Singular Terms, Ontology and Identity', *Mind* 65 (1956), 433–454, especially 446.

[16] Gottlob Frege is also sometimes taken to hold that a proper name has the sense of a definite description. This attribution is based on examples he gives of the sense of particular proper names. I think that there is textual reason to believe that he did not hold that the sense of proper names is always purely descriptive. See his *Begriffsschrift* (1879), section 8, in *From Frege to Gödel*, ed. Jean van Heijenoort (Cambridge, MA: Harvard University Press, 1981); my 'Introduction' in *Truth, Thought, Reason*; and my 'Sinning Against Frege', *Philosophical Review* 88 (1979), 398–432; reprinted in *Truth, Thought, Reason*.

that focused on *communal language*.[17] It was frequently observed that different people associate different descriptions with proper names, even though they seemed to share usage of the name. Attribution of radical ambiguity in the name (which Russell claimed) was not plausible, again if one focused on communal linguistic usage and meaning. Further, it was never clear how an 'associated' definite description was to be determined on a given occasion.

Wittgenstein, Strawson, and Searle fashioned accounts that held, with Russell, that the meaning and reference of names are fixed by description. They loosened the relation between names and associated descriptions. They maintained that the descriptions can form a shifting cluster, and that some of the descriptions can reside in the individual's linguistic community.[18]

This view, and the whole tradition of thinking that the reference of a name is fixed primarily by description, came under sustained, persuasive criticism from Donnellan and Kripke. They developed examples in which reference succeeds even though the individual lacks descriptive resources to determine a name's referent, or in which the descriptions that the individual has apply differently from the name. Some examples also showed that invoking a communal repository of descriptions does not suffice to explain successful reference.

For example, Kripke noted that the standard description of Jonah (as the prophet to Ninevah who spent three days in a whale) is not fully correct, and is almost certainly insufficient (in its correct components) to determine semantically a unique referent for the name. Yet the name has a unique referent. Kripke pointed out that the whole community that uses the name might—for long periods of time—not know enough about Jonah to distinguish him descriptively from other individuals. Merely taking him to be a prophet to Ninevah, even if correct, need not single him out from all other individuals. Despite lack of an adequately individuating description, the individual and community can speak about an individual by using the name.[19]

Kripke and Putnam developed parallel criticisms of descriptivist accounts of natural-kind terms. They showed that the *representata* of natural-kind terms are not determined by descriptions that ordinary people use to teach others to recognize natural kinds. The *representata* of natural-kind terms need not be fixed even by descriptions available to whole communities.[20] The issues

---

[17] Russell and Frege were more concerned with individuals' linguistically expressed knowledge than with communal linguistic meaning. Frege's case was more complex in that he gave great weight to scientific communities in his account of sense. Even so, he was not primarily concerned with what we now think of as communal linguistic meaning. In cases like ordinary proper names and demonstratives, he focuses on the individual's knowledge, not on communal linguistic meaning. See my 'Introduction', in *Truth, Thought, Reason*.

[18] Wittgenstein, *Philosophical Investigations*, sections 79, 87; P. F. Strawson, *Individuals*, chapter 6; Searle, 'Proper Names'.

[19] Kripke, *Naming and Necessity*, lectures I and II. On Jonah, see pp. 67–68, 87, 160 ff. See also Donnellan, 'Proper Names and Identifying Descriptions'.

[20] Kripke, *Naming and Necessity*; Putnam, 'Is Semantics Possible?'

regarding reference by names and demonstratives have counterpart issues regarding indication by predicate expressions.

These developments supported a new picture of linguistic reference and indication, in an important range of cases. It is uncontroversial that linguistic reference and indication depend on individuals' psychological abilities. The individual must have minimal mastery of the grammar of names, some sensitivity to usage of natural-kind terms, some ability to fit these expressions into a network of perceptual, cognitive, and grammatical capacities. But the new picture showed that a large burden of *linguistic representation* is carried by causal relations that the individual bears to the environment and, often, to other speakers, with their own causal relations to the environment. The individual need not be able to describe these relations.[21]

This picture does not require the individual to be in cognitive control of conditions that determine reference of names or natural-kind terms. It does not require the individual to be able to represent, much less know, conditions that make objective reference (or indication) possible. The picture points in a different direction from that of Individual Representationalism.

The change in the theory of linguistic representation did not, however, lead to rejection of Individual Representationalism. In fact, many philosophers adapted Individual Representationalism to the causal picture of reference.

The main ground for this state of affairs lies in the fact that the picture centered on language. The psychology that underlies language use is complex. Wittgenstein's influential reflections had highlighted ways in which even such simple-seeming devices as naming or pointing are embedded in a complex system of capacities. Philosophers had been drilled to appreciate the psychological and social complexity of linguistic understanding.

The objectivity of language use must connect objective representation to linguistic competence. Linguistic competence requires a background of complex psychological abilities. In explaining conditions for such competence, it was easy to reinsert the lever to objectivity that Individual Representationalism demands. It was often assumed that even if an individual need not master a specific description in order to refer with a proper name, the individual must be able to

---

[21] For example, in using the name 'Jonah', an individual relies on a chain of connections through other speakers to the historical figure. Neither the individual nor the community *has to* have a distinguishing description of the historical figure. An individual user need not be able to describe the causal-historical chain. A child could use the name but lack the sophistication to describe a chain. What determines the referent is not a description under the control of the individual, but the chain itself, and the minimal linguistic competence needed to participate in it. There seems no prospect that such competence accords with descriptivist theory.

The positive picture, of a causal-historical chain connecting a name with its source, has never been developed into systematic theory. This situation may be inevitable. The range of causal relations that might make reference possible may not form a unitary explanatory kind. Some relations are perceptual. Many go through memory. Some go through communication with other people. Some are mediated by theory to experiment. Causal chains can branch or be diverted. For a fine development of this last point, see Gareth Evans, 'A Causal Theory of Names' (1973), in *Collected Papers* (Oxford: Clarendon Press, 1985).

represent *general* conditions for referring to kinds of things. To represent bodies, for example, one would have to be able to represent general conditions for reidentification.

Language sometimes loomed even larger. It was not just that the particular devices for reference highlighted by critics of descriptivism presuppose a network of linguistic and cognitive abilities. Many philosophers gave language a more global role in accounts of objectivity. They maintained that objective reference is possible only for beings that have a language. Quine, Davidson, Dummett, and others urged this view.[22]

Even where the focus on language was not backed by a doctrine that having a language is necessary for representing the physical environment, the focus encouraged philosophers *not to reflect on* perception. It is clear, especially from the examples that Donnellan, Kripke, and Putnam gave, that the causal picture of representation ultimately hinges on perceptual relations to linguistic *representata*. Perception is the natural starting point in reflection on origins of objective representation. Yet neither Donnellan, nor Kripke, nor Putnam showed specific interest in perception in making or following up on their breakthroughs. Their attention to language was nearly undivided.[23]

The lack of focus on perception in mainstream philosophy between 1955 and 1985 had broad consequences for the way anti-descriptivist theories of reference and mental representation developed. In fact, perception was seen by many as made possible by language. If a reasonable and informed conception of perception had been central in mid-twentieth-century philosophy, the discoveries about linguistic reference and mental states would, I think, have come more easily. And

[22] It may be implicit in some of Kripke's work. See Saul Kripke, 'A Puzzle about Belief', in A. Margalit (ed.), *Meaning and Use* (Dordrecht: D. Reidel Publishing Company, 1979). I see no evidence of Individual Representationalism in Putnam or Donnellan. None of these philosophers discusses the view explicitly. They concentrate on language. They have little or nothing to say about objectivity, perception, or mind. I believe that it is a great weakness in this area of the philosophy of language that so little has been done by the original theorists or their successors to relate their work to mind. The failure to reflect on perception is especially striking, inasmuch as the empirical, context-dependent reference central to the key examples is grounded in perception.

[23] Donnellan, 'Proper Names and Identifying Descriptions', section VIII, appeals to perception in his argument against descriptivist theories of reference. But he does not remark on the general role of perception in primitive empirical reference.

In his Dewey Lectures in 1994, Putnam does say a lot about perception: Hilary Putnam, 'Sense, Nonsense, and the Senses: An Inquiry into the Powers of the Human Mind', *The Journal of Philosophy* 91 (1994), 445–517. But Putnam does not cite a single work in the psychology of perception. What he says about the science suggests lack of sophistication, and even serious misunderstanding. Most of Putnam's philosophical remarks about perceptual representation are metaphorical. He regards perceptual representations as 'interfaces' 'between' the perceiver and the world, and he disapproves of postulating such 'interfaces'. The metaphors are not explained. Putnam may hold some kind of naive realism, which avoids appeal to states with representational content. Such a view is incompatible with what is known about perception. Putnam's discussion is so vague and metaphorical that it makes no serious contact with scientific knowledge. For criticism of similarly misinformed philosophical views about perception—one of which (McDowell's) Putnam praises—see my 'Disjunctivism and Perceptual Psychology'.

understanding of the empirical origins of objectivity would have been attained more readily.

The Kripke–Donnellan points about reference of names have obvious analogs for perception. An object can be seen even though the perceiver could not perceptually distinguish the object—given looking angle and background knowledge—from a lookalike that might have been substituted for the object. Perceptual reference is not carried out purely by perceptual categories in the perceiver's repertoire.[24] Perceptual reference is compatible with being wrong about most of the salient properties of the perceived object. The color, shape, sortal type, and position of an object can be misperceived, all at once, while the object is perceived. Here we have a clear analog of a standard point about the use of names, natural-kind terms, and so on.

Focus on language, illuminating in itself, distracted the founders of the causal picture of reference from origins of objectivity prior to language use. Like Strawson, they failed to exploit Strawson's insight into the relation between non-descriptive aspects of reference and perception.

INDIVIDUAL REPRESENTATIONALISM AND
ANTI-INDIVIDUALISM: AGAIN

Anti-individualism, recall, is the claim that the natures of many mental states constitutively depend on relations between an individual and a subject matter beyond the individual. For mental states that represent empirically, the relations must include causal relations. The causal picture of reference shows how the referents of some of an individual's terms can be determined even though the individual cannot describe the referent or the mechanism by which the referent is determined. Anti-individualism maintains an analogous view: an individual need not be able to explicate his or her own mental contents, or describe the individual–environment relations that help determine the contents of representational capacities.

Anti-individualism goes much further than the causal picture of reference. It applies to states of mind, not just linguistic reference. It claims that the representational natures of mental states are constitutively dependent on the environment. And it applies not only to a small range of representational devices, but nearly to the whole range.

Individual Representationalism survived the demise of sense-data theories. It survived the demise of logical positivism, behaviorism, and descriptivism.

---

[24] This point is, of course, Strawson's. It probably played some role in the overthrow of descriptivism. See P. F. Strawson, *Individuals*, chapter 1 and the first two pages of chapter 4. But Strawson concluded that perception must be supplemented by criteria in thought. Strawson's work centered on articulating these criteria. I argue in subsequent chapters that no such criteria are necessary for perception to represent physical objects and their properties. Strawson's Individual Representationalism prevented him from exploiting his insight.

It survived the emergence of causal pictures of linguistic reference. It even survived the development of anti-individualism.

Individual Representationalism retains a presence in current philosophical work. It guides most philosophical remarks on the problem with which we started—determining conditions under which representation of a mind-independent subject matter is possible.

In mainstream philosophy in the second half of the twentieth century, Individual Representationalism is most prominently developed by Strawson, Quine, and Davidson. In the next two chapters, I discuss these figures in some detail. I want simply to evoke them now.

Strawson thought that if it is to be intelligible that an individual can engage in objective reference to bodies as localized in space, the individual must have criteria for individuating bodies. He also held that the individual must have a conception of veridical and non-veridical mental states, and a conception of a comprehensive spatial framework.

Strawson's views depend partly on residues of positivism. Strawson thought that unless an individual has procedures for verifying general attributes of objects in at least the simplest cases of reference to bodies, an individual's representing the physical environment would be unintelligible. Strawson embedded this view in a neo-Kantian framework. Strawson's work engendered a train of broadly neo-Kantian variations.

Quine dealt verificationism its death blows. Yet he maintained one of its central tenets—that meaning is, if anything, confirmation procedure. Quine maintains an official scepticism, indeed eliminationism, about meaning and representational states. But his sceptical position begins with the same consideration that supports Individual Representationalism for the positivists and Strawson. Quine took the necessary connection between meaning and confirmation procedure to indicate that objective representation of a physical world would require, at a minimum, linguistic abilities necessary to understand simple analogs of scientific confirmation procedures.

A reason why Verificationism, even after its demise, could provide support for Individual Representationalism was that the most prominent objections to it seemed not to affect its application to the empirical *roots* of representation. Verificationism had received rough treatment for its inability to explain meaning in theoretical science. Quine had claimed that it overlooked holistic aspects of confirmation. Others had shown that it failed to distinguish metaphysics from scientific theory.

To many, these difficulties seemed not to apply to less theoretical empirical representation. To many, it remained plausible that to engage in simple empirical representation of the physical world, one must be able to understand procedures for confirming the presence of basic attributes of the entities represented. These procedures were called 'criteria for individuation or reidentification'. The idea was that even though theoretical representations could not command such criteria, the most primitive ones could. The individual needed, for example, to determine in a general way when objects are the same and when different. To count as representing objectively, the individual must be able to understand and apply such criteria.

Quine, like Strawson, highlighted a capacity to individuate referents. He believed that it is unintelligible to attribute representation of anything at all, unless an individual is taken to have linguistic resources to express conditions of individuation. He held that an individual must learn to 'divide' reference into individuated packages. Mass-like representations were supposed to approximate pre-individuative experience. Strictly speaking, according to Quine, no objective reference occurs until a linguistic individuative apparatus is developed. The individuative apparatus includes logical devices including quantifiers. Quantifiers, like 'every' and 'some', are needed to express general principles of individuation, identification, and reidentification.

Quine's claim that having language is necessary for objective reference, and his insistence that mastering an array of logical operations is necessary for having language, deeply influenced Davidson. Unlike Strawson and Quine, Davidson did not postulate a proto-objective stage of reference.[25] He maintained that reference to physical bodies is full blown from the beginning. But, like Strawson and Quine, he required that the beginning include an individual's ability to represent general criteria, or some basic principles, of individuation, identification, and reidentification. With Strawson he further required a capacity to represent a seems/is distinction. Specifically, he required that the individual be able to represent a distinction between true and false belief. With Quine he required that the individual be able to speak a language and interpret the language of others.

All these philosophers follow Frege in holding that objective representation begins at a sophisticated intellectual level. All focus either on language or on thought that can formulate general conditions or principles. All require a capacity to represent in general form some preconditions for objectivity.

Strawson, Quine, and Davidson deny the *autonomy* of ordinary perceptual representation of, and as of, the physical environment. One must understand exactly what is encompassed by this denial if one is to understand what is wrong with the form of Individual Representationalism that dominated the second half of the twentieth century.

I believe that a limited holism is correct about linguistic and propositional representation. I accept Wittgenstein's point that linguistic reference depends on complex background conditions. I accept Frege's point that inferential capacities determine the logical forms of sentences and of the propositional contents of representational states. I think that much of what Strawson, Quine, and Davidson write about interrelations among linguistic and cognitive capacities is true and insightful. I think that to refer to a particular in perception or perceptual belief, one must have some attributive that is veridical of the particular.[26]

---

[25] Sellars preceded Davidson on this point.

[26] I argue for this point in 'Five Theses on *De Re* States and Attitudes', section III.

The basic mistake in this work is to hyper-intellectualize minimal conditions of objective representation. The accounts of objective representation begin at too high an intellectual level. They err in taking objective representation, particularly in perception and perceptual belief, to depend on capacities to represent general conditions on objective representation.

There is overwhelming empirical evidence that perception, in both humans and non-linguistic, even pre-propositional, animals operates independently of such capacities. Objective perceptual representation of, and as of, environmental entities does not depend on having propositional attitudes at all, much less propositional attitudes sophisticated enough to think general conditions on objectivity. Perceptual belief requires inferential capacities. But it draws content from perception. The required inferential capacities do not connect perceptual belief to abilities to represent general conditions on objectivity.

A kind of holism obtains even among perceptual capacities. Perception of any one entity constitutively depends on capacities to perceive others. For example, perception as of one spatial relation or shape is not possible apart from a capacity perceptually to attribute others.

Similarly, perceptual modalities normally depend on other modalities. Most perceptual modalities (for example, vision) represent in ways that are not fully independent of other perceptual modalities (touch or hearing). Perception also utilizes efferent information that derives from action and proprioception.

It is true, and uncontroversial, that perception and perceptual belief can be influenced and enriched by higher-level cognitive capacities. Perception and perceptual belief are not 'autonomous' in that limited sense.

The 'autonomy' lacking in these examples is not the same as the autonomy that the later forms of Individual Representationalism deny. What they deny, as a constitutive matter, is that elementary forms of objective empirical representation—those of perception and perceptual belief—can *occur* without being supplemented by higher-level representational capacities. The higher-level capacities have the content of general principles about conditions of objectivity.

What is at issue is whether the natures of perception and perceptual belief are constitutively dependent on a capacity *in the individual's psychology* to represent *general* conditions of objectivity. The forms of Individual Representationalism that dominated the second half of the twentieth century claimed that the most elementary types of empirical representation are constitutively impossible unless they rely on higher-level representational capacities of the individual.

Among second-family views, there are many positions on development. Some views (Frege's, for example) postulate a development that begins with representation of a mind-dependent or perspective-dependent entity. But usually an initial subjective representation is *not* postulated. Often the initial stage is world-oriented, but marked by the subject's inability to segment, categorize, or refer to the main macro-attributes of the physical environment. Other forms of Individual Representationalism do not postulate a development. They propose conceptual analyses that reveal an order of dependence, but they make no empirical claim about development. Others hold that there is no conceptual order of dependence from subjective or proto-objective to objective. They hold that representation of physical objects and their properties is present, conceptually and developmentally, as soon as any representation is.

Although second-family views differ about development, they agree on the constitutive condition required if objective representation of significant environmental entities is to be possible. All maintain that if empirical thought and perception of, and as of, such entities is to occur, the individual must be able to represent general conditions or understand general principles of objectivity. The individual must do the objectifying.

There is little argument in second-family Individual Representationalism for this requirement. There is little argument for requiring the various specific compensatory *apparati*. The claims are usually presented as conditions on intelligibility and as obvious common wisdom. I will discuss only a few representative second-family Individual Representationalists. In Chapter 6, I discuss Strawson and Evans. In Chapter 7, Quine and Davidson. In Part III, I develop a positive alternative.

6 Neo-Kantian Individual Representationalism: Strawson and Evans

Kant is a primary source of inspiration for Individual Representationalism. First-family phenomenalism was inspired by Kant as well as by Berkeley and Mill. Kant's strictures on rationalism and his account of schemata for the categories inspired the positivist insistence on criteria for verification. Piaget's stages of child development make liberal use of Kantian conceptions. Second-family Individual Representationalism was even more deeply influenced by Kant. In particular, Strawson's appeal to a comprehensive spatial organization as condition for identifying physical individuals—particular bodies—and his account of the role of reidentification of physical bodies in achieving objective reference extrapolate, respectively, from the Transcendental Aesthetic and the Refutation of Idealism passages of *Critique of Pure Reason*.

In this chapter I center on one strand of twentieth-century neo-Kantianism. I begin with some brief remarks about Kant. Then I discuss second-family neo-Kantian Individual Representationalism in Strawson and Evans.

KANT

Kant's dictum 'Intuitions without concepts are blind' suggests that reference via intuition (roughly perception) is possible only when supported by concepts, which are elements in propositional thought.[1] The dictum has been taken to restrict reference. Kant is frequently read as holding that perceptual reference to a physical world requires concepts of substance, causation, spatial location, self.[2]

---

[1] Immanuel Kant, *Critique of Pure Reason*, A51/B75.
[2] For example, H. W. Cassirer, *Kant's First Critique* (London: George Allen & Unwin Ltd, 1954) straddles the inaccurate account of the dictum. On one hand, he gives direct aid to the misinterpretation that I am discussing. He does so by interpreting intuition as 'mere occurrences of sense impressions in the mind' (p. 56), and then claiming that apart from understanding in virtue of which sense impressions are referred to consciousness in general, 'no proper awareness of anything is possible' (p. 118), and that 'in the absence of original acts of understanding, there can be no

The reading of Kant's dictum is certainly incorrect. There is textual evidence that Kant means by 'blindness' not lack of perception, but lack of self-conscious understanding. Kant's remark occurs in the explanation of conditions for cognition (*Erkenntnis*). 'Cognition' is a technical term. A cognition is an objective conscious representation whose (actual) objective validity can in principle be established through argument, by the individual with the cognition.[3] Cognition requires an ability to argue something about a representation. Kant's dictum attributes blindness to intuitions relative to obtaining cognition, in this demanding sense. It does not say that perception is impossible without concepts.

Animals and human babies probably lack concepts *of representations*. They certainly cannot carry out justifications with regard to them. The dictum takes no position on whether they can represent mind-independent entities. It takes no position on the perceptual capacities of animals that lack concepts.

More broadly, I believe that in the first *Critique* Kant is not primarily concerned with conditions on representing the physical world. He explains conditions on an ability self-consciously to *justify* representation of a world *conceived* as mind-independent.[4]

Kant is well known for giving conditions for the possibility of experience. Like 'cognition', 'experience' (*Erfahrung*) is a technical term. Kant explains it in terms of empirical cognition.[5] So having an experience in this technical sense requires an ability to establish something about it. In holding that one can have experience only if one is capable of self-consciousness and capable of unifying experience under categories like cause, Kant is not proposing that higher animals and young children lack experience in an ordinary sense, because they lack self-consciousness and lack reflective access to an account of warrant (an argument for objective validity).

---

consciousness of anything objective ... ' (p. 138). On the other hand, Cassirer characterizes the transcendental nature of Kant's account in such a way as to make it virtually irrelevant to accounts of actual sense perception. This characterization provides, I think, an inaccurate account of Kant's transcendental standpoint. Cassirer uses it to exonerate Kant from empirically untenable claims. Cassirer does not clarify how his construal of Kant as requiring understanding of sense impressions for consciousness of anything objective avoids empirical difficulties. Although the matter is not entirely clear to me, Cassirer seems to interpret Kant as an Individual Representationalist. See pp. 124, 132, 199.

[3] Kant, *Critique of Pure Reason*, A89/B122.

[4] The interpretational issue is large and complex. Kant does sometimes seem to mix points about reference with points about cognition, in his demanding sense of 'cognition'. Some of this mixing can be seen not to conflict with my main line of interpretation, if one attends carefully to the distinction between Kant's empirical realism and his transcendental idealism. Independence of perception from conception is admissible for Kant only from his empirical realist point of view. In any case, I believe that Kant's main topic *is* cognition in the demanding sense. There are passages that indicate very clearly, including passages late in his career, that he attributed to animals intuitions of, and probably as of, physical entities. He thought that animals lack concepts, as well as self-consciousness and cognition in the demanding sense. I hope to develop these interpretative matters elsewhere. Here I just caution against over-reading Kant's dictum. The dictum definitely does not claim that intuitions require concepts in order to intuit.

[5] Kant, *Critique of Pure Reason*, B147.

Kant says things that suggest such a doctrine. But the central project of the first *Critique* does not depend on it. Evidence from Kant's lectures indicates that he thought that animals, which he regarded as lacking concepts, have empirical intuitions (perceptions) of physical entities.[6] I believe that Kant was not deeply concerned with minimal conditions on representation of the physical world. Kant tried to account for mature epistemic states, and for what is needed to show that such states are instances of cognition. Cognition and experience are assumed to be epistemic states of beings capable of deliberation and of science.[7]

In Kant's system the claim that intuitions without concepts are blind does not mean that without concepts, without propositional thought, an individual lacks perception of, and as of, physical entities. It means merely that without concepts perception cannot yield scientifically based cognition. Blindness for Kant is not literal inability to see a physical world. It is inability to understand and justify, from a meta-perspective, the objectivity of empirical judgment.

Kant's misunderstood dictum and the general caste of his epistemic doctrines inspired positions on conditions for objective reference. Many neo-Kantians hold that animals have only sensitive reactions to the physical world that function for their own good. Animals are held to lack perception of, and as of, specific physical entities because they lack required conceptual categories. Much of the inspiration for this approach to objective reference has been mediated and amplified by Strawson's work.

STRAWSON—TWO PROJECTS

In understanding what follows, it is important to distinguish two projects. The first is the one that I have been discussing: the project of *explaining minimal constitutive conditions on objective representation* of the physical environment. Objective representation comprises accurate representation of physical entities *as* having specific physical characteristics. The second project is that of explaining constitutive conditions for having a *conception* of mind-independent entities *as* mind-independent. I call this second project that of *explaining conditions for our conception of objectivity*.

---

⁶ I intend to discuss this matter in other work.

⁷ For intuitions to yield *cognition*, they must be associated with concepts. From the empirical realist point of view, I think it very doubtful that Kant claims that intuitions must be associated with concepts to yield *reference* to the physical environment (as opposed to cognized or understood reference). From Kant's transcendental idealist point of view, intuitions and concepts *constitute* physical entities, as we cognize them. Being a physical entity, from the point of view of a transcendental account of cognition, is *explained* in terms of intuitions and concepts. From this point of view, physical entities are potential patterns of representation that conform to certain canons for explaining empirical experience. From this idealist point of view, human bodies, rocks, planets, trees, animals, as we cognize them, are *all* constitutively dependent on concepts as well as intuitions.

It is part of the very formulation of the second project that one has a concept of mind. The claim that one has a conception of mind-independent entities *as* mind-independent entails that one has a concept of mind. An ability to hold that physical entities are independent of one's mind, and everyone else's mind, requires a capacity for self-consciousness. Thus appeal to self-consciousness is no big step within the second project. It is already present in our ordinary *conception* of objectivity. The second project tries to understand elements of our adult conceptual scheme. That scheme includes, uncontroversially, concepts of mind as well as concepts of a mind-independent world.

By contrast, the first project tries to explain minimal conditions on representing physical entities. It does not presuppose that to represent physical entities, one must have a concept of mind. The claim that to represent physical entities, one must have a concept of mind is a substantive claim. It is not entailed by the very formulation of the problem.

Similarly, the second project can assume, uncontroversially, that we have conceptions of causation, of error, of a comprehensive spatio-temporal framework, of linguistic capacities and structures, and so on. Its task is to explain the role of these capacities in our *understanding* of objectivity. The first project cannot make free use of these conceptions. If it introduces them, it must show that they are part of the minimum constitutive conditions on representation of the physical environment.

Strawson's main project is, like Kant's, not to account for minimal conditions on representing physical entities. It is to account for our *conception of objectivity*. Strawson aims to 'exhibit some general and structural features of the conceptual scheme in terms of which we think about particular things'.[8] He takes this conceptual scheme to include thoughts not only about physical individuals (bodies) but also about ourselves, and about the independence of physical individuals from minds. He takes self-consciousness to be included in the conceptual scheme.[9] When he discusses identifying reference to particulars, he usually presumes a background of sophisticated self-conscious thought and often a context of linguistic communication.[10]

Strawson holds that a necessary feature of a conceptual scheme that identifies particulars is that it include reference to material bodies as occurring in a comprehensive spatial framework. He also maintains that to understand the physical world as independent, we must recognize that reference to all other particulars (events, stuffs, property instances) are in a sense parasitic on reference to material bodies.

---

[8] Strawson, *Individuals*, 2; see also p. 12. I provide page numbers both to this edition of *Individuals* and to the currently more widely available edition (London: Routledge, 2002). I cite page numbers in this latter edition in brackets. In this case: [15]; see also [24].

[9] Ibid. 2, 24, 27, 55, 61, 72–74 [15, 35, 38, 65–66, 69, 79–83]. See also P. F. Strawson, *The Bounds of Sense: An Essay on Kant's Critique of Pure Reason* (1966; London, Routlege, 1989), 89, 91, 98.

[10] Strawson, *Individuals*, 2–3, 5 ff. [15–16, 17 ff.]. Strawson lays aside the assumption of linguistic communication (p. 51 [60]), but reinvokes it elsewhere.

In preparing to justify these views, Strawson poses a question that is prima facie ambiguous between the first and second projects. He asks:

Could there exist a conceptual scheme which was like ours in that it provided for a system of objective and identifiable particulars, but was unlike ours in that material bodies were not the basic particulars of the system? When I say, 'Could there exist such a scheme?' I mean 'Can we make intelligible to ourselves the idea of such a scheme?'[11]

This formulation is not specific. Making intelligible to ourselves the idea of such a scheme leaves open what the scheme includes, beyond 'providing' for objective, identifiable particulars that are not material bodies. Thus, as far as this formulation goes, we might be trying to make intelligible to ourselves a scheme that is completely unreflective but yet makes reference to objective particulars other than material bodies. Is the scheme taken to include self-consciousness and a seems/is distinction?

Strawson answers this question two pages later:

The limit I want to impose on my general question is this: that I intend it as a question about the conditions of the possibility of identifying thought about particulars distinguished by the thinker from himself and from his own experiences or states of mind, and regarded as actual or possible *objects* of those experiences. I shall henceforth use the phrase, 'objective particulars' as an abbreviation of the entire phrase, 'particulars distinguished by the thinker &c'.[12]

Here Strawson makes it clear that his question concerns the second project. He is investigating a *conception* of objectivity, marked by an antecedent ability to distinguish one's experiences from the entities experienced. Many other passages show clearly that Strawson is primarily concerned with finding necessary connections within our adult, reflective conception of objectivity.

Notably, Strawson speculates just after the passage just quoted that the limit that he imposes may not be a limit at all. He sympathizes with the idea that there can be no such thing as an identifying thought about particulars, if the thinker cannot distinguish between his own states and the objects of his experience. Here he shelves the issue. Nevertheless, much of what Strawson goes on to write, particularly in the second half of the book, concerns conditions under which thought about particulars is possible—the first of the two projects. Strawson enters this territory without emphasizing or exploring differences between the two projects.

Despite focusing mainly on the second project—that of understanding conditions for having a concept of objectivity—Strawson influenced others who explicitly and primarily pursue the first project. Much post-Strawsonian work in this area is hampered by a failure to think clearly about the differences between the two projects.

---

[11]   Strawson, *Individuals*, 51 [60].
[12]   Ibid. 52–53 [61].

A symptom and perhaps even a cause of this lack of clarity lies in Strawson's fateful abbreviation announced in the passage quoted above. 'Objective particulars' does not ordinarily mean 'particulars distinguished by the thinker from himself and from his own experiences or states of mind, and regarded as actual or possible *objects* of those experiences'. Commonly 'objective' would be taken to indicate a property of particulars. 'Objective particular' might be taken to mean 'a particular that is objective—independent of any individual's states of mind'. Strawson's abbreviation encourages a conflation of his own project regarding our conception of objectivity with the first project regarding objective representation itself.

The main reason why Strawson's work influenced others who were concerned with conditions for objective representation lies in his own commitments. He sometimes moves, without comment, from an account of our *conception* of objectivity to points that bear directly on conditions for objective reference. In some cases, these moves seem to constitute an unnoticed slide, greased by unstated background assumptions. In others, Strawson explicitly commits himself to Individual Representationalism about minimal conditions for empirical reference to the physical environment.[13]

In the first three chapters of *Individuals*, Strawson stays largely focused on the project of giving conditions for having our conception of objective representation. In some sections, however, he slides between the two projects. And in the second half of the book, he concentrates primarily on the first project—the project of explaining minimal conditions for objective representation. When he addresses this project, he sometimes just carries over commitments made in his main project, without exploring whether those commitments remain plausible regarding minimal conditions on objective representation.

In chapter 1, he writes: 'Hence, as things are, particular-identification in general rests ultimately on the possibility of locating the particular things we speak of in a single unified spatio-temporal system.'[14] The reference to *possibility* here should be noted. The idea is that there *is* a unified spatio-temporal system. In our sophisticated adult maturity, we can reflectively 'make sense of'—give a rational explanation of—particular identification by reference to this system and to the places in it occupied by ourselves and other particulars. Particular-identification rests on facts known within our mature conceptual scheme. In that scheme we can marshall that knowledge to give explanations. Strawson's quoted claim concerns conditions for articulating our conception of objective representation.

Later in the book, however, Strawson offers a different formulation:

particular identification was shown to rest in fact on the use of expressions which, directly or indirectly, embody a demonstrative force; for such identification rests upon

---

[13] See, for example, P. F. Strawson, 'Entity and Identity' (1976) and 'Reference and its Roots' (1986), both in *Entity and Identity and Other Essays* (Oxford: Clarendon Press, 1997).

[14] Strawson, *Individuals*, 27 [38].

the use of a unified framework of knowledge of particulars in which we ourselves have a known place.[15]

Here Strawson discusses particular identification *tout court*, not within our adult conceptual scheme. (He does not use his misleading technical term 'objective particulars' here.) Strawson is not focused on making intelligible our conception of objectivity. He is focused on explaining identification of particulars. Here he holds such identification to depend not just on the *possibility* of an intelligible explanation in terms of a spatio-temporal framework. He holds that it depends on *actually using the reference to that framework* and *knowing* one's place in it. Strawson writes as if this much stronger claim was established in the first half of the book, where he was discussing a very different matter—conditions for understanding our adult conception of objectivity. Here Strawson takes a position on the project of understanding conditions for objective representation.

I believe that Strawson argues successfully that actual use of demonstrative-like representation is necessary for identifying particulars. I believe that he nowhere successfully argues that identifying particulars, even particular bodies in space, depends on using a comprehensive spatial framework—much less on knowledge of one's place in such a framework. These are commitments that Evans and other followers champion, as if Strawson had established them. Many of these positions also maintain that to identify a particular in a demonstrative way one must *know* which particular one identifies. I will return to this issue.

Strawson makes commitments within the project of accounting for constitutive conditions on objective representation that have no serious grounding. Some of them seem to result from unacknowledged slides from parallel commitments within the project of accounting for our *conception* of objective representation. I will discuss some of Strawson's commitments in the former project, beginning with passages in Strawson's commentary on Kant.

STRAWSON ON KANT

The slide from discussing conditions on a conception of objectivity to discussing conditions on objective reference occurs in Strawson's exposition of Kant. In expounding the Second Analogy, without any argument, Strawson counts it an insight of Kant's to reduce the problem of discovering 'what is necessary to make a temporal succession of experiences (or perceptions) perceptions *of* an objective reality' to the problem of discovering 'necessary conditions of the possibility of distinguishing . . . time relations between objects which the perceptions are to be taken as perceptions of . . . and time-relations between the members of the

---

[15] Strawson, *Individuals*, 115 [118].

(subjective) series of perceptions themselves'.[16] This is to reduce the problem of explaining minimum conditions on experience of objective reality to the problem of explaining necessary conditions on our *conception* of the relation between perceptions and their objects—an aspect of the problem of explaining our conception of objectivity.

Strawson is primarily interested in our mature conceptual scheme. Yet he expounds Kant (mistakenly, I think) on the presumption that perceiving physical entities depends on conceptualizing the distinction between perceptions and physical entities. Such a presumption would exclude children and animals, which probably lack a conception of their perceptions as such, from perceiving physical entities as having specific physical attributes. Such a view would be high-handed and hyper-intellectualized. Strawson probably believed this view. But his failure to argue for it or to call attention to its consequences suggests that he slides carelessly between the project of explaining conditions for our conception of objectivity and the project of accounting for conditions on perceptual representation of, and as of, physical objects.

The same slide resides in Strawson's discussions of Kant on experience. When Strawson introduces the notion of experience in his exposition of Kant, he does not give it the technical explanation that Kant does. He uses it as if it is a completely ordinary notion, glossing it simply as 'the way things appear to us'.[17]

The issue of what to count as experience bears on Strawson's approving exposition of Kant's account of conditions for the possibility of experience. Strawson expounds Kant's view that 'experience' requires unity of consciousness. Both Kant and Strawson construe unity of consciousness as a capacity for self-consciousness—an ability to add 'I think' to representations.[18] Strawson holds that the ability to recognize particulars as being of a general kind requires an ability to refer different experiences to a single thinking subject. This latter ability is said to preserve a distinction between a particular recognized and recognition of the particular. In sum, the capacity to ascribe experiences to a single subject, and a conceptual capacity to distinguish between the way things seem and the way things are, are jointly supposed to be necessary for having experience.[19]

This argument would need more discussion than Strawson provides if the notion of experience did not, virtually as a matter of terminology, exclude the perceptions and perceptual beliefs of animals and children, as Kant's does.

---

[16] Strawson, *Bounds of Sense*, 124. Strawson makes it clear that the latter project presupposes empirical self-consciousness.

[17] See ibid. 15 ff. Strawson appears to use the term 'experience' in the same ordinary sense in his exposition of Kant's Second Analogy, quoted above. The one hint of construing experience in a more honorific sense occurs in an off-hand remark (p. 60): 'there is no experience worth the name, certainly no knowledge, without concepts, without thoughts.' Even here, I think that he is expressing a substantive view rather than a technical notion of experience.

[18] Ibid. 93, 98, 100–102. See Kant, *Critique of Pure Reason*, B132–134, B138; Strawson, *Individuals*, 75 [81–82].

[19] Strawson, *Bounds of Sense*, 100–102, 110–111.

Common sense and empirical science support the view that animals and young children have perceptions and beliefs about bodies. Yet there is no evidence that all these individuals have conceptualized a seems/is distinction or can think thoughts of the form 'I think . . . '. Strawson starts with a liberal, common-sense notion of experience. He gives arguments that do not nearly suffice to reach their conclusions, unless the notion of experience in their premises is taken in a narrower sense.

The view that an individual must be able to make sense of each of these conditions is perhaps plausible in an account of a conception of objectivity. These requirements cannot be assumed in an account of objective representation—more specifically, an account of the capacity of perception, or even perceptual belief, to represent physical particulars, including bodies, as having specific physical characteristics.

STRAWSON ON SOLIPSISM

In *Individuals* Strawson rejects taking a 'true' solipsist to be someone who believes that there is no external world (a philosophical solipsist). He writes: 'The true solipsist is rather one who simply has *no use* for the distinction between himself and what is not himself.'[20] Similarly, he writes:

I shall mean by non-solipsistic consciousness, the consciousness of a being who has a use for the distinction between himself and his states, on the one hand, and something not himself or a state of himself, of which he has experience, on the other; and by a solipsistic consciousness, the consciousness of a being who has no use for this distinction.[21]

Strawson identifies a conceptual scheme that makes a meta-distinction between experiential states and entities in the physical environment with a non-solipsistic consciousness. A scheme that has no use for the distinction marks a solipsistic consciousness. One way of lacking a use for the distinction is to lack the wherewithal to draw it. Strawson's explication suggests a very pure form of Individual Representationalism. The individual is required to be able to represent a precondition on objective representation in order to avoid solipsism. The precondition is that there is a distinction between an individual and his states (presumably experiential states), on one hand, and objects of experience, on the other. The claim is that avoiding solipsism depends on being able to represent a seems/is distinction, or being able to employ a meta-point of view that distinguishes experiences from objects of experience.

---

[20] Strawson, *Individuals*, 66 [73]. Strawson is careful to indicate that the 'true' solipsist, on his characterization, would not be a philosophical solipsist, and would not think of himself as a solipsist.
[21] Ibid. 61 [69]. Strawson is cautious about exactly what sort of reference to the observer's standpoint is necessary to avoid solipsism. See also pp. 74–80 [81–86].

Strawson's terminology suggests that he thinks that an ability to draw such a distinction is a condition on reference to a physical world. Whether or not Strawson intends this position, his terminology *entails* that lacking the capacity to take up a meta point of view, an individual thinker is, by default, a solipsist. If Strawson had regarded objective representation as a default position, he could not have introduced his terminology in this way.

Strawson's explication entails that children and animals who cannot represent a distinction between experience and objects of experience, and who therefore have no use for the distinction, are solipsists. They count as solipsists because they do not think of physical entities *as* mind-independent. Since 'solipsist' is a term with antecedent meaning—not a neologism—such a view needs argument, not merely definitional, or explicational, characterization.[22]

Animals and very young children almost surely cannot draw the distinction that Strawson requires. Yet they are in no sense solipsists. Through perception they represent—in some cases have beliefs about—the physical environment.

Strawson's characterization of solipsism suggests that the natural bias for a cognitive system is to be subjective. Strawson does not announce this view. His explication, however, whether intentionally or not, entails that animals that lack a meta-point of view are solipsists: if they cannot explain why they are not solipsists, they are solipsists. Strawson's explication nurtures Individual Representationalism.

STRAWSON ON FEATURE PLACING

Strawson takes representation of material bodies to rest on a more primitive type of thought. He calls this type 'feature placing'. Feature-placing notions include analogs of mass terms, property-indicating adjectives, and event terms. Examples of feature-placing thoughts are it is raining, there is water here, here is green, there is roundness. The key idea is that feature-placing thoughts are not accompanied by principles for distinguishing or reidentifying particulars of the given type. They lack what Strawson calls 'conceptual resources for identifying reference'. The features that are 'placed' are universals.[23]

The account of feature placing is part of a theory of introduction of representation of certain *kinds* of particulars into discourse or thought.[24] Strawson intends to illumine conditions under which certain *kinds* of particulars, most importantly

[22] If 'solipsist' is taken to have no other meaning than that stipulated by Strawson, this aspect of Strawson's position does not entail Individual Representationalism. Meanings do not work that way, however.

[23] Strawson, *Individuals*, 208–216 [202–209], and chapter 7. Substantially the same account is given in 'Particular and General' (1953–1954), in *Logico-Linguistic Papers* (London: Methuen and Co. Ltd, 1971). And a version of the account shows up in 'Reference and its Roots', 137. I later discuss what Strawson takes these 'conceptual resources for identifying reference' to involve.

[24] Strawson, *Individuals*, 136, 198, 204 [137, 193–194, 198–199].

material bodies, can be talked or thought about. He proposes a separable theory of conditions under which particulars can be represented on specific occasions. He thinks of this latter theory as being about conditions for introducing identified particulars into a proposition.[25] The feature-placing theory itself is a theory about conditions for engaging in certain *types* or *forms* of discourse or thought.

One can certainly isolate a form of thought that involves the conceptual counterparts of mass terms, event terms, and ordinary adjectives, and that decries the contextual presence of mass types, event types, and property types. One can also conceive of these feature-placing thoughts in the absence of abilities to enumerate or reidentify instances. Feature-placing thought is logically separable from thought as of bodies. Strawson is right on these points. He is further right to maintain that the ability to reidentify material bodies is an ability that is not employed in feature-placing thoughts.

Strawson is careful not to claim that the 'transition' from feature placing to material-body representation corresponds to a temporal order of learning. He avoids making empirical claims about order of development.[26] What I question is his claim that feature placing constitutes a level of thought in terms of which introduction of reference to material bodies is to be explained. The order of explanation that he envisages depends on a conception of objective reference that I believe is endemic to Individual Representationalism.

Strawson's larger idea is to provide an explanation of, and a conceptual basis for, 'introduction' on contextual occasions of particulars, through identifying reference to them. The basis is supposed to be feature placing. The larger explanation then cites an idealized transition from feature placing to the representation of particulars, especially material bodies. The explanation is supposed to illumine constitutive factors in both kind introduction and representation of particulars, especially material bodies.

Strawson explains the feature-placing level of thought in terms of a 'naming-game':

Playing the naming-game may be compared with one of the earliest things which children do with language—when they utter the general name for a kind of thing in the presence of a thing of that kind, saying 'duck' when there is a duck, 'ball' when there is a ball &c.[27]

The naming-game is conceived as lacking conceptual resources for identifying reference to the corresponding particulars. There is no identifying reference to

---

[25] Late in the book, Strawson explains his notion of *introducing a particular into a proposition*: 'One "introduces a particular" into a proposition if one makes an identifying reference to that particular in that proposition' (*Individuals*, 203 [198]).

[26] Ibid. 216 [209]. In this respect Strawson is more circumspect than Quine. As we shall see, Quine makes empirical commitments on order of learning. Strawson calls his own conceptual explanation 'speculative'. Despite their putatively 'conceptual' character, I believe that Strawson's speculations are at odds with empirical considerations. I think that Strawson's 'explanatory' points are incorrect, and the empirical order of learning is sometimes the reverse of his conceptual order of explanation.

[27] Ibid. 212 [206].

particulars in any of these forms of discourse or thought—as Strawson conceives them. I want to make some general points about the feature-placing form of thought and about the order of explanation that Strawson proposes.

Strawson does not regard the feature-placing form of thought as about the contents of an individual's mind. He seems to take features to be stuff types, event types, or other 'universals' (such as shapes) that are instantiated in the physical environment. However, he regards spatio-temporal adverbs in expressions of feature-placing thoughts (adverbs such as 'now' and 'here') as vague and gestural rather than genuinely referential. He maintains that they cannot identify definite spatial regions or temporal intervals.[28]

In fact, Strawson regards the apparent representation of instances of stuffs, events, and properties as equally gestural and indefinite. He conceives this primitive level of thought as conceptually prior to thought about material bodies in a way that anticipates Quine's conception of alleged pre-individuative stages of language.

As noted, Strawson does not regard feature-placing thought as introducing any *particulars* at all. It does not introduce particular events (in it is raining). It does not introduce particular expanses of stuff (in there is water here). It does not introduce instances of properties (such as instances of greenness or roundness in here is greenness or there is roundness).[29] He distinguishes between feature placing and representation of *any* particulars, including particular instances of the universals that are placed. He writes: 'Feature placing does not bring particulars into our discourse.' So placing is *not* representation of instances of the features (universals) that are placed. Feature placing represents universals. But, in placing the universals, no particular instance of the universal is represented.[30] There is feature placing, representation of particulars that are material bodies, and representation of particulars that are not material bodies. Feature placing is, according to Strawson, conceptually prior to *both* sorts of representation of particulars. Representation of universals is supposed to be conceptually prior to representation of particulars.

The position just described is a delicate one. What distinguishes feature placing for mass notions (water, gold) and event notions (raining) from representing a particular instance of some water or gold, or a particular event of raining? Why is representation of such particulars not effected through designation of such instances when the relevant feature is localized to places and times through indexicals such as here and now? Strawson seems to think that an arbitrariness or lack of specificity accompanies feature-placing thought. He seems to think that representing even particulars other than material bodies requires resources that

---

[28] Ibid. 222, 228, 230 [216, 221, 223].
[29] Ibid., chapter 7. I distinguish between an instance of a property and a surface or body that has the property.
[30] Ibid. 209 [203]. See also 211–215 [205–209].

feature placing lacks. He implies that having criteria of distinctness is necessary for representing any particulars at all.[31]

There are certainly logical forms that might model feature-placing discourse, forms in which no element in the discourse has a form that makes reference to particulars. Formally, one could regard feature-placing discourse as consisting of present-time and present-place operators that operate on predicates, such as 'is water' or 'is raining': 'there is (the universal) water now/here.' The quantifier ranges only over universals. 'Now' and 'here' are, respectively, tense and place operators that do not explicitly refer to time or place. The sentence is true if and only if the universal is instantiated at the time and place of utterance. This truth condition quantifies over universals, instances of universals, times, and places. But one can stipulate that the sentence whose truth conditions are given quantifies (represents) only universals.

The ontological commitments of the meta-explanation of the truth conditions of the sentence need not be the same as the ontological commitments of the sentence whose truth conditions are explained. Strawson's idea can perhaps be captured by maintaining that feature-placing discourse has the ontological commitments of the object-language sentence, not the sentence that gives meta-theoretic semantical explanation of its truth conditions.

I think that the foregoing is a coherent semantical explication of a kind of discourse. I do not think that it could possibly be a basic form of discourse or thought. Let us bracket time and place operators. Any such discourse or thought must derive its representational powers from its relation to perception. Perception is necessarily and constitutively a relation to particulars with causal powers. The relevant perception is of instances of water, or events of raining, or instances of greenness (or green particulars). So representational relation to particulars must precede—in the order of explanation of meaning, representational content, and reference—any discourse or form of thought that refers empirically to universals but avoids explicit reference to particulars. So the operator discourse or form of thought must be an *abstraction* from a more basic form. The more basic form perceptually refers to particulars and perceptually attributes features (such as *water* or *red*) to those particulars.[32]

---

[31] Strawson, *Individuals*, 211–213 [205–207]. For Strawson, representation of material bodies requires having criteria for distinctness *and* reidentification.

[32] An anonymous reviewer complained that the argument in this paragraph has a gap, citing the possibility that in perceiving instances of water or color, it does not, or might not, 'make sense' that a given particular instance of water or color is 'the same again'. I think that this criticism is mistaken. The argument does not depend on any premise about making sense of 'sameness again'. So there is no such gap in it. As will become clear as the work proceeds, it is not constitutively necessary for perception of particular instances of water or color (hence of being in a perceptual state with the representational content that liquid or that red color, where the 'thats' single out the perceived particular liquid or the perceived red color instance) that the individual or the individual's psychological resources be capable of 'making sense' of reidentification of the same particular on another occasion. The 'making-sense' requirement is vague, but redolent of individual representationalist assumptions. I do think that perception of *bodies* constitutively requires a capacity to track the bodies as the same on other occasions. But perception of instances of

Strawson nowhere explains why he thinks that in feature-placing thought, general concepts can apply to features that, as a matter of fact, are instantiated in space. What allows such application? Why does he not take primitive feature-placing thought to be about sense data, or at any rate not specifically to concern the physical world? It is because he assumes that perception is of elements in the physical environment. But perception is clearly constitutively of concrete particulars, and thus has singular elements in its representational content.

Strawson offers no theory to back his view of the allegedly basic feature-placing form of discourse, one that indicates universals without making reference to particulars. He provides no account of how the discourse has any relevance to conditions in the physical environment. He does not explain what, in the absence of a mastery of a stable comprehensive framework of spatial reference, makes spatial 'placing' possible. I believe that had he pursued these questions, he would have been led to reflect more seriously on perception. He might have had deeper insight into the nature and application of both general concepts and singular referential devices.

As things stand, Strawson postulates a level of thought that is more primitive than thought about not only material bodies but all particulars. The level is supposed to provide an explanatory basis for introduction of these levels of thought. I have argued that feature placing in thought must depend representationally on feature placing in perception, and that feature placing in perception already involves perception of (and perceptual representation as of) particulars— instances of the features. So feature placing in thought must involve thought of particulars.[33]

I have been discussing Strawson's conception of an idealized feature-placing stage of thought. Let me now discuss, briefly, the supposed idealized conceptual transition from this stage to the stage in which particulars are thought about. Among particulars, Strawson regards material bodies as especially important.

Strawsonian features does not carry any such requirement. And perception of such instances does not constitutively require perception of or as of bodies. The point of the argument in the text is to show that basic feature-placing capacities cannot lack singular elements whose function is to single out, perceptually, particular instances of the features. I think that feature-placing capacities are possible, and probably actual, in the animal kingdom. Contrary to Strawson, however, a feature-placing form of representation that lacks any singular elements is not a possible *basic* form of feature-placing representation.

[33] While representation of bodies appears to be developmentally basic for human perceptual systems, it is likely that not all perceivers can perceive bodies as such. Thus feature-placing systems probably exist. As I have argued, they all involve perceptual reference to particulars. There are probably perceptual systems, even perhaps visual systems, that represent instances of colors, events, masses, but not bodies. There is some evidence that a phase in the first micro-seconds of visual processing in humans involves feature placing that then normally serves perceptual representation of (and as of) bodies. See Anne Treisman, 'Feature Binding, Attention, and Object Perception', in G. W. Humphreys, J. Duncan, and A. Treisman (eds.), *Attention, Space, and Action* (Oxford: Oxford University Press, 1999). But such feature placing appears to be linked in humans, from the beginning of development, with representation as of bodies. The main point of this section is that contrary to Strawson's conception of feature placing, perception and thought guided by perception are of, and as of, particulars.

According to Strawson, the key element that is missing at the feature-placing stage and that makes thought of particulars possible is the *adoption* of 'criteria' for individuation. For thought that represents bodies, there must also be adoption of criteria for reidentification. Strawson explains the transition from feature placing to representation of *particulars* in discourse and thought as follows:

Though feature-placing sentences do not introduce particulars into our discourse, they provide a basis for this introduction. The facts they state are presupposed, in the required sense, by the introduction of certain kinds of particular. That there should be facts statable by means of such sentences as 'There is water here', 'It is snowing', is a condition of there being propositions into which particulars are introduced₁ by means of such expressions as 'This pool of water', 'This fall of snow'. In general, the transition from facts of the presupposed kind to the introduction of the particulars for which they supply the basis involves a conceptual complication: it involves the adoption of criteria of distinctness and, where applicable, criteria of reidentification for particulars of the kind in question, as well as the use of characterizing universals which can be tied to a particular of that kind.[34]

Adopting *criteria* of distinctness and, for material bodies, criteria of reidentification is required *in addition to* just having the characterizing universals (pool of water or body or cat). I believe that Strawson holds that being able to use universals in predication as attributives requires having criteria of distinctness. Feature placings of universals, even those that sound like 'duck' or 'water', are not true attributives, in Strawson's view. What enables one to have characterizations of universals *that guide identifying reference to particulars* (and attribute the universals to particulars)—as opposed to merely feature placing—is having criteria of distinctness.

Strawson writes further of the relevant transition as applied to the special case of thought about bodies. This transition requires criteria for reidentification:

Operating with the idea of reidentifiable particular cats, we distinguish between the case in which a particular cat appears, departs and reappears, and the case in which a particular cat appears and departs and a different cat appears. But one could play the naming-game without making this distinction. Someone playing the naming-game can correctly say 'More cat' or 'Cat again' in both cases; but someone operating with the idea of particular cats would be in error if he said 'Another cat' in the first case, or 'The same cat again' in the second. *The decisive conceptual step to cat-particulars is taken when the case of 'more cat' or 'cat again' is subdivided into the case of 'another cat' and the case of 'the same cat again'.*[35]

According to Strawson, this subdivision is made possible only through possessing general criteria for reidentification. The criteria of distinctness and reidentification that mark the supposed transition from feature placing to representing material bodies are supposed to be conceptual. The individual is supposed to

---

[34] Strawson, *Individuals*, 209 [203]. The subscript on 'introduced' is Strawson's way of distinguishing particular introduction from kind introduction.

[35] Ibid. 213–214 [207]. The italics are Strawson's.

know these criteria, at least implicitly. I discuss such criteria two subsections hence. The point to note here is that the explanatory transition that Strawson postulates is the addition of a conceptualized type of propositional knowledge about conditions of particular identity, and more specifically of material-body identity and continuity over time. The addition supplements a more primitive conceptualized thought about stuff-, event-, and property-universals. Feature-placing thought lacks criteria of distinctness and criteria of reidentification. The transition constitutes an intuitive augmentation of objectivity, a better-understood system for characterizing the world as it is. Strawson takes reference to material bodies as such to occur only when this transition is effected—only when thinkers know and apply conceptualized criteria for identification and reidentification.

Strawson believes that reference to particulars other than bodies (stuff instances, events, property instances) is parasitic on reference to bodies. He also believes that reference to a particular of *any* type is explanatorily posterior to feature-placing reference purely to universals. And he thinks that the key to explaining the transition to reference to particulars lies in a requirement that the individual know criteria for distinctness—and, in the case of material bodies, criteria for reidentification.

Strawson proposes an idealized order for understanding components of our conception of objectivity. Perhaps the order can be illuminating for some purpose. Strawson regards it as an explanatory ordering of our practices of reference. From this latter prospective, it is deficient.

Many animals *perceive* bodies and other particulars as such, but lack propositional attitudes altogether—certainly propositional attitudes capable of having the representational content of criteria. I shall discuss evidence for this view in Chapters 8–10. Let us suppose for now that the view is correct. The perceptual capacity of these animals consists partly in an ability to single out bodies from a background, locating them in space, to perceive them in relation to other bodies, and to track them over time.[36] The capacities operate under principles that *we* can understand and use in explaining them. But they themselves cannot understand, formulate, or conceptualize principles or criteria for discriminating, locating, and relocating.

A capacity to *think* of bodies as bodies, and to think of other particulars as being of specific types, can rely on these perceptual capacities by incorporating perception into propositional thought. Incorporating perception into propositional thought involves utilizing perceptual modes of presentation within propositional structures and patterns of propositional inference. The inferential patterns need not conceptualize *principles* for perception formation, tracking, or

---

[36] I believe that a capacity to reidentify bodies through intervals of not experiencing them is *not* a necessary condition on perceiving bodies as such. There is, however, empirical reason to believe that several lower (pre-propositional) animals—baby chicks, other birds, many lower mammals, as well as primates, do have this capacity. See Chapters 9–10.

inference. For example, the relevant perceptual systems enable a perceiver to distinguish one body from other bodies perceived at a given time, or over time. The thinker need not be able to think about *conditions* under which bodies are the same or different. In order to use perceptual concepts to distinguish bodies as same or different, the thinker need not understand principles that the perceptual system operates under. It is enough to be able to track sameness and difference of particular bodies perceptually, and to incorporate this ability into a propositional structure by carrying out propositional inferences that utilize body concepts.

In many species capable of thought, thought about bodies is not posterior to any other sort of thought, in the order of development. It is not conceptually explained in terms of adding propositionally mastered and known criteria for reidentification to a more primitive level of thought. It is itself the most developmentally primitive level of *thought*. It rests on non-propositional perceptual capacities that themselves incorporate capacities for tracking and reidentifying particulars. The principles governing the laws in which these capacities are embedded are not propositionally available to the individual thinkers. No general criteria or principles need be represented, conceptualized, understood, or otherwise grasped, even implicitly. No general criteria need even be representable, much less known, by the individual.

In some animals, including human infants, representation of bodies as such is developmentally basic in both perception and empirical thought. In fact, there is evidence that in human infants, thinking in mass-like ways emerges later than thought as of bodies.[37]

I believe that the order just sketched is the actual order of development in human beings and many other animals. Because perception is the developmental basis for representational content in thought, and because perception constitutively involves representation of particulars as having specific attributes, empirical thought and discourse inevitably represent particulars at the most fundamental level. This point applies to empirical representation, not only of bodies, but of particular instances of all attributes. The idea that the most primitive form of representation in thought is a representation of universals with no representation of particulars is incompatible with the fact that perceptual representation lies at the basis of empirical representation in thought.

Strawson's explanatory order is mistaken. Representation of particulars together with attribution of attributes is basic to perception and to empirical thought. Representation of universals *alone* in empirical contexts must derive from abstraction from or generalization from representation of particulars as falling under universals. Feature-placing discourse, as Strawson characterizes

---

[37] G. Huntley-Fenner, S. Carey, and A. Salimando, 'Objects are Individuals but Stuff Doesn't Count: Perceived Rigidity and Cohesiveness Influence in Infants' Representation of Small Numbers of Discrete Entities', *Cognition* 85 (2002), 203–221; Spelke, 'Principles of Object Perception'. Although Strawson does not claim that the feature-placing form of thought occupies a prior temporal stage in child development, he clearly thinks this view plausible. There is strong empirical ground to reject the view.

it, is discourse that abstracts from or suppresses explicit reliance on perceptual and empirical-conceptual capacities to refer to particulars in the physical environment. One can explain such discourse, as I did in the account of tense and place operators, so as not to allow it to represent particulars explicitly. But such discourse is possible only through abstraction or suppression. Perceptual reference to particulars is basic in the order of explanation of empirical representation and in the order of development in humans and other animals.

When we reflectively think about methods of tracking and reidentifying *bodies* through perception and empirical thought, we recognize that such methods are more complex than *perceptual* means of identifying masses or simple events. The key addition in complexity is a capacity to reidentify over time. So conceptualizations of the *principles* governing the capacities, including perceptual capacities, that underlie singular thought about material bodies are more complex than conceptualizations of the principles that govern singular thought about masses or simple events. Here, at one level of reflection removed, Strawson's conception of relative complexities of the two types of thought is sound. It does not follow that singular thought as of bodies is to be *explained* in terms of the introduction of criteria for reidentification into a simpler form of thought. The root mistake in Strawson's conception of singular thought as of bodies lies in his conception of the role of *criteria* in making singular thought about bodies possible. Perceptual tracking, and tracking in empirical thought, does not require the individual perceiver or thinker to have criteria (as contents of any psychological states) that explain or make sense of the tracking. To think that having criteria is required for tracking or otherwise thinking about bodies is an expression of Individual Representationalism. To the contrary, one can think of bodies as bodies without being able to think principles governing one's doing so.

STRAWSON ON PARTICULAR-IDENTIFICATION IN THOUGHT

I turn now to Strawson's account of conditions under which particulars are represented in specific contexts. This account concerns particular-identification, or what Strawson calls introduction of particulars into propositions, in thought or discourse. For him, it is to be distinguished from feature placing.

Strawson made two fundamental, correct points that are relevant to understanding constitutive conditions on objective representation of particulars in thought and language.

One is that descriptive representation cannot be sufficient of itself for representing physical particulars. Strawson argued that demonstrative-like reference has to underlie and mediate purely descriptive representations of physical particulars.[38]

---

[38] Strawson, *Individuals*, chapter 1, and pp. 114–117 [117–119].

This point seems to me deep and correct. I have nothing but admiration for Strawson's development of it.

The other fundamental point is that representation of, and as of, bodies must be associated with some capacity to represent spatial relations in a spatio-temporal framework.[39] This point requires subtle handling. How it applies in an account of our conception of objectivity is different from how it applies in an account of objective reference. Nevertheless, Strawson, following Kant, is surely right to place it at the center of any account of representation of bodies. It is, I think, impossible to represent bodies as such without being able to represent specific spatial properties and relations as such. And it is impossible to have a conception of bodies as mind-independent without having some spatial conceptions that one associates with those bodies.

Strawson develops both points within his primary project—that of explicating our adult conception of objectivity—and also within his secondary project—that of explaining conditions for objective representation. But Strawson makes further, less salutary commitments that severely constrain the project of explaining conditions on representing bodies. I want to discuss two of these further commitments.[40]

The first is a requirement on representation of particulars in a specific context. The commitment is the claim that to engage in singular reference in propositional thought to a particular, one must *know* which particular one is thinking about. Strawson writes:

A sufficient, but not necessary, condition of the full requirement's [requirement for demonstrative hearer identification] being satisfied is—to state it loosely at first—that the hearer can pick out by sight or hearing or touch, or can otherwise sensibly discriminate, the particular being referred to, knowing that it is that particular.[41]

Strawson does not take the stated condition to be a necessary condition, because one need not *perceive* a particular that one knows an identifying fact about. He does regard knowing some such identifying fact as necessary in both the perceptual case and in the case in which the individual does not think of the particular by way of a perceptual demonstrative. Knowing an identifying fact might involve connecting the referent to demonstratively expressed, perceptually based knowledge of another referent:

It seems that the general requirements of hearer-identification could be regarded as fulfilled if the hearer knew that the particular being referred to was identical with some particular about which he knew some individuating fact, or facts, other than the fact that it was the particular being referred to. To know an individuating fact about a particular is to

---

[39] Strawson, *Individuals*, 13, 24, 26 [25, 35, 36–37].

[40] Strawson's contributions to understanding constitutive conditions on objective representation are usually ancillary to his main project of understanding our conception of objectivity. But both contributions and mistakes are, with close reading, discernible as positions within the first project as well.

[41] Strawson, *Individuals*, 6 [18].

know that such-and-such a thing is true of that particular and of no other particular whatever.... This, then, is the general condition for hearer-identification in the non-demonstrative case; and it is obvious that if a genuine reference is being made, the speaker, too, must satisfy a similar condition.[42]

Strawson later takes these hearer-conditions to apply to speakers and to individual thinkers.[43]

The general condition on singular reference is that the hearer must know an individuating fact about the particular referent:

The identifying introduction of either a particular or a universal into discourse entails knowing what particular or what universal is meant, or intended to be introduced, by the introducing expression. Knowing what particular is meant entails knowing... some particular fact which suffices to identify that particular, other than the fact that it is the particular currently being introduced.[44]

To require identifying knowledge as a condition on thought about particulars is, in current philosophy, immediately jarring. Developments in understanding how reference works that came after *Individuals* showed that it is not a necessary condition for thinking about a particular (whether a person, or body, or event) that one know an individuating fact about it. For example, an individual can think about a person through a proper name and lack any individuating knowledge of the person.[45]

Strawson lays down the knowing-which requirement as a general requirement. But my primary interest is in its application to perception and to propositional attitudes immediately grounded in perception—attitudes like non-inferential perceptual beliefs. The requirement may seem more plausible as applied in this restricted domain.

Strawson makes his knowing-which requirement more specific. He requires an individuating definite description. Under the heading of considering conditions of 'introducing a particular into a proposition', he elaborates as follows:

---

[42] Ibid. 11 [23].

[43] Ibid. 11, 51 [23, 60].

[44] Ibid. 189 [185–186]. See pp. 184–189, 198, 61 [181–186, 193, 69]. It is clear from these passages, which invoke knowledge of *facts*, and from many other passages (for example, those that discuss logically adequate criteria) that Strawson thinks of knowledge of which object is represented as *propositional* knowledge, not mere perceptual know-how. I owe this cautionary point to Tony Brueckner. And it appears from many of these same passages that Strawson requires the *individual thinker*, speaker, or hearer to have the relevant knowledge. (See the section POSTLUDE: STRAWSON ON CRITERIA IN IDENTIFICATIONAL REFERENCE.) On these points, see also the next three quotations displayed in the text.

[45] Donnellan, 'Proper Names and Identifying Descriptions'; Kripke, *Naming and Necessity*, lecture I. Strawson writes: 'One cannot significantly use a name to refer to someone or something unless one knows who or what it is that one is referring to by that name. One must, in other words, be prepared to substitute a description for the name.' This requirement, later clarified to require an individualizing definite description, is defeated by examples supplied by Donnellan and Kripke.

But we are now considering, not simply what he says, but the conditions of his doing what he does by what he says. For him to be referring to just one particular, it is not enough that there should be at least one particular which his description fits. There must be *at most* one such particular *which he has in mind*. But he cannot, for himself, distinguish the particular which he has in mind by the fact that it is the one he has in mind. So there must be some description he could give, though it need not be the description he does give, which applies uniquely to the one he has in mind and does not include the phrase, 'the one I have in mind'.[46]

Strawson allows that the description might depend on 'demonstratively in-dicatable features of the situation of reference'. But he adds again that the identifying description 'must not include a reference to the speaker's own reference to the particular in question'.[47]

I believe that part of the intent of this requirement is that the individual not be allowed to represent the particular simply by a demonstrative-marked description like 'that body'. The individual needs to be able to give a further identifying answer to the question 'which body?'. A possible answer could be 'the body presently in that place' or 'the most salient body that I am pointing at'. But the remark about features of the situation seems to me to indicate Strawson's belief that a simple that F must be supplemented.[48] He clearly rules out supplements like the F that I have in mind. This exclusion seems to me also intended to exclude the F that I am currently perceiving.

Strawson motivates the requirement that the individual have a description that applies uniquely to the particular. He does so by appealing to the antecedent

---

[46]   Strawson, *Individuals*, 184–185 [181–182].

[47]   Ibid. 185 n. [182 n.].

[48]   Although I will not go into this point here, I believe that allowing That F to count as an identifying description would be incompatible with Strawson's attempt to account for the asymmetry between subject and predicate, a major and long-standing project through Strawson's career. (See also Strawson, 'Particular and General'; 'Singular Terms and Predication', *The Journal of Philosophy* 58 (1961), 393–412; 'The Asymmetry of Subjects and Predicates' (1970), in *Logico-Linguistic Papers*; and 'My Philosophy', in *The Philosophy of P. F. Strawson*, ed. P. K. Sen and R. R. Verma (New Delhi: Indian Council of Philosophical Research, 1995).) Grammatical subjects of sentences or thoughts are supposed to contain a complete proposition. See Strawson, *Individuals*, 194, 197–198, 216–217 [190, 192–193, 210–211]. I think that Strawson would have regarded The unique F that is here or That F there as requiring, respectively, knowledge that there is a unique F and it is here, and that there is an F at the place where I am pointing. (See especially p. 194 [190].) I think that he would not have regarded That F as containing within itself a genuine proposition: There is a unique this, and it is F. He would have asked 'a unique this?—what particular is intended?' The invocation of place or a relation to one's pointing is supposed to answer such a question. (Note that appealing to the object to which one is pointing is not question-begging in the way that appealing to the object of one's perception or the object of one's demonstrative reference in thought would be.) I believe that Strawson's requirement that subject terms in thought be expandable into propositions is a mistake. I think that perceptual demonstratives guided by perceptual attributives are non-conceptual partly because they *cannot* be thus expanded into propositions. See Chapter 11 below. *Subject terms in perceptual thought* often rely essentially on perception. They cannot in general be expanded into propositions available to the subject's representational powers. Sometimes reference by subject terms in thought is no more elaborated than reference in perception, though the whole thought must be capable of figuring in propositional inferences, whereas whole perceptions need not be.

requirement that the individual be able to answer the question '*which* particular he was then referring to'. This requirement is that the individual know what particular he was thinking of. And *this* requirement is claimed to be a condition on making a genuine identifying reference.[49]

Strawson summarizes:

in order for an identifying reference to a particular to be made, there must be some true empirical proposition known in some not too exacting sense of this word, to the speaker, to the effect that there is just one particular which answers to a certain description.[50]

The identifying introduction of either a particular or a universal into discourse entails knowing what particular or what universal is meant, or intended to be introduced, by the introducing expression. Knowing what particular is meant entails knowing . . . from the introducing expression used, some empirical fact which suffices to identify that particular, other than the fact that it is the particular currently being introduced.[51]

Postulating identifying *knowledge* as a condition on successful singular thought is unacceptable even in the case of perceptual thought. An individual in a psychological experiment could have sufficient reason to doubt whether what is in fact a perceived body is illusory. The individual—perhaps unwarrantedly, perhaps hesitantly—could go on thinking about the body that he or she is in fact perceiving. In such a case, the individual could think of the particular through perception, but lack knowledge of an identifying fact.[52] The key point is that perception can succeed in picking out particulars independent of knowledge— either knowledge of identifying descriptions or knowledge of criteria.

Strawson's apparent view that it would be 'question-begging' to rely on a demonstrative-marked description like <u>that F</u> in satisfying the identifying de- scription requirement (see note 48) is also mistaken. Reference does not have to answer questions. It just has to use perceptual competencies and causal relations to determine entities in the environment.[53]

---

[49] Ibid. 186 [183].

[50] Ibid. As regards the exclusion of a description of the form <u>that F</u> (that body), note Strawson's quantification of the singular element with widest scope: 'to the effect that there is just one particular which answers to a certain description'. See also ibid. 194 [190], where Strawson rephrases 'that person there' as 'there is just one person there where I am pointing' in order to bring out the identifying fact (description). Although demonstratives are allowed in the description, they apparently cannot be employed with a minimum descriptive element (a sortal) simply to pick out the object. They cannot be so employed as a sufficient fulfillment of the requirement of an identifying description. Description is required to be somehow 'informative' in articulately individualizing the particular that is thought about. See note 48.

[51] Ibid. 189 [185–186].

[52] We can imagine that the individual is not sophisticated enough to believe some more complicated hypothetical proposition (such as <u>the material body that I am seeing, if there is one, is green</u>). To be able to perceive and think about a particular, individuals need not be capable of such meta-descriptions. Examples of children are again worth bearing in mind. As indicated earlier, I believe that Strawson would also regard such descriptions as question-begging—in the way that <u>the material body that I have in mind</u> would be.

[53] An individual could perceive and think of an entity that is perceived as a body, but that is in fact a flash of light or a hologram. I do believe that any successful perception must be guided by *some*

Strawson's requirement that one know which entity one is thinking of in singular thought may have stemmed from a conflation of two notions of knowing-which. What is minimally required for successful singular thought about a particular is surely some competence to single it out in some way or other. The view that singular thought requires knowing-which in this minimal sense is nearly truistic. The means that the representational competence relies upon can be perceptual. The means can depend on certain types of competent interlocution with others. These means need not carry with them identifying propositional knowledge.

Such competencies should not be conflated with propositional knowledge (knowledge of a 'fact') that identifies or individuates the particular. Such knowledge would be knowing-which in a stronger sense. The competencies that single out the particular need not involve knowledge of some proposition that uniquely picks out the particular—in the sense that the knowledge entails warranted true belief that distinguishes that particular from every other.

Whether conflating these two notions of knowing-which played a role in Strawson's thinking is unclear to me. His requirement of knowledge of an individuating 'fact' certainly indicates a requirement of individuating propositional knowledge in the stronger sense. His arguments for his requirement tend to be off-hand.[54] At any rate, the requirement is mistaken. A version of the strong interpretation of the requirement was taken up by Evans, as we shall see.

STRAWSON ON CRITERIA FOR REPRESENTATION

Strawson's second commitment regarding singular representation of, and as of, bodies is that we must have adopted criteria for distinctness and criteria for reidentification. This commitment is separable from the knowledge- and identifying-description requirements. One could drop the requirement that one be knowledgeable in applying an identifying description in any given case of particular identification. One could further drop the requirement that one apply a true, uniquely identifying proposition—whether knowledgeably or not—in a given case. There would remain for Strawson the requirement that one have propositional criteria for individuating and reidentifying bodies, if one is to think about bodies. As we saw in the section on feature placing, Strawson requires

accurate perceptual attributive. See my 'Five Theses on *De Re* States and Attitudes', section III. In hologram or flash-of-light cases, the accurate attributive might be some generic shape attributive. Again, I believe that a description of the form that G (where G indicates a closed shape) would not suffice to meet Strawson's requirement of an identifying description. See notes 48 and 50. Even if it did, Strawson's knowing-which requirement fails because successful singular reference in perceptual thought does not require warrant or even belief. See the example, in the text, of the psychological experiment.

[54] As I indicate shortly, Evans makes similar mistakes in his elaboration of 'Russell's Principle'. He engages in a similar hyper-intellectualization of the knowing-which requirement.

adoption of criteria of distinctness, as conditions on thinking of *any* sort of particular. For the special case of thinking of particular bodies, Strawson further requires adoption of criteria of reidentification.

In discussing conditions on having a concept of objectivity in a mature conceptual scheme, Strawson claims that reidentification of stable points of reference (ultimately, bodies) is a condition on having a comprehensive spatio-temporal representational framework. He then adds that a condition on reidentification is that there *be* general criteria for reidentification:

I have argued that a fundamental condition of identifying reference without dependence on alien types is the possession of a common, comprehensive and sufficiently complex type-homogeneous framework of reference. I have claimed that this condition is satisfied in the case of material bodies, and not generally in other cases. But earlier . . . I asserted that a condition, in turn, of the possession of a single, continuously usable framework of this kind, was the ability to *re*identify at least some elements of the framework in spite of discontinuities of observation: that is to say, one must be able to identify some particular things as *the same again* as those encountered on a previous occasion. Evidently the ability to do this entails the existence of general criteria or methods of reidentification for different kinds of particular.[55]

Similarly, Strawson writes:

Now it might further be said that it makes no sense to say that there logically could be reidentifiable particulars in a purely auditory world, unless criteria for reidentification can be framed or devised in purely auditory terms. And if this is correct, as it seems to be, we have the conclusion that the conditions of a non-solipsistic consciousness can be satisfied in such a world only if we can describe in purely auditory terms criteria for reidentification of sound particulars.[56]

In both passages, Strawson is discussing conditions on having a use for a distinction between mind-independent objects and experiences. The last sentence requires a capacity to frame criteria for reidentification of particulars. These are requirements on having, and presumably understanding, our mature conceptual scheme that includes a *concept of objectivity*.

Later in the book, however, Strawson takes a further position. He does not just require that there *be* a method of identification and reidentification that *can in principle* be described or explained in the form of general criteria. He does not just require that one have criteria of reidentification if one is to explain, in one's mature conceptual scheme, the distinction between mind-independent bodies and experiences. As we have seen, in discussing his account of the 'transition' from feature-placing thought to thought that represents particulars, Strawson requires the *adoption* and the *having* of criteria of distinctness as a condition for representing particulars at all—at least representing them in thought. In the basic case

---

[55] Strawson, *Individuals*, 45–46 [55].
[56] Ibid. 65 [72–73].

of representing particular bodies, he requires adopting and having criteria of reidentification.[57]

Sortal concepts attribute sortal universals to particulars. A sortal universal 'supplies a principle for distinguishing and counting individual particulars which it collects'. Strawson adds that a sortal universal 'presupposes no antecedent principle, or method, of individuating the particulars it collects'.[58] According to Strawson, the *concept* of a sortal universal ϕ 'incorporates . . . criteria for identification of particulars[ϕ]s'.[59] It follows for Strawson that having a sortal concept, the type of concept that fundamentally and necessarily guides thought to particulars, requires *having* criteria of identification. Having concepts of bodies, and having concepts for specific kinds of bodies, require also having criteria for reidentification.

Having criteria for reidentification means being able to represent, and being disposed to accept, general propositional verification principles for counting a continuously existing body in space as the same over time. Strawson takes having criteria to be a constitutive condition on both identification and reidentification of particulars.

The assumption that the individual has to be able to know, or at least represent as such, relevant conditions for identification and reidentification is, in my view, not even plausible in an account of our *conception of objectivity*. I do not accept the idea that having a use for a conceptualized distinction between mind-independent objects and one's own experiences requires having criteria for drawing the distinction. I think that at most *reflectively understanding* the distinction *in some depth* requires having criteria. An individual could have learned the concept of objectivity without being able to explain how he or she distinguishes mind-independent entities (conceived as such) from experiences (conceived as such). I need not pursue this matter here. I am primarily concerned with Strawson's requirement on representation of bodies. It certainly cannot be assumed that an individual must be able to represent relevant conditions for identification or reidentification in order to engage in objective reference.

More specifically, an individual need not be able to represent general criteria for identification or reidentification in order to refer to bodies as bodies and as having specific physical attributes, in perception or even perceptual belief. Individuals can perceive and perceptually think of particulars without being able to represent conditions or methods by which they do so. Individuals can perceive and perceptually think of bodies as bodies, without being able to

---

[57] Strawson, *Individuals*, 210, 213–214 [204, 207–208]; see also p. 63 [70]. Strawson's requirement that one have criteria as a condition of engaging in objective representation is a holdover from verificationism. The very meaningfulness of the practice of engaging in objective representation is supposed to depend on having criteria for determining and 'verifying' such representation.

[58] Ibid. 169–170 [167–168].

[59] Ibid. 227 [220]. Strawson adds, p. 227 [221], that criteria for distinctness or reidentification are 'implicit in the meaning' of relevant sortal terms. He seems to think that they are available for being made explicit through reflection.

represent criteria for identification or reidentification. As will become clear in Chapters 7 and 9–10, the types of shapes and continuities that human beings and other animals in fact rely upon are not immediately accessible even to adult reflection.

Strawson does not discuss perception in itself, independently of any association with propositional thought. Earlier I quoted the following passage from early in *Individuals*:

A sufficient, but not necessary, condition of the full requirement's being satisfied [the requirement on identifying reference to particulars] is—to state it loosely at first—that the hearer [speaker, or thinker] can pick out by sight or hearing or touch, or can otherwise sensibly discriminate, the particular being referred to, knowing that it is that particular.[60]

The condition of knowledge is carrying the weight here. The knowledge must include knowledge of an identifying description. And one must have, and presumably also know at least implicitly, a general criterion for individuation. Strawson does not consider a simpler idea. He does not consider the idea that one could single out a particular by perceiving it, without any help from propositional thought or propositional knowledge. He does not consider the idea that propositional perceptual thought might simply capitalize on perceptual reference to particulars. Such thought would embed the perceptual capacity in a network of propositional inferential capacities. But it need not accompany perception with successful, much less knowledgeable, identifying reference that goes beyond the singling-out of particulars present in perception. And it need not associate the perceptual thought with conceptualized general criteria for identification or reidentification. It would be enough to use perceptual know-how, without having the capacity to conceive of how the perceptual identifications and reidentifications operate. There would *be* general methods of identification and reidentification. But those need not be conceptualized or adopted. Strawson never gives this line of thought the slightest consideration.

Strawson's failure to discuss the alternative just outlined derives from conviction that another viewpoint is correct. The basis for Strawson's view on primitive objective representation is his assumption of second-family Individual Representationalism. On this assumption, if an individual is to form a perceptual belief about particular bodies as bodies, he or she must be able to think conditions that make that ability possible. General constitutive conditions must be conceptualized by the individual. The relevant constitutive conditions are conceptualized as criteria for identification and reidentification. Strawson holds that this constitutive condition for one's content's referring to bodies as such must be conceptualized and must be reflectively accessible to the individual. Strawson's view also has an epistemic dimension: the individual must know which particular body is identified; and the individual must know conditions for identification and

---

[60] Ibid. 6 [18–19].

reidentification. All of these assumptions are, I think, mistaken. My main point here is that they are not argued for.[61]

POSTLUDE: STRAWSON ON CRITERIA IN IDENTIFICATIONAL REFERENCE

Strawson's views on criteria change slightly over the course of his career. My discussion has centered on his position in *Individuals* (1959). Given his focus on conceptual schemes and the nature of communal discourse, Strawson is not always explicit about whether given *individual thinkers* must have relevant criteria, or about what form criteria must take in individual minds.

Many passages that I have cited can appear to be compatible with the view that some individuals engage in a community's referential practices without having conceptualized criteria. On such a view, individuals might rely on others in the community who do have such criteria.[62] This more communal position is similar to the view that Kripke attributes to Wittgenstein (see Chapter 4).

To such a view I object that objective reference, even to bodies as such, not only does not depend on the individual's being able to think relevant general principles that represent fundamental general conditions for objective reference. Objective reference does not even depend on relying on others in a community who have criteria that represent such conditions.

I know of no clear evidence that Strawson held the more social view about identifying reference to basic particulars through demonstratives and basic sortal predicates (for example, the predicate body). In Chapter 2 of *Individuals*, he discusses the need for 'availability' of criteria while reflecting on the capacities of a single 'being'.[63] There is no suggestion of a communal background. More importantly, Strawson indicates that the requirements on introducing particulars (fundamentally bodies) into *discourse*—the criteria— are *applied* in introducing particulars into a *proposition*. That is, the criteria are applied in identifying reference to particulars on particular occasions. The requirement of possession of a criterion is discussed as a necessary supplement to the capacity to pick out individuals through knowing some identifying fact about them.[64] These passages render the social interpretation of Strawson very doubtful.

In 'Particular and General' (1953–1954), Strawson writes: 'We bring a [specific] particular into our discourse only when we determine, select, *a point of application* for such criteria, only when we mention, refer to, something to which

---

[61] For reasons to doubt this epistemic internalism, see my 'Perceptual Entitlement'.

[62] In 1959 Strawson did hold a communal-dependence position regarding proper names. It should be noted that proper names whose referents depend on relations to others do not yield identifying reference.

[63] Strawson, *Individuals*, 63 [71].

[64] Ibid. 206 [200–201].

these criteria are to be applied . . . '.[65] The specific individuating knowledge that picks out specific particulars in particular contexts clearly must be for Strawson, as I argued before (see note 44), both propositional and *applied by* the thinking individual. The general criteria of identity, distinctness, and reidentification that back up and are 'applied' along with this individuating knowledge appear equally to be assumed by Strawson to be applied by individuals who engage in relevant identifying reference.

It is completely clear that Strawson regards the criteria as propositional and conceptual. As noted earlier, he claims that criteria of identity, distinctness, and reidentification are implicit in the meaning of sortal universal terms and 'incorporated' into sortal universal concepts.[66] There is no suggestion that individuals can use sortal concepts in picking out particular bodies while lacking the capacity to think the general criteria. So, when Strawson writes of identifying reference to material bodies as requiring an 'adoption' of criteria, a 'readiness to operate' with criteria, and an 'application' of criteria,[67] he appears to be writing of propositional criteria thinkable by each individual who engages in identifying reference to bodies.

Later, in 1976, Strawson modifies his terminological position slightly. He emphasizes a view that he already held in *Individuals*: that basic sortals must be used in any general principles of identification, so a criterion cannot be applicationally more basic than a basic sortal. He reserves the term 'criterion of identity' for principles that give conditions for applying non-basic sortals.[68] So basic sortals like body are not associated with what he calls 'criteria'. But the change appears to be mainly terminological. Strawson does not give up the idea that in applying a basic sortal (for example, body), one must be able to apply general principles of identity or reidentification. He rejects the priority of general principles over basic sortals in an individual's identifying reference. But he does not reject the necessary applicability of the relevant principles.[69] The applicability appears to be required of each individual thinker.

EVANS ON STRAWSON

The slide in Strawson between a theory of our conception of objective representation and a theory of objective representation gained momentum in the work of

---

[65] 'Particular and General', 36.

[66] As for propositionality, there are the repeated remarks that criteria are general and that they have logical properties. The remarks about incorporation of criteria into the basic sortal concepts (for example, for bodies) are in *Individuals*, 226–227 [220–221]. On the conceptual nature of criteria of identity, distinctness, and reidentification, see also *Individuals*, 214–215 [207–208].

[67] Ibid. 209, 218, 220, 206 [203, 211, 214, 200–201].

[68] Strawson, 'Entity and Identity', 39–44. The view about lack of priority of criterial principles over basic sortal predicates is expressed in Strawson, *Individuals*, 169–170 [167–168].

[69] See Strawson, 'Entity and Identity', 39–40.

his followers, initially and strikingly in Evans's work.[70] Unlike Strawson, Evans focuses almost entirely on explaining objective reference—not our conception of objectivity. Yet, in expounding Strawson, Evans sometimes transmutes Strawson's formulations of the latter project into formulations of the former. Evans correctly states Strawson's project this way:

If someone has a conception of a world, something whose existence and operations are independent of his experience of it, must he thereby conceive of a system of spatial relations in which both he and the phenomena he experiences has a place?[71]

He then remarks: 'This question can be put another way.' He restates the question as follows:

We can imagine a series of judgements 'Warm now', 'Buzzing now', made by a subject in response to changes in his sensory state, which have no objective significance at all. But we can imagine a similar series of judgements, prompted by the same changes in the subject's sensory state, which do have such a significance: 'now it's warm', 'Now there's a buzzing sound'—comments upon a changing world. What is involved in this change of significance?[72]

These questions are not at all the same. The first falls within the project of explaining our *conception* of objectivity. The second falls within the project of explaining objective reference itself. Evans's identification of the two projects turns Strawson's slide into a plunge.[73] Evans transforms Strawson's main project into a completely different one, without seeming to realize that he is doing so.

---

[70] I discuss Evans's work because it forms a paradigm of thought influenced by Strawson. It is both systematic and detailed, at least in some of its central formulations. Evans died before completing the book on which my discussion centers. He appears to have contemplated making changes. So criticism applied to the published book may, in some cases, not be applicable to the book that Evans would have written had he lived to complete it.

[71] Gareth Evans, 'Things without the Mind: A Commentary upon Chapter Two of Strawson's *Individuals*' (1980), in *Collected Papers* (Oxford: Clarendon Press, 1985), 249. I am taking this somewhat ambiguous formulation in a way that correctly paraphrases Strawson's stated project. If the clause 'something whose existence and operations are independent of his experience of it' is not supposed to gloss how the person's conception conceives the world, but merely what a world in fact is, then the quotation misstates Strawson's intent, and assimilates Strawson's project, right from the start, to one that investigates objective reference rather than our conception of objectivity. I think it more probable that Evans is correctly characterizing Strawson's project, and then, in the quotation about to be cited, engaging in the conflation that Strawson's work sometimes invites.

[72] Evans, 'Things without the Mind', 249. The passage continues: 'In particular, if "Now it's warm" is interpreted as a report on the world prompted by experience, must it be tantamount to: "now it's warm here"?' Evans is anticipating his view that objective reference requires a conception of oneself and others as occupying a comprehensive, allocentric spatial framework.

Given that Evans (like Strawson) reasons entirely about conditions for objective reference in terms of conditions on judgments (propositional capacities), he like Strawson rules out, almost from the beginning, the possibility that objective reference occurs in pre-propositional, pre-judgmental forms. As we shall see, Evans does provide an account of pre-propositional representation that rules out this possibility. I argue against the account in the next subsection.

[73] Evans conflates the two projects in other places. See 'Things without the Mind', 252–256—where he goes from a correct statement of Strawson's project on p. 252 to a misleading statement of what it would take to fulfill it on pp. 253 and 256. There are also passages where Evans states Strawson's project

Many philosophers followed Evans in concentrating on conditions for objective representation, and in maintaining with Evans and Strawson versions of second-family Individual Representationalism. They simply assumed that Evans, Strawson, or Kant had established that objective representation requires a supplementary array of conceptual abilities. In fact, no strong argument was ever given for such an assumption.

I have emphasized the slide between the two projects because it lends a spurious plausibility to claims that objective representation requires concepts that fund our *conception* of objectivity. Nearly all of Strawson's and Evans's remarks about objective reference take for granted the presence of self-consciousness in the individual. They also take for granted a conception of objectivity and an array of meta-concepts about the independence of physical entities from experience. Given such context, it is easier to think that objective representation *requires* mobilizing a conception of what one is doing. It suggests the need for a conception of oneself and one's place in a spatio-temporal framework. It suggests the need for an ability to distinguish oneself and one's states—the realm of the subjective—from physical entities—the realm of the objective.

Evans develops more fully than Strawson an account of the conceptual abilities that are alleged conditions on representing the physical world. Because of this focus, Evans's Individual Representationalism is more integral to his philosophy than Strawson's is to *his* philosophy. So Evans's views are more directly and fundamentally vulnerable to criticisms of Individual Representationalism.[74]

Evans holds that idioms that attribute singular reference in perceptual belief 'have their home in the activity of interpreting, or making sense of, the speech of others'.[75] While there is perhaps a narrow sense in which this claim is true, the claim illustrates Evans's concentration on perception's relation to thought, especially thought expressed by language. Evans's discussion of perception almost totally ignores the science of perception. No empirical theory of perception or

entirely correctly—for example, pp. 261, 249. A similar conflation or unargued slide occurs in John McDowell, *Mind and World* (Cambridge, MA: Harvard University Press, 1994), 54. McDowell is similar to Strawson, and dissimilar to Evans, in being primarily focused on the problem of explaining our *conception* of objectivity.

[74] In what follows, I highlight Evans's requirements on spatial representation. There are other aspects of his views that run in the same direction. For example, he believes that to attribute the property of materiality to bodies, an individual must be able to 'make sense' of such properties. This making sense is supposed to require having a propositional 'learned' theory of primitive mechanics—including such principles as conservation of matter and competition for occupancy of space. See 'Things without the Mind', 269–270. I believe that all of this is backwards. Perception itself represents materiality, by being causally associated with bodies and by being accompanied by anticipations of continuity and so on—where these anticipations are pre-propositional. The individual need not be able to theorize about the attributes represented in perception and perception-based thinking. See Chapter 10, the section PERCEPTION AND BODY.

[75] Gareth Evans, *The Varieties of Reference* (Oxford: Clarendon Press, 1982), 129–130. The assumption pervades the book. Evans was remarkably insulated from the science of perception. See the relation between *The Varieties of Reference*, chapters 2, 4, 5 (especially 5.5), on one hand, and chapter 9, on the other. See also his chapter 6, note 1.

perceptual belief gives language anything like the prominence that Evans gives it
in his discussion. To assume that perceptual belief is to be understood in terms of
linguistic understanding is to be out of step with the empirical study of perception
and perceptual belief. Empirical psychology attributes—on the basis of considerable evidence—perception and perceptual belief to non-linguistic animals and
children.

Evans's account of constraints on objective reference divides into two parts. In
the first, he maintains that perception has representational content with objective
reference only if it is associated with certain concepts that support demonstrative
propositional thought. In the second, he argues that one must have certain
conceptual abilities to have singular thoughts involving demonstrative reference
to particulars. I begin with the first part.

EVANS ON CONSTRAINTS ON OBJECTIVE REFERENCE IN PERCEPTION

Evans does not discuss perception in any depth.[76] He does take strong positions.
His account begins by postulating a notion of informational state. An informational state is not in itself perceptual. It makes no objective singular reference to
particulars in the physical environment on its own. It becomes perceptual when
combined with a propositional-conceptual framework that is supposed to be a
necessary condition on there being perceptual states.[77]

An informational state carries information about a particular object a—and is
of a. An informational state is *of a* if it is caused by a and 'has to be' evaluated for
accuracy, at the time the state was produced, by reference to whether a satisfies its
representational content.[78]

According to Evans, an informational state can be *of a* without having a
singular content that represents (or misrepresents) a.[79] In such cases, the particular entity a causes the informational state and the state has to be evaluated for
accuracy with respect to a; but a is not singularly represented.[80]

There is an incoherence in Evans's specification of informational content. He
takes the content of an informational state not to involve singular elements that

---

[76] Evans distinguishes, I think rightly, between perception and conception. But he thinks that
perception of particulars is impossible without conception and propositional abilities. I discuss this
view below. Evans's position that perception cannot represent physical particulars unless it is
associated with conceptual thought has been influential. See Christopher Peacocke, *A Study of
Concepts* (Cambridge, MA: MIT Press, 1992); McDowell, *Mind and World*; and Fred Dretske,
Naturalizing the Mind (Cambridge, MA: MIT Press, 1995). Peacocke has since changed his mind.

[77] Evans, *The Varieties of Reference*, chapters 5 and 6. See also 'Things without the Mind', 261 ff.

[78] Evans, *The Varieties of Reference*, 125, 128.

[79] Ibid. 125 note 10, 128–129.

[80] Ibid. 124–125, 128. Evans allows that two informational states can embody the same
information, even though they have different (representational or intentional) content—if they stem
from the same particulars and properties (pp. 128–129). He also holds that an informational state may
be of nothing (p. 128).

represent any particular entity. He holds that an informational state, and its content, can be *of* a particular without there being any element of the content that represents the particular. He formulates the content of an informational state as a conjunction of open sentences—such as 'Red(x) & Ball(x) & Yellow(y) & Square(y) & OnTo-pOf(x,y)'—or as an existential quantification of such a conjunction.[81]

Evans thinks that either of these forms of content can be *of* a particular, even though they have no singular element that represents the particular. This view is incompatible with his account of *ofness*. The contents that he cites are not *of* any particulars at all. The second clause in his explication of *ofness* is that to be of a particular, a content has to be evaluated for accuracy, at the time the state was produced, by reference to whether the particular satisfies its content. This condition cannot be met by any empirical informational content of the sort Evans cites.

Take particulars *a* and *b* that either the open-sentence form of content or the existential-quantification form is supposed to be *of*. It is simply not the case that at any time the content 'has to be' evaluated for accuracy by reference to whether *a* and *b* satisfy its representational content. The content is veridical if *any* pair of particulars satisfies the open sentence or existential quantification. *a* and *b* do not have to figure in evaluating its accuracy.[82]

Perhaps Evans intends the content of the informational state to be evaluated for accuracy by reference not only to whether an object or objects must be used in evaluating the content, but also whether the object or objects that *cause* the state

---

[81] Ibid.; p. 125 for the first formulation; pp. 127–128 for the second.

[82] The difficulty is not the result of a mere slip. It bears on fundamental, I think fundamentally mistaken, aspects of Evans's view. The problem emerges in Evans's peculiar remarks on photographs: 'A photograph should not be said to represent, e.g., that *a* and *b* are such that the former is *r* to the latter—at least, not in the way in which a painting may be said to represent, e.g., that Christ is on the cross. We see, here, the need for a distinction between, on the one hand, an *a*-representation (i.e. a species of particular-representation, in a specification of whose content mention of *a* would figure: something which represents, or misrepresents, *a*), and, on the other, something which, without being an *a*-representation, is a representation *of a*.' See *Varieties of Reference*, 125 n. Evans means not merely that the photograph does not contain a name of the entity it is *of* (a name like 'Christ'), but that it is not *about a* or *b* at all, and contains no indexical or demonstrative singular element at all. Being 'of *a*' is just deriving causally from *a*. See p. 128. Yet, Evans wants to retain enough representational content for perception (unaided by thought) and for photographs to give them a logical form and to claim that they must be evaluated by reference to relevant particulars. Here again, Evans's view is incoherent.

Evans's conception of photographs as not representing and not being about the particulars that they photograph seems to me to be directly incompatible with the representational function of photographs. They are pictures that represent the particular things photographed. They do not just represent conditions that are instantiated somewhere or other in the world. The accuracy of the photograph is judged with respect to the very particulars that it photographs. So the representational content of the photograph must have accuracy conditions that make actual singular reference to those very particulars. The existential quantificational or open-sentence forms that Evans offers do not fit either his own formulations or the representational function of the cases he discusses. Although photographs are representational only parasitically, because we made cameras to produce them, and although perceptions are not parasitic in this way, the two are analogous in that their representational function requires context-dependent singular elements in their representational contents.

must be used in evaluating the content.[83] But then the content of the informational state that he offers—most obviously, in the existential generalization case—
simply does not correspond to this way of evaluating content for accuracy. One
could supplement the content to read: $(Ex)(Ey)(Red(x) \& Ball(x) \& Yellow(y) \&$
$Square(y) \& OnTopOf(x,y) \& Causes(x, \text{this very state, now}) \& Causes(y, \text{this}$
$\text{very state, now}))$.

On this supplementation, there is a singular contextual reference ('this very
state') to the informational state itself. This line is implausible for some of the
reasons that Russell's sense-data analysis was implausible. Singular reference to
the informational state is less plausible than singular reference to the particulars
in the world.

Another way of accommodating the causal condition is to reject the existen-
tially quantified formulation, and let the free variables in the free-variable
formulation apply to particulars that cause the state. Then the representational
content *does* represent particulars, contrary to Evans's account.

The basic difficulty is similar to the difficulty for Strawson's account of
feature placing.[84] Evans tries to keep reference to particulars out of the representational content of informational states. As with Strawson and feature placing,
Evans allows representation of universals, but not of particulars. The sort of
representation that Evans tries to explain is sensory, if not sensory-perceptual.
Accuracy of the representational content depends on the relation of the content to
the particulars that cause it. Both perception and sensory–causal relations are
relations between particulars. They are relations between the particulars that
provide the information and cause the informational state, on one hand, and the
particular informational state (in a particular organism and particular context)
that is caused, on the other. If the informational state is to be taken to have
representational content with accuracy conditions at all, and if the representational content is supposed to correspond to psychological function and capacity,
there is no reasonable way to exclude elements that refer to particulars (as
opposed to types or universals) from the *basic* content of the state. For the
psychological function and competence associated with the state must be reflected in the basic representational content of the state. And the accuracy of the
representational content depends on the particulars that cause the state. So the
basic content must make reference to such particulars. Basic accuracy conditions
cannot reasonably be understood purely in terms of universals. Evans makes a
version of Strawson's mistake.

Evans's view of informational content is distorted by his conviction, following
Strawson, that singular reference depends on a background of intellectual

---

[83] Evans's statement of how the definition of *of-ness* relates to his truth conditions is either
ambiguous or not specific enough to provide a clear interpretation. Here I am trying an
interpretation suggested by Alex Radalescu.

[84] Although he does not credit Strawson, Evans accepts Strawson's view of the primitive, pre-
referential, pre-predicational status of feature-placing languages. See Gareth Evans, 'Identity and
Predication' (1975), in *Collected Papers*, 30–33.

abilities. Perceptual states represent particulars and are evaluable for veridicality by reference to those particulars and their properties. The representational contents of perceptual states—and indeed any state that is *of* a particular even in Evans's sense—must contain contextually applied singular elements.

Evans takes an information link between subject and object to be the 'core idea' of a perceptual state.[85] He thinks that the core must be supplemented with conceptual, propositional abilities to make perceptual representation possible.[86] More specifically, he thinks perception must be supplemented by conscious propositional thought if an individual is to make any reference at all to spatially located entities.[87]

---

[85] Evans, *The Varieties of Reference*, 144.

[86] Ibid. 145–151, especially 148 ff. Evans invokes what he calls the Generality Constraint as part of the supplement. For brief discussions of the Genarality Constraint, see p. 196 n. 112 and p. 206 n. 131. I believe that Evans not infrequently draws conclusions that are said to be consequences of the Generality Constraint that do not follow from it at all.

Evans imposes several other requirements on perceptual representation of a particular in space. These requirements are interpretations of 'knowing what it is'. They include requirements of knowing the particular to be of a given sort, having certain general spatio-temporal representational abilities, and being able to locate the particular. See p. 149. Evans seems to assume that spatio-temporal abilities must be perceptual, but cannot be *purely* perceptual. There is no argument for this latter assumption. It is incompatible with a massive amount of empirical work. In due course, I shall discuss these requirements.

[87] See ibid. 157–159. Evans presupposes that conscious experience is necessary for objective perceptual reference to particular objects in space. Peacocke, *A Study of Concepts*, 90 ff., accepts this claim of Evans's. In various other places in the book, he follows Evans in not allowing singular reference except through the aid of propositional thought. (He has since changed his mind.) In that book, Peacocke doubts that there could be a creature with perceptions that have non-conceptual, representational content, but that lacked concepts, hence lacked propositional thought. He alludes to 'strong arguments' that indicate that reidentification of places over time requires thought, and that a spatial map requires first-person thought. No argument in the book is given for why such reidentification could not be effected by processing of perceptual representations—for example, in perceptual memory, in lower animals that lack conceptual thought (propositional attitudes). In fact, there is (and was then) massive empirical reason to think that such cases occur. See Chapters 9–10. In a cognate passage in 'Scenarios, Concepts, and Perception', in T. Crane (ed.), *The Contents of Experience* (Cambridge: Cambridge University Press, 1992), reprinted in *Essays on Nonconceptual Content*, ed. Y. H. Gunther (Cambridge, MA: MIT Press, 2003), 124, Peacocke provides the argument he seemed to have in mind. There Peacocke writes: 'I doubt that we could ever justify the attribution of genuinely spatial content to an organism's states, of a kind going beyond [mere sensitivity to higher-order properties of stimulation patterns] unless the subject were on occasion to employ states with these contents in identifying places over time. . . . Identification of places over time requires that states with scenario content contribute to the construction of a cognitive map of the world around the subject. It is, in turn, highly questionable whether we can make sense of the subject engaging in such construction unless he employs at least a rudimentary form of first-person thought, that is, unless he possesses at least some primitive form of first-person concept. . . . On the approach I am advocating, then nonconceptual content is not a level whose nature is completely explicable without reference to conceptual content at all.' The appeal to a 'cognitive map' in the second sentence, though not explained, suggests the demand of an allocentric scheme—a demand with no real argumentative support. The main difficulty with the passage lies in the next to last sentence. The claim in this sentence simply begs the question. So there is no real argument in this passage either. It is possible that Peacocke was relying in the appeal to 'identification' on views about conditions for identification that derived from Strawson and Evans, and that I criticize in the text. Egocentric indexes occur in perception; but first-person concepts, which are constitutively associated with propositional thought, do not. Peacocke appears to be following Evans and Strawson in requiring thought to provide genuine spatial content, as well as singular reference.

Evans provides no developed argument for the requirement. He simply states that conscious perceptual experience of objects in space requires that the subject have conceptual demonstrative thought that depends systematically on the informational properties of perceptual states about those objects. Evans provides only off-hand considerations to support this claim.

I think that Evans relies on two lines of unelaborated argument for the view that conscious propositional thought must back perception if an individual is to make perceptual reference to particular spatially located entities. One centers on consciousness. The other centers on a distinction between what an individual does and what the individual's brain does.

The first argument goes as follows. Thought (which Evans firmly associates with *propositional* attitudes) is necessary for consciousness. Consciousness is necessary for objective perceptual representation. So propositional thought is necessary for objective perceptual representation.[88]

The conclusion of the argument is unacceptable. There is wide and deep empirical support for the view that certain animals—honey bees and jumping spiders, for example—that show no evidence of having propositional attitudes nevertheless engage in objective perceptual representation. Their perceptions attribute specific environmental attributes to environmental particulars. Their perceptual capacities exhibit numerous perceptual constancies. So the conclusion is mistaken.[89]

What of the argument's premises? The first premise is unargued, and extremely implausible. Feelings like pain are types of consciousness. Some animals that lack thought very probably feel pain.[90] The second premise is also unsupported and implausible.[91] It is doubtful that any sort of consciousness is necessary for perceptual representation of entities in the environment. We know that some bees and spiders have perceptual representation of environmental entities. We do not know that they are conscious. Similarly, in certain human pathologies, patients who appear to lack conscious perception of certain particulars are able to pick them out visually. Such patients group the particulars as having specific attributes, and exhibit perceptual constancies with respect to them.[92]

---

[88] Evans, *The Varieties of Reference*, 157–158. This argument is not stated, but enough is said to suggest that Evans relies on it.

[89] I discuss these points in greater detail in Chapters 8–10.

[90] There is independent empirical evidence for the separability and sometimes separation of consciousness from propositional thought, even in human beings. See Ned Block, 'Consciousness, Accessibility, and the Mesh between Psychology and Neuroscience', *Behavioral and Brain Sciences* 30 (2007), 481–499. See my comment, 'Psychology Supports Independence of Phenomenal Consciousness', ibid. 500–501.

[91] For attempted support of the second premise, see John Campbell, *Reference and Consciousness* (Oxford: Clarendon Press, 2002). The premise is widely rejected in psychology. See pp. 374–376 below.

[92] See M. A. Goodale and A. D. Milner, *The Visual Brain in Action* (Oxford: Oxford University Press, 1995); W. Prinz and B. Hommel (eds.), *Common Mechanisms in Perception and Action* (Oxford: Oxford University Press, 2002). I think that it is not known whether blindsight is conscious. It could be phenomenally conscious, but the conscious states could be inaccessible to perceptual thought. (See Block, 'Consciousness, Accessibility, and the Mesh between Psychology and

Evans's second argument for the claim that perception of objective matters requires propositional thought goes as follows. Informational states that are perception-like but that do not serve thought are correctly attributable to the brain, but not correctly attributable to the individual perceiver. Genuine perceptual representation is constitutively attributable to an individual perceiver. If and only if perception-like informational states are connected to propositional thought in an individual psychology can those states be correctly attributed to an individual perceiver. So genuine perceptual representation must be connected to propositional thought in an individual psychology.[93]

The idea behind the second premise is that informational states that are attributable *merely* to the brain or to some subsystem of the individual are not perception in the ordinary sense. The distinction between processing in modular subsystems and representation by an individual is an important one. With minor qualifications, I accept the second premise. However, the first and third steps of the argument are not given any support. Empirical considerations count against them.

The science of visual perception applies not only to humans but to lower mammals, birds, fish, some insects. With respect to many of these animals, there is no evident explanatory gain in attributing propositional thought to them. No behavior is illuminatingly explained in terms of propositional inference. Are the visual perceptions of these animals therefore attributable only to their brains (or to some psychological subsystem) and not to the whole animal?

I see no reason to accept such a position. Visual perceptions guide activities of eating, navigating, mating, and so on. These are clearly activities of the whole animal. It is common, natural, and, I think, correct to attribute perceptions to the whole animal, not just its brain or visual system, in explaining such activities. An insect, bird, or rat perceives a moving solid or a color, and moves toward it. Standard perceptual and ethological accounts attribute perceptions to whole animals in these cases. For many of these animals, there is massive empirical

Neuroscience'.) Or the states could be flat-out unconscious. What is known is that blindsight exhibits spatial perceptual constancies with respect to specific particulars and perceptual attributions. These perceptual representations seem not to be available to conscious propositional thought. So the separation of perception from conscious thought in blindsight has an experimental basis.

[93] Evans does not explicitly give the argument set out in the text. His discussion, which is meant to support the argument's conclusion, conspicuously lacks the needed 'only if'. Evans's remarks do, however, suggest the argument. See *Varieties of Reference*, 158, 227. These remarks appear to be developed by McDowell. McDowell places an armchair constraint on the science of perceptual psychology. Evans suggests that the sort of representational states that can be attributed to a whole person requires the presence of thought. One might infer from this suggestion that the perceptual states postulated in perceptual psychology are simply unconscious 'informational' states (in Evans's sense) that can be attributed only to the brain or to subpersonal aspects of the perceptual system. McDowell follows this train of reasoning. In 'The Content of Perceptual Experience', *Philosophical Quarterly* 44 (1994), 190–205, he develops this view into an interpretation of the nature of the empirical psychology of vision. The interpretation holds that mainstream psychology of visual perception is not about human perception, ordinarily so-called—perception by human or other individuals. McDowell's interpretation rests on several striking, very elementary misunderstandings of the science. I discuss these matters in 'Disjunctivism and Perceptual Psychology'. For more on the science, see Chapters 3 and 8–9.

support for taking them to have perceptual states, and no support at all for taking them to have propositional thought. Such animals perceive physical particulars as having some of the specific physical attributes—such as spatial location and spatial relations—that the particulars in fact have.[94] So the first and third premises appear to be mistaken.

I believe that Evans seriously misdraws the line between what is attributable to the whole perceiver and what is attributable *merely* to its brain. He gives no rationale for his position. Any armchair argument that holds that animals that lack propositional attitudes cannot perceive physical particulars as having specific attributes is empirically unacceptable.

I do believe that there are certain notions of proprietary ownership of psychological states that hinge on consciousness. If bees are not conscious, they lack a certain *type* of ownership of their visual states. There remains, however, a functional distinction between, on the one hand, those end products of perceptual systems, perceptions, that are attributable to the whole animal, as actions like eating would also be, and, on the other hand, processes like registration of light arrays and digestion that are functionally attributable only to the animal's subsystems.

Moreover, it appears very likely that many animals with *conscious* perception lack propositional thought. Conscious perceptions are certainly attributable to such animals, not just to their brains or other subsystems.

The primary points here are two. First, there is no reason to think that the notion of whole-animal perception is to be explained in terms of the notion of propositional thought. Second, there is no reason to think that the notion of consciousness is to be explained in terms of the notion of propositional thought. Sensory phenomenal consciousness appears not to depend on rational powers, even in humans.[95] There is no ground, empirical or apriori, to believe that animals that lack propositional thought cannot perceive physical particulars as having specific physical attributes.

Evans's offhand remarks about whole-animal perception make no acceptable case for his sweeping view on the relation between whole animal perception and thought. They make no acceptable case for the first part of Evans's account of objective representation. The first part is the claim that an animal's perception has representational content with objective reference (specifically to particulars in

---

[94] For more on individual perceivers and subsystems, see Chapter 9, the section PERCEPTION AS THE INDIVIDUAL'S. See also Chapter 3, notes 43 and 57; Chapter 8, note 97; and Preface, note 1.

[95] For empirical evidence that strongly suggests that phenomenal consciousness is to be distinguished in humans from consciousness associated with access to rational powers, see Ned Block, 'Two Neural Correlates of Consciousness', *Trends in Cognitive Sciences* 9 (2005), 46–52. Block discusses further evidence in 'Consciousness, Accessibility, and the Mesh between Psychology and Neuroscience'. Block first draws the distinction between phenomenal consciousness and access consciousness in 'On a Confusion about a Function of Consciousness', *Behavioral and Brain Sciences* 18 (1995), 227–247. An earlier isolation of phenomenal consciousness occurs in Thomas Nagel, 'What Is It Like to Be a Bat?', *The Philosophical Review* 83 (1974), 435–450. See also my 'Reflections on Two Kinds of Consciousness', in *Foundations of Mind*.

space as having specific physical properties and as being in spatial relations) only if it supports propositional thought. I believe that this claim has not been given any serious support.

EVANS ON DEMONSTRATIVE, PERCEPTUAL THOUGHT

The second, more developed part of Evans's account of conditions on objective reference maintains that to have *thoughts* involving demonstrative reference to physical particulars, an individual must have certain specific conceptual abilities and specific types of knowledge. Here the topic is not perception but perceptual belief or perceptually based thought. Evans develops a view that requires relatively high-level abilities as conditions on demonstrative reference in perceptual belief.

Like the first part of Evans's account, the second is guided by the view that linguistic understanding is a model for understanding perceptual belief.[96] As indicated earlier, I think that the focus on linguistic expression of perceptual belief distorts the account of perceptual belief.

I shall lay out, in a series of steps, Evans's view of conditions on demonstrative, perceptual thought. Then I evaluate these steps and the conclusions that they lead to.

Evans holds that the representational contents of thoughts must be understood in terms of conditions on truth that those contents place on their subject matter.[97] These conditions have a structure that marks inferential capacities of the thinker. I accept this conception of representational content in propositional thought.

The first distinctive step in Evans's account consists in an interpretation of what it is to have a thought with representational content. He begins with a move that closely parallels the move that I criticized in Strawson in the section STRAWSON ON PARTICULAR-IDENTIFICATION IN THOUGHT. The move begins, as does Strawson's, with the claim that to make a judgment about an object, 'one must *know which* object is in question'.[98] Evans calls this condition 'Russell's Principle'. As Strawson does, Evans then interprets this knowing-which condition, as applied to singular thought about particulars, in a strong way.[99]

Evans begins the move of giving the strong interpretation before he thinks he has begun it. The acceptable idea that propositional representational contents are conditions on truth is transmuted into the more dubious formulation (which Evans counts 'truistic') that thinking a thought of the form a is G entails 'knowing

---

[96] This commitment drives Evans to require a considerable degree of *understanding* of the concepts and ideas involved in carrying out reference in perceptual belief. See *The Varieties of Reference*, 92, 129–132. Understanding, of any sort that goes beyond minimal competence with relevant concepts, develops after most perceptual belief has already developed.

[97] Ibid., for example, 103.

[98] Ibid. 64.

[99] Evans is aware that he gives Russell's Principle a contentious interpretation. See ibid. 73–76.

what it is to be the case that' a is G.[100] More generally, in thinking a representational content with certain truth conditions, one must 'know what it is' for these
truth conditions to hold.

I think that these formulations are not truistic at all. They constitute a hyper-
intellectualized description of the competence involved in thinking a thought.
Having the minimal propositional competence necessary to think <u>a is G</u> does not
obviously require knowing what it is to be the case that a is G, unless these latter
words are given a particularly de-natured construal. Having concepts and being
able competently to think with them is not the same as *knowing* or *understanding*
conditions for their application, unless these latter expressions just *reduce* to
being able competently to apply the thoughts or concepts. As we shall see, Evans
does *not* reduce the apparently intellectualized construal of his phrase 'knowing
what it is to be the case that' to any less controversial construal.

Evans maintains a necessary condition on thinking a thought, or holding a
belief, of the form <u>a is G</u> (where '<u>a</u>' is any singular term, context-dependent or
not). The condition is that the subject have discriminatory 'knowledge': 'the
subject must have a capacity to discriminate the object of his judgment from all
other things.' To think about a physical object, the individual must 'know what it
is' to be that particular object, or know which object the thought is about.[101]

The intended meaning of this requirement is not immediately evident. Evans
explicitly notes that he does not just follow colloquial usage in developing the
relevant conception of <u>knowing-which</u>.[102] He seeks to refine that core notion
through theory. Evans's understanding of the requirement of discriminatory
knowledge emerges in detailed "theoretical" accounts of particular cases. I
shall discuss some of his restrictions as the view is developed.

Evans's account of singular reference in thought parallels Strawson's account
of identification of particulars, or what Strawson called 'introducing a particular
into a proposition'. Although Evans credits Russell with Russell's Principle, he is
clearly developing Strawson's notion of knowing-which as a condition on iden-
tificatory singular reference in thought to particulars. Evans thinks that the notion
<u>knowing-which</u>, or discriminatory knowledge of a particular from 'all other
things', can be initially grounded by considering *three basic types of sufficient
conditions* for having the relevant discriminatory knowledge: one can perceive an
object at the present time; one can recognize it if presented with it; and one can
know a distinguishing fact about it.[103]

---

[100] Evans, *Varieties of Reference*, 105–106.

[101] Ibid. 89.

[102] Ibid.

[103] Ibid. The reader should not simply accept that perception of an object is sufficient for
discriminatory knowledge, as Evans claims. The knowledge is clearly meant to be propositional.
But individuals can perceive particulars without having propositional capacities. Even individuals
who perceive and form beliefs directly from the perceptions do not always have propositional
knowledge. Perception is sufficient for reference, but not for knowledge. Hence it is not sufficient
for knowing-which in anything like Strawson's or Evans's senses.

To fulfill the requirement of knowing which object one is referring to, it is not enough, for Evans, that an individual have a perceptual memory of the object. An individual cannot fulfill the requirement merely by discriminating the object through remembering it through a past perception of it, and then forming a perceptual belief regarding it based on conceptualization of the perceptual memory. Any such belief must be backed by *further* discriminating abilities.[104]

This striking position is announced right at the beginning of Evans's discussion of the discriminatory knowledge that is supposed to be required for singular reference to particulars in thought. After mentioning the three cited cases, each of which is supposed to be sufficient for discriminatory knowledge, Evans presents the following example as a paradigm case of lacking the relevant discriminatory knowledge.

Suppose that an individual perceives a steel ball one day and then perceives another, similar-looking steel ball the next day. Suppose that some physiological defect blocks memory of the first perception. Suppose that the individual has a memory that derives causally from the perception of the ball on the second day. And suppose that the individual has no further way of discriminating one ball from the other. The individual does not realize that he saw a similar-looking ball before the second one. Then, according to Evans, the individual lacks the necessary discriminating knowledge to think about the second ball, the one that his memory is in fact connected to. According to Evans, <u>That ball that I once perceived is F</u>, or more simply <u>That ball is F</u> (where the demonstrative is guided by memory), is not a possible thought for the individual.

This position is not plausible. The individual's memory derives from one ball and not the other. It is not clear why this memory does not suffice to enable the individual to think about that ball. Evans claims that 'theoretical considerations' back his position. The only relevant consideration that Evans ever advances is his highly restrictive construal of Russell's Principle.[105]

As noted, Evans cites three types of knowledge that he regards as sufficient for making singular reference to particulars in thought. It appears that he regards it as necessary for singular reference to objects in the environment that it be backed by one of these three types.[106] I will discuss Evans's views on singular reference in thought backed by the first of these three types of knowledge—knowledge of a particular object based on present perception of it. Evans's restrictions on singular reference in perceptual thought are restrictive in ways that echo the strange restrictiveness of his view about memory of the steel balls. Evans's interpretation of Russell's Principle includes a particularly determined elaboration of Individual Representationalism.

---

[104] On the strictures on memory, see ibid. 89–91.

[105] For what I think is a largely correct criticism of Evans's account of related matters, see Marleen Rozemond, 'Evans on *De Re* Thought', *Philosophia* (1994), 275–298.

[106] This view is suggested by the way Evans introduces the cases and calls them a trichotomy. See *The Varieties of Reference*, 89 note 2. It is also suggested by the fact that he discusses no other types of singular reference to empirical environmental objects.

EVANS ON CONDITIONS FOR REPRESENTING KINDS
AND PARTICULAR OBJECTS

Like Strawson, Evans places conditions both on representing kinds or universals
in thought through attributives and on representing particulars. General attributives must guide singular demonstrative reference. So some of the conditions on
thinking the attributives are also conditions on thinking the singular demonstrative elements.

I begin with Evans's account of representation of kinds. Evans introduces the
notion of a *fundamental ground of difference*. For every kind of object, there is a
general answer to the question 'what differentiates that kind of object from
others?' in a way that is basic to objects of the relevant kind. For material objects,
Evans holds that this question is partly answered, relative to a time, by citing the
position occupied by the object and the kind of object it is. For example, what
differentiates a stone from other objects, at a given time, is its being a stone and
being in a particular place.

These points seem broadly correct. They are metaphysical points about kinds
themselves, not points about conditions on representing kinds. Evans uses these
points in his account of representing kinds. He explains the notion of a *fundamental
Idea* in terms of a fundamental ground of difference. One has a fundamental Idea of
an object if, and presumably only if, one can think of it as the possessor of the
fundamental ground of difference that it in fact possesses.[107] Having a fundamental
Idea requires having a capacity to *generalize* about the kind. For example, having the
fundamental Idea of stones is being able to think of stones as differentiated from
other objects at a given time by being a stone and being in a particular place.

Evans claims that the fundamental Idea of objects that are G must enter into
knowing what it is to be a G. Knowing what it is to be a G is necessary for
thinking thoughts of the form ...G... So to think a thought with the concept
G one must have a *general conception which constitutes general knowledge of
the conditions* that differentiate Gs from all other kinds of objects. This idea
seems to develop Strawson's notion of a criterion of distinctness.

Evans elaborates this claim as follows:

For there is no thought about objects of a certain kind which does not presuppose the idea
of *one* object of that kind, and the idea of one object of that kind *must employ a general
conception* of the ways in which objects of that kind are differentiated from one another
and *from all other things*. A conception of a state of affairs involving a G is such in virtue
of its being a conception of a state of affairs involving an object conceived to be
distinguished from other objects by some fundamental ground of difference appropriate
to Gs, and hence as distinguishable, or differentiable, *by citing a fact of this kind*.[108]

---

[107] Evans, *Varieties of Reference*, 106–107. Evans uses 'idea' to apply to representational contents
that can be either singular or predicative, but that must distinguish particular objects. He uses
'concept' to apply to representations of properties. See ibid. 104.

[108] Ibid. 108. My italics, except on 'one'.

A parallel explication applies to what is involved in knowing what it is for an object to be object *a* (referred to by demonstrative Idea a̱). If a̱ is a fundamental Idea, then having that Idea and knowing how to apply it to object *a* suffices. If the subject's idea a̱ is not a fundamental Idea, the subject must know what it is for a proposition of the form a̱ = ḇ to be true, where ḇ represents an arbitrary object and is a fundamental Idea. (Hence ḇ indicates the fundamental ground of difference for objects of the kind that a̱ indicates.) In other words, the individual must know what it is to identify object *a* by means of some fundamental Idea (either the idea a̱ itself, or some other idea ḇ that enters into a known identity proposition with a̱), where the fundamental Idea represents object *a*. Again, it is worth noting that this knowledge is *general* knowledge.

Evans claims that this requirement on knowing what it is for an object to be object *a* is evident. He continues: 'So we can take the subject's Idea-of-the-object, a̱, to consist in his knowledge of what it is for an arbitrary proposition of the form a̱ = ḇ to be true.'[109] Evans requires knowledge of what it is for an *arbitrary* thought of a given form, bearing specifically on a fundamental ground of difference, to be true. This requirement pervades his account, and seems to motivate it.[110]

Let us consider how these requirements are instantiated for general kind concepts that apply to bodies and for singular perceptual demonstratives that apply to bodies. According to the requirements, to think of something as a body, one must know what it is to be a body. To know what it is to be a body is to know that bodies are differentiated from other objects by being a body and occupying a given space at a given time. To think about a particular body—for example, by forming the perceptual belief that moving round shape is green, an individual must know what it is for that moving round shape to be identical with a particular body. And that knowledge again requires the generalized propositional knowledge that bodies are differentiated from other objects by being a body and occupying a given space at a given time. The individual must classify relevant objects in a way that involves knowing the fundamental ground of difference.[111]

---

[109] Ibid. 110.

[110] Ibid. 108–112. Evans's editor, John McDowell, states that Evans was worried about the entire postulation of fundamental Ideas. McDowell suggests replacing the notion with the notion of knowing, for idea a̱ and concept G̱, what is to be an arbitrary object *of an objective order* to be object *a*, or to be a G̱. See *The Varieties of Reference*, 264–265. McDowell takes this knowledge to involve a *conception* of objectivity. This replacement invokes abilities that are even more sophisticated than those Evans required. So I see the suggestion as a step backward. Both requirements postulate concepts that are not available to young children or animals. Young children and many animals nevertheless represent the physical world in perception and, in some cases, in perceptual belief.

[111] Evans later weakens his requirement, to claim not that the individual must know what it is for the demonstrated object to fall under its fundamental sortal, but only that the individual know how to discover what sortal the object falls under. The weakening is motivated by the possibility of seeing some object half-buried in the sand and discovering what it is only on pulling it out. See ibid. 178. This weaker requirement still demands of the individual the conceptual resources to know the generalization involved in fundamental grounds of difference. I think that there is no reason to believe that individuals with perceptual beliefs must be capable of such general knowledge.

Are these requirements sound? They are hardly self-evident. They are not supported by any further account about why they must obtain.[112] The requirements are instances of the view that to use a concept, one must know a general criterion that explicates what entities it applies to. That is, one must know the fundamental general conditions under which objects (or, as I prefer, particulars) of the relevant kind are the same or different. Evans applies this requirement to demonstrative, perceptually guided, singular representations. He allows that singular reference can occur in which no fundamental idea occurs in the thought. But such thought is supposed to be possible only because one knows identities that connect these singular references to would-be singular references guided by fundamental ideas. This view is not self-evident. For the case of singular representations, it was under attack in philosophy even at the time Evans wrote.[113]

It seems that an individual can apply a concept in perceptual-demonstrative belief, while being unable to conceive of the fundamental general conditions for being an instance of the kind that the concept applies to. Similarly, an individual can have a perceptual belief about a particular without having the generalizing capacities necessary to know the ground of difference associated with the particular. Evans's view constitutes hyper-intellectualization at several turns. I want to outline some dimensions along which this requirement is doubtful.

As I have noted, Evans's talk of 'knowing what it is' for a type of proposition to be true suggests a relatively high level of understanding. Understanding, beyond minimum competence in conceptual *use*, is not present in the perceptual beliefs of higher animals and very young children. Animals, children, and many human adults seem to lack the general propositional knowledge that Evans requires. Yet there is ample empirical ground to think that they have perceptual beliefs that attribute physical kinds (for example, *rigid body*). Evans requires that they have 'a general conception of the ways in which objects of that kind are

---

[112] At one point (*Varieties of Reference*, 149) Evans claims to have argued that if our thoughts conform to his Generality Constraint, they 'would need' to fall under these requirements. But he never provides such an argument. The Generality Constraint is the principle that, with provisos regarding the appropriateness of predicates to their subject matters, if a subject can be credited with the thought that a is G, then he must have the conceptual resources for thinking the thought that a is J for every property-conception J that he has. Similarly, the subject must be able to think that $\overline{b \text{ is } G}$ for every individual (particular)-conception (or idea) b that the thinker has (pp. 100–105). I doubt, on empirical grounds, that the Generality Constraint is in general true. It seems to me probable that some thought is sufficiently compartmentalized in some individuals that the individual cannot think all thoughts that result from otherwise grammatically permissible permutations of all thought-components that the individual has. But let us grant the Generality Constraint for the sake of argument. In fact, Evans never argues from the Generality Constraint for the requirements discussed in the text. He argues only that the requirements 'enable us to see how our thinking can conform to the Generality Constraint' (p. 111). In various other places, Evans misemploys the Generality Constraint—maintaining that theses follow from it that do not follow. For example, in ibid. 104–105, he cites Donnellan's work as a prime example of running afoul of the Generality Constraint. But nothing in Donnellan's work is shown to be incompatible with it. Sometimes Evans seems to conflate the Generality Constraint with Russell's Principle.

[113] I have in mind the accounts of singular reference by Kripke and Donnellan. See Chapter 5.

differentiated from one another and from all other things'. This requirement leans on and develops Strawson's requirement of criteria.

One should reject such a requirement. Much ordinary cognition, particularly perceptual cognition, derives from instinctive extensions from paradigms or salient exemplars, rather than from general *conceptions* of differentiating principles that govern arbitrary instances of a kind. These extensions are subindividual and probably subconceptual. The principles governing such extensions need not be *conceived by the individuals* in whose psychologies the extensions are carried out. The extensions are the result of many interactions between psychology and the environmental patterns in evolutionary history. That is why the extensions match attributes in the environment. Concept formation is often the product of such subindividual, subconceptual tendencies. Concepts mark abilities. The abilities can be explained by principles that apply to subconceptual processes and causal relations to the environment. The principles need not be known, represented, or even thinkable by the individual (even "implicitly").[114]

Similarly, in the application of singular representations, the individual can pick out particulars in perception and perceptual belief without being able to produce representations that indicate how the particulars are distinct from all others. No propositional generalization that distinguishes an entity or type of entity from other objects or types is needed. The individual picks out particulars by relying on causal relations with them, and by applying general attributives that guide the contextual applications. The general attributives are often products of the sort of molding discussed in the previous paragraph.

These sources of doubt can be made more specific. Evans requires for objective representation an understanding of what it is for a proposition to be made true by the fundamental kinds that are attributed. This requirement rules out an alternative without argument. According to the alternative, the individual need not know general fundamental, criterial application conditions. The individual need only have recognitional know-how. The recognitional know-how enables the individual to respond perceptually and conceptually to relevant environmental kinds (for example, *rigid body*). The response is unique to the kinds, among the kinds in the environment that figure in explanations of the individual's needs and activities (principally, biological needs and activities). The individual's representational states and capacities are constitutively determined by this combination of (*a*) causal and practical relations to environmental attributes with

---

[114] I use scare quotes here because 'implicitly' is a term used to express a number of different ideas. I intend the term here to mean an unconscious state that is nevertheless the individual's (not a subindividual psychological state). Some may think that *subindividual* psychological states have the content of principles that govern them. I believe that such claims are almost always mistaken. Although I discuss such claims and notions of implicit representation in Chapters 9 and 10, I do not, *in this discussion of Evans*, oppose the idea that subindividual states have the contents of principles. Here I oppose *individual* representationalist views. Such views place requirements on representation by individuals. In Chapter 9, the section PERCEPTION AS OBJECTIFICATION, I argue that not even perceptual systems, much less individuals, "implicitly" represent principles governing the formation of objective (accurate) perceptual states.

(*b*) the way the individual discriminates those kinds. The individual's perceptual and conceptual responses are possible despite lack of mastery or representation of general, criterial individuating conditions. These points are applications of anti-individualism regarding perception.

The recognitional know-how consists in psychological competencies governed by general principles, which concern how contentful states operate under relevant conditions. These general principles are psychologically real in the weak sense that they explain why transformations in the psychology occur as they do. But the principles are not the representational content of any psychological state. I think that there is no clear sense in which they are known, even tacitly or implicitly—beyond the fact that the contentful states are present in the psychology and principles governing their operation are genuinely explanatory. I know of no reason to think that the, in general, individuals have states with the representational content of the principles.

The ability to *conceive* of objects as being of certain kinds, and the ability to pick out particulars in *thought*, may make heavy use of perceptual attributives and perception of particulars. The attributives express capacities for perceptual grouping. The principles of perceptual grouping and perceptual reference need not be conceptually available to the individual thinker. It is enough for the conceptual abilities to use the perceptual abilities, while fitting them into a framework of propositional inference.

Perceptual grouping discriminates a kind from other kinds in an environmental context. Discrimination does not depend on being able to think a criterion, or a fundamental idea, associated with representation of the kind.

There is empirical reason to believe that the possibilities just described correspond to the way perception and perceptual belief regarding the environment are actually determined. Perceptual belief that involves concepts of bodies does require some competence in localizing objects in space, tracking them in time, and applying general kind-attributives to them. On this point, Evans, like Strawson, is entirely right. Even the ability to *perceive* bodies as such requires some competence in locating and tracking them.

Two issues are in question. One is whether all or even some of these competencies that touch on these fundamental elements in the individuation of bodies need be conceptualized by the individual, as Evans maintains. The other is whether conceptual abilities that are needed must take the forms that Evans requires them to take.

These issues can be made more specific by reflecting on the requirement of an ability to track a particular over time. A certain sort of tracking is crucial in an individual's ability to perceive and have perceptual beliefs as of bodies. A sound basis for this requirement is that some such capacity is necessary for an individual to be representing bodies instead of events. Both bodies and events are in the individual's environment. Both figure in macro-explanations of individuals' basic biological needs and activities. Individuals perceive both. So some difference in ability is necessary if one is to be able to represent one instead of the other. Bodies are perceptually distinguishable partly and fundamentally through their continuity of boundary integrity over time. An ability to track by way of such continuity is a basic differentiating ability. Tracking the movement of bodies is one common realization of such an ability. Tracking a single unmoving object over some lapse of time is another.

These tracking abilities need not be coded conceptually. They need not be represented. There need be no state with representational content of the principles governing the tracking. The abilities need not reside in a conceptualized criterion for reidentification or in a generalized fundamental idea of the sort that Evans postulates. There *are* principles governing the cognitive system and perceptual systems. The perceptual system can be explained as operating according to these principles. Conceptualizations of perceptions could inherit tracking capacities that operate according to such principles. No state of either the individual or the individual's subsystems need have such principles as its representational contents (even unconsciously). I shall return to these matters in Part III.

EVANS ON SPATIAL REPRESENTATION IN THOUGHT

Since spatial representation lies at the heart of fundamental ideas for nearly all empirical kinds, particularly bodies, I want to dwell on Evans's conception of constitutive conditions for spatial representation.

Evans holds, plausibly, that to refer to physical objects in perceptually based demonstrative thought, an individual must be able to locate objects in a space—to perceive and conceptualize spatial relations among objects—and to track such objects over at least short periods of time.[115]

The spatial ability must take a specific form. Representation of space in perception, in perceptual thought, and in perception-guided action must be in an *egocentric framework* of reference. That is, spatial relations must be represented in a framework in which there is an origin or anchor point at the position of the individual perceiver, or some part of the individual. And the origin must be of direct relevance to the individual's needs, motivation, or perspective.[116]

I want now to discuss Evans's application of Russell's Principle to spatial representation. I will discuss Evans's restrictions on referential discrimination in thought that represents spatial relations and spatially located particulars. Evans's requirements can be divided into those that apply to general abilities and those

---

[115] Evans, *The Varieties of Reference*, 174–175; see pp. 161–163.

[116] The statements of the requirement and the explication of the notion of egocentric framework, both of which I accept, are mine. I believe that Evans would have accepted the explication. The requirement is *almost* explicit. Evans is not explicit on the modal element in the requirement, but that element is implied. See ibid. 153–156, 161 ff. Evans does not discuss temporal frameworks. I believe that a full elaboration of his position from this point onward would make parallel points for them.

that apply to the exercise of general abilities within singular reference on a particular occasion.

I begin with Evans's requirements on reference to particulars on particular occasions. Evans maintains that to think about a particular perceived object, the individual must be able to locate the object in an egocentric spatial framework (locate it in relation to himself), or to locate it in some practical way.[117] As discussed earlier, Evans thinks that the individual must individuate the object by being able to apply a fundamental idea to it. Evans takes this requirement to elaborate the general requirement that one must know which object one is thinking about in a way that distinguishes it from all other objects. Thus Evans holds that perceiving an object does not suffice in itself to pick out physical entities for thought. On each occasion, perception must be supplemented by a fundamental idea and by spatial localization of the object in practice or through thought.[118]

I have already criticized the requirement of having a fundamental idea. I believe that the localization requirement is even more obviously unacceptable in its restrictiveness. There are many cases in which an individual can see an object and yet be unable to locate it with respect to his own position. Clearly, individuals can think about objects thus perceived. One can see and think about a star or comet through light that is refracted by the atmosphere. One might have seriously mislocated the object with respect to one's own position and have no practical way of locating it correctly.[119] Similarly, one can see an object by means of a mirror (without knowing about the mirror) or through refracting prisms. One might mislocate it and not be in a practical position to correct one's error. One can still think about the object. Evans's requirement is so obviously mistaken that I will not pause over it. I cite it as a striking example of his tendency to place overly restrictive conditions on the ability to pick out an object in perception or thought.

I turn now to requirements on representation of objects in perception and perceptual belief that center on more general abilities. Some of these requirements are entirely plausible. As noted, Evans holds that to think about particular physical bodies, one must be able to perceive and conceptualize spatial relations among them and track them over at least short time periods.[120]

Evans also holds that perceiving and conceptualizing spatial and temporal relations among objects requires that the individual be able to localize objects in egocentrically centered frameworks.[121] That is, locations of objects and spatial relations among them must be represented by the individual, at least some of the time, within a framework that has an anchor or origin that has two characteristics.

---

[117] Evans, *Varieties of Reference*, 171–174.

[118] See ibid. 149.

[119] This sort of counter-example was given by Christopher Peacocke, *Sense and Content* (Oxford: Oxford University Press, 1983), 153 ff.

[120] Evans, *The Varieties of Reference*, 174–175, 161–163.

[121] Ibid. 153 ff., 161 ff.

It indexes the individual's own position at a given time. And it is associated with the individual's perspective, needs, and motivations in an immediate way: the origin position is privileged with respect to aspects of the individual's psychology.

These requirements seem to me plausible, with the caveats about hyper-intellectualization regarding knowing entered earlier. A relation between a capacity for perception-based reference to bodies and a capacity for spatio-temporal organization seems constitutive. Egocentric frameworks of some kind are a necessary feature of any perception. And egocentric *spatial* frameworks are necessary to spatial perceptual representation. Egocentric frameworks figure centrally in agency.[122]

Evans places a further condition on reference to bodies in perceptual thought. He requires that the individual be able to relate egocentric spatial frameworks to an allocentric spatial framework, a framework whose origin is not egocentric, and independent of that individual's position.[123]

The support that Evans offers for the requirement is diagnostically interesting. So I shall give it detailed attention. When Evans introduces the requirement, he associates it definitionally with the notion of thinking 'objectively' about a public space.[124] An ability to transcend an egocentric point of view is certainly one *type* of objectivity. However, Evans engages in a slide similar to the one I attributed to Strawson. Soon after his introduction of the requirement, without remarking on any transition, Evans writes that one must attribute this capacity to relate an egocentric spatial framework to an impersonally represented spatial framework to 'anyone who has the ability to think about an objective spatial world at all'. Evans adds that this capacity is necessary for the subject's egocentric space to be a *space* at all.[125] Understood this way, the requirement is not at all definitional. It is extremely doubtful.

Evans gives two argument sketches to support the view that one *must* be able to connect an egocentrically anchored spatial framework to an allocentric framework. Here is the first:

nothing that the subject can do, or can imagine, will entitle us to attribute such a representation to him [a representation of a spatial world] if he cannot make sense of the idea that *he* might be at one of the points representable within his map. We say that the subject thinks of himself as located in space (in an objective world that exists independently of him, and through which he moves); only if this is so can the subject's egocentric space be a *space* at all. But what does this thinking of himself as located mean

---

[122] I discuss egocentric frameworks in some detail in 'Memory and Persons'. See also Chapters 9–10.

[123] I think that Strawson demonstrated in chapter 1 of *Individuals* that even allocentric frameworks depend for their ultimate grounding on some demonstrative applications that are framed within an egocentric framework. For example, the allocentric system of longitude for the earth has Greenwich, England, at its origin. But determining where Greenwich and the earth are ultimately depends on association of the names with perceptually based beliefs about the place. Perceptual beliefs are framed egocentrically. Egocentric anchors do not figure in the longitude system itself. Zero longitude is an allocentric index. But the whole system has its content grounded in egocentrically framed context-dependent applications in thought.

[124] Evans, *The Varieties of Reference*, 162.

[125] Ibid. 163; see pp. 150 ff., 168, 173.

except that the subject can in general regard his situation 'from the objective point of view'? And this means that in general he has the ability to locate his egocentric space in the framework of a cognitive map.[126]

Every step of this sequence seems to me to be unsound. To have an egocentrically anchored spatial framework, it is certainly necessary that an animal be able to keep track of objects, spatial positions, and spatial relations. Normally, perhaps always, this tracking will be of moving objects, made possible through the animal's sensitivity to its own movement. The ability of the animal to track what is in fact its own movement is an ability to relate different egocentrically anchored spatial frameworks to one another. This egocentrically indexical tracking need not involve a capacity of the animal to think of itself (or perceive itself) at all. Egocentric spatial indexing in perception or perceptual thought is not thinking about oneself. It is indexing a position. It is not plausible that an animal's having the ability to track objects, spatial positions, and spatial relations requires that the animal represent itself. It is also not plausible that the animal need be able to 'make sense' of a modal claim, or even of a prediction, regarding hypothetical but non-actual shifts of egocentric point of view.

Evans further requires that an individual think of itself as located on an allocentrically anchored map if the individual is to have any spatial representation, even an egocentric spatial representation, at all. This requirement seems to be an unsupported assertion. Neither the requirement that one be able to think about oneself as located nor the requirement that this thinking be worked out on an allocentrically anchored cognitive map is given any support in the quoted passage.

It seems entirely possible that an animal have only egocentrically anchored spatial representations used navigationally and systematically related to one another in series as the animal moves. The series would be governed by principles that the animal cannot represent. This ability could contribute to formation of perceptual beliefs about spatial objects and properties. There is ample evidence that some animals' perceptions and perceptual memories involve egocentric spatial frameworks related in these ways. In some of these cases it is an open empirical question whether the abilities are associated with allocentric frameworks.[127] There is no incoherence in this empirical position. There is no evident reason why what holds for perception cannot hold for perceptual belief.

[126] Evans, *Varieties of Reference*, 163.

[127] Fred C. Dyer, 'Spatial Cognition: Lessons from Central-Place Foraging Insects', in R. P. Balda, I. M. Pepperberg, and A. C. Kamil (eds.), *Animal Cognition in Nature* (San Diego: Academic Press, 1998). Dyer claims that bees' use of *landmarks* in navigation does not involve allocentric maps. He claims that the perception and perceptual memory involved in this particular navigational task use only egocentric spatial frameworks. This position is empirically controversial, and I believe that more current views weigh against Dyer's. (See Chapter 10, note 136, below.) But it is certainly an empirically and conceptually coherent position. For more general discussion along the same lines as Dyer's, see Sue Healy, Zoe Hodgeson, and Victoria Braithwaite, 'Do Animals Use Maps?', in K. J. Jeffery (ed.), *The Neurobiology of Spatial Behaviour* (Oxford: Oxford University Press, 2003). For more on this issue, see Chapter 10 below.

Evans's requirement that the individual 'make sense' of something in order to be credited with thought (or perception) about spatial subject matters suggests the Strawsonian slide between a conception of objectivity (making sense of a reflective conceptual scheme) and representation of objective environmental entities as having specific physical characteristics. The requirement that one conceptualize conditions that make one's thought possible as a condition on the thinking constitutes an extremely strong version of second-family Individual Representationalism. No such requirement has been given apriori or other arm-chair support.

Objective representation of, and as of, spatial subject matters derives from competencies whose content constitutively depends on systematic relations to the physical environment. Evans's requirement that objective reference derive from a capacity to *make sense* of conditions for objective reference is the root mistake of second-family Individual Representationalism. Perceptual anti-individualism helps undermine the mistake.

Evans's second argument sketch goes as follows:

the network of input-output connections which underlie the idea of an egocentric space could never be regarded as supporting a way of representing space (even egocentric space) if it could not be brought by the subject into coincidence with some such larger spatial representation of the world as is constituted by a cognitive map. For instance, the subject must be able to think of the relation in which he stands to a tree that he can see as an instance of the relation in which (say) the Albert Hall stands to the Albert Memorial. That is, he must have the idea of himself as one object among others; and he must think of the relations between himself and objects he can see and act upon as relations of exactly the same kind as those he can see between pairs of objects he observes. This means that he must be able to impose the objective way of thinking upon egocentric space.[128]

The argument begins with the idea that spatial representation in thought requires that one associate egocentrically anchored representation of spatial relations with a non-egocentrically anchored representation of spatial relations. It requires that one's thought represent spatial relations between an egocentrically anchored position and some other object or position as being the same kind of relations as relations between two objects or positions, neither of which is represented through an egocentric anchor. This is the first point in Evans's reasoning.

This point is supposed to entail ('That is') a second point. The second point is that the individual must have an idea of himself (or herself) as one object among others.

These two points, in turn, are supposed to entail or be equivalent to ('This means that . . .') the view that the individual must be able to impose an allocentric representation of space on egocentrically anchored representations of space.

---

[128] Evans, *The Varieties of Reference*, 163.

This argument fails at each step. Let us consider the first step. I believe it to be true that in utilizing any reasonably rich, egocentrically anchored spatial framework, the individual's system of spatial representation can compute (by triangulation, for example) spatial relations between objects or positions neither of which is indicated egocentrically. For example, if, from position e_1 I see and think about an object x at a certain distance 45 degrees to my right and another object y at a certain distance 45 degrees to my left, I should be able to determine the approximate distance between the two objects. And I should be able to determine the approximate relation between the distance from me to object x and the distance from me to object y. This determination depends on computational transformations in the perceptual system. If the transformations are to be regular, all the principles governing the three distance relations must attribute roughly the same metric properties (or be ordinally comparable), and must employ the same geometrical principles.

The ability to rely on such visual transformations in thought could, as far as the argument has shown, always employ an egocentrically anchored framework. The computations between positions or objects neither of which is egocentered could always require an egocentering somewhere in the framework. Evans may have conflated the need to be able to compute spatial relations between relata neither of which is egocentrically indexed *within* an egocentric framework with the alleged need to compute whole frameworks allocentrically—without any egocentric anchor.

In actual use of egocentrically anchored spatial maps, the "triangulating" computations just discussed are supplemented by a further ability. As the individual thinker/perceiver moves, the egocentric position moves. The individual can connect a new egocentrically anchored perceptual map to earlier egocentrically anchored maps, held in memory. Let us consider a case of movement. Suppose that an individual starts at an egocentrically referred-to position e_1. Then the individual moves to the position of object x (so that the position of x coincides with the position indicated by a new egocentric anchor $\underline{e}_2$). Suppose that the individual can, from there, see object y but cannot see the position earlier marked by $\underline{e}_1$. Suppose that from memory the psychological system can compute the distance and direction of e_1. So, when the individual moves to the position of y, it can return to e_1 even if it cannot see the objective from the position of y (marked now by $\underline{e}_3$). By maintaining connections in memory between different egocentrically anchored maps, the individual can represent and navigate a space without ever using an allocentric map. I discuss such cases in Chapter 10.

Evans claims that the individual must be able to think of egocentrically anchored spatial relations as being of exactly the same kind as spatial relations between objects or positions neither of which is egocentrically anchored. What does it mean to think of these relations as being 'of exactly the same kind'? Consider triangulation within a single egocentric map. Suppose that this triangulation is used in thought that makes use of overlapping, remembered egocentric maps to guide movement. The use in thought of a specific distance relation that is always dependent on (or abstracted from) the use of an egocentric map would seem to count as thinking a relation as being of exactly the same kind. If it does count, then there is the foregoing counterexample to Evans's claim. The counter-example would undermine the requirement of allocentric frameworks to represent spatial relations. If the case does not count, then Evans has begged the question by not explaining why.

Thus Evans gives no reason to maintain that spatial relations one of whose relata has an egocentric anchor, on one hand, and spatial relations none of whose relata have an egocentric anchor, on the other, have to be treated (in thought) in *exactly* the same way. He gives no reason to think that the individual *must* be able to abstract somehow from the differences. It would seem enough that the spatial relations are computed under the same geometrical principles. Of course, the egocentrically anchored positions are associated with different motivational or other psychological implications in the individual's representational system. To claim that the individual or the individual's psychology must be able to abstract from such differences and treat the relations as exactly the same—thus eliminating egocentric markers from a map—is in effect to beg the question at issue.

Let us turn to Evans's second step. The second step is supposed to follow from the first. The second step is that the individual 'must have the idea of himself as one object among others'. (This is a Strawsonian transmutation of a condition for a *conception* of objectivity into a condition for objective representation.) Even if the first step were to be granted, the second does not follow. Evans gives no further argument for the second step. Thinking of a relation between spatial positions in the same way whether or not one of the relata are egocentrically indicated does not entail being able to think in both an egocentric way and a non-egocentric way of an entity (in this case, oneself) that *occupies* space. The framework for thinking can be entirely egocentric.

Moreover, it does not follow from having an egocentric (or indeed, allocentric) spatial framework that an individual can think of himself or herself at all. An egocentric anchor, in either thought or perception, can index a spatial position. The index of the position carries motivational and perspectival implications—ego-relevant implications. It need not present the individual thinker or perceiver at all. Even less need it be associated with any capacity of the individual to represent itself in thought as itself.

It seems to me wildly hyper-intellectualized to maintain that to represent entities in spatial relations, in perception or in empirical belief, an individual must conceive of itself as one object among others. Developmentally, it is clear that individuals can think about the physical world before they can think about themselves and their relations to other aspects of the world. There is empirical evidence that many animals and young children utilize egocentrically anchored spatial frameworks in propositional thought, but lack an ability to think about themselves from a first- or third-person point of view. Whether or not this is empirically true, nothing that Evans says shows it to be impossible—or known from the armchair not to be true.

Evans's view on this second step tracks a position of Strawson, but from outside Strawson's framework. Strawson claimed that we must view ourselves from an impersonal point of view as physical beings if we are to 'make sense' of a first-person point of view.[129] His arguments occur within a richer framework than Evans's. Strawson tries to account for our *conception* of objectivity. Evans tries to account for minimal conditions necessary to represent a space 'at all'. In this context, Evans's transition from his first step to his second is a long leap.

Evans's conclusion is that the individual must be able to impose the objective (allocentric) way of thinking upon egocentric space. I have shown why this conclusion is ungrounded. All the foregoing criticisms bear on Evans's claims as armchair constitutive requirements on the possibility of egocentrically anchored spatial representation in thought. In fact, there is empirical reason to think that allocentric spatial representations may not be uncommon, even among lower animals that lack propositional thought. They are certainly not unique to human representation. Allocentric spatial maps with origins on the sun, stars, or nest appear to occur in numerous types of animals.

A similar point applies to allocentric temporal schemes. Egocentrically grounded temporal representations are needed for the timing of any activity. But many animals capable of objective perceptual representation have allocentric temporal systems that figure in their memories and in guiding activity. Many temporal schemes are keyed to the rhythms of nature. The circadian cycle, seasonal cycles, and internal bodily rhythms ground various allocentric schemes of temporal representation, which are connected to the fundamental perceptual and actional egocentric schemes of temporal representation.[130]

There is empirical controversy (see notes 127 and 130, and Chapter 10, notes 135–137) over whether particular navigational systems—for example, the system for using landmarks in certain arthropods—are allocentric or egocentric. There is no controversy in the sciences over whether it is intelligible to attribute allocentric systems as well as egocentric systems to lower animals, or whether it is intelligible to attribute spatial and temporal egocentric representational systems without attributing allocentric systems. Nothing in Evans's arguments show why these points about spatial perception do not carry over to spatial perceptual thought. Evans's claims lack force, and are prima facie controverted by science.[131]

---

[129] See Strawson, *Individuals*, chapter 3. I do not endorse Strawson's claim, but it is challenging. Evans's transmutation of the claim into a requirement on objective reference (as opposed to a requirement on the individual's 'making sense' of his own objective reference) seems to me clearly false.

[130] See Charles R. Gallistel, *The Organization of Learning* (Cambridge, MA: MIT Press, 1990), chapters 3–5, 8–9; R. Menzel, U. Greggers, A. Smith, S. Berger, R. Brandt, S. Brunke, et al., 'Honey Bees Navigate According to a Map-Like Spatial Memory', *Proceedings of the National Academy of Sciences* 102 (2005), 3040–3045.

[131] Andrea Bianchi pointed out that Evans may have implicitly appealed to the Generality Constraint to make the argument work. That constraint cannot help one get from step one of the argument to step two. For being able to represent spatial relations egocentrically does not guarantee that one can think of oneself (or otherwise represent oneself). The Generality Constraint operates only

Whether allocentric maps accompany egocentric frameworks is an empirical matter. It is not an apriori necessity for perception or propositional thought.

In requiring an allocentric framework for objective spatial representation, Evans requires that spatial relations be indicated in a way that represents a *general precondition* on spatial reference. Relations between an individual and a space (a space independent of any egocentrically indexed perspective on it) are certainly constitutively necessary for that individual to have spatial concepts or indeed spatial perceptual attributives. But Evans fails to give a reason for holding that for an individual to have thoughts with spatial representational content, the *individual* must be able to *represent* this precondition on spatial representation in a generalized way that abstracts from egocentric elements in the representation. Evans's attempt to support such a conclusion is a typical instance of second-family Individual Representationalism.

Evans thinks that if one does not attribute supplementation of an egocentrically anchored spatial framework for representing space, the attribution of spatial representation is subject to deflationary reduction. The reduction that Evans envisions is to some sort of sensory system that lacks veridicality conditions regarding a physical environment.

This worry is unfounded. There are indeed fundamental differences between perceptual systems and belief systems, on one hand, and non-perceptual sensory systems, on the other. These differences do not hinge on individuals' being able to represent in thought ('make sense of') general conditions that are essential for objective representation. There are capacities in perceptual systems that figure essentially in the formation of perceptions as of the physical environment and that function to distinguish the physical environment from surface stimulations. These capacities constitute a form of objectification. They are not accessible to the individual perceiver. The objective representation involved in perception can be appropriated in thought, even though the individual does not represent counterparts of these capacities. The individual need not do the objectifying himself.

---

on the representations in thought that an individual has. It cannot indicate which representations an individual must have. An egocentric index is not itself a mode of presentation of oneself. One could skip the second step, however. The idea would be that, by the Generality Constraint, if one can think with an egocentrically indexed spatial framework, one can think with the same spatial framework with a non-egocentric representation of a spatial position substituted for the egocentric index. And one might hold that the result of the substitution is an allocentric representational network. Of course, this argument could not show that allocentric spatial representational networks are necessary in *perception*, since the Generality Constraint applies only to thought. But, even as it stands, the argument would be very doubtful. Although egocentric indexes are representational, they are not like ordinary singular terms that can be the subject terms in thought. They do not seem to be the sort of representational items that are open to free substitution. So the applicability of the Generality Constraint to egocentric indexes (which I am not sure Evans regarded as *terms* in thought) is very doubtful, and would require special argument. In fact, spatial representational frameworks can be inherited from perception by thought. And empirically it is nearly certain that some animals have egocentric spatial perceptual abilities that are not linked to allocentric spatial mapping abilities. So I believe that we have a *modus tollens* argument that the Generality Constraint cannot require apriori, or otherwise from the armchair, that every egocentric spatial representational system in perceptual thought must be linked in the same animal with an allocentric spatial mapping system.

Objectification is carried out in the subsystems of perceptual systems. I elaborate these points in Chapter 9.

Evans's account of spatial representation is unusual in its system and detail. Its basic ideas are, however, broadly Strawsonian. These ideas are shared by many neo-Kantian accounts of representation. Such accounts require greater sophistication and more conceptual control over the represented subject matter than is warranted. Although Evans is an anti-individualist, his account is shaped by residues from individualist and descriptivist habits. These are habits of requiring, as a condition on representing the environment, that the individual make more of a contribution to the underpinnings of objective representation than is necessary. They are simultaneously habits of underestimating the role of the environment in determining the nature of psychological abilities. Evans ends up assigning the individual subject the role of conceptually representing some of the conditions on objective representation. His anti-individualism is miscast in individual representationalist form. Evans's development of Russell's Principle is one of the most elaborate versions of second-family Individual Representationalism. Scrutinized closely, it is seen to lack any force.

NEO-KANTIAN INDIVIDUAL REPRESENTATIONALISM: SUMMARY

Strawson's work produced a train of variants on neo-Kantian Individual Representationalism. Strawson contributed directly to four main themes. He developed all of these themes primarily within his project of accounting for our *conception* of objectivity. Because Strawson blurred lines between that project and the project of accounting for constitutive conditions on objective representation, many post-Strawsonian philosophers, like Evans, developed Strawsonian themes within this latter project without serious argument.

One Strawsonian theme is the alleged need to locate objective representation within representation of a comprehensive spatial framework. This theme led to the requirement in Evans and others that the individual must have an allocentric scheme of spatial representation in order to engage in any spatial representation.

A second theme is the idea that to represent objectively, one must be able to represent a contrast between the objective and the subjective—a seems/is or appearance/reality distinction. This idea was abetted by the idea, sometimes attributed to Wittgenstein, that a given form of representation is not intelligibly attributed unless one can also attribute a contrasting form of representation.[132]

A third theme is often taken to be a corollary of the first and second. This is the idea that to represent objectively, one must be able to track oneself and one's point of view through space, and be capable of self-consciousness.[133]

---

[132] Evans, 'Things without the Mind'.

[133] McDowell, *Mind and World*, 54. See also various articles in J. L. Bermudez, A. Marcel, and N. Eilan (eds.), *The Body and the Self* (Cambridge, MA: MIT Press, 1995); Evans, *The Varieties of Reference*, chapter 7.

A fourth theme is the idea that to represent a type of entity, one must be able to represent criteria for the application of the representation, or criteria for being that type of entity. Such criteria were commonly associated with a means of determining or verifying the presence of entities of that kind. We have seen Evans's development of this theme, both in criteria for being a material body and in criteria for being the same body over time.[134]

A further theme in neo-Kantian second-family Individual Representationalism is less indebted to Strawson and more directly indebted to Kant. This is the idea that to represent objectively, or alternatively to represent bodies, one must be able to represent causal relations, or force, as such.[135] There is substantial evidence that arthropods represent spatial relations as such, but no evidence that I know of that they represent causal relations as such, much less think propositionally of them as such.[136] There is evidence that apes, birds, chickens, and other animals perceptually represent bodies as such, but no evidence that I know of that all of them represent causation or force as such.[137]

I believe that armchair argument cannot show that separating these representational abilities is incoherent. Whether or not individuals that represent bodies as bodies also represent causal relations is an empirical matter. I will not discuss accounts that center on causation. I think that most such accounts have weaknesses similar to those that I criticized in this chapter.

I have not surveyed the vast neo-Kantian post-Strawsonian literature, as expression of second-family Individual Representationalism. There are many versions of the view that to represent the physical environment as having specific

---

[134] Strawson, *Individuals*, 11–12 [23–24]; David Wiggins, *Sameness and Substance* (Oxford: Blackwell, 1980). In the updated version, *Sameness and Substance Renewed* (Cambridge, Cambridge University Press, 2001), p. xiii, Wiggins weakens his commitment to criteria in a salutary way.

[135] See Christopher Peacocke, 'Intuitive Mechanics, Psychological Reality and the Idea of a Material Object', in N. Eilan, R. McCarthy, and B. Brewer (eds.), *Spatial Representation* (Oxford: Basil Blackwell, 1993); John Campbell, *Past, Space, and Self* (Cambridge, MA: MIT Press, 1995), 30–32. I discuss the former work in Chapter 10, the section PERCEPTION AND BODY.

[136] R. Wehner, 'Spatial Vision in Arthropods', in H. Autrum (ed.), *Comparative Physiology and Evolution of Vision in Invertebrates: Invertebrate Visual Centers and Behavior* (Berlin: Springer Verlag, 1981); R. Stimson Wilcox and Robert R. Jackson, 'Cognitive Abilities of Araneophagic Jumping Spiders', in R. P. Balda, I. M. Pepperberg, and A. C. Kamil (eds.), *Animal Cognition in Nature* (San Diego: Academic Press, 1998); T. S. Collett, 'Peering: A Locust Behavior for Obtaining Motion Parallax Information', *Journal of Experimental Biology* 76 (1978), 237–241; P. H. Brownell, 'Prey Detection by the Sand Scorpion', *Scientific American* 251 (1984), 86–97; C. R. Gallistel, 'Animal Cognition: The Representation of Space, Time and Number', *Annual Review of Psychology* 40 (1989), 155–189.

[137] M. D. Hauser, 'Expectations about Object Motion and Destination: Experiments with a Non-Human Primate', *Developmental Science* 1 (1998), 31–38; I. M. Pepperberg and F. A. Funk, 'Object Permanence in Four Species of Psittacine Birds', *Animal Learning and Behavior* 14 (1990), 322–330; L. Regolin, G. Vallortigara, and M. Zanforlin, 'Detour Behavior in the Domestic Chick: Searching for a Disappearing Prey or a Disappearing Social Partner', *Animal Behavior* 50 (1995), 203–211; L. Regolin and G. Vallortigara, 'Perception of Partly Occluded Objects by Young Chicks', *Perception and Psychophysics* 57 (1995), 971–976.

physical properties, an individual must represent general constitutive preconditions on objective representation. I have discussed only prominent examples.

Some neo-Kantian developments of individual representationalist themes do not derive from Strawson. Some come from verificationism. Some take their inspiration from Frege's remarks regarding criteria for identity.[138] Some pick up themes from the later Wittgenstein.[139]

I turn next to another tradition of second-family Individual Representationalism. Again, the tradition overrates the role of individuals' representations of conditions on objectivity in making objective representation possible. Again, the tradition underestimates the force of perceptual anti-individualism in undermining hyper-intellectualized requirements on primitive objective representation. This tradition has a different surface form from the Strawsonian tradition. But its philosophical deep structure is similar. The tradition is prominently represented by Quine and Davidson.

---

[138] See Michael Dummett, *The Interpretation of Frege's Philosophy* (Cambridge, MA: Harvard University Press, 1981).

[139] Robert Brandom, *Making It Explicit* (Cambridge, MA: Harvard University Press, 1994).

7 *Language Interpretation and Individual Representationalism: Quine and Davidson*

An important tradition of second-family Individual Representationalism centers on language. The chief representatives of this tradition are W. V. Quine and Donald Davidson. I begin with Quine.

Quine claims that the notions of meaning, reference, and representation lack objective status. He argues that attributions of representational content are indeterminate. He views psychology and semantics as less factual than natural science.

In *The Roots of Reference*, Quine pursues a separable line. He elaborates an account, polished through his career, of the development of, and conceptual priority among, referential devices.[1] According to the account, human children begin with undifferentiated, not truly referential, sensory and sentential equipment; by learning certain linguistic devices, they become able to carry out genuine reference to environmental entities. This account is meant as a contribution to psychology and linguistics, whatever their factual status. It can be evaluated on its merits, apart from the indeterminacy theses.[2]

The indeterminacy theses and the developmental and conceptual-priority accounts rest, however, on a common mistake. They fail to recognize certain connections between natural sciences and the sciences of psychology and linguistics. In particular, they fail to recognize connections between biological explanations, which indicate ecological relations between the basic needs and pursuits of animals and their environments, and psychological explanations of perception, which use the relevant ecological relations to help determine both perceptual *representata* and perceptual kinds. Biology sets out for perceptual psychology an array of candidates for perceptual *representata*. The array is the

---

[1] W. V. Quine, *The Roots of Reference* (La Salle, IL: Open Court, 1973); see also 'The Scope and Language of Science' (1957), in *The Ways of Paradox* (New York: Random House, 1966); and 'Speaking of Objects' (1958), in *Ontological Relativity and Other Essays* (New York: Columbia University Press, 1969).

[2] I include under 'indeterminacy theses' the thesis of the indeterminacy of meaning and the thesis of the inscrutability of reference. These theses are set out in Quine, *Word and Object*, chapter 2; 'Ontological Relativity' (1968), in *Ontological Relativity and Other Essays*; and many other places.

range of things in the environment that the individual interacts with. This array is fixed in natural science. Perceptual psychology then determines through theory and experiment what the *representata* of various animals' perceptual states actually are. Perceptual kinds, in turn, help determine the meanings and *representata* of linguistic expressions.

These points about relations between sciences are corollaries of anti-individualism regarding perception. The representational contents of an individual's perceptual states constitutively depend not only on an individual's discriminatory capacities and perspective, but on a background of causal relations between environment and individual. What the states are *causally related to* helps fix what they are perceptions of, and as of. The causal relata are partly *circumscribed* by their figuring in explanations of the individual's basic biological needs and activities—eating, mating, navigating, fighting, fleeing, parenting.[3]

Consider how this point applies to a simple visual capacity for determining location. Through a type of processing called '*convergence*', a visual system can determine location simply from the directions the eyes are pointing (which fixate a given point) and the distance between the eyes. In understanding perception of entities at particular locations, one must specify what attributives the perceptual system applies to entities at the fixation point. Perception does not just single out positions where sight lines intersect. It perceives concrete particulars at such locations, and attributes specific attribute types to such particulars. There are many kinds and properties instantiated at any location from which the two eyes receive light. Those instances of types, in the relevant positions, both that the individual can discriminate *and* that are of some potential environmental relevance to individual biological function, needs, and activity help constitutively determine the types that the individual's perceptual system attributes to concrete particulars that an individual perceives.[4]

I will apply these points to Quine's two lines of argument. Both lines assume that kinds that natural sciences represent have no privileged status in determining the kinds represented in psychology or semantics.

QUINE'S STARTING POINT: THE ARGUMENT FROM
DEFAULT NEUTRALITY

I begin with Quine's explanation of the psychological development of representation. Quine assumes a default neutrality among various possible referents. He thinks that since a pattern of behavioral responses can be taken to be equally a pattern of responses to all of these possible referents, there is no ground to take the referent of a piece of language to be any one of the possibilities. As alternatives to bodies, he considers as possible referents masses, light arrays,

---

[3] For fuller development, see my 'Perceptual Entitlement', section I.

[4] See Chapter 8, the section PERCEPTION AND THE ENVIRONMENT: THE 'DISJUNCTION PROBLEM'.

temporal stages of objects, instances of universals, undetached object parts, and so on. He believes that each of these entities is *discriminated* when any of the others is discriminated.

What is present and compatible with a pattern of discriminative response is not the only relevant factor in determining perceptual and linguistic *representata*. Biological explanations of animal pursuits advert to bodies as obstacles, mates, prey, predators, offspring, and so on. None of Quine's contrived entities is central in explaining individual functioning with respect to basic biological needs and activities. They are not on a par with bodies, and their attributes, in determining the natures and contents of perceptual states for most perceivers. Explanation is not default neutral among them.

Quine claims that the representational contents of psychological states exhibit an indeterminacy 'over and above' inductive indeterminacy in the natural sciences. This claim, like the default neutrality in his developmental account, derives from overlooking the methodology of explanations of perceptual capacities. It overlooks the fact that perceptual content is constrained by the subject matters of ethology and zoology. These accounts relate animals to key environmental entities that figure in their needs and activities.[5]

In both the quasi-empirical account regarding development and the reasoning about indeterminacy, Quine takes the child to have a sense of the externality of the world in early stages of language learning. He claims, however, that there is no genuine reference to anything until certain linguistic structures are learned.

The main argument for a pre-referential linguistic stage rests on the claim that in the absence of linguistic abilities that explicitly make relevant distinctions, any attribution of representation or attribution to physical particulars is gratuitous. Perhaps Quine believes that this claim undercuts the natural idea that reference in language is underwritten by antecedent reference and attribution, or grouping, in perception. In any case, he believes that reference and attribution occur only with the advent of language. The argument from gratuitousness is a variant on the point, made by Wittgenstein, that ostension without stage-setting is unspecific.[6]

Here is an early statement of Quine's view:

I will grant that the linguist may establish inductively, beyond reasonable doubt, that a certain heathen expression is one to which natives can be prompted to assent by the

---

[5] Noam Chomsky criticizes Quine's thesis of the indeterminacy of translation in 'Quine's Empirical Assumptions', in Donald Davidson and Jaakko Hintikka (eds.), *Words and Objections* (Dordrecht: D. Reidel, 1969). Chomsky correctly targets Quine's assumption that indeterminacy in the human sciences is 'over and above' any indeterminacy in the natural sciences. Donald Davidson defends indeterminacy by assimilating it to scales of measurement—Fahrenheit and Centigrade, for example. See 'A Coherence Theory of Truth and Knowledge', in E. LePore (ed.), *Truth and Interpretation* (Oxford: Blackwell, 1986), 313; reprinted in *Subjective, Intersubjective, Objective*, 137–157. This defense underplays the point and degree of Quine's radicalism. Quine holds that different translations of a sentence can be incompatible—they assign some of the same sentences incompatible truth values—and yet can be equally best. Different scales of measurement are fully compatible at each attribution.

[6] Wittgenstein, *Philosophical Investigations*, the opening sections.

presence of a rabbit, or reasonable *facsimile*, and not otherwise. The linguist is then warranted in according the native expression the cautious translation 'There's a rabbit,'.... 'Lo, a rabbit,' 'Lo! Rabbithood again,' insofar as the differences among these English sentences are counted irrelevant. This much translation can be objective, however exotic the tribe. It recognizes the native expression as in effect a rabbit-heralding sentence. But the linguist's bold further step, in which he imposes his own object-positing pattern without special warrant, is taken when he equates the native expression or any part of it with the *term* 'rabbit'.

It is easy to show that such appeal to an object category is unwarranted even though we cannot easily, in English, herald rabbits without objectification. For we can argue from indifference. Given that a native sentence says that a so-and-so is present, and given that the sentence is true when and only when a rabbit is present, it by no means follows that the so-and-so are rabbits. They might be all the various temporal segments of rabbits. They might be all the integral or undetached parts of rabbits. In order to decide among these alternatives we need to be able to ask more than whether a so-and-so is present. We need to be able to ask whether this is the same so-and-so as that, and whether one so-and-so is present or two. We need something like the apparatus of identity and quantification; hence far more than we are in a position to avail ourselves of in a language in which our high point as of even date is rabbit-announcing.[7]

Quine applies the point of this passage to child development:

For though ... the child has learned the trick of using the utterances 'mama' and 'water' strictly in the appropriate presences, or as means of inducing the appropriate presences, still we have no right to construe these utterances in the child's mouth as terms, at first, for things or substances.

We in our maturity have come to look upon the child's mother as an integral body who, in an irregular closed orbit, revisits the child from time to time ... But the mother, red, and water are for the infant all of a type: each is just a history of sporadic encounter, a scattered portion of what goes on. His first learning of the three words is uniformly a matter of learning how much of what goes on about him counts as the mother, or as red, or as water.... They are all on a par: Hello! More mama, more red, more water. Even this last formula, which treats all three terms on the model of our provincial adult bulk term 'water', is imperfect; for it unwarrantedly imputes an objectification of matter, even if only as stuff and not as bits.[8]

Quine makes a fundamental mistake at the very beginning. He is right that it does not *follow* from utterances that occur when and only when rabbits or rabbit *facsimiles* occur that the utterer mentions rabbits. But he just assumes that the only relevant evidential consideration is the history of black-box utterances in the

---

[7] Quine, 'Speaking of Objects', 2; in *Quintessence*, 91–92. Quine claims that the situation is worse than he represented it. He believes that even segmenting the sentence to isolate 'rabbit-announcing' as a general term is unsupported by evidence. Note the similarity of language in this passage to the passage I quoted from William James, Chapter 4, note 3, above.

[8] Quine, 'Speaking of Objects', 7; in *Quintessence*, 95. There is a nearly identical passage in Quine, *Word and Object*, 92.

presence of rabbits. He thinks that if this evidence does not warrant unique attribution of a referent or a meaning, such attribution is gratuitous.

Quine does not confront the natural view that the semantics of language is initially determined by perception. He does not consider how perceptual representational content—hence perceptual singular reference and perceptual attribution—are established. I believe that his assertions about child development are empirically untenable. They certainly do not address relevant questions.

Language initially gets its meaning and reference from perception. Perceptual reference and content are evidentially determined through a combination of the individual's discriminatory capacities and facts about what discriminated environmental elements enter into the individual's basic biological pursuits. Bodies are more basic to biological explanations of most animals' pursuits than temporal stages, undetached spatial parts, or instances of universals (all as such). So bodies have prima facie priority in determining perceptual referents and contents. Most of the alternatives that Quine uses to suggest gratuitousness are ruled out by these sorts of considerations. Some are ruled out on narrower empirical grounds as well.

Quine postulates a pre-referential, pre-individuative stage. He thinks that the stage is pre-referential because in it individuals refer to no environmental entity, even though they have sensory systems and rudimentary language. Quine thinks that the stage is pre-referential because it is pre-individuative—no types of entities are appropriately isolated from others.

The simplest bit of language in the pre-referential stage is said to be the one-word *observation sentence*. Quine defines 'observation sentence' for a single speaker as follows: 'If querying the sentence elicits assent from the given speaker on one occasion, it will elicit assent likewise on any other occasion when the same total set of receptors is triggered, and similarly for dissent.'[9] Observation sentences are conditioned responses to direct stimulation. Their association with concurrent stimulation is said to be essential to acquiring them prior to language.[10] Examples of sentences at this stage are 'Dog!' and 'Red!'

These sentences are said to be 'unstructured'. Quine writes: 'all the baby learns is to say his word when appropriately irritated and not otherwise.'[11] He means not merely that the sentences consist of a single word. He means that they lack even an implicit logical form or structure. He thinks that there is no prior

[9] W. V. Quine, 'Empirical Content' (1981), in *Theories and Things* (Cambridge, MA: Harvard University Press, 1981), 25. Quine discusses changes in the definition over the years in *Pursuit of Truth* (Cambridge, MA: Harvard University Press, 1990), 2–6, 40–44. The initial account is in *Word and Object*, 40–46; see also *Roots of Reference*, 39. Quine recognizes that given background information, a speaker may withhold assent from any sentence—for example, if there is warning that special conditions are producing illusion. See *Word and Object*, 40–42. Quine brushes this issue aside, claiming that some sentences ('Red!') have less scope for intrusive collateral information. I think that this notion of scope is illusory. Collateral information presents a serious problem for his notion observation sentence. I do not press the objection here.

[10] Quine, *Pursuit of Truth*, 5.

[11] Quine, *Word and Object*, 91–92; a cognate passage occurs earlier, in 1958, in 'Speaking of Objects', 6–8. See also *Pursuit of Truth*, 7.

referential ability in the language user that the language can be mapped onto.[12] He holds that the same one-word expressions have structure, and succeed in carrying out reference to specific entities in the environment, when and only when the individual acquires an auxiliary linguistic apparatus that we shall discuss in due course. Only then can 'Dog!' be construed as having the structure 'That's a dog'. In the supposed pre-referential stage, observation sentences are simply whole linguistic responses to stimulation.

Quine holds that the meaning of an observation sentence is its *stimulus meaning*. The stimulus meaning of a sentence for a speaker is the range of types of stimulations that would elicit the speaker's assent to the sentence, paired with the range of types that would elicit the speaker's dissent.[13] Quine takes this account to spell out the empirical content of the sentences.

Quine takes stimulations of utterances of observation sentences to be nerve-ending triggerings—proximal stimulations, not distal stimulations. He rejects appeal to entities in the distal environment as factors in individuating the meaning of observation sentences.

Many issues surround the claims just rehearsed. They figure in four projects: an account of translation and communication, an account of reference, an account of empirical psychology, and a theory of evidence and knowledge. I believe that there are basic errors in this sequence that bear in different ways on these projects.

INTERLUDE: EVANS'S CRITIQUE OF QUINE ON REFERENTIAL INDETERMINACY

Evans criticized Quine's thesis of referential indeterminacy. Quine never replied. Although the criticism has been regarded as telling in some circles, I think it ineffectual. Discussing some of its shortcomings will highlight genuine grounds for rejecting Quine's thesis. Readers indifferent to Evans's objections can skip this section.

Evans accepts Quine's view that referential indeterminacy infects the (supposed) stage of unstructured one-word sentences. He agrees with Quine that there is no reference or predication at this stage. He thinks, however, that reference and predication depend constitutively on different linguistic phenomena from those that Quine proposes. Specifically, he thinks that sensitivity to certain word compounds involves or depends on a sensitivity to object boundaries. He thinks

---

[12] See also W. V. Quine, 'Propositional Objects', in *Ontological Relativity*. There Quine supports a deflated attribution of attitudes to animals. He writes: 'the cat wants to get on to the roof... what the cat wants is a simple matter of superposition with respect to the roof, by whatever name' (pp. 146–147). The ensuing account omits representational content for the cat's state, and thus does not connect with perceptual psychology.

[13] Quine, *Word and Object*, 31–35, 44; *Pursuit of Truth*, 3–4, 16 ff.

that such sensitivity demands explanation in terms of predication, reference, and identity conditions. He holds that Quine's requirement of quantification and various other linguistic competencies is not necessary. In fact, Evans claims that his favored apparatus of compound linguistic structures 'alone' gives sense to the notion of a predicate's having an extension. And he maintains that the specific semantics of such predications is determinate, contrary to Quine's indeterminacy claims, once the relevant compounding and sensitivity to boundaries shows up in linguistic behavior.[14]

Quine and Evans are *primarily* mistaken in what they agree on. Their primary error lies in ignoring the role of autonomous perception in providing a representational grounding for language. Both believe that linguistic structures are the source of specific representation—that is, the source of attribution or singular reference with respect to specific *representata*. To the contrary, specific representation occurs in perception, prior to language, indeed prior to propositional thought. Such representation is both phylogenetically and developmentally independent of language. Words' initial *representata* derive primarily from perceptual attributions that the words are linked to.

Strawson, Evans, Quine, and Davidson are right to insist that words are not parts of propositional sentence structures unless they are part of a grammar of compound structures that partly reflect inferential structures. But the extensions of many words do not depend primarily on that compounding. The words' extensions hinge on their connections to antecedent, perceptual representational abilities that themselves have specific *representata*. So certain words initially take over extensions of perceptual attributives. But they are *words* (where the words are associated with concepts, and the sentences in which they occur are associated with propositional representational contents) only through systematic grammatical/inferential relations to other words. Reference, indication, and attribution are in place before language or thought, hence before the compounding that Evans champions. Constitutively speaking, the compounding figures primarily in certain representational relations' being *linguistic*, or *propositional*.

So Evans disagrees with Quine over the solution to a pseudo-problem. The pseudo-problem is that of explaining how, and which, linguistic devices make linguistic reference and predication possible. It may be of help in understanding Quine, however, to see how, even given this mistaken frame of agreement, Evans's objections to Quine fail.

Evans postulates a language that contains expressions $G_1, G_2 \ldots G_n$ that when uttered as questions are assented to when material objects of various kinds are presented to a speaker. These might be expressions like 'Rabbit', 'Rabbit parts', 'Human Body', and so on. The language also contains expressions $F_1, F_2 \ldots F_m$ that are assented to when various general features are presented. These might be

---

[14] Evans, 'Identity and Predication', 27–33. The claim that compound linguistic structures 'alone' give sense to the notion of a predicate's having an extension, and (later) for 'introducing objects and their properties into semantics' (p. 29) occurs on p. 28. See a similar claim, pp. 39–40.

expressions like 'White', 'Bloodstained', 'Warm'. Evans also postulates combinations among the *F*-type expressions and between *G*-type and *F*-expressions. (He holds that there are no combinations among *G*-type expressions alone.) Finally, Evans postulates two types of negation that occur in the combinations. One is an 'internal' negation that turns out to be predicate negation. The other is sentential negation.[15]

The discussion of Quine is marred from the beginning by Evans's failure to recognize the inductive, counterfactual aspect of Quine's evidential base. Evans claims that assent to 'Red' at a relevant stage of language use leaves us with no idea of what entities satisfy the predicate. To illustrate the claim, he considers the affirmative utterance of 'Red Water' in response to some drops of red ink having fallen into a pool. Attempting to explain his agreement with Quine on the indeterminacy of reference for very simple fragments of language, Evans writes:

But which object is it, even roughly, whose satisfaction of the predicate 'Red' makes the remark true? Is it the whole pool, or just the water immediately diluting the ink, or one of the indefinitely many intermediate alternatives? The language provides us with no way of answering these questions, to which we must somehow find an answer if the construction is predication.[16]

The rhetorical questions betray an oversight. They have answers, from Quine's point of view, within the framework in which they are asked. Stimulus meaning encompasses *would-be* assent and dissent relative to all possible stimulations. Repeated empirical testing can in principle show some among the alternatives to be better than the others. Such testing could in principle determine whether the boundaries of application of 'Red Water' coincide with the boundaries of the whole pool, the water 'immediately diluting the ink', some intermediate quantity, or perhaps each of them. For example, by isolating the water immediately diluting the ink from the rest of the pool and asking 'Red?', one might find that the term applies to the isolated water. Using appropriate gestures, one might succeed in indicating to the speaker a contrast between the boundaries of the isolated water and those of the whole pool. Such a contrast might elicit dissent from the expression in response to the latter. (Or it might not.) Similarly, for the intermediate quantities. Even supposing that one finds a unique quantity that counts as red, Quine would hold that indeterminacy remains as to what 'Red' applies to. As I shall explain, Quine's indeterminacy is *not about* the spatial

---

[15] Evans, 'Identity and Predication', 33–34. Sentential negation is exemplified by 'Not(Rabbit, Bloodstained)'—possibly translating: 'It is not the case that a bloodstained rabbit is here.' Internal negation is exemplified by 'Rabbit not-Bloodstained'—possibly translating: 'A rabbit is here that is not bloodstained.' I think that despite his attempt not to do so, Evans begs questions against Quine in interpreting internal negation as predicate negation. I waive these difficulties here. Throughout his article Evans criticizes Quine for claiming that prior to introduction of his individuating apparatus, one cannot discern predication in the language. Of course, I agree with Evans in opposing this view, though I do not endorse his arguments. I do not agree with Evans's view that predication is forced only by presence of explicit word compounds.

[16] Ibid. 32.

boundaries of the entity or entities that satisfy predicate expressions. This under-estimation of the power of inductive testing in Quine's account is closely associated with the failure of Evans's main objections to Quine.

Evans sets out to show that the indeterminacy postulated by Quine can be resolved without appealing to Quine's apparatus of quantification, identity, and so on (which I shall discuss in detail later in this chapter).[17] Evans claims that the indeterminacy can be resolved given the apparatus of combination and negation that he sets out.

Evans cites compounds 'F_1G' ('White Rabbit') that can be dissented to even when 'F_1' and 'G' are separately assented to, and even when there is apparent spatial overlap between what, in the environment, causes assent to each. Evans notes that one might get such results if a foot of a proffered rabbit is white, but the rabbit is otherwise brown, or if brown rabbits are so situated that the rabbit-sized confluence of their contiguous white tails is white.[18]

Similarly, Evans cites compounds 'F_2G' ('Bloodstained Rabbit') that elicit assent as long as there is some overlap of application between 'F_2' and 'G', and compounds 'not-F_2G' that elicit assent only given the complete absence of the F-feature from the entire exposed surface of the relevant G-object.

Further, Evans cites triple compounds like 'F_2F_1G' ('Bloodstained White Rabbit') that require some principle explaining the different ways in which 'Blood-stained' and 'White' relate to the boundaries of 'Rabbit'. 'Bloodstained' requires only some incidence of blood on a rabbit surface, whereas 'White' requires nearly complete coverage of whiteness on the surface.

Evans believes that what is required to explain such behavior in response to such compounds is that 'the F-feature be distributed in a characteristic way in relation to the boundaries of a *single* object whose presence prompts [assent or dissent to relevant] queried G-terms'.[19] He thinks that the sensitivity to object boundaries exhibited by such assent–dissent behavior supports taking the com-pounds to represent material objects and their properties, as opposed to the possible non-standard construals of representation that Quine proposes—rabbit parts, temporal rabbit stages, abstract objects, and so on.

Elaborating on this view, Evans emphasizes the 'sensitivity of these sentences to the distribution of features . . . within the confines of a single rabbit'. He holds that good explanation takes 'G' ('Rabbit') to carry 'a particular set of identity conditions—a particular divided reference'. Evans thinks that the sensitivity to boundaries uniquely fixes the identity conditions. In accord with his Individual Representationalism, he holds that correctly attributing kind predicates to a speaker requires attributing 'systematic mastery' of the 'identity conditions' of

---

[17] Of course, I think that indeterminacy is resolved independently of either apparatus. Here I argue just that Evans does not show that it is resolved given his apparatus, and given the background of agreement with Quine that I have just criticized.

[18] Evans, 'Identity and Predication', 34.

[19] Ibid. 34.

the entities to which the predicate applies. In the particular case, he thinks that we 'have to suppose that the surface of the rabbit stuff upon which the incidence of the white feature is relevant to the truth of the judgement "White Rabbit", must genuinely be a boundary that separates a single rabbit from things that are distinct'.[20] He claims that the behavioral evidence shows one must sort situations into those in which the same rabbit is involved in all parts of compound sentences and those in which the same rabbit is not involved in all parts.[21]

In the latter part of his article, Evans argues against Quine's proposals for accounting for the behavioral evidence by attributing non-standard, but equally good, translation schemes beyond those that attribute as *representata* middle-sized bodies, such as rabbits. I will cite the main points he makes against Quine's proposal for (non-standardly) taking 'G' to apply to groups of rabbit parts.

Evans's argument consists in knocking down some non-starter ways of applying the non-standard, rabbit-part semantics. For example, he asks how the non-standard semantics is to construe 'F_1' ('White') in its combination with 'G' ('Rabbit'). He first holds that we must amend the satisfaction condition that would hold that 'White' applies to something if and only if that something is white. He says that individuals' dissent to 'White Rabbit' when shown a brown rabbit with a white foot would show that on such a satisfaction condition 'Rabbit' could not apply to rabbit parts. For there is certainly a white rabbit part present (the rabbit foot).[22]

Evans then proposes an emendation: 'White' is satisfied by something if and only if that thing is a part of a white rabbit. The white foot of a brown rabbit is not part of a white rabbit. Evans notes that this emendation is not right, for it confines the application of 'White' to rabbit parts. So assents to 'White' in the presence of white huts would not be accounted for.

Evans's counter-argument then leaps to the conclusion that there is no way to find an acceptable satisfaction condition for 'White' on the non-standard scheme. His discussion of this conclusion is extremely unclear, and his formulations are manifestly sloppy in ways that are not easily made right.[23] I believe that his argument against Quine is unsound from the start.

I noted earlier that Evans's initial attempt to support Quine's position on the simplest one-word sentences showed that he underestimated the inductive, counterfactual testing power that is present in Quine's notion of evidence, in stimulus meaning. A corollary of this point is that it is part of Quine's conception that an individual's sensitivity to spatial boundaries can be discerned through repeated tests. In fact, it is *part of Quine's conception of the non-standard translation or*

---

[20] With one exception, all quotations cited so far in this paragraph are from 'Identity and Predication', either p. 34 or p. 35. The exceptions are the quotations regarding mastery of identity conditions. These occur on pp. 39–40.

[21] Ibid. 38.

[22] Ibid. 42.

[23] Ibid. 42–44, especially the first full paragraph p. 43.

semantical schemes that they accord with the sensitivities to boundaries that standard schemes (that attribute ordinary macro-objects) capture.

Significantly, Evans does not accurately describe the non-standard scheme that traffics in rabbit parts, rather than rabbits. Evans systematically fails to mention that Quine's non-standard scheme attributes *undetached* rabbit parts.[24] These are parts not only not detached spatially from other parts. They are parts not detached from the characteristic grouping of parts that form rabbit shapes (more specifically, rabbits). I think that it may be part of Quine's conception that in some cases the non-standard scheme can take 'Rabbit' to apply to some proper subgroup of undetached parts. But in many cases he takes the term to apply, on the non-standard scheme, only to the particular plurality of parts that make up a rabbit shape. One might think that that plurality, so grouped, just *is* the rabbit. Quine holds, rightly I think, that a language that represents the parts and a language that represents only rabbits do not represent exactly the same entities. They have different ontologies.

A similar point applies to Quine's other non-standard schemes. Taking 'Rabbit' to apply to instances of rabbithood is to introduce a different ontology (an abstraction and its instances) from the ontology of rabbits alone. Similarly with rabbit-fusion, temporal rabbit stages, and so on. In each case, the ontology requires a capacity of speakers to recognize rabbit boundaries. For example, commitment to rabbit fusion is like commitment to macaroni as a whole scattered stuff. To master a term meaning 'rabbit fusion', one must be able to recognize characteristic packets of rabbit, somewhat as one recognizes characteristic pieces of macaroni. But such a capacity to recognize pieces does not entail that one speaks of the pieces, *per se*, in one's language. The non-standardness of the scheme consists not in an inability to recognize the packets, or even in an inability to pick out contextually through language such packets by their spatial boundaries. Speakers of non-standard language would not be deficient in these respects. The non-standardness consists in introducing a stuff-like totality into the ontology, and in a mass-like treatment of the term. Analogous remarks apply to other non-standard schemes.[25]

With these points in mind, let us go back over Evans's discussion of cases in his objection to the non-standard, rabbit-parts scheme. Take the compound 'F_1G' ('White Rabbit'). The compound can be dissented to in the presence of both a rabbit and white rabbit parts (those in a brown rabbit's foot).[26] Clearly, the dissenter is not referring to the white undetached rabbit parts in the foot. From

[24] Quine, *Word and Object*, 52–54.

[25] Evans takes his objections to the rabbithood and rabbit-fusion ontologies to be especially decisive. See 'Identity and Predication', 40–42, 47. In my view, even in these cases, he misunderstands Quine's conception in ways that completely undermine his objections. I will not discuss Evans's objections to each of the non-standard schemes. I continue to focus on the rabbit-part scheme, as Evans mostly does.

[26] Evans also cites a confluence of contiguous white tails of different rabbits. This case is irrelevant, since the contiguous tails could easily be determined to be detached from one another.

the point of view of the non-standard scheme, the dissenter would *assent* to the sentence if it were applied to those. Those parts are not relevant to interpreting the utterance. Which parts are? By inductive testing in the way I discussed in the case of the red water, one can in principle determine that the relevant undetached parts—those that are referred to in the context—are those that make up the full rabbit shape. The semantics of the sentence, on the non-standard scheme, is that it is true if and only if a sufficient (quite large) number of *that* plurality of undetached rabbit parts are white.

Consider again the compound 'F_2G' ('Bloodstained Rabbit'). On the non-standard scheme, this compound elicits assent (and is true) if and only if any visible number of the same plurality of undetached rabbit parts is bloodstained. Similarly, 'not-F_2G' elicits assent (and is true) if and only if there are no exposed members of the relevant plurality of parts that are bloodstained. As with 'White Rabbit', 'Bloodstained Rabbit' depends on isolating a particular plurality of undetached rabbit parts—the plurality that makes up the whole rabbit shape. But, in Quine's system, this isolating capacity can be tested for inductively. It is reflected in stimulus meaning. The difference in behavior between the two sentences lies purely in the different semantics of 'White' and 'Bloodstained'. I will return to this semantics. For now, it is enough that 'White' requires nearly all parts of a relevant plurality to be white, whereas 'Bloodstained' requires only at least one visible part of the relevant plurality to be bloodstained. The key issue concerns what parts are relevant. Quine's view makes this a testable matter. What he thinks is not testable, given the apparatus introduced so far, is whether the speaker is speaking of undetached rabbit parts or rabbits. There is an ontological difference, even if the undetached parts are those that coincide with the whole rabbit.

Evans's triple compound can be treated similarly. 'F_2F_1G' ('Bloodstained White Rabbit') can be given a semantic explanation only if, as Evans claims, one attributes a capacity to relate 'Bloodstained' and 'White' to the boundaries associated with 'Rabbit'. But I have already indicated how Quine's account allows for and can test for just such a capacity.

In Evans's direct argument against Quine's non-standard scheme, Evans centers on the semantics of 'White'. He thinks that the non-standard scheme must amend the following satisfaction condition for 'White': that 'White' applies to something if and only if that something is white. He believes that dissent to 'White Rabbit' when shown a brown rabbit with a white foot shows that 'Rabbit' could not apply to rabbit parts, if 'White' were given the standard satisfaction condition. But this belief is a consequence of the same mistake that we have been discussing. To understand the dissent, one needs to determine which parts are being responded to in the context. Quine's system enables the semanticist to carry out such determination empirically. The relevant parts are not the foot parts but the plurality of parts that make up the whole rabbit shape. There is no need for emendation of the satisfaction condition for 'White'.

Evans makes two fundamental mistakes in his objections to Quine. One mistake is to think that Quine cannot account for determination of boundaries within stimulus meaning. The other, more important mistake is to think that determining boundaries is determining identity conditions.[27] Relevant spatial boundaries can normally be determined inductively. Such boundaries are fixed by stimulus meaning. What is not fixed is just which of those entities that are associated with the relevant boundaries are being referred to, or predicated. Particular rabbits, particular instances of rabbithood, particular packets of rabbit stuff, particular pluralities of undetached rabbit parts, particular temporal slices of rabbits, can all be associated with the same spatial boundaries. But the ontological commitments of the expressions just listed are different. Quine holds that boundaries are determined by the evidence fixed by stimulus meaning, but that ontological commitments are not fixed. Evans's objections to Quine are rendered ineffectual by his failure to understand this point. Many others have followed Evans in these mistakes.

COMMUNICATION AND EVIDENCE: QUINE'S NOTION OF THE EMPIRICAL

I will briefly discuss Quine's views on communication and evidence before confronting his views on relations between stimulus meaning and reference, and his views on psychology.

Quine takes observation sentences to be associated initially with stimulation of conditioned response. He holds that the sentences' direct association with concurrent stimulation is essential if the child is to acquire them without prior language.[28] Besides the directness of connection to stimulation, he advertises intersubjective agreement, given the same stimulation, as a key feature of observation sentences.[29]

In mid-career Quine noticed a problem for this view. Stimulation is triggering of sensory receptors. No two speakers share nerve-ending receptors. So they cannot literally share stimulus meaning or respond to the same stimulation. Even the idea of similarity in stimulus meanings presupposes homology of receptor nerve endings. For understanding communication, it clearly does not matter whether such homologies obtain.

Quine's last of several responses to this problem was to declare that for purposes of communication, it does not matter that stimulus meaning is not intersubjective. To communicate via observation sentences, it is enough for

---

[27] The conflation is very explicit in Evans, 'Identity and Predication', 36, lines 9 ff.

[28] Quine, *Pursuit of Truth*, 5.

[29] Quine, *Roots of Reference*, 37; *Pursuit of Truth*, 3. In fact, in *Word and Object*, 43, Quine defines degree of observationality in terms of *intersubjective* similarity of stimulus meaning for occasion sentences—sentences that elicit changes between assent and dissent in response to changes of stimulation over short periods of time.

each speaker to match stimulations with an interlocutor's utterances. If fluency of interchange results, that is the best one can do. On this view, stimulus meaning is not shared among speakers.[30]

Quine maintains that we can 'do without' assuming sameness of stimulus meaning or sameness of stimulations in the account of communication. He appeals to each person's 'projecting' his stimulus meaning[31] onto the sentences of another through 'empathy'.[32]

What Quine does not note is that these points amount to admitting that he has no account of communication at all. His notion of stimulus meaning plays no role in explaining what it is to communicate successfully, to get another person's communication right, to translate correctly—even at the most 'determinate' levels. Quine sees empathy as key to learning language and communicating, and calls it 'uncanny'. Indeed. His account does literally nothing to explain why such projections are successful, or even what their success consists in.[33]

Quine invokes epistemological considerations to motivate taking surface stimulations as the basis for his account of stimulus meaning. He cites a primary interest in the 'flow of evidence' and confidence in the role of nerve-ending triggerings as being the starting point of an account of such evidence.[34] The epistemological account that Quine envisages is an explanation in empirical psychology. For, at least according to some of his more colorful pronouncements, he wants to replace epistemology with empirical psychology.[35]

On Quine's view, nerve-ending triggerings are the basic evidence for scientific theory. They begin the 'flow of evidence'. He sees the test for scientific theory as lying in 'prediction of stimulation'.[36] He admits the oddity of the phrase. His idea remains fundamental to his deflationary view of epistemology. Prediction 'is' anticipating certain stimulations that one puts oneself in the way of: 'What we are doing when we amass and use circumstantial evidence is to let ourselves be actuated as sensitively as possible by a chain of stimulations as they reverberate through our theory, from present sensory stimulations, via interanimation of sentences.'[37]

---

[30] For this last position, see Quine, *Pursuit of Truth*, 39–44.

[31] W. V. Quine, 'Epistemology Naturalized', in *Ontological Relativity*; and *Roots of Reference*, 1–4.

[32] See Quine, *Pursuit of Truth*, 42–43.

[33] For further criticism of Quine's and Davidson's approaches to communication, see my 'Comprehension and Interpretation', in Lewis Hahn (ed.), *The Philosophy of Donald Davidson* (Chicago: Open Court Publishers, 1999).

[34] Quine, *Pursuit of Truth*, 41–42.

[35] See Quine, 'Epistemology Naturalized', 75 ff.; *Theories and Things*, 72. I think that empirical psychology cannot replace epistemology. The two enterprises are complementary and interwoven, but their legitimate aims and vocabularies differ. For a sympathetic account of Quine's views on relations between epistemology and psychology that suggests a more nuanced position than Quine's most famous pronouncements, see Richard Foley, 'Quine and Naturalized Epistemology', *Midwest Studies in Philosophy* 19 (1994).

[36] Quine, *Pursuit of Truth*, 1–2.

[37] Quine, *Word and Object*, 18; see also p. 22; *Ontological Relativity*, 75; *Roots of Reference*, 37 ff.

One can certainly describe matters in Quine's way. Nerve endings are stimulated when evidence is acquired. Reference to them is part of the causal story of perception. This way of describing matters, however, fails to connect to the use of evidence in science.

Evidence is something one can refer to, share, check. No scientist appeals to stimulations of his or her nerve endings as evidence, nor would such stimulations be of interest to other scientists who do not know or care whether they have the same patterns of nerve-ending firings. There is no reason to think that confirmation theory will ever take individuals' nerve-ending stimulations as a significant *kind* in understanding the marshaling of evidence. Our notions of evidence, justification, and warrant are not to be understood in such terms. Quine's account of evidence is a scientistic fairy tale.[38]

On Quine's account, each scientist would have his or her own idiosyncratic evidence. No scientist who was not also an anatomist could characterize his or her evidence, and even this characterization would have to rest on evidence other than those nerve-ending firings. The account provides no explanation of why scientists take each other seriously. A consequence of these points is that Quine does not have, in stimulus meaning, an acceptable notion of empirical evidence or content with which to state his indeterminacy theses.[39]

A fault line in Quine's account of evidence is the uneasy relation between the notion of sensory stimulation, which carries no immediate implications regarding the individual's representational point of view, and notions like observation, experience, evidence, assent, and being about the passing scene—which do carry such implications. This fault line is worth examining. It marks failures in Quine's notion of the empirical. The fault line runs through the psychological territory that he sees the child as becoming emancipated from when the child breaks through to objective reference to physical objects. What is the lay of this land?

Quine is aware of the need to connect evidence to a representational perspective. He speaks of the common effective core in a total stimulation of receptors that is similar 'by the subject's lights'. He glosses this phrase in terms of

---

[38] Davidson makes parallel criticisms of Quine, emphasizing lack of connection between sensory causes and justification that evidence provides. See Davidson, 'A Coherence Theory of Truth and Knowledge', 311–312. See also his 'The Very Idea of a Conceptual Scheme', in *Inquiries into Truth and Interpretation* (Oxford: Clarendon Press, 1984). Davidson sees his attack as applying to reliance on any intermediary between objects in the physical world and the subject's belief—not specially on nerve-ending triggerings. In 'Perceptual Entitlement', I criticize Davidson's views. Perceptual states, which are certainly not beliefs, are epistemically relevant and contribute to epistemic warrant.

[39] One might concentrate entirely on the discipline that is supposed to replace epistemology—empirical psychology. Here there is a causal story that goes from environmental entities, perhaps through light or sound, to triggerings of sensory nerve endings (the first causal stage in the individual), to perceptions, to perceptual beliefs, to theory. Something like this causal chain is Quine's guiding picture—except that he skips the perceptions. I discuss weaknesses in Quine's account of perceptual psychology in succeeding sections.

perceptual similarity. Yet he explains perception, like observation, in terms of responses to conditioning.[40]

Perception and observation are, however, not simply responses to nerve-ending triggerings. Perceptual states are, according to common sense and psychology, type-individuated as representational states with veridicality, or accuracy, conditions. They are states whose nature depends on relations to environmental attributes in terms of which their accurate representations are explained. Perception is not perception if it cannot be accurate or mistaken. This fact plays an implicit role in Quine's theory.[41] Yet he provides no clear explication of it.

Stimulus meaning is the range of stimulations that would prompt assent paired with the range of stimulations that would prompt dissent. Stimulus meaning is supposed to be an adequate surrogate for the meaning of observation sentences.[42]

Assent entails commitment to truth. Here the account appears to connect with correctness conditions. Yet the only conditions cited in the account are effects of proximal stimulations on individuals' nerve endings. Quine intends that there be no account of correctness conditions that bear on the physical environment. The view that stimulus meaning accounts for the meaning of observation sentences involves a commitment to welding the meaning of a sentence to assent to the sentence in response to nerve-ending-firings. It is unclear how there is room for error in assent to (the meaning of) the sentences.

Clearly, it is possible for stimulations to prompt assent even though they do not derive from any objects of perception in the environment: the stimulations could be artificial. The official account provides no materials to account for correctness or error in assent. One is disposed to assent or dissent when one is so disposed. Correspondingly, the account provides no correctness conditions for perception, and says nothing to explicate perceptual error.

Had Quine been pressed in these ways, perhaps he would have agreed that assent to one-word sentences is surrogate assent: it need not have correctness conditions. He might also have said that perception has no correctness conditions until it is connected to a language that can individuate such conditions.[43] I think that this view is empirically untenable. I discuss it later.

Quine's account of evidence centers on stimulations of nerve endings. His account fails to explain either linguistic communication or the communicability

---

[40] Quine, *Roots of Reference*, 16–19; *Pursuit of Truth*, 2–4.

[41] Quine allows himself repeatedly to speak of the child's seeing red, portions of the scene, or surfaces of physical objects, even before the child can refer to objects. He takes stimulations as 'presenting', and observation sentences as affirming, conditions in the physical environment. See *Roots of Reference*, 37–38, 56, 81; *Word and Object*, 30–31, 91 ff.; 'Things and their Place in Theories', in *Theories and Things*, 4–5; *Pursuit of Truth*, 23. These are what might be termed 'informal' expository passages, meant to lend color to the official theory. Quine systematically ignores most of what is central in the psychology of perception in very young children and non-human animals.

[42] Quine, *Word and Object*, 42.

[43] See Quine, *Word and Object*, 41–44, 5–8. These passages can be interpreted in other ways. Compare p. 44 with p. 43.

and shareability of evidence. It fails to account for correctness conditions of perception. It fails to explain the relevance of evidence and perception to the physical environment. It fails to account for the empirical content of observation sentences, because it fails to account for correctness conditions that mark either a capacity for error or a relevance to the physical environment. Quine's behaviorist predilections seriously limit his notion of the empirical.

I have belabored these issues in the foundations of Quine's philosophy because they are relevant to evaluating his account of objective reference. I consider this matter next.

BEFORE OBJECTIVE REFERENCE: THE PRE-INDIVIDUATIVE STAGE

Quine proposes a deflationary explication of meaning and reference. In his account of the first stage, however, he does not always confine himself to his official account. One can view these departures as picturesque metaphor. They indicate, I think, an ambivalence in his view of the initial one-word-sentence stage of meaning. Quine gave more scope to such departures over the course of his career.

Quine uses various phrases that suggest more objectification in the initial stage than he officially allows. He writes of the child's learning how much of 'what goes on about him' counts as thus and so.[44] He claims that child and adult see red (where this appears not merely to be a matter of sensory irradiations).[45] The child and the mother view the scene from their 'unlike vantage points'.[46] He writes of the child's finding the proper direction in the scene.[47] He takes up Strawson's phrase in calling the one-word stage a matter of feature placing.[48] He indicates that the truth of a one-word sentence depends on what visible points lie on Fido or on milk and what ones do not: the visible points are in space beyond the child's boundaries.[49] One-word sentences 'herald' the presence of milk, Fido, dog, chair (all entities beyond the individual's surfaces); and stimulations are taken as 'presenting' entities in the physical environment.[50] Quine takes some

[44] Quine, 'Speaking of Objects', 7; in *Quintessence*, 95. Quine warns against taking his remarks to entail objectification of matter or stuff. See the quotation at note 8 above. He does not warn against taking them as indicating objectification of other attributes beyond the child's surfaces. One can just barely hear the phrase 'about him' as referring to the child's boundary, but I do not think that this is the natural construal of the phrase; and I doubt that it is Quine's construal.

[45] Quine, *Roots of Reference*, 37–38.

[46] Quine, 'Things and their Place in Theories', 8.

[47] Ibid. 43.

[48] Quine, *Pursuit of Truth*, 24. Both Quine's examples (breezes, cool air, sunshine) and Strawson's indicate that features are not placed inside individual's surfaces.

[49] Quine, 'Things and their Place in Theories', 4.

[50] Ibid. 5. Elsewhere Quine again writes of stimulations as 'presenting' entities in the physical environment. See *Word and Object*, 30. These locutions can, of course, be deflated to mean that the entities are among the causal sources of the stimulations. However, the language of 'heralding' and 'presenting' (like 'focusing on the scene') enables Quine to trade on the natural sense that the import of these one-word sentences, at the alleged beginning of meaning, goes beyond surface stimulations.

one-word sentences to 'affirm movement'.[51] He refers to the child's instinctive 'sense of externality'[52] and to an instinctive 'body-mindedness' of the child.[53]

I will center on Quine's remarks about truth and truth conditions in these variances from official doctrine. Assent—an element in stimulus meaning—entails, ordinarily speaking, commitment to the truth of what one assents to. Quine clearly takes unstructured observation sentences to be true or false.[54] What are their truth conditions?

Sometimes Quine toes the behaviorist line. He holds that in the first stages of language learning, the child assents only to the presence of the stimulations; and the sentence is made true by such presence.[55] As we have seen, as officially interpreted, it is not clear how such assents could be false.

---

[51] Quine, *Word and Object*, 31.

[52] Quine, 'The Scope and Language of Science', 219: 'The most primitive sense of externality may well be a sense of the mother's reinforcement of likenesses and contrasts in the first phases of word learning. The real is thus felt, first and foremost, as prior to language and external to oneself. It is the stuff that mother vouches for and calls by name.' This early appeal to a sense of externality is again strikingly similar to William James's attribution from birth of an undifferentiated sense of 'the universe' in *Principles of Psychology*, ii, chapter 17. See Chapter 4, note 3, above.

[53] Quine, *Roots of Reference*, 54, 56. Quine places more emphasis on a child's 'sense' of objectification and the child's body-mindedness in *Roots of Reference* than before. By the time he wrote this book, he had read some developmental psychology, especially that of Bower, which he footnotes. See ibid. 54. See T. G. R. Bower, 'The Object in the World of the Infant', *Scientific American* 225/4 (1971), 30–38. Ironically, the experiments that impressed Quine were subsequently called into question, on methodological grounds. The *results* are now by and large substantiated, and greatly enriched, by further experimental work. For discussion of the Bower results and of subsequent criticism and development, see R. Baillargeon, E. S. Spelke, and S. Wasserman, 'Object Permanence in Five-Month-Old Infants', *Cognition* 20 (1985), 191–208; also E. S. Spelke, 'Principles of Object Perception', *Cognitive Science* 14 (1990), 29–56. Quine nods toward the apparent fact that infants perceive material bodies. He makes minimal concessions to appearances, however. While admitting that children are 'body-minded', he interprets the segregation of bodies by allegedly pre-individuative children as compatible with being just a feature of a mass-like orientation. See *Roots of Reference*, 54 ff., 81 ff. In resisting the idea that plurals suffice to evince individuation, Quine takes empirical evidence not to differentiate between the hypothesis that bodies are represented as such and the hypothesis that bodies are grouped as aspects of certain salient types of masses—clumpy ones. Similarly, Quine takes the fact that children perceive objects as having definite, bounded shapes as insufficient to show that they single out bodies as particular objects. He would maintain that the shapes could simply help the child distinguish different types of portions of what goes on. So he continues to believe that young children cannot refer to particular bodies. His basic views about objective reference remain constant through his career.

[54] Quine, 'Things and their Place in Theories', 3–4; *Roots of Reference*, 39; *Word and Object*, p. 44. In *Word and Object* more generally, the translation of observation sentences, including one-word ones, is based on matching affirmative and negative stimulus meanings, which is in effect, for Quine, to match truths with truths and falsehoods with falsehoods. See *Word and Object*, 57, 92.

[55] This view is close to the surface in *Word and Object*, 41–44. There Quine writes, 'the philosophical doctrine of infallibility of observation sentences is sustained under our version. For there is scope for error and dispute only insofar as the connections with experience whereby sentences are appraised are multifarious and indirect . . . there is none insofar as verdicts to a sentence are directly keyed to present stimulation.' He then immediately writes that directness of being keyed to stimulation is a matter of degree. Interpreting this passage is difficult, given his remark that immunity to error, like observationality, comes in degrees. It is not clear that he thinks that either is ever absolute, even at the one-word stage. But it would seem to be (apart from tongue slips), if the stimulus meaning of a one-word observation sentence gave its entire meaning and hence, in effect, entailed its

Frequently Quine runs a different line. He takes one-word sentences to affirm movement. He writes that such sentences as 'Fido!' are true or false depending on 'what visible points are on Fido . . . and what ones are not'.[56] Movement and the visible points on Fido are in the physical environment, not at the individual's sensory nerve endings. The truth of the sentence, as Quine explains it, depends on environmental conditions beyond the individual's surfaces.

Quine's intimations of objectification in one-word sentences are not matched by his official doctrine. As remarked earlier, it is possible for stimulations (say, artificial ones) to prompt assent, even though they do not derive from anything perceived in the distal environment. There is nothing in stimulus meaning to indicate the environmental conditions under which the sentence is true or false. On the account of 'Fido!' quoted in the previous paragraph, the truth of the sentence depends on the arrangement of the distal environment. Yet nothing in stimulus meaning bears on such an arrangement.

Quine's account lacks an explanation of what it is about the sentence that makes possible its being true or false. Stimulus meaning is the only meaning Quine accords to the sentence. Stimulus meaning does not account for truth conditions that Quine himself associates with the sentence. Truth conditions, truth, and falsity become relevant to the account once assent and dissent become relevant. Assent, dissent, truth, and falsity are present, on Quine's own account, even in stimulus meaning.

The point that there is nothing in stimulus meaning that bears *on the arrangement of the distal environment* may seem to be a criticism that applies only to Quine's auxiliary remarks—those suggesting objectification at the one-word stage. Perhaps he could simply withdraw the remarks about the arrangement of the distal environment. Perhaps he would count them a picturesque but misleading anticipation of what is to come in an individual's development. On the official core doctrine, no objectification at the one-word stage needs to be accounted for. There is more to the criticism, however.

truth conditions. In 'Things and their Place in Theories', 3, he characterizes development toward objective reference as 'beginning with the flat conditioning of simple occasion sentences to stimulatory events . . .'. One page later, Quine indicates that the truth conditions of one-word sentences, *presumably at the initial stage*, are not fully accounted for by reflection on meaning explained in terms of 'flat conditioning' of assent to proximal stimulation.

One could remove from Quine's technical, quasi-behaviorist notion of assent any association with truth or falsity. One could take 'assent' to be a relaxed, positive-seeming response. Then it would be doubtful whether Quine is talking about sentences, meaning, or the like at all. It is only by trading on some basic notions clearly relevant to language use ('sentence', 'assent', 'meaning', 'truth condition') that Quine can claim that his deflationary behaviorist account has any relevance to his purported *explananda*. As noted, Quine never suggests doubt that one-word sentences are true or false.

[56] Quine, 'Things and their Place in Theories', 4. See also *Roots of Reference*, 43.

TRUTH CONDITIONS AND STRUCTURE

Assent is an integral part of Quine's notion of stimulus meaning. Stimulus meaning is the only sort of meaning that he attributes to sentences at the first stage. Attribution of assent presupposes attribution of truth or falsity. Quine raises no doubt that the sentences are true or false. If sentences can be true or false, they have truth conditions. Quine's notion of stimulus meaning does not explicitly explain *any* sort of truth condition. There is an incoherence in Quine's account of observation sentences that is analogous to the incoherence in Evans's view of the information content of perception.

Quine counts one-word sentences, in the initial stage of language learning, *unstructured*. I believe that insofar as they have truth conditions, they must have structure. I argue for this conclusion over the next five paragraphs.

Quine's initial one-word sentences are true or false. Hence they have truth conditions. The truth condition of a sentence is an aspect of its meaning.[57] Quine's one-word sentences are occasion sentences. The truth or falsity of occasion sentences depends on (varies with and is explained in terms of) particular elements in a context.[58] So the truth conditions of the initial one-word sentences depend on particular elements—particulars—in contexts.

The truth conditions of occasion sentences, hence initial one-word sentences, also depend on patterns that are repeatable in different contexts. For example, in relying on the counterfactual 'A would assent to sentence G under stimulation S', one presupposes that stimulation type S could be repeated in a context different from one in which it occurs, and then another instantiation of it in another context would (other things being equal) still produce assent.

So the truth conditions, hence one aspect of the meaning of the initial one-word sentences, must include at least two factors. One factor marks the possibility of particularistic contextual instantiation (that marks a particular context or some particular element in a context). The other factor marks the repeatable element that is instantiated. For example, the first element might mark a context in which the individual is caused to assent or dissent, or perhaps the particular

---

[57] The stimulus meanings of one-word sentences do not give truth conditions for the sentences. So, by the first three steps of the argument, just given in the text, an aspect of the meaning of one-word sentences is not given by their stimulus meanings. So either the stimulus meaning of a one-word sentence must be supplemented with another sort of meaning that constitutes its truth conditions, or stimulus meaning must be shown ("implicitly") to entail truth conditions—if all aspects of the meaning of a one-word sentence are to be rendered explicit. Quine could deny that the sentences have truth conditions as an aspect of their meaning. Then his invocation of assent and his explicatory remarks would be illegitimate, along the lines discussed earlier.

[58] This step does not follow from the definition of occasion sentences in Quine, *Word and Object*, 35–36, which concerns only assent and dissent. The step *is* an evident consequence of Quine's views, given that occasion sentences are taken to be true or false. The point of taking assent to vary with context is to allow that truth or falsity varies with context. In 'Things and their Place in Theories', 3, Quine takes one-word sentences to be occasion sentences and explicates them as sentences true on some occasions of utterance and false on others.

firings of nerve endings in that context; the second element might mark the patterns of stimulation in the sentence's affirmative stimulus meaning, patterns that could be repeated, or not, in another context.

These elements are structural because their effects on truth conditions differ. A stimulation pattern can remain the same as the context of stimulation varies.

Since the interplay between these factors must be represented in the truth conditions of Quine's one-word sentences, and since the truth conditions are an aspect of their meaning, one-word sentences must have structure in an aspect of their meaning. Thus 'Rabbit!' has such structure. The particularistic factor could be entirely implicit and dependent on context for its activation—for example, through a gesture or reliance on deliverances of the perceptual system.

I will illustrate the point, more concretely, by reference to the informal remarks by Quine that I criticized in the preceding section. (Note that the argument that one-word sentences must have semantical structure is independent of Quine's remarks.) Quine writes that the truth of the unstructured sentence 'Fido' depends on what visible points are on Fido and what ones are not.[59] This *being on* relation is general and repeatable. So there is an element of generality in the truth conditions. The truth of the sentence, however, also depends on particular elements in the scene at hand—not purely on the general arrangement of the world. Quine discusses visible points and Fido's surface. Visible points are points within causal range of the eyes in the relevant context. They are particulars. Since the truth of a pre-individuative observation sentence depends on particulars in the context, the utterance has a context-dependent element in its truth conditions.[60]

The argument is not deflected by appealing to the operator formulation that we discussed with respect to Strawson's feature placing. For the attachment of a context-dependent operator (like a present-tense operator) to a cross-context expression—yielding something like 'Fidohood now!'—still constitutes a truth-conditional structure.

One might reply that just as the operator structure does not correspond to references to particulars and attribution of attributes that occur in the meta-theoretic explanation of its truth conditions, so a one-word, unstructured sentence need not have a structure that corresponds to a structured meta-theoretic explanation of *its* truth conditions. The claim would be that the structure need be only in the meta-theory, not in the sentence itself.

The fundamental objection to Quine's view that his one-word sentences are unstructured is, however, not a point about meta-theoretic explanations of truth conditions. The fundamental objection is that insofar as one-word sentences are applied to the environment, as Quine clearly assumes they are, the use of the sentences depends on applications of perceptual capacities. Perceptual capacities necessarily and constitutively involve both a capacity to single out particulars specific to a context (the particulars perceived) and a capacity to group those

---

[59] Quine, 'Things and their Place in Theories', 4.

[60] I call this an 'ability particular' element. See my 'Five Theses on *De Re* States and Attitudes'.

particulars under general types (attribute attributes to the particulars)—types that can be discriminated in a variety of contexts. Perception involves a context-dependent element and a general repeatable element. Since the use of one-word sentences ultimately depends on perception, any structure that abstracts from the capacities involved in perception cannot reflect the linguistic and psychological capacities that are fundamental in use of the sentences. So an account that treats the one-word sentences as unstructured cannot be basic. Quine's associating assent and truth with his pre-individuative sentences is incompatible with assigning them only stimulus meaning and denying them structure.

THE PRE-INDIVIDUATIVE STAGE: PROXIMAL STIMULATION AND THE PHYSICAL ENVIRONMENT

Let us return to Quine's views on objectification in language development and language interpretation. A major feature of Quine's account of linguistic meaning is his taking stimulus meaning to be grounded in proximal stimulations, not relations to the distal environment. Quine supported this position throughout his career.[61] All his expositions of the point are terse. Here is one of the fuller ones:

> I remain unswerved in locating stimulation at the neural input, for my interest is epistemological, however naturalized. I am interested in the flow of evidence from the triggering of the senses to the pronouncements of science. My naturalism does allow *me* free reference to nerve endings, rabbits, and other physical objects, but my epistemology permits the subject no such starting point. *His* reification of rabbits and the like is for me part of the plot, not to be passed over as part of the setting.[62]

The terseness of Quine's remarks hinders clear separation of issues. There is certainly a point to psychology's giving proximal stimulation a central place in its account of how perception and empirical thought are formed. The theory of vision accords proximal stimulation an important role. But grounding meaning and reference in proximal stimulation requires much more support than Quine provides.

Excluding physical objects and their properties from the setting within which reference is explained amounts to giving the entities referred to in biological explanations of animal activity no priority in an account of reference. On my view, bias toward environmental macro-entities—notably including bodies—*is* part of the setting.

Given that for Quine meaning resides at the surface of the individual, there is a problem about how the individual moves from proximal meaning to objective reference. Here we unearth a root of Quine's Individual Representationalism.

---

[61] He did so against persistent, long-standing opposition from Donald Davidson.

[62] Quine, *Pursuit of Truth*, 41–42. See also *Word and Object*, 31; *Roots of Reference*, 38.

Quine gives a second reason for centering on nerve-ending firings in a theory of empirical meaning.[63] He claims that one should take stimulation rather than rabbits to prompt assent because stimulation can remain the same while the rabbit is supplanted by a counterfeit, and the rabbit can remain the same while stimulation varies in prompting dissent rather than assent. He concludes that in experimentally equating uses of sentences, it is stimulations 'that must be made to match, not animals'.[64]

The force of these considerations depends on what 'experimental' enterprise is at issue. It is true that proximal stimulation can cause assent or dissent even as distal causes vary. It is true that initial registration of stimulation is the beginning of the causal account in the psychology of perception. These reasons do not, however, even begin to show that an account of the empirical content of sentences should ground itself in representation of proximal conditions.

I have indicated that considerations regarding both the 'flow of evidence' and translation/communication do not support Quine's choice. As regards accounts of empirical content and the roots of linguistic reference, the considerations are equally unpersuasive.

Counterfeit rabbits and rabbit illusions should not be on an equal footing with rabbits in accounting for veridicality conditions of either perception or sentences. The point of a theory of perception is to account for representational success—for perception. Similarly, an account of the meaning of sentences, insofar as assent and dissent play a role in the account, must—even on Quine's view—take the veridical cases to have a certain priority. So perceptual content and the empirical content of sentences should not take illusory and veridical cases as on equal footing.

Conversely, differences in stimulation and differences in angle of perspective are certainly relevant to understanding perceptual content and the empirical content of sentences. But, to enter into an account of reference, these must be associated with distal properties or objects that remain constant across such variations. Such association is necessary to account for perceptual constancies, which I believe are at the heart of the psychology of perception and the roots of

---

[63] Quine, *Pursuit of Truth*, 37–44.

[64] The full rendering of this argument by Quine for focusing on proximal stimulation goes as follows: 'It is important to think of what prompts the native's assent to 'Gavagai?' as stimulations and not rabbits. Stimulation can remain the same though the rabbit be supplanted by a counterfeit. Conversely, stimulation can vary in its power to prompt assent to 'Gavagai' because of variations in angle, lighting, and color contrast, though the rabbit remain the same. In experimentally equating the uses of 'Gavagai' and 'Rabbit' it is stimulations that must be made to match, not animals' (*Word and Object*, 31). Anyone can agree with Quine's two premises. These premises are supposed to support the conclusion that stimulations not animals must be made to match in 'experimentally equating uses' of the two sentences. It is not evident why the premises support the conclusion at all.

Again, perceptual psychology explains the formation of perceptions from proximal stimulations. The fact that perceptual psychology gives proximal stimulations a place in its account of the formation of perceptions (hence representations) does not show that accounts of *shared evidence, shared meaning, or the* first stage of language use *need make any reference to proximal stimulations. Individuals could share evidence, meaning, and objective reference without having comparable nerve endings.*

objective reference. Proximal stimulations in themselves are of little interest to a theory of perception or reference. Nerve-ending firings without environmental relevance are no sort of meaning—perceptual or linguistic.

Strawson postulates a feature-placing stage. Quine hypothesizes a stage of undifferentiated representation of masses, or a stage that lacks divided reference. Neither view is given serious argumentative support.

Strawson's feature placing externalizes the sense data invoked by Russell, Broad, Price, and Ayer. Quine's undivided reference updates William James's idea that representation begins with a sense of the undifferentiated world whole. Evans follows Strawson in taking representations of general types to precede representations of instantiations of the types. In all these cases, a type of representation is postulated that lacks what each author regards as representation of fundamental environmental particulars and their attributes.

The view that I believe is correct, and massively supported by empirical science, is that prior to language, perception in infants and many animals represents particular bodies and other environmental entities as having specific physical attributes. Language builds on prior objective representation. In centering on language, Quine's account of objective reference begins too late.

Quine says little about perception. In the remarks (discussed earlier) that suggest that some objectification occurs at the one-word stage—even if the objectification has not penetrated into the language—he assumes that the child sees the distal environment.[65] Yet he explains perception in terms of responses to conditioning by proximal stimulation.[66] There is no explanation of the 'focus' on the distal environment that Quine associates with perception.

Perception is not just response to nerve-ending triggerings. It can be correct or incorrect. Nothing in Quine's account explains correctness conditions or the distal focus that he takes to be present in early perception. On his official account, childhood would be an experiential muddle. On this account, language can be mapped onto no prior representational ability.

In a passage I quoted earlier, Quine writes:

We in our maturity have come to look upon the child's mother as an integral body who, in an irregular closed orbit, revisits the child from time to time . . . But the mother, red, and water are for the infant all of a type: each is just a history of sporadic encounter, a scattered portion of what goes on.[67]

These are empirical claims. Quine gives no empirical support for them. He gives no reason to believe that the ability to perceptually group bodies by way of attributes of such bodies is posterior to some neutral position, or some feature-placing or mass-attributing ability.

---

[65] Quine, *Roots of Reference*, 37–38, 56; *Word and Object*, 30–31; *Pursuit of Truth*, 23; 'The Scope and Language of Science', 219.

[66] See Quine, *Word and Object*, 6–7; also 'Natural Kinds', in *Ontological Relativity*, 123–128; *Roots of Reference*, 16–19; *Pursuit of Truth*, 2–4.

[67] Quine, 'Speaking of Objects', 7; in *Quintessence*, 95. See also *Word and Object*, 92.

In fact, empirical evidence runs contrary. There is substantial empirical evidence that, for human children, perception as of integrated bodies is prior to perception as of masses, qualitative scatters, and so on. Children segment bodies by their spatial characteristics and by their coherence in motion from as early as the first weeks of life—as soon as vision has adequate powers of resolution. Tracking bodies in motion centers on rigid, closed forms, as distinct from masses. Children find masses and stuffs less salient than bodies. They attribute mass kinds only after they perceive and perceptually group relatively rigid, bounded bodies, moving continuously.[68] Quine's assumption that mass-like or feature-placing representations are either developmentally prior to representation of bodies, or equally likely, is empirically mistaken.

DIVIDED REFERENCE: THE SUPPLEMENTAL LINGUISTIC APPARATUS

I turn from the supposed pre-individuative stage to Quine's account of the development of objective reference. Given that Quine sees the pre-individuative stage as mass-like, or as massively undifferentiated, it is natural for him to regard objective reference as *dividing reference*. Reference must be divided to individuate particulars—especially bodies—of general types.

Quine's view of individuation is rooted in the logical tradition that flows from Frege. Frege required that one have a criterion for determining the identity of an object. He imposed the requirement in his enterprise of reducing numbers to logical objects. He does not discuss it in relation to perceptual belief.[69] Quine applies it quite generally. His slogan 'No entity without identity' extends the Fregean requirement beyond numbers to all entities. Quine takes this slogan to require that an individual be able to represent the general conditions under which objects of any given kind are the same or different, if the individual is to represent an entity of that kind at all.[70]

For Quine, divided reference consists in an ability to individuate objects as being of certain kinds indicated by sortal predicates—predicates like 'apple', 'chair', and 'dog': 'To learn "dog" we have to learn more than presence. We have to learn also the individuative force of the term, the division of reference. We

[68] See Spelke, 'Principles of Object Perception'; N. Soja, S. Carey, and E. Spelke, 'Ontological Categories Guide Young Children's Inductions of Word Meaning', *Cognition* 38 (1991), 179–211; Susan Carey, 'Speaking of Objects, as Such', in G. Harman (ed.), *Conceptions of the Mind: Essays in Honor of George A. Miller* (Hillsdale, NJ: Erlbaum, 1993); Susan Carey, 'Does Learning a Language Require the Child to Reconceptualize the World?', *Lingua* 92 (1994), 143–167; Huntley-Fenner, Carey, and Salimando, 'Objects are Individuals but Stuff Doesn't Count'. The experiments are controlled to address Quinean responses. See Chapter 10.

[69] Frege, *The Foundations of Arithmetic*, section 62. Whether Frege would have imposed his requirement beyond mathematics is not clear. I believe that he thought that it had special importance to a theory of the numbers within his logicist project.

[70] W. V. Quine, 'Speaking of Objects' (1958), in *Ontological Relativity*, 27; and 'On the Individuation of Attributes' (1975) in *Theories and Things*.

have to learn what to count as one dog and what to count as another.'[71] According to Quine, the child must *learn* when there is one dog and when there are two. Only then can it single out an object rather than merely respond to an instance of a feature or portion of the scene. Learning sortals, and learning when there is one dog and when there are two, are said to require acquisition of supplementary linguistic abilities.

Specifically, the ability to individuate is supposed to depend on mastering a linguistic apparatus of plurals, identity, negation, pronouns, and quantifiers (expressions like 'some' and 'every').[72] Sortals are needed to demarcate objects into kinds. Negation, plurals, identity are needed to formulate discrimination of one object from another. Pronouns are needed to link different identifications over time, and for quantification. Quantification is needed to formulate general principles of identity.

In understanding this view, it is helpful to see how Quine applies it. One might think that a child's mastery of plurals would suffice to indicate mastery of individuation of particular bodies. Quine holds that if one has only the child's sensory capacities and its use of plurals to go on, there is insufficient basis to attribute an ability to individuate objects. As we have seen, he believes that it would be gratuitous to attribute individuative ability rather than a tendency to find among masses some sort of 'clumpiness' that calls for what are in fact plural constructions. A clumpy mass would be a scatter of 'portions of the scene', where each portion is in fact a material body. For example, when a child is exposed to apples, and uses the plural form 'apples', the reference might be mass-like. The term might be 'applicable to just so much apple as is taken up in apple heaps'. 'Apples' would be a subcase of 'apple', as 'bright red' is of 'red'.[73] Another way of putting Quine's idea is that in the absence of supplementary linguistic devices, 'apple' could be distinguished from 'pear' as rigatoni is distinguished from macaroni—in terms of shapes of clumps within a larger mass.[74]

One might think that a child's perception of shape might yield representation of bodies. Again, Quine would object that the child might not have learned individuation. Shape might be important for distinguishing dogginess—taken as a smallish mass of dog. Quine thinks that perceptual representation of shape

[71] Quine, *Roots of Reference*, 55.

[72] Quine, *Word and Object*, 93–95; *Ontological Relativity*, 32–33; *Roots of Reference*, 55, 84–101; *Pursuit of Truth*, 23–28.

[73] Quine, 'Speaking of Objects', 8–9; *Word and Object*, 93. As noted, Quine tends to describe representation in the pre-individuative stage in mass-like terms. *Word and Object*, 51 ff; *Roots of Reference*, 54 ff., 81 ff.; *Theories and Things*, 7–8. Sometimes he appeals to Strawson's feature-placing idea. Despite his predilection for mass-like descriptions, Quine's fundamental position is that none of these descriptions is better than any other. Any specific attribution of a scheme of representation or reference is gratuitous: *Roots of Reference*, 82; 'Speaking of Objects', 8–9; *Word and Object*, 93.

[74] This development of the point occurs in Carey, 'Does Learning a Language Require the Child to Reconceptualize the World?'

does not entail an ability to individuate—the ability to represent one dog body as opposed to two. One could treat shape as simply segmentation of the scene.

A complementary position applies to singular expressions for particular bodies. One might think that because the child can perceive Mama as a bounded object, an expression like 'Mama' that consistently links up with this object represents that object. Quine holds that until the individual has an apparatus of individuation that involves quantification, pronouns, sortals, negation, identity, and so on, there is no ground to take 'Mama' to refer to a single object. There is no basis for distinguishing singular terms from general terms. He writes:

'Mama' and 'Fido' are singular terms, though our categorizing them as such is a sophisticated bit of retrospection that bears little relevance to what the learning child is up to. 'Animal', 'dog', 'apple', 'buckle', and 'body' are general terms, retrospectively speaking, and what makes them so is the built-in individuation.

In these examples the objects are bodies. The general terms are true of bodies, and the singular terms 'Mama' and 'Fido' designate bodies, one apiece. Nevertheless, those two singular terms were learned as observation sentences in the same way as other observation sentences, such as 'red' and 'water' and 'it is raining', that do not designate bodies. Recurrence of Mama or Fido was recurrence of a recognizable circumstance, like recurrence of red or rain. Thus the learning of these singular terms had nothing distinctive to do with objective reference. It is rather the learning of the first general terms, as we now call them, that may be said to bring the child a step nearer to our patterns of objective reference, because of the individuation.

Individuation is initially the one feature that distinguishes general from singular: 'dog' from 'Fido'. Their difference of role in predication is not significant at first, because the way of learning the predication 'Fido is a dog' or 'Fido is an animal' is not significantly different from the way of learning 'A dog is an animal' or 'Snow is white'.

'Snow', 'water', 'white', and 'red' can be learned in the simple manner of 'Fido' and 'Mama'. These all start out on a par, with no thought of designation and no premium on bodies. The early individuative terms, on the other hand, are general terms for bodies.[75]

Quine's point is that the distinction between singular and general terms cannot be reasonably attributed to the child until the child 'divides reference'. Since objective reference is supposed to depend on a distinction between singular and general terms in *language*, objective reference to physical objects, or indeed any entities, is supposed to depend on divided reference. As I indicated at the end of the preceding section, empirical evidence weighs against Quine's invocation of this mass-like (or default neutral) pre-individuative stage. It also tells against perception's depending on language for picking out particulars, including bodies.

Quine holds that dividing reference requires learning when, *in general*, there are two bodies rather than one. He assumes that it is gratuitous to attribute a general ability to mark off particular bodies from one another unless the individual can mark them off via an ability to represent generalizations—via linguistically *representing general* conditions under which bodies are individuated and

[75] Quine, *Roots of Reference*, 85.

differentiated. It is not enough to be able to mark the difference between one apple and two in any (appropriate) *given* context. These assumptions constitute a form of Individual Representationalism.

There are two assumptions here. One is that the ability must represent generality, in the sense indicated. The other is that it must be learned. Quine holds that the individual must learn a linguistic apparatus of sortal predicates, negation, plurals, identity, pronouns, and quantifiers.

Quine goes to some lengths to avoid giving the impression that mastering this apparatus requires mastery of symbolic logic. One only needs to be able to distinguish an object of a given sort from a different contemporaneous object, to treat an object as a focal point of different properties, to track it and differentiate it from others over time, including when observation of it lapses, and to understand or know general principles governing these abilities. Quine claims that all of these abilities and the corresponding general principles must be expressible in the individual's language if the individual is to engage in objective reference.

The philosophical and empirical issues center on whether relevant abilities must be at the intellectual level that Quine requires, and whether they must be learned.

QUANTIFICATION

The most distinctive aspect of Quine's account of the emergence from a supposed pre-individuative stage is his insistence on a role for an ability to express quantification in language. Quantification is the genus of operations that invoke number—some, all, every, any, there is, most, few, several, and so on.

An obvious question about Quine's insistence on a role for quantification in explanation of reference is whether singular terms (or their counterparts in perception or thought) could suffice without quantification. The question is pressing with respect to demonstrative-marked terms. Quine holds that quantification is needed to formulate general principles of identity and individuation. Requirement that the individual represent general conditions of individuation is the hallmark of second-family Individual Representationalism. Quine's version of the view is especially pure.

Quine initially invoked quantifiers in a project to regiment the language of science. He argued that quantification is needed because some theories invoke unnamed objects. In some cases, theoretically postulated objects are not nameable, because there are non-denumerably many of them.[76]

---

[76] Quine, 'On What There Is'; *Philosophy of Logic* (Englewood Cliffs, NJ: Prentice Hall, 1970), 14–16; 'Existence and Quantification' in *Ontological Relativity*, 95. See also 'The Scope and Language of Science'. Quine's method of elimination of singular terms assumes that science uses only context-independent predicates, involving no demonstrative or indexical elements. The method

Quine maintained that singular terms can be eliminated from the language of science. His method of elimination assumes that science uses only context-independent predicates, containing no demonstrative or indexical elements. The method purports to capture uniqueness of application in Russell's manner, using quantifiers, identity, and logical connectives.

Kripke and Donnellan showed that individuals refer to objects even though they lack context-free predicates that are uniquely true of the object. This point suggests that Quine's method cannot apply in an entirely general, context-free manner. His method requires that scientists can describe all particulars that are referred to in science in context-free ways. Such descriptions are supposed to differentiate particulars in context-free ways—say, in terms of their spatio-temporal coordinates. It is doubtful that this condition can be met even in physics.

Formulations of science in which singular terms are eliminated presuppose a framework, for example, a spatio-temporal framework, whose coordinates must be established by demonstrative or indexical means. Such demonstratives and indexicals cannot be eliminated in terms of quantifiers and predicates free of demonstrative elements.[77]

Quine's arguments that science needs quantification and can eliminate singular expressions are, in any case, irrelevant to determining whether quantification is necessary to objective reference.[78] Science builds on abilities that are already in place. Some of these abilities do not need to carry out the tasks in science that Quine argues quantification is needed for. Children do not need to represent non-denumerably many numbers or spatial points in order to count or to represent spatial relations.[79]

In a brilliant article, Strawson argues that singular terms *must* be part of the initial stages of learning a language that contains general predicates that apply to empirically apprehended particulars. He argues that to learn predicates of particulars, one must learn them by 'direct confrontation'. One must connect them to experiences. Experience is of particulars and is expressible only through

---

depends on capturing the singularity of singular terms in Russell's manner—eliminating singular terms in favor of quantifiers, identity, and logical connectives. Kripke and Donnellan showed that individuals can refer to objects even though the individuals lack non-demonstrative predicates that are uniquely applicable to the objects. See Kripke, *Naming and Necessity*; Donnellan, 'Proper Names and Identifying Descriptions'. So the elimination is not always possible. Even canonical formulations of science in which singular terms are eliminated presuppose a framework—for example, a spatial framework—whose coordinates must be established ultimately by demonstrative or indexical means.

[77] Strawson articulates the point. *Individuals*, chapter 1. See note 76.

[78] Yet Quine occasionally appeals to them, even in the context of discussing conditions for objective reference in child development. See *Pursuit of Truth*, 27–28.

[79] Sometimes Quine appears to regard quantification as implicit in a child's use of relative pronouns. See, for example, *Pursuit of Truth*, 27. The idea is that once a child has general terms and relative pronouns, it is referentially committed to those values of the relative pronouns that the general terms must be true of if the child's beliefs or assents are to be true. But this view does not suffice to show the presence of quantification. If the antecedents of such pronouns are singular terms, quantification is not needed. Demonstrative singular reference seems to precede quantification.

demonstrative identification of particulars. Demonstrative identification of particulars is the hallmark of singular reference.[80]

What interests me here is Strawson's appeal to context-dependent singular identification. The core of the argument, in my view, is the appeal to singular context-dependent identification as guided by particular perceptual experiences. Mastering predications or attributions to particulars presupposes such an ability, regardless of whether the ability is expressed in language.

Even if singular reference is necessary to objective reference, might not quantification also be necessary? Quine argues that the individuative apparatus must include quantification. He discusses simple sentences like 'Fido is a dog'. He holds that prior to quantification, such sentences remain at a pre-individuative stage, approximating a response to a clump within a scattered mass of dogginess. Quine maintains that more is needed for objective reference:

> Even at this stage, however, the referential apparatus and its ontology are vague. Individuation goes dim over any appreciable time interval. Thus consider the term 'dog'. We would recognize any particular dog in his recurrences if we noticed some distinctive trait in him; a dumb animal would do the same. We recognize Fido in his recurrences in learning the occasion sentence 'Fido', just as we recognize further milk and sugar in learning 'Milk' and 'Sugar'. Even in the absence of distinctive traits we will correctly concatenate momentary canine manifestations as stages of the same dog as long as we keep watching. After any considerable lapse of observation, however, the question of identity of unspecified dogs simply does not arise—not at the rudimentary stage of language learning. It scarcely makes sense until we are in a position to say such things as that in general if *any* dog undergoes such and such then in due course that *same* dog will behave thus and so. This sort of general talk about long-term causation becomes possible only with the advent of quantification or its equivalent, the relative clause in plural predication. Such is the dependence of individuation, in the time dimension, upon relative clauses; and it is only with full individuation that reference comes fully into its own.

> With the relative clause at hand, objective reference is indeed full blown. In the relative clause the channel of reference is the relative pronoun 'that' or 'which', together with its recurrences in the guise of 'it', 'he', 'her', and so on. Regimented in symbolic logic, these pronouns give way to bound variables of quantification. The variables range, as we say,

---

[80] Strawson, 'Singular Terms, Ontology and Identity', especially p. 446. Strawson further held that no meaning can be attached to the idea that predicates of particulars are learned as predicates of demonstratively identified particulars unless the language contains singular expressions used for making demonstratively identifying references to particulars. Strawson allows that a regimented language of science might eliminate singular terms. He maintains that any such language must depend upon another language that contains demonstrative singular terms from which the scientific language was learned.

I think that Strawson does not show that any language that contains general predicates that apply to particulars must presuppose a *language* that contains singular demonstratives. Certainly, the identifications to which Strawson appeals need not be via *expressions* in a language. Perhaps if the notion expression is given a liberal enough interpretation, Strawson's view can be sustained. Strawson's basic idea here seems to me to be deep and right.

over all objects; they admit all objects as values. To assume objects of some sort is to reckon objects of that sort among the values of our variables.[81]

I lay aside the comparison between learning 'Fido' and learning 'Milk' as occasion sentences. I concentrate on the argument for the necessity of quantification in making reference to (or 'assuming') objects of some sort.

The argument features the individuative role of tracking objects. I assume that some tracking ability is necessary for objective representation of, and as of, bodies. Let us even assume, for now, that tracking through 'lapses of observation' is necessary. The key transition in the argument occurs in these sentences:

After any considerable lapse of observation, however, the question of identity of unspecified dogs simply does not arise—not at the rudimentary stage of language learning. It scarcely makes sense until we are in a position to say such things as that in general if *any* dog undergoes such and such then in due course that *same* dog will behave thus and so.

Quine assumes that the argument from default neutrality establishes a need for linguistic individuative apparatus. He argues that the tracking necessary for objective reference to bodies must apply after lapses of observation and for unspecified dogs. The question of identity of an object tracked through time is supposed to make sense only when the *individual* can *generalize* about the behavior of dogs. The generalizations must not be schematic or substitutional (notions I will discuss directly). They must be *quantificational*. And they must determine identity, individuation, or reidentification. Such generalizations are to be applicable by the individual independently of any particular tracking context.[82]

In other words, Quine assumes that unless the individual can generalize through quantification over 'unspecified' objects of relevant sorts, there is no sense to the question of identity over 'considerable lapses' in observation. That is, there is no sense to attributing to the individual a capacity to track identity over time, where the capacity can be accurate or inaccurate in particular trackings.

This step simply begs the question as to whether quantification is necessary for objective reference to (or as of) bodies. It is not self-evident that to engage in such reference, or even in tracking through lapses of observation, that an individual must be capable of such generalization. A dog returns to its buried bone. Why must it be able to think generalizations about bone behavior if it is to perceive and remember a particular bone? The dog's actions must be explainable by general

---

[81] Quine, *Theories and Things*, 7–8. Even in this passage (pp. 5–8), Quine seems flexible about the role of quantifiers in objective reference. Sometimes he seems merely to regard quantification as epitomizing objective reference. Since he thinks that objective reference is indeterminate, the issue of the conditions on such reference has a certain insubstantiality for him. He might be seen as simply counting quantification an important attribute of objective reference but as shrugging his shoulders over whether it is necessary to objective reference. By contrast, he usually seems to count quantification a necessary element in any objective reference. I expound Quine's view in this latter way.

[82] For other passages that state or presuppose such a requirement, see Quine, *Word and Object*, 93, 115 ff.; *Roots of Reference*, 82; *Pursuit of Truth*, 24–25.

principles, or under general routines. But why must it be able to *represent* the generalizations?

Quine's appeal to 'unspecified dogs' is a holdover from his view that in science quantification is forced only in cases where one lacks singular representations for entities that one wants to theorize about. There is a more ordinary point to the idea that to be able to refer to particulars as being of a kind, an individual should be able to represent other entities of the kind. An ability to make objective reference to entities of a kind must be a repeatable, general ability. The ability to attribute the kind must apply to instances of the kind. But it need not be tied to any specific instances. So at any given time, the individual must be able to attribute the kind to instances that are not singled out at that time. These points are consequences of having a 'general', that is, repeatable *ability* to attribute a kind.[83] Quantification might seem to correspond to the generality involved in this ability to attribute the kind in various contexts.

The appearance is deceptive. Ability to attribute a kind in various contexts does not entail or require ability to generalize quantificationally over entities of the relevant kind. It does not follow from having an ability to attribute a kind to an entity (whether in thought or in perception) that one is able to make the attribution without singling out the entity *in the attribution*. The individual need not be able to represent generalization. It need not be able to quantify over anything. Quine provides no argument here that to be able to represent unspecified dogs by having an attributive dog, one must be able to attribute the kind *dog* without singling one out. He begs the question.

General, repeatable representational abilities are necessary for any representation or reference. Such abilities do not entail ability to think general principles that bear on reidentification—to be able to settle questions of identity and reidentification in the abstract. They do not even require an ability to generalize, either quantificationally or schematically. I see no reason to believe that reidentification over lapses in observation makes sense only when conjoined with quantification or schematization over 'unspecified' objects. The key to all these points is to distinguish a general ability from an ability to represent generality. An ability to engage in objective reference or representation must involve general abilities and be explainable in terms of general principles. It need not involve an ability to represent or think generalizations.

A more specific line of reasoning probably figured in Quine's thinking that in the special case of representing something as a body, one must be able to engage in quantification—a capacity to represent generality. This line centers on constitutive conditions that are special to attributing the kind *body*.

A certain empiricist conception of sensory representation, including perception, maintains that what is truly perceived is limited to what can be immediately and fully apprehended in the moment of sensory representation. Thus a genuinely

---

[83] Equivalently, the points are a consequence of what it is to represent something (whether in perception or in thought) as being of a kind.

sensory representation could incorporate look, feel, sound, taste, but not anything further. This conception often insisted that the supposed immediate apprehension was infallible. Infallibility and immediacy were important in traditional empiricist responses to scepticism. They played a large role in sense-data theories discussed in Chapter 4.

Representation of body cannot be regarded as perceptual according to this traditional conception. In the intended, narrow sense of 'fully', one cannot fully apprehend a whole body. One cannot immediately apprehend a body's backside. Indeed, on this conception, one cannot immediately apprehend whether it has a backside. Bodies are distinguished from events and momentary instantiations of features in persisting through time. It is natural to assume that some tracking requirement that corresponds to this persistence is a constitutive condition on representation as of bodies. The traditional empiricist conception of sensory representation, including perception, holds that one cannot fully apprehend a body because one cannot perceive its past or future, or all its parts. Given the requirement of "full" apprehension, the tradition concluded that no representation of, or as of, body can be sensory or perceptual. Representation of body must enter at a higher level. Such a level might be conceptual, linguistic, or some other sort of representation that is not confined to a sensory or perceptual modality.

This empiricist conception of sensory representation yielded a further reason why any representation of, or as of, body cannot be perceptual. The idea is that a representation as of body must involve some correlation between touch, sight, and motor capacities. Touch in itself is supposed to be insufficient, because it cannot distinguish between one's sensations and what is sensed. Vision is supposed to be insufficient, because it cannot take in solidity, backsides, past, or future. Representation as of a body has to involve integration of visual representation of figure with representation of solidity and backsides through a touch system. It was assumed that any such integration must be intermodal, hence not a matter of immediate apprehension—of a "look", "feel", or the like. Representation as of body must also integrate with memory and anticipation. Of course, empiricists added that any such intermodal correlations must be learned. So representation of, and as of, body is supposed to be possible only at a higher level than the level of sensory-perceptual modalities.

As I will explain later, I believe that nearly every claim in this empiricist conception is mistaken. I first indicate how aspects of this conception might have affected Quine's reasoning about representation of body. Of course, Quine had no interest in infallibility or in maintaining foundational conceptions of experience. He would not have agreed with some of the claims just outlined. But I believe that this tradition influenced his thinking.

As the displayed quotations in recent pages illustrate, in introducing the need for a representational apparatus of individuation and reidentification, Quine consistently appeals to the difference between the sensory effect of 'momentary' 'manifestations' and the representation of body that must take single bodies to endure beyond the moment. He thinks of the effect of sensory experience as a history of 'sporadic encounter'.[84] Only what can be imprinted in relatively brief encounters can be in the meaning or content of sensory experience. Given this assumption, it is natural to conclude, as Quine does, that nothing in perceptual representation can be relevant to whether an entity is the same or different over time.

Quine does allow that 'as long as we keep watching', we concatenate the individual representations as representations of something that is the same.[85] But, as soon as something goes out of view, no approximation to identification over time can, on his view, be maintained. So, to track bodies over time, one needs some supplementary apparatus in one's representational repertoire. The supplemental apparatus must, on the empiricist conception, be non-sensory and non-perceptual. Quine claims that the relevant supplementary apparatus must include generalizations that constitute principles or criteria for reidentification. He claims that such generalizations are available only through language.[86]

What is wrong with the empiricist conception just sketched? The mistakes begin with the initial assumption about what can be a *perceptual* representation. The assumption is that the perceptual is limited to what can be immediately and fully apprehended in the moment of sensory representation. What is it to be immediately and fully apprehended in the moment? The assumption is never clearly articulated. Its meaning emerges in what it excludes. It excludes representation of, and as of, body. Whether a body has a backside cannot, on this conception, be apprehended in the moment. Similarly, for functional representations—mate, food, in most cases even danger.

These ideas trade on blurring a distinction between different notions of immediacy and full apprehension. In an ordinary sense, one can immediately and fully apprehend something as a body or something as food. It is not evident that it takes extra time, beyond the moment of viewing, to see a body, or to see something as a body. It is true that we do not see a body's backside. But a requirement on seeing a body that one see its backside is not plausible. It would seem that we can see a body and see it *as having* a backside (or as a full three-dimensional body), even in a moment. It cannot be a requirement on seeing a body as a body that one see it existing over times longer than it takes to form a perception. It is hardly evident that one cannot see a body as a body—without supplementing vision with language or other representational apparatus.

---

[84] Quine, *Word and Object*, 92.
[85] See Quine, *Theories and Things*, 7–8. He allows a pre-individuative subject a capacity to concatenate momentary impressions of dogginess as indications of 'the same dog'. I think that his doctrine is not compatible with taking this allowance to be literal. The allowance is part of Quine's proclivity toward picturesque departures from official doctrine. Or perhaps Quine allows such talk because he believes that representation at this stage is a bleary approximation to genuine representation—'one of degree'. See note 81.
[86] I know of no passages in which Quine appeals to the empiricist view that representation of bodies must be intermodal, hence not sensory or perceptual.

The empiricist idea rests on a special, extreme conception of immediate and full apprehension. Underlying the initial empiricist assumption about what can count as a primitive perceptual representation is the idea that perceptual *meaning* or *content* is entirely dependent on what is contained in the momentary registration of stimulus. This view is not evident or even plausible. As we shall see in Chapters 9 and 10, it is contradicted by science. One sees a body and sees it as a body in the time needed to form a perception.

Perceptual content depends on ability. Such ability—hence content—depends on patterns of interactions with the environment that go beyond what is determined in any given, momentary stimulus registration. The ability involves patterns of application and dispositions, governed by formation principles, that project beyond what is available in the registration of stimuli in a moment. Even the look of a thing, in the sense of 'look' relevant to the representational content of perceptual primitives, depends on abilities that use cues in the registration of stimulus to project, fallibly, beyond that registration. Perceptual content is not fully determined by what is contained in a momentary stimulus.

The idea that meaning and content depend on patterns of use and on capacities to use short-term registration of stimulation as a basis for projecting beyond what is fully determined in the registration is a staple of late-twentieth-century philosophical thinking *as applied to thought and language*. A parallel idea applies to perception.

I think that in Quine's thought the initial empiricist assumption about what can be a perceptual primitive combines with the characteristic second-family intellectualist orientation to yield the view that perception needs supplementation by language or thought to yield representation of body. But the initial empiricist assumption is unargued and mistaken.

Of course, the initial empiricist assumption is even more restrictive than I have advertised it as being. The content of a visual representation of, and as of, a shape cannot depend purely on what is contained in a momentary registration ('apprehension') of stimulus. Perceiving something as a square surface from an angle that is not straight on requires abilities to allow for angle. These abilities are governed by perceptual formation principles that connect momentary stimulus registration with patterns of application and dispositions that carry beyond the moment. Similar points apply to nearly every environmental attribute that is attributed in perception.

One cannot infer from the fact that a representation's content requires a capacity to project beyond what is fully determined in registration of a stimulation, taken strictly by itself, that the representation is non-perceptual. Perception *always* requires such a capacity. The empiricist assumption offers an impossible conception of perception. It then invites one to supplement perception, thus conceived, with non-perceptual, higher-order representation.

This way of thinking is a residue of requirements of foundational completeness and infallibility that are central to the sense-data tradition. When one gives up the assumption that sensory experience provides complete and infallible apprehension of what is sensed or perceived, as Quine and nearly all philosophers after the mid-twentieth century do, there remains no clear motivation for the restrictions implicit in the initial empiricist assumption about perceptual representation. The conception of sensory experience as complete (no missing of backsides!) and infallible (no illusions!) motivates the view that not only bodies but all instances of physical environmental attributes cannot be represented in sensory experience, including perception. But, short of these extreme assumptions, the use of a notion of "complete" apprehension to rule out bodies, or other denizens of the physical environment, as possible objects of primitive perceptual representation seems unmotivated.

Quine never spells out his motivations. I do not know whether he clarified for himself exactly what he was assuming about perception, and exactly why representation of bodies requires supplementary, non-perceptual criteria, comprised in quantified, general representation. In any case, the cursory justifications that he gives do not stand up to scrutiny, philosophical or scientific.

Once the empiricist assumption is scrutinized, the claim that to represent bodies, one needs a capacity to think criteria or principles of individuation and of reidentification over time loses its superficial plausibility. Let us start not with endurance over time, but with backsides. In visual perception, one normally cannot see backsides. (Mirrors allow exceptions.) Normally, one receives no visual stimulation from an object's backside. Still, part of the perception of a body as a body is a projection from cues in a stimulus to a visual representation as of three-dimensionality. The content of the perception depends on formation laws or law-like patterns that make such a projection. The individual is disposed to anticipate certain further would-be visual stimulations that depend on the three-dimensionality of a body. For example, under appropriate stimulus conditions an animal or child shows surprise if certain visual stimulations are followed by further ones that indicate a two-dimensional surface instead of a three-dimensional solid. The dispositions associated with such surprise are constitutive concomitants of the capacities governed by formation principles regarding visually perceiving something as a body. The formation principles need not be representable by the individual. They simply describe and explain the laws that operate in forming perceptual representational states.

Similar points apply to representation of bodies as entities that commonly endure in time.

Bodies are distinguished from events and momentary instantiations of features in persisting, and maintaining generic structure, through time. Because events as well as bodies figure in an animal's basic biological needs and activities, representation as of bodies constitutively requires some capacity to track bodies over time. The tracking requirement applies to perception, perceptual anticipation, and perceptual memory. It does not motivate requiring non-perceptual types of representation (beyond capacities for perceptual anticipation and memory) as a constitutive condition on representation as of body.

For example, a constitutive condition on visual representation as of body is that the representation be associated with visual perceptual anticipation (relative to memory preservation of recent perception) of certain sorts of continuation. If a child or animal sees a body as such, and the body suddenly disappears, the child or animal will be surprised. If a child or animal sees a body as such, and then is blocked from view by the insertion of an occluder, the child or animal will be surprised if the body is not there when the occluder is removed. Similarly, a 2-month-old child is surprised if a body that passes behind a barrier does not emerge from behind the barrier on the path and at the velocity that it exhibited when it passed behind the barrier. Particular types of retinal-level shrinkage and expansion (caused by the body's passing behind the barrier and then re-emerging) are necessary to produce the surprise reaction. Similarly, a child is surprised if first one body is hidden by a screen and then, when the screen is removed, two bodies are there.[87]

The capacities associated with such types of surprise are constitutive concomitants of the capacities governed by formation principles—principles that describe and explain visually perceiving as of body. Both the principles and the capacities can be perceptual (assuming that they include a role for perceptual anticipation and perceptual memory). The capacities need not involve use of representations in propositional thought or language. They need not include a capacity to *represent* generalizations, as long as the formation of the perceptions, perceptual memories, and perceptual anticipations are governed by appropriate general formation principles.

Thus Quine's easy inference from a tracking requirement on representation as of body to the conclusion that representation as of body requires a linguistic (or any other) capacity for quantified generalization appears ungrounded. Perception's meeting a tracking requirement on representation as of bodies does not require a capacity to conceptualize principles or criteria for reidentification. All perception constitutively requires resources for perceptual anticipation and memory. Such capacities are realized in animals that lack language and, to all appearances, propositional attitudes.

As I indicated (note 86), Quine does not appeal to the traditional empiricist idea that representation as of body is necessarily intermodal. But this idea is worth discussing for its own sake.[88] The intermodal integration of visual, tactile,

---

[87] P. Kellman and E. S. Spelke, 'Perception of Partly Occluded Objects in Infancy', *Cognitive Psychology* 15 (1983), 483–524; E. S. Spelke, R. Kestenbaum, D. J. Simons, and D. Wein, 'Spatio-Temporal Continuity, Smoothness of Motion and Object Identity in Infancy', *British Journal of Developmental Psychology* 13 (1995), 113–142; A. Aguiar and R. Baillargeon, '2.5-Month-Old Infants' Reasoning about When Objects Should and Should Not Be Occluded', *Cognitive Psychology* 39 (1999), 116–157; A. Aguiar and R. Baillargeon, 'Development in Young Infants' Reasoning about Occluded Objects', *Cognitive Psychology* 45 (2002), 267–336; Karen Wynn, 'Addition and Subtraction by Human Infants', *Nature* 358 (1992), 749–750.

[88] Empirical evidence suggests that *at least some* integration of visual, tactile, and proprioceptive capacities is not learned. It is part of a natural maturation process, realized early in a child or animal's development. A. N. Meltzoff and M. K. Moore, 'Imitation of Facial and Manual Gestures by Human

proprioceptive, and actional representational capacities in animals and infants, even assuming (plausibly) that they are integrated with respect to body representation, does not settle the question. The question is whether there is something *constitutive* of body representation that requires that *it* be intermodal, hence not strictly perceptual. As I use the terms, being intermodal does not require being conceptual (being a component in propositional structure), much less being linguistic. So the issue does not bear directly on second-family Individual Representationalism or on Quine's specific views. Still, I think it important that representation as of body need *not* be purely intermodal, even if it is always associated with further intermodal representations as of body. A representation as of body can be, say, visual-perceptual.

Perceptual representation is, I think, always in fact associated not only with perceptual memory but with actional representation. But, of course, it does not follow that perceptual representation is itself memorial, intermodal, or actional.

Visual representation as of body may always be associated with touch or proprioceptive representations through intermodal representations as of body. Again it does not follow that visual representation cannot itself be body representation. In fact, modality-specific perceptions as of body are common.

What is constitutively necessary for such representation is that the law-like patterns privilege states that specify attributes that are specific to bodies, among biologically relevant candidates for representation. And, of course, formation patterns must yield genuine perceptual representation.

Thus a visual perception as of a body is commonly associated with anticipation of a touch representation as of solidity. But there is evidence of *visual* anticipation of solidity. Infants are surprised when objects that they are exposed to seem to pass through one another.[89] The visual perception as of solidity does not constitutively require intermodal association.[90]

Neonates', *Science* 198 (1977), 75–78; A. N. Meltzoff and R.W. Borton, 'Intermodal Matching by Human Neonates', *Nature* 282 (1979), 403–404; M. Myowa-Yamakoshi, M. Tomonaga, M. Tanaka, and T. Matsuzawa, 'Imitation in Neonatal Chimpanzees (*Pan troglodytes*)', *Developmental Science* 7 (2004), 437–442.

[89] Baillargeon, Spelke, and Wasserman, 'Object Permanence in Five-Month-Old Infants'. In Chapter 10, the section PERCEPTION AND BODY, I propose that representation as of solidity (visual or otherwise) is not *constitutively* necessary for representation as of body, though the two are almost always linked. The example is meant just as illustration.

[90] For an excellent critical discussion of Quine and the empiricist conception of perception that is broadly congenial with mine, see Susan Carey, *The Origin of Concepts* (Oxford: Oxford University Press, 2009), chapters 2 and 3. Carey highlights an *intermodal*, inferentially rich representation as of body that is non-linguistic and non-propositional, but not specifically perceptual. Thus she emphasizes that at a certain level of intermodal psychological organization—below the propositional and above the perceptual—body representations play a significant role in human and animal cognition. I certainly agree. However, she frequently states that object representations are non-perceptual—seeming to generalize over all object representations (pp. 33–36, 40–46, 60, 63, 94, 115; there is some apparent inconsistency on this matter, see p. 72). In this and subsequent chapters, I will take object (or body) representations to be perceptual, allowing that there are also higher-level object (or body) representations that are non-perceptual. In fact, in Chapter 10, the section PERCEPTION AND BODY, the subsection BODY REPRESENTATION AS ORIGINATING IN PERCEPTION, I argue specifically against the explicit

I have focused on showing that perceptual representation as of bodies does not constitutively require a capacity to represent quantified principles of individuation or re-identification. There is empirical reason to think that children develop production and comprehension of quantifiers only after they have mastered sortals, only after they have mastered the distinction between count nouns and mass terms, and only after they have mastered reidentification of objects under sortal classifications. Mastery of sortals, mastery of the mass-count distinction, and mastery of reidentification under count sortals occur near the end of the first year of life. Perceptual representation as of bodies in human children occurs much earlier. Pronouns are among the earliest words. They cross-reference singular expressions long before they serve as bound variables for quantifiers on sortals.[91] The ability to generalize quantificationally appears to be a separate

---

view of Carey's colleague, Elizabeth Spelke, that all body representations are post-perceptual. Carey's writing that object representations are non-perceptual may amount to no more than imprecise writing (meaning only that the object representations that she focuses upon are post-perceptual representations). But I think that the writing is at best misleading. She argues that 'representations of object cannot be stated in the vocabulary of perception' (p. 63; compare also p. 97). It is clear that Carey is mainly focused on intermodal, inferentially rich object representations, which are indeed not strictly perceptual. But her formulation is entirely general, seemingly applied to all representations as of objects.

It is clear that Carey is focused on the correct point that representations as of objects are not reducible to representations as of *spatial and temporal properties and relations* (pp. 60, 94, 97, 103, 115, 171, 195). In fact, she sometimes explicitly takes such non-reducibility to be a *sense* of "non-perceptual" (pp. 115, 171, 195). But there is no such *sense* of "non-perceptual". Perceptual primitives are in no sense *defined* as spatio-temporal primitives. Perceptual primitives certainly include color primitives, which are also not reducible to spatio-temporal primitives. It is a substantive question whether perceptual primitives include object or body representations, even *given* that such representations are not reducible to primitives that are as of spatio-temporal properties and relations. I believe that that substantive question has been settled affirmatively. Body representations are outputs of modality-specific (for example, visual) perceptual systems. The facts that body representations are attributed when objects are out of view and that they are not reducible to spatio-temporal primitives do *not* show that such body representations are never perceptual representations. I discuss this matter further in Chapter 10, the subsection cited just above. In conversation, Carey indicated that she does think that there are primitive, modality-specific perceptual representations as of body. So perhaps the passages that I have cited are simply misleading.

It is worth noting that it is also incorrect to characterize *perceptual* representations as those that are the outputs of modular processes—as some interpretation of Jerry Fodor's admirable *Modularity of Mind* have suggested. Carey herself departs from this characterization, but sometimes politely treats her difference with it as merely terminological. See, for example, *The Origin of Concepts*, 94. To the contrary, whether the characterization is correct is a substantive issue. It is clearly incorrect. There are modular processes that are not perceptual. Syntactic processing and the formation of the intermodal, core-cognition representations that Carey centers upon are examples. Incidentally, accessibility to consciousness certainly does not prevent representational *states* from being perceptions. It is the processing within modular perceptual systems that is thus inaccessible, not necessarily the products of the processing.

[91] Carey, 'Does Learning a Language Require the Child to Reconceptualize the World?', 143–167; P. Bloom, 'Syntactic Distinctions', *Child Language* 17 (1990), 343–355; Soja, Carey, and Spelke, 'Ontological Categories Guide Young Children's Inductions of Word Meaning'. Carey, in particular, is sensitive to Quinean reinterpretations of the data. In one respect, I think that she concedes more to Quine's alternatives than is warranted. She thinks that the fact that infants perceive by categorizing with bounded shapes 'does not bear on' Quine's thesis. She takes the rigatoni–macaroni reply (above) to require that one produce further evidence. I believe that this mass-type reply is much weaker than

and later stage in the development of language. I believe that there is no reason for Quine's insistence on mastery of quantificational generalization as a necessary condition for objective reference to bodies as such. There is empirical reason to think that it is not necessary.

Objective reference to bodies as such occurs in perception among neonate children and a variety of animals, to be discussed later. It is taken up into language-learning from perception. It is constitutively independent of, and developmentally prior to, quantification.

FURTHER ELEMENTS IN QUINE'S INDIVIDUATIVE APPARATUS

Besides quantification, Quine requires, as a condition on objective reference, a linguistic mastery of sortals (roughly, nouns that take plural form), negation, identity, and relative pronouns. Quine holds that objective reference occurs only with acquisition of an ability to distinguish bodies through sortals.[92] Sortals differentiate bodies from qualities and masses. Negation and identity formulate discrimination of one object from another. In addition to their role in quantification, relative pronouns link different identifications over time. The key item in this list is sortal predication.[93] Quine invokes the other abilities because he regards them as necessary for the individuative capacities that he thinks are necessary for using sortal predicates.

It is true that to refer to bodies (and to bodies as bodies), an individual must be able to single out bodies. Quine assumes that an individual must be able to articulate these abilities. He thinks that the individual must be able to represent, think, or be capable of formulating general principles for distinguishing one object of a given kind from another, and hence one object from two. This is why he insists that an individual be able to represent identity and negation. The individual must be able to represent identity, not merely to pick out a particular. The individual must be able to represent differentiation—through negation of identity—not merely represent different objects in given contexts. The individual must have criteria for reidentification and be able to think principles for reidentifying or differentiating objects of a given sort over time.

she suggests. Infants can be shown to have perceptions as of solid bodies, as distinct from masses. If bodies are already distinguished in perception—for example, through capacities to track them in motion—and there is no ground to attribute a default mass-portion picture to the child, then Quine's appeal to a mass-like interpretation of plurals has no force. For perceptual segmentation of bodies antedates language, let alone plurals in language. Similarly, if bodies are already distinguished in perception, the fact that shape is used to distinguish types of masses is irrelevant. For such distinctions already depend on perceptually distinguishing pieces of macaroni from pieces of rigatoni. The pieces are bodies.

[92] Quine, *Roots of Reference*, 85.

[93] Quine, 'Speaking of Objects', 8 ff.; *Word and Object*, 91 ff.; *Roots of Reference*, 85; 'Things and their Place in Theories', 4–5.

Like Strawson, Quine holds that representation of, and as of, bodies is necessary to representation of, and as of, any other type of particular. I want to look at further passages in which Quine holds that the ability to represent, and even to articulate in language, general principles for reidentification is necessary to engaging in any reference. I bracket Quine's view that the generalization must be quantified. As far as the present discussion is concerned, it could be purely schematic.[94] Here is one such passage:

For the very young child, who has not got beyond observation sentences, the recurrent presentation of a body is much on a par with similarities of stimulation that clearly do not prompt reification. Recurrent confrontation of a ball is on a par at first with mere recurrent exposure to sunshine or cool air: the question whether it is the same old ball or one like it makes no more sense than whether it is the same old sunbeam, the same old breeze. Experience is in its feature-placing stage, in Strawson's phrase. Individuation comes only later.

True, an infant is observed to expect a steadily moving object to reappear after it passes behind a screen; but this all happens within a specious present, and reflects rather the expectation of continuity of a present feature than the reification of an intermittently absent object. Again a dog's recognition of a recurrent individual is beside the point; the dog is responding to a distinctive odor or other trait, unavailable in the case of qualitatively indistinguishable balls. To us the question whether we are seeing the same old ball or just a similar one is meaningful even in cases where it remains unanswered. It is here that reification of bodies is full blown.[95]

This last suggestion that objective reference to physical objects is meaningful only when the question of sameness of object can be raised independently of specific answerable cases is elaborated more fully in the passage that we discussed earlier:

After any considerable lapse of observation, however, the question of identity of unspecified dogs simply does not arise—not at the rudimentary stage of language learning. It scarcely makes sense until we are in a position to say such things as that in general if *any* dog undergoes such and such then in due course that *same* dog will behave thus and so.[96]

Quine goes on, from the previous passage, to hold that deciding issues of identity requires constructing the simplest account in one's 'overall scheme of things':

Our venerable theory of the persistence and recurrence of bodies is characteristic of the use of reification in integrating our system of the world. If I were to try to decide whether the penny now in my pocket is the one that was there last week, or just another one like it,

---

[94] For the distinction between quantificational and schematic generalization, see my 'Logic and Analyticity', *Grazer Philosophische Studien* 66 (2003), 199–249. Schematic generalization is distinguished in having an open place fillable by linguistic or conceptual singular terms. Quantificational generalization represents the holding of a single attribution of multiple entities in a subject matter. Perceptual systems contain neither schematic nor quantificational generalization.

[95] Quine, *Pursuit of Truth*, 24–25.

[96] Quine, 'Things and their Place in Theories', 7–8.

I would have to explore quite varied aspects of my overall scheme of things, so as to reconstruct the simplest, most plausible account of my interim movements, costumes, and expenditures.[97]

Quine assumes in these passages that his argument from default neutrality establishes a pre-individuative stage. The failure of this argument is the fundamental deficiency in these passages. Infants perceive and track bodies as bodies long before they can think the generalizations that Quine requires.[98] There is no reason to think that their perception of bodies and attribution to them of the kind *body* is anything less than 'full blown', unless 'full blown' just means 'accompanied by an ability to generalize'.

The quoted passages evince three more unarticulated assumptions that deserve comment.

First, Quine assumes that for young children and animals, issues of reidentification do not 'arise' after considerable lapses of observation. I believe that there is no reason to require long-term memory as a condition on representing bodies as bodies. Attribution of <u>body</u> through visual perception can be established independently of the role of such attribution in long-term memory, and independently of a capacity to track objects out of view. Segregating a body from a surround, having continuity anticipations, and tracking a body in view, under appropriate attributional principles, is, I think, sufficient.

Animals retain expectations over a wide variety of search times. Birds, squirrels, dogs, monkeys, apes track bodies over months without intervening observation.[99] The idea that issues of reidentification do not 'arise' for these animals needs support that Quine does not give.

---

[97] Quine, *Pursuit of Truth*, 25. The passage continues: 'Perhaps such indirect equating and distinguishing of bodies is achieved by some other animals to some extent. Perhaps a dog seeking a ball that disappeared fairly recently in one quarter will not settle for a similar ball at an unlikely distance. However that may be, it seems clear that such reification of bodies across time is beyond the reach of observation sentences and categoricals. Substantial reification is theoretical.' This last speculation is striking. Despite life-long adherence to the view that reidentification makes sense only in a context of a language with quantifiers, Quine may, late in life, be signaling a step toward open-endedness. I discuss this idea below.

[98] Susan Carey makes this point with Quine as target in 'Does Learning a Language Require the Child to Reconceptualize the World?'

[99] See Baillargeon, Spelke, and Wasserman, 'Object Permanence in Five-Month-Old Infants', 204–206; N. S. Clayton, D. P. Griffiths, N. J. Emery, and A. Dickinson, 'Elements of Episodic-Like Memory in Animals', in A. Baddeley, J. P. Aggleton, and M. A. Conway (eds.), *Episodic Memory: New Directions in Research* (Oxford: Oxford University Press, 2002); Charles Menzel, 'Progress in the Study of Chimpanzee Recall and Episodic Memory', and Bennett L. Schwartz, 'Do Nonhuman Primates Have Episodic Memory?' both in Herbert S. Terrace and Janet Metcalfe (eds.), *The Missing Link in Cognition: Origins of Self-Reflective Consciousness* (Oxford: Oxford University Press, 2005). The Clayton et al. article describes ingenious experiments in which scrub jays cache perishable and non-perishable food packets and keep track of where they stored each food type and how long ago. There is independent evidence that birds perceive bodies as such. The Clayton experiments show a capacity to track bodies over periods of 100 hours. The results do not depend on whether the birds have episodic memory—roughly, whether they remember the caching *events*. It is enough that they track duration of presence of the objects in the various hiding spots.

The second unstated assumption in the quoted passages is that expectations of animals and children regarding reappearing objects can be understood in terms of a specious present in which the individual expects only the reappearance of a stimulus or quality.[100] This assumption is based on two important mistakes.

One mistake is the assumption that tracking by infants and animals can be accounted for in terms of a specious present. Infants and many animals can remember the presence of a hidden body behind the screen for substantial periods of time. The youngest infants can remember a body, when it fails to reappear on the other side in continuous motion, for ten seconds or more. Few times in search experiments with infants require more memory than this.[101] In other animals, which cache food over months, the same difficulty is more dramatic. The invocation of a specious present that spans such times has no empirical support and would be incompatible with numerous results about memory, search, and perceptual tracking.

The other mistake is the assumption that tracking fixes on a distinctive stimulus or quality. Infants and many non-human animals do not track by expecting qualities or specific proximal stimuli. They track bounded, closed, relatively rigid three-dimensional figures—bodies. The specific shape, color, and ordinary sortal kind are strikingly unimportant in tracking during the first twelve months of human life.[102] The tracking follows the most basic element that is specific to an integrated body.

Of course, any tracking of bodies must be by way of representating *some* further attributes. At any given time, the visual system represents the approximate concrete shape (color, texture, and so on) of a seen body. But much perceptual tracking cannot be explained as response to the stability of any one specific shape property. It cannot even be explained in terms of smooth changes among such properties. Primitive tracking in infants allows for large, sudden changes in shape as long as motion maintains a closed figure and a continuous speed and direction. Similarly, color, ordinary sortal type, and so on can change even as a body is visually tracked. Primitive tracking also allows for large sudden changes in color and shape of *stationary* entities, as long as they are viewed continuously.

A certain generic topological property must be preserved if a body is to be tracked. The body must be bounded; it cannot scatter into pieces. Outline-hugging properties must be deformations that maintain boundedness and coherence. These more abstract properties are computed automatically in the visual

---

[100] Piaget proposed similar deflationary explanations—in terms of a phenomenalistic feature-continuity of an activity in a specious present. He applied these explanations to the kinds of cases (objects passing behind barriers) that Quine refers to. Piaget, *The Construction of Reality in the Child.*

[101] Baillargeon, Spelke, and Wasserman, 'Object Permanence in Five-Month-Old Infants', 204–206.

[102] Claes von Hofsten and Elizabeth S. Spelke, 'Object Perception and Object-Directed Reaching in Infancy', *Journal of Experimental Psychology: General* 114 (1985), 198–212; Baillargeon, Spelke, and Wasserman, 'Object Permanence in Five-Month-Old Infants'.

system. Even at the earliest stages of infant vision (and vision of many other animals), bodies are tracked not by a distinctive trait or odor, but by the generic topological property that distinguishes macro-physical bodies.[103]

Quine's third assumption constitutes the core of his position. The assumption is implicit in his claim that the traits that the dog relies upon are unavailable in the case of qualitatively indistinguishable objects, and in the point that the question of identity is for us meaningful even in cases where it remains unanswered. The assumption is most nearly explicit in the remark, in the second passage, that the question of identity scarcely makes sense 'until we are in a position to say such things as that in general if *any* dog undergoes such and such then in due course that *same* dog will behave thus and so'. The third assumption is that for representation of bodies as such to be meaningful, the individual must be able to raise questions about identity, individuation, and reidentification *in general form*, applicable independently of any particular tracking context.[104] This is the basic assumption of second-family Individual Representationalism.

THE BASIC ASSUMPTION

The assumption that to engage in objective representation as of bodies, an individual must be able to represent and apply general criteria for identity, individuation, and reidentification is the primary form of second-family Individual Representationalism that underlies Quine's positive views about conditions for objective reference. Quine offers no argument for this assumption. He simply claims that it is unintelligble to attribute a capacity for objective reference to a particular object or body, unless the individual has such criteria.

This assumption is shared by Quine, Strawson, and Evans. They all assume that an individual can represent bodies only if *the individual* can represent individuation and reidentification in *general* form, through some criterion for individuation. The idea is that constitutive conditions determining objective reference must be representable by the individual in general form if the individual is to represent basic attributes of the physical environment. Principles governing objective reference must be under representational control of the individual in that the individual must *make sense of* conditions for objective representation.

In fact, Quine, Strawson, and Evans require that the individual *know* conditions under which one *succeeds* in individuating entities. The individual must know constitutive conditions of objective representation if it is to be intelligible to suppose that the individual engages in objective representation. The

---

[103] I discuss in Chapter 10, the section PERCEPTION AND BODY, how perceptual systems distinguish bodies from generic spatial properties.

[104] Other passages in Quine that state or assume such a requirement: *Roots of Reference*, 82; *Word and Object*, 93, 115 ff.

assumption of these requirements is so deeply embedded in these philosophers' standpoints that they do not discuss them, much less argue for them.[105]

I would like to sharpen a sense of the vulnerability of this shared basic assumption. There are two key features of the assumption. One is a requirement that capacities necessary for objective reference or representation be capacities for representation of *generality*. The other is the requirement that the *individual* be the *executor* of the representational capacities that make objective reference or representation possible: the *individual* must represent constitutive conditions of objective reference.

The requirement of generality in representation is implicit in the requirement of *criteria* of individuation. The generality need not be strictly quantificational (although Quine imposes this requirement). The generality must, however, cover schematically, or in the content of the representations themselves, fundamental conditions determining individuation and objectivity. Thus, in representing identity and negation, the individual represents general conditions of sameness and difference. Kind attributives are supposed to be associated with a capacity to represent general conditions under which instances of a kind are the same or different.

The second key feature of the basic assumption is the requirement that the individual be able to understand, in the sense of being able to think, principles (criteria) that distinguish objective representation from mere reaction, sensory responsiveness, or the like. The assumption excludes the possibility that a perceptual subsystem might operate under principles that describe conditions that make objective reference or representation possible—even though neither the individual nor the perceptual subsystem has states with the representational content of such principles.

Both the requirement of generality and the requirement that the individual execute the objectifying capacities are undefended and, I believe, mistaken. Let me first return to the requirement of generality.

In Quine's hands—and in Evans's—criteria for individuation seem to be intended as criteria for individuating an object from all other objects.[106] There seems to be no clear reason to hold that a capacity for objective reference or

---

[105] Thus, for example, in his article on Quine's *Roots of Reference*, Strawson criticizes Quine's placing quantification at the center of his account. Strawson assumes with Quine that *learning* characteristic modes of individuation is the critical step in the development of objective reference. He shares the unargued view that objective reference requires a learned understanding of criteria for individuation. Strawson does not say how criteria can be formulated without quantification. But I believe that they could be conceived as schematic rather than quantified. In this article, Strawson discusses the project of accounting for objective reference, as distinguished from that of accounting for our conception of objectivity. See 'Reference and its Roots', in *The Philosophy of W. V. Quine* (La Salle, IL: Open Court Publishing Company, 1986); reprinted in Strawson, *Entity and Identity and Other Essays* (Oxford: Clarendon Press, 1997). Evans provides more discussion, mainly under the rubric of Russell's Principle. I believe, as I argued in Chapter 6, that this discussion is largely question-begging.

[106] In his later work, Strawson's notion is less absolute. See 'Entity and Identity'.

representation needs such a degree of context-free individuation. It is true that objectivity is greater, the greater the independence of a point of view from provincial matters. Objectivity in theoretical physics strives for frame-free laws. Yet there is no evident reason why the primitive beginnings of objective reference or representation need be so magisterially general. Once this relatively obvious point is firmly realized, one can ask how much discrimination, and what sort of discrimination, is necessary for minimal objectivity. Suppose that a kind of entity need not be distinguishable from literally all other (actual or possible) kinds. What sort of discrimination is necessary if an individual is to refer to a physical particular, or represent it as having specific physical attributes?

An individual's perceptual capacities are individuated partly through causal and practical relations that the perceiver's perceptual system bears (normally in its evolutionary history) to elements in the environment.[107] Those attributes of the environment that play a role in biological explanations of the animal's needs and activity are candidates for discrimination. The perceptual system must be able to discriminate an attribute from other attributes that are also candidates. It need not be able to discriminate any of the candidate kinds or properties from kinds or properties that play no role in the explanation of the individual's basic biological pursuits. To refer perceptually to a particular as of a given kind, the individual must rely on a perceptual system that exercises a capacity to discriminate instances of the kind from other environmentally and explanatorily relevant kinds. And the particular must be in the relevant causal relation to an exercise of such a capacity. The relevant perceptual capacities need only be in play in particular perceptual contexts, embedded in a particular environmental context.

General conditions of individuation or objectification need not be representable in the psychology, even unconsciously. The individual need not be able to think principles that explain the operation of a perceptual system. Indeed, the perceptual system itself need not have them as representational contents of its states or processes. It need only form states with perceptual representational content in a way that is explained by the principles. The system must operate under such principles. Its activities must be explainable as involving transitions that are explainable under such principles. But neither the individual nor the individual's representational subsystem need have capacities to represent principles in language, thought, or perception. Usually neither the individual nor the subsystems have contents that can constitute the representational principles under which they operate. Perception itself, including the subindividual processes that form perceptions, *represents* no general principles or conditions, and cannot represent its own representations.

Thus kind- and property-discrimination constitutively depends on causal/practical relations to elements in an environment. It depends on subindividual capacities in perceptual systems that are governed by formation principles. It

---

[107] See my 'Disjunctivism and Perceptual Psychology'; 'Perceptual Entitlement'.

does not constitutively depend on an individual's having general descriptive abilities to represent preconditions that determine what it is to be a given kind or property.

The second main requirement that Individual Representationalists impose is that representation of constitutive conditions of objective representation be imputable to the individual. This requirement can be seen to be unnecessary through the same resources that show the requirement of generality to be unnecessary. Conditions of individuation or objectification need not be representable by the individual, even "implicitly". The perceptual system must operate in ways that meet such conditions. But neither it nor the individual represents them. Some of the conditions for a sensory system's *being* a perceptual system depend on subindividual, modular capacities that separate proximal stimulation from probable environmental antecedents. But the individual need not be able to represent such conditions on objective empirical representation in language, thought, or perception. The conditions that make an individual's objective empirical representation possible need not be, and commonly are not, under the representational control of the individual.

The foregoing remarks sketch a radically different picture of the psychological grounds of objective empirical representation from the picture offered by individual representationalists. The picture lessens the reliance on descriptive capacities in favor of causal relations in determining representational capacities. This shift allows the nature and exercise of capacities for objective representation to depend more on historical relations to the environment and on causal relations in a particular context, and less on representation of generality, to account for capacities to engage in objective representation.

Of course, all sensory responses are responses to environmental factors. These responses have been shaped by evolution to accord well with animal need. But not all such responses count as objective reference or representation. Many can be accounted for purely in terms of responses to proximal stimulation that co-varies with distal conditions that affect the animal's life and capacity for reproduction. Objective representation consists in animal capacities that ground non-trivial explanatory appeal to states with veridicality conditions regarding elements in the environment. There must be a distinction in the animal's capacities between mere response to proximal stimulation and objective representation. The precise nature of an animal's discriminative capacities bears on whether the capacities can represent objective entities. It is this line of reasoning that led many, including Quine, to appeal to higher cognitive or linguistic capacities in the individual as a condition on objective reference.

However, such appeals hyper-intellectualize objective reference. By assuming that to have objectifying capacities, an individual must be able to represent conditions that constitute objectification, the appeal fails to recognize that objectification can be carried out in perceptual subsystems of the individual. The perceptual system can itself systematically distinguish proximal stimulation from distal stimulation. It can form representational states that are not simply read-offs from the stimulus array. It can achieve perceptual constancies that track distal properties through a great variety of proximal conditions. The individual need not be able to represent principles of objectification. The perceptual system, memory system, and action systems can operate under such principles in such a way as to 'make intelligible' attributing *to an individual* an objectifying capacity— perception.

Let me illustrate this point. Quine acknowledges that dogs bury bones and return long afterwards to disinter them. He maintains that they cannot refer to such bones as bodies because they lack the language to say such things as that if any body is buried, it will tend to stay put. This position is not well motivated. A dog can see the body as a body. Perhaps the dog can remember it even over long periods.[108] Suppose that it is known that the dog's perceptual system locates seen bone-shaped objects in space and that the dog anticipates continuity of such objects. Suppose that the dog tracks bodies' movement behind barriers in something like the way children do. Suppose that it is known that the dog can use a memory map rather than an odor or other beacon in finding the bone. These matters can be tested. Most of these suppositions have some empirical support. For the sake of argument and illustration, suppose that they are correct. Then it could be correct, and is certainly intelligible, to maintain that the dog perceptually refers to the bone, perhaps as an edible body, and remembers it as such. The dog may not be *thinking* propositionally at all. The dog acts in ways explained by generalizations like 'any buried bone is likely to stay where it is'. Its perceptual and intermodal capacities are exercised by perceptual anticipations that are governed by such principles. But it need not be able to represent such principles, or any generalizations at all. It need not be able to represent general conditions of its own psychological operations. Even its perceptual, actional, and memory systems need not represent generalizations or general conditions. They need only form perceptions, anticipations, memories according to such conditions, and explainable under such principles.

Whether a dog reidentifies the bone as the same body is an empirical question. For there to be an affirmative answer, it is not necessary that the dog be able to represent general principles of reidentification, or 'make sense' of reidentification. Perception individuates the bone. It singles out one bone from all others, not descriptively but through its causal–perceptual relation to it. Dogs can perceptually track moving bodies in view. A question is whether the dog's perceptual memory preserves the singular element in the perceptual representation. If the dog perceptually tracks the particular over time, or uses a remembered map in finding the bone, in addition to a capacity to respond to a type in the same way— matters that can be tested—the dog can reidentify a buried particular. The dog need not show any further capacity to differentiate the bone from other bodies or

---

[108] I think it empirically plausible that the bone is perceptually represented as a body of a certain shape and size and that, either in the dog's perceptual and actional systems, or in its actional system alone, the bone is represented as edible.

to raise general questions about identity and difference regarding particulars. It would already display tracking and reidentification.[109]

Late in life, Quine reworked the passages that we have been discussing. He distinguished between perceptual identification, on one hand, and 'full reification' or 'full reference', on the other. This distinction might be regarded as a sign of late flexibility in Quine's view. Still, the flexibility does not change the basic picture. Here is the passage:

As Donald Campbell puts it, reification of bodies is innate in man and the other higher animals. I agree, subject to a qualifying adjective: *perceptual reification.* . . . I reserve '*full* reification' and '*full* reference' for the sophisticated stage where the identity of a body from one time to another can be queried and affirmed or conjectured or denied independently of exact resemblance. Such identification depends on our elaborate theory of space, time, and unobserved trajectories of bodies between observations. Prior recognition of a recurrent body—a ball, or Mama, or Fido—is on a par with our recognition of any qualitative recurrence: warmth, thunder, a cool breeze. So long as no sense is made of the distinction between its being the same ball and its being another like it, the reification of the ball is perceptual rather than full. A dog's recognition of a particular person is still only perceptual, insofar as it depends on smell.[110]

Despite opening the door to 'non-full' reference in perception, this passage involves the oversights discussed earlier. First, perceptual tracking of bodies in the visual perceptual systems of mammals cannot be assimilated to sensory response to smells, breezes, warmth. Nor does perceptual tracking depend on 'exact resemblance'. Quine's deflationary conception of perception, as response to a simple quality, has not changed in any fundamental way. Second, the requirement that the individual *make sense* of reference as a condition on engaging in 'full' reference, as distinguished from engaging in degenerate reference (or no reference), is the basic assumption of second-family Individual Representationalism. Quine gives no argument for it. Of course, there is a difference between an individual that perceptually tracks a body and an individual that can query, affirm, deny a distinction between identity and exact resemblance. But Quine has not shown that this difference bears on the nature of reference, or on kinds or degrees of reference. I think it bears on kinds and degrees of remove from perceptual reference. It also bears on a difference between having representational capacities and understanding them.

---

[109] It is controversial both whether non-human animals have long-term memory of particular *events* (roughly whether they have *episodic* memory). There is less controversy over whether non-human animals can remember particular perceived objects. I think it beyond question, empirically, that dogs *perceptually* track bodies as such. My main points are (*a*) that the requirement that the dog be able to represent the problem in order to be counted as tracking a particular at all has no rational or empirical basis, and (*b*) that there are empirically supported alternatives. See Clayton, Griffiths, Emery, and Dickinson, 'Elements of Episodic-Like Memory in Animals'.

[110] I owe Dagfinn Föllesdal for calling my attention to this passage. See Paolo Leonardi and Marco Santambrogio (eds.), *On Quine* (Cambridge: Cambridge University Press, 1995), 350.

IDENTITY AND RESEMBLANCE

Quine's emphasis on the distinction between identity and exact resemblance deserves further discussion. A distinction between identity and resemblance is implicit in the postulation of perceptual tracking. An individual tracks the same body over time, in motion, behind barriers. Perceptual theory assumes that the individual tracks a given body, not simply keeping track of a resemblance among possibly the same but possibly different bodies. What motivates thinking that individuals are tracking particular, identical bodies?

A key motivation lies in understanding the nature of perception, particularly as this understanding is elaborated by anti-individualism about perception. Perception is constitutively of concrete particulars, particulars with the power to cause perceptual states. It would make no sense to take (sense) perception to be of attributes in the abstract. In experiments that show an individual discriminating a three-dimensional body from a surround and tracking it over time—perhaps in motion, or behind barriers—the alternative account is not that the individual perceives only some abstract shape or kind and tracks a quality. The alternative is that the individual perceives an instance, or a series of instances, of a property or kind—not a single instance of the kind *body*. Or the alternative could be that it is indeterminate whether the individual is tracking a single body or a series of instances of some property or kind. The alternatives are unmotivated and yield a less simple, less explanatory perceptual theory.

One can distinguish empirically an individual's tracking a single instance of a body from the individual's tracking a single instance of some other attribute. So the real issue is distinguishing between tracking a single instance of a body from perceiving several distinct exact-resembling instances of the kind *body*.

Given that science establishes that an individual has perceptual states—states marked by perceptual constancies—the individual need not have any further capacity to distinguish individuals from types. Perception cannot be of types alone. It always involves the individual's perceptually attributing types to particulars. So the question is, again, whether, prior to the individual's acquiring linguistic devices for expressing general criteria for sameness and difference of instances of a type, a postulation that attributes to an individual perception as of a series of instances of a given type is always an equally good postulation as one that attributes perception as of a single instance of the type. These postulations are not commonly, much less always, equally good.

In the first place, perception itself often distinguishes between qualitative lookalikes. Different particulars can be in different places or at different times, both seen but otherwise indistinguishable. Such differentiation occurs in tracking of bodies in motion. An individual expects one body to continue along its path and emerge from a barrier. The individual is surprised when two exactly similar bodies emerge if only one body disappeared. An individual can perceptually attend to one body, tracking it, while giving little attention to other simultaneous-ly perceived bodies.[111]

In the second place, and more fundamentally, differentiating between the scientific postulations depends to a large extent on the individual's non-representational relations to kinds in the environment—assuming, of course, that the individual has perceptual capacities. What perceptual states constitutively are depends on patterns of interaction between individuals and particular instances of actual kinds in the environment. Perceptual psychology individuates perceptions in a way that accords with the actual, causally relevant facts in the environment, as described by other sciences. Take, for example, motion of solid bodies through space and time. Perception functions partly to enable an individual, and species, to track things in carrying out its basic activities. Mating, predating, navigating, depend on continuity of particular bodies through time. Perception tracks such matters, insofar as a perceiver has the discriminatory and objectifying capacities to do so.

The motion that perception tracks is in fact the motion of *single* integrated bodies. Perception of a succession of very short-term instances of the kind *body* in different positions along a continuous path is not perception of anything in motion, and does not correspond to any biologically relevant environmental kind. Perceptual anti-individualism maintains that perceptual kinds are determined through interaction with relevant kinds in the environment. The relevant envir-onmental kind here is diachronic—motion of bodies. For a perceptual system to match such a kind, it must track an identical individual in motion. Thus the type of explanation provided by perceptual anti-individualism prima facie favors attribution of perceptual tracking of a particular instance of the kind *body* over attribution of serial perception of different instances of the kind. The alternative of taking individuals to track a series of instances fails to account for patterned and functional interaction with the kind *bodily motion*.[112]

The alternative of taking individuals to be doing something indeterminate between tracking a single body and representing a series of instances of the kind fails to take perceptual competence to be individuated in terms of actual biologi-cally relevant patterns in the environment—here, bodily motion. Only if there were independent reason to think that representation of particulars is problematic and needs supplementation would such alternatives have any claim on serious consideration. In fact, no such independent reason has been given. So perceptual anti-individualism motivates the natural bias toward attributing a perceptual

---

[111] Again, tracking itself does not depend on resemblance, unless resemblance consists in whole-body integration. Differences in color, shape, and ordinary macro-kind are unimportant to primitive motion tracking. Infant and animal observers are unsurprised by changes through motion or behind barriers, as long as an integrated body emerges on a similar trajectory at a similar speed.

[112] Of course, perceptual anti-individualism does not hold that all perceivers track bodies. Whether a particular perceiver tracks bodies is a specific empirical matter. The point is that if empirical considerations seem to support attribution of perceptual tracking as of bodies, perceptual anti-individualism helps indicate why such attribution, as opposed to attribution of a series of perceptions of resembling particulars, is warranted.

capacity to track particulars, including bodies, over time. The perceptual capacity does not need supplement from the Quinean apparatus.

To try to account for motion tracking by maintaining that it is neutral as to whether the same particular is in motion loses explanatory power that lies in connecting kinds of perceptual states with biologically relevant patterns in the environment. There is no relevant pattern in the environment that consists of a series of particulars replacing one another along trajectories that single bodies move upon. So perception cannot be regarded as neutral between the pattern of single-body motion and a pattern of different particulars replacing one another along the same trajectory. Perceptual representation is individuated in terms of relations to patterns in the environment that are important to the perceiver's biologically basic needs and activities, patterns with which it interacts and which it discriminates. That is the nature of perceptual tracking.

The points that I have made with respect to tracking bodies in motion apply to tracking non-moving bodies, whether behind occluders or remaining in view.[113] The fact that perception is necessarily of particulars, together with the fact that perceptual kinds and patterns are individuated in terms of kinds and patterns in the environment that figured in forming the perceptual kinds and patterns, motivate taking perceptual tracking to track identical particulars over time. The individual need not be able to formulate a distinction between tracking a resemblance of different particulars and tracking a single particular. The nature of perception and the nature of perceptual tracking ground perceptual tracking of identical particulars over time.

Tracking in perception can be integrated with longer-term memory and application of such memory in action. For example, perceptual tracking can be integrated with pursuing prey behind obstacles, or in responding to a parent or mate after an absence, or in acting in a proprietary way toward a stash. Often such integration is connected to the animal's use of relatively specific spatial representation that requires singular positional or landmark reference. These capacities can often be shown to connect perception and use of spatial representation to find a formerly perceived entity. The spatial representation's content involves fixing particular spatial positions. The representational content of perceptions and perceptual memories that use spatial representation—in navigation, parenting, mating, predation, stashing—commonly depends on facts about the movement or continuation of particulars in space over time. Often the best account of an animal's memory treats it as an extension of perceptual tracking that holds the object in view, or of perceptual tracking that follows an object, in a short-term

---

[113] I believe that for an individual to be able to represent bodies as bodies, it is not *constitutively* necessary that an individual reidentify them through lapses in observation. See Chapter 10. Many psychologists as well as philosophers assume this requirement. The requirement is not clearly motivated. I believe that perceptual tracking itself counts as reidentification, and helps distinguish attribution of bodies from attribution of events and other particulars that are relevant to the individual's (or species's) biologically basic functions. However, many animals share a capacity to track entities behind obstacles.

way, behind obstacles. Best empirical explanations can support an account of the connections between such capacities, without needing to rely on evidence that the individual has general criteria for distinguishing tracking a particular from just responding again to a type.

The view that the individual may just be tracking a quality or type trades on a tendency to assimilate perception to mere sensory response. It is often correct to understand behavior of an animal as a sensory response to any stimulus with a given quality, regardless of what particular instantiates the quality. If such sensory discrimination were all there is to contrast with propositional thought, there might be some plausibility in the individual representationalist claim that tracking particulars requires an ability to formulate a distinction between identity and resemblance. My response to this view has depended on a distinction between perception and mere discriminative sensitivity. Perception is necessarily and constitutively of particulars as having certain attributes. I discuss the basis for this distinction in Chapters 8–9.

Quine is not a philosopher whom one tends to think of as hyper-intellectualizing a subject matter. Still, in this case, the charge applies. Like Strawson and Evans, he postulates conditions on objective representation that are far more sophisticated than are warranted.

The conditions Quine places on objective representation are incompatible with empirical knowledge. There is substantial empirical evidence that perceptual representation specifically as of bodies occurs widely among animals, and from the very beginning of infant development.[114]

Children perceptually track bodies in motion by tracking their bounded, relatively stable three-dimensional figures. Tracking occurs over various stretches of time and behind barriers. In the absence of motion, bodies are perceptually segmented from a surround and grouped as three-dimensional, bounded, relatively rigid wholes. Perception of shapes as three-dimensional has developmental priority. Studies of non-human visual systems are less abundant,

---

[114] Spelke, 'Principles of Object Perception'; R. Baillargeon and J. DeVos, 'Object Permanence in Young Infants: Further Evidence', *Child Development* 62 (1991), 1227–1246; E. S. Spelke, K. Brelinger, J. Macomber, and K. Jacobson, 'Origins of Knowledge', *Psychological Review* 99 (1992), 605–632; E. S. Spelke, 'Initial Knowledge: Six Suggestions', *Cognition* 50 (1994), 431–445; Gallistel, 'Animal Cognition'; Hauser, 'Expectations about Object Motion and Destination'; Pepperberg and Funk, 'Object Permanence in Four Species of Psittacine Birds'; Wolfgang Wiltschko and Roswitha Wiltschko, 'The Navigation System of Birds and its Development', in Russell P. Balda, Irene M. Pepperberg, and Alan C. Kamil (eds.), *Animal Cognition in Nature* (San Diego: Academic Press, 1998); Regolin and Vallortigara, 'Perception of Partly Occluded Objects by Young Chicks'; Regolin, Vallortigara, and Zanforlin, 'Detour Behavior in the Domestic Chick'; Michael F. Land, 'Visual Tracking and Pursuit: Humans and Arthropods Compared', *Journal of Insect Physiology* 38 (1992), 939–951. One of the important developments in understanding mammalian vision in the last two decades has been recognition that some basic operations for representing objects in space occur in the early stages of visual processing, requiring less apparatus even within the visual system than had previously been thought. Most such processing is unconscious. See, for example, Mary A. Peterson, 'Object Perception', in E. Bruce Goldstein (ed.), *Blackwell Handbook of Perception* (Oxford: Blackwell, 2001). The simplicity of the most primitive object-segmenting operations suggests that similar object-discerning operations occur in many non-mammals.

but baby chicks, other birds, monkeys, apes, and other animals are similar in this regard.[115]

Evidence and theory have grown since Quine wrote. But even in his time, Quine ignored substantial, specific evidence that perceptual systems of a wide variety of pre-linguistic animals, including human infants, are geared to enabling individuals to distinguish and track middle-sized, integrated bodies. For a man who allied with science on so many other issues, Quine showed remarkably little interest in the empirical psychology of perception. He, along with most other prominent philosophers in the second half of the twentieth century, thought that it was possible to explain objective empirical representation without thinking seriously about perception.

Most of Quine's confidence lies not in argument, but in assumption—particularly the assumption of a requirement on intelligibility. This is the requirement that the individual must be able to represent in general form basic conditions on objective representation, if objective representation by the individual is to be intelligible to the scientist. This requirement is not self-evident. It is responsibly ignored in empirical psychology. I think it safe to count it mistaken.

DAVIDSON ON CONDITIONS FOR OBJECTIVE
EMPIRICAL REPRESENTATION

Donald Davidson avoids postulating a stage of pre-individuative representation. An individual's *first* representations are supposed to be representations of objects in the environment. Although Quine is more equivocal on the matter, as we have seen, his official position is, strictly speaking, the same. For Quine, one-word sentences are not vehicles of reference. Davidson's view is, however, front and center, whereas Quine's is mixed with externalized residues from the sense-data tradition.

Davidson emphasizes that there is no progression from the *subjective* to the objective. The subjective, properly so-called, is formed within a context of objective reference.[116] Davidson presents this view with great emphasis. But here also he is anticipated by others. The initial stages in Quine and Strawson are not subjective. They are just limited. In fact, not one of the major late-century philosophers postulates an initial *subjective* stage of the sort championed by Wundt, Piaget, Cassirer, Russell, early Carnap, and the sense-data theorists.

---

[115] Spelke, 'Principles of Object Perception'; Baillargeon and DeVos, 'Object Permanence in Young Infants'; Spelke et al., 'Origins of Knowledge'; Gallistel, 'Animal Cognition'; Hauser, 'Expectations about Object Motion and Destination'; Pepperberg and Funk, 'Object Permanence in Four Species of Psittacine Birds'; Regolin, Vallortigara, and Zanforlin, 'Detour Behavior in the Domestic Chick'; Regolin and Vallortigara, 'Perception of Partly Occluded Objects by Young Chicks'.

[116] Donald Davidson, 'Three Varieties of Knowledge' (1991), in *Subjective, Intersubjective, Objective*, 219.

Davidson's position has the advantage of not being committed to empirically false armchair claims about developmental progression. But the position is committed to an extremely restrictive view of the possibilities of explaining development. Its larger claims remain incompatible with empirical knowledge.

On some occasions Davidson doubts the coherence of stages of objective representation, suggesting that developmental psychology may be impossible. On other occasions, he allows for stages, but shows no interest in them.[117] His official view allows only a simple dichotomy: either there is mere sensory discrimination with no genuine representation, or there is propositional thought about objects in the physical environment. Propositional thought is said to depend *constitutively* on language, and even on being in a communicative relation with another.

For our purposes, Davidson differs from Quine mainly in rejecting proximal stimulation as the ground for explanations of meaning and reference. The causal relations that ground explanation of representation are distal. In this respect, Davidson's work is further from behaviorism and British empiricism and, I think, closer to the truth.

Nevertheless, Davidson's work inherits the Individual Representationalism of Quine and Strawson. He shares their basic assumption. The assumption is that to engage in objective reference, or representation of the physical environment, an individual must be able to think general criteria for applying representations. That is, the individual must be able to represent some basic conditions that make objectivity possible. *In the subject's own representational capacities* there must be a mirroring of some constitutive preconditions of objective representation, if objective representation is to occur.

Citing his agreement with Quine in rejecting an analytic/synthetic distinction, Davidson places relatively loose demands on the notion of criterion. Reference depends on multiple empirical criteria, no one of which is indubitable or decisive. But some group of criteria must be true of the objects represented. They must be generalizations about the 'nature' of those objects. They play a role in explaining application. They must be believed by the individual.[118]

Davidson's account of criteria is less specific than the accounts of Quine and Strawson. Davidson agrees, however, with their emphases. For example, he holds that to represent a body, one must have general beliefs about temporal continuity of bodies—criteria for reidentification.[119]

Davidson's most insistent point about criteria is that they be *general* beliefs— and beliefs about *natures*, or beliefs about *what it is to be* an F. The beliefs that

---

[117] See Donald Davidson, 'The Emergence of Thought' (1997), in *Subjective, Intersubjective, Objective*, 128, 134.

[118] See Donald Davidson, 'Epistemology Externalized' (1990), in *Subjective, Intersubjective, Objective*, 195; 'Rational Animals' (1982), in ibid. 98; 'The Emergence of Thought' (1997), 124; 'The Problem of Objectivity' (1995), in *Problems of Rationality* (Oxford: Clarendon Press, 2004), 10–11, 17.

[119] Davidson, 'The Emergence of Thought', 124.

make objective representation possible must be general beliefs. Davidson follows Quine in the view that the individual must represent general criteria in quantificational form. (See the section QUANTIFICATION above.) So quantificational structure is necessary for objective representation.[120] The requirement that an individual have such criteria, and even believe them, is always stated without argument.

The element in Davidson's Individual Representationalism that is broadest and most characteristic of his work is the requirement that to engage in objective representation, an individual must have of a concept of objectivity. Davidson associates, sometimes identifies, a concept of objectivity with a concept of truth as applied to propositional belief. He understands such application to require that the individual have not only beliefs, but a concept of belief, and beliefs as of beliefs.[121] This requirement is a variant on the requirement, imposed by Strawson, that the individual have an ability to represent a distinction between <u>seems</u> and <u>is</u>.

Sometimes Davidson argues for these views. I will discuss the arguments shortly. On some occasions, however, he elides a crucial distinction. He sometimes slips, without comment, from 'believes' to 'holds true'; and then glosses 'holds true' as entailing 'has the concept of truth' and 'knows that the belief may be true or false'. These are conceptual slides, masking substantial steps that need argument. Holding beliefs does not entail that one know or believe anything about beliefs. Holding beliefs does not obviously entail that one have a concept of truth that applies to beliefs or to representational contents.

'Understand the truth conditions' is another phrase that blurs distinctions. There are different types and levels of understanding. Having propositional attitudes with truth-conditional content requires having reapplicational and inferential competencies that constitute a low-level type of understanding. Understanding truth conditions *as* truth conditions, even understanding representational content as having *any* attribute, is another matter. Being able to engage in thought and inference is not the same as having meta-beliefs about beliefs and applying meta-concepts like truth to them. Having a perspective *on* the contents, making reference to them, and thinking of them as true or false, or thinking about

---

[120] Davidson, 'Rational Animals', 98–99, 101; 'The Emergence of Thought', 124 (the requirement that to think about a cat one must have beliefs about 'what a cat is'); 'The Problem of Objectivity', 13; 'What Thought Requires' (2001), in *Problems of Rationality*, 139–140; 'Epistemology Externalized', 195. Davidson requires quantification in the last two passages. In the last passage Davidson writes: 'Possession of a concept already implies the ability to generalize since the point of a concept is that it is applicable to any item in an indefinitely large class.' This argument is clearly fallacious. One can have a conceptual ability to think about any instance of the concept, as instances come up individually as candidates for application, without being able to collect the instances under a generalization. Ability generality does not entail quantificational generality. Ability generality also does not entail schematic generalization—which involves propositional *representation* of generality that allows any relevant substituends into the schemas.

[121] Davidson, 'The Problem of Objectivity', 4, 7–8, 10–11; 'Three Varieties of Knowledge', 209; 'The Emergence of Thought', 129–130, 124; 'Epistemology Externalized', 202; 'Thought and Talk' (1975), in *Inquiries into Truth and Interpretation* (Oxford: Clarendon Press, 1984), *passim*, but especially p. 170.

inferential connections as sound or unsound, is a decidedly different sort of understanding from low-level competence understanding. The former is a second-order understanding.

It cannot be *assumed* that a capacity to believe that *p* involves a capacity to believe the content *p* is true. Having the concept <u>truth</u> involves having an ability to group as truths certain propositional representational contents, where those contents are represented as propositions or as representational contents. It is hardly evident that having a belief entails such an ability.

Davidson needs to argue that it does. For it is prima facie possible that a being could have beliefs but lack the capacity to think about representational contents, or beliefs, and to think of some of them as true and of others of them as false. Believing and disbelieving constitutes one level of cognitive activity. Holding beliefs about such attitudes and their success or failure constitutes another level. It is not even plausible that belief requires a concept of truth and a concept of propositional representational content as such. It is also not plausible that having beliefs requires having a concept of belief—an ability to think about beliefs as such. Prima facie, and I think in fact, propositional attitudes—not to say objective perceptual states—emerge before a second-order capacity to hold beliefs about them.

DAVIDSON'S TWO ARGUMENTS

Davidson gives two primary arguments for requiring these higher-order abilities as necessary conditions on objective representation. One is an argument from surprise. Davidson claims that to have beliefs, a being must be capable of surprise. This claim seems fairly plausible. Ordinary beliefs, as well as perceptions, are associated with anticipations that may not be realized. For example, if a person has a belief that *that* is a solid body, and reaches out to touch it, and there is only a feel of thin air, there will be surprise. The individual anticipates feeling a solid body. If solidity is not felt, the individual is surprised. Surprise in this sense requires having representational content.

This ordinary notion of surprise is different from merely being startled, which could be a matter of reflex and which could involve no representational elements at all. In Davidson's sense and one ordinary sense, a worm is startled if one grabs it, but it is probably not surprised.

Davidson invests his notion of surprise with further special meaning, however. He uses it in the special sense that if an individual is surprised, the individual has a *conception of a mistaken belief and a conception of objective truth*. There is no argument for this augmentation of the ordinary first-order notion of surprise to a second-order notion.

Davidson claims that 'it is clear' that if one is surprised, one has reflective thoughts. He claims that surprise requires awareness of a contrast between what one did believe and what one now believes. This awareness involves belief about belief—belief that the earlier belief is false.

These claims beg the critical question. It is certainly *not* 'clear' that if an individual is surprised, the individual has reflective thoughts. Davidson's claims may introduce a special notion of surprise. Then it would be completely unclear that belief requires surprise in that sense. Or the claims may introduce an unargued transition between an ordinary 'first-order' notion of surprise and a higher-order notion requiring reflective thoughts. The transition needs argument. Davidson gives none. He simply skates over the distinction.[122]

The distinction figures significantly in developmental psychology and animal ethology. The facile move from objective representation to a representation of objectivity is, of course, reminiscent of similar moves by Strawson and Evans discussed in the previous chapter.

Davidson's second argument for requiring a concept of objectivity as a condition on objective reference is more elaborate. A capacity by an organism to discriminate a property in the environment does not entail that the organism represents that property. Amoebae discriminate heat and at certain temperatures move away from it. Plants are sensitive to light and grow toward it.

It would be explanatorily unilluminating and unnecessary to invoke representational notions to explain such phenomena. Any notion of representation that one invoked could easily be reduced to other notions that are not in any ordinary sense psychological. The phenomena can be explained in terms of surface stimulation and physiological or cellular responses, together with a gloss on the evolutionary and ecological functions of such reactions.

---

[122] Davidson, 'Rational Animals', 102–104. See also 'The Problem of Objectivity', 7. In the latter passage, Davidson holds that having beliefs requires a capacity for surprise, and then slips without comment from requiring a capacity for surprise to requiring awareness of the possibility of surprise. This is another move from a prima facie first-order notion to an apparent second-order notion. Again the move begs the question.

Understanding the early development of representing *psychological* attributes is not very far advanced. For some years, empirical work has suggested that higher animals like chimps, and children at roughly age 3, have beliefs but no beliefs about beliefs. See, for example, Michael Tomasello and Josep Call, *Primate Cognition* (Oxford: Oxford University Press, 1997); Daniel Povanelli, *Folk Physics for Chimps* (Oxford: Oxford University Press, 2000); H. Wimmer, G.-J. Hogrefe, and J. Perner, 'Children's Understanding of Informational Access as a Source of Knowledge', *Child Development* 59 (1988), 386–396; H. Wimmer and M. Hartl, 'Against the Cartesian View on Mind: Young Children's Difficulty with Own False Beliefs', *British Journal of Developmental Psychology* 9 (1991), 125–138; H. M. Wellman and J. D. Woolley, 'From Simple Desires to Ordinary Beliefs: The Early Development of Everyday Psychology', *Cognition* 35 (1990), 245–275; A. Gopnik and J. W. Astington, 'Children's Understanding of Representational Change, and its Relation to the Understanding of False Belief and the Appearance–Reality Distinction', *Child Development* 59 (1988), 26–37; P. Mitchell, *Introduction to Theory of Mind: Children, Autism and Apes* (London: Arnold, 1997). This line has been recently questioned by some researchers who regard concepts of propositional attitudes as, in effect, innate in young children, and perhaps in apes as well. I believe that this questioning has so far rested on confused conceptualization. I will not discuss the matter here. Suffice it to say that it is an *empirical* question whether having beliefs always goes with having beliefs about beliefs, and that there is some empirical reason to maintain a negative answer.

For an individual to have representational states—thoughts or perceptions with definite representational content—there must be some non-arbitrary fact or ground that fixes what those thoughts are about. Whatever is representationally discriminated in basic cases is an attribute with instances that regularly causes the representational state and to which the individual reacts differentially. But this condition alone does not get us very far. In the case of vision, it does not by itself distinguish among patterns of photons, light arrays, retinal surface stimulations, and various types of distal stimulations from the environment. In physiology, the bacterium's response to light is explained in terms of proximal stimulation. There is certainly no explanatory power in giving explanations of its present activity in terms of representation of the objective physical environment. Response to proximal stimulation together with functionally relevant causal connections between environment and such responses suffice for explanation of the organism's sensory reactions and capacities. One needs to appeal to something more than causal interaction with the environment to ground an account of representational relations to specific elements in the distal environment.

Davidson cites points like these. He then maintains that the only way to ground a specific content for representational states is to appeal to a communication situation in which a speaker and interpreter are fixed on a common entity in the distal environment.[123] Thus, not only an ability to speak a language, but actually being interpreted by another person, is supposed to be necessary for having a concept of objectivity. And having a concept of objectivity is supposed to be necessary for representation of, and as of, the physical environment.

I think that Davidson's conclusion is unacceptable. It is particularly unacceptable as a conclusion of armchair argument. The idea that genuine representation in perception, or even in thought, conceptually requires that an individual actually enter into a dialog with another person is not sanctioned by common sense, much less science.

Davidson's drawing the conclusion is sometimes nothing more than a leap. Sometimes he makes an unsupported claim that his conclusion provides the best explanation of objective representation. Davidson does, however, sometimes provide intermediate considerations that purport to bolster the key transitions in the argument.

Davidson tries to justify such transitions in two ways. One centers on the notion of error or mistake. Davidson rightly insists that where there is representation, it must make sense to speak of a mistake. He adds that the mistake must be 'a mistake not only as seen from an intelligent observer's point of view, but as seen from the creature's point of view'.[124]

---

[123] Donald Davidson, 'The Second Person' (1992), in *Subjective, Intersubjective, Objective*, 118–119; 'Epistemology Externalized', 201–203; 'Three Varieties of Knowledge', 212–213; 'The Problem of Objectivity', 8–9; 'The Emergence of Thought', 124–130; 'What Thought Requires', 142–143.
[124] Davidson, 'The Problem of Objectivity', 8.

He notes that a worm that eats poison has not made a mistake in the relevant sense. It has not mistaken one thing for another, but simply reacted to stimulus in a way that is bad for it. This much seems correct. Davidson then interprets making a mistake 'as seen from the creature's point of view' in a second-order way. He holds that the creature itself must be able to regard its representation as mistaken. Davidson characterizes this ability as an ability to apply the concepts of truth and falsity. This unexplained move to a second-order characterization again begs the question. The only reasonable requirement is that the creature must have a representational point of view or perspective that can itself incur mistakes. Worms probably lack representational capacities, as opposed to merely sensory capacities. Hence worms probably lack a representational point of view.

The notions of correctness and error in representation already have a grip on perceptual representation. They are fundamental to explanation of perceptual states in empirical science and common sense.[125] They gain grip in the context of the perceptual constancies embedded in animal perceptual systems and in the context of the use of perception to fulfill animal needs in the animal's environment. No second-order representations are needed to make intelligible first-order representation in perception or perceptual memory. A mistake 'as seen from the creature's point of view' is simply a non-veridical perceptual (or other type of) representation by the creature. I develop these points in Chapters 8–10.

Davidson offers another line of support for the view that objective representation requires a concept of objectivity, which in turn is supposed to require engaging in linguistic communication. He claims that there are no intrinsically natural similarity classes for non-human animals, or for humans, apart from language. He claims that the similarity classes that we use when we are inclined to attribute representations are natural for *us*. He maintains that 'it begs the question to project our classifications on to nature'.[126]

Davidson holds that there are no representational similarity classes that are not established through interpersonal linguistic usage. Thus he holds that it is illegitimate to take animal sensory states to represent particulars as having specific attributes. He holds that all animal sensory states could just as well be taken to be responses to *any* intervening causal conditions, or to stimulations of nerve endings, as to elements in the environment.

Davidson maintains that justifiably to fix on an object of representation in interpreting another being, there must be a certain triangulation in interpersonal linguistic interaction. The causal line linking the utterance and reception of a sentence between the two people (where the two respond to the sentence similarly) constitutes one leg of the triangle. The causal line that fixes one's own line of sight and the causal line that fixes the other's line of sight form the other two legs. The triangle is closed where the two lines of sight intersect. There one finds the object of representation. There, as opposed to elsewhere in the chain causing

---

[125] For more detail, see my 'Disjunctivism and Perceptual Psychology'.
[126] Davidson, 'Epistemology Externalized', 142.

mental states. Even the content of one's own sense of similarity, of one's own representations, is supposed to derive from and only from such communicative triangles.[127]

The fact that a speaker and an interpreter respond to the same objects and properties in the distal environment is supposed to ground the attribution of definite objects of representation. The speaker and interpreter respond to different light arrays, different surface stimulations, and so on. But objects in the environment are triangulated upon in explaining the causal ancestry of their responses. Distal environmental entities and attributes form a non-arbitrary ground for attributing representations of, and as of, those entities. Davidson holds that in the absence of such triangulation through *actual linguistic interpretation*, there is no non-arbitrary ground for determining what mental states are about. In the absence of an interpreter, there is supposed to be no non-arbitrary way to fix what would count as similarity of response to a purported cause.

Davidson writes:

> For this reason we cannot resolve the question of the contents of mental states from the point of view of a single creature. This is perhaps best seen by thinking about how one person learns from another to speak and think of ordinary things.... The role of the teacher in determining the contents of the learner's attitude is not just the 'determine' of causality. For in addition to being a cause of those thoughts, what makes the particular aspect of the cause of the learner's responses the aspect that gives them the content they have is the fact that this aspect of the cause is shared by the teacher and the learner. Without such sharing, there would be no grounds for selecting one cause rather than another as the content-fixing cause. A non-communicating creature may be seen by us as responding to an objective world; but we are not justified in attributing thoughts about our world (or any other) to it.[128]

Davidson holds that there are 'endless' equally good causal explanations of perceptual belief, if one abstracts from attributions of perceptual beliefs based on the *linguistic* usage of the believer.[129] Each explanation would dictate a different content of the perceptual belief.

Davidson notes that in earlier work I responded to such a point that we have no idea how to characterize the various patterns that would cause a perceptual belief, apart from appeal to macro-objects in the distal environment. I held that in alternatives like taking the beliefs to be about photons or surface stimulations,

---

[127] Davidson, 'The Second Person', 118–119; 'Epistemology Externalized', pp. 201–202. The premises of this reasoning are never spelled out. Davidson may think that unless there is a check from another person on one's own sense of similarity, there is no non-idiosyncratic, non-private way of verifying one's inclinations. And a public content requires such verification. I dispute both premises.

[128] Davidson, 'Epistemology Externalized', 202–203. The fact that Davidson thinks that at least two individuals must represent conditions of objectivity does not prevent him from being an Individual Representationalist. He thinks that for either individual to represent the physical environment as having specific physical attributes, the individual must represent general conditions on objectivity.

[129] Davidson, 'What Thought Requires', 142.

'the descriptions would have to be complicated in ways that have never been fully articulated'.[130] Davidson replies that such descriptions would be complicated for us, but not necessarily complicated for the creature with the perceptual system.[131]

This reply underestimates the force of my point. The relevant descriptions in terms of perceptions of, and as of, macro-objects are not haphazard, conventional ways of talking. They are integrated into systematic explanations, not only in common sense, but in empirical science—for example, in zoology and the psychology of vision. As noted in discussion of Quine, perceptual psychology uses kinds indicated in biological explanations of animals' needs and pursuits. Perceptual psychology embeds law-like explanations of the formation of perceptual states in biological explanations of animal–environment interactions. The psychological explanations attribute representational states to non-linguistic creatures. Many such explanations are detailed and scientifically impressive. No one has shown how to recast them, or how to produce alternatives, so as to attribute representation of things like photons, surface stimulations, or the like. It appears that such recasting would be complicated in ways that undermine the viability of alternative explanations. So Davidson's claim that there are 'equally good' alternative descriptions-cum-explanations is completely unsupported and prima facie quite untrue. Like Quine, Davidson failed to appreciate the power of scientific explanations of perception, particularly vision. They both thought that they could understand primitive empirical representation without serious reflection on what is known scientifically about perception.

The role that Davidson gives to triangulation in linguistic interpretation is filled much earlier in the ontogeny and phylogeny of the mental. Relevant triangulation already occurs in perception. Triangulation operates at two levels of abstraction.

The first level derives from the fact that perception is a sensory capacity that is functionally available to (or attributable to) the whole animal. In this regard, perception contrasts with various proprioceptive feedback mechanisms. For example, the sensors that yield contraction of the blood vessels or that regulate muscle tone are not functionally available to the whole animal. The movement of the blood vessels and relevant shifts in muscle tone are not movements by the animal, but *only* movements of its parts (unlike an animal's movement of a paw). A consequence of the whole-animal feature of perception is that it is integrated with explanations of whole-animal need and whole-animal function, including animal activity. Animals' basic activities are those like finding a mate, catching prey, fleeing predators, navigating around obstacles, finding home, eating, protecting offspring, and so on. Biological explanations of these activities make essential reference to kinds of objects, properties, and relations in the physical environment. Individuation of representational states in perception are fitted to these explanations of activity. So explanation of animal need and activity by

---

[130] See my 'Cartesian Error and the Objectivity of Perception', 126–127.
[131] Davidson, 'Epistemology Externalized', 201–202; 'What Thought Requires', 142.

appeal to animal perception relies on an empirically grounded default presumption toward individuating perceptual states in terms of the attributes in the environment that the animal can discriminate, and whose discrimination helps explain whole-animal activity and fulfillment of whole-animal needs. Similarity of response with other animals has a natural scientific basis—inasmuch as our perceptual states and our basic needs and activities are explained by reference to interaction with similar attributes and patterns in a shared environment.

Thus there is triangulation among the explanatory objectives of biological explanations of whole-animal activity, explanatory objectives in explaining whole-animal sensory response to proximal stimuli, and comparison of such responses across animals of a given species or across species that share similar perceptual systems. This first-level of triangulation does not suffice to ground objective representation. It is, however, a necessary framework for such grounding. It privileges environmental macro-entities as candidates for being objects of representation, *if* explanation in terms of representation is justified.

This privileging emerges in the practice of perceptual psychology. The first thing that a psychologist of animal vision asks is how the animal's vision aids the animal in coping with its environment. It is certainly not apriori that representational forms of explanation apply to any given type of animal. When they do apply, however, they integrate animal perception with animal activity. Recasting theory in other terms would complicate not only perceptual psychology but various biological sciences.

I believe that Davidson fails to appreciate the resources of perceptual anti-individualism. He holds that a perceptual object is a cause of the perceptual state that is discriminable by the individual. This claim leaves open a wide range of causes that the animal reacts to differentially. It also considers perception (apart from language and belief) in an artificially impoverished way. Only when perceptual anti-individualism is understood in a realistic explanatory context is this range narrowed to macro-entities in an animal's physical environment.[132]

The first level of triangulation—among grounds of different types of explanation—is necessary but not sufficient to ground understanding of objective perceptual representation. Many animals interact with the environment, but lack perception or any other kind of representation. Thus the paramecium ingests its food (whereas only its gut digests it) and reverses the direction of its swimming in response to its heat sensors. An earthworm eats, burrows into the soil, and so on. But these animals do not perceive or otherwise represent their environment. Their sensory discriminations link their movements to environmental contingencies that are, by and large, good for their survival and reproduction. But whole-animal

---

[132] See my 'Perception', *International Journal of Psychoanalysis* 84 (2003), 157–167; and 'Perceptual Entitlement', especially sections I and II. See also my 'Social Anti-Individualism, Objective Reference', *Philosophy and Phenomenological Research* 67 (2003), 682–690, reprinted in *Foundations of Mind*.

activity is not linked to objective perceptual representation of the physical environment.

Explanation of an animal's occurrent sensory discriminations and occurrent behavior can center on responses to proximal stimulation. A paramecium sensorily responds to the temperature of its surfaces. No appeal to perceptual representation of the environment is needed.

A distinguishing feature of perception is a kind of triangulation that occurs in sensory perceptual systems. Such triangulation is pre-representational, pre-perceptual. It underlies perceptual constancies. Perceptual constancies are capacities systematically to represent a given particular or attribute as the same despite significant variations in proximal stimulation—despite a wide variety of perspectives on the particular or attribute. Such constancies are explanatorily associated with systematic filtering mechanisms that yield sensitivity to a single environmental particular or attribute. For example, a perceptual system might enable an animal to represent a body's size as the same even as the retinal image, the body's immediate effect of proximal stimulation, grows or diminishes. Or a perceptual system might produce an individual's perceptual states that represent a degree of brightness or a color shade as the same even though the illumination of the object, hence the spectral properties of the light intensity available to the retina, vary dramatically.

A literal triangulation underlies the perceptual capacity *convergence* that I mentioned near the beginning of this chapter. Convergence is a way of coming to represent location (hence distance) relative to viewer position—and achieving location and distance constancies. The length of the line between the foveas of the two eyes is fixed. The fovea of each eye is aimed in a certain direction. Any fixation point, where the angles of sight of the two eyes meet, creates a triangle. If a visual system can track the angles of direction, relative to the line connecting the eyes, it has information sufficient to determine the distance and location of the fixation point (with respect to the viewer). Given two angles and the length of a side, the distance and direction of the fixation point can be determined by elementary geometry. It is convenient to discuss the angle between the two lines of sight (at the fixation point). Again, this angle can be determined from the two angles that the eyes are pointing in. Distance varies inversely with the size of this angle at the fixation point, given the direction in which the eyes point. Systems that employ convergence have access to extra-retinal sensory cues regarding directions the eyes point. The distance between the eyes is, in effect, hardwired into the system. There is substantial evidence that the visual systems of humans and many other animals operate in accord with such computations. Explanations of distance perception by convergence do not refer to background propositional belief, much less language.[133]

---

[133] C. von Hofsten, 'The Role of Convergence in Visual Space Perception', *Vision Research* 16 (1976), 193–198; Palmer, *Vision Science*, 204–206. Many species' visual systems, including humans', employ several ways for determining distance.

Perceptual constancies, illustrated by convergence, are present in the perceptual systems of numerous human and non-human animals. They are most prominent in visual systems, but also occur in hearing and touch. These constancies constitute capacities to differentiate attributes in the physical environment from proximal stimulation and from various other causes of perceptual states. Perceptual psychology provides rigorous explanations, in these terms, of perceptual representational formation operations in a wide range of animals, including many that lack language and propositional attitudes.

The triangulation problem—often called the 'Disjunction Problem'—that Davidson discusses to motivate his appeal to linguistic communication is not a serious problem.[134] It has long been solved in perceptual psychology. Discriminated elements in the environment are the *representata* of perceptual representation because various 'triangulations' already occur within perceptual systems. Which attributes and particulars are perceptually represented is determined empirically. The subject matters of perceptual belief are constrained by the subject matters of perception. As I have indicated in discussing Quine, the relevant represented attributes are determined by combining considerations regarding discriminative capacities in perception (particularly perceptual constancies) with ecological considerations regarding what attributes figure in ecological explanations of animals' basic biological pursuits. Triangulations in linguistic communication are not needed to provide a non-arbitrary ground that fixes what perception and perceptual belief represent.

Here again we see the striking failure in second-family Internal Representationalism to reflect on perception in an informed way. Davidson is like Quine, Strawson, Evans, and most other Strawsonians, including living ones, in trying to account for empirical representation without any serious scientific understanding of perception.

Let us return to Davidson's second argument for requiring a concept of objectivity as a condition on objective reference. I remarked that this argument contains a large leap. The leap is from contrasting earthworms with representers to claiming that the only ground for the contrast lies in representers' actually entering into linguistic communication.

Davidson tries to support the leap in two ways. One features the notion of error. The other features the idea that there are no natural pre-linguistic 'senses of similarity' that could ground attribution of representational content. These two lines of thought are very characteristic of Individual Representationalism.

Davidson claims that there is no sense to the idea that an earthworm can make a mistake from its own point of view. I think that this claim is correct. The idea is, of course, not that the worm's point of view is subjectively infallible. Davidson plausibly holds that it has no *representational* point of view. Davidson's Individual Representationalism lies in his requirements on what it takes to achieve

---

[134] I return to the Disjunction Problem in Chapter 8.

representation. The relevant requirement is that to engage in objective representation, or even to have any representational point of view at all, an individual
must represent constitutive conditions on objectivity. For Davidson, the key
elements of objectivity that must be represented are representations themselves,
truth and falsity, belief, and independence from belief. Davidson holds that these
elements come together only in linguistic interpretation.

A realistic perceptual anti-individualism shows why such requirements are
unnecessary and hyper-intellectualized. Empirical accounts of perceptual systems indicate how individuals can engage in objective representation without
representing conditions on objectivity. Differentiation between the proximal and
the subjective, on one hand, and entities in the wider environment, on the other, is
effected in the subsystems of perceptual systems. The distinction need not be
represented by the individual. Such a view of representation of the distal environment, independent of language, is not threatened by Davidson's arguments.
The arguments beg the question.

Like Quine, Davidson claims that there are no pre-linguistic senses of similarity or natural classifications that can be justifiably attributed. On their views, in
dealing with 'foreigners' (animals, children, other adult humans), one must
regard it as a wide-open question what kinds they find natural—what similarity
classes they use—until one matches reactions in *linguistic* behavior. We must
regard as prima facie idiosyncratic the kinds and similarity classes that *we* regard
as natural. Only when we find others reacting similarly *in linguistic contexts* can
we rationally attribute a set of shared representational classifications.

Like Quine, Davidson underestimates the dependence of psychology on
biological sciences. Primitive perceptual categories are closely connected to
attributes that are relevant to explaining animals' basic biological needs and
activities. Given that animals can discriminate these attributes, and given that
animals have perceptual subsystems that differentiate, in exercises of perceptual
constancies, between proximal registration and environmental attributes, there is
a rich, natural framework for attributing perceptual and other representational
kinds to non-linguistic beings.[135]

DAVIDSON ON BELIEF

A striking feature of Davidson's views is that, quite intentionally, he gives no
place to perception as a representational capacity. He maintains that there is
sensation and belief, but nothing in the causal, psychological, or justificatory
orders in between. Sensation, for Davidson, amounts functionally to nothing
more than sensitivity to stimulation. Belief is propositional, and is supposed to
entail a conception of truth.

---

[135] The distinction is not made by the perceptual subsystem's representing it.

Most of Davidson's account centers on conditions for *belief* about an objective world. Davidson correctly takes belief to be a *propositional* attitude. He thinks that having states with representational content requires meeting conditions for having beliefs—hence conditions for propositional attitudes.[136] Since he holds that belief necessarily represents an objective subject matter, he maintains that constitutive conditions for objective representation are the same as constitutive conditions for having belief. Davidson holds that these conditions include having concepts of belief, of propositional content, and of objectivity—and having capacities to express these concepts in language.

I have located primitive objective representation in perception. I have shown that Davidson has given no reason to think that representation of environmental particulars as having specific attributes requires any of the second-order representations that he invokes.

Some animals that seem to lack belief or any other propositional attitude perceptually represent environmental particulars and attributes. That is, there is no current ground to think that propositional attitude psychology applies to these perceivers. So Davidson's view that objective representation requires belief appears to be mistaken.

The criticisms already presented are the fundamental ones. I want, however, to remark on individual representationalist accounts of *conditions for having perceptual belief*, focusing on Davidson's account.

Might not the supplemental capacities postulated by second-family Individual Representationalism be required for having *propositional* capacities—including perceptual belief?

The objectivity present in perceptual systems of various animals is a very low-level type. Some might insist that "true empirical objectivity" begins only with propositional attitudes. They might hold that having perceptual beliefs requires having supplemental beliefs, along lines required by second-family Individual Representationalism. Thus one might require that for an individual to have propositional attitudes regarding the physical environment, the individual must represent a seems/is distinction, or have criteria for applying concepts, or have a battery of linguistic capacities.

---

[136] Davidson usually states his conditions as conditions on having beliefs or having concepts— which he regards as necessarily components or aspects of propositional attitudes or propositional contents. He allows no pre-propositional representational states. He sometimes states his conditions as conditions on mental content, intentionality, or intensionality. See Davidson, 'A Coherence Theory of Truth and Knowledge'; 'The Emergence of Thought', 128–130; 'Epistemology Externalized', 202–203; 'Three Varieties of Knowledge', 212; 'What Thought Requires', 138; 'Rational Animals', 99, 101; 'Thought and Talk', 163. In one passage (see 'What Thought Requires', 136) Davidson writes that animals recognize individual people and other animals, distinguish among various kinds of animals, and see and hear all sorts of things. Most of the rest of his work suggests that he thinks that this convenient way of speaking means that they have sensations that correlate well with these distal matters, without representing them through some mental content. In fact, on the next page (p. 137) he assimilates such discriminations to conditioned differential responses.

The objectivity of perceptual systems is certainly a primitive type of objectivity. It is true that propositional attitudes yield a higher level of objectivity. What is pure dogma in the preceding reasoning is the claim that having propositional attitudes requires the supplementary paraphernalia that second-family Individual Representationalism requires. No reason has been given for holding that to have *perceptual beliefs*, an individual must represent a seems/is distinction, represent the unity of the self, represent a comprehensive space, have criteria for applying concepts, or have a battery of linguistic capacities.

Prima facie, what is needed to have beliefs is a capacity to make use of propositional logical form—to carry out propositional inference. No constitutive connection between this capacity and the requirements set forth by Individual Representationalism has ever been drawn. The representational objectivity of perceptual belief, and the conceptualization of perception, seem to derive from embedding perceptual abilities in systems of predication and inference.

Although perceptual representation of a physical environment appears to occur in animals that lack propositional attitudes, belief remains a distinct and important form of representation. I will briefly discuss what Davidson has to say about it.

Davidson claims that belief is a fundamental propositional attitude in the sense that one cannot have other propositional attitudes unless one has beliefs. I accept this claim.

I think that I have shown that Davidson has failed to make it plausible that having belief requires having a concept of belief, a concept of objectivity, or various other second-order concepts. Empirical belief obtains its subject matter and substantial aspects of its representational content from perception. Clearly, perception need not—cannot—represent conditions for its own objectivity. Belief need not either.

Davidson holds that having a language requires a second-order interpreter's perspective on the language. Thus linguistic understanding is to be construed in terms of applying, or at least having the resources to apply, a truth theory. Even these positions seem to me hyper-intellectualized. In fact, they are hyper-intellectualized in much the way that Davidson's accounts of representation and belief are.[137]

Davidson sometimes disclaims any psychological significance to the use of a truth theory in accounting for linguistic interpretation and linguistic understanding. However, his accounts of belief and of having a language require that an individual at least have the conceptual capacities necessary to use a truth theory. Davidson holds that having a belief requires having a concept of belief and a concept of objectivity (through a concept of truth). He thinks that having belief requires having a language partly because he thinks that having a language requires a capacity for interpretation. And he takes interpretation to involve the application of second-order capacities systematized and rationalized in a Tarskian truth theory as applied to language.

---

[137] See my 'Comprehension and Interpretation'. See also my 'Predication and Truth'.

I believe that there is no ground to think that having a language requires a capacity for interpretation in this sense. In early stages of language learning, children seem to lack the higher-order capacities needed to have such a theory. Davidson gives no conceptually based argument for thinking that an empirical developmental theory along these lines must be wrong. The key point here is conceptual. Understanding language does not apriori require understanding that it is language, that sentences are true or false, and so on. It is enough on hearing or reading sentences to form beliefs expressed by them, to carry out inferences in ways that depend on sentential structure, and so on. A second-order interpretative perspective on this activity is a further matter.

Suppose that neither having belief nor having a language requires having second-order propositional attitudes—attitudes that employ the concepts of truth, objectivity, belief, and so on. What is the relation between having beliefs and having a language? Davidson holds that having beliefs requires having a language and being interpreted by another. His main argument for this position depends on arguing that having belief, even having representational content, requires a capacity for linguistic interpretation and requires being interpreted. Since this argument fails, Davidson's main argument that having belief requires having a language fails.

Davidson sometimes invokes a second argument. It is that having propositional content requires mastery of a network of inferential relations, and this network can be mastered only through mastery of linguistic structures.[138] I accept the first premise, and will return to it. I think that the second premise has been given no good support.

There are probably many beliefs that non-linguistic animals cannot have. It does not follow that non-linguistic animals are incapable of making simple inductive, deductive, or means–end inferences, applying perceptual concepts to perceivable entities, forming beliefs about spatial relations among perceptually identified objects, or forming beliefs about social relations among con-specifics, or about tools whose use they have mastered. Reflection on experiments in cognitive ethology with apes supports the view that apes engage in propositional reasoning—not conditioned responses, not instinctive tropes, and not mere manipulation of images or other non-conceptual representations deriving from perception. There is considerable empirical reason to think that best psychological explanations of the activity of apes attribute propositional capacities.[139] Davidson's arguments from the holistic nature of belief content do not show

[138] Davidson, 'Rational Animals', 97–99; 'The Emergence of Thought', 123–129; 'What Thought Requires', 135–137.

[139] Tomasello and Call, *Primate Cognition*; Povanelli, *Folk Physics for Chimps*; Richard Byrne, *The Thinking Ape* (Oxford: Oxford University Press, 1995); Marc D. Hauser, *Wild Minds* (New York: Henry Holt, 2000). Some of this literature is not meticulous about distinguishing propositional activity from other types of activity loosely called 'thinking'. Some experiments do, however, test propositional reasoning. Here it is enough to remark that Davidson's arguments do not even confront the empirical research.

that such empirical explanations must be mistaken. It seems plausible, indeed supported by explanations in cognitive ethology, that some higher animals have beliefs without language.

Although Davidson's main theses about conditions for having beliefs seem to me poorly supported and mistaken, I think that some of his holistic requirements on having beliefs are sound. The representational content of propositional attitudes has propositional structure. To have mental states type-identified by propositional structure, an individual must be able to use the structure. The structure must ground explanations of psychological processes. Using the structure entails making inferences that hinge on it. It also entails applying these inferences to meet theoretical and practical ends, commonly in response to perceptions or to emotional needs.[140]

Davidson is right to hold that one of the main sources of our grip on what propositional attitudes an individual has is our locating the attitude in a network of abilities that fall under rational norms. These include norms of practical rationality, norms of theoretical or common-sense rationality, norms of inference, and so on. It is not necessary that the individual always fulfill these norms, of course. But there must be enough complexity in the individual's psychological capacities to ground explanation that invokes propositional content, and norms attendant on propositional attitudes.

Notions of propositional truth and falsity become applicable when representation is embedded in a system of propositional inference, and when questions of rational and other epistemic norms for inference and belief formation are apropos. Having a language and having a concept of objectivity are not necessary conditions for having propositional attitudes. They are conditions on certain types of understanding. Propositional capacities emerge before any capacity to understand them as such.

The representational content of elementary perceptual beliefs depends on perceptual representation. Such beliefs use the representational content of perceptions and fit it into propositional networks.[141] Perception alone, however, provides only a limited array of representational types. For vision, there are perceptual representations as of spatial relations, size, shape, motion, color, bodies, and perhaps some functional representations—danger, predator, mate, shelter.[142] The development of true natural-kind concepts, many functional concepts (for complex artifacts), psychological concepts, modal concepts, concepts in pure mathematics, and even moderately theoretical concepts of common sense and natural science—all employ content that is not simply inherited from perceptual systems. I believe that such concepts are held in place and partly made

---

[140] This argument is mine. The argument in the next paragraph glosses argumentation that Davidson does give.

[141] See my 'Perceptual Entitlement', especially the last sections.

[142] It is a delicate empirical question whether such functional attributives occur only in representational actional systems or in perceptual systems as well.

to be what they are through explanatory, reason-giving inferential relations among propositional contents that contain them. A limited holistic inferential ability is constitutively necessary for having the relevant concepts.

Holism is not, however, confined to propositional representation. Holism is inevitable in perception. Perceptual organization is inevitably temporal, and almost inevitably spatial.[143] Consider what is involved in being able to perceive entities as entering into spatial relations. A perceiver could not possibly be capable of only a solitary spatial perceptual representation-type. Perceiving entities as being in spatial relations requires relating one position to another, shorter distances to longer ones, the upper and lower half of a line, one direction to another, lines or edges to planes or surfaces, planes or surfaces to volumes, and so on. Similar points apply to perceptual temporal representation.

A limited perceptual holism is also made inevitable by perceptual constancies. To represent an attribute from various perspectives is to perceive instances of the attribute in perceptually different ways. These different ways are marked by different perceptual representational contents. Constancies are capacities of a perceptual system to relate the different representational contents to one another, functioning as perspectives on the same particular or attribute. Each perceptual constancy constitutes a local perceptual holism—a capacity to relate different perceptual representations to one another systematically, under perceptual principles.

Perceptual representation is constitutively capable of correctness and error. These notions are species of notions of veridicality and non-veridicality. The latter notions apply to any type of representational state. Truth and falsity of propositional attitudes are special cases of veridicality and non-veridicality. Like holism, veridicality is not confined to propositional attitudes.

In any case, there is reason to believe that apes and other animals have the holistic network of inferential abilities required to have propositional attitudes about facts and goals relevant to their lives. Language enriches and accelerates development of propositional attitudes. It is not a precondition. Even less is it a precondition for perceptual representation.

LANGUAGE-CENTERED INDIVIDUAL REPRESENTATIONALISM:
SUMMARY

Like Strawson, Davidson requires as a constitutive condition on objective representation that an individual be able to represent a seems/is distinction. Strawson develops the point by distinguishing between how things appear in perceptual belief and how they really are. Davidson concentrates on the application of a concept of truth. He regards such application as implying a capacity to represent a

---

[143] See Chapter 10.

distinction between what one believes and the truth, which in turn implies that one's beliefs might be wrong.[144]

Like Strawson and Quine, Davidson requires as a condition on objective representation as of bodies that the individual be capable of thinking criteria. Strawson and Quine center on individuation and reidentification of bodies. Davidson agrees broadly with their strictures. The shared view is that unless general conditions for objective application are representable in the subject's system of beliefs, objective representation is impossible, in fact unintelligible.

Quine and Davidson differ from Strawson in focusing on linguistic interpretation. They claim that, lacking certain linguistic abilities, an individual cannot represent physical entities as having specific physical attributes. Quine offers the most detailed account of the supplementary apparatus. He highlights quantification because he regards the capacity to formulate general principles about conditions for being objects as a condition on representing objects. In this regard, Quine is a quintessential second-family Individual Representationalist. Davidson accepts Quine's constraints. He elaborates conditions under which one individual interprets another in linguistic communication. These conditions include being able to formulate a theory of truth and being in actual communicative/interpretative relations with others.

The influence of Quine and Davidson's lingua-centrism has been comparable to the influence of Strawson's neo-Kantianism. Many philosophers have tried to build an account of objective representation out of uninterpreted sounds, or uninterpreted syntax (whether a language of thought or a publicly expressed language), together with behavior and individual–world relations.[145]

No argument has shown that objective representation depends on language. Proponents usually just assert that intelligibility requires accepting conditions on objective representation that they propose. All such positions are hyper-intellectualized.

To represent an objective world, it is enough that the individual perceive. Perceiving involves having certain subindividual competencies that systematically filter contextually idiosyncratic elements in a signal from elements likely to bear on environmental reality. The perceiver need not be able to *represent* these distinctions. Even individuals capable of perceptual belief need not be able to form beliefs about a distinction between how things seem and how they are, or between true and false belief. Perceptual belief in higher animals and very young

---

[144] See Davidson, 'The Emergence of Thought', 129.

[145] Kripke's Wittgenstein, Putnam's model-theoretic arguments for a kind of indeterminacy of meaning, and Lewis's functionalism are examples of work that is influenced by the Quine–Davidson model. See Kripke, *Wittgenstein on Rules and Private Language*; Jerry A. Fodor, *The Language of Thought*; Fodor, *Concepts* (Oxford: Clarendon Press, 1998); Hilary Putnam, 'Models and Reality', in *Philosophical Papers*, iii (Cambridge: Cambridge University Press, 1983); *Reason, Truth, and History* (Cambridge: Cambridge University Press, 1981), chapters 1–2; David Lewis, 'Psycho-Physical and Theoretical Identification', *Australasian Journal of Philosophy* 50 (1972), 249–258; 'Radical Interpretation', *Synthese* 27 (1974), 332–334.

children need not be associated with beliefs about beliefs or about truth and falsity. It is enough that their perceptual beliefs incorporate perceptual represen-tation into a system of predication and propositional inference. Meta-beliefs about beliefs or about perception are not a constitutively necessary condition on having perceptual beliefs. No armchair argument can show them to be.

The notion of a criterion, which figures in both Strawsonian and Quinean traditions, received various explications. The explications became more cautious and more liberal as the century drew to a close. But, under all explications, Individual Representationalists maintained that to represent physical reality an individual must be able to represent some general preconditions for such representation.

It is, of course, true that something in the capacities of an individual must make the representation indicative of a specific attribute if the individual is to be able to represent that attribute. But the *individual* need not be capable of *representing* principles or conditions that fix representations on a given attribute. The individual's non-representational relations to the environment together with perceptual constancies in the individual's perceptual system can help fix the natures of objective representations. The perceptual capacities operate under general principles and are formed by conditions in the physical world. The individual need not be capable of (even implicitly) formulating such principles or conditions. It is enough that the individual's psychological capacities operate in accord with such principles and be explained in terms of them. It is enough that the individual be in relevant causal relations to conditions in the environment that help determine representational content of his psychological states.

Requiring language as a condition on objective representation is perhaps the most hyper-intellectualized of all the proposals in the Individual Representation-alist tradition. The idea that in accounting for objective representation one can ignore perception until language is in place is very far removed from an empir-ically reasonable account of origins of objectivity. In Part III I develop the conception of such origins that I have been gesturing toward.

A RETROSPECTIVE ON INDIVIDUAL REPRESENTATIONALISM

In this and the preceding three chapters, I have expounded and criticized two families of Individual Representationalism. Given their dominance in philosophy and in intellectual culture, it is perhaps surprising how little the various views have to recommend themselves. They are supported by little genuine argument. Once the views' claims are explained in the light of an alternative, they are seen to lack force.

Individual Representationalism is vulnerable to a realistic perceptual anti-individualism. Once one reflects on constitutive conditions for having perceptual representation, it becomes clear that the requirements imposed by Individual Representationalists are overblown.

Individual Representationalism is also subject to empirical scientific objections. Many of these objections derive from the impressively mature science of perceptual psychology. Some derive from developmental psychology and from cognitive ethology. These sciences indicate that human babies and many other animals perceive macro-physical particulars and perceptually group them under specific macro-physical attributes. Empirical accounts of this phenomenon are supported by a large body of sophisticated and frequently replicated evidence.

The developmental and conceptual stories told to support Individual Representationalism now seem quaint and out of step with a solid body of scientific knowledge. Some of the problem lay in the fact that early in the twentieth century, the relevant sciences had not matured. But that excuse is not available to most second-family Individual Representationalism. Some of the problem lay in philosophy's preoccupation with language and other high-level cognitive phenomena. Much of it lay in hubris and ignorance with regard to psychology, and lack of appreciation of the relevance of biological sciences to psychology and semantics.

I have emphasized the main differences between my view about origins of objectivity and those of the Individual Representationalists. I want to review these differences as a basis for reflection on similarities. Reflection on what Individual Representationalism got right about objective representation may enhance understanding.

Individual Representationalists maintain that some constitutive conditions on objective representation must be *represented* by the *individual*, if the individual is to engage in objective representation. I have claimed that there is a primitive but robust type of objective representation in which individuals represent no preconditions on objective representation. The capacities for objective representation are made possible by subindividual separation of the environmental from its surface effects, and by determination of representational content through non-representational interactions between individuals and the environment.

Nevertheless, I think that many of the conditions that Individual Representationalists postulated, other than the distinctively individual representationalist ones, were on the right track.

It will be recalled from Chapter 4 that Russellian versions of the sense-data tradition require, as a condition on representing physical reality, that the individual be able to construct descriptions of the form the cause of these sense data. Underlying this mistaken condition is a sound requirement that objective empirical representation be constitutively determined through causal relations between particulars and sensory states.

In effect, Russell captured the causal condition on particular representational encounters. Perceptual anti-individualism expands this point. It maintains that repeatable, representational attributives are constitutively determined by patterns of causal encounters.

This latter point about the way patterns of causal relations enter into the nature of objective empirical representation is anticipated in Carnap's Individual Representationalism. Carnap held that objective environmental physical patterns were reflected in laws or counterfactual relations among sense data. Appearances and sense impressions are not normally perceptually represented, nor are they normally evidence (data) for knowledge. Underlying mistaken appeals to sense data as objects of perception is a sound sense for the way that law-like patterns in the physical environment are reflected in patterns among representational states.

These patterns remain constant while individuals' experiences vary. The patterns are coded in the formation laws and law-like processes. The general character of these laws and processes help constitutively determine kinds of representational states. They help determine the specific representational content of objective representation and help make that content objective. Perceptual constancies in effect recapitulate, within an individual's psychology, physical regularities that hold constant through the proximal stimulations and the perspectival stream of perceptual representations.

The foregoing examples of constitutive conditions on objective representation involve relations between individual and environment. Of course, the distinctively individual representationalist conditions are psychological. Individual Representationalists were right to look to something in the individual's psychology that distinguishes representation of an objective subject matter from mere sensory responsiveness that is causally linked in reliable ways to an objective world. Their specific constitutive conditions often have correct analogs.

Strawson's requirement that the individual be able to represent a seems/is distinction and Davidson's requirement that the individual be able to represent beliefs and sentences as true or false are cases in point. These requirements are hyper-intellectualized. In perception, the separation and link between environment and surface effect occurs at subindividual, subrepresentational levels in the individual's perceptual system. (In non-perceptual sensory systems, the two are never separated, and the link occurs only externally.) But the requirements that Strawson and Davidson impose on individuals have analogs in subrepresentational aspects of perceptual systems.

There is no such thing as a perceptual representation of a perception, in the same perceptual system, as a seeming or as false. Still, the requirements of Strawson and Davidson have analogs in subindividual filtering mechanisms that underlie objectification in perception. The filtering mechanisms in effect distinguish between what is idiosyncratic and what reflects perception-independent patterns in the environment. This filtering is a non-representational analog of the distinctions that Strawson and Davidson postulate.

Perception does not represent appearances. Fundamentally, it represents environmental conditions that matter to the individual's basic activities. Perceptual representational contents constitute the perceptual perspective of, and, when conscious, the appearance to, the individual. Perception does not represent proximal stimulation. Such stimulation is informationally registered at an early stage in the formation of a perceptual representation. Perception does not represent meta-conditions such as truth, accuracy, objectivity, mind-independence—much less falsity, inaccuracy, subjectivity, mind-dependence. The appearance/reality distinction is the functional product of perceptual competence.

What Strawson and Davidson get right is that some capacity to distinguish environmental reality from effects on the individual that do not reflect such reality must be present in the individual's psychology if the individual is to engage in objective empirical representation.

A similar pattern emerges in individual representationalist requirements on conditions necessary for representing specific environmental kinds. From a very general perspective, Quine and Strawson make two mistakes in their requirements on representing bodies as such. First, their respective requirements of competence with logical relations and with comprehensive allocentric spatial frameworks are hyper-intellectualized. Such hyper-intellectualization is closely associated with requiring representation of generalities about constitutive conditions on objectivity—criteria. Second, they require abilities to discriminate bodies from all other kinds, not just kinds that are relevant to the individual's basic activities and needs in the individual's normal environment. Still, some of the requirements proposed by Quine and Strawson find analogs at lower representational levels.

Strawson's postulation of a deep connection between body representation and spatial representation is correct. Representing attributes like shape, and representing spatial localization, and spatial relations are constitutive concomitants of representing bodies as such. An individual visually perceives particulars as bodies by having perceptual capacities that are differentially sensitive to three-dimensional shapes whose integrity is maintained over time. The spatial representation can be of a local, egocentrically anchored space. It need not be the comprehensive space of mature objective thought.

Quine's requirement that an individual be able to distinguish one body from two has a lower-level analog. To represent anything as a body, the individual and system must be able to perceptually distinguish bodies when more than one body is perceived. However, there need be no analog of negation or plurals, much less a mastery of identity thoughts, or of quantification and general principles of counting.

Strawson's and Quine's postulation of criteria have lower-level analogs. To perceptually represent bodies as such, an individual and the individual's perceptual system must be able to distinguish bodies from events, colors, and shapes, since these attributes also occur in the normal environment, and figure in biological explanations of the individual's basic needs and activities. The individual and the system need not be able to distinguish bodies from *all* other kinds.

Strawson and Quine are correct to maintain that representing bodies as bodies requires an ability to track a body over time. The perceptual formation operations that make localization and tracking possible are complex and non-trivial and will be discussed further in Chapter 10. Again, however, there need be no capacity to think general principles for reidentification.

I give two more examples of how individual representationalist requirements find less intellectualized analogs.

First, Strawson and Evans maintained that self-consciousness is constitutively necessary for being able to engage in objective representation.[146] A lower-level analog is the fact that spatial and temporal representational frameworks in perceptual representation are constitutively anchored egocentrically. (I argue in Chapter 10 that temporal frameworks are constitutively necessary to perceptual representation, and spatial frameworks almost are.)

A perceiver's position is the origin of whatever spatial coordinate system the scene's elements are represented within. This origin is constitutively privileged, not only in that it is the standpoint of the perception, but also in that it has certain practical and perspectival ego-implications in the individual's psychology. For example, the perceiver is equipped with capacities to protect itself if the position of its perceptual standpoint is threatened.

Egocentric anchors figure in *representation* of spatial and temporal *relations*. The distance of a perceived object is computed as a relation between the perceiver's position and the position of the object. The timing of an event or act is measured with respect to the present time marked in a given perceptual state.

The anchor positions are not represented as a perceived entity is represented. They are indexed, not perceived. They are a part of perception's representational apparatus, even though they are not perceptual objects, much less objects of perceptual attention. The indexing is normally not conscious. Nonetheless, there is here a primitive analog of self-consciousness, inasmuch as the anchoring has the *ego* implications mentioned above. Ego enters not as perceived or as an object of consciousness, but as origin of perspective and locus of agency.

Second, there is also a lower-level analog of Strawson's and Evans's self-tracking requirement. If an individual is to track the position or motion of a perceived object, the individual's perceptual system must be able to distinguish position or motion of the egocentric position from that of the perceived object. Such a capacity is necessary to motion and distance constancies. Similarly, in timing ego-relevant events and activities, an individual must be able to track where its present is in a temporal ordering, temporal cycle, or temporal interval. The tracking ability need not involve tracking the perceiver's body in the sense of representing it, any more than an egocentric anchor need represent the perceiver, as opposed to the perspectival origin of the perceiver. The tracking need not involve any sort of consciousness, much less *self*-consciousness. The tracking must, however, have an *ego*centric element. For the tracking carries with it the implications for agency, need, and perspective that mark egocentricity. These

---

[146] Both claimed further that an ability to track one's own body through space is a necessary condition for self-consciousness.

implications constitute a primitive ancestor of self-consciousness and self-representation.

The preceding reflections indicate that individual representationalists had a largely sound conception of important constitutive elements in objective representation. They erred in requiring that the individual be able to represent these elements.

PART III

We must . . . not recoil . . . from examining the humbler animals. In all things of nature, there is something of the marvelous.

Aristotle, *Parts of Animals* I 5, 645ᵃ16–17

8 *Biological and Methodological Backgrounds*

man didn't necessarily eat his way through the world but by the act of eating and maybe only by that did he actually enter the world, get himself into the world: not through it but into it, burrowing into the world's teeming solidarity like a moth into wool by the physical act of chewing and swallowing the substance of its warp and woof and so making, translating into a part of himself and his memory, the whole history of man or maybe even relinquishing by mastication, abandoning, eating into it to be annealed, the proud vainglorious minuscule which he called his memory and his self and his I-Am into that vast teeming anonymous solidarity of the world from beneath which the ephemeral rock would cool and spin away to dust...
William Faulkner, *Intruder in the Dust*, chapter X

Instinct is the actual germ of the mind.
C. O. Whitman, 'Animal Behavior', in *Biological Lectures from the Marine Biological Laboratory of Wood's Hole, Mass.* (Boston: Ginn and Company, 1899)

In the remainder of the book I elaborate a view of constitutive conditions on empirical objective representation. This chapter sets stages. By discussing some attempts to reduce representational notions to biological notions, I try to develop clearer understanding of representational phenomena. The discussion issues in a distinction between biological functions and representational functions, and a distinction between biological norms and representational norms.

I argue for a use for the (or a) notion representation that is distinctive to psychology. By focusing on actual explanation in science, I rough out one border of a psychological kind, *representation*. I argue that certain psychological explanations are not special cases of biological explanations. Psychological explanations have a distinct explanatory paradigm. Psychology depends on there being systematic, functional pre-representational causal relations with the environment. But it discovers its own kinds. One of them is the kind *representation*.

In this chapter and the next, I also develop a specific conception of *perception* that indicates a significant, explanatorily relevant kind. I develop this conception by contrasting perception with *non-perceptual sensory discrimination*. Delineating each kind, *representation* and *perception*, depends on delineating the other.

In delineating the kind *perception*, I discuss relations between perception and action. Action is constitutively more primitive than perception. I believe that biologically basic actions—eating, navigating, mating—along with whole-animal biological needs figure epistemically and constitutively in background conditions for perception, representation, and empirical objectivity.

The chapter ends with examples of explanation in perceptual psychology that are distinctive of psychology and that invoke the kinds *representation* and *perception*.

DEFLATIONARY CONCEPTIONS OF REPRESENTATION;
BIOLOGICAL FUNCTION AND REPRESENTATIONAL FUNCTION

In discussing Individual Representationalism, I used an intuitive notion of representation. A mental state is representational if it has veridicality conditions and is *as of* entities in a subject matter.[1] Nearly any sort of state can be *regarded* as having veridicality conditions. An automatic water pump's operations in clearing water out of the hold of a boat can be construed as having veridicality conditions: the pump functions to keep water out of the boat; it represents the water level in the hold as above a certain threshold; so it starts pumping. A state of the pump can be regarded as having a veridicality condition that is fulfilled if water in the hold is above the threshold. One can even take the pump to *want* to keep the boat clear of water, to *believe* that there is too much water in the hold, to *decide* to start pumping, and to decide to stop when the benchmark is met.

The latter construal is easy, but perverse. It is imposed on events better explained without invoking psychological states. Even the former, less-psychological invocation of representation and veridicality conditions is not needed to explain the pump's functions and operations.[2]

I have assumed a distinction between cases in which the notion of representation applies to a subject matter and cases in which it is simply imposed on a subject matter. Underlying this assumption are epistemic considerations regarding explanation. What states are well explained in terms of states having veridicality conditions? What explanations appeal non-trivially to states with veridicality conditions?

---

[1] As explained in Chapter 2, this 'as of' locution applies to the representational content of a state. Such contents include contents of modular states that are not imputable to an individual. So the locution does not entail anything about something's seeming to an individual. The locution functions as a reminder that the content may not be veridical. A content may not even refer to or indicate anything.

[2] I write here *tout court* of explanations of events and states, which are temporally bound instances, because the explanations that interest me key on *basic*, *constitutive* natures of psychological events or state instances—and on the law-like patterns in which those natures figure. It is common to think of explanations of events or states *relative to aspects* or *features* (properties, relations, kinds) of those events or states. I accept this way of thinking, and simply take the relevant aspects or features to be constitutive ones. No aspects of pumps' operations are genuinely explained by reference to any representational aspects of those operations. There are no such aspects, in my sense of 'representational'.

I think that there are definite answers to these questions. Representational states figure in explanatory enterprises that are not in any evident way replaceable by explanatory enterprises in non-representational terms. There are types of understanding that are not attainable apart from attribution of representational notions. My primary goal for the remainder of this work is to explicate the notion of perceptual representation in a way that indicates its distinctive place in our knowledge of the world.

In this section I discuss some deflationary views about representation. According to these views, representation is to be assimilated to notions that have no *distinctive* theoretical relation to psychology as it is ordinarily understood.

I mention one deflationary view only to lay it aside. On this view, treating something as engaging in representation is merely a matter of a 'stance', with more or less practical or instrumental value.[3] On such a position, there is no objective kind, *representation*, that can be discovered through normal scientific investigation. On such a position, there is no more *theoretical* reason to treat an individual as having beliefs or perceptions than there is to treat a vending machine, or a planetary system, as representing something. It is all a matter of practical convenience or optional attitude toward the phenomena. I pass over this view because it ignores explanatorily relevant distinctions in science. Explanations in science (and common sense) appeal to representational states as real kinds.

Some philosophers and psychologists apply the term 'representation' to the products of the sensitivities of all or nearly all living things. Roughly, a state 'represents' something if it is differentially sensitive and responsive to it. Often a teleological condition is added—that the sensitivity and responsiveness are biologically functional for the individual. I call explications of representation along these lines the 'Deflationary Tradition'.[4]

There is nothing wrong with a broad notion of differential sensitivity and responsiveness that is associated with function. Such a notion describes the sensory capacities of many organisms, including the sensitivities of plants. One can use any term to express such a notion that one likes, including 'representation'. Many biologists and psychologists, and some philosophers, do use the term 'representation' in this way.

What I doubt about this tradition is an additional claim. This is the claim that the foregoing notion is the only scientifically respectable notion of representation and that there is no significant difference in kind between this notion and any notion of representation employed in psychological explanations. Proponents of

---

[3]   See Daniel C. Dennett, 'Intentional Systems', *The Journal of Philosophy* 68 (1971), 87–106; *The Intentional Stance* (Cambridge, MA: MIT Press, 1989).

[4]   Artifacts can be counted as capable of the discrimination as well. Artifactual functions can count as fulfilling the function requirement. I believe that my conception of representation can be extended in similar ways. But the level of artifactual competencies will have to be very different from the level described here. I do think that the derivative character of artifacts' functions complicates application of psychological notions to artifacts. I bracket these issues.

such a view hold that the only relevant notion of representation has its home in biology.

Thinkers in the Deflationary Tradition often claim that representation and objectivity are matters of 'degree'. They hold that all living things, or at least all animals, represent objectively to some 'degree'.[5] They apply their notion of representation to sensitivities of extremely simple organisms, and sometimes plants and non-living artifacts, such as thermometers. Implicitly or explicitly, they doubt that there is a notion of representation distinctive to psychology.

I believe that what I call the 'Deflationary Tradition' uses the term 'representation' so liberally as to debase it. The appeals to differences in degree ignore explanatorily relevant distinctions, both in common sense and in empirical science. The *term* 'representation' that they invoke has no distinctive philosophical, scientific, or explanatory interest. The term misleads, by drawing interest that accrues from interest in distinctively psychological phenomena, whereas the term is applied to numerous phenomena that are not, even remotely, distinctively psychological. From an explanatory point of view, the term could be dropped in favor of other notions, notions of sensitivity or discrimination, or co-variation, or causal co-variation, or structurally isomorphic causal co-variation, or information-carrying—together with the notion of biological function. The term 'representation' has been given significances in this tradition to fit into explanations that do not need the term at all.

These views issue a challenge to explain notions of perception and representation that have some specificity and explanatory substance, and that render non-trivial and philosophically interesting the questions about objective representation that began this book.

Accounts of representation that are this liberal and deflationary trivialize the issue over Individual Representationalism that we have been discussing. If representation is conceived in these ways, it is trivial that objective "representation" of the physical world does not require the capacities that Individual Representationalists invoke to explain such "representation". If objective representation is simply functional co-variation with physical attributes, or functional sensory discrimination, criticism of Individual Representationalism would be uninteresting. On such conceptions, one does not need philosophy to realize that simple organisms that lack capacities required by Individual Representationalism "represent" the environment.

Criticism of Individual Representationalism that rests on such deflationary conceptions would elicit a serious and reasonable question whether the criticism simply changes the subject.[6] Faced with criticism that uses such conceptions of perception and representation, Individual Representationalists could plausibly

---

[5] See Ruth Garrett Millikan, *Language, Thought, and Other Biological Categories* (Cambridge, MA: MIT Press, 1984), 86.

[6] Some philosophers reject Individual Representationalism because of allegiance to deflationary conceptions of representation. I think that deflationary conceptions talk past traditional views.

protest that they use richer notions in their claims. Relative to those notions—they might hold—their claims stand.

More specifically, the issues discussed by Individual Representationalists concern conditions under which perception or thought can attribute specific physical attributes to physical particulars. These issues seem, prima facie, very far from the sensitivities of plants to light, or of bacteria to magnetic fields. Perception and thought have well-entrenched places in common-sense and psychological explanation. Assimilating the types of attribution involved in these psychological phenomena to the responsiveness of plants to the environment, and then calling differences a matter of degree, trivializes, or even ignores, the issues that Individual Representationalists were concerned with. Deflationary conceptions of representation are unilluminating in confronting those issues. They are insufficiently sensitive to distinctive features of psychological states.

In fact, much of the impetus behind second-family Individual Representationalism was to distinguish between genuine objective representation and low-level deflationary analogs and surrogates. Individual Representationalists repeatedly claimed that the difference lies in the fact that in the case of the low-level analogs, individuals lack the ability to represent or 'understand' what they are doing. Or they claimed that such individuals cannot represent general principles governing their competencies, or cannot follow rules. Or they claimed that such individuals lack the language to differentiate themselves from thermometers, plants, amoebae. Then Individual Representationalists pointed out that we have linguistic abilities, meta-abilities, or abilities to generalize. The distinction between genuine objective representation and fake, surrogate representation is supposed to be explained by Individual Representationalism. The doctrine is supposed to be explanatorily necessary if objective representation is to be distinguished from mere stimulus-response, mere groping in the dark. Underlying invocations of a supplementary apparatus is the assumption that unless fundamental *general* conditions that make objectivity possible are represented *by the individual*, it is impossible to distinguish genuine representation from the surrogate representation of a thermometer or amoeba.

I believe that there are differences in psychological kind between amoebae and human beings that do bear on the issues that Individual Representationalists discussed. I think, however, that their diagnosis of the differences is mistaken. I believe that *no* reasonable general notion of representation is distinguished by the requirements of Individual Representationalism. In fact, I think that no individual representationalist position is supported for *any* notion of representation. Criticism of Individual Representationalism does not depend on overstretched, deflationary conceptions.

Still, dissatisfaction with deflationary conceptions as the only conceptions of representation seems to me to be reasonable. There is an explanatorily relevant kind, *representation*, that is psychologically distinctive. Before isolating this kind, I want to reflect further on deflationary conceptions of representation.

First, some background. A strand of thought in philosophy, and in the methodological writings of some psychologists and biologists, aims to show that psychology's notions are scientifically respectable. This strand seeks respectability by assimilating explanatory notions of representation to biological or informational notions.

In psychology, the strand derives from scientists' working out from under the shadow of behaviorism. In philosophy, there are similar attempts to "naturalize" the notion of representation. Both groups try to show that their appeals to cognitive notions are respectable by assimilating them to notions in biology or in information theory that are not mentalistic.[7]

Naturalization projects in philosophy proceed in a spirit of trying to save representation from 'mystery' or 'miracle'.[8] Promoters of such projects suggest that representation 'may prove permanently recalcitrant to integration in the natural order'.[9] They see themselves as saving representation from such darkness by reducing it to notions in sciences other than psychology, particularly natural sciences. Alternatively they think that rescuing the notion depends on giving it sufficient conditions for representation in other scientific terms. No reasons beyond the apocalyptic ones just mentioned are given for insisting on these types of reduction. These attitudes are prevalent among philosophers, even today.

I find such rescue missions in philosophy quaint and the parallel moves in psychology retrograde. Each approach is out of sync with empirical knowledge and practice. Neither approach captures, or even reflects on, what is distinctive about certain powerful and successful explanations in psychology, specifically perceptual psychology.

Promoters of "naturalizing" projects are driven, I think, by misconceptions of science. These misconceptions breed misconceptions of mind. The notion of representation—of reference and attribution that can be correct or incorrect and that helps type-individuate kinds of psychological states—is entrenched not only in common-sense explanation but in scientific explanation in psychology. There

---

[7] For an example of a psychological meta-theory that uses 'representation' in this broad way, see Gallistel, *The Organization of Learning*, chapters 1–2. For further discussion, see Chapter 10 below, especially the sections on mathematical capacities, spatial capacities, and association–computation–representation. An example of a philosopher who tries to reduce representational notions to information-theoretic notions alone is Fred Dretske, *Knowledge and the Flow of Information* (Cambridge, MA: MIT Press, 1981). In later work, Dretske supplements this account by invoking the notion of biological function. See Dretske, 'Misrepresentation', in R. J. Bogdan (ed.), *Belief, Form, Content, and Function* (Oxford: Oxford, University, Press, 1986); *Explaining Behavior* (Cambridge, MA: MIT Press, 1988); and *Naturalizing the Mind*. I discuss Dretske's views below. A philosopher who firmly distinguishes between informational content and representational content is Peacocke, *Sense and Content*, 6 ff. I do not, however, accept all the distinguishing features that he cites. I do not accept the fourth alleged difference, which implies that for an individual to have experiential representational content, the individual must have concepts. Peacocke no longer holds this view.

[8] Dretske, 'Misrepresentation'. See also *Naturalizing the Mind* and *Explaining Behavior*.

[9] Jerry A. Fodor, 'Semantics, Wisconsin Style', in *A Theory of Content and Other Essays* (Cambridge, MA: MIT Press, 1990), 32. Dretske and Fodor are strongly influenced by Quine's "naturalism", cited in Chapter 7.

is nothing unnatural or supernatural about such explanation. Some of the relevant psychology is well-supported, mathematically rigorous, mature science. There is no basis, even a prima facie one, to the worry that psychological notions are invitations to mystery or miracle. Even if there were such basis, the role that these notions play in powerful empirical science would undermine it.

The bogeyman of Cartesian dualism is repeatedly and tiresomely invoked as ground for "naturalizing" the notion of representation. Cartesian dualism depends on detailed and subtle argumentation. In particular, it depends on argumentation about whether one can intuitively discern *all* of a psychological state's nature or essence. Neither common-sense psychological explanation nor scientific psychological explanation is committed to such argumentation, one way or the other. They are committed to entities needed to make their explanatory claims true. I know of no good ground for thinking that these explanatory claims must be twisted into the mold of biological or information-theoretic explanation, or any other explanation in the natural sciences, in order to be explanatorily successful.[10]

Determining the place of representational kinds in the wider order studied in the natural sciences need not take the simple forms that philosophical reductionists require. It is enough to find systematic connections between the psychological and natural sciences. There is nothing in psychological explanation that conflicts with the natural sciences. There is a large and growing set of connections among biological, neural, computational, and cognitive-perceptual explanations.

Philosophers in the last half-century repeatedly warned about dire consequences that would ensue if their favored solutions to philosophical problems about the relation between psychological notions and other notions were not accepted. These warnings are a way of insuring a special role for philosophy in saving science and common sense from themselves. I think that such warnings constitute a characteristically late-twentieth-century form of philosophical hubris. They present philosophy as rescuer for ailing common sense or bumbling, unreflective science, rather than as queen of the sciences. In this respect they are less grandiose than claims for the old all-encompassing metaphysical systems. They nonetheless arrogate to philosophy a role that the actual intellectual products of the claims cannot sustain.

None of the foregoing is meant to imply that there are no hard questions about the mind–body problem or about relations between the psychological and natural sciences. There is much to be said about how the notion of representation fits into a wider domain of explanations—causal and teleological explanations, chemical, neural, macro-biological, information-theoretic, engineering, and semantical explanations. My point is that these issues should be approached in an

---

[10] I discuss these matters in more detail in 'Individuation and Causation in Psychology'; and 'Intentional Properties and Causation', in C. MacDonald and G. MacDonald (eds.), *Philosophy of Psychology: Debates on Psychological Explanation* (Oxford: Blackwell, 1995); 'Mind–Body Causation and Explanatory Practice', in J. Heil and A. Mele (eds.), *Mental Causation* (Oxford: Oxford University Press, 1993); and 'Postscript: "Mind–Body Causation and Explanatory Practice"'; all printed or reprinted in *Foundations of Mind*.

exploratory spirit, free of strong preconceptions of how they *must* be answered. The notion of a representational state cannot reasonably be taken to be prima facie defective or in need of supplement or help. It has long earned its explanatory keep. What philosophy can do here is to clarify, explore, connect.

An antecedent commitment to reduction is ungrounded ideology, not an expression of science or reason. Once the rescue rhetoric is dropped, there remains an issue for inquiry. Is reduction of the sort expected by the Deflationary Tradition possible? Reductions are a legitimate type of explanatory unification. Occasionally reductions succeed. In principle, representation might be somehow reducible to other notions. I believe, however, that trying to reduce representation and veridicality to something more "naturalistically acceptable" is probably pointless and hopeless. At any rate, the reductionistic proposals that have been made so far seem to me hopeless.

Notions like representation earn their keep in science, and to a large extent in common sense, by figuring in successful explanation. Successful explanation is marked in the usual ways by yielding agreement, opening new questions, making questions testable and precise, engendering progressive improvement in theory and experimentation. Mainstream work in perceptual psychology displays these features. As I outlined in Chapter 3 and shall explain in more detail at the end of this chapter and in Chapters 9–10, the central mode of explanation in this science takes representational state and transformation that produces representational states to be *the* central explanatory notions. Explanation of the formation of states that can be representationally successful or unsuccessful—perceptually accurate or illusory—is the central organizing theme of the science. The explanations of such states center on law-like patterns of formation of representational states. One could hardly have better epistemic ground to rely on a notion than that it figures centrally in a successful science.

Indeed, it is hard to see how one *could* explain vision—accurate perception—without these notions. I know of no reason to think that this theme will be displaced or that these notions—or what they apply to—will be reductively explained in other terms. I think that the notions of veridicality and representation—and notions like perceptual state, belief, propositional inference—are scientific primitives. I will discuss philosophical reduction on the assumption that these notions are scientifically acceptable. Our questions are whether they can be reduced to other scientific notions, and exactly what these notions come to. I turn to a modicum of detail.

Nearly everyone agrees that representation is to be distinguished from what Grice calls 'natural meaning'. A particular state of type T *naturally-means* a state instance or property instance G if and only if there is some relatively reliable counterfactual supporting relation between instances of T and instances of G that cause instances of T.[11] This notion approximates common notions of T's carrying information about G, except that it adds the causal component. There are several

[11] Paul Grice, *Studies in the Ways of Words* (Cambridge, MA: Harvard University Press, 1989), 213–214.

such notions—statistically regular co-variation, counterfactual dependence, or lawful dependence—that I shall loosely call 'information-theoretic notions'. It is widely recognized that this range of notions is too generic to capture a psychologically relevant notion of representation. Natural meaning holds among too many things—tree rings and age, smoke and fire, the angle of smoke and the direction of the wind. Even most authors in what I call the 'Deflationary Tradition' balk at resting with such a general notion of representation.

One reason for balking is that information-theoretic notions do poorly in accounting for veridicality and error—the key notions associated with representation. Error is a type of failure or shortcoming. Failure is not extractable from causal, statistical, or law-like notions that underlie both natural meaning and information-theoretic notions. Abnormality and interference with regular processes are not in themselves errors or even failures. Moreover, perceptual veridicality is not always correlated with regularity. A perceptual state can be veridical even if its veridicality is unusual. Information-theoretic notions by themselves offer no prospect of accounting for error. Their applicability is neither sufficient nor necessary for the applicability of such notions as perceptual representation.

A common move among reductionists is to supplement information-theoretic notions, or other notions of differential responsiveness, with a notion of biological function. It is said that a state represents certain properties if it has the *function* of naturally meaning them, or giving information that correlates with them, or otherwise being differentially responsive to them. There are many explications of the notion of biological function. But the differences are not important for present purposes.[12] An advantage of the teleological notion of function is that it has a natural association with success and failure. It is common to hold that misrepresentation is a matter of failure to fulfill a function. The idea is to explain error in terms of failure to fulfill biological function, and to explain veridicality in terms of fulfillment of biological function.

Perceptual systems and some of their states surely have biological functions. Further, biological function is relevant to understanding both the content of perceptual states and their relation to actions that serve biological needs. (See the section PERCEPTION AND THE ENVIRONMENT: THE "DISJUNCTION PROBLEM" below.) I believe, however, that the connections between perceptual representation and biological function are more complex and less direct than they are portrayed in the Deflationary Tradition.

Some problems are internal to particular programs. For example, Dretske starts with a notion of information-carrying that requires that representation have a high likelihood of corresponding to its object, at least in normal circumstances. But representation can in principle be quite unreliable, even in normal

---

[12] For collections of articles that develop various conceptions of biological function, see Colin Allen, Marc Bekoff, and George Lauder (eds.), *Nature's Purposes* (Cambridge, MA: MIT Press, 1998); and David J. Buller (ed.), *Function, Selection, and Design* (Albany, NY: SUNY Press, Series in Philosophy and Biology, 1999).

circumstances. An animal's representation of danger might be reliably inaccurate but still serve the animal's biological needs. Phenomena that are counted representational by deflationists are often very unreliable but still fulfill biological functions.[13]

This problem led some deflationists to jettison strictly informational elements, and any appeal to reliability, in favor of *some* differential responsiveness to normal conditions backed by biological function. Millikan's work presents a sophisticated version of this approach. She separates representation from information-carrying, from reliability, and from causal relations. The following example illustrates the view.[14]

Bacteria have sensors that respond to magnetic fields. Under certain conditions, moving in response to those fields leads bacteria to areas in a pond that are beneficial to them because the areas have less oxygen. The function of the sensory registration and movement is to enable the bacterium to move toward oxygen-poor locales. But the bacterium is not causally sensitive to oxygen or oxygen poverty, and the bacterium's states and movements are more reliably and more informationally correlated with magnetic forces than with oxygen or oxygen poverty. Millikan notes this split and uses it to criticize views that connect representation with causation, reliability, or information-carrying. She holds that intuitively the bacterium represents oxygen poverty.[15]

I think that this view is *not* intuitive. Whatever "representation" the bacterium might be seen as engaging in surely must be sensory. But the bacterium has no causal sensitivity to—hence no capacity for sensing—oxygen or oxygen poverty. I believe that Millikan's view amounts to a stipulation about how she intends to use 'representation'. The word 'representation' is to apply to certain normal conditions relevant to biologically functional relations between the animal's states and elements in the environment. I see no reason to use 'representation' that way. Everything in the example can be explained using the notion of biological function (with respect to oxygen poverty), normal environmental conditions, and sensory discrimination (with respect to magnetic forces). Adding an odd use of the term 'representation' contributes nothing to explanation, and does not independently illuminate representation.

The example illustrates the fact that connections among causation, information, and biological function are not simple. Whether these notions can be brought together in a more illuminating way seems to me an open question.

---

[13] For discussions of this problem, see Peter Godfrey-Smith, 'Misinformation', *Canadian Journal of Philosophy* 19 (1989), 533–550; and 'Indication and Adaptation', *Synthese* 92 (1992), 283–312; Ruth Garrett Millikan, 'Biosemantics', *The Journal of Philosophy* 86 (1989), 281–297, and 'Compare and Contrast Dretske, Fodor, and Millikan on Teleosemantics', *Philosophical Topics* 18 (1990), 151–161, both in *White Queen Psychology and Other Essays for Alice* (Cambridge, MA: MIT Press, 1993).

[14] The example was introduced by Dretske, in 'Misrepresentation'. He treats the example differently, but I believe that Millikan is right that the separation of causal/informational factors from functional factors in the example raises difficulties for Dretske's view.

[15] Millikan, 'Biosemantics', 92 ff.

There is, however, a *root* mismatch between representational error and failure of biological function. The key deflationist idea in explaining error is to associate veridicality and error with success and failure, respectively, in fulfilling biological function. Biological functions are functions that have ultimately to do with contributing to fitness for evolutionary success. Fitness is very clearly a practical value. It is a state that is ultimately grounded in benefit of its effects for survival for reproduction.[16] Explanations that appeal to biological function are explanations of the practical (fitness) value of a trait or system. But accuracy is not *in itself* a practical value. Explanations that appeal to accuracy and inaccuracy—such as those in perceptual psychology—are not explanations of practical value, or of contributions to some practical end.

Deflationist theories are part of a long, failed tradition of assimilating truth and accuracy to contribution to practical success, and falsity and inaccuracy to practical failure. Error need not be a failure or frustration of *any* independently identifiable biological function. Representational success need not fulfill any biological function.

It is repeatedly said that the biological function of a sensory state is to 'detect' the presence of some distal condition (perhaps a predator). Given this claim, any failure of correlation with the distal condition is *in itself* a biological failure at some level of explanation. But *in itself* detection does literally *nothing* to contribute to fitness.[17] It is the causal properties of the detecting state in affecting *responses* that contribute.

I do not doubt that biological functions can involve detection relations to distal conditions. I do doubt that biological functions, as ordinarily understood, ever reside strictly in detection by itself, or in mere correlation with distal conditions (see note 17). A biologically more accurate description would be that the function is to initiate some sequence of states that ultimately issues in some response to the distal condition. Sensory states that are predator detectors, for example, have the biological function of initiating a chain of avoidance behavior, given further states and conditions, with respect to the predator. It is this initiation, not the detection *per se*, that contributes to biological success.

---

[16] Millikan develops considerable complexity underlying this point. She is sensitive to the fact that sometimes serving a *larger* biological function can issue in reliable failure. Most sperm fail to end in insemination, but producing lots of sperm can fulfill a primary biological function. She also shows that fulfilling certain derivative biological functions can be bad for the individual and species. See 'Truth Rules, Hoverflies, and the Kripke–Wittgenstein Paradox', *The Philosophical Review* 99 (1990), 323–353, also in *White Queen Psychology and Other Essays for Alice*, 227.

[17] This distinction between different types of explanation is repeatedly fudged in descriptions of the biological functions of states. See David Papineau, *Reality and Representation* (Oxford: Blackwell, 1987), 87: 'The biological function of a given belief type is to be present when a certain condition obtains: that then is the belief's truth condition.' Being present when a certain condition obtains cannot *in itself* be a contribution to biological success. Detection can be an aspect of a state whose biological function is not to detect *per se* but to cause fit response to whatever is (perhaps normally) detected.

We can certainly correctly regard the state as a detector. Detection is, however, not *in itself* a biological function, as 'biological function' is standardly understood. Detection failure is not in itself a failure of biological function. It is the contribution to *response*, and ultimately to fitness, not the detection *per se*, that is biologically functional. Detectors were selected, not because they were accurate in detecting a condition, but because they tended to contribute fit responses, including fit behavior, with respect to the condition. Such initiation may be maximally beneficial to biological success, at *every* level of biological explanation, even when the initiating state occurs and the distal condition is not present (and not detected).

For example, suppose that the avoidance mechanism functioned to increase strength and agility—in avoiding the predator—even in cases in which the animal engaged in avoidance behavior, because of a misrepresentation as of a predator, when no predator was present. Suppose that in each case, whether or not the predator is present, the avoidance mechanism contributes to the animal's fitness for avoiding predators. Then, although the ultimate *raison d'être* for the mechanism might be absent in a given case, there would be *no* biological sense in which the mechanism failed to fulfill a biological function when it effected avoidance behavior in cases where the distal condition was not present. The biological function is to contribute to a fit response to the predator—which entails contributing to avoiding predators. Failure of accuracy need not be failure to realize *any* biological function. Functioning in interacting successfully with respect to a beneficial or detrimental distal condition is not the same as accurately detecting the condition.[18] Attempts to explain failures of representational accuracy as failures in realizing a biological function face this problem. The problem is another aspect of their conflating representational issues with the practical issues that underlie biological functions.

Although accuracy in perception, and correlation with environmentally beneficial matters in sensory registration, usually contribute to fitness, they are not *in themselves* contributions to fitness. When they do contribute, it is not the accuracy *per se* that makes the contribution. The tendencies of the state to produce efficient response to *need* or, more precisely, tendencies to produce evolutionary fitness—not the veridical aspects of the state—make the contribution.

There is no question that biological structures that underlie perceptual and cognitive systems evolved and were selected for. These structures were selected for not because they are or underlie representational systems *per se*—systems for

---

[18] Millikan shows that some analogy of inaccuracy can be functional in normal conditions. She points out that sperm fail to impregnate most of the time, and that, for small creatures, protective coloration fails to protect most of the time. See note 16. In these cases a larger *practical biological* function is not fulfilled. It does not follow that in all cases of reliable detection failure a larger biological function is not fulfilled. My general point is that one cannot assimilate issues of accuracy and inaccuracy to issues of practical use. Functioning to be accurate is not *in itself* a biological function, at any level. Biological functioning is not a semantical matter. It is a practical matter, a matter of fitness for procreation.

accurately representing the world (to within some degree of accuracy). They were selected for because they yielded results that were good enough to further fitness. Evolution does not care about veridicality. It does not select for veridicality *per se*. Being fitted to successful evolution is a matter of functioning well enough to contribute to survival and reproduction. Well enough often coincides with veridicality. But even coincidence is not identity. Biological explanations of function explain a different feature of reality than do explanations of veridicality and error. Biological explanations of sensory registration and function, on one hand, and psychological explanations that center on accuracy, on the other, are different types of explanation.

The explanatory content and goals of theories of perception and belief are not the same as those that underwrite biology. Explaining the way veridical and non-veridical representational states arise, given proximal stimulation, is a different explanatory enterprise from that of explaining any states in terms of their *biological* functions—their contributions to fitness. So biological explanations cannot reduce explanations whose point is to explain accuracy and inaccuracy of representational states. Since what they explain is different, the former cannot take over the job of the latter.

Psychological explanation in terms of representational states, which places veridicality in a special explanatory position, is a distinctive type of explanation. I shall illustrate this point in some detail in the last section of this chapter.

A non-vacuous appeal to veridicality conditions in psychological explanation requires evidential support independently of the fact that there is causally based co-variation with external conditions that have a biological function. One needs specific ground for making veridicality (accuracy, truth) a theoretical notion, both in understanding the phenomena and in explaining the occurrence of psychological states. This is just what perceptual psychology does.

The fact that biological functions of sensory systems are relatively close to representational functions makes psychology possible. The fact that biological functions are not the same as representational functions helps make psychology independently interesting.

A further problem for deflationary theories of representation is they have not offered a reduction that is even approximately co-extensive with *distinctively psychological* notions of representation that are employed in scientific explanations. Every known explication of representation in terms of functional information, or functional sensory discrimination, or functional correlation, applies too broadly. Such explications apply just as well to discriminative responses of plants, very low-level organisms, and very low-level regulatory processes, as to what is more normally counted representation. For example, registration of light or dark in amoebae or planaria for phototaxis meet most deflationist conditions for representation. A reptile's body heat varies with the heat of the sun striking the body. Internal registrations, or encodings, of such variations contribute functionally in various physiological regulations of bodily operations. So these organisms and response mechanisms "represent" their environment.

It would be a misleadingly broad use of 'representation' to maintain that the amoeba represents light or that the reptile's body represents heat, and then suppose that such "representation" had anything much to do with accuracy of representation in psychology.[19]

More importantly, any such usage cannot claim to capture the type of representation that is of *independent* scientific, or other cognitive, interest—and that cannot be *trivially* explained in other terms. Many in the Deflationary Tradition engage in such usage. Some claim that no further notion of representation is acceptable. I believe that not distinguishing functional sensitivity from a narrower range of phenomena, which are representational in a traditional, more distinctively psychological sense, misses fundamental psychological kinds.

There exists a kind *representation* and a type of scientific explanation of processes involving this kind that are systematically overlooked by deflationists as well as Individual Representationalists. This point will be fundamental to the rest of the argument in this book. I want to develop just an aspect of the point here in discussing deflationist accounts of representation in philosophy.

Dretske addresses the breadth-of-application problem. He hopes to distinguish *mental* representation from low-level functioning sensitivity. He thinks that only in mental representation is there grouping or categorization. Grouping and categorization are, of course, not notions that are admissible in his deflationist account. So he must explain them in other terms. Dretske distinguishes mental representation from low-level sensory discrimination by claiming that in cases of mental representation the individual can *learn*.[20]

---

[19] It is, of course, acceptable to say that a reptile's body carries *information* that correlates with heat, in the technical sense that it varies with heat in a statistical, even nomological, way. Such variations are *functional* in that they are capitalized upon in the animal's physiology. One *can* call such correlation 'representation', in a very broad sense. But no representation in any distinctively psychological sense is involved. A similarly broad use of 'representation' applies to artifacts. Of course, the states of a phonograph cartridge are intentionally made to vary with variations in sound frequencies, and indeed with the musical events created by an orchestra. What "representation" there is in these artifactual cases, in the narrower, more normal usage of the term, resides in our use of the co-variations. The moving magnet in the cartridge enables us to represent the orchestra's sounds. We use it as an instrument to that end. The cartridge does not represent—or perceive—anything autonomously. It represents the music only for us.

Even in literature that clearly takes information as statistical correlation, the phrase '*information about*' is often misleadingly used. A tree's bending is not *about* the force of the wind, but the former carries information that correlates with the latter. Philosophy, the biological sciences, and the human sciences are rife with talk that has only statistical and functional content, but that suggests a distinctively psychological representationality.

[20] See Dretske, *Knowledge and the Flow of Information*, 'Misrepresentation', *Explaining Behavior*, and *Naturalizing the Mind*, chapter 1. Dretske assumes that mental representation can occur only in a psychology that also involves propositional attitudes, or propositional thought. He thinks that exercises of sensory capacities that are not backed by propositional thought cannot group or categorize. They are mere sensory reaction. See *Naturalizing the Mind*, 18. Here he explicitly follows the Individual Representationalism of Gareth Evans, criticized in Chapter 6 above. This development casts in a less favorable light Dretske's earlier work on perception, which I find more congenial than the reductive work that begins with *Knowledge and the Flow of Information*. Dretske's earlier work occurs in *Seeing and Knowing* (Chicago: University of Chicago Press, 1969). The first section on 'non-epistemic seeing' is original and illuminating. Dretske holds that S sees$_n$ D if and only if D is

I think that this idea does not work. I discuss it as an instance of one of the more sophisticated attempts to explain a distinctively psychological notion of representation in terms already used in the natural sciences.

Dretske does not elaborate his conception of learning. He says only that learning is 'a process in which there is a more or less permanent modification of [an ability in the system]'.[21] It is, of course, necessary for his reductionist project that the notion of learning not import representational notions. Some conceptions of learning in psychology, natural ones, explicitly utilize representational notions.

The most common non-representational conception of learning derives from behaviorism. This conception counts any non-peripheral, relatively permanent, adaptive modification of behavior, associating either two sensory inputs or a sensory input and a response, as learning.[22] This conception distinguishes learning from sensory fatigue, injury, disease, and maturation. Sensory fatigue is distinguishable in being relatively temporary, as well as in being peripheral. Injury and disease are not adaptive. Maturation is more difficult to distinguish, at least in practice.[23] Maturation is marked by relative uniformity across members of a species, independent of vicissitudes of individual sensory stimulation. Its causal sources are primarily internal and are not linked to the nature of the

---

visually differentiated from its immediate environment by S. ('Seeing$_n$' means 'non-epistemic seeing'.) The account has the merit of not maintaining that beliefs are necessary to engage in non-epistemic seeing. He holds that 'visual differentiation' of D is constituted by D's *looking some way* to S, and looking different from its immediate environment (p. 20). Dretske makes some illuminating further remarks about visual differentiation, which I will not discuss.

I am unsure how Dretske regards the relation between this early view and the later views that I discuss in the text. The notion of a look is not clarified. It suggests conscious mentality. If the suggestion is intended, then it is an open question whether, say, bees see anything in Dretske's non-epistemic sense. This consequence would count against the theory. I think that consciousness is constitutively neither necessary nor sufficient for perception. If a look is understood simply in terms of the specifically visual effect of light (light's encoding) in the individual's sensory capacities, then non-epistemic seeing occurs in the sensory capacities of molluscs and amoebae. Grouping, or perceptual attribution, is a constitutive aspect of perception. Dretske does not discuss this aspect with respect to non-epistemic seeing. I believe that his non-epistemic seeing does not correspond to visual perception, but it certainly overlaps.

In my view, what is excellent about this early work is its persistent defense of the position that there is a type of seeing that does not require belief, at least in particular cases. Dretske does not argue, as I do, that human seeing does not require even a *capacity* for belief. I think that Dretske's later work errs both in its attempts at reduction of representational notions and in its maintaining that perceptual grouping (attribution) depends on having propositional capacities.

[21] Dretske, *Knowledge and the Flow of Information*, 144. I will not discuss Dretske's account of concepts. The account centers on the notion of extracting digital information from an analog sensory base. I think that, in the relevant sense, digital information is present in perceptual as well as conceptual representation. I think, however, that Dretske is right to regard (relatively) analog information as an important element in understanding perceptual representation.

[22] I owe Randy Gallistel for conversation on several of the following points about learning.

[23] Dretske's explication does not distinguish learning from these latter phenomena, but perhaps it can be adapted to do so.

stimulus in the way that learning is. On this conception of learning, habituation as well as various forms of association count as learning.[24]

There are at least two general difficulties with such conceptions of learning. One is that the distinction between central and peripheral modifications is not psychologically principled. The distinction relies on an anatomical criterion for a psychological notion.

A second difficulty is that the associationist–behaviorist cast of the conception is inadequate to account for quite a lot of learning in reasonably complex animals. Association and conditioning are not adequate theoretical bases for accounting for learning. As far as is now known, much learning cannot be accounted for except in representationalist terms. If one allows representation into one's account of learning, the notion of learning will be worthless for reduction of representation. If one is to avoid this difficulty by appealing to some intermediate conception of learning, between classical associationist and representationalist conceptions, one must spell out the relevant conception. Dretske does not do so.

There is also a specific difficulty with the *application* of the conception of learning that we have been discussing. The anatomical criterion excludes plants from the learners because there is no "center" in which modifications can reside. As noted this exclusion does not appear to be principled. A similar problem arises for the lowest animal-like organisms. The distinction between center and periphery is not easily applied to organisms like amoebae. Modifications that otherwise would be counted as instances of learning—on this conception—appear in these simple organisms. For example, habituation-like modifications that are relatively enduring and that are distinguishable from mere fatigue are inducible in protozoa. An analog of trial and error associative learning occurs in paramecia. Over time, the paramecium exhibits a reduction of average time for escape from a tube-maze.[25]

Appeal to the lack of clear distinction between peripheral and central parts of protozoa to exclude them from the learners is, as mentioned, not psychologically principled. Moreover, such a move just postpones the basic difficulty. There are slightly higher animals to which the central/peripheral distinction does apply that

[24] For general discussion in this tradition, see W. H. Thorpe, *Learning and Instinct in Animals* (London: Methuen, 1963). I oversimplify the account. The account is elaborated to exclude certain central modifications that are intuitively not learning—such as the transient waning reflex, which is more concerned with response than stimulus.

Habituation is, roughly, decrease of responsiveness not due to sensory adaptation or effector fatigue, injury, or maturation.

Thorpe appeals (circularly) to experience in his official definition of experience (p. 55), but his account can be read as not depending essentially on representational notions.

[25] J. W. V. French, 'Individual Differences in *Paramecium*', *Journal of Comparative Psychology* 30 (1940), 451–456; Thorpe, *Learning and Instinct in Animals*, 184–189. The general point that I develop was made with a wealth of detail and in application to numerous species by H. S. Jennings, *Behavior of the Lower Organisms* (1906; Bloomington: Indiana University Press, 1962). All such organisms adapt to local circumstances through reaction to stimulation. Some of the adaptation is relatively permanent. See also J. D. Carthy, *An Introduction to the Behaviour of Invertebrates* (London: George Allen & Unwin Ltd, 1958), 2, who makes the same point: On the most common non-representational conception of learning, probably all invertebrate animals can learn.

also exhibit habituation and modification of behavior through trial-and-error association. Flatworms and snails exhibit habituation and trial-and-error association that straightforwardly meet the requirements of this conception of learning.[26]

I think that anyone who hoped to draw an interesting distinction between biologically functional information-carrying and some more psychologically distinctive kind of representation would not draw it just below snails and flatworms. So it appears that a notion of learning suitable to the reductionist enterprise does not distinguish deflationary "representation" from representation. Dretske's appeal to learning does not appear to capture any antecedently interesting notion of psychological representation. It still applies too broadly. A non-representationalist type of learning is not *sufficient* for distinctively psychological representation.

A further difficulty with Dretske's appeal to learning is that no capacity for learning, even learning understood in the broad associationist way that we have been discussing, seems *necessary* to being able to represent objectively. A perceptual system could be as innately constituted and as hard-wired as one pleases and still engage in perception. Perhaps there are no such perceptual systems in nature. All known organisms seem capable of adapting in response to sensory input. Even if some sort of learning is actually associated with all perceivers, learning does not seem part of the explanation of the distinction between perception and other sorts of sensory discrimination.

The existence of a distinct type of theorizing that uses a normal notion of veridicality, not merely a matter of biological success, is evident in the explanatory practice of perceptual psychology. The most advanced explanations of this type occur in *visual* psychology. This science operates on an explanatory paradigm that makes attribution of perceptual states, with specific representational contents and veridicality conditions, fundamental to its explanations. I discuss this paradigm in the last section of this chapter and in Chapter 9, the section PERCEPTION AS OBJECTIFICATION. There I highlight the roles of non-deflationary representational notions.[27]

---

[26] See Thorpe, *Learning and Instinct in Animals*, 201–208.

[27] I have not discussed the quasi-deflationist account of representation of Jerry Fodor. Fodor tries to do without biological–functional notions in his explanation of content. Fodor thinks that his explanation is needed to make representational notions scientifically respectable. See *A Theory of Content and Other Essays*. He claims that his theory gives only a sufficient condition. I think that it must apply to real cases. I evaluate it with that point in mind. Fodor tries to account for representation and error in terms of certain supposed asymmetrical relations among supposed laws between elements in the environment and tokenings of mental symbols. In many cases of "higher" representational states, laws are clearly lacking—even on the most liberal conception of law. Moreover, the only known laws or law-like patterns that are relevant to understanding representation (perception) are themselves formulated in representational terms.

I think that Fodor's discussion is very remote from any actual theorizing about representational phenomena.

As a small aside: in one case, what I see as a difficulty Fodor regards as a strength. He explains failures of representation in terms of subjunctive conditionals holding between *non-instantiated* properties (such as the supposed properties of being a unicorn or being phlogiston) and occurrences of states. Invoking non-instantiated properties in a reductive explanation of a science seems to me a metaphysical fudge. Natural science invokes no such properties. Such invocation does nothing toward reducing or "naturalizing" the notion of representation. I think that the notion of non-instantiated property is best understood *in terms of*

In psychology, reductionism about representation has been motivated by behaviorism, or other fear of seeming to be insufficiently scientific. In philosophy, reductionism has been motivated by "naturalism"—the idea that properties recognized by natural sciences are all the properties science should recognize. Psychology has transcended behaviorism without reduction. Naturalism does not connect well with actual scientific explanation. It has yielded little of scientific or philosophical value. I will proceed on the assumption that notions of perception and representation have a place in scientific explanation. They do not need reduction to be scientifically acceptable. For all that is now known, they are *irreducible explanatory* notions.

REPRESENTATIONAL FUNCTION AND NATURAL NORMS

Explanatory practice in psychology grounds appeal to representational states. Such states are type-individuated partly in terms of their conditions for being veridical. For example, a perceptual state is the type of perceptual state it is partly by virtue of being a state that purports to pick out various particulars in a scene and to attribute to those purported particulars such attributes as being cube-shaped, being green, being in certain directions and at certain distances. If there are particulars causing the perceptual state in the right way and those particulars have the attributes that are attributed, the perceptual state is veridical.

Veridical perceptual states are in one way successful. Non-veridical perceptual states are in one way failures. The relevant notions of success and failure are not those of biological success and failure.[28] Such success, however, entails fulfillment of some sort of function.

Whatever function is fulfilled in cases of representational success (and frustrated in cases of representational failure) is not a biological function. Perceptual accuracy does not necessarily or constitutively contribute to biological success. Perceptual error can fail to hinder, or it can even contribute to, survival for mating. More basically, perceptual error is not necessarily or constitutively a failure to contribute to fulfilling either generic biological function or specific *zoological/ ethological* functions. Nature selects not for veridicality but for fitness advantage.

Perceptual accuracy *is* constitutively a representational success. Perceptual error *is* constitutively a representational failure. So representational success and failure are not fulfillments or frustrations of biological functions. The function fulfilled by representational success, by perceptual veridicality, is not a biological function.

The relevant function associated with representational success and failure is also not a design function associated with artifacts, since perceptual states are not

---

representation. But my central point is that the notion representation has earned its place in science, and does not need philosophers to vindicate its respectability.

[28] They are certainly not the successes or failures of tryings or literal aimings. The successes and failures do not even attach to acts. Perceptions are not acts, much less intended acts.

artifacts and are not designed for being veridical. So the function associated with representational success and failure of perceptual states is distinct from both biological function and artifactual function.

I call the type of function constitutively associated with representational success *representational function*.[29] Examples of representational success are veridicality, truth, making veridical (for example, in realizing subintentional actional representations), making true (for example, in realizing intentions), preserving truth (in inference), and so on.

Perceiving is a type of veridical representation. The representational function of a perceptual system is to represent veridically. Veridical perception is necessarily and constitutively a kind of success for a perceptual state or perceptual system. It is fulfillment of a kind of function. Non-veridical perception is necessarily and constitutively a kind of failure—not necessarily biological failure, as we have seen, but representational failure. This is a failure to fulfill a central representational function of perception. Veridical representation, more specifically accurate representation, is the *representational function* of perceptual states and perceptual systems. The notions <u>perceptual state</u> and <u>perceptual system</u> are partly teleological notions. The point also applies to notions of belief and inference.[30]

Given that veridicality and non-veridicality cannot be reduced to success and failure (respectively) in fulfilling biological function, we must recognize a type of function that is not a biological function—a representational function. Not all functions that figure in scientific explanation are biological functions. It is a narrow and perverse vision of the science to assume that explanations in representational terms (or in terms of veridicality conditions) must, on pain of mystery or miracle, be reduced or reconstrued in biological terms.[31]

---

[29] For fuller discussion, see my 'Perceptual Entitlement'.

[30] It is a mistake to think that this notion of teleology is attenuated. Any state constitutively associated with success or failure has a constitutive teleological and functional aspect in the fullest sense of 'teleological' and 'functional'. Many philosophers are so in the habit of associating functions with biological functions that representational functions are thought of as functional, if at all, only in a stretched sense. Some philosophers think that unless belief, or perception, is taken to be a product of an individual's immediate purposes, it cannot count as teleological except in an extended sense. Such habits and thoughts are out of perspective. Any perception or belief undergoes a certain type of failure if it is not veridical. Failure is not meeting standards associated with purposes or functions. Purposes are not relevant. So failures of perception and belief are cases of falling short of standards associated with functions. The relevant functions, representational functions, are constitutive of perception and belief. Of course, perceptions or beliefs—veridical and non-veridical ones—can fulfill other functions, for example, biological functions.

[31] One can see an analogous error not only in philosophy but among characterizations of psychology by popularizers. See Steven Pinker, 'So How *Does* the Mind Work?', *Mind and Language* 20 (2005), 19: 'The subject matter of psychology is the functioning of the brain.' Pinker does not connect his apparent view that biological function is the only type of function relevant to psychology with actual explanations in, say, vision science. As I have been emphasizing, biological function has several roles to play in the explanatory methods of psychology. But the central mode of explanation in vision science—at the representational, as opposed to the neural level—gives veridicality a central position that his account does not even seriously address. Accounts of biological function help explain a framework within which representational psychology operates. But psychology is not biology in disguise.

The roles for both biological and representational functions are constitutively associated with success, and such functions ground explanations of success. Biological function grounds explanations of fitness, or successful survival for mating. Representational function grounds a distinctive sort of explanation: explanations of approximately veridical perception—and of failures of approximate veridicality—of the environment, and explanations of attainment of perceived goals. Biological and psychological explanations are different but complementary.

Empirical science has found that explanations that make essential explanatory reference to representational states are fruitful. The science of the formation of visual states takes states type-individuated in terms of their representational content to be basic—both in what is explained and in the principles used to explain such formation. The explanation takes perceptual states with representational contents as primitives in the explanations. The laws and kinds of the explanation essentially involve representational contents, which set veridicality conditions. These explanations therefore utilize an explanatory kind constitutively associated with a function. The explanations have a teleological element.

Again, this conclusion does not derive from assuming that veridicality *per se* is favored in evolution. Biological functions contribute to an individual's or group's survival for reproduction. Biological functions are not representational functions. The conclusion that perception has a representational function does not derive from reflection on the biology underlying perception. It derives from reflecting on the nature of explanatory kinds in perceptual psychology. Having veridicality conditions is a constitutive feature of a perceptual state; and inaccuracy is constitutively a kind of representational failure of a perceptual state. A primary function of a perceptual system is to perceive. Perception is veridical representation. Failure to produce veridical representation is a failure to fulfill that function.

We know empirically that there are perceptual states with such accuracy conditions. There is extensive empirical support for explanations in which the representational aspects of perceptual states are explanatorily central. And there are explanations that give perceptual and other representational states a causal role in engendering animal action, and in causing further psychological processes. Such explanations evince the existence of perceptual states. So they support the claim that there are representational states that have representational functions.

Thus it is empirically determined that there *are* perceptual systems. But, as I maintained in Chapter 3, the section GENERAL GROUNDS FOR ANTI-INDIVIDUALISM, it is apriori that a function of a perceptual state is to be veridical. It is apriori that a function of a perceptual system is to yield accurate perceptual states. A perceptual state undergoes failure or shortcoming if it is inaccurate. From the point of view of psychology, whether there *are* any perceptual states or perceptual systems is an empirical matter. But it is apriori that where there are perceptual states or systems, their representational function is to be accurate, or to yield accurate perceptual states.

The fundamental mode of explanation in the perceptual psychology of vision is to explain ways in which veridical representations of the environment are formed from and distinguished from registration, or encoding, of proximal stimulation. Veridicality, fulfillment of representational function, is the central *explanandum* of visual psychology. Illusions are explained as lapses from normal representational operation, or as the product of special environmental conditions.[32] Visual psychology explains visual perception. It explains *seeing*. Seeing is fundamentally veridical visual representation.[33]

Explanations in visual psychology take specifications of perceptual states with veridicality conditions as primitives. There is nothing unnatural about taking perceptual representation as an unreduced primitive in science or common sense. Explanations make basic reference to perceptual states by way of reference to conditions on successful representation—representational content. So representational function is associated with both *explanans* and *explanandum* in the science of visual perception.

Representational function is constitutively associated with certain norms. Success in fulfilling functions is, in a broad sense, a *good* for the system and for the representer, *relative to the function*. Goodness here just is success. The heart's beating efficiently is a good for the heart relative to its function of pumping blood. Veridical perception is a good for the perceptual system, relative to its function of producing veridical representation.

Where there are fulfillments of functions, there are *standards* for fulfilling them. Here 'standard' applies to a level of fulfillment, as it does in the phrase 'standard of living'. In this usage, a standard need not be set, imposed, required. A standard of living can be high or low, and need not depend on anyone's setting it or recognizing it.

Some levels of fulfillment are standards that are also *norms*. A *norm* is a standard or level of possible performance that is in some way adequate for fulfillment of a function or purpose.[34] For every function, it is apriori that there are various norms in this sense.

Some norms are *natural norms*. By 'natural norm' I do not mean naturalistically reducible norm. I mean a level of performance adequate to fulfill a function or a purposiveness, and that constitutes an explanatorily relevant kind, independently of any individual's having a positive or negative attitude toward the function or the norm. Specifically, the applicability of natural norms is independent of any individual's setting or acceding to them—accepting them as applicable. Usually, natural norms are also independent of any individual's appreciating

---

[32] For more on the role of veridicality in explaining perception, see my 'Disjunctivism and Perceptual Psychology' and 'Five Theses on *De Re* States and Attitudes'.

[33] In Chapter 9, the section PERCEPTION AS REPRESENTATION, I support this remark that seeing *is* veridical visual representation. I criticize alleged examples in which accurate visual representation is supposed not to be seeing.

[34] From the *Oxford English Dictionary*: '**Norm 12. a.** A definite level of excellence, attainment, wealth, or the like, or a definite degree of any quality, viewed as a prescribed object of endeavour or as the measure of what is adequate for some purpose.' I think that the level of measure of adequacy does not have to be *viewed* in order to be in place, or in order to be a norm.

them—or having them as the representational content of any state, however dimly or implicitly.

There are natural norms constitutively associated with representational functions, as well as natural norms constitutively associated with biological functions. I think that for every function, it is apriori that there are various natural norms associated with it.

There are natural norms for perceptual representation. The primary natural representational norm that is constitutively associated with perceptual capacity is to perceive things as they are—to form *veridical* perceptual representation. Veridical perception fulfills perception's primary constitutive representational function. A second natural representational norm constitutively associated with perception is to perceive as well as the perceptual system can, given its natural limitations, its input, and its environmental circumstances. A third natural norm for perception is to be reliably veridical. A fourth is both to be reliably veridical and to perceptually represent as well as possible given the perceptual system's natural limitations, its input, and its environmental circumstances. The first norm, that of perceiving veridically, constitutes a baseline against which the other natural representational norms for perception are constituted.

Perception is not knowledge. None of these perceptual norms is an epistemic norm. But the fourth of these norms is an ancestor of the primary epistemic norm for belief—epistemic warrant. In fact, it is an aspect of epistemic warrant (epistemic entitlement) for perceptual belief.

The same considerations that indicate norms for fulfilling the primary constitutive representational function for *perception* also indicate norms for fulfilling the primary constitutive representational function for *belief*—production of *veridical* propositional representation. There are also representational natural norms for belief and belief-formation that are analogous to just-cited representational norms for perception. Such norms are associated with believers whether or not they know or care about them. They are norms constitutively associated with the nature and basic function of belief.

The second norm mentioned—that of perceiving as veridically as possible given the system's natural limitations, input, and environmental context—is relevant to explaining one type of psychological well-functioning. Not all psychological well-functioning is a matter of biological efficiency. There is psychological well-functioning that is to be explained in terms of meeting representational norms.[35]

Here I emphasize again that some standards for fulfilling the representational function of perception, natural norms, are set by the nature of the kind (in this case, *perception*) itself. Some of these natural norms—veridical representation and the capacity-and-circumstance-relative norms—are, I think, apriori knowable from knowing what perception is.

---

[35] See my 'Perceptual Entitlement'. For the distinction between representational norms for perception that do and do not require reliability, see p. 533 in that article.

In this respect, natural norms for perception are analogous to natural norms for deductive inference, and some natural norms for belief. In none of these cases is the norm prescribed by social authority or by any individual agency. Nor need the norms be appreciated by anyone if an individual is to fall under them.

Basic natural representational norms of deductive inference, norms of perception formation, and norms of belief formation are constitutively associated with the representational function of the respective enterprises. Each such enterprise fails if certain standards regarding veridicality are not met. Each has a representational function that is distinct from whatever biological functions the enterprise also has. The basic representational function of deductive inference is or includes not violating certain formal procedures that necessarily preserve truth. The basic representational function of perception is accurate representation of subject matters that are presently sensed. The basic representational function of belief is true propositional representation. As noted, perception and belief are subject to other representational norms that are constitutively associated with this basic function—norms for representational well-functioning, given the natural limitations and circumstances of the individual.

In philosophy, norms are often associated with morality, or with intentional, intellectual, or social action. The notion of norm that is apriori associated with representational function is more generic. Not all norms concern fulfillment of an agent's aim, much less intention.

Norms of deductive inference are not primarily concerned with fulfillment of agent aim or purpose. They are standards for fulfilling the representational function of deductive inference—preserving truth by drawing inferences that are explainable as according with certain formal rules. These standards hold regardless of an individual's aims, purposes, or intentions, as long as the individual engages in deductive inference.

Norms for truth and epistemic warrant, which are constitutively associated with belief, further exemplify norms that are apriori associated with representational function, but that do not depend on agent aim or purpose. All these norms are representational natural norms. I believe that neither the psychology of perception, belief, and inference, nor the epistemology of any kind of belief or inference, can be understood without reference to representational natural norms. None of these norms depends on being set, or acceded to, as goals or standards by individuals.

The tendency to associate norms with moral or other intentional action has the consequence that norms are usually assumed to be associated with some ability to appreciate or be guided by the norms, on the part of individuals who fall under them. Such internal replication is often taken as a condition on falling under norms. Such an assumption is reminiscent of the way conditions of objectivity are required, by Individual Representationalists, to be mirrored in individuals. At least dimly appreciating norms is taken to be a necessary condition on falling under them, just as at least unconsciously representing conditions of objectivity is taken to be a necessary condition on engaging in objective representation. The idea is that falling under a norm does not make sense unless the individual can represent, appreciate, sense, or be at least subliminally guided by the norm—internally. Here we have analogs of the hyper-intellectualization that dominated discussions of objective representation.

Norms that constitutively involve some capacity to appreciate the norms—for example, moral norms—are, I think, special cases. Moral norms are crucially important for human beings. But they are not typical norms.[36] Most types of norms need not be representable, or sensed—much less set or acceded to—by individuals that fall under norms. Most norms need not be the representational content of any state of a system or individual that falls under the norms.

An individual's perception falls under representational norms for successful formation of perceptual states, given the individual's perceptual capacities. Natural norms apply even if an individual cannot understand or be guided by them.

An individual's beliefs fall under the norm of veridicality or truth, and norms of epistemic warrant, whether or not the individual knows or cares about the norms. Similarly, for norms applicable to deductive inference. Natural norms apply even if an individual cannot understand or be guided by them, as long as the individual has the relevant *kinds* of capacities—perceptual capacities, capacities for belief, capacities for deductive inference.

The notion of a natural norm is not purely descriptive. It does not specify statistical normality. It is a level of performance that constitutes adequacy in fulfilling a function or a type of purposiveness, where the level and function constitute explanatorily relevant kinds. The notion need not be associated with prescription, responsibility, or sanction. It need not be associated with appreciation of the norm or guidance by it. A generic notion of "should" nevertheless applies to functioning well, within the limits of the individual's, or system's, capacities.

The heart should beat efficiently relative to its biological function. A perceptual system should form veridical perceptual states, and a perceptual state should be veridical, relative to its representational function. A perceptual system should form perceptual states that are as nearly and as frequently veridical as its natural limitations and its environmental circumstances allow, relative to its

---

[36] Conditions of applicability for moral norms are, of course, controversial. I think that moral norms are natural norms: Their applicability does not depend on any individual's setting them or acceding to them. An important respect in which moral norms differ from the biological and representational norms that I have been discussing is that, at some level of abstraction, they must be representable by individuals to whom they are applicable. They require some meta-representational capacities. An individual who does not understand the difference between right and wrong does not fall under moral norms: moral failures and successes are not possible for that individual. Still, I think that moral norms are similar to biological and representational natural norms in that the applicability of the norms to an individual depends only on the individual's having certain capacities or being of a certain kind, not on acceding to the norms. Moral norms are *reflexive* in that they require some understanding of the norms, but natural in that their applicability does not require acceptance by anyone. Examples of reflexive norms that are also not natural norms are rules of etiquette and norms for a style of landscape gardening.

representational function. Performances of the system that do not meet these norms are failures in some respect.

In primitive agency, indeed in all agency, an agent should act so as to maximize fitness ('should', relative to a biological norm). Action that does not maximize fitness constitutes a failure to realize biological norms associated with biological function. Some agency falls under representational norms as well as biological norms. In agency guided by perceptual representation, an agent should act so as to meet its represented goals, as they are represented (where 'should' is relative to a representational norm). Performance that does not satisfy the representational contents of acts and goals constitutes failure, relative to the representational norm constitutively associated with representational agency.

Natural norms for perception, deductive reasoning, perceptual belief, primitive agency, and agency guided by perception or perceptual belief do not depend on any individual's setting, appreciating, or acceding to the norms. Such norms do not depend on intention, convention, or rational agency. The norms apply whether or not anyone recognizes them. Many natural norms applicable to representational states are constitutively associated with representational function.

If one eschews associations with 'prescriptive' or 'guiding' norms, one can distinguish a notion of norm that is important for understanding not only perception, perceptual belief, and epistemic warrant, but also much action.

Explanation guides us to what kinds there are. Psychological explanation makes extensive reference to representational kinds. Natural norms are constitutive aspects of the system of representation that blooms from the root of perceptual objectivity.[37]

THE LOWER BORDER OF PERCEPTION: SENSORY INFORMATION REGISTRATION AND PERCEPTION

I have highlighted a distinction between representational perceptual states and states that function merely to register, or encode, sensory information. In this section, I begin to elaborate one side of this distinction. I develop the notion of perception in some detail in Chapter 9. Here I focus on the contrasting notion.

Organisms like bacteria, amoebae, paramecia, worms, molluscs, clams are differentially sensitive to various attributes in the physical environment. They *discriminate* those attributes. Their sensory capacities carry information. They function to respond in certain ways, given this information. These organisms can discriminate light, heat, magnetic force, and so on. Responses to such

---

[37] I think that it would be just as big a mistake to try to reduce representational states to natural norms as it is to try to reduce them to biological functions. Fortunately, such a view is less tempting to most philosophers and has no traction among scientists. Recognition of the primitive explanatory nature of representational kinds is long overdue. Natural norms are a corollary of representational kinds, neither reducible to them, nor the basis of reduction of them.

discriminations function to enable them to live, move, and reproduce in their environmental niches. These sensory capacities are not perceptual.

Anatomical specializations for sensing emerge in very simple organisms. Many such specializations and their associated sensory systems are retained in more complex animals. The capacity of our retinas to register, or encode, the spatial pattern and spectral properties of light is not itself perception. The sensitivity of various systems to saccadic eye movements is not perception. These cases also do not instantiate representation in the sense that I am developing.

I believe that the distinction between mere sensory information registration and perceptual representation is basic for understanding not only perception but also representation, in a non-deflated sense, and objectivity. I take as a working hypothesis that representation begins with perception.[38] *Perception is the most primitive kind of (non-deflated) representation.* It is certainly a very primitive form, close to the origin of representation, and, as I shall argue, of objectivity.[39] '*Representational*' in a non-deflated sense applies to a type of state with veridicality conditions, where such conditions could, in principle, ground non-trivial explanation. The hypothesis is that the lower border of perception is also the lower border of representation in this sense.

I believe that neither representation in this sense nor perception reduces to carrying information, or any other sort of sensory discrimination, together with biological functions.

Let me review how I use relevant terms. If a state or condition A is a regular, or nomological, or counterfactually supported consequence of a state or condition B, or if A is differentially sensitive to B (regardless of how reliable the sensitivity is), I say that A *carries information* that correlates with B.[40] Different notions of information-carrying derive from the different alternatives. The differences are not important for present purposes. In this broad sense, smoke carries information about fire. We can add to this list of alternatives common causal dependence if we like. Let us do so. So far, we are using notions that are *in no sense distinctively psychological*.[41] The notion of information is fundamentally one of statistical correlation. I broaden the notion to include nomic and causal notions.

---

[38] For further discussion, see my 'Reflections on Two Kinds of Consciousness'.

[39] See my 'Perceptual Entitlement'; Reflections on Two Kinds of Consciousness'; 'Disjunctivism and Perceptual Psychology'; 'Perception', *International Journal of Psychoanalysis*, 84 (2003), 157–167.

[40] In *Knowledge and the Flow of Information*, 63, Fred Dretske states a very strong version of this type of condition. A signal r carries the information that s is F is defined as: the conditional probability of s's being F, given r (and given certain background conditions) is 1. For discussion of less stringent versions, see Peter Godfrey-Smith, 'Indication and Adaptation', and *Complexity and the Function of Mind in Nature* (Cambridge: Cambridge University Press, 1996).

[41] Loose use of 'information' to suggest representationality in a distinctively psychological sense is the bane of the biological and human sciences. Phrases like 'information about' mix the strictly statistical notion with a notion of representation. This mix promises insights into ordinary notions of representation that simply rephrasing so as to stick to the strictly statistical content shows to be doubtful, and often flatly illusory. See note 19 above.

Some states that carry information that correlates with other states, and are causally dependent on them, have a function that capitalizes on such dependence. Broadly speaking, such states have such a function by virtue of having been selected through evolution, or perhaps designed as artifacts, partly because of the causal roles that they play given the information that they carry. Let us say that such states *functionally carry information*.

Since I think that only functional carrying of information is relevant to understanding the sensory systems of organisms, I call functional carrying of information '*information registration*' (equivalently '*functional encoding*'), thus supplementing the pure notion of carrying information that I started with. The sensing of light by amoebae and the sensing of up or down in an earthworm are sensory registrations of information. Registration of proximal stimulation in the relevant sensory capacities carries information that statistically correlates (usually highly) with further environmental conditions. This further relation need not, however, affect the explanation of sensory capacities themselves. The further relation concerns the statistical, nomic, counterfactual, or causal relations between the sensory states and the environmental conditions. So the individuals and their sensory systems are causally connected to the environment and functionally explained in terms of values the environment has for the individuals' fitness. Nothing in the individual's capacities, however, distinguishes (*a*) environmental causes that figure functionally in the individual's basic needs and activities from (*b*) sensory registration (or functional encoding) of proximal causes—from the surface effects of the environmental causes.

Where there is perception, there is sensory information registration. That is, where there is perception, there is functional, causally based, usually high, statistical correlation, between a type of state impacted by surface stimulation (and that encodes surface stimulation), on one hand, and a type of stimulation, on the other. Sensory information registration *per se* is not a type of perception or a type of representation, as I use the terms. Perception is a sensory capacity for objectified representation. Representation is a condition constitutively associated with veridicality conditions—for example, perceptual accuracy. Some sensory information registration neither meets conditions for objectification nor has any constitutive or non-trivial explanatory association with veridicality conditions. I discuss these points about perception in Chapter 9. I make them here only for orientation.

I have argued that biological function bears no constitutive relation to veridicality conditions. Biological explanation, including explanation of functional sensitivity to environmental conditions, is not psychological explanation. Relevant psychological explanation centers on kinds that have veridicality conditions. Biological functions are explained in terms of contribution to fitness for reproduction. Non-vacuous appeal to veridicality conditions in psychological explanation requires independent support not provided by biology alone.

Independent support lies in the explanatory practice of perceptual psychology, especially visual psychology. This science uses an explanatory paradigm that makes attribution of perceptual states, with specific representational contents and veridicality conditions, fundamental to its explanations. The science uses a type of explanation that explains perceptual states that have veridicality conditions and that can be seeings or illusions. It also appeals to perceptual states and transformations of perceptual states in its explanations. The explanations are fundamentally, and not just adventitiously, explanations of states with accuracy conditions, as well as the causal processes that form such states.

Biological and information-theoretic forms of explanation can be applied to perceptual systems. But an additional form of explanation is empirically explanatory. The theory takes the form discussed in Chapter 3 (the section THE SHAPE OF PERCEPTUAL PSYCHOLOGY).

Explaining representational success and failure—explaining how animals perceive veridically to the extent that they do—is a source of challenging and illuminating theory. The stability of this science and the empirical fruitfulness of its results constitute good ground to believe that it describes distinctive psychological kinds—*perception* and *representation*.

Applying this type of explanation to many sensory systems would be uninformative and misleading. It would add nothing to explanations in sensory physiology. The light sensors in Euglena (flagellated protozoa), sensitivity in paramecia to certain concentrations of sodium chloride, the contact sensors in flat-worms, shadow sensors in molluscs, proprioceptive feedback on self-motion in dragonflies, the hearing of the pocket gopher (which cannot localize sounds) seem to be non-perceptual sensory systems.[42] Applying the representational form of explanation to these sensory systems is unilluminating and dispensable.

Accounts of the sensory systems of worms and molluscs could have turned out empirically to require perceptual categories. In fact, there is no explanatory value in invoking such categories. Good explanation centers on discriminative sensitivity to proximal stimulation, weightings of registrations of such stimulation from different bodily sensors, capacities for adaptation or conditioning, neural pathways, and biological functions of the system.

Veridicality does not enter systematically or non-trivially into explaining these sensory systems. We do not need a notion of representation or a notion of perception to explain a paramecium's or a snail's sensory system. We do need states with veridicality conditions to explain vision in mammals and many other animals.

---

[42] Accounts of these cases can be found respectively in: N. Tinbergen, *The Study of Instinct* (1951; New York: Oxford University Press, 1969, with new introduction), 21; Jennings, *Behavior of the Lower Organisms*, 47–54; Dan R. Kenshalo, Sr, 'Phylogenetic Development of Feeling', in Edward C. Carterette and Morton P. Friedman (eds.), *Handbook of Perception* (New York: Academic Press, 1978); Bernhard Möhl, 'Sense Organs and the Control of Flight', in Graham J. Goldsworthy and Colin H. Wheeler (eds.), *Insect Flight* (Boca Raton, FL: CRC Press, Inc., 1989); Rickye S. Heffner and Henry E. Heffner, 'Evolution of Sound Localization in Mammals', in Douglas B. Webster, Richard R. Fay, and Arthur N. Popper (eds.), *The Evolutionary Biology of Hearing* (New York: Springer-Verlag, 1992).

The terms 'perception' and 'representation' are part of a distinctive and powerful form of psychological explanation. *Representation* and representational content are most basically associated with kinds of states that are constitutively associated with veridicality or non-veridicality. As we shall see, issues of veridicality enter both into the explanatory kinds and into the basic paradigm for explanation.

Described from the point of view of anatomy and physiology, there is a continuum between an amoeba's sensitivity to light and human vision. Described from the point of view of explanations of the visual systems in mammals and other relatively complex animals, perceptual representation is a distinctive kind of psychological state. Explanations in the sciences provide the best basis for judging what kinds there are. Perceptual states, and representational states more generally, are distinctive, explanatorily relevant kinds.

In this chapter's last section, and in Chapters 9–10, I focus on the explanatory kinds invoked in perceptual psychology. Here I have just sketched an important distinction and maintained that differences in scientific explanation support drawing the distinction.

PERCEPTION AND THE ENVIRONMENT: THE 'DISJUNCTION PROBLEM'

The explanatory strategy distinctive of perceptual psychology postulates perceptual representation of particulars and attributes in the *physical environment*. The details of empirical explanation support the postulation. Many of the capacities in the visual system, for example, are explainable by taking perceptual states to be type-individuated in terms of representations as of distal matters. Capacities for distance perception, exemplified by the triangulation involved in convergence, are examples. These points instantiate anti-individualism about perception.

As I indicated in discussing Quine in Chapter 7, there is a further element in the postulation of representational relations to the environment. Such postulation integrates representational explanation with prior explanations in zoology and ethology. An animal's needs and activities are explained in the context of its functional relations to macro-elements of its environment. Animals eat, mate, move around obstacles, procreate, attack, flee, and so on. Where there are capacities explicable in terms of representation that derives from transformations that in effect distinguish between proximal stimulation and elements in the environment, an account of perception plays a role in explaining animal activity and other animal responses to the environment. Perceptual kinds mesh with the kinds invoked by zoology and ethology to ground explanation of animal activity. This fact provides further empirical support for taking elements in the environment to figure in the individuation of perceptual–representational kinds of states.

The range of objects of perception, and the environmental grounds for explaining constitutive conditions for a state's having the perceptual content it has, are constrained by factors beyond the animal's discriminative capacity (which leaves open too wide a range to determine what an animal perceives and how). The range is also constrained by the needs and activities of whole individuals—eating, predating, mating, navigating, fleeing, parenting, nesting, and so on. The science of perception explicitly leans on such a constraint.

I do *not* hold that for each perceptual state there is some specific need or activity that is distinctive to its representational content. Individual functional responses that fulfill needs and activities in an environment that figured in molding a perceptual system set a framework for determining perceptual content. They help exclude irrelevant alternatives (time slices of rabbits and so on). I believe that even perceptual states that we humans do not share with other animals, such as perception of sounds that express words and grammatical constructions, are constitutively related in this broad sense to antecedent needs and functions of the individual. The content of phonetic perception is broadly constrained and framed by antecedent functional interactions with the environment.

The needs and activities that help set the framework for determination of perceptual content are understood in zoology as biologically functional for individuals. Functions of *individuals* are subcases of biological functions, subcases that contrast with functions of an organ or a sensory system. Functions of organs or systems are the subcases of biological function most frequently discussed in philosophy. The notion of whole–individual function seems to me to stand near the basis for understanding the most primitive form of individual action. It is this notion that figures in explanations that coordinate animal perception with animal needs and activities.[43]

Whole animal (or organismic) function is constitutively associated with an individual's basic biological functional responses to the environment—eating, navigating, mating, parenting, and so on. These responses, usually activities, are functional according to the most commonly cited sense of biological function. Roughly, their existence is explained by their contribution to the individual's survival for mating.[44] They are distinctive in being functions of the whole individual—not the individual's subsystems. Fulfilling these functions—successfully engaging in these activities or other, non-active functional responses—contributes to the individual's or species' fitness for survival for mating.

When a sensory system has the objectifying capacities that mark it as perceptual, the representational content of its perceptual states is constitutively

---

[43] See the section PRIMITIVE AGENCY below.

[44] See Larry Wright, 'Functions', *The Philosophical Review* 82 (1973), 139–168. There are other notions of function that figure in biology. See Robert Cummings, 'Functional Analysis', *The Journal of Philosophy* 72 (1975), 741–765; Paul E. Griffiths, 'Functional Analysis and Proper Functions', *British Journal of the Philosophy of Science* 44 (1993), 409–422; Peter Godfrey-Smith, 'Functions: Consensus without Unity', *American Philosophical Quarterly* 74 (1993), 196–208. The Cummings notion bears no clear relation to teleology. For present purposes, it seems to me unnecessary to discuss various conceptions of biological function. I use the standard Wright-like notion, which *is* associated with teleology in biology, as a foil to compare and contrast with the notion of a representational function.

constrained by aspects of the environment that figure, or figured, in relevant individuals' functional responses to the environment in fulfilling basic needs and activities. The environmental framework set by such responses limits relevant alternatives for perceptual representational contents and their *representata*.

As noted, these responses need not be responses of the very individual with the perceptual system. Typically, they are functional responses by individuals in the prehistory of the evolution of the perceptual system. In fact, as I argue in the section PRIMITIVE AGENCY below, the responses normally are those of ancestors that do not even have perceptual systems. The interactions with the environment that are involved in these responses are fulfillments of individual functions, whether active or not.[45] Where perceptual objectification is present, the specific range of attributes in the environment that an individual perceptually represents—and the range of representational contents specifically as of those attributes—are constrained by causal interactions with the environment, explained in ethology and zoology. The key interactions are those that figured in molding the perceptual system shared by relevant individuals.

In actual fact, these interactions are evolutionarily *antecedent*, *agential* fulfillments of *biological* functions. The fully general constitutive conditions, however, allow for artifactual perception by non-living individuals. Hence the relevant functional individual responses need not be by living individuals. So it is not constitutive of perception that relevant individual–environmental interactions be studied in biology. The fully general constitutive conditions also allow for non-agential functional responses (see note 45). And they allow the relevant responses to occur not in the evolutionary prehistory of the perceptual system. The responses can be potential responses by newly synthesized individuals, as long as the perceptual system is connected with responses to a relevant environment.

Apart from science fiction, theology, and science's copying nature, however, the framework for perceptual reference and perceptual representational content is set by organisms' responses to the environment in fulfilling individual biological functions, in the evolutionary prehistory of the perceptual system. The context for perceptions' having objects and representational contents is set and constrained by the environment in which such responses occur, and by the environmental

---

[45] I discuss the constitutive matter in 'Memory and Persons', section 3. There I maintain that perception bears a constitutive relation, somewhere in the determination of its content, to *action*. Although animal perception is always in fact associated with animal action, I am now content to regard constitutive constraints on the range of perceptual referents, perceptual contents, and perceptual kinds, as deriving from causal relations with the environment through whole-animal, functional interaction with the environment—whether this be a matter of agential interaction or passive need-based interaction. I suppose that having certain emotions, and certain functional non-active responses, are biological functions of individuals. As before, the interaction could occur in the evolutionary (or design) prehistory that formed the animal's capacities before the individual animal existed. I am more impressed than previously with the fact that the causal structures of perceptual constancies suffice by themselves to solve most aspects of the Disjunction Problem. Only some of the most philosophically contrived 'disjuncts' are ruled out only by the role of zoological and ethological relations to the environment.

attributes that ground explanations of those responses. I develop this point in the remainder of this section, and in the section PRIMITIVE AGENCY below.

A problem that has exercised those who try to find reductive explanations of the notion of representation is called the *Disjunction Problem*. This is the problem of explaining conditions on representation that show that representation applies to one set of attributes rather than equally well to a set of alternative attributes. Philosophers concerned with the problem ask why a perception that intuitively represents a body does not equally represent a light array. Or it is asked why a frog's perceptual representation that seems to be as of moving objects might equally well be as of flies, bee-bees, features, stuffs, instances of abstract entities, undetached parts of objects, or temporal slices of objects. The challenge is to explain conditions on representation that show why representations represent one range of entities rather than other entities that co-vary with, and in many cases play a role in causing, the representation.

I have commented on versions of this problem in discussing Quine's and Davidson's Individual Representationalism. In his argument for indeterminacy, Quine appealed to gratuitousness in choosing among various ranges of *representata*. Davidson raised a version of this problem by claiming that the natural similarity classes of one individual cannot be assumed to be the same as those of another. Dretske and Fodor dramatized versions of the problem in their projects to render representation naturalistically acceptable.

All these philosophers pose the problem with no reference to specific empirical work in psychology. Their versions of the problem are correspondingly artificial. The Disjunction Problem is largely an artifact of reductive programs, detached from explanations in perceptual psychology, which privileges macro-attributes in the environment as perceptual *representata*.

As we have seen, Quine thought that he had an argument that showed empirical psychology to be indeterminate. The others implicitly assume that their accounts are prior to empirical work that postulates representation with specific representational content. I think that in all cases, a failure to reflect seriously on actual empirical psychology and its relation to parts of biology—together with insufficient reflection on anti-individualism about perception—renders struggles with the Disjunction Problem pointless.

Let us look at an example. What attributes are represented by a frog's vision?

Philosophically contrived entities like undetached fly parts or temporal slices of flies are excluded from being represented as such by the fact that they are not kinds that ground biological explanations of the frog's needs and activities. I believe that undetached fly parts can probably further be ruled out by tests of frog attention. Similarly, for cases like instances of body fusions, insofar as representation of them as such differs from representation of bodies as such. The methodology of perceptual psychology excludes such alternatives. Psychological explanation is framed to fit with explanation in zoology and ethology. These entities do not ground such biological explanation. Animals' basic activities are not explained in terms of their interactions with such entities. Biological explanations of animal activity refer to macro-particulars and macro-attributes that are of some eco-logical importance to the animal's functions. Perceptual psychology gains empirical strength by fitting in with these antecedent non-representational empirical explanations.

Even apart from artificial contrivances, it is often asked whether a frog's visual system specifies bee-bees, flies, light arrays, sense data, moving bodies, or what not. Most of these issues can be solved experimentally.

Given that the frog has a *perceptual* visual system, with capacities for percep-tual constancies such as distance perception, there is empirical reason not to take the representations to be as of light arrays or sense data. The constancy capacity *convergence*, for example, occurs in many simple animals like frogs. Such constancies bypass the proximal elements in stimulation and bypass intermediate causal factors (those in the causal chains between entities at fixation points and the eyes) to fix on the position of a distal object of vision.

A frog's visual system lacks perceptual groupings like bee-bee. There is no explanatory value in taking a frog's perceptual system to represent human artifacts as such.

It is unlikely that empirical considerations support attributing to a frog's perceptual system a representation as of a natural kind (like fly). Attributives that apply specifically to natural kinds as such seem to require an openness to a distinction between surface properties and underlying natures, an openness frogs cannot be expected to have. Empirically, it is unlikely that a frog's visual system represents flies or mosquitoes as such.

There is some empirical support for taking the frog's perceptual system to have a perceptual attributive like moving body of such and such a size and shape. (One can test whether frogs are capable of distinguishing animate from inanimate bodies.) Having such an attributive would depend on being able to distinguish bodies from events and shapes. I discuss these matters in Chapter 10, the section PERCEPTION AND BODY. There is empirical reason to believe that frogs have perceptual capacities to track bodies by their rough shapes and sizes under various conditions, including movement.[46]

There are other perceptual attributives, like edible, whose presence in the visual or actional systems of frogs can be empirically supported. Such func-tional attributives surely depend on perceptual application of other attributives for physical attributes (such as size, shape, motion, being a body). The frog sees something as edible by seeing it as a moving body within a certain size range.

A reason to take functional attributives like edible to be psychologically parasitic on attribution of the physical properties is that similar principles for discerning bodies, size, motion, color, and so on govern visual systems among different species. For example, a wide range of species perceive the location

---

[46] David Ingle, 'Perceptual Constancies in Lower Vertebrates', in Vincent Walsh and Janusz Kulikowski (eds.), *Perceptual Constancy* (Cambridge: Cambridge University Press, 1998).

(hence distance) of objects by convergence. (See Chapter 7 and below.) Systems that rely on convergence capitalize on the geometry implicit in light's arriving from a given object to different eyes at different angles. Perceptual subsystems for producing perceptual states that represent location, body, size, motion, color are common to different species. By contrast, representations as of functional attributes, such as *edibility* or *danger*, are likely to apply to instances of food or danger in more species-bound ways. What counts as food varies more from species to species than what counts as motion, color, or shape. The attributive edible—whether it is an action attributive or a perceptual attributive—is grounded in a species-specific response to types of perceptual discrimination that occur across many species.[47]

Experiment might support distinguishing fly-shaped bodies from the bodies of other types of edibles. An animal's visual system might have different types of food representation (parasitic on size–shape motion representations) that *correspond to* different types of bugs—if the frog could be found to respond differently to the different types. These are empirical matters.

I have made two points about the Disjunction Problem. One is that generic features of the methodology of explanation in perceptual psychology and consti-tutive features of perception support attributing representations of, and as of, common macro-attributes in the environment. Given the methodology of percep-tual psychology, as aiming to dovetail with biological explanations of animals' needs and activities, and given specific constitutive aspects of perceptual systems—perceptual constancies—most of the candidates proposed as candi-dates for perceptual objects are summarily excluded. Philosophical contrivances (abstractions and temporal stages) are ruled out because they do not ground relevant biological explanations. Entities like light rays, surface stimulations, and sense data are ruled out by the nature of the perceptual constancies.

The second point is that more specific empirical–explanatory considerations rule out representation of, and as of, certain attributes as possible referents—bee-bees, flies *qua* natural kinds, and perhaps stuffs.

Underlying the methodological aspect of the first point is the deep role of perception in guiding animal life. Since perception guides action, it is not surprising that perceptual kinds mesh with animal activities.

An animal perceives something as prey and pursues it. It perceives something as shelter, a landmark, or an obstacle, and navigates to it, by it, or around it. It perceives something as a mate and moves toward it. Shelters, landmarks, obstacles, mates have characteristic shapes, sizes, ways of moving that enable a perception to guide such activities.

---

[47] I think it an open question whether functional attributives like danger, edible, and mate occur only in the action systems of simple animals that have perception, or in their perceptual systems as well. This is obviously an empirical issue. For discussion of representations in action systems, see Marc Jeannerod, *The Cognitive Neuroscience of Action* (Oxford: Blackwell, 1997).

Coordinating explanation of perceptual representation with antecedent biological facts requires, of course, that psychology determine empirically that an animal's sensory capacities are *perceptual*, hence representational. Explanations that attribute *perceptual* systems to animals contrast with explanations of the simplest organisms' sensory discriminations and responses.

Bacteria can discriminate light from dark and move to where there is a paucity of oxygen. Nothing in their sensory capacities segments out the entities that have the attributes that they need (oxygen-poor water). Their sensory systems simply register information (functionally encode information) associated with proximal stimulation. The organisms simply react to conditions on their bodily surfaces. These reactions are reliably correlated with environmental conditions that fulfill the organism's needs. Negative response to light is regularly correlated with oxygen poverty. Such response is functional because low light intensities tend to correlate with oxygen-poor habitats. But bacteria do not perceive anything. They simply react to proximal stimulation. They sense light. They register it. They respond. Explanations of the capacities of bacteria are not enriched by invoking perceptual reference or perceptual attribution.

Similarly, amoebae are sensitive to aspects of the physical environment. Some aspects of their lives—eating of cysts, for example—may hinge on bodies. Other aspects may depend more on fluids, chemicals, and stuffs. Their activities and functions are explained in sensory physiology and zoology partly in terms of their relations to environmental conditions. Yet amoebae do not represent or perceive anything. Their sensory capacities can be fully explained in terms of their discriminations among and responses to proximal stimulation. This proximal stimulation is functionally connected to environmental conditions that are important for the organism. But nothing in the amoeba's sensory system distinguishes such conditions as perceptual *representata*.

Certain molluscs are sensitive to sudden shading of light. The sensitivity is not even directional. It can be explained purely in terms of the aggregate effects of light on the mollusc's sensors. Responses to these shadings function to protect molluscs from danger. The mollusc does not perceptually represent danger, shadows, movement, or anything else. There is no non-trivial explanatory invocation of veridicality conditions. The mollusc simply responds in a discriminative way to surface stimulations that are functionally correlated with environmental situations relevant to animal need.

In all three cases, the organism's sensory capacities link causally with environmental macro-attributes that bear on the organism's needs or activities. The sensory capacities do not represent those attributes. They simply react to surface stimulation that is sufficiently correlated with environmental attributes for the reaction to be beneficial for the animal.

If an animal's activity is to be explained partly in terms of perceptual states, the animal must meet conditions for having a perceptual system, as distinguished from a sensory system that merely registers, or functionally encodes, information. Reciprocally, perceptual explanation and candidates for perceptual representational contents (and their *representata*) are constrained by environmental kinds with which organisms interact in fulfilling their needs and pursing their activities. I think that a type of agency is phylogenetically more primitive than perception. I want to discuss this type and some aspects of the way perception coordinates with agency.

PRIMITIVE AGENCY

In the previous section, I appealed to a notion of individual function, paradigmatically that of individual animals. The notion of animal or organismic function seems to me to stand near the basis for understanding the most primitive form of action. Primitive animal action is the main ground of constraints on perceptual psychology from zoology and ethology. I will argue in this section that animal action is phylogenetically and constitutively prior to perception. It, and other individual functional responses, commonly constrain perception through instances of interaction with individuals' environments in which the individuals lack perception, or any other representational capacities, altogether.

Whole animal function is exemplified by basic biological activities—eating, navigating, mating, parenting, and so on. These activities are functional in the most commonly cited sense of biological function. Roughly, their existence is explained by their contribution to the individual's survival for mating, or perhaps in some cases the species' survival. See note 44. They are distinctive in being functions of the whole individual—not the individual's subsystems, organs, or other parts. Fulfilling these functions—successfully pursuing these activities—contributes to the individual's survival for mating.

There are, I think, further natural functions, other than the narrowly biological ones, that can be associated with whole organisms. There is a notion of a naturally flourishing life in which (beyond surviving long enough for mating) an animal lives out a life that realizes its natural capabilities, with relatively little misfortune. Such a notion of flourishing would be the counterpart of a decent standard of living. Early death and exceptional deprivation, hardship, or disease would lower the level of flourishing, and count as limiting fulfillment of the sort of animal function that consists in full or normal realization of the animal's life course and natural biological capacities. Lower levels of flourishing count as relative failure of the animal to live a life that is normal and natural for that animal.

Such a conception of animal function is naturally derivable from reflection on biological facts about species and individuals. I focus here on the standard notion of biological function, as applied to whole animals, because I understand it better in its relation to animal agency. A fuller account would encompass both notions of function.

Non-representational relations of an animal to its environment in the fulfillment of animal needs and activities play a definite role in the determination of the natures of its perceptual representational contents.[48] Such relations ground the explanatory methodology of perceptual psychology—motivating it to relate its explanations to biological explanations, particularly explanations in zoology and ethology. Those relations figure in the constitutive determination of perceptual content. So the relations ground both the epistemology of perceptual psychology and the ontology of perceptual kinds. What range of attributes a type of animal *perceptually* discriminates is partly determined by what its needs and activities are—or what the needs and activities of its evolutionary ancestors were. In this mix of needs and activities, activities are surely primary in setting the preconditions for determination (epistemic and constitutive) of perceptual kinds. In actual fact, the agency involved in predating, eating, navigating, mating, parenting, and so on forms the primary ground for constraining the attributes whose discrimination is central to perceptual content and perceptual kinds. Primitive agency forms a background for understanding both representation and representation-as in perceptual systems—hence for understanding perceptual kinds. Primitive organismic agency is phylogenetically prior to perception. It occurs in animals that demonstrably lack perception in the sense that I will elaborate.

Primitive agency constitutes a large topic, bookworthy in itself. I just sketch an orientation.

Action theory in philosophy has, in the last half-century, been almost as hyper-intellectualized as perception theory. Usually discussion begins with cases involving desire, intention, will, and then focuses on subcases of intentional action. There is nothing in itself wrong with this focus, of course. But often it is assumed that such approaches encompass all action.[49]

Animal action begins earlier. Much of it is pre-intentional, even pre-representational and pre-perceptual. Origins of agency precede those of perception and representation. Even *representational* agency precedes intention and belief, not to say meta-evaluation.

We distinguish firmly between an animal's actions, on one hand, and both things that happen to the animal and processes that occur within the animal, on the other. There are conceptual difficulties and borderline cases here. But the distinction invites and rewards reflection.[50]

A spider pursues, jumps on, bites, and eats its prey, approaches and inseminates its mate, navigates around an obstacle, or runs across its web. These actions are distinguished from processes occurring only within the spider. The spider

---

[48] As always, these relations might go back through the formation of the animal's capacities in its evolutionary prehistory. They might thus depend on needs or activities of previous animals that figured in this formation.

[49] See Donald Davidson, 'Psychology as Philosophy' (1974), in *Essays on Actions and Events* (2nd edn., Oxford: Clarendon Press, 2001), 229; see also Donald Davidson, 'Agency' (1971), in ibid. 46.

[50] Some work in this direction can be found in Brian O'Shaughnessy, *The Will* (Cambridge: Cambridge University Press, 1980), i–ii. See especially the chapter 'The Sub-Intentional Act' in volume ii of the first edition.

ingests; its stomach digests. Only subsystems operate in the circulation of body fluids, production of protein, semen, or wastes.

Lower animals, even some simple organisms that are not animals, engage in action in a broad sense. An amoeba's ingesting its food is action. Digesting its food is not. A paramecium's swimming forward or backward is, I think, action. The plasmolysis that causes shrinking of the paramecium in highly concentrated solutions is not. The crawling of a tick toward a heat source is active and attributable to the whole organism. Protein transfer through its membranes is not.

Amoebae, paramecia, ticks, and more complex organisms lack perception. Since they cannot perceive a goal or objective, their actions are not engendered by perceptual representation. They simply act in response to sensory stimulus. The most primitive whole-organism agency is pre-perceptual.

The ethological literature has developed a complex taxonomy of *orientation*. Both the concept of orientation and the taxonomy are sources for philosophical reflection in understanding primitive agency.

Orientation is taking, or moving into, a position by an organism in relation to its surroundings. Orientation places an organism in its characteristic bodily positions (right side up for a starfish, four feet on the ground for a dog), or in areas of its habitat in which it can thrive.[51]

Not all orientations are actions. But some are. Growth toward the light is an orientation that is not an action. A fish's swimming toward its prey is an orientation that is an action.

Active orientations constitute a large subclass of primitive actions. Active orientations are actions that have specifically to do with locomotion (as opposed to eating, mating, and so on).

Orientations that are directional reactions by freely motile organisms are called *taxes*. I will return to taxes. First, I want to rough out a contrast subclass within orientation. The nomenclature for non-tactic orientation is somewhat varied. One common one is as follows.

Bending movements by plants and sessile animals are *tropisms*. In many cases, tropisms are nothing more than oriented growth. I lay tropisms aside. They are mostly either non-active movement or at best borderline cases of active movement.

Another subclass of non-tactic orientation is kinesis. *Kineses* are non-directed, non-directional locomotory movements by organisms, in which speed and frequency of turning depend only on the intensity of the stimulation. Kineses occur when organisms are incapable of detecting the direction of a stimulus gradient, and when response to the stimulus produces a reaction whose direction is not determined by the direction of the stimulus. The organism responds to change in intensity of the stimulus by changed rate of locomotion (orthokinesis) or turning (klinokinesis). These changes tend to lead towards or away from the source of the stimulus, even though the

---

[51] Gottfried S. Fraenkel and Donald L. Gunn, *The Orientation of Animals* (Oxford: Clarendon Press, 1940), 1.

organism is incapable of movements whose direction is directed with respect to the stimulus. There is a random, non-directional character to the movements.

For example, simple organisms, such as paramecia, move by the beating of their cilia in a liquid. When they are stimulated by heat or contact, the beatings reverse. At a fixed distance of reversal, the swimming turns in a new forward direction. The *turning*, the change in direction, is not related to the direction of the stimulus. Relative to the stimulus, it is random—except that it is not directly back toward the stimulus. With sufficient turnings, such movement tends to put the paramecium in a more advantageous position. Yet the turning movement is undirected in the sense just indicated.[52] Such turnings after reversals are not taxes. They are a type of kinesis.

Let us return to taxes. Taxes occur when an organism is oriented with respect to the stimulus source and travels in a direction that depends on the direction of the stimulus source. *Taxes* are directional movements with respect to stimulations in the environment. They require sensory capacities that are directional. Usually determining direction depends on there being two or more locations of sensory receptors on the body of the organism. Directional movement is usually achieved by some mechanism in the animal for simultaneous differentiation of intensities of stimulus registration in different bodily sensors.[53]

True taxes are widespread in flagellate, single-cell eukaryotic organisms.[54] Such organisms are capable of moving toward or away from a stimulus source, subsequent to internal differentiations between stimulus intensities in different areas of the body. There are signs of simple specialization that allow a distinction between sensory and response regulators, even in these very simple organisms.[55] The responses in these unicellular organisms are not the direct physical or

---

[52] The case derives from the classic work of Jennings, *Behavior of the Lower Organisms*, 44–54. I oversimplify the paramecium's behavior. With respect to chemical stimulants, its turning behavior is less random than with respect to contact. Similar descriptions apply to planarians and to bacteria, whose rate of movement and frequency of turning depend on the intensity of light, and whose direction of turning is random, relative to the stimulus. See also Fraenkel and Gunn, *The Orientation of Animals*, 43 ff. For more on the distinction between taxes and kineses, see M. J. Carlile, 'Taxes and Tropisms: Diversity, Biological Significance and Evolution', and J. Adler, 'Chemotaxis in Bacteria', both in M. J. Carlile (ed.), *Primitive Sensory and Communication Systems* (London: Academic Press, 1975); R. Campan, 'Tactic Components in Orientation', in M. Lehrer (ed.), *Orientation and Communication in Arthropods* (Basel: Birkhauser Verlag, 1997).

[53] Carlile, 'Taxes and Tropisms', 14 ff. Positive phototaxis steering can be achieved through a single receptor's responding to shading by the cell body. Reorientation occurs until the receptor, located at the front of the cell, receives maximum stimulation. This type of capacity occurs in Euglena. The basis of positive phototaxis is differentiation between intensities at a single receptor at successive times. Direction is derived from temporal rather than spatial diversity of stimulations.

[54] True taxes in prokaryotes are rare or absent, because the small size of the prokaryotic cells does not admit of much diversity on the cell body or of sufficient capacity to register the small differences that must be differentiated. Carlile, 'Taxes and Tropisms', 23.

[55] Judith van Houten, 'Chemoreception in Microorganisms', in Thomas E. Finger, Wayne L. Silver, and Diego Restrepo (eds.), *The Neurobiology of Taste and Smell* (2nd edn., New York: John Wiley & Sons, 2000).

chemical effects of the stimuli. They depend on the condition of the organism and are produced by the release of forces characteristic of the organism.

Each of the primary physical parameters is used by some organism in orienting within its environment. In fact, each physical parameter is used by some *unicellular* organism. There are sensory capacities associated with light, magnetic fields, chemical mixes, heat, electricity, mechanical contact, gravity, and sound. One dimension of classification of taxes is the type of sensory stimulant that leads to a relevant orientation. There is photo-taxis, geo-taxis, chemo-taxis, thermo-taxis, and so on. The taxes are further classified by the aspect of movement that is affected by the stimulus, and its relation to the stimulus.[56]

What does all this have to do with primitive agency? I think that some of these types of taxis, even in very simple organisms, are instances of primitive agency. The paramecium's swimming through the beating of its cilia in a coordinated way, and perhaps its initial reversal of direction, count as agency.[57] I will discuss, conjecturally, what drives and grounds the judgment that agency is to be found at this very primitive level.

It is natural, and in a sense correct, to regard primitive agency as "just reaction". Certainly, primitive agency does not involve will or intention. It is not intelligent. Much of it is not very flexible. In fact, even among birds and lower mammals, inflexible, automatic, instinctive agency is probably the most common type of whole-animal agency. Instinct-based action depends on a chain of reflexes and is certainly not intelligent or flexible.

In the case of unicellular organisms, such as paramecia and amoebae, it is easy to declare such cases to be borderline, or below the level of any reasonable conception of agency. Even in eukaryotic, unicellular organisms, however, there is some specialization of sensory and response mechanisms, and some coordinated whole-animal responses to stimulation that issue from capacities characteristic of the organism.[58]

---

[56] For discussion of different taxes, see Fraenkel and Gunn, *The Orientation of Animals*, and Tinbergen, *The Study of Instinct*. For one of the early descriptions of various taxes, see Jennings, *Behavior of the Lower Organisms*. (There are studies of taxes that go back earlier.) The point that unicellular organisms are responsive to all stimuli that higher animals are responsive to is made on p. 261. For a classic account of two basic types of taxis, see Gottfried Fraenkel, 'Beiträge zur Geotaxis and Phototaxis von Littorina', *Zeitschrift für wissenschaftliche Biologie* 5 (1927), 585–597; translated in C. R. Gallistel, *The Organization of Action: A New Synthesis* (Hillsdale, NJ: Lawrence Erlbaum Associates, 1980). Gallistel gives a rich exposition of various mechanisms involved in animal action. He seems to take a hierarchy of simpler mechanisms to underlie all action. This picture is surely accurate for primitive agency in relatively complex animals. I believe, however, that even unicellular organisms exhibit primitive agency. There is no evident hierarchy of mechanisms in these cases, but there is a minimal specialization for certain capacities such as self-propulsion, reversal, and eating. This specialization allows scope to the idea that there is a type of coordination in the active behavior of the whole organism.

[57] The klino-kinetic turning seems less clearly a coordinated functional activity than, say, the default swimming. It contrasts with the reversal in that its direction is unrelated to the direction of the stimulus. At any rate, I find it at best unclear whether this aspect of the paramecium's behavior is action.

[58] Houten, 'Chemoreception in Microorganisms'.

The notion of primitive individual action is, I think, driven by examples. The swimming of a fish or paramecium, carried out by the thrashing of a tail or the beating of cilia in still water, is, I think, an example of an organism's acting. The paramecium is not just being moved around by its environment. The movement is broadly functional. A significant contribution to the movement comes from within. And the movement often involves whole-organism coordination between central capabilities and peripheral systems. Similar points can be made about organisms' eating, mating, and so on.

I think that the relevant notion of action is grounded in *functioning, coordinated behavior* by the *whole organism*, issuing from the individual's *central behavioral capacities*, not purely from subsystems. Coordination is meant to imply that the behavior must issue from central capacities, in effect coordinating subsystems, or coordinating central capacities with their peripheral realizations. The schematic account in this paragraph is not a definition. It nevertheless guides my conception and helps unify the examples.

The notion of *behavior* here is vague, and would reward more development. I take it as primitive. Plants are usually not construed as exhibiting behavior. Animals and certain other very simple organisms are.[59]

Behavior is not merely movement caused by physical forces on the organism. It is not merely the occurrence of processes in the cells or other subsystems of the organism. It is to be distinguished from growth, maturation, and certain peripheral reflexive responses to stimulation. At the lower levels of agency, it is always related, in ways that I shall discuss, to whole-organism biological functions.

I believe that notions of behavior and primitive agency apply beyond whole, individual organisms. Very close analogs of the notion of individual primitive agency, the notion that I will develop here, are applicable to the agency of groups. Behavior and agency are necessarily imputable either to individuals or to groups of individuals acting in concert. I discuss individual *organisms*, and groups of individual organisms, leaving aside issues about robots and such.

The behavior and agency of a group of organisms are often vivid and evident. The operations of a swarm of bees, or an army of ants, or a herd of water buffalo, or a pack of wolves or orcas, are often functioning, coordinated, and the product of the whole group. Cooperative interaction is part of the nature of the group activity. A conception of group primitive agency is just as important to understanding primitive agency in nature as is a conception of individual primitive

---

[59] Perhaps Venus Fly Traps are borderline cases, or even special exhibitors of behavior. For a description of bacterial "swimming" that provides some basis for seeing bacteria as agents, see Houten, 'Chemoreception in Microorganisms'. For a useful discussion of the generic kind *behavior*, see Ruth Garrett Millikan, 'What is Behavior? A Philosophical Essay on Ethology and Individualism in Psychology', in *White Queen Psychology and Other Essays for Alice*. Millikan's emphasis on function in individuating behavior is valuable, at least insofar as one is concerned with primitive organismic behavior. The main error in her account is that it is much too inclusive. It includes maturation and growth. It also includes peripheral changes such as sweating and protein transfer that are not imputable to the individual. There are loose uses of 'behavior' that include such peripheral changes perhaps. No serious science counts maturation or growth as behavior.

agency. I think that sketching the latter notion, however, will give us enough to do. So I focus on *individual* organism behavior, and ultimately on *individual* organism agency.

A lot of behavior is active. Yet not all broadly functional behavior is active or action.

Reflexive stress or *schreck* reactions are behavior but not actions. They constitute passive behavior. The shock responses of small organisms are not active. A deer's helpless freezing in headlights or out of fear of a predator need not be active. Helpless writhing in pain is behavior that is not agency.

Such non-active behavioral reactions can be functional. They typically serve the animal's needs. These sorts of behavior function to shut down all other behavioral systems. In active behavior, sometimes an action will inhibit other types of behavior; but its function is not to arrest or shut down the individual's central behavioral capacities. So *schreck* reactions and helpless writhing are not coordinated behavior that issue from the individual's central behavioral capabilities. They involve a shutting-down of central behavioral capacities.

An animal's shivering in the cold, or its coughing or sneezing, is perhaps an instance of behavior. But it is not an instance of active behavior. Such events can be functional. Shivering engenders heat. Coughing and sneezing have expectorant functions. They are functional, but they are operations of peripheral systems that are not normally products of coordination with central behavioral capacities. They are reflexive, peripheral processes. Ordinarily, they are not instances of agency, although of course they can be, as when an individual coughs intentionally. If they are types of behavior, they are normally not active behavior.

It is unclear to me why these passive types of behavior count as behavior—and hence are imputable to the whole individual. I conjecture that the explanation has to do with the fact that either the process engages the individual's whole body— as *schreck* reactions, writhing, and in a sense shivering do—or the process is the product of a subsystem that is closely associated with the animal's anatomical center—as coughing and sneezing are, and knee jerks are not.[60]

Not all behavior fulfills whole-animal functions. Although most behavior in the simpler organisms fulfills some function, not all *instances* of primitive agency fulfill functions. In a rage or under the influence of some disease, an animal can run in circles or off a cliff. An animal can eat a poisonous plant. Running and eating remain acts by the whole animal. Normally, the point of a *type* of activity, in non-pathological cases (as in the case of eating poison), is explicable by reference to purpose or function.

There are *types* of non-pathological primitive agency that do not obviously fulfill larger biological functions. Idly, non-intentionally, drumming one's fingers, or the unconscious coordinated swaying to rhythmic sound by an animal,

---

[60] In understanding ordinary language involved in attributing processes to individuals rather than their subsystems, it is perhaps important that these processes involve animals' heads. These points seem not to have any *theoretical* power.

can be active. It is not evident what function it performs. Certainly it need not realize any of the basic biological functions. These cases seem, however, to be instances of more generic types of agency that do fulfill biological functions—moving one's fingers, moving one's body. Most primitive agency, even specifically described, has obvious functions. All primitive agency, generically enough described, has a whole individual function. It is in this broad sense that primitive agency is *functioning*.

All behavior is imputable to individuals, as distinct from their subsystems. As I have indicated, not all behavior is active. Yet the distinction between what is imputable to the whole organism, perhaps as well as to certain subsystems, and what is imputable *merely* to subsystems, is a key element in the active/passive distinction. Action must be a whole-organismic affair: it issues from central capabilities of the individual. (Again, I lay aside action by groups of individual organisms.) Active behavior is distinguished from the reflexive responses of muscle twitch and the classical reflex arc. In these cases, movement is imputable purely to the organism's subsystems.

In relatively complex animals, the classical reflex arc does not even go through the central nervous system. It is not available to central coordinating agency. Similar points can be made about muscle spasms, the firing of neurons, saccades by the eyes. Such events are normally not imputed to individuals. But even shivering, coughing, sneezing—processes that are normally imputed to individuals (sometimes as well as subsystems)—are distinguished from active behavior because, normally, the processes are not a product of coordination with central behavioral capabilities of the individual.

In the cases of larger animals, there is usually a fairly clear distinction between central and peripheral processes that correlates roughly with an anatomical distinction between processes that are controlled by the central nervous system and processes that are not. One can make a start at analogous points even for simple organisms like paramecia that lack a central nervous system. Eating involves a unitary process that involves the whole organism (eating itself, and rotation of the animal body so that the side that has the gullet opening faces the food), as well as operations that are imputable purely to its subsystems (expansion of the gullet). By contrast, protein transfer through the membranes of the paramecium is not a process that engages the unified behavior of the whole animal.

The role of specialized anatomical structures in distinguishing active and passive processes probably goes beyond that of the central nervous system. For example, eating is often distinguishable from photosynthesis—also a source of energy production—by the existence of certain specialized anatomical structures. The paramecium has a gullet, a chamber in which digestion occurs. No plant has a gullet. Protein transfer through cell membranes and absorption of light or other sources of energy occur in all cells. There is no coordination among structures within the organism in these cases.

Still, I doubt that the contrast can be made plausibly on a strictly anatomical basis. The fact that the whole paramecium is eating probably carries more weight than any view of it as being a coordination of anatomical subsystems. The centrality of the capabilities is often signaled by some sort of coordination. But one cannot read off the relevant type of whole-organism coordination from physiology and anatomy.

I am not convinced that anatomical specialization is even necessary, much less sufficient. The amoeba's anatomical specializations for feeding are minimal. What is necessary is functional behavior that issues in a coordinated way in the realization of central capabilities of the individual. Photosynthesis lacks such coordination. It is carried out equally in individual cells across the plant. The amoeba's eating exhibits relevant coordination, even though there may be no relevant anatomical or physiological coordination of *subsystems*, as there is in the paramecium.

I doubt that there is an independent criterion for whole-individual agency. Again, the fact that the amoeba is eating seems to carry as much weight in the judgment that the eating is active rather than passive behavior as the fact that there is coordination with the individual's central capabilities. Anatomy and physiology can sometimes guide what counts as a central capability, but not always. As I indicated earlier, I think that our understanding of these matters is probably partly guided by an antecedent list of whole-individual functions that already embody conceptions of activity by the whole, individual organism—eating, navigating, mating, and so on.

Functioning, coordinated behavior by the whole organism, issuing from the individual's central behavioral capacities, need not engage—coordinate—all an individual's capacities, of course. Ordinary absent-minded, non-reflexive, unintentional scratching by humans does not. Eating does not. The requirement is that the process be imputable to the individual and that it involve some behavior that is the natural product of the individual's central capabilities.

There are always borderline cases. Still, the notions of whole-organism organization of behavior issuing from central behavioral capacities and whole-organism function, together with a list of paradigm cases, seem to me to provide a beginning at understanding the relevant notion of primitive agency. Let me add a few comments to what I have already said.

Primitive whole-organism agency often involves whole-organism *control*, but does not require it. Ducking an approaching missile can be an action even if it is against one's own attempt to inhibit the ducking. I assume that the ducking is not a peripheral reflex in the classical sense. It is guided by perception.[61] Such ducking seems not to be under the individual's control.

---

[61] If one is on a wheel and one knows that a knife thrower will accurately miss one's head if one remains stationary, one still might move one's head at the approaching knife—to one's own peril. The example is Sean Foran's.

A more fundamental reason against taking control to be central to primitive agency is that with respect to the simplest organisms, the notion of control has little grip.

Primitive whole-organism agency also does not require a *capacity to shape or guide* whole-organism movement past the point where the stimulus is registered.[62] Various types of instinctive behavior are inflexible and chain-reflexive, but still count as action. The male grouse will copulate with a stuffed grouse, male grouse, or dead grouse, if it sees any of these as assuming the relevant female mating position. The male grouse's copulation activity is released by a single stimulus or single perception. The instinctive behavior does not derive from an inability to distinguish visually between the sexes, or between live and dead grouses. It is just that the instinctive behavior overrides these distinctions, once the key stimulus is received.[63]

The grouse is guided by visual perception. This capacity is inessential, however. Whole-organism instinctive behavior that counts as agency need not be guided, or capable of being guided, by perception at all. Nestling thrushes, which are initially blind, strenuously gape to be fed when the nest is jarred. The direction of gaping is not influenced by the jarring. They stretch their necks vertically upward, oriented by a proprioceptive sense of gravity. The activity is initiated by the jarring, but is not shaped by or oriented to the jarring in any way. Yet the behavior is whole animal and active.[64] Of course, the examples from very simple organisms, such as the paramecium and the tick, make the same point.

Some accounts of agency center on an animal's use of perceptual stimulation. Not all primitive action is direct response to stimulation, let alone perception. Swimming is the normal condition of paramecia, eels, and fish. They do not need present stimulation to keep them going. Activity may change without

---

[62] I have long been indebted to a remark by Harry Frankfurt for my interest in primitive animal action. See Harry G. Frankfurt, 'The Problem of Action' (1978), in *The Importance of What We Care About* (Cambridge: Cambridge University Press, 1988). Frankfurt remarked that a spider acts when it walks, but does not act when its legs are moved (in anatomically the same way) by an external agent. I think, however, that Frankfurt's own account of action is incorrect. Frankfurt explicates the notion of action in terms of guidance of behavior by the individual during the behavior. He does not develop his notion of guidance. But his view seems vulnerable to both the ducking example and the examples of instinctive behavior, such as the grouse's, that I am about to discuss. Action does not require *guidance by the individual* during the act (or even before the act). Intuitively the grouse's action and the ducking are guided by the individual's perception. But the action is not under the control or guidance of the individual in this sense: the individual could not monitor or adjust it, given the initial perceptual input. These matters need development, of course. I have invoked, tentatively, the more liberal notion of coordination, with allowances for questions as to whether the notion applies straightforwardly to action by very simple organisms. The key notion is issuance from central behavioral capabilities of the individual.

[63] Tinbergen, *The Study of Instinct*, 36. Tinbergen's tentative definition of 'instinct' is 'a hierarchically organized nervous mechanism which is susceptible to certain priming, releasing, and directing impulses of internal as well as of external origin, and which responds to these impulses by coordinate movements that contribute to the maintenance of the individual and the species' (p. 112).

[64] Ibid. 85–87. I doubt that the proprioceptive sense that yields the orientation to gravity here counts as perception. Whether or not this is correct, there is no perception of any objective (the food) of the activity of gaping.

external stimulation. Action even by very simple organisms does not require occurrent stimulation. A hydra's periodic movement tends not to be in response to present stimulation. A hydra can be resting attached to a water plant or the side of a glass container. After a few minutes, it contracts, bends into a new position, sets its top on a surface, and extends its bottom upward (head over heels, so to speak). It moves in a slow cartwheel-like motion about its environment, increasing its chance of finding food. Rates of movement depend on hunger.[65]

Some instinct-based action derives from release of pent-up energy and has no further function for the animal. Many animals act without exogenous stimulation. For example, famously, Lorenz's hand-reared starling periodically performed an elaborate fly-catching routine in the absence of flies, having never trapped a fly in its life.[66] The periodic movement of hydra seems also to be endogenously driven.

Examples of more hierarchical endogenous behavior production illustrate ramifications of the same point. Hungry cats have been observed to catch, kill, and eat a half dozen mice, then kill a few more without eating them, then catch more without killing, then sit in the attitude of lying in ambush with head lowered, not attacking but intently watching mice, some of which crawl over their paws.[67]

Neither the function nor the environmental object of an animal's agency need be represented by the organism. The cyst that the amoeba ingests is not represented by the amoeba. Nothing is. Much animal agency is pre-perceptual and pre-representational. Lorenz's starling was presumably capable of visual perception of prey, but the action is not shaped by perception of anything. Whether the starling hallucinates prey when it engages in its endogenously driven fly-catching behavior is an open question. There are active routines that are not the result of *unusual* damming up of motivational energy (as was the case with Lorenz's starling), but simply of ordinary endogenously driven instinctual behavior. The nearly perpetual swimming of fish and the nearly constant flapping of the wings of small birds are examples.

All activity of the simpler organisms and much activity of more complex animals are not guided by perception. Where such activity is a response to sensory stimulation, it is backed by non-perceptual sensory capacities that register information. All the active behavior of amoebae, paramecia, hydra, ticks, and molluscs, most of the active behavior of moths, spiders, shrimp, fish, and snakes,

---

[65] Jennings, *Behavior of the Lower Organisms*, 189 ff., 261, 285 ff.

[66] 'It would fly up to an elevated look-out position . . . perch there and gaze upwards continuously as if searching the sky for flying insects. Suddenly, the bird's entire behaviour would indicate that it had spotted an insect. The starling would extend its body, flatten its feathers, aim upwards, take off, snap at something, return to its perch and finally perform swallowing motions. . . . there were really no insects to be seen' (Konrad Lorenz, 'A Consideration of Methods of Identification of Species-Specific Instinctive Behaviour Patterns in Birds' (1932), in *Studies in Animal and Human Behaviour*, i, trans. R. Martin (Cambridge, MA: Harvard University Press, 1970)). See also Lorenz, 'The Establishment of the Instinct Concept' (1937), in ibid.

[67] See Konrad Lorenz (who cites the work of Paul Leyhausen), *The Foundations of Ethology* (1978), trans. K. Z. Lorenz and R. W. Kickert (New York: Springer-Verlag, 1981), 135–136.

and some of the active behavior of birds and mammals are not guided by perception.

Much exogeneously stimulated animal action derives not from perception but from sensory registration of information—from sensory discrimination that can be adequately explained as functional responses to surface stimulation. The animal's sensory discriminations are linked to the biologically important aspects of the environment purely in a causal, information-theoretic way that has functional value for the life of the organism. Although the organism acts, both the environmental stimulants and environmental objectives lie outside its purview. It acts blindly in the fullest sense. Blindly, but functionally and often efficiently.

When perception sets an object for animal action, agency reaches a new level of sophistication. The animal itself perceptually represents the goal that the action fulfills.[68]

If an animal can perceive, it has some perspective on its objectives. Much agency by animals with perception, like copulation by the grouse, remains dominated by instinctual patterns that are not intelligent or shaped by the animal, let alone reasoned. Nevertheless, since perceptual representation is constitutively the whole animal's representation, and since perception enables an animal to fix its goal, action guided by perception derives from a perspective in a way that action in response to mere sensory registration does not.

With animal agency guided by perception, a primitive type of *psychological* agency is commonly in place for the first time. Acting on a perception requires distinguishing elements of the perceptual representation to act upon. Perception *per se* is not normally an act. But the direction of perceptual attention is an act. In fact, it is a primitive type of *psychological* act. Selective orientation of the whole individual to aspects of what it perceptually represents is empirically demonstrable at relatively low levels of animal activity.[69] Such selective perceptual orientation, or perceptual attention, is, I think, the most primitive sort of psychological agency.

Perhaps another type of psychological act that emerges at this stage is the setting of a goal. The direction of attention serves the setting of a goal for which the actional system then forms an actional representation. Perhaps some goals are

---

[68] Sean Foran, 'Animal Movement' (manuscript; extracted from his UCLA dissertation 'Animal Movement' (1998)), highlights the role of perception in animal movement. I think that he is onto the more sophisticated type of animal agency that is guided by perception. I believe, however, that his notion of animal movement either blurs the distinction between pre-perceptual agency and perception-guided agency, which I think so important, or simply applies to the more sophisticated type. The case of the nestling thrushes and the case of endogenously engendered action seem to me to pose problems for applying his account to all animal agency. Similarly, for the cases of activity in very simple organisms. Despite these differences, I have found Foran's original paper a source of stimulation. I read the paper in draft several years ago, and have returned to it, in later drafts, several times since.

[69] The attention need not be conscious. For development of the point, see Goodale and Milner, *The Visual Brain in Action*, 181 ff.; also D. Ingle, 'Selective Visual Attention in Frogs', *Science* 188 (1975), 1033–1035. On the other hand, there are delicate issues here involved in distinguishing individuals' directing attention and the grabbing of attention by a stimulus.

set passively, but those set pursuant to directing attention can, I think, be set actively.

Psychological agency need not *be* a piece of coordination. But it is one of the wellsprings of centrally coordinated behavior. Attention and setting a goal are psychological acts that are active partly because they function in initiating or coordinating active bodily behavior.

A new aspect of agency that emerges when agency is associated with perception is a primitive type of objectification. This type of objectification in action derives from the objectification that is constitutive of perception. I will discuss perceptual objectification in some detail in Chapter 9. The animal perceives its goals, and the action is directed toward a goal represented through the animal's perception. Such goal objectification is missing from action engendered by registration of information based on response to mere bodily stimulation.

To develop how this element relates to norms, let us return to the notion of function. I remarked that at least under relatively generic descriptions, primitive agency has biological functions. The agency is biologically functional roughly in the sense that the existence of the activity is explained by its contribution to the individual's, or the individual's group's, fitness.

As emphasized in this chapter, the section REPRESENTATIONAL FUNCTION AND NATURAL NORMS, success in fulfilling a function is a *good* for the system or for the agent of the activity, *relative to the function*. The heart's beating efficiently is a good relative to the heart's function to pump blood. The amoeba's ingesting a cyst is a good for the amoeba, relative to the relevant function.

There is, of course, nothing moral about such goodness. The goodness lies merely in success in fulfilling function.

The application of the notion of goodness here is not comparative, like applications of assessing a level of quality. A knife is a good knife not merely through fulfilling its function, or through being adequate with respect to its function.[70] It must fulfill its function in a better than minimal way. The use of 'good' as applied to the knife is comparative. In the present non-comparative use of the notion of goodness, any fulfillment of function is a good, a success, relative to the function, in our generic sense.

Let me review our previous discussion of norms.

Where there are functions, it is apriori that there are *standards* for fulfilling them. A standard, in this sense, is a level of fulfillment. A standard need not be set, imposed, required, recognized, or even recognizable by any individual.

Some levels of fulfillment are standards that are also *norms*. A norm is a standard or level of possible performance that is in some respect adequate for fulfillment of a function or purpose.

Some norms are *natural norms*. Natural norms are norms that constitute an explanatorily relevant kind, independent of any individual's setting or acceding

---

[70] As Judy Thomson has pointed out.

to them. Commonly, natural norms are independent of *any* attitudes regarding them. It is apriori, I think, that for every function there are various natural norms.

Here we have a momentous structural feature of the world. Wherever there is teleology—that is, wherever there is function or purposiveness—there are standards for realizing the function or the end state of the purposiveness. One level of fulfillment is, of course, full realization. But there are, I think, always other natural levels of fulfillment, relative to the nature, capacities, and circumstances of those things that have the function. I believe that this basic scheme applies to a wide range of phenomena—to all biological organisms and their subsystems, to artifacts, to animal agency, to perception and belief, to inference, to knowledge, and to morality. Some basic norms or standards associated with an enterprise— natural norms—are set by the nature of the enterprise itself, not by choice or convention.

Some natural norms concern primitive, pre-representational agency. In the section REPRESENTATIONAL FUNCTION AND NATURAL NORMS, I remarked that biological functions and natural biological norms are associated with primitive, pre-representational agency. The tick's crawling fulfills biological functions, and fulfills or fails to fulfill standards of adequacy in performance for fulfilling those functions. The efficiency of a tick's navigation to a blood source occurs at a given level of performance relative to various standards—ideal standards like straight, shortest distance walking; realistic standards like the straightest route available given the terrain and given a tick's best navigational capacities. Such routes mark minimal expenditure of energy in the acquisition of food. The tick's action is associated purely with biological functions and biological norms.

Biological functions and biological norms are not the only sorts of function and norm that are relevant to explaining the capacities and behavior of some animals. Given that veridicality and non-veridicality cannot be reduced to success and failure (respectively) in fulfilling biological function, we must recognize a type of function that is not a biological function, a *representational function*. The basic representational functions concern representational success—veridicality, truth, making veridical, preserving truth, and so on.

Once primitive agency is supplemented and guided by perceptual representation, agency is associated with representational functions as well as biological functions. Correspondingly, biological natural norms associated with agency are supplemented with representational natural norms. The representational natural norms concern relations between action and *perceptual representational content*. An action can be more or less successful in fulfilling the representational content that represents the action or its goal. Representational functions and representational natural norms come into play.

Any agency guided by perception has, in addition to biological functions, functions associated with representation. The biological function of action is to do something that contributes, however indirectly, to fitness or survival for mating. Perception's basic baseline representational function is to represent veridically: perception undergoes a type of failure if it is inaccurate. The simplest representational function of action guided by perception is to make veridical the actional representation that maps out the action. A frequently related representational function is to fulfill through an action a perceptually set goal. The action is to fit the representational content that maps out the action, or the goal.

Representational agency can meet or fail to meet various levels of adequacy of performance relative to fulfilling its representational functions. It may meet or fail to meet various natural representational norms. An individual falls under such norms as a consequence of engaging in representational agency, agency with a representational function. The simplest natural norm associated with representationally successful agency is fulfilling the action's representational function— meeting the action's representational goal by making the action's representational content veridical. There are less demanding norms that are specializations of this simplest norm. I have in mind such norms as acting as well as possible, relative to the action's representational function, given interfering factors in the circumstances and given the agent's capabilities. Both the primary simple norm and the less demanding specializations are natural representational norms attaching to agency guided by perception.[71]

An individual need not understand or be *guided* by the norms, or by any other general principles, even though general principles help explain the individual's actions. Basic natural norms apply to such agency even if an individual cannot understand or be guided by them. An action can be evaluated regarding how well it fulfills the representational content that represents its goal and action. The norms, standards for success, *are set by the kind of enterprise or capacity involved*: agency guided by perception.

Let us look at a low-level example of representational agency and its relation to natural norms. A spider may perceive another spider as prey of such and such a shape and size, and at such and such a distance. The spider and its actional system may set the prey (represented as such) as goal. It does so only if it has perceptual capacities to perceive the goal. The actional system may represent the target as the objective of a jump with a certain distance and direction. There are norms regarding how well the spider succeeds, given the action and objective *as represented by the spider*. What counts as success in the action is determined by the actional system's representation of the action and its relation to the objective.

---

[71] What I am calling the simplest norm is essentially an instrumental norm. An act that falls under this norm always falls under more global norms that concern the same act and its goal. For example, an act that fulfills the agent's representational content can be evaluated under biological or other practical norms, such as whether it contributed to the individual's evolutionary fitness, or the individual's flourishing. Of course, when more sophisticated global practical norms—such as moral norms—are in place, an instrumentally successful act and its goal may or may not meet those more sophisticated norms. All these issues arise only once agency is supplemented by perceptual representation—thus once agency becomes constitutively associated with representational functions and representational norms.

The norms that figure in such explanations are low-level natural representational norms that concern efficiency. As with actions that are not associated with representational content, the natural norms for representational agency are set by the function of the enterprise. There are two interrelated differences between representational agency and the most primitive, pre-representational agency. One is that a function of the action, its representational function, is to meet conditions partly set by *representational content*. Success in fulfilling *this* function is success in meeting a standard set by a representational enterprise of the animal, not merely by norms associated with biological functions.

The other difference is that natural norms for successful action work off objectives set by the agent. The agent does not act blindly. It sets its goals and represents them. The *agent* perceives, and it acts to carry out actions and to fulfill goals that it represents. Action coordinates with perception.

Of course, at low levels of representational agency, the notions of function, good, and norm are not parts of the representational content. The animal does not represent functions or norms. It does not set its goals *as* good, or *as* good for it, or *as* its own.[72] It does not reason about its goals. It lacks propositional intentions. Still, just as some norms for perceptual success are antecedents of norms for epistemic warrant, norms for representational agency are antecedents of norms for practical rationality.

As with perception, so with representational agency: veridicality is part of the basis of the system. The notion of goodness, or success, in fulfilling function and the notion of a norm for fulfilling a function are more primitive than notions of representation and veridicality. Teleology is more primitive than representation. But, once functions of agency and norms for agency become associated with perception and *representational* agency, veridicality joins goodness in being central to the practical domain. Representational functions and norms associated with such functions become constitutively associated with actional psychological kinds. Here, I think, is the most primitive level at which ancestors of two members—veridicality and goodness—of the traditional philosophical trinity join forces as explanatory kinds. The basic type of representational success for perception is veridicality. The basic type of representational success for agency is doing what one sets out to do. Doing what one sets out to do is making an actional representational content veridical through one's action. Individuals' being guided to goals through appreciation of norms, evaluating goals, and evaluating norms themselves, come later.

In the remainder of this chapter and in the next, I return to our key contrast—that between *perception* and *sensory discrimination that merely registers information*.

---

[72] Also, low-level representational agents do not represent their representations or representational contents. Hence they do not represent them as veridical. There is, of course, an egocentric element in the structure of goal oriented action, but this is not the same as an individual's representing the goal as his/her/its own.

PERCEPTUAL PSYCHOLOGY AND THE DISTINCTION BETWEEN
SENSORY INFORMATION REGISTRATION AND PERCEPTION

In this section, I discuss examples of empirical theories of some specific processes in visual perception. The examples are intended to provide a sense for
distinctively psychological, non-trivial explanations by reference to states individuated partly in terms of representational content with veridicality conditions.

The examples should contribute to better understanding of two matters. First,
the examples elaborate the distinction between (*a*) mere sensory registration
(functional sensory information encoding), explained in biological and information-theoretic terms, and (*b*) perception, explained in distinctively psychological
terms—terms that make non-trivial explanatory use of an appeal to states with
veridicality conditions. Second, the examples provide the background for a more
fundamental account of the distinction between sensory registration and perception, set out in Chapter 9.

Explaining the examples requires some detail. I have tried to discuss the detail
in ways that are accessible to readers not familiar with the science. The detail is
there to help fix ideas.

In Chapter 3, the section THE SHAPE OF PERCEPTUAL PSYCHOLOGY, I outlined the
basic problem and the explanatory shape of visual psychology. Let me recall the
main points of that account.

The primary problem of the psychology of visual perception is to explain how
visual systems form perceivers' visual perceptual states of, and as of, the physical
environment from the input that they receive. In other words, the primary
problem is to explain how individuals accurately perceive particulars as having
specific physical attributes. Although accurate perceptions are the primary *explanandum*, perceptual illusions are also explained. Both the primary problem
and solutions to it rest on a distinction between mere sensory registration and
representational states. The science that solves instances of this problem makes a
non-trivial, distinctively psychological, appeal to states with accuracy conditions,
or veridicality conditions. It therefore makes non-trivial explanatory appeal to
representational states.

The initial, psychologically relevant effects of proximal stimulation are the
initial inputs into the perceptual system. Such inputs are registrations of stimulations—functioning, causally based, statistical correlations that encode the impact
of stimulations. The outputs are perceptual states with representational content as
of specific entities in the physical environment. The states and their contents can be
accurate or inaccurate. The initial effects of proximal stimulation are specified in
information-theoretic terms. They could be described in representational terms, but
no non-trivial explanatory ground indicates that they should be so described.

For visual perception, the primary initial effects of proximal stimulation are
the results of stimulation of the retinal receptors. Such effects can be mapped on a
two-dimensional grid. Each minimum area of the grid is a sensory registration by
a retinal receptor. Each such registration is the causal product of a given light

intensity that stimulates that receptor. Each such registration contains information that correlates with the light intensity.

The primary proximal stimulation for the visual system is the spatial pattern and spectral properties of the light striking the retina. As noted, the first registration of such stimulation is the primary initial input into visual perceptual systems. Further input includes proprioceptive information regarding eye movement or other bodily movement. Further input comes from other parts of the individual's psychology—from other senses (such as touch or hearing), from actional systems, and even from conceptual sets, for individuals that have propositional attitudes.

I shall largely ignore these other sorts of input here. There are several reasons why this focus on the primary input (light arrays) is justifiable. Many of the processes in the visual systems of animals that have propositional attitudes are carried out independently of those attitudes. Some are carried out before top-down input is available. Conceptual input seems often to occur at late stages in the sequence of visual processing—*high-level vision*—after the basic percepts are already formed.[73] The visual systems of human infants are well developed before infants have acquired any of the propositional attitudes that are contingent to human culture. More broadly, many of the basic forms of visual processing appear to be shared between animals that have propositional attitudes and animals that lack them. The basic capacities and transformations in human vision are shared by most mammals.

Bracketing input from proprioception and other non-visual sensory systems is a more delicate matter. Input from other senses is always relevant to the formation of visual perceptual states. Some of the most intense research in vision science currently focuses on ways input from other senses, especially input that is "at odds" with visual input, affect formation of visual perception. Still, many of the basic processes can be understood as operating on their own, in a default mode. The effects of most proprioceptive and tactile input, for example, can be included at later stages of explanation. Similarly, for input from actional systems.

So for purposes of illustration—and in actual fact—the form of many primary processes in visual systems can be understood by focusing on registration (functional encoding) of proximal stimulation of the retina by arrays of light intensities. The primary problem of the theory of vision can be simplified for our purposes: it is to explain formation of both veridical visual perception and perceptual illusion, given various types of retinal stimulation.

---

[73] The late stage of interface between visual processing and conceptual input is called 'high-level vision'. For work on this interface, see Shimon Ullman, *High-Level Vision: Object Recognition and Visual Cognition* (Cambridge, MA: MIT Press, 1996). For more on the limited nature of input from conceptual resources in many basic types of visual processing, see Pylyshyn, 'Is Vision Continuous with Cognition?' Ordinary language condones such remarks as: 'She perceived the x-ray as showing cancer.' In such cases perception is indeed supplemented with background propositional knowledge and belief. What ordinary language calls perception is a hybrid of perception proper and belief. Ordinary language blurs psychological kinds here.

The initial sensory state registers a pattern and spectral properties of light. The initial state is not a perceptual state. The individual does not perceive this light pattern. Nothing in the system perceptually represents the array. The initial sensory state registers or functionally encodes proximal stimulation, without in any way privileging an environmental source.

The initial registration of input is information theoretic, not perceptual. The initial sensory state is a two-dimensional registration or encoding of the pattern and spectral properties of light striking the retinal surfaces. Proximal stimulation by the light causes this sensory information registration. The primary problem of the theory of vision then is to explain how, given this initial input, visual systems form perceptual states, both veridical and illusory ones, that represent particulars in the distal environment as having specific attributes. A key aspect of this problem is that effects of proximal stimulation on the sensors of a perceptual system *underdetermine* both *representata* of perception and the nature of the perceptual state that represents such *representata*. The same stimulations could have been produced artificially, or from other distal conditions than those that normally produce them. In such cases, there are perceptual illusions. Moreover, nothing in the immediate effects of the stimulation, taken strictly in themselves, determines *representation* of one possible distal cause as opposed to another.

The primary problem for perceptual psychology is difficult and interesting, because it is simultaneously the *underdetermination problem*. This is the problem of explaining how the system represents, often veridically, specific environmental conditions, given that its input only registers, functionally encodes, proximal stimulation that underdetermines such conditions. The effects of proximal stimulation in themselves underdetermine the perceptual states as well as the environmental causal antecedents that are the putative *representata* of perception.[74] So, to arrive at a representational state that privileges as *representatum* one of many possible environmental antecedents of the registration of sensory input, the system must have default settings, or a default range of possibilities for learning. In each case, it must in effect make bets on one among many possible causal antecedents of proximal stimulation.

The initial sensory state (whether taken synchronically or diachronically) registers, or functionally encodes, an array of light intensities, without privileging a distal source. As noted, this registration constitutes a two-dimensional informational array corresponding to the array of light that impacts retinal receptors.

By contrast, spatial scenes are represented three-dimensionally. The representational content of a perception of those scenes can attribute three-dimensional characteristics. No two-dimensional array can uniquely determine a three-dimensional array. Thus the registration of a pattern and spectral properties of light in

---

[74] In the cases of touch and proprioceptive perception, the *representata* are frequently not distal, as they are in visual perception. Where there is perception in these sensory systems, versions of the underdetermination problem still arise.

the initial sensory state underdetermines both the distal situation and the perceptual representation of the distal situation.

The theory of vision must account for how information registered from the proximal stimulation is transformed into fallible but often approximately accurate perception as of three-dimensional distal conditions. Somewhat metaphorically, we might call perceptual systems' conversion of the registration of proximal stimulation into veridical perception of, and as of, entities in the distal environment *the systems'* solution to the underdetermination problem.

Transformation of information that correlates with a two-dimensional array into a perception as of a three-dimensional distal scene is an important instance of a perceptual system's solving the underdetermination problem. But the problem takes other forms. For example, the light intensities that impact the retina are a combination of surface color, or reflectance, and illumination. Registration of such intensities underdetermines surface color. Yet many visual systems reliably represent surface color, or reflectance.

The science of vision attempts to explain ways in which perceptual systems solve instances of the underdetermination problem. Explanation has been rich and often backed with substantial mathematical detail. In sum, science accounts for a set of processes that lead from registered information that correlates with proximal stimulation to perceptual states that represent specific environmental conditions, even though those conditions are only one among many physically possible causal antecedents.

Perceptual systems have developed so that their representational states tend to correlate with the likely causal antecedent, in the systems' formative environment, of the given proximal stimulation. There is a many–one mapping from the distal, environmental cause to proximal stimulus, and a one–many mapping from proximal stimulus to the environment. But there is something like a one–one mapping from proximal stimulus to distal environmental cause that is most likely to have generated that proximate stimulus. Now this latter fact is common between non-perceptual sensory systems and genuine perceptual sensory systems. Nature molds all sensory systems—perceptual and non-perceptual—to be likely to respond to environmental conditions that are beneficial to animals' functions. Perceptual systems are distinctive in the *way* that this likelihood is determined. The beginning of understanding this way lies in reflecting on the formation principles. The full account of this distinctive way cites a type of objectification, which I elaborate in Chapter 9.

To explain perceptual processes that overcome the underdetermination problem, perceptual theory postulates what in Chapter 3 I called *formation principles*. Formation principles describe formation laws: laws that determine transformation of sensory registrations—sensory states that correlate highly with a type of stimulation—into perceptual representational states with representational content. Formation principles also describe laws that lead from one type of perception (perception as of edges and surfaces) to another (perception as of solids), where again the first type underdetermines the second.

The formation principles describe law-like regularities, in the perceptual system, that reflect or mirror law-like regularities in the distal environment. The law-like regularities in transformational processes among states in the perceptual system, described by formation principles, are analogs of distal (sometimes statistical, sometimes law-like) regularities and kinds in the environment, instances of which figured causally in forming the perceptual system. In individual cases, the analogies are relatively clear and straightforward. In effect, the perceptual system has incorporated, through causal interaction with the distal environment over centuries, analogs of environmental laws and regularities. The formation principles describe laws of perception formation that reflect constitutive determination of perceptual representational kinds by the distal regularities and kinds. They illustrate anti-individualism regarding perception.

The principles are computational in the sense that they are computable. They describe quasi-algorithmic, quasi-automatic transitions in the perceptual system in ways that enable one to model perceptual systems on a computer.[75] The states that are described and explained, however, have representational content. There is no evidence that the principles, with their mathematical content and their specifications of mathematical operations and perceptual states, are the form or content of any states in the perceptual system. The formation principles are not "accessible" to the system. They are not represented in the system. The principles describe law-like patterns according to which one set of psychological states is transformed into another. (See the exposition of the notions of *computational* transformations and *computational* theory in Chapter 3, the section THE SHAPE OF PERCEPTUAL PSYCHOLOGY.)

Of course, the formation principles have only inductive force. They yield at best a high *likelihood* that the representational contents of the perceptual states are veridical. The environmental patterns that have been encoded by the patterns of psychological transformation do not, in every instance, underlie the causation of particular given registrations of light intensities. The perceptual states that ensue from transformations of psychological states are thus fallible. Some perceptual states thus formed are non-accidentally veridical. If the environmental conditions that the principles mirror and capitalize on are the sources of a specific kind of perceptual state, then, barring interference, malfunction, or abnormal conditions, some instances of the state are veridical. These instances are paradigmatic for the theory. Errors are explained as malfunctions of or interferences with the system, perhaps from antecedent anticipation or emotion. Or they are explained as effects of noise or limitations of acuity. Or they are explained as the results of special environmental conditions that fool the perceiver by producing the very registrations of proximal stimulation that under more favorable circumstances yield veridical representation.

---

[75] They are *quasi*-algorithmic in that it is recognized that noise and other interferences—even some that can cause malfunction or breakdown in the perceptual system—can prevent the formation operations from fitting the principles. Some specific allowance for such elements is made in the laws. But the laws are not probabilistic.

Let us turn to examples of transformations in visual systems. I discuss four examples. Each is a transformation from a source of information that underdetermines the result. So each example illustrates the role of formation principles in explaining formations of perceptions. Each exemplifies the explanatorily non-trivial invocation of states with representational content (and veridicality conditions) that distinguishes this psychology from biology.

The first two examples illustrate a law-like transformation from *non-perceptual* sensory registration to perceptual states with a representational content. Those examples illustrate the distinction between sensory registration and perception, and correspondingly the distinction between non-representational sensory states and representational ones. The existence of a science that makes systematic explanatory use of the distinction is the best possible reason to accept it, and to take perceptual states as *representational* in a psychologically distinctive sense.

Convergence

Let us reconsider *convergence*, one of the ways visual systems determine distance.[76] Determination of distance, indeed location, by convergence is a competence that capitalizes on the geometry of binocular vision.[77] The two eyes converge on or fixate a point in space when both are aimed at the point. The angle formed by the two

[76] Standard theory currently attributes to the human visual system as many as twelve basic capacities for determining distance and depth, each capacity with its own informational cues and forms of transformation. Combinations among these capacities and input from other senses complicate distance and depth determination further. Recent work suggests that the division into roughly a dozen basic capacities is probably artificial, and the number of types of cues that provide absolute or relative distance and depth information may be much greater.

[77] A basic understanding of convergence is present in Descartes (René Descartes, *The Dioptrics in Philosophical Writings: Descartes* (1637), ed. E. Anscombe and P. T. Geach (Indianapolis: Bobbs Merrill, 1971). Descartes's description of the geometrical transformations involved in convergence is basically right. Bishop Berkeley ridicules Descartes in a deliciously arrogant and mistaken passage, which I owe to Susan Carey:

But those *lines* and *angles*, by means whereof mathematicians pretend to explain the perception of distance, are themselves not at all perceived, nor are they, in truth, ever thought of by those unskillful in optics. I appeal to any one's experience, whether, upon sight of an *object*, he compute its distance by the bigness of the *angle* made by the meeting of the two *optic axes*? Or whether he ever think of the greater or lesser divergence of the rays, which arrive from any point to his *pupil*? Nay, whether it be not perfectly impossible for him to perceive by sense the various angles wherewith the rays, according to their greater or lesser divergence, do fall on his eye. Every one is himself the best judge of what he perceives, and what not. In vain shall all the *mathematicians* in the world tell me, that I perceive certain *lines* and *angles* which introduce into my mind the various *ideas* of *distance*; so long as I myself am conscious of no such thing. (George Berkeley, *A New Theory of Vision and Other Select Philosophical Writings* (1732; New York: E. P. Dutton & Co., 1919))

Berkeley assumes, mistakenly, that any explanation of processes in the formation of visual states must be carried out by the *individual perceiver*, or must be thinkable by the individual, and must be directly available to the individual's consciousness. In fact, the computations are in the descriptions of laws offered by 'mathematicians', or perceptual psychologists. They describe the laws of transformation in visual systems. The changes occur below the level of consciousness, and they are not acts imputable to individuals.

lines of sight (the *vergence angle*) varies systematically with the distance between the observer and the fixated point. Fixating a close object yields a larger angle. Fixating a more distant object yields a smaller vergence angle. Suppose that the lines of sight fixate a point straight ahead at eye level, then, given the distance between the two eyes and the angle between the intersecting lines of sight—the vergence angle—the distance of the point can be determined. The smaller the angle, the greater the distance. See Figure 8.1.

Given that the eyes can point in other directions than straight ahead at eye height, the vergence angle does not uniquely determine distance. The actual geometry involved is more complicated. To see why, imagine that the two eyes point neither up nor down, but only in the plane that extends parallel to the ground at eye height. Consider the circle drawn through the two eyes and the fixation point that is straight ahead. If the eyes fixate any other point in front of the eyes lying on the circle, the same vergence angle will be produced. That is, the same vergence angle is formed when the sight lines fixate the point directly in front of the viewer, and at other points to the left, or right, at a slightly closer distance. Hence, unless information deriving from the directions in which the eyes point is available to the system, distance is still not determinable.

In addition to the vergence angle, convergence operations in vision rely on what is called the *version angle*. The version angle is formed by the intersection of the line between the fixation point and a point midway between the two eyes (called 'the *cyclopean eye*'), on one hand, and the line that runs straight ahead at eye level, on the other. It is roughly the direction in which the two eyes are pointed.[78] Given that the distance between the two eyes is constant and given that both vergence and version angles can be determined from endogenous information available to the visual system, the location, and hence the distance, of fixation points, where lines of sight of the two eyes cross, are computable from geometrical principles. The same geometrical principles also apply outside the plane at eye level, though some additional psychological complications arise at extreme angles up or down.

Experiments have shown that visual systems rely on proximal information regarding vergence and version angles, together with the distance between the eyes to determine distance and location of distal causes of proximal information.[79]

Of course, none of this geometrical computation determines, by itself, that anything is seen at the relevant fixated location. Proximal stimulation underdetermines distal objects *seen* at that location. Proximal stimulation may be abnormal, and illusions may occur. So the location, hence distance, of *perceived*

---

[78] Strictly, of course, to fixate a point the two eyes point in different directions. The relevant direction is set by the line from the midpoint between the two eyes and the fixation point.

[79] Of course, as the distance grows, the increments between successive angles become smaller. Eventually, the increments may be too fine for actual visual systems to resolve. For descriptions of convergence, see Hofsten, 'The Role of Convergence in Visual Space Perception'; Palmer, *Vision Science*, 205–206. See Marr, *Vision*, 111 ff.

objects, relative to the viewer, are underdetermined by proximal stimulation itself. A given location hence distance can be determined for many textures, shapes, kinds of entity, all of which produce very different proximal stimulations. A red circle, blue square, and moving rough textured black body—each producing different proximal stimulations—can each be attributed the same distance and direction (location).

Convergence is one of the simplest *constancy* capacities. It yields location and hence distance constancy, relative to an egocentrically indexed origin. Perceptual constancies are key to understanding the nature of perception. I return to their significance in Chapter 9.

I have described convergence in a way that refers to fixating points and entities occupying such points, in the environment. But a visual system has access to such facts only through accessing information in proximal stimulation or endogenous sources. The aim of psychological explanation is to explain how representations as of environmental entities are formed from proximal and endogenous input that underdetermines the environmental situation. The theory must describe convergence in a way that accords with the actual situation of visual systems.

A simple redescription is as follows. The constant distance between the two eyes is coded into transformational processes. The fixation point of the two eyes is determined as follows. There is only one central point in the fovea of each eye. Each eye can be pointed in one direction at a time. The two lines marking those directions intersect at one point. The visual system has information that statistically correlates strongly with the angle of each eye and the stimulation registered at the center of each fovea. So (given the length of a line and two angles of a triangle) the visual system has sufficient information to determine the location, hence distance, of the fixation point—the position of the represented object. A perceptual representation as of a *representatum* at a given location, hence distance, relative to the viewer is formed from this information in accord with the relevant geometrical principles.[80]

Attributives indicating attributes of the *representatum* that is located at the distance and position determined by convergence are formed from the sensory input in areas surrounding the centers of the foveas. Formation of such attributives is governed by further formation principles.

The formation principle governing convergence describes a transformation that yields a representation of distance from this input. It is fallible. If either or

---

[80] The assumption that there is exactly one relevant point of sensory registration in the center of each fovea is an idealization. Determining exactly how the triangle's lines are determined is less straightforward than the description in the text suggests. There is, for example, an empirical question whether the matching points in the two foveas vary from context to context, or are fixed. Current empirical evidence strongly suggests that the pairings of points in the two foveas that are struck by light lines proceeding from the same distal point in space are fixed, and do not vary from context to context. See J. M. Hillis and M. S. Banks, 'Are Corresponding Points Fixed?', *Vision Research* 41 (2001), 2457–2473. If the suggestion holds, the computation involved in principles governing convergence would be substantially simpler than it otherwise would be.

CONVERGENCE

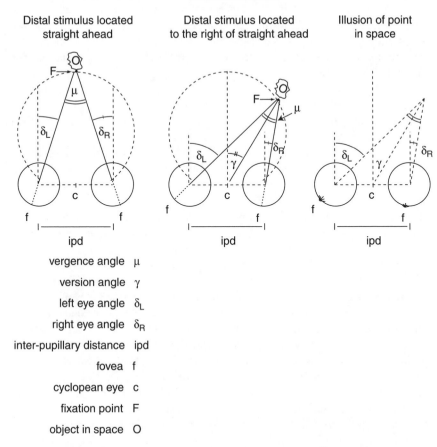

vergence angle   μ

version angle   γ

left eye angle δ_L

right eye angle δ_R

inter-pupillary distance   ipd

fovea   f

cyclopean eye   c

fixation point   F

object in space   O

FIGURE 8.1 Distance and location from convergence. Convergence is a way of establishing the location of an entity that is fixated by both eyes. It is a proto-typically geometrical constancy. It is an evolutionarily very old constancy mechanism. Given a constant distance between the two eyes, and proprioceptive information about the direction in which each eye is pointed, the distance and direction (hence location) of the fixated point, where the lines of sight of the two eyes meet, can be computed. The vergence and version angles are illustrated in the diagram. Convergence operates even when there is merely an illusion of an entity in space. The diagram depicts convergence in the plane at eye level. Convergence determines location for vision up or down as well.

both registrations at the centers of the foveas do not derive from an environmental object, but are the product of abnormal stimulation, then the representational content is inaccurate as regards the presence of a *representatum* at the represented distance.

Lightness Constancy

Let us consider a second example of a transformation that in effect solves an instance of the underdetermination problem. The transformations underlying determination of the lightness of a surface are more complex than those that underlie convergence. But they are among the best-understood aspects of the visual system.[81] *Lightness constancy* is a capacity to see surface lightness as approximately the same despite large differences in proximal stimulation that correlate with large differences in surface illumination.

This capacity requires no background knowledge. It occurs in the visual systems of many animals that surely lack propositional attitudes. Many animals, including perhaps all mammals, many birds, and some insects, can perceive an achromatic surface (one that is white, black, or some shade of gray) as having the same lightness despite large variations in illumination of the surface. Such variations normally cause large variations in proximal stimulation.

Individuals can see a white page with black print on it as roughly the same shade of white whether it is illuminated by a desk lamp or by bright sunlight. Outdoor light is more than one hundred times brighter than illumination from the lamp. In sunlight, the black print reflects many times more light into the eyes than the white page when illuminated by the lamp. Yet most mammals, including humans, can see the white as the same shade indoors and outdoors.

The transformations that underlie lightness constancy center largely on responses to ratios of light intensities at what are called luminance contours. A *luminance contour* is a sudden, sharp discontinuity between adjacent registrations (adjacent functional encodings) of light intensity by receptors in the eye.

---

[81] For an account of lightness constancy, see Palmer, *Vision Science*, 122–133. For more background, see Hans Wallach, 'Brightness Constancy and the Nature of Achromatic Colors', *Journal of Experimental Psychology* 38 (1948), 310–324; E. H. Land and J. J. McCann, 'Lightness and Retinex Theory', *American Journal of Optical Society of America* 61 (1971), 1–11; A. L. Gilchrist, 'Perceived Lightness Depends on Perceived Spatial Arrangement', *Science* 195 (1977), 185–187; Irving Rock, *The Logic of Perception* (Cambridge, MA: MIT Press, 1983), 279; A. L. Gilchrist, 'Lightness Contrast and Failures of Constancy: A Common Explanation', *Perception and Psychophysics* 43 (1988), 415–424; D. H. Brainard, W. A. Brunt, and J. M. Speigle, 'Color Constancy in the Nearly Natural Image. 1. Asymmetric Matches', *Journal of the Optical Society of America* A/14 (1997), 2091–2110; J. M. Kraft and D. H. Brainard, 'Mechanisms of Color Constancy under Nearly Natural Viewing', *Proceedings of the National Academy of Sciences USA* 96 (1999), 307–312; E. H. Adelson, 'Lightness Perception and Lightness Illusions', in M. Gazzaniga (ed.), *The New Cognitive Neurosciences* (2nd edn., Cambridge, MA: MIT Press, 2000); A. D. Logvinenko and L. T. Maloney, 'The Proximity Structure of Asymmetric Surface Colors and the Impossibility of Asymmetric Lightness Matching', *Perception and Psychophysics* 68 (2006), 76–83; I. K. Zemach and M. E. Rudd, 'Effects of Surround Articulation on Lightness Depend on the Spatial Arrangement of the Articulated Region', *Journal of the Optical Society of America* A/24 (2007), 1830–1841; M. E. Rudd and I. K. Zemach, 'Contrast Polarity and Edge Integration in Achromatic Color Perception', *Journal of the Optical Society of America* A/24 (2007), 2134–2156. A sophisticated overview is A. Gilchrist, C. Kossyfidis, F. Bonato, T. Agostini, J. Cataliotti, X. Li, B. Spehar, V. Annan, and E. Economou, 'An Anchoring Theory of Lightness Perception', www-psych.rutgers.edu/~alan/theory3. The following description slightly condenses and modifies an account of lightness constancy that I give in 'Disjunctivism and Perceptual Psychology'.

A luminance contour is thus an immediate sensory effect of proximal stimulation. If a series of spatially adjacent receptors, which register spatially adjacent light intensities striking the retina, produce a pattern of registrations of sharply different, adjacent levels of light intensity, receptors produce a luminance contour. The averaged ratio between sharply different light intensities along relatively local lines of registration is a primary starting point for the transformations that lead to perceptions that exhibit lightness constancy. The visual system is known to undergo changes that are determined by computation of such ratios. See Figure 8.2.

The light intensity that stimulates a receptor is a combination of the *reflectance* of a surface and the *illumination* of the surface. Luminance contours are the immediate effect, the sensory registration or functional encoding, of proximal stimulation. Luminance contours are thus produced by a combination of surface reflectances and surface illumination. The receptors can respond only to light intensities. Lightness constancy depends on an ability in the perceptual system to separate surface reflectance from illumination. This is a separation of the primary perceptual *representatum* (surface reflectance, which is *roughly* the lightness of the surface) from another less important distal factor (illumination) in causing the proximal stimulation. Lightness constancy is a capacity to fix on achromatic surface reflectance—lightness of the surface itself—despite differences or changes in illumination. The distinction between surface reflectance and surface illumination is not in the proximal stimulation itself, or in the immediate effect of the proximal stimulation on the receptors. The distinction must, in effect, be drawn by the visual perceptual system. The proximal stimulation and its first registration in the visual system underdetermine the relative contributions of the different distal causes.

A fact about the environment facilitates a solution to the visual system's problem of separating surface reflectance (the distal property that is usually most useful to the animal and the one whose perception we are concerned with) from the illumination of the surface. This is the fact: some types of discontinuity in light intensity are usually caused by discontinuities in reflectance; other types are usually caused by discontinuities in illumination.

The discontinuities in light intensity in the environment that are due primarily to changes in illumination are called *illumination edges*.[82] Illumination edges are distal conditions. Shadows, reflections on glossy surfaces, slight differences in surface orientation toward the light source, and focused light sources, such as spotlights, cause illumination edges. Other discontinuities in light intensity are due primarily to changes in the reflectance of a surface. These changes are called *reflectance edges*—changes in the reflected light due to either sharp changes in

---

[82] Thus I use 'contour' for changes in encodings of light intensity *in the visual system* and 'edge' for an environmental condition. The term 'luminance edge' is sometimes, in the literature, used in the way that I use 'luminance contour'. And in 'Disjunctivism and Perceptual Psychology', I used 'luminance edge' in that way. But I think it easier to follow the discussion if 'edge' is reserved for the distal condition and 'contour' is introduced for the pattern of registrations in the visual system.

the lightness of the surface itself (stripes of a zebra) or sharp changes in the orientation of a surface (such as an edge of a cubic block). Much of the solution to the underdetermination problem in the case of lightness constancy derives from separating reflectance edges from illumination edges. The two types of distal cause must be separated on the basis of registrations of differences of light intensity by different receptors.

The problem is solved by virtue of the visual system's operating in accord with certain formation principles. Such principles specify what perceptions are formed given relevant registrations of light intensities—in particular, luminance contours. The law-like formation processes described by formation principles are, of course, not infallible in yielding veridical perceptions. Yet they are usually reliable in normal circumstances. I will discuss only one of several cooperating formation principles under which mammalian vision operates.

This principle centers on the degree of sharpness of the luminance contour. In the absence of contrary information, the visual system forms a perception as of a reflectance edge (rather than as of an illumination edge) in response to a *sharp* luminance contour. Recall that a luminance contour is a pattern in the retinal image, not a distal condition. Reflectance edges and illumination edges are distal environmental conditions.

The formation process described by the principle tends to yield veridical separation of illumination from reflectance, because in the actual environment illumination edges—deriving, for example, from shadows or spotlights—tend to be fuzzy. Reflectance edges tend to be sharp.[83] When sharp changes occur along a luminance contour in the sensory registration, the principle dictates formation of a perception as of a reflectance edge.

The formation process can yield illusions. A sharp-edged spotlight trained on a surface of uniform reflectance will yield a misperception as of a reflectance edge instead of an illumination edge—unless some further clue betrays the presence of the illumination.

Principles governing the sharpness or fuzziness of luminance contours are not the only principles involved in operations within a capacity for lightness constancy. Further principles, not discussed here, involving perceived distance of surfaces, and more specific principles governing luminance ratios also play a role in most known visual systems capable of lightness constancy. The principle that I have explicated, however, illustrates how the undifferentiated information available in initial registrations of light intensities (the registration of proximal stimulation) can be combined with "privilege conferring" formation laws to overcome a version of the underdetermination problem.

Overcoming underdetermination through reliance on differences in retinal registrations to separate environmental reflectance from environmental illumination is in itself a perceptual constancy. In this case, the process constitutes a

---

[83] Fuzziness is associated with gradual change in luminance. Sharpness is associated with relatively sudden change in luminance.

ILLUMINATION VS. REFLECTANCE EDGES

Increasing sharpness

FIGURE 8.2 A factor in lightness constancy. Determining the lightness of a surface hinges on distinguishing reflectance properties of the surface from illumination on the surface. This task is facilitated by distinguishing reflectance edges from illumination edges. Because sharp luminance contours in the retinal image are statistically more likely to correlate with reflectance edges than with illumination edges, it would benefit veridical vision if formation laws took sharp luminance contours to generate perceptual representations as of reflectance edges. In fact, they do. In the illustration, note how the surfaces to the left are more naturally seen as involving a shadow on the surface, whereas the surfaces further toward the right are more easily seen, than those to the left, as involving either a change in reflectance (white to grey) of the surface, or an edge that constitutes a break in the surface plane.

transition from sensory registration to perception. Thus this aspect of lightness constancy is an *independent* perceptual constancy: its operation does not depend on any other perceptual constancy.

The full lightness constancy capacity in humans is more complex than the capacity I have described, which is only a component in the full capacity. As noted above, the full lightness-constancy capacity utilizes distance perception to refine the perception of lightness and to deal with environmental situations that the operations on luminance contours alone could not resolve. Representation of distance is the product of other constancies—involving three-dimensional spatial representation. But the simplest types of lightness and color constancy are primitive. These types are components operating within the more complex capacity, components that can be modified by information (including perception) coming from other components. These primitive types do not depend on the perceptual system's exercise of other perceptual constancies. In particular, they do not depend on spatial perceptual constancies.

The formation principle that I cite in this example describes and explains a law-like process that tends to yield veridical perceptions of distal conditions. The explanatory principle that describes and explains the process makes non-trivial reference to representational states with veridicality conditions. The principle also describes a significant type of lightness constancy, which is a type of objectification typical of perception. The principle describes a formation process that effects a systematic separation of (as of) environmental elements from registration of merely proximal stimulation. I elaborate the relation between such perceptual constancies and objectification in Chapter 9.

Planar Slant from Planar Surface Texture

Here is a third example of a law-like transformation from one state of the perceptual system to a further state underdetermined by the first.[84] The transformation determines *planar surface slant from planar surface texture*. Surface slant is the angle away from the plane perpendicular to the line of sight. Thus the transformation proceeds from two-dimensional information that correlates with a two-dimensional surface to representation of three-dimensional attributes of the surface. See Figure 8.3.

Suppose that one looks front on at the surface of a white sheet of cardboard about a meter away. The white sheet has several circles drawn on it. The circles are regularly spaced and are roughly of the same size. Suppose that one slants the cardboard surface backwards so that the top slants away—and away from the upright position—at, say, a 60-degree angle from vertical. The cardboard slants so that instead of being perpendicular to the line of sight, it is closer to being flat. The center of the cardboard remains one meter away; the top is, of course, farther away.

The images of the circles projected on the retina will be distorted by the perspectival angle. Thus, relative to the images projected on the upright, unslanted cardboard, the *shape* of the images caused by the circles that are farther away on the cardboard surface will be increasingly flattened ellipses. Their projected image sizes will be smaller. And the density of these images per retinal area will be greater. The visual systems of many animals capitalize on such geometrical facts to produce fairly accurate perceptions as of planar slant.

Proximal stimulation and registration of such stimulation underdetermine the facts about surface slant. The relevant sensory registration is a product of a combination of the actual shapes of the circles and the slant of the surface. A systematically non-uniform array of ellipses on a surface perpendicular to the line of sight could produce proximal stimulation (and registration of that stimulation) that are indiscernible at a given time from the stimulations produced by a regular array of circles on a slanted surface. Such a straight-on surface could exhibit increasingly flattened, smaller, and more densely distributed shapes, from bottom to top. Such patterns seen straight on can produce the illusion as of a slanted surface, if other cues are minimized.[85]

---

[84] This account is drawn primarily from David C. Knill, 'Surface Orientation from Texture: Ideal Observers, Generic Observers, and the Information Content of Texture Cues', *Vision Research* 38 (1998), 1655–1682; 'Discrimination of Planar Surface Slant from Texture: Human and Ideal Observers Compared', *Vision Research* 38 (1998), 1683–1711. For very elementary exposition, see Palmer, *Vision Science*, 234–236. I have transposed the present exposition from a slightly more detailed account in 'Disjunctivism and Perceptual Psychology'.

[85] It is a confusion to hold, as some philosophers do, that 'in one sense' in the condition in which the surface is slanted, one sees something as elliptical, as well as perceiving the circles as circular. Normally, no elliptical shapes are seen, and the circular shapes are in no sense misperceived as elliptical. What is true is that one perceives the circles as circular in an 'elliptical way'—in a way that bears some phenomenal comparison to perceiving ellipses as elliptical straight on. The phenomenology—and the way in which the circles are perceived as circular (the representational content)—are associated with the elliptical shape of the proximal stimulations on the retinal surface.

The formation principles describe law-like transformations that produce perceptual representation that privileges representation as of a slanted surface with regularly distributed textural elements over representation as of a straight-on surface with irregularly distributed textural elements. The formation principles describe a default bias toward a regular array of textural elements. The formation principles are mathematically specific, and closely fitted to empirical evidence about what slants are perceived from what proximal stimulations deriving from what types of arrays of textural elements.[86]

The formation principles describe transformations that start with registrations that carry information correlated with the *shape*, *size*, and *density* of the surface textural elements (the circles). These registrations constitute a two-dimensional *image*. Given these registrations that correlate with (or possibly represent) two-dimensional shapes, sizes, and distributions, the formation principles describe transformations that in effect bet in favor of these patterns' deriving from regular distributions of surface textural elements in the world, and against these patterns' deriving from irregular distributions. Irregular distributions would yield illusions of the sort described above. The bet yields a perceptual representation as of a surface as being at a specific backwards slant and as having an array of circles—regular in size and distribution—as elements of surface texture. The overall computational principle describes a transition from a two-dimensional image to a perception as of surface slant in three-dimensional space.

'*Image*' is a term that can be used for either a non-perceptual pattern or a representational content. I use it, here and throughout unless context indicates otherwise, in accord with its technical use in the science.[87] On this usage, the term does *not* imply representational content, though it can allow for it. An example of a *non-representational* image is a two-dimensional pattern of retinal registrations of light intensities. A given pattern might constitute a pattern of luminance contours that are caused by, and that informationally and reliably correlate with, circles. The luminance contours are the first sensory effects of the light patterns emanating from a pattern on a surface. The image is a two-dimensional pattern of registrations that also reliably correlates not only with circular figures on the page but also with a pattern of light intensities that strike the retina. Such a pattern is a non-representational two-dimensional *image*. Computational explanation of the perceptual constancy regarding slant begins with a two-dimensional image that is probably non-representational.

---

[86] The transformation utilizes three primary parameters computable on registrations that amount to a two-dimensional image. The transformation allows for distortion of *shape* of textural elements by taking the foreshortening of these elements as being in the direction of surface tilt by an amount proportional to the cosine of the slant of the surface relative to the line of sight. The transformation allows for distortion of *size*-elements in the image by scaling textural elements so that the relative size of images of the elements is inversely proportional to the distance of the elements from the eye. The transformation allows for change of *density* of texture distribution by making transformations that accord with the principle that an increase in average density is roughly proportional to an increase in distance.

[87] The term 'image' is often used in the science for the light array falling on the retina. I usually use it to apply to the first registration or informational encoding of this array.

SLANT FROM TEXTURE

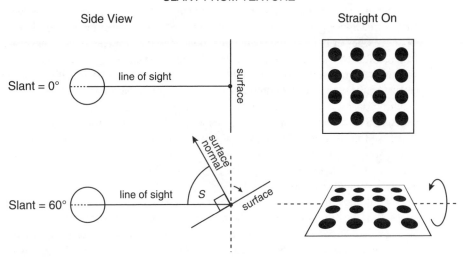

FIGURE 8.3 Surface slant from surface texture. The lower surface illustrates how the foreshortening of the circular textural elements, which cause elliptical images on the retinal receptors, is perceived as slant of the surface away from the viewer. Regular surface textures are statistically more likely in nature. The formation laws work off of such regularity and tend to yield veridical perception of slant and of the actual shape of the figures on the surface. The diagram also illustrates the possibility of illusion. When surface textures are irregular in certain ways, they cause retinal stimulation that, by the formation rules, yields inaccurate perception of slant. That is, unslanted surfaces are perceived as slanted and vice versa.

It was not part of the work on slant from texture that I described to determine whether the images that correlate with surface texture (the effects in the psychology of the closed figures on the surface) are non-representational registrations of light intensities, or, on the contrary, already perceptual states. For example, it is possible that sharp luminance contours are first used by lightness constancy operations to yield perception as of figures on surfaces. So the luminance contours would be inputs to processes that yield perceptions as of reflectance edges that bound two-dimensional figures that are in fact the circles or other closed figures on a surface. Then these primitive *perceptual* representational states could be input into the processes that lead to the formation of perceptions as of slant. Thus the input into the process that yields slant from texture—and slant constancy—could begin either with input of a non-perceptual retinal image or with input of a perceptual state as of a set of closed figures in a texture—input that is the prior product of a perceptual process realizing a more primitive constancy, lightness constancy.

I do not know whether it is known whether the initial input into the process for determining slant from texture is a *non-representational image* (consisting of two-dimensional arrays registered in the retinal image) or whether, on the contrary, the input is a *representational image* (the content of a perceptual state as of a two-dimensional figure, perhaps derived from lightness constancy operations). That is, I do not know whether it is known whether the inputs into this perceptual constancy (this particular form of slant constancy) are merely non-perceptual sensory registrations or are, rather, perspectival aspects of low-level perceptions as of two-dimensional patterns. Either possibility is compatible with the form of the transformation.

For purposes of understanding the form of the explanation, the answer does not matter.[88] The nature of the starting point does not matter for our illustrative purposes. The example illustrates how formation principles explain a solution to underdetermination. The example also illustrates how formation principles attribute to the visual system fallible, specific, representational commitments regarding the physical environment.

Psychological theory is not advanced enough *always* to locate clear transition points from the non-perceptual to the perceptual. What is clear from the theory is that there are such transitions. For the transformational story begins with two-dimensional retinal sensory registration and ends with visual perceptions as of attributes in the physical environment. The transition is marked by perceptual constancies. No perceptual constancy is involved in registration of light arrays, to which all visual perceptual constancies trace back.

Again, the transformations in planar slant from planar texture depend for their reliability in producing veridical perception on the pattern of surface textures being *homogenous*: distributions of shapes, sizes, and densities of textural elements are statistically about the same in any surface region. Patterns that cause illusion are not homogenous.

Any given textural image (or sensory registrations that can be mapped as a two-dimensional array) that is produced by the textural pattern described above is in itself consistent with either a slanted surface with homogeneous pattern or a straight-on surface whose non-homogenous objective pattern of textural elements matches the foreshortening, scaling, and density images projected by the slanted surface. The patterns of transformation described by the formation principles yield accurate perception only if a textural pattern in the environment is homogeneous. Relative homogeneity is a feature of a large class of surface textures. The fact that homogeneity is more common than lack of homogeneity makes possible reliable determination of slant from texture by many visual systems in many circumstances.

It is widely believed that it is an environmental fact that homogeneity is a common feature of surface textures. Assuming this belief to be true, the relevant fact is mirrored in perceptual states and in transformations that form those states. The claim that such mirroring is constitutive is basic to perceptual anti-individualism. The nature of perceptions as of slant, and the nature of the law-like patterns

---

[88] Some law-like formation transformations (and their corresponding formation principles) proceed purely from non-perceptual states to perceptual states. Some proceed from one type of perceptual state to another. Some proceed from mixtures.

of transformation, are constitutively dependent on connections to deep regularities in the environment.[89]

Depth from Convexity of Image Regions

I conclude this chapter with one more example of a transformation from lower-level information (possibly perceptual, possibly not) to perceptual representation that is underdetermined by the input information. This example illustrates a radicalization of the anti-individualistic methodology presupposed in all mainstream explanations of perception formation: the nature of the perceptual representation and of formation laws for perception depend on patterns in the environment that are independent of perception.

In 1953, Egon Brunswik, a perceptual psychologist, proposed that the perceptual meaning of perceptual states is type-individuated partly by reference to attributes and regularities in the physical environment. Specifically, he proposed that Gestalt cues reflect statistical regularities in the environment, and that understanding perceptual content and processing could benefit from studying statistical patterns in the environment, and between the environment and proximal stimuli.[90]

Brunswik's pursuit of this line of investigation is quaint in its simplicity, lack of technological wherewithal, and lack of specific formation principles.

Time has shown, however, that his method was pregnant with research possibilities. Brunswik took frames from the movie *Kind Hearts and Coronets* and traced edges (borders of dramatic changes in lightness) in the frame images. These edges were supposed to approximate the edges registered as luminance contours in the visual system's image, or the edges perceptually represented, in human vision. Then he measured, by hand, distances between roughly parallel edges in the frame images. Finally, knowing what the images correlated with in the physical world, he and his collaborator made judgments about which edges belonged to the same objects. They found that the closer parallel edges in the images were to each other, the more likely they corresponded to parallel edges of a given surface in the environment. He argued that the Gestalt grouping rule of proximity of similars was empirically plausible because it had a statistical basis in natural environmental scenes.

---

[89] Again, I oversimplify the character of the laws of perception formation. There is research on how the three cues—shape, size, and density—are weighted. Density is the least reliable cue and is relied upon least. The foreshortening cue, regarding shape, is weighted most heavily of the three cues in most contexts. There are physical bases for the relative weightings. Clearly, these largely innate weightings of the different cues depend on the relative likelihoods in the physical world (in which the system evolved) of certain types and degrees of regularity in textural patterns on physical surfaces. The case of a surface with regular circles on it is geometrically much simpler than most surfaces in nature. Statistical principles apply to regularities of shape, size, and density of all sorts. See Knill, 'Discrimination of Planar Surface Slant from Texture: Human and Ideal Observers Compared', and my 'Disjunctivism and Perceptual Psychology', 17–18.

[90] E. Brunswik and J. Kamiya, 'Ecological Cue-Validity of "Proximity" and of other Gestalt Factors', *American Journal of Psychology* 66 (1953), 20–32.

The technology to study such patterns in detail was not available to Brunswik. The development of powerful computers and sophisticated statistical methods aids pursuit of his suggestion in an empirically fruitful way. The statistical relation between attributes in natural scenes and cues available to the visual system is now intensively studied by Brunswik's method. See Figure 8.4.

Let me sketch a modern realization of Brunswik's method.[91] Numerous digital photographs of natural scenes were collected, along with a spatially co-registered distance map: a laser range finder determined the distance of each scene point corresponding to each pixel. The edges in these photographs were identified, and hundreds of thousands of local regions on either side of the edges were classified on the basis of local convexity. Analysis of these images established that convex photographic image regions are statistically more likely to correspond to occluding figures than to grounds in the scene. Also, analysis showed that large depth intervals are more likely when the nearer of two surfaces is convex than when it is concave.

The assumption of scientists who work in this area is that the foregoing statistical relations hold because figures partly occluding the grounds tend to be convex. Objects tend to be convex. There is no apriori mathematical reason why the shape of an image region should provide a cue to depth relations in the scene.[92] But the shapes of actual objects in natural scenes with which animals (including humans) systematically interact, in evolution and in experience, comprise the basis for the existence of this depth cue. The deep regularity in the environment that determines perceptual kinds appears to be that most bodies and masses are convex.

Whether correlations between shape and depth relations that occur in the natural environment are capitalized upon in visual processing can be tested. If statistical patterns in nature associating depth and convex shapes are matched by perceptual estimations of depth based on convexity cues, there is reason to believe that the natural patterns have been incorporated into visual processing.

It has long been known that local convexity of image regions affects individuals' perception as of ordinal figure-ground relations.[93] More recently, it has been established that such cues carry veridical ordinal (non-metrical) depth information.[94] But it has been assumed that the depth information is *purely* ordinal: x is occluding y—but how much distance separates x and y (the depth

---

[91] The modern methodology is described in E. P. Simoncelli and B. A. Olshausen, 'Natural Image Statistics and Neural Representation', *Annual Review of Neuroscience* 24 (2001), 1193–1216; W. S. Geisler, J. S. Perry, B. J. Super, and D. P. Gallogly, 'Edge Co-Occurrence in Natural Images Predicts Contour Grouping Performance', *Vision Research* 41 (2001), 711–724; C. C. Fowlkes, D. R. Martin, and J. Malik, 'Local Figure-Ground Cues are Valid for Natural Images', *Journal of Vision* 7 (2007), 1–9; W. S. Geisler, 'Visual Perception and the Statistical Properties of Natural Scenes'.

[92] Depth relations are to be understood as the separation between two points along or near the line of sight. This definition is the standard one used by the vision research community. The computer-science community, by contrast, uses 'depth' to refer to the distance between the viewer and a point in the scene. The vision-science community refers to that quantity as distance.

[93] G. Kanizsa and W. Gerbino, 'Convexity and Symmetry in Figure-Ground Organization', in M. Henle (ed.), *Vision and Artifact* (New York: Springer, 1976).

[94] Fowlkes, Martin, and Malik, 'Local Figure-Ground Cues are Valid for Natural Images'.

between x and y) is left completely open. This assumption has been challenged through use of natural scene statistics and tests on human perceivers.

Observers are given stimuli that yield images of two surfaces in depth. Binocular disparity (one of the primary sources of information for determining relative distance) represents a metric depth interval between the surfaces. The silhouette of the near region is sometimes convex, sometimes concave, sometimes neither. For a fixed amount of binocular disparity, more depth is perceived between two surfaces when the silhouette of the near surface is convex than when it is concave. That is, changing the shape of a near surface's silhouette can change how much depth is perceived as being between the surfaces. When the cues from binocular disparity and cues from convexity are consistent, the distance between nearer and farther regions is perceived as greater.[95] When cues from binocular disparity and convexity are inconsistent, less depth is perceived.

The convex regions in the retinal image that encodes light arrays were statistically related to the depth between occluding surfaces in natural scenes. Since, statistically, depth varies with local convexity of regions in the image, it is reasonable to suppose that representation of, and as of, the *absolute* metric distance between seen surface x and seen surface y can capitalize on this statistical relationship. Given that human performance in estimating depth correlates with these statistical facts, when disparity is held constant, empirical evidence supports the view that the statistics regarding local convexity of regions *in the retinal image* is an informational basis for perception of *absolute* depth relations between the corresponding surfaces in the environment.[96] This result is a very striking and surprising product of the natural-scenes statistics methodology. The result suggests that visual systems utilize a wide range of brute statistically relevant environmental facts as cues for indicating and attributing basic environmental attributes.

The pursuit of this methodology, indeed all mainstream visual psychology, realizes anti-individualist principles. The representational contents of perceptual states, and of law-like patterns in formation of perceptual states, derive from patterns of causal relations between environment and individuals. These patterns of causal relations track attributes, and statistical or law-like patterns, in the environment. The perceptual state types—particularly their accuracy conditions—and the types of formation transformations are type-individuated partly through causal relations to environmental attributes and environmental statistical or law-like patterns. The attributes and patterns are coded into the representational kinds and formation laws of perceptual systems.

The details of these four explanations in vision science are less important than their overall shape. The examples illustrate the type of scientific explanation that

---

[95] The cues are consistent, intuitively, when binocular disparity and convexity agree on which surface is in front. Otherwise, the cues are inconsistent.

[96] J. Burge, C. C. Fowlkes, and M. S. Banks, 'Natural Scene Statistics Predict How the Figure-Ground Cue of Convexity Affects Human Depth Perception', forthcoming.

indicates the existence of two important psychological kinds: *representational state* and *perceptual state*.

The more generic kind, *representational state*, is a state with representational content. Representational content has two primary roles in the science. One is to constitute specific veridicality conditions and ways of referring to, indicating, and attributing elements in the environment. The other role is to help individuate specific kinds of psychological state.

All the examples illustrate a type of explanation that is distinctively psychological. The non-trivial explanatory invocation of perceptual states type-individuated partly in terms of veridicality conditions is distinctively psychological. The invocation is not a gloss on a more basic form of explanation, easily couched in other terms. The examples illustrate a non-deflationary conception of representational state.

In view of these explanations, and many more like them, it is not an empirically acceptable position to maintain that states with representational content are outside the purview of science, or that they need some explanation in other terms. Explanations that appeal to representational perceptual states are the most precise and fundamental explanations in a well-entrenched and rapidly developing science. Deflationism about representation has no basis, empirical or apriori.

Views that maintain that perception is a relation that involves no state with veridicality conditions, or that there can be no explanatorily relevant psychological kind in common between veridical perceptions and perceptual referential illusions, have long been unreasonable on empirical grounds.[97] Such positions lack empirical

---

[97] This latter view is called 'Disjunctivism'. It is one of the philosophical views, mentioned in the Preface, that are commonly propounded without serious understanding of relevant science. This particular view is incompatible with scientific knowledge.

For example, some naive realist versions of disjunctivism postulate a primitive relation of consciousness to the environment that is supposed to 'provide a semantic foundation for' perceptual representation. The relation is supposed not to involve any representational content and supposed to make possible perceptual demonstrative representations of objects. It is said that only postulation of such a non-representational consciousness relation can explain how perceptual experience can make it possible to think of objects. On such a view, the (non-representational) content of the perceptual state *consists in* the objects and properties in the scene perceived. Alternatively, the state is *purely* a relation whose only relata are the individual perceiver and the entities perceived. The more general view that naive realism instantiates, disjunctivism, maintains the following: there is never any perceptual state *kind* in common, or at least no explanatorily relevant (psychological/mental) perceptual state in common, between a veridical perceptual state instance and a perceptual referential illusion, even if the two state instances have the same proximal stimulation and are phenomenally indiscernible. These counterintuitive claims are not accompanied by serious engagement with perceptual psychology. The science of perception is commonly claimed to be compatible with disjunctivism because it is just study of the brain, or of mere information processing— not of perception in any ordinary sense. Hence, on this view, the science is not directly relevant to understanding reference or warrant, in perception or empirical thought. The erroneousness of such claims is, I think, clear from the discussion of the science in Part III of this book. See especially Chapter 9, note 3.

In fact, both referentially successful perceptual demonstrative applications and referentially illusory perceptual demonstrative applications are explained in science without invoking a prior, unexplained consciousness relation. I think that the idea of any conscious relation to environmental objects that lacks representational content—that is, the idea of consciousness of environmental objects that lacks perspectival veridicality conditions—does not correspond to any *possible* capacity. (See my 'Five Theses on *De Re* States and Attitudes', section I.) Perceptual psychology explains a *mental* or

DEPTH FROM CONVEXITY
Task:
Which side appears to be in front?

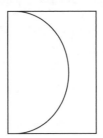

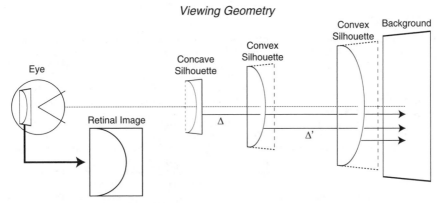

FIGURE 8.4 Depth from convexity. Look at the uppermost figure. If you had to choose which side is closer, which would you choose? Although the bias is not strong, a majority of the time people choose the convex side as the nearer side. The lower part of the diagram illustrates the fact that one can receive the same retinal image regardless of whether a surface is convex or concave, and regardless of the depth relationships between nearer and farther surfaces. But it has been shown that convex retinal image regions are statistically more likely to derive from near surfaces than from far surfaces. The visual system capitalizes on this environmental fact as one of its means to represent the depth order of and the distances between visible surfaces. Here the visual system relies on purely statistical environmental facts—not on geometrically determinable facts—to determine approximate depth relations (a geometrical fact).

psychological perceptual kind (not brain states or mere informational states), whose instances are often but not always conscious, and that can be common between instances of veridical and referential–illusory perception. Such kinds can be the same, whether they are veridical or referentially illusory, if they derive from the same type of proximal-stimulation registration by the same formation laws. For more on the points in this paragraph and the next, see Chapter 9, the sections PERCEPTION AS THE INDIVIDUAL'S and PERCEPTION AS REPRESENTATION.

Individuals' *veridical* perception is scientifically explained as the product of causal relations that derive from normal, specified distal environmental conditions that cause specified proximal stimulations (by, for example, well-known laws of optics) whose sensory registrations in turn initiate specific formation processes that (under the formation laws) yield specific kinds of perceptual states. The formation processes yield perceptual illusions, including referential illusions, in specifiable cases where proximal stimulation registration stems from specifiable abnormal stimulatory conditions, distal or proximal. These abnormal conditions are among the physically possible conditions that are undetermined by proximal-stimulation registration. The same attributional *type* or *kind* of perceptual state can be veridical or illusional if instances of the kind are formed by the same formation laws from the same type of proximal-stimulation registration. This possibility is guaranteed by the underdetermination of distal conditions by proximal-stimulation registration. Similarly, the same perceptual constancies can be realized in cases of both perceptual success and perceptual referential illusion. The most basic, explanatorily relevant *kinds* of perceptual state—the *attributional* kinds of perceptual state marked by the perceptual attributives, not including the different occurrent singular perceptual applications—can on different occasions be veridical or illusory. In such cases, the differences between veridicality and illusion lie in state *instances*—in different occurrent context-bound applications of perceptual demonstratives and of perceptual attributives. The different applications yield perceptual-referential and perceptual-veridicality differences because of different *distal* causal antecedents of the same type of proximal-stimulation registration—which can cause the *same attributional kind* of perceptual state, under the same formation laws. Allowing for noise, interference in the perceptual system, and malfunction, and abstracting from occurrent, context-bound elements in the veridicality conditions of perceptual states, what *kind* of perceptual state is formed (what general attributive elements are part of the state's representational content) depends only on the antecedent psychology of the individual, the formation laws, and the registration of *proximal* stimulation. Such kinds of perceptual state figure in the formation laws specified in perceptual psychology. The principle articulated two sentences back is the Proximality Principle. See my 'Disjunctivism and Perceptual Psychology'.

As I emphasized in that paper (and contrary to what some responses to the paper allege), I believe that there are other ways of classifying perception—for example, in terms of veridicality or non-veridicality. But the key explanatory kinds in the science satisfy the Proximality Principle. I wrote: 'Disjunctivism claims that there is no common, explanatory kind in common between cases of perceptual referential illusion and cases of perceptual belief in which perception is referentially successful. Whether one individuates application tokens in terms of their distal causes is, I believe, not fundamental. I believe that there is a natural and defensible understanding of representations marking such events that accords with human and animal fallibility: One's perceptual belief could have been based on illusion if abnormal conditions had been substituted, indiscernibly, for the actual causal conditions. But even if applications were object-based, the same explanatory perceptual state kind (and the same belief kind) would have been involved' (ibid., note 70; see also sections V–VII).

As noted in Chapter 9, the section PERCEPTION AS THE INDIVIDUAL'S, a lot of perceptual singular reference is not conscious. That is one reason why consciousness cannot explain reference. It is true that there is so far not much of a *science* of consciousness. But many of the kinds of perceptual states that are postulated by the science of perceptual psychology and that can be *common* between veridical perceptual state instances and state instances that are referential illusions are conscious. Indeed, the consciousness of the respective state instances would be consciously indiscernible. That is another reason why consciousness cannot explain perceptual reference. Where consciousness figures in perceptual processes, its role in perceptual *reference* must be explained through the causal account of representational state formation as applied to particular state instances with particular *distal* causal chains. Contrary to the view described in the first paragraph of this note, conscious relations to objects in perception are not prior to or independent of the process of representational state formation. Vision science does not countenance postulating a relation to the environment prior to or independent of its causal–perceptual account. Such postulation adds nothing, relevant to explanation of reference in perception or perceptual belief, to the detailed, causal accounts that the science already provides.

An example of the view criticized in this note is John Campbell, 'Demonstrative Reference, the Relational View of Experience, and the Proximality Principle', in R. Jeshion (ed.), *Essays on Singular Reference* (Oxford: Oxford University Press, forthcoming). Campbell's essay contains several serious misrepresentations of my views and of vision science that I will not discuss here. For discussion of other accounts of conscious perceptual experience that also show lack of touch with scientific work, see my 'Disjunctivism and Perceptual Psychology'.

bases for overturning empirically well-entrenched science. Such positions are untenable and irrelevant, through their isolation from scientific knowledge.[98]

Scientific explanations of the sort illustrated in this section mark a distinction between functional information registration and representational states with veridicality conditions. Veridicality and failure of veridicality have a role in perceptual theory that is different from, and much more specific than, identifications of accuracy with biological success, and inaccuracy with biological misfortune. The account of the formation of states with representational content—in explanations of perceptual processes and capacities—marks the kind *representational state*, properly so-called. Subspecies of this kind are studied in perceptual psychology. The explanations illustrate the lower border, in perception, of perhaps the most important generic psychological kind—*representational state*.

The examples also illustrate invocation of the more specific psychological kind, *perceptual state*. They illustrate how formation principles describe transformations in which the earlier state (in the causal order of processing) underdetermines the later state. All illustrate how laws of transformation, described by formation principles, complete determination of the later psychological state. In all the examples, the product of a transformation is a perceptual state with veridicality conditions that attribute specific environmental attributes. In some cases, the initial states are non-perceptual. In others, the transformation begins with states that include perceptual states and ends with further perceptual states.

The examples illustrate how the perceptual state that is the product of a transformation depends constitutively on relations to laws or deep regularities in the physical environment. The *details* of the laws are not constitutive. What are constitutive to perceptual-state kinds are the causal relations to environmental attributes, and the individuation of laws of formation of instances of perceptual-state kinds by deep statistical or law-like regularities in the physical environment that are specifically relevant to attributes being represented. The perceptual state as of lightness depends constitutively for being what it is on causal relations to lightness, or to attributes systematically related to lightness.

The examples illustrate exercise of perceptual constancies. The formation transformations can produce a range of perceptual states all indicating and attributing the same environmental attribute. Each state derives from significantly different registration of proximal stimulation. For example, a perceptual state that attributes a given distance to a particular is produced by convergence. A

---

[98] Another way naive realist views can be seen to be incompatible with science lies in noting differences of modes of presentation despite sameness of environmental attributes perceived. For a striking demonstration of the point, which relies on differences of modes of presentation that derive from differences in degree of *attention* to the same distal particulars and attributes, see M. Carrasco, S. Ling, and S. Read, 'Attention Alters Appearance', *Nature Neuroscience* 7 (2004), 308–313; M. Carrasco, 'Covert Attention Increases Contrast Sensitivity: Psychophysical, Neurophysiological, and Neuroimaging Studies', in S. Martinex-Conde, S. L. Macknik, L. Martinez, J.-M. Alonso, and P. U. Tse (eds.), *Progress in Brain Research* vol. 154: *Visual Perception, Part 1* (Amsterdam: Elsevier, 2006).

range of other perceptual states, each attributing the same distance, can be caused by different proximal stimulation, deriving from very different sorts of particulars. Similarly, perceptual states attributing a given degree of lightness, or a given slant, are formed by perceptual constancies—despite large variations in proximal stimulation. Different representational contents represent a given attribute in perceptually different ways, each corresponding to a different perspective on a single attribute.

Some of the examples, certainly those that concern convergence and lightness constancy, illustrate transformation from non-perceptual sensory registration to perceptual states. The natures of perceptual states are partly fixed by representational content with veridicality conditions. These transformations cross a border between sensory registration and perceptual representation. Some of the examples may illustrate transformation, under formation principles, from input that *includes* perceptual states to output that is a perceptual state. But all illustrate a type of explanation that marks out a certain species of representational state, reference to whose veridicality conditions is integral to the scientific explanation. The species of representational state is a *perceptual state*.

In Chapter 9, I discuss demarcations of psychological kinds that such explanations signal.

9 *Origins*

A **perception** *that relates to the subject as a modification of its state is a* **sensation** *(sensatio); an objective perception is a* **cognition** *(cognitio). The latter is either an* **intuition** *or a* **concept** *(intuitus vel conceptus). [Intuition] is immediately related to the object and is singular . . .*
Immanuel Kant, *Critique of Pure Reason*, B376–377

The basic fact of perception is distal focusing . . . Distal focusing is the result of an ecological generalization process on the part of the responding organism. The generalization takes place over the range of concrete variants in the proximal mediation patterns of the distal variable.
Egon Brunswik, *Perception and the Representative Design of Psychological Experiments*, chapter II

In this chapter and the next, I elaborate a conception of sense perception as a distinct psychological kind. This kind grounds scientific as well as common-sense explanation. I discuss how human psychology and animal psychology implicitly apply this conception to distinguish sensory registration of information from perceptual representation.

I believe that this distinction forms the lower border of both representation and objectivity. Perceptual representation is where genuine representation begins. In studying perception, representational psychology begins. With perception, one might even say, mind begins. With these two kinds, *perception* and *representation*, a rudimentary objectivity also originates. These origins have phylogenetic, developmental, and constitutive dimensions.

Numerous texts in psychology sport titles like 'Sensation and Perception'. The titles advertise an important distinction. Explications of the distinction are disappointing. Often it is said that sensation is raw data, whereas perception involves interpretation of data. The terms 'data' and 'interpretation' are rarely glossed. These terms are at best metaphorical. Each is misleading. Sensation does not play the role of data or evidence. Thinking that it does is the primary mistake of the sense-data tradition. Perception does not involve interpretation. In perception, no one, indeed nothing, takes sensation as an object to be interpreted. To attribute literal interpretation to a perceptual system is to engage in the most elementary, confused homunculus thinking. At best, the interpretation metaphor suggests, correctly, some accrual of "meaning" in transitions from sensation to perception. Both terms—'data' and 'interpretation'—are, however, more misleading than helpful.

Another common way to draw the distinction is to say that perception is active whereas sensation is passive. Of course, perception is not a type of individual agency. It is the product of subindividual processing. Even in sensation, processing usually occurs.

A tradition in psychology, stemming from Kant, does better. It characterizes perception as a type of *conscious objective sensory representation.* Unlike perception, sensory information registration is not objective. In my sense of 'representation', it is not representation either. The Kantian tradition assumes that perception both represents particulars and groups them by attributes.[1] It assumes that both the particulars and the attributes are in the environment. I will develop a conception of perception suggested by this tradition.

Perception is a type of *objective sensory representation by the individual.* From the Kantian characterization I drop the association with consciousness. I think that perception can, and apparently does, occur without any sort of consciousness. I justify this difference in the next section, and subsequently. My reference to an individual is only an apparent addition. Kant assumed, correctly, that consciousness is constitutively attributable to individuals. Probably in contrast to Kant, I take the individual's constitutive role in perception not to be grounded in consciousness. The italicized characterization marks the key similarities to the Kantian tradition.

I regard this characterization as constitutive. It speaks to the *nature* of perception, what it fundamentally *is*.[2] For reasons that will emerge, the characterization gives necessary but not sufficient constitutive conditions. I next discuss each notion in the characterization—<u>by the individual</u>, <u>sensory</u>, <u>representation</u>, and <u>objective</u>.

---

[1] Kant, *Critique of Pure Reason*, A320/B376–377. See the quotation heading the chapter. Kant's notion of representation (*Vorstellung*) is, as intimated, in one respect broader than my notion of representation. It applies to non-perceptual (non-objective) sensory states that I do not count as representational because they lack non-trivial veridicality conditions. Another difference may concern consciousness. Kant asserts that unconscious representations (*Vorstellungen*) exist. But I know of no evidence that he countenanced *objective* unconscious perceptual representations. There is ample evidence that there *are* objective, unconscious perceptual states, imputable not to modular subsystems, but to individuals. I discuss some of this evidence in the next section. Certainly, Kant required empirical intuitions to be conscious. The conception of perception that I elaborate is the rough counterpart of Kant's notion of an *objective perception that is a present empirical intuition, except* that I do *not* limit objective perception to conscious perception. (Kant characterizes intuitions as conscious (B376–/B376–377).) In the next section, I cite evidence that perceptual constancies occur in unconscious perceptual states of individuals. Kant's idea that intuition is singular corresponds to the idea that perception has a representational function of singling out particulars. Kant's idea that perception functions to attribute types is signaled, not in his definition, but in his notion of a predicate in intuition. See B278. Kant's introduction of the notion of the sensory occurs at A19–20/B34.

[2] In the section PERCEPTION AS OBJECTIFICATION AS OPPOSED TO PERCEPTION AS EXTRACTION OF FORM below, I discuss a related but wider conception of perception, associated with pattern discrimination. Although I think that this wider conception isolates a psychological kind, I think it an incorrect conception of perception.

PERCEPTION AS THE INDIVIDUAL'S

Perception is constitutively attributable to individuals. I focus on individual organisms, tabling issues about animal groups, corporations, and robots. An individual perceives particulars, or perceives as of particulars, as being certain ways. Perceptions and perceptual states that are attributed to an individual are always also attributable to the individual's perceptual system, a subsystem of the individual. Any visual perceptual state of an animal, for example, is also a state of the animal's visual system. Many processes that occur in perceptual systems, however, are not attributable to individuals. Transformations of sensory information into perceptions and transformations among perceptions are almost never attributable to the individual. The individual does not make them occur; they are not conscious or accessible to consciousness; they are not exercises of the individual's central capabilities. But, necessarily and constitutively, *individuals* perceive. Perceptual states, as distinct from transformations by which they are formed, are the individual's. Individuals perceive as a result of perceptual states' being formed in their perceptual systems. Perceptual states are realizations of individuals' capacities. I think that this claim is apriori.

I do not claim that *all* perceptions are perceptions by an individual. I claim that necessarily and constitutively, some perceptions in an individual's perceptual subsystem are perceptions by the individual. And I claim that all perceptions, including any that are not strictly attributable to the individual, serve perception by the individual. Fundamentally, it is the individual that perceives.

This point is not just a quirk of usage. It signals something important about the role of perception in psychological explanation. It is deeply embedded in the methods and assumptions of perceptual psychology.[3] The fact that *individuals*

---

[3] In Chapter 6, notes 93–94 and surrounding text, I discussed a line of thought deriving from Evans and McDowell according to which perceptual psychology is about some topic other than perception by individuals. See also Chapter 3, note 43, and Chapter 8, note 97. This claim is sometimes repeated to this day, among a (fortunately) small circle of philosophers, in order to maintain that the science is compatible with some particular philosophical ideology—often disjunctivism. The science is sometimes said to be only about 'brain processes' or subindividual (or subpersonal) 'modular states', or subindividual 'information processing'. Vague characterizations like these represent the science as not being about what it manifestly *is* about: perception by individuals. The science is a psychological science, not a brain science—though it leaves open whether all psychology just describes brain states in psychological terms. Some of the brain mechanisms that underlie the psychological transformations described by the science—especially transformations that occur early in perceptual processing—are being discovered. But very little is known about the basis in the brain for even some of the most central types of perception—perception of color, location, shape, and so on. As I have indicated, the key states are not merely informational states. They are representational in a strong, non-trivial sense. The *processing events* described by the science are indeed subindividual. But many, perhaps most, of the *representational products* of these processes, products specified in the science as both antecedents and products of formation processes, are perceptual states in the ordinary sense—individuals' perceptual states. Such states are commonly conscious. The methods of the science rely on some perceptual states' being conscious. Human subjects are commonly asked to report what they see, or to report which of two things has some perceptible property to a greater extent. Psychological theory then (within limits) matches theoretical accounts of the attributional aspects of the representational perceptual state—whether this be an illusion or a veridical perception—to the

perceive and have perceptual states is basic to the explanatory roles of the notions perception and individual.

Why is there a constitutive relation between perception and individual?[4] There are at least two grounds for the relation.

One resides in the connection between perception and whole animal, or individual, function—paradigmatically individual agency. In Chapter 8, I discussed the role of whole-animal function in setting a framework for individuation of perceptual states. Primitive agency by individuals is in place before perception evolves. Eating, mating, navigating are types of primitive agency by individual organisms that biology explains as a salient subset of whole-animal biological functions. Such agency is part of the pre-representational interaction between individual and environment that sets a context in which functional aspects of pre-perceptual sensory discrimination are explained.

Patterns of bi-directional, pre-representational causation also provide a baseline from which perceptual capacities are individuated and explained. Interactions between individual organisms and environment help determine the range of causes of sensory discrimination that are candidates for being *representata* of perceptual states (given that perceptual capacities are in place).[5] What types of entities can be *representata*, and what causal relations between environmental entities and sensory states help determine perceptual states' representational content, are both constitutively limited by the nature of pre-representational individual function.

One of the grounds for this constitutive relation between individual and perceptual kinds is that perceptual kinds constitutively figure in individual functions—in fulfilling needs and guiding action. Perception is not agency. But perception helps type-individuate a level of agency at which individuals can represent goals of, obstacles to, or threats to their activities, and act accordingly. Perceptions single out particulars that action aims for or aims to avoid. Perception may also serve passive realizations of individual functions, such as freezing or becoming fearful.

Since individual function, particularly agency, is attributable to individuals, and since individual function constitutively constrains its representational content, perception must be perception by individuals if it is to ground the explanatory role that these constitutive content-constraining relations fit it for.

---

subjects' reports. Theories of animal perception and action take perceptual states, as described in the science, to be ordinary states of animal perception—more clearly specified and more rigorously explained. Strange as it is to have to assert it: perceptual psychology is about human and animal perception. Claims that vision science is not concerned with *individual*, including *human*, visual states—the seeings and visual illusions that *individuals* undergo—show an unfortunate willingness to write about the science despite lack of the most elementary understanding of it.

[4] I thank Michael Bratman for raising questions during my Kant Lectures at Stanford University in October 2006 that led me to think beyond where I had been.

[5] See the discussion of the Disjunction Problem in Chapter 8 and the discussions of Quine's argument from gratuitousness and Davidson's argument from triangulation in Chapter 7.

To put the point another way: perceptual states are constitutively (partly) dependent for their representational content, not only on the environment's causally impinging on individuals, but on individuals' fulfilling basic whole-animal functions. The constitutive ground for this latter dependency lies partly in the role that perception and perceptual kinds play in explaining realizations of individual biological function—centrally, individual activity. Perception is constitutively a way of representing goals, obstacles, and threats for individuals. If perception is to ground this explanatory role, it must be attributable to individuals.

One must distinguish explanations of function from explanations of operation. The particulars and attributes referred to in accounts of individuals' realizing basic functions are just as privileged in explaining *realizations* of the biological *function* of *non-perceptual* sensory capacities as they are in explaining *realizations* of the biological *function* of perceptual capacities. Macro-conditions in the distal environment are privileged in both cases. Explanations of the *operation* of pre-perceptual sensory capacities can, however, focus on surface registrations of proximal stimulation. There is no need to advert to the environment in explaining the operation of such capacities. There is no need for a *representational* explanation of non-perceptual sensory capacities. By contrast, psychological explanations of the *operation* of perceptual capacities postulate a systematic, structured filtering of the effects of proximal stimulation that distinguishes information likely to be relevant to specific distal environmental features and that yields representational states. Such accounts signal perception.

I elaborate this idea in the section PERCEPTION AS OBJECTIFICATION. The present point is that there is antecedent pressure to privilege the distal environment. The pressure derives from the role of individual function in biological explanation of the function of *all* sensory capacities. This pressure affects the form of the psychological account of the *operation* of sensory capacities *if*, but also *only if*, there is something in the operation of the individual's sensory capacities that indicates a privileging of specific elements in environment over the immediate effects of proximal stimulation, where that 'something' is fruitfully explainable in terms of representational states. The account of the *operation* (as distinct from the function) of sensory discrimination incorporates facts about the environment that are relevant to individuals' functional relations to the environment, if the individual's sensory capacities ground distinctively perceptual explanations.

I mentioned a second ground for there being a constitutive relation between perception and individuals. Being a locus of perceptual representation just *is* being an individual with a representational perspective. The objectification and representational content involved in perception constitutes a point of view on environmental *representata*. Representational perspectives or points of view are constitutively attributable to individuals.

Psychology tries to explain how the representational perspectives of individuals are formed. Perceptual kinds ground this type of explanation. To play this role, they must be attributable to individuals.

This second basis for a constitutive relation between perception and individuals is, I think, not independent of the first. Being an individual with sense-perceptual capacities and a perspective on a subject matter implies some connection to individual–functional interactions with the subject matter.[6]

The presence of a representational perspective involves a further type of agency, in addition to acting on the environment. As indicated in Chapter 8 (the section PRIMITIVE AGENCY), the presence of a perceptual perspective that guides action or realization of need virtually guarantees a capacity for attention. To act on something perceived, something in the perceived array must be selected to be acted upon.[7] The same point has overwhelmingly likely, though perhaps not necessary, application to use of perception in realizing non-active individual functions. Direction of attention is selective orientation of the whole individual to aspects of what it represents. Direction of attention is a type of psychological agency. Hence it is attributable to the individual.

Being an individual with representational perspective does not entail that the individual is an agent with respect to all aspects of the perspective. Sensory states are the effects of (mainly) exogenous causation. Individuals do not form their sensory states, perceptual or non-perceptual, although they may put themselves in positions to receive such states.

Let us compare perception and non-perceptual sensory information registration with respect to attributability to individuals.

Certain types of non-perceptual sensory systems harbor only sensory states that are not attributable to individuals: they are not sensings by individuals. For example, sensory states in subsystems that regulate muscle tone, body temperature, and vascular constriction are never attributable to the individual. Proprioceptive registrations of saccades by the eyes are normally not attributable to individuals.

On the other hand, some non-perceptual sensory states are commonly attributable to individuals. A snake or tick senses warmth; a fish or mammal feels pain. Although unicellular organisms, like amoebae and paramecia, are special with respect to the distinction between individual and subsystem, it is still natural, I think, to regard paramecia as sensing (without consciousness) light or chemical mixes—as well as swimming. Paramecia do not transfer proteins into their bodies.

---

[6] I think that an individual or species could lack this capacity, yet have perception. But I think that the representational contents of the individual's perceptual system would still have to be explained, however indirectly, in terms of some use of the sensory discriminations in individual–environment interactions—in agency or in fulfilling needs. The interactions could, for example, be those of evolutionarily antecedent individuals from which the perceptual system evolved. See Chapter 3, Chapter 10, the sections on spatial and temporal representation, and Chapter 8, the section PERCEPTION AND THE ENVIRONMENT: THE 'DISJUNCTION PROBLEM'.

[7] It is probably not the case, however, that perception of particulars requires attention to the particulars. See, for example, F. F. Li, R. VanRullen, C. Koch, and P. Perona, 'Rapid Natural Scene Categorization in the near Absence of Attention', *Proceedings of the National Academy of Sciences of the United States of America* 99 (2002), 9596–9601.

More complex animals make the individual/subsystem distinction delicate in other ways. Sea urchins have numerous motor organs. Moveable spines may serve as legs or as means of defense. Among the spines are jaw-like organs known as pedicellariae, each borne on a moveable stalk. These jaws are sensitive to contact. They open and close, seizing foreign objects. The relevant sensory capacity is likely to be non-perceptual.

In these reactions, each organ may operate as an independent individual. If a piece of the shell bearing a single spine or pedicellaria is removed, the organ reacts to stimuli broadly in the same way as when it is connected with the whole animal. The sea urchin is made up of a colony of nearly independent structures. It has been called a republic of reflexes. The organs are not, however, entirely independent. They are connected by a nervous system that determines *some* coordination among the spines, and other sorts of integration.[8] In many cases among the simpler animals, the distinction between an individual and a colony is not immediately obvious. Still, it is natural to regard the urchin as sensing contact that causes reaching for prey and eating it.

The foregoing remark provides the key to understanding attribution of non-perceptual sensory states to individuals. Where a sensory state, non-perceptual or perceptual, can initiate action by the individual, it is attributable to the individual. The biologically basic actions—eating, navigating, mating, and so on—support regarding the animal as the agent in fulfilling or failing to fulfill its functions. Sensory states that are integral to accounts of the initiation of such actions are attributable to the individual. Where sensory states merely regulate internal processes, they are not thus attributable.

I think that all perceptual states are part of a sensory system constitutively associated with individual functions—paradigmatically, with individual agency. A perceptual state is constitutively part of a system some of whose states are attributable to individuals. The representational content of all perceptual states is partly but constitutively fixed by causal relations that derive from functional interrelations between individuals and environment. Moreover, perceptions are constitutively part of a perspective. And perspectives are constitutively attributable to individuals.

Non-perceptual sensory states bear a looser constitutive relation to being attributable to individuals. If such states are factors in action, or occur in subsystems that cause action or behavior, they tend to be attributable to individuals. If they are not central factors in *individual* functions, they tend not to be attributable to individuals. Non-perceptual sensory states, *per se*, lack the constitutive connection to individual function in determining their identities that perceptual states have.

---

[8] Jennings, *Behavior of the Lower Organisms*,. 234–235; Thorpe, *Learning and Instinct in Animals*, 194–195. 'Republic of reflexes' is an epithet coined by J. Van Uexküll, 'Über Reflexe bei den Seeigeln', *Zoologische Biologie* 34 (1897), 298–318.

Although some sensory systems figure directly in explaining action or other realizations of individual function, not all do. Of course, all sensory states that occur in individuals are part of a system—the whole organism—that has individual functions. So there may remain a constitutive relation, even though not all sensory states need be part of a system that has any *direct* relation to individual functions. Sensory states that regulate heart rate, vascular constriction, lubrication of eyes are examples.

Consciousness is constitutively a state of an individual. When a sensory state, perceptual or non-perceptual, is conscious, it is attributable to an individual. I believe, however, that consciousness is not the basic factor in determining what in a perceptual system is an individual's and what is merely a subsystem's. This matter is associated with consciousness's not being a necessary condition on perception.

Being conscious is not necessary for a non-perceptual sensory state to be attributable to an individual. The sensory states of many of the organisms that we have been discussing are not conscious.[9] A tick's sensing of warmth is imputable to the tick, not merely its subsystems. Such sensing is integral to the tick's action, its crawling toward a food source. There is little chance that ticks are conscious.

More importantly, there is considerable evidence that *individuals*, not merely subsystems, have unconscious *perceptual* states. So there is reason to doubt that consciousness is constitutive either to the individual/subsystem distinction or to perception. This conclusion will be more firmly supported once I discuss the objectivity of perception. Here I sketch three considerations against holding that perceptual states that are imputable to individuals must be conscious.

First, blindsight patients perceive environmental conditions. The perception involves perceptual constancies—including motion, location, and size constancies. The perception guides action. There is strong reason to believe that some of these patients lack phenomenal consciousness in the relevant perceptions. An important feature of these cases provides one of several reasons to reject any necessary connection between *attention* and consciousness. Standard attentional paradigms are fulfilled in blindsight cases. Attentive perception is successful; consciousness is missing.[10]

---

[9] Two broad notions of sensation occur in the history of psychology. One applies merely to a sensory registration of information that correlates causally and statistically with proximal stimulation. Sensations in this sense are states that lie at the beginning of physiologically or psychologically represented causal processes that lead into a specialized sensory system. The initial sensory registration of light arrays in mammals' visual systems is an example of sensation in this sense. Such sensory states need not be conscious. The other notion of sensation bears some constitutive relation to conscious feeling. Conscious pain is an example. Sensations in both senses can be sensory registrations. To avoid inviting confusion, I tend to use 'sensory state' rather than 'sensation'. 'Sensory state' has no usage that is as firmly associated with consciousness as one of the uses of 'sensation' is.

[10] For an overview of blindsight, see L. Weiskrantz, *Blindsight* (New York: Oxford University Press, 1986). For more recent accounts that discuss blindsight and attention, see R. W. Kentridge, C. A. Heywood, and L. Weiskrantz, 'Attention without Awareness in Blindsight', *Proceedings: Biological Sciences* 266/1430 (1999), 1805–1811; R. W. Kentridge, C. A. Heywood, and L. Weiskrantz, 'Spatial Attention Speeds Discrimination without Awareness in Blindsight', *Neuropsychologia* 42 (2004), 831–835; James Danckert and Yves Rossetti, 'Blindsight in Action:

Blindsight is just one of many types of dissociations between different aspects of brain/psychological systems. In several other cases—for example, in proso-pagnosia and extinction-neglect syndromes—there is evidence for unconscious perception. In most cases, the perceptual state is clearly imputable to the individual. It meets conditions for perception; in particular, perceptual constancies are exhibited. And it is almost surely unconscious, according to every plausible conception of unconsciousness.[11]

A second set of considerations that strongly suggests that perception by individuals need not be conscious derives from what is known about animal perception. As I shall indicate later in this chapter, some arthropods clearly have perceptual capacities. Bees and certain spiders visually perceive color, shape, motion, spatial location, and so on. They exhibit associated perceptual constan-cies. Whether bees and spiders are phenomenally conscious is unknown. These cases are not *known* to illustrate individual perception without consciousness. But the epistemic situation supports not taking consciousness to be constitutive of individual perception, or of the individual/subsystem distinction. Since percep-tion can be confidently and firmly attributed to bees and spiders without knowing whether they are conscious, it is at best questionable that their perception or (more generally) individual-level psychological states constitutively require con-sciousness. The dissociation cases make the point more directly.

Third, certain states in early vision (states in the first micro-seconds of visual processing) may count as perception by the individual, but fail to be conscious. Again, such states exhibit perceptual constancies. Certain complex, pre-attentive, pre-conscious categorizations occur but are not available to conscious report. Whether they are phenomenologically conscious is not known. Perception occurs and figures directly in guiding action. At the level of conscious *access*, individ-uals are oblivious to what they perceive.[12]

What Can the Different Sub-Types of Blindsight Tell Us about the Control of Visually Guided Actions?', *Neuroscience & Biobehavioral Reviews* 29 (2005), 1035–1046.

[11] For overviews, see Daniel L. Schacter, Mary Pat McAndrews, and Morris Moscovitch, 'Access to Consciousness: Dissociations between Implicit and Explicit Knowledge in Neuropsychological Syndromes', in L. Weiskrantz (ed.), *Thought without Language* (Oxford: Clarendon Press, 1989); Martha J. Farah, 'Visual Perception and Visual Analysis after Brain Damage: A Tutorial Overview', in C. Umilta and M. Moscovitch (eds.), *Attention and Performance XV: Conscious and Nonconscious Information Processing* (Cambridge, MA: MIT Press, 1995), 37–75; reprinted in N. Block, O. Flanagan, and G. Güzeldere (eds.), *The Nature of Consciousness* (Cambridge, MA: MIT Press, 1998). See also Bruce T. Volpe, Joseph E. Ledoux, and Michael S. Gazzaniga, 'Visual Processing of Visual Stimuli in an "Extinguished" Field', *Nature* 282 (1979), 722–724; M. Verfaellie, W. P. Milberg, R. McGlinchey-Berroth, L. Grande, and M. D'Esposito, 'Comparison of Cross-Field Matching and Forced Choice Identification in Hemispatial Neglect', *Neuropsychology* 9 (1995), 427–434; James P. Morris, Kevin A. Pelphrey, and Gregory McCarthy, 'Face Processing without Awareness in the Right Fusiform Gyrus', *Neuropsychologia* 45 (2007), 3087–3091.

[12] See Steven J. Luck, Edward K. Vogel, and Kimron L. Shapiro, 'Word Meanings Can Be Accessed but not Reported during the Attentional Blink', *Nature* 393 (1996), 616–618; Stanislas Dehaene, Lionel Naccache, Guryan Le Clec'H, Etienne Koechlin, Michael Mueller, Ghislaine Behaene-Lambertz, Pierre-François van de Moortele, and Denis Le Bihan, 'Imaging Unconscious Semantic Priming', *Nature* 395 (1998), 597–600; Etienne Koechlin, Lionel Naccache, Eliza Block,

For these reasons, I do not count consciousness constitutive of perception—or of the individual/subsystem distinction. Consciousness is not required for perceptual reference.

I take being an individual-level psychological state—and the constitutive relation of perception to individuals—to be rooted in two other attributes.

Individual function, paradigmatically agency, is one root of the constitutive attributability of perception to individuals. Representational perspective in perception is another root. Perceptual perspective is less pervasive in nature than agency is. But it is present in animals—bees and some spiders—in which consciousness is not known to be present. Consciousness is certainly sufficient for constitutive attributability to individuals. Perhaps it is a necessary and sufficient mark of individuality, though not of perception, for certain *types* of individual. That issue can be left to when more is known of consciousness.

PERCEPTION AS SENSORY

Perception is a *sensory* capacity. It is a discriminative capacity whose states are formed from causal impacts.

Sensory discrimination is discrimination of causes. To *discriminate* a *type* of causal impact is to co-vary with and respond differentially to that type, as part of a larger functioning system. To discriminate a *particular* is to respond to the causal impact of an instance of a type that is discriminated. Individuals discriminate many types of causal impacts when they discriminate one type. When an organism or sensory system discriminates light from dark, it also discriminates certain types of stimulations of its surfaces from other types.

Sensory discrimination serves biological function. Organisms' sensory capacities—perceptual or non-perceptual—have a generic *biological* function. The sensory system contributes to fitness. Sensory systems also have more specific functions, in enabling the individual to act effectively or in regulating aspects of the individual's life. Again, these are biological functions: such action contributes to fitness. As argued in Chapter 8, *perceptual* sensory systems have another type of function—*representational* function. They function to yield perception— to enable the individual to represent correctly through sensory mechanisms.

The notion of a sensory capacity has causal implications. What is perceived causes the perception. What is *sensorily* registered in a non-perceptual way

and Stanislas Dehaene, 'Primed Numbers: Exploring the Modularity of Numerical Representations with Masked and Unmasked Semantic Priming', *Journal of Experimental Psychology: Human Perception and Performance* 25 (1999), 1882–1905; René Marois, Do-Joon Yi, and Marvin M. Chun, 'The Neural Fate of Consciously Perceived and Missed Events in the Attentional Blink', *Neuron* 41 (2004), 465–472. The distinction between conscious access and phenomenological consciousness alludes to Ned Block's work that supports the distinction. See Chapter 6, note 95.

(perhaps both proximal stimulations and distal stimulations) causes the registration. These points seem to be apriori.

In both cases, a normal cause can be absent. Receptors of a non-perceptual system sensitive to light could be stimulated by a distal source quite different from the source that the sensory system has the evolutionary function of responding to. Analogously, a perceptual state could be caused by artificial stimulation of receptors, or by stimulation from an abnormal environmental condition. When perceptual systems are causally impacted either by artificial stimulation or by abnormal environmental conditions, perceptual processes are still set in motion. In both perceptual and non-perceptual sensory cases, abnormal conditions can undermine fulfillment of function—whether this be biological function (in either case) or representational function (in the perceptual case).

So a sensory state can fail to connect with its normal environmental cause. A notion of normal cause figures in explicating both what types of causes non-perceptual sensory states discriminate and what perceptual states represent there being.

The causal sensitivity of sensory systems serves discrimination. Relevant variations in causal input cause systematically different registration of information, or perceptual states with different representational content.

The differences between mere sensory states and perceptual states do not lie in their being functionally related to causation, even normal causation. They lie in the nature of the capacities.

Although the notion of a sensory capacity is constitutively associated with responsiveness to causal impacts, such responsiveness does not make a system a sensory system. Oil is causally responsive to fire, but no state of the oil is a sensory state. A plant is sensitive and responsive to light and carbon dioxide, but plants do not have sensory systems. A system of empirical theory and propositional inference is responsive to causal impacts on a perceptual system. An individual's system of empirical theory and inference is not a sensory system.

The notion of a sensory system is a functional notion. A sensory system is a system of an entity capable of behavior. Plants are not capable of behavior. Oil is not either. Behavior is a difficult scientific notion. I sketched some points about it in Chapter 8. But I will not try to explicate it in depth. Although not all behavior is active, I believe that the notion behavior applies only to individuals capable of agency.[13]

An individual's system of empirical theory is perhaps necessarily associated with behavior. But it lacks another feature of sensory systems. A sensory system is partly marked by its responsiveness to a particular modality of stimulus. For example, a visual system is responsive to light; an auditory system, to sound; a

---

[13] As noted in Chapter 8, the section PRIMITIVE AGENCY, some behavior is passive. Passive behavior is usually understood either in terms of interruption of active behavior—like stress or *schreck* reactions—or in terms of occurrences like sneezing that are generated by peripheral subparts of the individual.

touch system, to mechanical contact. Systems of belief and inference are not modality specific. Lower-level intermodal systems of representation, such as those that mediate perception and action, are also not modality specific.

There are other differences between sense-perceptual systems and systems of empirical theory that derive from the role of the individual in carrying out propositional inferences in the latter type of system. I will not develop these differences here.

Some objective sensory *representational* systems are not perceptual. Perceptual memory, anticipatory representation of action that derives from perception, and sense-perceptual imagination are all representational capacities that make essential use of sensory material. They can be modality specific. Distinguishing these capacities from perception is delicate. Roughly, none of these capacities is causally controlled by present sensory stimulation, and none functions to represent by processing present sensory stimulation. They are also psychologically marked as representation as of past or future, or as fictional representation. They do not form their sensory representational states in a systematic way from present effects of proximal stimulation. And none of these capacities marks their *representata* as causally present.[14]

Boundaries of the present are empirically determinable. But perceptual memory, including short-term perceptual memory, is a capacity for forming or preserving representations from perceptions that are already formed. Thus perception mediates between registration of proximal stimulation and perceptual memory. Moreover, perceptual memory functions to represent entities perceived in the past, and to represent them as being in the past. Anticipatory sensory actional representation is commonly mediately related to perception by perceptual memory. It represents its *representata* as being in the future. Sensory imagination is not committal on whether at least some aspects of its representational contents have *representata*, past, present, or future. It too is not immediately controlled by present sensory stimulation. It has further endogenous sources.

Present purposes do not demand a detailed account of relations among perception, perceptual memory, sensory representational anticipation, and sensory representational imagination. Representational capacities for memory and anticipation prevent our characterization of perception as *a type of objective, sensory representation by the individual* from providing a *sufficient* constitutive condition on perception. Perceptual memory and sensory representational anticipation are forms of objective, sensory representation by the individual. They are not forms of perception.

I have said enough, however, to locate perception among other operations of sensory representation. *Perceptual* systems are specific types of sensory systems. The features that distinguish them from *non-perceptual, non-representational* sensory systems are our main topic.

---

[14] Of course, perception can represent something in the distant past—as in astronomical observation. It nevertheless functions to be *controlled* by present stimulation.

PERCEPTION AS REPRESENTATION

Perception is constitutively a representational competence. Representational competencies are constitutively capable of veridicality or failure of veridicality. So a constitutive condition on perception is that it be capable of veridicality or failure of veridicality—accuracy or inaccuracy.

Veridicality conditions—conditions for accuracy—partly constitute what a perceptual state is. Perceptual states are type- (or kind-) individuated by such conditions. Thus a perceptual state as of a particular's being round is the kind of perceptual state that it is, inasmuch as it is accurate if and only if it singles out (perceptually) a round particular. Perceptual accuracy is success in fulfilling perception's representational function. So singling out a round particular is fulfilling the state's veridicality conditions, and its representational function. It is perceiving accurately. A perception as of a particular's being round is a generic kind of perceptual state.

Again, a perceptual state is the kind of perceptual state that it is by virtue of its conditions of veridicality—conditions that must be fulfilled if the perceptual state is to be a veridical perception. Representational contents set—indeed constitute—these conditions. Representational contents are abstract kinds that fix conditions under which a psychological state is veridical.[15] Representational contents constitute the perspective that the individual has on a subject matter. They also help mark—type-individuate—kinds of psychological state and particular states. Thus representational contents help individuate perceptual state kinds and perceptual states.[16] The representational contents are aspects of the kind of state a perceptual state is.

---

[15] A long dispute in philosophy centers on whether perception involves representation*s*, plural. Representations, conceived as they are conceived in the dispute, are particulars, often with qualitative or phenomenal characteristics, that serve to represent the world as *vehicles* or *instantiations* of content. Sense data, conceived as mental particulars, are proto-typical representations in this sense. I believe that much perception involves such mental particulars, but I avoid entering the dispute. I think that the dispute would be better focused on questionable psychological, representational, and epistemic roles that such representations have been given. My discussion, however, does not assume that there are such mental particulars, over and above the perceptual state instances. (See Chapter 2, the sections REPRESENTATION and REPRESENTATION-AS AND REPRESENTATIONAL CONTENT.) I think that psychology, so far, has made little *essential* use of mental representations in the disputed sense. Although perceptual psychology does discuss representations, perhaps in something like this sense, most psychological explanation relies essentially only on the existence of occurrent perceptual states and events that are of certain representational kinds and that have certain structural features. The kinds are representational contents. Perceptual representational contents are simultaneously ways of representing, types of perceptual state (or occurrence), and veridicality conditions with certain structural features.

[16] Kinds come in different levels of grain. Kinds of perceptual state indicated in psychological explanation tend to be those type-individuated by ability-general, attributional representational contents. These are the categorizational or grouping elements in perception—the attributional elements that represent (indicate) attributes in the environment. These contents contrast with the elements that serve to single out particulars—context-bound or occurrence-based elements. I discuss these matters, and the points about representational content that follow, in greater detail in 'Disjunctivism and Perceptual Psychology', especially section VII, and in 'Five Theses on *De Re* States and Attitudes'. The ability-general aspects of perceptual representational contents type-

Perceptual representational contents commonly represent attributes approximately, within some range. Thus states represent a distance *plus or minus*. I shall bracket this point and engage in idealization.

Perceptual representational contents are necessarily and constitutively structured. This claim derives from apriori considerations about perceptual veridicality conditions. All perception must have representational content that has both general and singular elements.

I start with general elements. Perceptual states necessarily represent what is perceived—the referents, or purported referents, of perception—as being a certain way. Perception types, characterizes, groups, attributes. It represents what is perceived by perceptually indicating certain *types* or *attributes*—such as roundness, being to the left of, being a body—and by attributing these types to particulars. Perception cannot indicate what is purportedly perceived except by way of some attribution of some purported property, relation, or kind.

This typing is of immediate semantical relevance, in that the particulars perceived can be accurately or inaccurately typed, grouped, or characterized. Aspects of perceptual representational content that function to group or characterize are general elements. I call them *perceptual attributives*. A perceptual attributive is an aspect of perceptual representational content that functions to indicate a repeatable type and to group or characterize purported particulars as being of that type. That is, a perceptual attributive *attributes* purportedly indicated types (attributes) to purportedly perceived particulars. A perceptual attributive is veridical of what is perceived if and only if what is perceived is of the type(s) indicated and attributed by the perceptual attributive.

The typing by general representational elements also marks repeatable perceptual abilities. The very notion of perceptual ability entails differential responsiveness to *types* of input. Perceptual response to a type of input characterizes or groups what is perceived as being of a certain type. Attributive aspects of representational content mark an aspect of general perceptual ability.

Perception is also constitutively as of particulars. Its content constitutively functions (representationally) to single out concrete particulars, not merely repeatables, or types. The particulars need not be events or material objects. They can be instances of properties or instances of relations. An individual, however, never perceives properties, relations, or kinds in the abstract. An individual perceives particular instances of properties, relations, or kinds—as being of certain types. Particulars are concrete in that they are localized in time. They (or in the case of some relation instances, their *relata*) have causal power. Veridical perception is only of what causes it.

---

individuate perceptual state kinds and perceptual states in a more fine-grained, more explanatory way than type-individuating them as the representation-as-of locution does. That is why in the text's preceding paragraph I count perceptual kinds individuated in the latter way 'generic'. See Chapter 2, the section REPRESENTATION-AS AND REPRESENTATIONAL CONTENT. Perceptual attributives are, I think, necessarily syntactically and semantically general. See 'Five Theses on *De Re* States and Attitudes'.

Perception's functioning to single out particulars is of immediate semantical relevance in that whether a perceptual state instance is accurate or not depends on whether there are causally relevant particulars and, if there are, whether those particulars are correctly characterized or grouped. Thus the representational content of perception constitutively has a singular element.

Singular elements in perception can fail to refer. But they function to perceptually represent concrete particulars—non-repeatable temporal entities that cause the perceptual state. The practical function of perception is to enable individuals to engage successfully with the particulars in their environment. The representational function is to represent those particulars accurately—to group them as instances of types that they in fact instantiate, within the representational means available.

Particulars cannot be perceptually represented in context-free ways. Perception depends on causal context as well as on perceptual attribution to represent particulars. So the singular element in perception must be context-bound. The singular element is a perceptual analog of occurrent uses of singular demonstratives in language. I call these singular elements '*singular perceptual applications*'.

Perception must always involve singular application of general abilities. The general abilities categorize or group. They function fallibly to indicate repeatable types and attribute them to particulars. So a perception—a representational perceptual state instance, or the content of a perceptual state instance—must always involve the context-dependent singular application of (general) perceptual attributives.[17] I believe that the foregoing structural points are apriori.

Neither the singular applications of attributives nor the attributives themselves need figure in propositional inference. I believe that perceptual content is not organized propositionally. The applicational and attributive elements in perceptual contents are organized in the structures of various magnitudes, most prominently spatial magnitudes (both topological and geometrical), though the groupings indicated in perceptual structures can be at various levels of abstraction.[18] A perceptual system can simultaneously represent a purported particular as square and as rectangular, or as a specific shade of red and as red.

I re-emphasize that perceptual representational contents—hence perceptual veridicality conditions—are conditions on successful perception, on fulfillment of perception's representational function. This point is incompatible with certain titillating philosophical construals of what is colloquially termed 'veridical hallucination'. Veridical hallucination is a genuine phenomenon, but I think that it is mislabeled. An example of the phenomenon is a person's visually hallucinating a large red cube when a large red cube just happens to be directly

---

[17] See my 'Postscript to "Belief *De Re*"'; 'Disjunctivism and Perceptual Psychology', especially section VII; and 'Five Theses on *De Re* States and Attitudes'.

[18] I return to the issue of perceptual organization in Chapter 11, the section THE UPPER BORDER OF THE PERCEPTUAL: PERCEPTION AND PROPOSITIONAL ATTITUDES.

in front of the person. The red cube could even have been a cause of the hallucination. The cube, through serendipity, could set up heat waves that affect a tumor in the brain that then causes a hallucination that just happens to "match" the red cube.

Some philosophers take such cases to exemplify perceptual states whose representational content are veridical, but that are hallucinations, not successful perceptions.[19] I believe that such views are mistaken. They are right to note the phenomenon. They are wrong to take it to show that perceptual states can have veridical perceptual representational content while not being (successful) perceptions. The relevant perceptual state instances are not veridical.

I think that there are no cases in which visual states, or states in other perceptual modalities, have (wholly) veridical representational contents but in which the states fail to be perceptions. Visual hallucinations, or visual referential illusions, can be veridical *of* entities that happen to be in the vicinity, and/or that even cause the hallucinatory states. The general attributive elements in such states might be veridical *of* lots of entities. But the application of the singular demonstrative element (or elements) in the representational content of the hallucinatory visual state fails (fail) to have a referent.[20] The demonstratives in the representational content of visual states refer to a particular only if the visual state is a successful perception of that particular. The reason for this point is that the referential conditions of a visual demonstrative are governed by the representational function of the visual system. Perceptual reference is singular reference through the visual system. The relevant hallucinations do not involve reference through the perceptual system. So the singular applications in the hallucinations fail to refer. Perceptual contents with singular applications that fail to refer are not veridical.

The point that the referential conditions of a visual demonstrative are governed by the representational function of the visual system is an instance of the more general point that the veridicality conditions constituted by perceptual representational content are conditions on successful perception.[21] What it is

---

[19] In 'Veridical Hallucination and Prosthetic Vision', *Australasian Journal of Philosophy* 58 (1980), 239–249, David Lewis holds that the content of a visual state can be veridical while the visual state is a hallucination. Christopher Peacocke, 'Demonstrative Thought and Psychological Explanation', *Synthese* 49 (1981), 187–217 (see pp. 209–210) holds a similar view. Lewis's paper contains ingenious cases that bear on when perception can occur through unusual, "prosthetic" channels. None of the cases, however, shows that the representational content of a hallucination can be veridical. I believe that the position of each author depends not only on missing the role of veridicality conditions of perceptual states in marking perceptual success, but also on mistaken views about singular reference in perception.

[20] Memory demonstratives might accompany a hallucination as of presence. For example, a memory demonstrative might apply to one's father, and one might hallucinate one's father as present. Then the memory demonstratives succeed. But the hallucination involves a reference as of a present body in a location in space that fails.

[21] I conjecture that the error in thinking that hallucinatory states can be veridical often derives from the view, which I criticized with respect to Strawson, Evans, and Quine, that perception cannot autonomously single out anything: singular reference depends on conceptual supplement.

for an occurrent perceptual demonstrative (singular application) in a representational content to pick out a particular just *is* for the perceptual state that is type-individuated by that representational content to be a *perception* of that particular. Perceptual (or hallucinatory) failures to perceive a particular entail failures of the singular elements in the state's representational content to secure a referent. So failures to secure a perceptual object (or a particular that is perceived) are failures of reference by perceptual singular applications (by occurrent perceptual demonstratives) in perception. These failures entail failures of veridicality. For veridicality in perception is representational success both in the occurrent singular applications of singular elements and in the attributional applications of perceptual attributives to the referents of the singular applications. So veridical hallucinations, understood as hallucinations with veridical representational content, are impossible. Perceptual kinds are constitutively associated with veridicality conditions, which are conditions on representationally successful perception. Perceptual-like hallucination is constitutively a representational failure.

Perceptual psychology's explanation of the formation of perceptual states with representational contents that set veridicality conditions provides the key ingredient in a scientific explanation of perceptual reference and perceptual illusion. The explanation explains by citing laws or law-like patterns of operation that lead from given registrations of proximal stimulation to perceptual states that specify particulars as having specific attributes. As explained in Chapter 3, the section THE SHAPE OF PERCEPTUAL PSYCHOLOGY, this key ingredient is supplemented with explanations from non-psychological sciences to yield relatively full explanations of veridical perception. In vision science, the idea is that when specific environmental conditions are realized and light from these conditions reaches relevant receptors in standard ways—where these ways are specifiable mainly by laws of optics—and where certain specifiable proprioceptive conditions are met, the formation laws will, barring various kinds of interference, yield a perceptual state that specifies particulars as being in those environmental conditions. Such perceptual states constitute veridical perception—veridical seeings.

For example, when a page full of regularly distributed circles is viewed straight on, the laws of optics can predict what sort of pattern of light intensities project onto retinal receptors. (See Chapter 8, the subsection PLANAR SLANT FROM PLANAR SURFACE TEXTURE). The formation principles describe laws that, barring interferences from outside the visual system, produce a perceptual state as of a surface perpendicular to the line of sight and with a regular distribution of circles. If the page is rotated backwards at a 60-degree angle, the laws of optics can again predict what sort of pattern of light intensities will project onto the retinal receptors. In this case, the psychological formation principles describe laws that yield a perspectivally different perceptual state (with a different attributional representational content) that is also as of a surface with a regular distribution of circles, but as being at a 60-degree slant backward from fronto-parallel orientation. (The representational content does not, of course, specify numbers, but contains a perceptual attribution that is veridical of 60-degree slants.) Both perceptual states are veridical inasmuch as the singular applications in the perceptual state instances are the effects of a (specfiable) causally normal causal chain that begins with light reflected from the specified distal condition, continues with the proximal-stimulation registrations, and proceeds thence through the formation laws to the perceptual state instance.

The explanations of the perceptual system's overcoming the underdetermination problem always suggest specific conditions under which perceptual illusions will occur. For example, under specifiable conditions in which the visual system is deprived of further cues (further sorts of registration of proximal stimulation that stem from other environmental conditions), a page with a straight-on slant and closed figures with a specifiable configuration of systematically different closed shapes can produce registration of proximal stimulation that, by the formation laws, will yield a misperception as of a surface slanted at 60 degrees with a regularly distributed set of circles. The specificity of the formation principles commonly implies the conditions under which other specific sorts of illusions occur. Of course, a proximal-stimulation registration that does not derive from a surface with closed figures on it at all can yield a referential illusion with specifiable attributional content: none of the singular applications succeeds in referring, and all of the attributions are vacuously non-veridical.

Perceptual psychology has yielded numerous specific explanations of veridical perception and perceptual representations. My example vastly understates the specificity and richness of the explanations. The explanations provide, I think, the first scientific explanations of representation—perceptual reference and veridical perceptual attribution.

Such explanations of perceptual veridicality and non-veridicality are hybrids. The *psychological* parts of the account contain the formation principles of perceptual psychology. They account for both (*a*) conditions in which underdetermination is overcome by the perceptual system and individuals perceive veridically, and (*b*) conditions in which perceptual systems yield misperceptions, and perceivers suffer perceptual misrepresentation. These psychological components of the explanation are joined with components from the natural sciences. For example, visual psychology relies on non-psychological explanations of how light is projected from types of environmental conditions onto a bank of sensory receptors. These not-distinctively-psychological explanations join psychological explanations to explain the veridicality or illusoriness of specific perceptual states. The combination of explanatory principles yields a scientific explanation of basic forms of perceptual reference and veridicality, and of basic forms of perceptual illusions. This type of account provides a vindication for psychology's individuating certain psychological kinds (perceptual kinds) in terms of representational content that sets veridicality conditions.

I have been discussing the constitutive aspect of perception that consists in the veridicality conditions set by the representational content of a perceptual state (type or instance). A closely related constitutive feature of perception—and of representational content—is that it is fallibly perspectival.

Representational perceptual content is to be strictly distinguished from entities that are perceived, indicated, or attributed. Like perception, which it helps type-(kind-) individuate, such content always constitutes a partial representation of, a perspective on, particulars perceived or attributes attributed. For any given particular or attribute, there are many possible (commonly actual) representational perceptual contents that correctly represent it. A particular can be perceived as being the same size in different ways, from different perspectives. That is of the essence of perceptual constancies.

Again, the representational content that helps type-individuate perceptual states is not the particulars perceived. Nor is it the repeatable types that are attributed. It consists in modes of presentation as of particulars, and modes of presentation as of attributes that are perceptually attributed.[22] The mode of presentation, or representational content, constitutes the individual's perspective and type-individuates states responsive to the input that produces that perspective. Even in veridical perception, perceptual states are individuated by fallible and partial perspectives on the particulars perceived.

There are scientific reasons why the contents of perceptual states do not consist of the particulars (instances of kinds, properties, relations) that are the environmental objects of perception. The content of a perceptual state helps type identify what kind of perceptual state it is. Of course, kinds can be individuated in many legitimate ways. But the kinds most significant for understanding how types of perceptual states are formed, and for understanding perceptual reference and perspective, are not individuated in terms of such environmental objects. I shall discuss two scientific reasons.

Here is one reason. In any given case, the kind of psychological perceptual state—including the kind of conscious perceptual state—that is formed (excepting the identity of the occurrence-based demonstrative singular perceptual applications, which will be discussed below) depends entirely on (*a*) the type of initial sensory state caused by proximal stimulation (the type of registration of proximal stimulation), (*b*) the psychological state of the individual at the time of the stimulation (or immediately afterwards), and (*c*) the psychological formation laws that govern causal transformations from registrations of proximal stimulation, transformations that form perceptual states. The psychological laws of formation allow for interference, including noise, and malfunction caused by internal factors other than the psychological ones described by the theory. So one

---

[22] The distinction between referent and mode of presentation derives from Gottlob Frege, 'On Sense and Reference' (1892), in *Translations from the Philosophical Writings of Gottlob Frege*. Frege applied the distinction to an ideal language of thought. An analogous distinction applies to perception. The import of the distinction is independent of particular ontological accounts of sense or representation. I think that all philosophically and scientifically reasonable accounts do and must find a place for a distinction that parallels Frege's. For explanation of why it is crucial to the science, see my 'Disjunctivism and Perceptual Psychology'.

could add as a fourth factor: (*d*) non-psychological internal states of the individual that might interfere with or otherwise affect the formation operations described by the formation principles. The laws of formation of perceptual states do not depend, in individual cases, on whether the registration of proximal stimulation has normal environmental distal antecedents. Thus what kind of state is formed and how the state presents the environment as being depends purely on these factors—registration of proximal stimulation, the individual's psychological states at the time of these registrations, and the laws of perceptual-state formation—allowing again for noise, interference, and breakdowns.[23] But any given type of registration of proximal stimulation, any given psychological and physical state of the individual perceiver at the time of the stimulation, and any formation laws that govern transitions from registrations of proximal stimulation to perceptual states are, together, compatible with both absence and presence of distal environmental objects of perception.

The retinal endings could be stimulated artificially or in some other way that produces referential illusions. The type of registration of *proximal* stimulation could still be the same as the registration of proximal stimulation that comes in the normal way from distal environmental objects. The same *kind* of perceptual state with the same *kind* of representational content is formed in either case. (And the resulting instances of conscious perceptual states would be consciously and sensorily indiscernible for the perceiver.) So the kind of perceptual state formed under the law-like formation principles is individuated in a way that takes the kind of perceptual state to be the same in referential and referentially illusory cases—as long as registration of proximal information, antecedent psychological set, and the laws of formation remain the same.[24] In the formation of types of perceptual state, the perceiver and perceptual system depend causally purely on registration of proximal stimulation and the internal states (psychological and otherwise) of the perceiver at the time of the stimulation. The kinds of perceptual

---

[23] Of course, as anti-individualism emphasizes, the perceptual kinds and the laws of transformations among the perceptual states depend on a background *pattern* of interrelations to distal environmental causes. But, at any given time, the perceptual-state attributional kinds formed in an individual's psychology—*given* a capacity for perception and *given* the laws governing that individual's perceptual psychology—depend entirely on the type of registration of proximal stimulation (together with the contemporary state of the perceiver and the laws governing those states). This last point, and the slightly more detailed version in the text, is what I call the Proximality Principle. The Proximality Principle is compatible with anti-individualism. See 'Disjunctivism and Perceptual Psychology', in which I discuss this principle and many of the points discussed in the remainder of the present section. See also Chapter 8, note 97.

[24] As I will make clear subsequently in the present section, the sameness of kind of perceptual state in this sense allows for differences in context-bound singular applications. These are occurrent or token differences, not differences in kind of perceptual state in the ordinary sense—or in the sense relevant to understanding laws governing formation of perceptual states, or perceptual perspective, or indeed epistemic warrant. The differences do bear on reference and veridicality. Whether a perceptual state instance is veridical or not, referential or not, hinges on how occurrent, context-bound singular applications are caused in particular contexts.

states that are formed depend causally, in individual cases, on the type of registration of proximal stimulation, not on the actual distal objects of perception.

For example, suppose that an individual accurately sees a round orange body (say, an orange) *as* a round orange body of such and such size. The same *kind* of perceptual state is formed—in the sense that the same attributions of color, shape, body, size occur—if the same *proximal* (largely retinal) stimulation is produced on the same perceiver, regardless of whether that type of proximal stimulation derives from a normal environmental source and yields veridical perception, or is produced in some abnormal way, so that no round orange body (and no relevant instances of the attributes *round*, *orange*, or *body*, and no instances of any other particular in the distal environment) is perceived. Perceptual states of the same attributional kinds—with the same attributional representational contents—are be produced in each case. Attributional kinds are the same. In the first case, a particular round body (the orange) is perceived. In the second case, no particulars are perceived at all: there is only a referential perceptual illusion as of a round orange body of such and such size. In both cases, a perceptual state that attributes the same attributes (*round orange body of such and such size*) in the same way— with the same *attributional* representational content—is formed.

An analogous point applies in exercise of perceptual constancies. If proximal stimulation is changed in appropriate ways on a given perceiver, perceptual constancies are exercised. The perceiver perceives *as of there being* a given environmental attribute under a wide range of proximal stimulations. It does not matter whether the registration of proximal stimulation derives from normal environmental particulars that are seen or (on the contrary) from artificial or otherwise abnormal sources that engender referential perceptual illusions—as long as the same *proximal*-stimulation registration in the *sensory receptors* initiates the perceptual processes.

Take size and color constancies. One can see a round orange body (say, an orange) as being of a given size whether it is close—causing stimulation of a substantial number of the retinal receptors—or farther away—stimulating a much smaller number of receptors. Size constancy is the capacity to see something *as of* the same size under very different proximal stimulations. Similarly, one can see the same orange body as the same shade of orange, whether the body is in natural white light or illuminated by green light. Color constancy is the capacity to see something *as of* the same shade of color under very different proximal stimulations. Now suppose that one sees the round orange body as being a round orange body of such and such a size. Suppose that one first sees the body up close and in a white light. Then (not given any further information) one sees the body much farther away bathed in green light. Suppose, finally, that the same type of proximal-stimulation registration that *had* derived from the body first near and then far is *later* reproduced but artificially, so that it does not derive from a relevant body, or any other perceived entity in the distal environment at all. The proximal-stimulation registration type PS_1 that derived from that actual round orange body that was relatively close to the perceiver produced a perceptual state instance as of a round orange body of such and such size. If PS_1 is later artificially produced, it will produce a perceptual state instance that represents as of a round orange body of such and such size, *and does so with the same attributional representational content*. That is, the attributional kind of perceptual state will be the same in the second case as in the first.

If the same body is located farther away and bathed in green light, the type of proximal-stimulation registration PS_2 will be different. It will produce a different perceptual state with a different representational content—a different way of representing than was produced by PS_1. But the different representational content makes an attribution as of a round body of the same size and same shade of orange as was formed from PS_1. The same attributes—of specific size, color shade, shape, and body—are attributed, but in different ways. The attributional kind of perceptual state formed from PS_2 will be different from the kind formed from the two occurrences of PS_1, even though both psychological state kinds (deriving from PS_2 and PS_1), in all occurrences, are perceptual states that represent as of a round body of a given size and a given shade of orange.[25] The representational contents, or ways of attributing those attributes, are different depending on whether the proximal stimulation is PS_2 or PS_1. The perceiver has different perspectives in attributing those attributes, and attributes them in perspectivally different ways. But, if PS_2 is produced artificially, so that no relevant body in the environment is seen, the same attributional kind of perceptual state will be produced, according to the laws of formation, with the same attributional representational content, as was produced when PS_2 derived from the orange body.

These points about the dependence of attributional kinds of perceptual state on kinds of proximal-stimulation registration (together with the formation laws and the antecedent psychological and physical state of the individual) are not matters of philosophical interpretation. They are matters of scientific fact.

The perceptual constancies are capacities (approximately) to track given environmental attributes under different environmental conditions that yield very different types of proximal stimulation. But exercises of the capacities are triggered even in cases where the proximal stimulations derive from no (environmental) objects of perception. Perception is not a referentially infallible capacity. The science explains perceptual illusion as well as veridical perception. Perceptual constancies, and the formation laws described by principles of perceptual

---

[25] Size constancy and distance constancy are in some respects closely related. When the same size is attributed despite different distances, a different distance is normally attributed. (There are, however, mechanisms for size constancy that do not depend on determining distance.) However, the attributes that are represented as constant are represented in different ways in the different cases. The point is intuitive: the body's size looks different, even as it looks to have the same size. Similar points apply to the attribution of a color shade. As noted in the text, the look is not a property of the environment, though it depends in normal cases on relations to the environment. In referential illusions, the look can be an aspect of perceptual attribution, even as the normal environmental relations are absent. And the perceptual constancies operate even under referential illusions.

psychology, work on states that contain attributions *as of* attributes in the environment. The constancies are exercised, and the law-like formation operations occur, even in cases in which no particulars are perceived (perceptually referred to)—in which no instances of the attributes that are attributed by the perceptual states occur in the situation in which the perceptual state is formed. The formation of perceptual states depends causally, in any given instance, on registration of proximal stimulation. The same attributional kind of perceptual state, with the same attributional representational content, can be caused by the same type of registration of proximal stimulation, whether or not the perceptual state has perceptual *representata*—whether or not it is a perception *of* anything at all.

To review: the first reason why psychology does not individuate each perceptual state in terms of particulars and attributes in the environment that are perceived on given occasions is as follows. Two occurrences of perceptual states can be instances of the same attributional kind of perceptual state, even though one occurrence is a veridical seeing and the other is a referential illusion (with no perceived particulars having the attributed attributes, and no perceived instances of the attributes). Science attributes the same attributional *kind* of perceptual state in cases of successful perception and cases of perceptual referential illusion—as long as proximal-stimulation registration is the same, antecedent states of the perceiver are the same, and formation operations through the perceptual system under formation laws are the same. The formation laws and the *kinds of psychological perceptual states that fall into the law-like formation patterns* concern perceptual states *as of*, not perceptual relations to the environment.

Of course, in a sense, veridical perception is one "kind" of state, and perceptual states that are referential illusions comprise another "kind" of state. This point invokes kinds that cut across the kinds of psychological state that enter into the psychological (formation) laws described by the best psychological principles that we have. The point is easily accommodated in the science. In fact, I set out the broad form of the explanation earlier in this section.

The account of *veridical* perception and perceptual illusion (including perceptual referential illusion) includes, not only the account of the formation of perceptual states from registrations of proximal stimulation, but an account of the further relations between distal causes and proximal causes. This account, discussed earlier in this section, is a hybrid of explanation in terms of psychological kinds and explanation in terms of physics and biology. The account of *veridical* perception of, and as of, the orange round body includes both an account of the formation of a psychological state from proximal-stimulation registration and an account of the causal relations, explained in optics and physiology, between orange round bodies and the sensory receptors of the perceiver. In any given case, the explanation of, say, a veridical seeing involves adverting to both psychological laws and non-psychological laws governing causal relations between distal environmental particulars and registrations on the perceiver's body. Thus, although seeing is in a sense a natural kind, it is a hybrid kind. It is a psychological state that, *in each instance*, depends for being a seeing on entities and causal relations beyond the psychology of the individual.[26]

The representational contents of perceptual states include context-bound applications—demonstrative *occurrences*. These applications' identities hinge on the particular contexts and particular times in which they occur. In referentially successful perception, these occurrent, demonstrative applications pick out environmental particulars (including instances of kinds and instances of properties). They do so by being caused by them in ways that go from the environmental particulars through proximal stimulations to proximal-stimulation registrations through formation operations to the occurrent perceptual states. In cases of referential failure in perception (and indeed other sorts of illusion), the proximal stimulation and proximal-stimulation registration are not causally connected in appropriate ways to environmental particulars.

Actual referential illusions occur on different occasions than do actual veridical perceptions. They have different context-bound singular perceptual applications in their respective representational contents. Since context-bound singular applications are part of perceptual representational contents, the perceptual representational contents of veridical perceptual state occurrences are always different from the representational contents of referentially illusory perceptual-state occurrences. These differences constitute different kinds of perceptual state *in a sense*. The different occasions can be associated with different distal sources of proximal information. In fact, every occurrent perceptual state has different applications from most other occurrent perceptual states (tracking is probably an exception). Even different perceptual state instances that are all veridical and all make the same attributions can have different context-bound singular applications in their representational contents.[27] *These* differences in representational content—however relevant to reference and veridicality—bear only on occurrent or token aspects of psychological states, not on their psychologically relevant attributional kinds.[28]

The foregoing discussion of perceptual constancies contains a second scientific reason why psychology does not individuate perceptual states in terms of particulars and attributes that are perceived on given occasions: Given attributes,

---

[26] Being a certain attributional kind of belief or perceptual state depends for being the kind of state it is on antecedent patterns of relations to an environment in which the perceptual system was formed. That point is central to anti-individualism. But such kinds do not depend in each instance, and in each occasion, on specific causal relations beyond the perceiver for being the kind of psychological states that they are.

[27] Exceptions relevant to each of the claims in the last two sentences are cases of tracking particulars—whether these are particulars like bodies or instances of properties like size and color shade. If an individual sees an object and later, *without* having tracked the object, sees the same object, unchanged as far as vision can discern, in the same circumstances (but not as the same object), the same attributions to the same object can be made, with different context-bound singular applications.

[28] See the discussion of the account of reference a few pages back, and the discussion of context-bound perceptual demonstrative applications (in perceptual representational contents) in the next few pages.

$F_1 \ldots F_n$, that are attributed *as* $F_1 \ldots F_n$ in two occurrences of perceptual states, the two occurrences of perceptual states can attribute $F_1 \ldots F_n$ *as* $F_1 \ldots F_n$ in different ways. And in having different representational contents in these attributional respects,[29] the two occurrences are different attributional kinds of perceptual state. The same attributes $F_1 \ldots F_n$ are attributed *as* $F_1 \ldots F_n$ but from different perspectives and with different representational contents, in exercises of the perceptual constancies. Two occurrences of perceptual states could both be veridical—as when an attribute and its instance are veridically tracked as the same, while perspectives change. Or the two occurrences of perceptual states could both be perceptual referential illusions: no particulars that are instances of any kinds, properties, or relations are perceived. Even in this latter case, perceptual constancies are exercised. The same perceptual constancies are at work whether an individual perceives entities in the environment or undergoes certain referential perceptual illusions, in which no particulars in the environment are perceived. The different ways of attributing attributes in perceptual constancies are aspects of different kinds of perceptual psychological states. The environmental attributes themselves are not fine-grained enough to account for the constitutively perspectival nature of perceiving, even laying aside cases in which perceptions in different modalities pick out the same particulars or attribute common attributes. Perceptual psychological kinds are individuated in such a way that what kind of psychological state occurs—certainly, what *attributional* kind occurs—causally depends, on particular occasions, purely on the type of registration of proximal stimulation, the state of the perceiver at or immediately after that stimulation, laws of perceptual state formation, and other non-psychological internal states of the perceiver.

Some philosophers postulate, as part of what is seen, "relational" properties between the perceiver and ordinary environmental entities.[30] Such postulations are meant to account for perspectival aspects of perception, evinced in exercises of perceptual constancies, while still placing such perspectival aspects among the particulars and attributes that are among the *objects* of perception. Sometimes these "relational properties" are identified with the "perspectival looks" of environmental objects. These "looks" themselves are supposed to be in the environment and are supposed to be seen. Call this position '*the first maneuver*'. Other philosophers postulate "looks" that are not subject to illusion as perceptual objects in cases that are normally taken to be illusions. *These* "looks" or "perspectival properties" are presumably not in any ordinary sense part of the environment. (I think it obvious that perception cannot be immune to illusion with respect to *any* environmental object.) The intent of these postulations is again to provide—in the "looks"—particulars and attributes that are *objects* of

---

[29] That is, in respects other than differences in context-bound demonstrative applicational differences (see notes 24 and 27).

[30] For discussion of specific proponents of the first two of the maneuvers about to be discussed, see my 'Disjunctivism and Perceptual Psychology'.

perceptions. These philosophers, who postulate "looks" as veridical objects of perception in cases normally taken to be illusions with respect to the environment, divide into two types. Some take the "looks" to be objects of perception only in cases that would ordinarily be called referential illusions. They maintain that in veridical cases, the perceptual state is individuated in terms of its environmental perceptual objects (the *second maneuver*). Others postulate the "looks" in all cases—making their positions a recrudescence to sense-data views (the *third maneuver*).

The first two maneuvers are in effect attempts to defend naive realism, at least about veridical perception. All these positions are incompatible with the science, and constitute outmoded ways of doing philosophy of perception.

The two scientific reasons given earlier work together against the first maneuver. One cannot account for perceptual perspective purely by postulating environmental perspectival relations to environmental objects, because perspectival differences and perceptual constancies occur even given proximal stimulation that yields perceptual referential illusions. Thus the perspectival differences occur even when there are no relevant environmental perspectival relations to environmental objects. A further difficulty for the first maneuver is that nothing in the science indicates that perspectival relations in the environment are *objects* of perception; they are not among the attributes and particulars that are perceived (*representata*). If they were, there would have to be a theory of conditions under which referential illusions with respect to *them* occurred and an underdetermination theory with respect to *them*. All environmental perceptual *representata* are underdetermined by registration of proximal stimulation. Perspectival properties that are most relevant to perception are aspects of perceptual states—ways of perceiving that are perspectives on the environment.

The second and third maneuvers are incompatible with the basic ecological orientation of the science. They amount to maintaining that perceptual reference is infallible: perception always succeeds in perceiving *something*—a "look" if not an environmental particular or attribute. No normal causal connection is postulated. These approaches postulate perceptual kinds and *representata* that ignore the basic problem of the science—to explain how perceptual systems overcome the underdetermination problem in cases of veridical perception, and to explain cases of illusion (including referential illusion) in terms of proximal stimulations that usually connect with environmental entities but sometimes do not. As noted earlier, even in cases of veridical perception, the entities in the environment are not fine-grained enough to explain attributional, perspectival differences in perception of the same attributes and particulars. All these attempts to defend explaining perception in terms of *representata* alone fail to make contact with how the science understands, and differentiates, perceptual *representata* and perceptual perspective, and how it explains perceptual causation and error.

To summarize and conclude: disjunctivism is the view that no explanatory kind of perceptual state is common between veridical perceptual states and referential illusions that are formed from the same registration of proximal stimulation (and that are often consciously indiscernible). Naive realist and other philosophical views of perception that maintain disjunctivism are incompatible with scientific knowledge.

Most disjunctivist views also maintain that no explanatorily relevant kind of perceptual state is common among cases where the same perceiver is given the same type of proximal-stimulation registration producing internally indiscernible perceptual states each of which is *veridical* of *different* (but indiscernible) environmental particulars. The idea is that veridical perception is *purely* a relation between a perceiver and the particulars perceived. On such views, since the state is nothing other than a referential relation between perceiver and environmental particulars, any difference in the environmental particulars perceived will leave no kind of perceptual state in common between the state instances.

For example, suppose that a perceiver accurately sees a round red ball against a white background. Then, during an eye-blink, the ball is exchanged for another round red ball that produces the same type of proximal-stimulation registration (and an indiscernible, conscious perceptual state instance). The new perceptual state instance is also veridical of the new ball. Most disjunctivist views maintain that there can be no explanatorily relevant kind of perceptual state common between the state produced before the blink and the state afterwards. The idea is that since veridical perception is purely a relation to environmental entities, and the entities are different, there are no explanatorily relevant perceptual state types—in particular, no representational state kinds—in common between the state produced before the blink and the state produced afterwards.

Such a view is again incompatible with scientific knowledge. Although the two state instances refer to different balls—and the states' contents have different token singular demonstrative applications—the kind of state formed (the attributional kind) is the same in all other respects. These are the respects that the *psychology* of perception centers on. The two instances of perceptual state are of the same kind in a basic, explanatory sense. Differences between the perceptual state *instances* depend on context-bound—token-bound, or instance-bound—differences, not differences in the *kind* of perceptual state that enters into (and is explained by reference to) the law-like formation operations described by principles of perceptual psychology. Differences in singular reference between the instances are marked by different context-bound (or token-, instance-bound) singular elements in the representational contents. There are different occurrent singular *applications* in the two perceptual state instances. Again, the differences in reference depend on differences in causal context—differences in the psychological state *instances* (before and after the blink). These differences in reference derive from different *distal* parts of the causal histories on the different contextual occasions. These differences bear on whether or not a particular is referred to, and which particular. But the *kind* of perceptual state that figures in the psychological laws is the same.

Consider again the example of perception as of an orange spherical body. The veridical perceptual state instance and the state instance that is a perceptual referential illusion as of an orange, spherical body differ in context-bound respects. The different perceptual state instances have different context-bound demonstrative applications (token differences) in their representational contents. The demonstrative singular application appropriately caused (through the perceptual formation processes) by the particular spherical orange body is referential. The demonstrative singular application in the representational content of the perceptual state instance that is caused by the same type of initial proximal-stimulation registration in response to the artificial proximal stimulation (with no appropriate causal antecedent in a distal environmental body) fails to refer to anything. The differences are those of occurrence-based or token elements in the states, or the states' representational contents.

Again, in a *certain* sense, these are differences in kind: one state instance is a seeing; the other is an illusion. But as for kinds that enter into the formation laws described by the science, they are of the same kind—the same attributional kind. The differences *in the states themselves* are purely context-bound, occurrent/ token differences. The differences in reference and veridicality hinge on those context-bound occurrent differences. With respect to kinds like seeing and illusion, the same kind of psychological state can be veridical or a referential illusion, or can be veridical of different (sensorily indiscernible) entities. Differences between veridicality and referential illusion depend on the full causal chain, including the distal parts of the chain, that leads up to the registration of proximal stimulation on the sensory receptors and then, through the operations of the perceptual system, to perceptual state instances—the ultimate effects of the chain. Relevant pairs of perceptual state instances that derive from the same proximal-stimulation registration, where one instance is veridical seeing and the other is referential illusion, are the same attributional kind of perceptual state: The two perceptual state instances are as of the same attributes, and (further) their ability-general (non-context-bound) modes of presentation in their representational contents—the perspectival ways of carrying out attributions, abstracting from occurrence-based, context-bound differences in perceptual singular applications—are the same. These are explanatorily relevant psychological kinds.[31]

Perceptual psychology attempts to explain the formation of perceptual states, conceived as representational states. Explanation adverts to detailed laws or law-like patterns of transformation that yield specific kinds of perceptual states. The principles governing formation laws (or law-like patterns) make reference not only to non-perceptual types of sensory states but also to perceptual states marked

---

[31] The difference between context-bound individuation and ability-general or attributional individuation is discussed at length in my 'Disjunctivism and Perceptual Psychology'. All the issues discussed in criticizing the view that the environmental particulars and attributes are the contents of perceptual states are discussed in detail in that work. See also my 'Five Theses on *De Re* States and Attitudes' for further, detailed discussion of the nature of perceptual states and representational contents.

by representational content. That is, the explanations take the representational states as participants in the formation processes. Some states enter in the formation of others. Thus reference to perceptual states with representational content that sets veridicality conditions and that constitutes perceivers' perspectives on the environment helps ground explanation in the science. Principles governing such patterns of transformation constitute an account of how perceptual states (whether veridical or not, whether successfully referential/indicational or not) are formed from registration of proximal sensory stimulation. As noted earlier, the science provides a constitutive component in scientific explanations of reference and failure of reference. The rest of such explanations refer to laws or law-like patterns of relations between types of distal entities and registration of proximal stimulation. These latter explanations are not distinctively psychological.

In Chapter 8, the section THE LOWER BORDER OF PERCEPTION: SENSORY INFORMA-TION REGISTRATION AND PERCEPTION, I held that the empirical success of perceptual psychology supports believing that it marks perceptual states as genuine kinds. I also held that the theory is a good guide to finding a division between perceptual states and non-perceptual sensory states.

In the cases of some sensory states—non-perceptual ones—saying that the states have veridicality conditions would add nothing explanatory to what is known about discriminative sensitivity and the biological function of the sensitivity. Invocation of veridicality conditions and perceptual perspective does not figure integrally in any explanation of these states. Veridicality conditions can be imposed. But invoking them gains no empirical traction, yields no empirical illumination. In such cases, there is no reason to believe that there are representational states.

Where theory that invokes states with veridicality conditions and associated perspectival capacities is empirically fruitful, there is reason to believe that there are perceptual states, hence representational states in a non-debased sense. Standard theory in perceptual psychology takes representational states, those with non-trivial veridicality conditions, to be explanatorily relevant psychological kinds, cuts in the world. I illustrated explanations that make non-trivial reference to law-like transformations involving states with representational content in Chapter 8, the section PERCEPTUAL PSYCHOLOGY AND THE DISTINCTION BETWEEN SENSORY INFORMATION REGISTRATION AND PERCEPTION. In their invocation of perceptual constancies and of states with representational content, such explanations are markedly different from explanations of non-perceptual sensory registration—the sensory encodings that correlate statistically with types of stimulus.

In sum, the main line of reasoning that takes the representationality of perception to be a guide to where representation and perception begin goes as follows. Explanations in perceptual psychology are powerful and fruitful science. Such explanations provide a good guide to finding explanatorily relevant kinds. Psychological accounts of the formation of perceptual states invoke representational states that have veridicality conditions, as illustrated in Chapter 3 and Chapter 8. The veridicality conditions are conditions for accuracy in representing environmental conditions beyond the sensory registration of proximal stimulation. Thus there is a transition from mere sensory registration to representation as of an environmental reality. The transition is marked by formation principles that concern states that specify aspects of the environment. I do not claim that this border is sharp. I claim that it is central to the science that there *is* a border and that the account of perception formation crosses it. At these border crossings, there are non-trivial explanatory invocations of states with representational content—states type-individuated partly by reference to their conditions for veridicality. Non-trivial explanatory invocation of states with representational content (hence veridicality conditions) is an epistemic guide to demarcating genuine represen-tational states from states on which veridicality conditions are imposed and have no explanatory value.

Such non-trivial explanatory invocation of states with veridicality conditions also guides demarcation of perception from mere sensory registration. Perception is constitutively representational—constitutively has representational content with veridicality conditions. Explanations in empirical psychology provide a refined method for distinguishing genuine perceptual representational kinds from sensory kinds that are neither perceptual nor representational. Since per-ception is the most primitive type of state that requires an explanation involving non-trivial appeal to states with veridicality conditions, it is the beginning of representation, conceived in a non-deflationary way.

What we need now is deeper understanding of what makes these explanations empirically fruitful. What are they getting at that yields empirical traction? What can we learn from them about what makes perceptual representation different from mere sensory registration of information? I think that we obtain insight by letting reflection on empirical theory be guided by reflection on the respect in which perception is *objective*.

PERCEPTION AS OBJECTIFICATION

I characterized perception as objective sensory representation by an individual. The notion of objectivity provides the most specific constraint on the type of sensory transactions that count as perceptual. It provides some insight, I think, into how representational accounts in perceptual psychology mark off a psychological kind. Perceptual objectivity helps mark a significant divide between the genuinely representational and the sorts of sensory response that need not be explained in representational terms—terms that invoke veridicality conditions. The perceptual side of this divide constitutes the beginning of the distinctively representational.[32]

---

[32] Two primary marks of mind are consciousness and representation. Science has not mapped relations between these marks. I think it highly likely that consciousness occurs without representation. There is already strong reason (discussed earlier in this chapter) that representation occurs without consciousness. Much more is known about representation than about consciousness. Representational psychology is a rich, growing science. A psychology of consciousness is still in the

The notions of representational content and objectivity are more general than perception. In their generic forms, they can, in a sense, be understood independently of understanding the notion of perception. But the ways in which these notions apply to perception—the forms that representationality and objectification take in perception—cannot be understood independently of understanding perception.

Understanding such generic notions as <u>representational content</u> and <u>objectification</u> depends on understanding *cases* to which the notions apply. Perception is a central case for both generic notions. The constraints that these notions place on perception should not be conceived in terms of classical conceptual analysis. There is reciprocity between understanding the two generic notions and understanding the notion of perception. One understands perception better by understanding explanations in terms of representational content and explanations in terms of objectification. One also understands representational content and perceptual objectification by reflecting on explanations in perceptual psychology. Perceptual constancies, the central instances of perceptual objectification, are not explicable independently of the notion of perception. Parallel points apply to reciprocity between the notions of representational content and perception.

In what way is perception *objective* sensory representation? Here I use 'objective' in a more specific way than the primary way in which I have been using it to apply to representation. In the primary way, I have simply meant *veridical* or *accurate*. Here I intend 'objective' to connote being a product of objectification. *Objectification* is formation of a state with a representational content that is *as of* a subject matter beyond idiosyncratic, proximal, or subjective features of the individual. The relevant subject matter is subject matter that is objective in one or both of the senses laid out in Chapter 2: the subject matter is mind independent, or it is constitutively non-perspectival. Basically, the subject matter is comprised of entities in the physical environment. Objectification, then, is the formation of a representational state that represents the physical environment, beyond the individual's local, idiosyncratic, or subjective features. So my question is: in what way is *perception* sensory representation that derives from objectification?

Objectification resides specifically in the ways perceptual systems overcome proximal stimulation's underdetermination of environmental *representata*, and sensory registration's underdetermination of perceptual representation of those *representata*. What makes perceptual psychology work—what makes explanation in terms of representational states with veridicality conditions fruitful—is the complexity, system, and structure in a sensory system's overcoming the underdetermination problem, described in Chapter 3. Overcoming that problem involves systematically neglecting aspects of sensory registration that are not likely

---

stage of groping for an explanatory method. Thus, at least as psychology is currently constituted, it is only a small exaggeration to say that psychology first gets an explanatory grip where representation begins. Phylogenetically, representation seems to begin among certain arthropods.

to correlate with relevant environmental conditions, and capitalizing on aspects that are likely to correlate, in order to form states that represent there being specific environmental conditions.[33] The formation principles describe and explain these patterns.

In effect, the transformation patterns systematically distinguish the merely proximal from the probably environmental. Such patterns constitute a type of *objectification*. They privilege, and separate out, specific types of environmental conditions, that are individual- and surface-independent and that are not privileged or determined by sensory information. Specification of mind-independent and constitutively non-perspectival physical entities is separated out from the individual's sensory registration—the functioning state that encodes proximal sensory information. Perceptual states are products of such systematic separation and privileging processes. The immediate effects of proximal stimulations are processed to provide a perceptual model of the world, as distinct from mere registration—from mere functioning statistically correlated, causally based encodings—of individuals' surface stimulations.

Objectification here hinges on distinguishing and contrasting, in the operations of the system, what concerns the individual's receptors and what concerns a receptor-independent reality—and doing so in an attribute-specific way. Recall the context in which candidate (relevant alternative) perceptual objects are determined. This is the environmental context in which candidates for perceptual objects are environmental types that the individual responds to in fulfilling basic individual biological functions. Given this context, a systematic distinction, carried out in modular operations within perceptual systems, between what concerns an individual's receptors and what concerns a receptor-independent reality constitutes a type of objectification. The distinction is between registrations on sensory receptors and representations of mind-independent, or perspective-independent, environmental reality.

Some very complex types of explanation of sensory-motor capacities center on receptor registration. There are explanations that attribute capacities to respond differently depending on what combination of surface receptors are stimulated, at what intensities, and at what locations on individuals' bodies. Extremely complex motor activity—for example, the salmon's navigation and other types of navigation to be discussed in Chapter 10—depends on quantitative transformations on these resources: types, intensities, and locations of sensory registration.

Such sensory registration, even together with the quantitative transformations, is not perception. It tends to correlate well with environmental conditions. It functions to enable the individual to respond to environmental conditions in a fine-grained way. But it can be fully explained in its *operation* without appeal to objectification. Relevant *operations* (as distinguished from functions) can be

---

[33] The presence of such filters is established empirically. I leave open whether distinguishing the environmental from initial sensory registration could take some other form.

fully explained without appeal to environmental conditions beyond proximal stimulation, and without appeal to representational states. The operation of such sensory registration does not depend on any distinction between surface sensory registration—including its location, intensity, and bodily distribution—and any specification of an independent environmental condition, as *contrasted* with the condition of surface-receptors. Accounts that postulate averaging or weighting of the effects of proximal stimulation do not attribute objectification, or perceptual representation.

Perception requires systematic transformations from sensory registrations to representational states that are distinctive to *specific* to environmental conditions. Perception requires that law-like patterns in these transformations lead systematically from very different arrays of sensory registration to a range of representational sensory states all of which are representations as of a given environmental attribute. Perception requires perceptual constancies.

Perceptual constancies are capacities for *objectification*. Objectification separates registration of surface stimulation that is local to individual and occasion from elements in that registration that are (according to formation patterns) representationally specific to attributes in the physical environment. Thus objectification separates local, idiosyncratic registrations from representations of individual-independent, occasion-independent, mind-independent, perspective-independent reality, beyond the individual.

Objectification of particulars is guided by this perceptual objectification of environmental attributes. Objectification of particulars consists in separating perceptual occurrences (applications) that refer to environmental particulars from occurrences in a registered sensory array.

"Distance" senses (vision, hearing) offer the most dramatic cases of objectification. But a sense that depends on mechanical contact (touch, proprioception) can also yield objective representation. In visual perception, relevant environmental conditions are almost always distal—at some remove from the sensory receptors. In touch perception, relevant environmental conditions are usually up against individuals' receptors. Touch is colloquially a contact sense. So not all objective perceptual representation yields representation of *distal* conditions.

It should be remarked that not all perceptual *representata* of touch systems are in contact with touch sensors. Mechanical contact can yield touch perception of entities at a distance.[34] Contact is the sensory mode, but the contact sense yields distal perception. Even in touch perception of, and as of, entities in direct contact with the sensors, there remains a distinction between sensory registration and states that represent as of environmental conditions. Perceptual constancies operate in touch perception. The *system* distinguishes specific environmental

---

[34] See discussion of the sand scorpion below, and note 52. Other cases of touch perception through intermediate media—for example, feeling the character of a surface by holding a stick whose far end passes across the surface—are often cited in the literature on touch.

conditions from the informational effects of proximal stimulation on the system's sensors.

A perceptual system, and a perceiver, gain access to environmental conditions only through registration of proximal stimulation—only through states that function to encode, in the sense that they have a high statistical correlation with, a type of proximal stimulus. If a perceptual system is to form accurate representations as of the environment from such registration, it must operate through processes that highlight those aspects of the registration that tend to be signs of specific attributes in the environment. That is, the perceptual system must distinguish specific patterns in the sensory registration that are likely to be adventitious in the context, or idiosyncratic to the subject, from patterns that tend to correlate with specific attributes that are independent of the idiosyncrasies of a particular causal transaction. The formation principles describe and explain stages of this process—the process that distinguishes the merely sensory from the probably environmental. Empirical psychology explains perception in terms of capacities that make this distinction in the formation of representational perceptual states.

This contrastive process is, I think, the primitive objectification distinctive of perception. Objectification lies in marking off states that are *as of* specific system-independent elements in the environment from states idiosyncratic or local to the perceiver. The principles that describe and explain perception formation are centered on this marking-off process. The process is carried out in numerous ways, each specific to some environmental entity. Objectivity is the product of separating what occurs on an individual's sensory surfaces from the significance of those stimulations for specific attributes and particulars in the broader environment. In this way, perception is the product of objectification.

Again, non-perceptual sensory capacities do not exhibit objectification. Non-perceptual sensory capacities do tend to correlate well with relevant environmental entities. Even unprocessed proximal stimulation does so. Proximal stimulation and registration of proximal stimulation carry information that usually is strongly statistically correlated with, and caused by, distal conditions. But the operations of non-perceptual sensory capacities can be explained without adverting to systematic separation of aspects of the proximal encoding as indications of specific aspects of environmental reality beyond the sensory surfaces. The explanation of non-perceptual sensory capacities need not appeal to objectification or to representational contents with veridicality conditions. In non-perceptual cases, correlation with environmental reality is purely a matter of the statistical, nomic, counterfactual, or causal relations between the sensory states and environmental conditions. Commonly, a general type of averaging and weighting system applies to all stimulations. There tends to be nothing in the mathematical transformations that varies with and is specific to different environmental attributes. By contrast, perceptual systems systematically distinguish states relevant to *specific* environmental attributes from surface registration of proximal stimulation.

Before developing the notion of objectification just sketched, I want to make some general remarks about it.

The objectivity of perception should not be denigrated because it is not the context-independent objectivity of theoretical science. Perception is inevitably from the perceiver's perspective. It is constitutively marked by egocentric representational frameworks. Such frameworks take their origins (spatial or temporal, for example) to be particular to the perceiver or some part of the perceiver. They mark the perceiver's present time or place. Moreover, such framework origins are essentially associated with motivational or perspectival matters for the individual. The framework origins of egocentric frameworks are motivationally or perspectivally significant for the perceiver.[35]

Despite its egocentric perspectival aspects, perception embodies a primitive type of objectivity: it refers to particulars in the environment; it attributes specific, indicated attributes to those particulars, sometimes accurately. Moreover, accurate perceptual reference, and accurate perceptual indication and attribution, depend on there being in the perceiver some explanatorily relevant capacity to distinguish contextually local sensory effects on the system from what is independent of the system. This capacity is distinct from merely responding to proximal stimulation in ways that are functionally valuable for the individual.

Perceptual objectivity is, of course, fallible. Any individual or perceptual system can be fooled into representing a natural distal situation as present when only artificial proximal stimulation occurs. The individual and system need not even be *capable* of detecting errors. A visual system might be unable to distinguish a body from a cleverly devised illusion. All an animal's perceptual systems, taken together, might be forever fooled by such illusions.

Perceptual objectification is carried out automatically and unconsciously. It is not intelligent. It is often not even exploratory. It is not an activity by the individual perceiver. It commonly occurs in specialized perceptual subsystems of individuals. The principles according to which the objectification is effected—and the laws or operations described by those principles—reside in the very structure of perceptual systems.

So, as Individual Representationalists required, there is something in *the individual's psychology* that counts as objectification and that makes possible the individual's objective representation. Individual Representationalism erred in requiring that objectification be effected by the *individual*. It erred where it required that objectification involve a *representation* of the distinction between items idiosyncratic to the sensory system and system-independent items.

The individual does not separate sensory surface effects from states that are probably relevant to specific environmental conditions. Modular, subindividual capacities of the perceptual system do that. The individual's perception is the beneficiary and product of objectification. It depends on an objectification

---

[35] For elaboration, see my 'Memory and Persons'.

already effected in the formation of the perception. Perceptual representation depends on objectification's occurring in the very production of the most primitive representational states attributable to system or individual. Objectification is a *subindividual* process.

Moreover, the separation of proximal stimulation from purportedly system-independent items in the environment is *represented* neither by the individual nor by the system. In perception, there is no representation of any distinction between subjective and objective.

The registration of proximal stimulation is not a seeing. It is not representational at all. So the separation is between non-representational registration of stimulation, on one hand, and specification of environmental attributes that are in fact independent of the perceptual system, or of any perspective, on the other. There is no such thing as a perceptual state that represents its own perception, or any other sort of representation in the system.

Even less is there a perceptual state that represents a representation as a seeming. Perceptual perspectives *are* seemings. Perceptual states do not represent themselves or their own modes of presentation. (In fact, I think that the foregoing is a constitutive truth.) Formation operations that separate registrations of proximal stimulation from specific purported environmental conditions—the operations that lead to objectification in perceptual systems—are subindividual and subrepresentational.

The preceding considerations ground my view that *objectified empirical representation precedes subjective representation* both constitutively and phylogenetically.

Sensory registration precedes empirical objectified representation, in both respects. But sensory registration is not representation. Veridicality conditions are not constitutive to registrations or to explanations of them. Sensory registration is not subjective representation.

Similar points apply to non-perceptual, phenomenally conscious sensory states. Phenomenal consciousness may or may not precede perception phylogenetically. I believe that neither phenomenal consciousness nor perception is constitutively necessary to the other. But non-perceptual phenomenally conscious sensory states are not in themselves types of representation. Conscious feels do not in themselves have non-trivial, constitutively associated veridicality conditions. So phenomenal consciousness is not in itself (that is, just by virtue of being phenomenal consciousness) representational. So priority issues between perception and non-perceptual conscious sensory states do not bear on whether objective representation is prior to subjective representation.

I see no other threats to the claim that objectified empirical representation is representationally basic. Representation of a perspective (for example, thoughts about one's perceptions or thoughts) and empirical representation of sensory items that are not a product of objectification (for example, thoughts of one's own particular, occurrent pains) arise only at higher levels. So, constitutively and phylogenetically, objective empirical representation of subject-matter-objective entities is prior to empirical representation of subject-matter-subjective entities. Perception lies at the lower border of empirical representation.[36]

Second-family Individual Representationalism erred in setting the conditions of objectification at too high a cognitive level. It required the perceiver to be able to conceptualize conditions for objectivity in propositional thought. The principles according to which the separation of the proximal-sensory from the environmental is effected—and the law-like patterns described by those principles—are *not* represented or representable, even "implicitly", in perceptual systems.[37] The principles describe psychological laws that effect the separation. The separation is the functional product of the operations of perceptual systems. To represent particulars as having specific physical attributes, the individual need not be able to represent a distinction between appearance and reality, or a distinction between true and false beliefs.

Representing such distinctions constitutes one type of objectification. It is not the type present at origins of objectivity. The type that concerns us is phylogenetically earlier and explanatorily independent. It is carried out in perceivers' subsystems, in ways not conceptually or consciously available to the perceiver. Perceptual systems realize the distinction, without depending on the perceiver to make it. The perceiver need not construct objectivity from more basic resources. The perceiver need not represent general principles, laws, or operations of objectification. (See notes 37, 39–40.) It is enough that a perceiver's perceptual system yields objective representation by systematically filtering effects of

---

[36] All perception is objective in the sense that it *functions* to be accurate of a mind-independent or perspective-independent subject matter. All perception is a product of objectification. Of course, not all perception is objective in the sense of being *accurate* with respect to such subject matters. As a constitutive matter, accurate perception is constitutively prior to inaccurate perception. For perception's representational function is constitutively explained in terms of representational success—accurate perception. Inaccurate perception is constitutively, as well as empirically, explained in terms of conditions that block representational success.

[37] *Principles* describe the transformations in general terms. The laws or operations are patterns in which given transformations are embedded. For some purposes, there is no harm in conflating principles with laws or operations. But doing so carries a danger that I will repeatedly warn against. The danger is that of thinking of the system as "holding", "accessing", or "using" the principles. The danger is not that of homunculus thinking. It is that of taking the system or individual as ("implicitly") having or containing *representations* of (that is, states with representational content specifying) laws or operations—or as having states with the representational contents of the principles. These ways of thinking are common in current philosophical and psychological work. They are mistaken in a pernicious and systematically misleading way. They are, in effect, a recrudescence to Individual Representationalism. I will discuss this mistake shortly. Psychologists state principles that describe laws or operations that embed or determine the transformations among representational states or representational contents instantiated in the system. The system or individual represents *representata* through representational contents. But in perception neither the system nor the individual represents, even implicitly, the laws or operations determining transformations among those representational states. Neither the system nor the individual (in perception) represents its own perceptual states, the transformations among them, or the principles governing such transformations, in the sense that neither system nor individual has any of these items as *representata* or as the representational contents of any perceptual states.

proximal stimulation that are adventitious from effects that are as of specific environmental attributes.

I have been emphasizing that Individual Representationalism was wrong to require, as a condition on objective empirical representation of the physical environment, that the individual be able to represent constitutive conditions on such representation. One might try to reduce the force of this point by claiming that Individual Representationalists erred only in not recognizing that relevant individual representation can be *implicit*. This idea misses the force of the criticism. Individuals need not be able to represent general conditions on objectivity implicitly, unconsciously, or potentially. They need not have the representational resources to do so.

The term '*implicit representation*' is used in various ways. Its main uses apply to unconscious representation or, more strongly, to unconscious representation that is beyond coming to consciousness.[38] There are psychological states that represent implicitly in these senses, perhaps including some perceptual states. I think, however, that none of the key elements in Individual Representationalism is vindicated by appeal to any conception of implicit representation.[39]

Representational contents of perceptual states represent neither relations between the states and the environment, nor constitutive conditions of objectivity.

An important feature of empirical accounts of perception is that the general principles, laws, or operations determining transformations among informational and perceptual states need *not* be represented in the perceptual system (or by the individual) in any way. General principles govern, and the laws or operations that they describe determine, operations of the system. Perceptual systems do not represent the principles, laws, or operations, except in the stretched and misleading sense that they fall under the principles and instantiate the laws and operations.

One reason to reject the idea that perceptual systems "implicitly" represent principles governing transitions within them is that no particular form of the principles is privileged in psychological explanation. Whether the mathematics in a transformation principle is formulated in one or another mathematically equivalent form is irrelevant to explanation. The fine-grained, specific mathematical forms used in quantitative explanations are not aspects of the system's perceptual representation. An individual or perceptual system no more implicitly represents laws determining, or principles governing, transformations of states than the solar system implicitly represents Kepler's or Newton's laws. In both cases, the laws are real. In neither case are they represented by elements of the subject matter governed by the laws.

---

[38] There are different notions of consciousness. I will not discuss these here. My remarks are intended to apply to uses of all notions of consciousness that I regard as acceptable. For more detail, see my 'Reflections on Two Kinds of Consciousness'.

[39] For more on my conception of implicit representation see the exchange in Christopher Peacocke, 'Implicit Conceptions, Understanding, and Rationality' and my 'Concepts, Conceptions, Reflective Understanding: Reply to Peacocke', both in Hahn and Ramberg (eds.), *Reflections and Replies*.

To represent "implicitly" the laws determining perceptual transformations, the system would have to have contents representing not only the mathematical operations contained in the laws. The system would also have to have contents that represent the perceptual states and contents that the laws incorporate. Perceptual systems do not have representational contents of, or as of, their own states or operations, even "implicitly". To perceive, individuals need not *represent* their own perceptual states or operations, even "implicitly".

Principles governing (describing and explaining) transformations among registrational and perceptual states differ from Kepler's or Newton's principles in that they govern *states with representational content*. This fact has encouraged the widespread tendency among philosophers and psychologists to say that the laws or principles are "implicitly" represented. I believe that this tendency usually embodies confusion. The principles are representational in that they govern laws involving representational states. But the principles' or even laws' being representational in these senses is quite different from being represented (being the *representata* of representations) in the system or by the individual perceiver—in any sense. The tendency to count such laws as implicitly represented in the individual is the result of combining unclear thinking, or deflationary notions of representation, with individual representationalist tendencies. The issue surfaces again later in this chapter, and in Chapter 10.

It is worth comparing and contrasting principles governing transformations in perceptual systems with principles and inference rules governing inferential transformations in thought. Embedded in the descriptive principles that help explain propositional inference are, at least sometimes, deductive inference rules that give the form of good inferences. That is, sometimes good deductive inferences are carried out under inference rules that set norms for good deductive inference; and principles governing inference sometimes represent such rules. If *either* descriptive principles governing propositional inference *or* the inference rules themselves are to be represented by an individual, the individual must have the conceptual capacity to think the principle (have the principle as the representational content of a thought) or specify the rule. Such a capacity would require concepts that indicate or refer to representational contents as such. For the descriptive principles generalize over states with propositional representational contents as such; and the inference rules schematically generalize—schematize—representational contents with specific logical forms, as such. The conceptual capacity to think such a descriptive principle or specify an inference rule would also require a capacity to conceptualize what it is to take an inferential step.

I believe that in the cases of *some* individual thinkers, neither descriptive principles that govern those individuals' propositional inferences nor the associated inference rules are represented, or even representable, in the psychologies of those individuals. For example, I believe that some animals engage in propositional inference and lack the conceptual resources to represent the inference rules that in fact govern their inferences. They lack the conceptual capacities to think about propositional representational contents or steps in inference—even unconsciously. It would be a confusion to say that such animals tacitly know or implicitly represent the inference rules. It is enough to say that the propositional inferences are psychologically real, and the inference rules really do figure in the explanations of the inferences—as well as set norms for whether the inferences are valid or not.

There is nothing about the *nature* of inference rules that *prevents* them from being representable, consciously or unconsciously, in an individual's psychology. There is no reason why any inference rule cannot be the content of psychological states in the psychology of a thinker. They could even be written out in some language of thought.[40] Clearly, inference rules are in fact specified in the psychologies of many humans. People often know what the inference rules are, can bring them to consciousness—perhaps with training—and specify them explicitly. They can, in principle, consciously appeal to such rules at each step in carrying out inferences. Perhaps all sufficiently mature humans have the conceptual resources to specify some of the rules by which they carry out inferences. But the mere fact that an individual engages in propositional inference does not entail that the rules are formulated anywhere, even implicitly, in the individual's psychology. I think that in the psychologies of many higher animals that engage in inference, the rules are the contents of no psychological states.

Principles governing transformations in *perceptual* systems are *not the contents* of any perceptual state in an individual. In this respect, perceptual principles are like the principles explaining deductive inference, and the deductive inference rules themselves, that occur in animals whose psychologies lack representational contents to specify those principles or rules. Descriptive perceptual principles help explain transformations in the perceptual system. They are psychologically real in that they specify patterns that occur in perceptual systems. But the content of the principles is not the content of any state in the perceptual system. There is no empirical reason to think that descriptive principles governing perceptual transformations are the representational contents of psychological states in individuals' perceptual systems—even unconsciously or implicitly. Of course, psychologists can make the principles the contents of their states. Human

---

[40] Christopher Peacocke, 'When is a Grammar Psychologically Real?', in A. George (ed.), *Reflections on Chomsky* (Oxford: Basil Blackwell, 1989), 118, claims that it is a consequence of the Lewis Carroll tortoise–hare point about inference that inference rules *cannot* be written down, on pain of regress. In 'Intuitive Mechanics, Psychological Reality and the Idea of a Material Object', Peacocke makes the weaker claim (his note 2) that inference rules *cannot always* be represented, on pain of regress. I think that both of these claims are mistaken. There is no general reason, beyond the psychological incapacities of individuals or species, why inference rules cannot *always* be represented or written down. They just cannot have the form or function of premises. Rules of inference have a form and function specific to them. But they are commonly written down in logical systems, for every case in which they are appealed to. And there is no reason *in principle* why they cannot occur as contents of states in a psychology, accompanying every step of every argument that relies on an inference rule. So the grounds for not attributing the content of rules to all individuals that engage in propositional inference are empirical, not apriori.

reasoners can often specify—implicitly or explicitly—the inference rules by which they infer. In such cases, the principles or inference rules are the contents of *thoughts*, not perceptual states.

The representational contents of perceptual states are partly determined by patterns of causal interrelations, usually in evolutionary history, with attributes in the environment. These causal relations ground explanations of individuals' basic biological functions, principally activities. Explanation individuates kinds of perceptual and actional states in a way that acknowledges the role of environmental attributes in these causal relations. The causal relations supplement the individual's discriminatory abilities to make perceptual content of the perceiver's states specific to attributes in the environment. Discriminative capacities play their role in an already highly structured environmental context. This is the insight of perceptual anti-individualism. Thus objectification in perception is partly beholden to environmental "context" for the nature of its representations and for what it can and does represent. Capacities for sensory discrimination cannot carry the full burden of making representation objective, or of determining what is represented.

To put the point differently: individuals' discriminatory abilities operate in a *restricted* context of environmental alternatives. To represent specific kinds, an individual need not be able to represent principles, laws, or criteria that segment off the kinds from all other kinds consistent with the individual's discriminatory abilities. It is enough that the individual have perceptual capacities that discriminate environmental attributes within ranges that have figured causally in the formation of the states and that are relevant to biological needs and activities.

This point generalizes a point made several times before: the perceiver need not be able to distinguish bodies from philosophically contrived stand-ins. The empirical explanation of the perceptual discriminatory ability counts these cases as irrelevant, non-alternatives.

Thus perceiving an instance of a shape as that shape requires an objectifying capacity. It requires a capacity to discriminate one shape from another. It further requires discriminating shapes from other *relevant* elements in the environment—such as colors, edges, textures. Perceiving bodies as bodies requires discriminating them from events and properties, including the shapes of the bodies. These are *relevant alternatives* in perceptual explanations because they also figure in explanations of individuals' biologically basic functions in fulfilling needs and activities, and because they are relevant to the individuation and formation of perceptual states. The *perceiver* need not be able to discriminate bodies from illusions, proximal stimulation, sensations, abstract kinds, undetached entity parts, and so on. For various empirical reasons, these attributes either do not figure in the causal account of the formation of perceptual states, or they do not figure in natural biological explanations of functional individual needs and activity. The perceiver's objectifying discriminatory abilities determine the nature and content of his perceptual abilities only within this larger environmental and ethological framework.

I turn now from general remarks about objectification to further elaboration of the sense in which perception is *objective* sensory representation. Objective sensory representation represents what is in fact a mind-independent, or perspective-independent, physical subject matter as having some of the attributes that it in fact has.

A perceptual system achieves objectification by—and I am inclined to believe *only by*—exercising *perceptual constancies*—given, of course, the background of relations to the environment through individual functions just sketched.[41] I have mentioned perceptual constancies before. I want to discuss them in more detail.

Perceptual constancies are capacities systematically to represent a particular or an attribute as the same despite significant variations in registration of proximal stimulation. (As always, such formulations are idealized and leave out elements of approximation that are ubiquitous in perceptual systems.) It is understood that these capacities cannot be explained simply as generalized weightings of registration of proximal stimulation. They must involve principles for forming representation of specific environmental particulars and attributes.

The intuitive idea of the constancies is that under different perspectives, a perceiver can represent a given particular or attribute as the same. Perceptual constancy is a theoretical notion. The explications that I give are not definitions. As definitions, they would be circular. The constancies are structured abilities to mark off *in perception* differences in registration of proximal stimulations, and differences in perspective, that correspond to differences in perception of, and as of, the same *representatum*. Differences in registrations of proximal stimulation that correspond to adaptation or desensitization do not count.[42] Processings of

---

[41] Perceptual constancies have been studied from Helmholtz onward. See Helmholtz, *Treatise on Physiological Optics*, especially volume ii, section 24; E. Hering, *Outlines of a Theory of the Light Sense* (1878), trans. L. M. Hurvich and D. Jameson (Cambridge, MA: Harvard University Press, 1964); K. Bühler, *Handbuch der Psychologie* I, 1 (Jena, 1922). The constancies figured prominently in the gestalt psychology of Wertheimer, Köhler, and Koffka. See Koffka, *Principles of Gestalt Psychology*, chapter 6; R. H. Thouless, 'Phenomenal Regression to the "Real" Object', *British Journal of Psychology* 21 (1931), 339–359. Egon Brunswik, whose quotation heads this chapter, worked on constancies in the 1920s through the 1940s, culminating in his *Perception and the Representative Design of Psychological Experiments* (1947; Berkeley and Los Angeles: University of California Press, 1956). See also David Katz, *The World of Touch* (1924), ed. and trans. Lester E. Krueger (Hillsdale, NJ: Lawrence Erlbaum, 1989). Interesting reviews of histories of studies of particular constancies are: Helen E. Ross and Cornelis Plug, 'The History of Size Constancy and Size Illusions', in Vincent Walsh and Janusz Kulilowski (eds.), *Perceptual Constancy* (Cambridge: Cambridge University Press, 1998); and Alan L. Gilchrist and Vidal Annan Jr., 'Articulation Effects in Lightness: Historical Background and Theoretical Implications', *Perception* 31 (2002), 141–150.

[42] M. J. Weissburg, 'Chemo- and Methanosensory Orientation by Crustaceans in Laminar and Turbulent Flows: From Odor trails to Vortex Streets', in M. Lehrer (ed.), *Orientation and Communication in Arthropods* (Basle: Birkhauser Verlag, 1997), 238: 'To be effective, sensory systems must take advantage of the information present in natural signals. Reliance on properties of odor pulses rather than average concentration is a manifestation of sensory systems well adapted to environment. Sensory systems must also filter out extraneous information to maximize signal to noise ratio.' Such screening does not constitute a perceptual constancy. The screening must be structurally specific to an attribute, and cannot be a weighting or averaging of sensory registrations.

proximal stimulation that are explainable in complex quantitative terms, but that do not involve specifically perceptual capacities, do not count.

Perceptual constancies show up saliently in behavior. They are recognized in empirical theory. They are the primary mark of perceptual objectification.[43, 44]

Perceptual constancies are commonly evinced by an individual's acting toward an attribute in the same way under a wide range of stimulations. Perceptually tracking the attribute involves coordinating different ways of attributing the attribute, all representing the same attribute *as* that attribute.

Various constancies occur in the visual perceptual systems of animals. *Size constancy* in a visual system is the capacity to represent an object's size as the same even as the stimulus from the object affects a smaller or larger proportion of the visual field—for example, while it moves closer to or farther away from the viewer. *Shape constancy* is a capacity to represent a given shape under various stimulus and perspectival conditions. A circular pattern can be seen as circular whether it is viewed head on or at an angle. A spinning irregular object can be seen as having the same three-dimensional shape even as the proximal stimulation that it causes changes significantly. *Distance constancy* is a capacity to

---

[43] Ernst Cassirer, 'The Concept of Group and the Theory of Perception', *Philosophy and Phenomenological Research* 5 (1944), 1–35—a translation of an article published in French in 1938—advocates the importance of perceptual constancies in understanding perception. This article, written after the second-family individual representationalist work by Cassirer discussed in Chapter 4, recognizes perceptual constancies in various animals and takes the constancies to be a primitive sort of objectification. Cassirer sometimes describes the constancies as *our* construction of reality out of appearances (whether the idealist formulation is intended, I do not know). He also hedges on whether reference to an object is realizable in perception apart from intellectual concepts and schemata. In these respects, his view remains individual representationalist. On the other hand, his recognition of constancies in many animals points beyond his older positions. In these respects, as in others, Cassirer was ahead of his philosophical contemporaries.

[44] I propose perceptual constancies as a mark of perception in 'Perceptual Entitlement', section II, and in 'Perception'. A recent philosophical work that independently takes perceptual constancy to be a mark of at least a primary group of perceptual abilities is A. D. Smith, *Perception* (Cambridge, MA: Harvard University Press, 2002). I saw Smith's book after developing my ideas in the mid- to late 1990s and after publishing the cited articles. Smith's use of perceptual constancies is different from mine. It is embedded in a predominantly phenomenological point of view that, in my judgment, cannot provide a fundamental account of perceptual representational content, unless it is supported much more fully by a discussion of the anti-individualist underpinnings of such content. The very notion of perceptual constancy that Smith uses is explained in phenomenological terms. This explanation takes the notion out of its explanatory context in psychological theory. Smith's notion of perceptual constancy does not apply in any case in which phenomenology is lacking. As noted in the section PERCEPTION AS THE INDIVIDUAL's above, there are numerous cases of perceptual constancies without phenomenal consciousness.

Still, Smith's book is a good one. The book is concerned mainly with the procrustean 'argument from illusion' that is supposed to show that we do *not* in the first instance make reference in perception to entities in the physical environment. I think that no modern psychologist would find the argument of much interest, and I believe that it does not provide a serious philosophical challenge. I agree with Smith's rejection of it. I agree, in particular, that the argument rests on an errant conception of perceptual object or perceptual reference. My reservations about his account of the argument concern his sympathy for disjunctivism—which is, as shown in my 'Disjunctivism and Perceptual Psychology', and the section PERCEPTION AS REPRESENTATION above, incompatible with scientific knowledge—and his appeal to 'intentional objects' (in the sense of Brentano).

represent a perceived entity as at a given distance, under various types of stimulation deriving from various types of entities perceived. *Motion constancy* is the capacity to represent an entity as in motion under such variations in proximal stimulation as those caused by the perceiver's being in motion or being still. *Color constancy* is the capacity to represent a color as the same under various conditions, including different illuminations.

Color constancy is widespread though far from ubiquitous in visual perceptual systems. All the spatial constancies are present in most animal visual perceptual systems.

The constancies are expressions of objectification. Not all selectivity with respect to registration of proximal stimulation constitutes the formation operation involved in a perceptual constancy. Some neglect or filtering of noise occurs in any well-functioning sensory system, perceptual or not. Non-perceptual sensory systems suppress some information in a signal to respond to information useful to the organism. Heightened responsiveness to aspects of a signal is one product of conditioning. All animals, no matter how simple, can adapt through habituation or conditioning. All such adaptation occurs under the pressure of objective circumstances. Adaptation in protozoa is as much under such pressure as learning in organisms with perceptual systems.

Genuine perceptual systems are distinctive in exhibiting structure and system in the formation operations and in the specificity of those operations to various environmental attributes. Systematic, repeatable, usually diverse principles for objectification fitted to specific attributes in the environment mark the competencies of a perceiver. These structures differ from the generalized weighting and averaging techniques characteristic of sophisticated non-perceptual sensory systems. Perceptual learning also differs from the serial, piecemeal, averaging adjustment to proximal stimulation in adaptive sensory systems that lack perception. Such structure, system, and specificity are marks of perceptual objectification.

Of course, the complexity, system, and structure must be explained as yielding perceptual states that are approximately accurate or inaccurate of environmental reality. Those are the primitive notions, not the notions that I am using to isolate and explicate them.

There are surely borderline cases between perceptual systems and sensory systems that merely register information. What is empirically striking is that different forms of explanation are fruitful in the two cases. For sensory systems that merely register information, explanations center on the discriminative sensitivity to proximal stimulation, the neural pathways of stimulations, the weighting among sensory registrations on different bodily sensors, the types of conditioning and adaptation, the role of stimulations in producing or modifying activity, the structural correspondences in the sensory system to environmental conditions, and the role of the system in species preservation.

One can count a sensory registration inaccurate if one wants. But doing so comes to no more than noting that the sensory state instance did not serve the organism's needs.[45] We do not need a notion of veridicality condition to explain a paramecium's or snail's sensory system. Veridicality conditions and perceptual constancies play no role in the explanation.

The biological and information-theoretic forms of explanation that apply to non-perceptual systems remain applicable to perceptual systems. But an additional type of explanation is explanatory, as well. This type appeals to representational content as marking conditions for veridicality—in this case, perceptual accuracy. Veridicality is success in fulfilling not a biological function, but a representational function.[46] Representational success and failure are not to be identified with biological or practical success or failure. Perceptual success (failure) is distinctive in fulfilling (or failing to fulfill) representational function. The applicability of this type of explanation is supported by the system and specificity found in the objectifying capacities present in the perceptual constancies.

The reader can get a fuller sense of perceptual constancies by reconsidering explanations in visual psychology sketched in Chapter 8, the section PERCEPTUAL PSYCHOLOGY AND THE DISTINCTION BETWEEN SENSORY INFORMATION REGISTRATION AND PERCEPTION. Convergence is one of several capacities for producing distance and location constancies. The account of the principles governing separation of lightness from illumination describes operations for producing lightness constancy—a simpler cousin of color constancy. The slant-from-texture account concerns both distance and surface-orientation constancies. The effect of image region convexity on perception of absolute, metric depth isolates a component in perceptual processing that yields depth constancies.

Perceptual constancies give empirical point to a distinction between perspective and subject matter. We have seen this distinction earlier, in the section PERCEPTION AS REPRESENTATION. Representational content or mode of presentation is to be distinguished from subject matter. Any perceivable particular, property, relation, or kind can be perceptually represented in many ways, constituting different perceptual perspectives on the *representatum*. In all cases of perceptual constancies, this multiplicity of perspectives on a given subject matter emerges. Constancies are the perceptual analog of Fregean informative identities. A given perceptual *representatum* (kind, property, relation, or particular) is represented as that *representatum*, even as it is presented in different ways, from different perceptual perspectives. These differences in perspective and representational content, or perceptual mode of presentation, are caused by variations in sensory registration of proximal stimulation.

Suppose that in the exercise of color constancy, I see as red a surface that is illuminated evenly by white light. Suppose that I see as the same shade of red a different surface that is illuminated unevenly by a blue light. Both surfaces look

---

[45] As emphasized in Chapter 8, mistake cannot be explained in terms of failures of biological function, or any other practical failure.

[46] See Chapter 8 and my 'Perceptual Entitlement', sections I and II.

to have the same color. I see them as the same color. But the ways the red shade looks to have that color are different. The same surface shade of red is presented, even in conscious experience, differently.[47] Thus, although the computations that lead to the two perceptual states are subindividual and unconscious, although they yield perceptual states that are *as of* the same color shade (and that will be seen that way without thinking), the constancy depends on capacities to coordinate different ways of representing the same color shade as that shade. Each mode of representation, each different representational content, indicates the same color shade. The individual perceiver perceives the different instances *as* instances of the same color shade through different modes of presentation of it, different representational contents (perceptual attributives) marking different types of perceptual states.

Of course, there are sometimes mistaken identifications in exercises of the constancies. There is perhaps no surprise or news for the individual that the colors attributed in exercises of perceptual constancies are the same, when they are the same. But when they are veridically perceived as the same, the sameness is not "logically" guaranteed; and sometimes perceptual errors occur. Veridical representation as of the constant color shade under different modes of presentation is a perceptual accomplishment. For the modes of presentation involved in perceptual constancies are different. The different ways in which a given color shade are perceived as the same shade are usually available to the individual's phenomenal consciousness.

The constancies emphatically do not depend on knowledge or conceptual understanding. Perceptual errors that occur in exercise of the constancies are not errors of judgment. Exercises of constancies, both veridical and erroneous, occur in simple animals that lack any such higher capacities. The perceiver, qua perceiver, need not *think* the identities. Rather, the perceiver perceives different instances of an attribute as instances of the same attribute; or the perceiver tracks a given particular as the same particular over time. The individual's capacity to capitalize on perceptual constancies depends, of course, on the individual's perceptual system's computational operations. The computations track both the invariant, constant element and some of the different elements that vary with stimulus conditions. Where a constancy centers on an attribute, different perceptual attributives, formed from different registrations of proximal stimulation, commonly indicate and attribute the same attribute. Where a constancy centers on a concrete particular, different singular perceptual applications (or a single application maintained in a trans-temporal file) refer to, or refer to there being, the same particular—even as attributions to the particular change.

---

[47] Often, as in this case, the difference in mode of presentation involves perception of, and as of, other environmental attributes. For example, one sees the color shade as the same, but one also sees the illumination of the surface as different. However, differences in modes of presentation of one attribute are not always associated in representation of, or as of, differences in other attributes. See Chapter 8, note 97.

Perceptually different representational contents, associated with different perspectives and caused by different proximal stimulations or indexed to different times, represent *for the individual and for the system* the same environmental attribute or particular. The different representational contents constitute different modes of presentation. They help mark or type-individuate different psychological states. But the different psychological states all represent the same *representatum* for the system and individual. So one of the most basic aspects of representation—the difference between the entity represented and the way of representing it, the representational content—is entailed by perceptual constancies.

Perceptual constancies are paradigmatic marks of objectification. I think that their presence in a sensory system is necessary and sufficient for the system's being a perceptual system. Their presence is certainly sufficient for perception and objectivity, at least given the environmental and individual–functional background discussed earlier in this chapter and in Chapter 8.[48] I conjecture that they are also necessary. Since they are not characterized independently of the notions <u>representation</u> and <u>perception</u>, one cannot use the notion <u>perceptual constancy</u> as an independent 'criterion' to determine when one has a case of genuine perceptual representation and when one has a case of non-representational sensory registration. Empirical theory must draw the distinction and identify cases of perceptual constancy. Still, it seems to me that in a rough, non-criterial way, perceptual constancies are necessary as well as sufficient for perceptual objectification and perceptual representation.

Sensory objectification can be intermodal—*non-autonomous* for a system. Objectification can occur when different sensory systems compensate for each other's limitations. So 'triangulation' occurs between different systems. Then objectified representation resides in intermodal systems of representation.

For example, vision can rely on the vestibular system to yield objectification. When exposed to a laterally tilted, fronto-parallel luminous line in a dark room, a human subject can perceive the slope of the line to a good approximation. When the head is laterally inclined, the vertical line projects an image on the retina quite different from the one it projects if the head is upright. If the visual system were to rely solely on the optic channel, even including proprioceptive information that correlates with eye movement (as it can in solving many other perceptual problems), it could not distinguish this situation from one in which the body remains upright but the line is tilted. Individuals can make this distinction. This capacity is usually called 'vertical constancy'. It is a purely intermodal

---

[48] The environmental background can figure proleptically, or potentially, as well as in evolutionary history. The point is that the perceptual constancies must be associated with some need or use associated with the nature of the system. It is in principle possible for an *individual* perceiver to lack such need or use, though such cases probably do not occur in nature. I do not require that there be spatial constancies. See Chapter 10, the section PERCEPTION AND ORIGINS OF SPATIAL REPRESENTATION.

constancy. The vestibular system combines with the visual system to yield the constancy.[49]

Many similar constancies occur in the touch system, which commonly relies on proprioception. For example, as one moves one's hand or arm over a corner of a chair, the corner is felt as being in the same place. The touch system relies on a continuing proprioceptive body image, onto which touch information derived from the movement of one's hand or arm is mapped. Here position constancy is achieved with respect to the surface of the corner of the chair, through the cooperation of the touch system with the proprioceptive system.[50]

These points bring out that a perceptual system need not be autonomously perceptual in all its perceptual aspects. Vision and touch often rely on proprioception to achieve constancies. Touch often relies upon vision. And so on. Still, many constancies are specific to the workings of single perceptual modalities.

I have centered on vision as a prime example of perception. Visual perceptual systems are the most impressively complex perceptual systems. They are also the most intensively studied. More is known about them than about other perceptual systems. But vision is not the only type of perception. Touch, hearing, and that grab-bag, proprioception, can exhibit autonomous perceptual capacities, and perceptual constancies, as well.

The touch system is capable of representing a given texture (say, the texture of velvet as contrasted with that of linen or even satin) as the same even though the texture is rubbed against different parts of the body. Different body parts have substantially different sensitivities. So the registrations of proximal stimulation in the different rubbings are quite different. The perception is nonetheless as of the same texture. This capacity is texture constancy. Active touch can identify three-dimensional shapes. It exhibits some of the geometrical perceptual constancies.[51]

Touch systems can yield representation of entities located at a distance. For example, the sand scorpion's system uses differences in timing of the arrival of vibrations through the sand to each of its eight legs to instantiate a computation of the location of a disturbance in the sand.[52] Spiders probably use such means to locate prey in their webs.

Hearing in many animals, notably owls and humans, is capable of relatively accurate localization of the source of sound in a single sensory representation. This capacity exhibits distance and location constancies. These constancies operate under principles analogous to forms of triangulation in binocular vision,

[49] N. Bischof, 'Optic-Vestibular Orientation to the Vertical', in H. H. Kornhuber (ed.), *Handbook of Sensory Physiology*, vol. VI/2, *Vestibular System Part 2: Psychophysics, Applied Aspects and General Interpretations* (Berlin: Springer-Verlag, 1974), 157.

[50] Katz, *The World of Touch*, 84. Body images are commonly representational. Here the term 'image' has its common-sense representational implications.

[51] Ibid. 85; R. L. Klatzky, S. J. Lederman, and V. A. Metzger, 'Identifying Objects by Touch: An Expert System', *Perception & Psychophysics* 37 (1985), 299–302; M. Taylor-Clarke, P. Jacobsen, and P. Haggard, 'Keeping the World a Constant Size', *Nature Neuroscience* 7 (2004), 219–220.

[52] Brownell, 'Prey Detection by the Sand Scorpion'; discussed in Gallistel, *The Organization of Learning*, 110–112.

such as convergence and disparity. Bats and dolphins emit high-frequency sounds that reflect off objects in the environment. The return echoes help to locate prey. For bats, the prey can be as small as insects.[53]

The chemical senses (smell and taste) seem largely to be non-perceptual sensory systems, unless they are supplemented by input from other sources. Constancies are not prominent in the workings of these senses. Although we humans can locate, map, and remember areas occupied by certain smells, these abilities seem to rely partly on homing capacities that are not perceptual, or on other senses or conceptual capacities. There is, I think, objectification in humans' determining quality and type of the taste of food or wine. The food is taken to have a taste, in addition to its producing a taste on the tongue. This objectification seems to depend on conceptual association and conceptual memory. I see no apriori reason why smell and sensory taste could not be largely perceptual systems. The reasons why they are not seem to be empirical.

The main reason why objectification is not prominent in olfactory systems lies in the changing and relatively amorphous character of the chemical blends carried in air or, for fish, in water. Proximal registration of a chemical blend, together with registration of intensity and distribution of registrations on the body, suffice for most purposes.

Under certain limited conditions, location constancy through single or relatively short-term sensory registrations, hence perceptual objectification, is in principle possible for olfaction.[54] Such conditions may well be realized in certain species. I think, however, that most animals that locate food or other targets by smell do so by the following technique, which does not make use of perception. They first register direction through intensities on one or another side of the body. Then they use a homing or beaconing technique that serially follows directional intensity (determined by relative intensities on one or another side of the body) of a favored odor to the target. This technique is widespread. It enables numerous animals to use a *non-perceptual* sense to locate targets. I discuss this homing technique three sections hence, and in Chapter 10, the section PERCEPTION AND ORIGINS OF SPATIAL REPRESENTATION.

With taste, the relevant chemical mixes are proximal ones, in the mouth. Would-be taste profiles, beyond what meets the surfaces of the mouth, do not

[53] A. N. Popper and R. R. Fay, *Hearing in Bats* (New York: Springer-Verlag, 1995); J. A. Simmons, 'Directional Hearing and Sound Localization in Echolocating Animals', in W. A. Yost and G. Gourevitch (eds.), *Directional Hearing* (New York: Springer-Verlag, 1987). For a more general discussion, see William A. Yost, 'Auditory Localization and Scene Perception', in E. Bruce Goldstein (ed.), *Blackwell Handbook of Perception* (Oxford: Blackwell, 2001).

[54] J. J. Hopfield, 'Olfactory Computation and Object Perception', *Proceedings of the National Academy of Science* 88 (1991), 6462–6466. See also J. J. Hopfield, 'Pattern Recognition Computation Using Action Potential Timing for Stimulus Representation', *Nature* 376 (1995), 33–36. For an overview of the exquisite complexity of the processing problems involved in this largely *non-perceptual* chemical sense, see R. I. Wilson and Z. F. Mainen, 'Early Events in Olfactory Processing', *Annual Review of Neuroscience* 29 (2006), 163–201; M. Stopfer, V. Jayaraman, and G. Laurent, 'Intensity versus Identity Coding in an Olfactory System', *Neuron* 39 (2003), 991–1004.

seem sufficiently important to animal well-being to have forced evolution of constancy capacities for determining such taste profiles in gustatory systems. At least, I know of no such capacities. Of course, distal profiles can be developed by supplementing taste with conceptualizations. We and perhaps other animals develop such objectification. But objectification seems not to reside in the sensory system itself.

Ordinary language sometimes portrays the taste of wine or the smell of banana as perception. Such cases are usually to be assimilated to belief and propositional memory derived from non-perceptual sensory states. The representation is not at the purely sensory level. The sensory system responds to certain types of proximal stimulation that in fact come from such things as wine or bananas. Discriminations can be either generic or fine-grained. But, except for the special cases noted with respect to smell, I know of no perceptual constancies in the gustatory or olfactory sensory systems themselves. Scientific accounts of their operations do not, for the most part, make non-trivial appeal to sensory states with veridicality conditions. I believe that ordinary language tends to blur natural psychological kinds.

A similar point applies to sensors of heat and cold in the skin. The stories here are complex. But these sensory systems seem not to be perceptual, or prominently perceptual. Like pain sensors, these sensors provide signals from proximal stimulation that register information that correlates with effects on the animal body. There is no systematic distinguishing between objective sources of information and sensory effects of conditions in the individual. The heat and cold sensors are sensitive to fast changes in heat and cold, to danger levels, and to relative differences in heat and cold stimulations. Constancy capacities are not prominent.[55]

I hope to have provided some understanding of objectification in perceptual systems, and of the way objectification helps distinguish those systems from non-perceptual sensory systems.

PERCEPTION AS OBJECTIFICATION AS OPPOSED TO PERCEPTION AS EXTRACTION OF FORM

The emphasis on objectification and the perceptual constancies as marks of perception is usefully contrasted with another conception. In the gestalt tradition and in occasional remarks by modern perceptual psychologists, it is sometimes said that perception is distinguished from sensory registration in that it involves

---

[55] See Kathleen Akins, 'Of Sensory Systems and the "Aboutness" of Mental States', *The Journal of Philosophy* 93 (1996), 337–372; Herbert Hensel, *Thermal Sensations and Thermoreceptors in Man* (Springfield, IL: Charles C. Thomas, 1982). Akins and her article helped spark my interest in sensory physiology and the variety of sensory systems.

extraction of form. I believe that this is an interesting conception, which is not quite adequate for interesting reasons.

Capacities to abstract from sensory cues in ways that function to respond to typical regularities, especially those of shape or motion, are striking aspects of perception. It is natural to group amodal completion along with perceptual constancy as a mark of perception. Amodal completion is a capacity to perceptually represent an entity as whole or completed, even though less than the whole entity causally affects the sensory apparatus. An example of amodal completion in vision is a capacity to see an entity as extended behind an occlusion, usually as complete as regards shape, texture, and color. Similarly, a capacity to perceptually anticipate the continuation of a path of motion is an extraction of form that goes beyond what is strictly present in sensory registrations. A similar phenomenon occurs in the perceptual projections and illusions associated with Kanizsa triangles.[56] The sensory capacity projects beyond what is strictly given in sensory registrations to represent, or register, typical regularities in the physical environment. See Figure 9.1.

Of course, even visual perception represents matters besides "forms"—color, for example. And the notion of extraction of form seems less relevant to some aspects of auditory and touch perception than it does to visual perception. So the conception of perception as extraction of form may not cover all cases.

Perhaps this difficulty could be overcome. I will not dwell on this issue, because I think that there is a more basic difficulty.

All the examples of extraction of form that I cited were described in perceptual terms—'perceptually represent', 'see an entity as', 'perceptually anticipate', 'perceptual projections and illusions'. In itself, this is no problem. The characterization need not be taken as a definition. It could simply cite what is paradigmatic and central about perception. Understood that way, the conception seems to me to be interesting. Such phenomena do mark central aspects of perception. But the extraction-of-form conception applies too broadly. There are cases of "extraction of form" that are not cases of perception.

---

[56] Kanizsa triangles are virtual triangles strongly suggested by surrounding configurations. The area of the triangle on a white surface usually appears whiter than the ground, even if it is not. See Gaetano Kanizsa, *Organization in Vision: Essays in Gestalt Perception* (New York: Praeger, 1979), chapter 1, 'Two Ways of Going Beyond the Information Given', and chapter 5, 'The Role of Regularity in Perceptual Organization'. For discussion of relations between amodal completion and the perceptual phenomena exemplified by Kanizsa triangles, see Palmer, *Vision Science*, 288–296. Neither Kanizsa nor Palmer proposes the characterization of perception presented here.

Palmer defines visual perception as 'the process of acquiring knowledge about environmental objects and events by extracting information from the light they emit or reflect' (p. 5). I find Palmer's invocation of knowledge too vague to be helpful. Visual perception often does not yield knowledge, even if one takes 'knowledge' to include non-propositional phenomena. I also find the notion of extraction of information too broad. Even the visual systems of simple animals whose eye cups cannot form images extract information from the light emitted by objects. Nothing in the definition helps one understand whether the information thus extracted is "about" entities in the environment. Nothing distinguishes perception from non-perceptual sensory registration in an illuminating way.

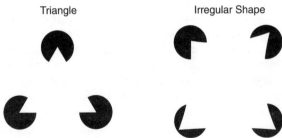

FIGURE 9.1 Kanizsa triangles and irregular figures. The figures illustrate amodal completion. The visual system tends to "fill in" the missing lines to produce white surfaces framed by the black figures. The irregular figure on the right illustrates that the phenomenon does not occur only with regular figures. The contour of the lines in the figure on the right are filled in as smooth best-continuations of the lines marked by the edges of the black figures. The white surfaces of the triangle and irregular figure tend to look slightly brighter than the surrounding white region.

Responses to continuities and regularities in the environment that are not full causes of sensory registration occur at low levels of pre-perceptual sensory registration. Imagine a very simple non-perceptual visual or touch system. The visual system is habituated to a luminance contour by being stimulated by light coming from the edge of a cube. (Recall that luminance contours are patterns of contrasting non-perceptual sensory registrations.) The touch system is habituated to the impress of a thin stick. A given pattern of neurons corresponding to the receptors repeatedly fires during habituation. Now suppose that the luminance contour is broken. Only the first two-fifths and last two-fifths of the light pattern coming from the cube's edge are allowed to affect the visual sensors that were affected before. Similarly, suppose that the stick is broken and only substantial parts of the stick are impressed on the skin, where those parts were impressed before. Then, in some situations, substantially the whole bank of neurons that fired in response to the original, unbroken stimulation will fire—even though only some of the corresponding receptors are stimulated. The sensory registration is substantially the same in broken and unbroken cases. In such cases, sensory registration engages in a kind of form completion. But the sensory registration need not yield sensory perception.

Pattern or form completion occurs at the most rudimentary sensory level. No representational content grounds explanation of the phenomenon. No objectification that distinguishes proximal stimulation from objective environmental affairs need be in play. Such a low-level sensory process can reasonably be construed as an extraction of form, unless the latter notion is supplemented to insure that representational contents and objectification are involved.

Retinotopic pattern matching and responsiveness to form at the level of retinal stimulation occurs in low-level aspects of many visual systems. For example, in some cases, the visual systems of bees respond to retinal impresses from the shapes of landmarks, without utilizing shape constancies, or other perceptual constancies. The bee flies to a position where it receives a stored retinal impress from a landmark. Then a further stage in its navigational procedure is triggered. In such cases, even if the retinal impress from the landmark is broken in some ways, the bee's sensory system will complete the sensory template. In such cases, no visual perception need be involved. The bee's visual system, in solving *this particular task*, does not form a visual representational model of any aspect of its environment. It relies purely on the prototypical retinal registration of proximal stimulation.[57] Such reliance could be counted an extraction of form. It is not visual perception.

PHYLOGENETIC DISTRIBUTION OF PERCEPTUAL SYSTEMS

I want to say a little about what is known about the perceptual systems of animals. These remarks may suggest the spread and primitiveness of perceptual objectivity.

Some arthropods have visual perceptual systems. Much of the work on the perceptual systems of arthropods concentrates on bees.[58] There is also remarkable work on the visual perceptual systems of locusts and spiders, principally jumping spiders. Bees have fairly good color vision, with color constancy. Bees, some spiders, locusts, and praying mantises have distance and location constancy. Bees and jumping spiders have size and motion constancy.[59]

---

[57] This description of the bee's visual capacities closely corresponds to what is known about bees' visual response to large distant landmarks. Bees do have visual perception. But many problems are solved by non-perceptual aspects of bees' visual systems. For discussion of vision in bee navigation, see Chapter 10, the section PERCEPTION AND ORIGINS OF SPATIAL REPRESENTATION.

[58] Ants rely largely on olfaction. I think that olfaction is in most respects not a perceptual sense.

[59] Georgii A. Mazokhin-Porshnyakov, *Insect Vision*, trans. R. and L. Masironi (New York: Plenum, 1969); 'Recognition of Colored Objects by Insects', in C. G. Bernhard (ed.), *The Functional Organization of the Compound Eye* (Oxford: Pergamon Press, 1966); Randolf Menzel, 'Spectral Sensitivity and Color Vision in Invertebrates', in H. Autrum (ed.), *Comparative Physiology and Evolution of Vision in Invertebrates: Invertebrate Receptors* (Berlin: Springer Verlag, 1979); Christa Neumeyer, 'Comparative Aspects of Color Constancy', in Walsh and Kulikowski (eds.), *Perceptual Constancy*; Wehner, 'Spatial Vision in Arthropods'; M. Lehrer, M. V. Srinivasan, S. W. Zhang, and G. A. Horridge, 'Motion Cues Provide the Bee's Visual World with a Third Dimension', *Nature* 332 (1988), 356–357; G. A. Horridge, S. W. Zhang, and M. Lehrer, 'Bees Can Combine Range and Visual Angle to Estimate Absolute Size', *Philosophical Transactions of the Royal Society London* B337 (1992), 49–57; M. Lehrer, 'Spatial Vision in the Honeybee: The Use of Different Cues in Different Tasks', *Vision Research* 34 (1994), 2363–2385; Miriam Lehrer, 'Shape Perception in the Honeybee: Symmetry as a Global Framework', *International Journal of Plant Sciences* 160 (1999), S51–S65; Stimson Wilcox and Jackson, 'Cognitive Abilities of Araneophagic Jumping Spiders'; Rainer F. Foelix, *Biology of Spiders* (Oxford: Oxford University Press, 1996), 87–92. Collett, 'Peering'; Karl Kral, 'Behavioral–Analytical Studies of the Role of Head Movements in Depth Perception in Insects, Birds and Mammals', *Behavioral Processes* 64 (2003), 1–12.

The visual systems of many birds have the basic spatial constancies, and in some species color constancies. Much of the study of the visual systems of birds centers on their navigation in homing and migration. Birds use not just vision but various other senses, such as olfaction and sensitivity to magnetic fields. Nevertheless, many birds have visual representation of spatial relations, involving spatial constancies. As mentioned before, object constancy occurs in chicks and various other birds.[60]

Work on the visual systems of reptiles, amphibians, fish, and cephalopods is more limited. Basic constancies utilizing spatial representations have, however, been demonstrated in the visual systems of frogs, fish, and octopi.[61]

The visual systems of non-human mammals are in fundamental respects similar to those of humans. They tend not to be as acute or as versatile. Nevertheless, they exhibit all the primary visual constancies that human vision does.[62]

I have concentrated on the phylogenetic distribution of *visual* perceptual systems. Although vision is the most impressive and thoroughly studied perceptual system, there are others. Many types of hearing—for example, in barn owls—exhibit location constancy. In owls, non-horizontal placement of the ears and inter-aural phase and time differences in reception of sound by the two ears make such localization possible. Human hearing operates under broadly similar principles for comparably accurate sound-source localization. The principles for parallax estimation resemble those used for localization by vision through convergence or disparity.[63] Similar sorts of localization occur in various sonar systems in bats, dolphins, whales, and other animals.[64]

Triangulation and timing are also used in touch sense-perceptual systems. As noted, the touch system of the sand scorpion uses differences in timing of the arrival of vibrations through the sand to each of its eight legs to instantiate a

[60] W. Wiltschko and R. Wiltschko, 'Magnetic Orientation and Celestial Cues in Migratory Orientation', in P. Berthold (ed.), *Orientation in Birds* (Basel: Birkhauser Verlag, 1991); P. Berthold, 'Spatiotemporal Aspects of Avian Long-Distance Migration', in S. Healy (ed.), *Spatial Representation in Animals* (Oxford: Oxford University Press, 1998); Pepperberg and Funk, 'Object Permanence in Four Species of Psittacine Birds'; Wiltschko and Wiltschko, 'The Navigation System of Birds and its Development'; Regolin, Vallortigara, and Zanforlin, 'Detour Behavior in the Domestic Chick'; Neumeyer, 'Comparative Aspects of Color Constancy'; Irene Maxine Pepperberg, *The Alex Studies* (Cambridge, MA: Harvard University Press, 2002), chapter 10; B. Pollok, H. Prior, and O. Guntrukun, 'Development of Object Permanence in Food-Storing Magpies (*Pica pica*)', *Journal of Comparative Psychology* 114 (2000), 148–157.

[61] Ingle, 'Perceptual Constancies in Lower Vertebrates'; D. Ingle, 'Shape Recognition in Vertebrates', in R. Held, H. Liebowitz, and H. Teuber (eds.), *Handbook of Sensory Physiology*, viii (Berlin, Springer Verlag, 1978); V. A. Braithwaite, 'Spatial Memory, Landmark Use and Orientation in Fish', in Healy (ed.), *Spatial Representation in Animals*.

[62] Hauser, 'Expectations about Object Motion and Destination'; E. S. B. Oucet and C. Thinus-Blanc, 'Landmark Use and the Cognitive Map in the Rat', in Healy (ed.), *Spatial Representation in Animals*; Neumeyer, 'Comparative Aspects of Color Constancy'.

[63] Georg M. Klump, 'Sound Localization in Birds', in Robert J. Dooling, Richard R. Fay, and Arthur N. Popper (eds.), *Comparative Hearing: Birds and Reptiles* (New York: Springer-Verlag, 2000).

[64] H.-U. Schnitzler and O. W. Henson Jr., 'Performance of Airborne Animal Sonar Systems I. Microchiroptera', in René-Guy Busnel and James F. Fish (eds.), *Animal Sonar Systems* (New York: Plenum Press, 1980); Arthur N. Popper, 'Behavioral Measures of Odontocete Hearing', in ibid.

computation of the location of a disturbance in the sand.[65] Thus distance and location constancies occur in touch systems. The less exotic touch systems of land mammals, including humans, that commonly rely on contact can yield texture and shape constancies.[66]

EXAMPLES OF THE SENSORY-REGISTRATION/PERCEPTION DISTINCTION

It may help in understanding objectification to consider in more detail some sensory systems, and aspects of sensory systems, that lack it.

Numerous sensory systems in human beings are not perceptual systems. The sensory systems that affect heart regulation, muscle tone, and vascular constriction; many sensory systems that effect balance; capacities to feel heat and pain; the registration of information by pain that functionally correlates with bodily damage (even location of bodily damage); and most or all aspects of the sensory systems for smell and taste: these are not perceptual or representational in the senses of these terms that I have been developing. These systems' operations can be fully explained as functional responses to proximal stimulation. There appear to be no perceptual constancies—no traction for perceptual as distinguished from sensory psychology. There are no systematic operations in these systems that are illuminatingly explained in terms of their systematically and structurally distinguishing aspects of sensory registration from specific aspects of environmental reality, or in terms of a capacity to get *representata* right.[67]

The issue of the localization of pain is more complex than these remarks suggest. The connection between a feeling of pain and a bodily location *in itself* seems to involve no perceptual constancies. I see no clear ground to count the feeling as either perceptual or representational, except in a deflationary sense of 'representational'. The feeling of location is surely there, and there are functioning practical connections between the feeling and taking care of the location of felt bodily damage. And, of course, we humans know conceptually a lot about where pains occur in the body. But *in itself* I think that the feeling of the location of pain is a functioning, causally reliable sensory registration. No constancies, no distinction between proximal stimulation and a perceptual object, appear to occur in the operations of the system. There is simply a functioning correlation between feeling and location. There is no explanatory need to invoke veridicality conditions or representational content.

---

[65] Brownell, 'Prey Detection by the Sand Scorpion'.

[66] See citations, note 51.

[67] Of course, more sophisticated representational systems—systems of belief, for example—can use non-perceptual systems to form objective representations. One can form beliefs about pain, the feel of muscle contraction, the smell of peanut butter, the qualities of the taste of a wine. These are not perceptual representations. Perceptual systems are sensory systems that have *within* them objectifying routines.

On the other hand, many animals probably associate the location of pain with a proprioceptive body image. Either innately, or as a very early result of learning, their systems map feelings of pain onto a continuing *representational* image of the whole body. Where this is so, at least the locational aspects of pain have, derivatively, a perceptual dimension. Still, the qualitative feeling *in itself*, including the feeling of location, is not, I think, representational. It does not in itself represent the pain (does not represent itself), or anything else.

As indicated, necessarily some aspects of every perceptual system are non-perceptual. A capacity to distinguish registration of proximal stimulation from environmental conditions requires operating on pre-perceptual registration. For example, certain aspects of vision register, or functionally encode, only the light that constitutes proximal stimulation.

Non-human animals exhibit a huge range of sensory systems that are in no respect perceptual. The sensitivity in paramecia to certain concentrations of sodium chloride, light sensors in Euglena, the contact sensors in flatworms, shadow sensors in molluscs, proprioceptive feedback on self-motion in dragon-flies, many aspects of the hearing of the pocket gopher (which cannot localize sounds) appear to be non-perceptual.[68]

In earthworms, light sensors are scattered over the worm's body. There is sensitivity to light and dark and to the direction of the light, depending on where on the body the light strikes. There is, however, no capacity to register even a non-representational image—a pattern of stimulus registration that correlates with a pattern of light intensities. There is no objectification in the earthworm's visual system.[69]

In tapeworms, the system for sensing light is more specialized. Simple eye cups provide information that functionally correlates with the direction of light. The discrimination depends on the effects of stimulation on different parts of the eye cup. The discrimination and response of the tapeworm to input through the eye cups can be completely explained in terms of the intensity and distribution of proximal stimulation registered on the eye cup.[70]

In neither case is there perceptual constancy. There is no explanatory need to attribute representation of distal attributes, as distinguished from registration of proximal stimulation.

Much of the sensory world is controlled by olfactory registration. Many species—from yeasts to ants, moths, and snakes, from mice to mongooses— find mates, food, nests through pheromones. In ants, signals regarding war, danger, and work routines are carried through pheromones. A *pheromone* is a

---

[68] Discussion of these cases can be found respectively in: Jennings, *Behavior of the Lower Organisms*, 47–54; Tinbergen, *The Study of Instinct*, 21; Kenshalo, 'Phylogenetic Development of Feeling'; Möhl, 'Sense Organs and the Control of Flight'; Heffner and Heffner, 'Evolution of Sound Localization in Mammals'.

[69] Jennings, *Behavior of the Lower Organisms*, 248; Fraenkel and Gunn, *The Orientation of Animals*, 73, 317.

[70] M. F. Land and D.-E. Nilsson, *Animal Eyes* (Oxford: Oxford University Press, 2002), 4.

chemical signal from an animal that consists of either a chemical compound or a relatively precise chemical blend. Not all chemical senses respond to pheromones, of course. Nearly all species capable of locomotion avoid noxious chemicals, whether or not these are pheromones.[71]

A certain homing or beaconing capacity is common in locomotion that responds to chemical stimuli, pheromones or not. The individual has a default type of motion. The individual is disposed to continue moving in a given direction when the intensity of the registration of an attractive chemical stimulus is high. When the intensity of registration of an attractive stimulus is low or a repellant stimulus is high, the organism changes direction.

In the simplest organisms such as hydra or paramecia, as we have seen in Chapter 8, both the initial movement and the change in direction in relation to the direction from which the stimulus comes may be random. Random default movement occurs in more complex organisms—for example, in many insects, including many flies. More complex animals, such as fish, utilize a steady zigzag as default movement, which serves as a systematic sampling technique. In all these cases, when a relevant chemical stimulation occurs, the organism holds course if the stimulus is positive, and alters direction if the stimulus is negative.

The most elementary organisms that operate according to these patterns lack directional sense. Hydra, amoebae, and paramecia are examples. Their orientations are purely kinetic: if the stimulant is noxious, change direction—any direction. If the stimulant is positive, hold course.

Sensory systems of slightly more complex animals, such as earthworms, respond to direction of a stimulus by determining where on the body more intense stimulations of a given kind occur. So motor state formation is explainable in terms of a simple computation on the distribution of sensory registrations. The animal's orientation is a *taxis*. It turns toward or away from the side of the body where the most intense registration of proximal stimulation occurs.

There are interesting subspecies of this sort of tactic orientation. In many cases, where the organism is given stimulation of approximately equal intensity from different sides of its body, its directional orientation is the average of the intensities of the two stimulations (tropo-taxis). In other cases, orientation is all or nothing. Thus, if the organism is given stimulations of approximately equal intensity from opposite sides of its body, it orients fully in the direction associated with exactly one of the proximal stimulations (telo-taxis).

The method of moving in a direction determined by relative intensities of proximal stimulation from odor plumes, positive or negative, on different sides of the animal's body is widespread among animals. If stimulus registration of a

---

[71] Thomas E. Finger, Wayne L. Silver, and Diego Restrepo (eds.), *The Neurobiology of Taste and Smell* (2nd edn., New York: John Wiley & Sons, 2000). In this book, see especially the articles: Judith van Houten, 'Chemoreception in Microorganisms'; Robert E. Johnston, 'Chemical Communication and Pheromones: The Types of Chemical Signals and the Role of the Vomeronasal System'; and Nancy E. Rawson, 'Human Olfaction'. See also Bert Hölldobler and E. O. Wilson, *The Journey of the Ants* (Cambridge, MA: Harvard University Press, 1995).

positive stimulus is stronger on a given side of the body than on the other side, the animal turns to the more strongly stimulated side.

This technique is basic to the simplest navigational systems. It is called *homing* or *beaconing*. The technique is evolutionarily very old. I illustrated the method by reference to olfactory chemical sensory systems.[72] But sensory/actional systems sensitive to all the physical types of stimulation use it. The method tends to result in animals' locating food, a mate, or just conditions for thriving (appropriate temperature or light, for example). Of course, the method is also used in defensive functions.

Sensory systems that operate through registration of proximal stimulation, including registrations of intensities on different body parts, are not perceptual systems. The sensory aspect of the homing method registers only the relative intensity and type of proximal stimulus on bodily locations. Such capacities do not involve perceptual constancies. There is no need in explaining them to invoke states with veridicality conditions. They are not cases of perception.

As noted, a direction for movement can be set by weighting or averaging the registration of stimulation on different parts of the body. In such cases, a formation of a state is explained as instantiating a computation on sensory registrations in the animal. The computation is on registrations of proximal stimulation. Various distributions of proximal stimulation could result, through weighting and averaging, in sensing and moving in the same direction. There is a kind of mimicking here of direction constancy. But in the absence of any genuine representation, marked by veridicality conditions not trivially replaceable by accounts in terms of functional registrations of information, there is no true perceptual constancy.

Despite presence of a computational transformation on sensory registration (on sensory statistical encoding of information that is functional for the individual), neither empirical explanatory practice nor philosophical meta-theory supports attributing representational states. Here we have computation *without* representation. The directional effect can be explained entirely in terms of weighted averaging on distributions of registrations of surface stimulation. There is no separation of an objective environmental condition from sensory registrations of proximal stimulation. The correlation is already so close that explanation in terms of the nature of the surface registrations suffices. No explanation of the operations of such systems would be enhanced by invoking states with veridicality conditions.[73]

---

[72] For an overview of olfaction in beaconing, see N. J. Vickers, 'Mechanisms of Animal Navigation in Odor Plumes', *Biological Bulletin* 198 (2000), 203–212. See also note 54 above.

[73] One gets a closer analog of perceptual constancy in simple systems in which computations on sensory intake and movements of a sense organ or movements of the head yield directional sense and directional behavior. There may be borderline cases here, but everything hinges on the nature of the internal transformations. (Certain types of combination of spatial and temporal distribution of sensory registration to determine direction are clearly not perceptual. See Chapter 8, note 55, for a simpler case that suggests this point.) The occurrence of genuine representation and genuine perceptual constancy

The power of these types of non-perceptual, non-representational sensory capacities in determining complex behavior is vividly illustrated by the homing behavior of salmon. At about age 4 years, salmon return to the stream where they molted.[74] They follow an olfactory trail in oceans, sometimes over a thousand miles, back to the home stream by swimming in a zigzag manner (vertically as well as horizontally) and responding to relative intensities of a specific series of chemical blends imprinted on the salmon's outward journey to the ocean. Salmon find home by zigzag swimming that follows odor plumes that match an imprinted sequence.

The amplitude of zigzags is related to the slope of the gradient across an odor plume. Where the gradient is shallow, the animals show larger amplitudes in their zigzags. As the gradient steepens, the turning rate increases and the amplitude of the turns decreases. So the fish swims more nearly in a straight line. The default movement, apart from any relevant stimulation, operates like a random sampling technique. Once an appropriate type of odor with a relevant level of intensity stimulates the animal's receptors, the animal orients in a direction of maximal intensity and holds course until the type or intensity falls off. Obviously, this is a highly developed successor of the klino-kinetic movement found in the paramecium.[75]

As noted, the generic homing capacity works not only with chemical compounds as stimulants. It also works with light, sound, heat, electrical-magnetic fields, mechanical contact, and so on. Every major physical parameter is capitalized upon as a source of sensory stimulation by some species or other. In each instance of the generic capacity, direction of movement is determined by type and intensity of stimulation on positions on the organism's body.

As the salmon case illustrates, the tasks solved by the homing capacity can be immensely complex. Yet such systems of sensory registration are not perceptual.

---

is not established by the fact that a computational transformation involving a variety of sensory registrations yields a single behavioral result. Explanation of the transformations may not be enhanced by appeal to representation—states with veridicality conditions. For example, if there is no significant distinction between spatial distribution and timing of initial sensory registration, on one hand, and informational correlation with the environmental attribute (direction), on the other, the contrastive feature of perceptual objectification is absent. Then invocation of representational content is explanatorily trivial and dispensable. Genuine directional constancy must be embedded in formation operations specific to environmental attributes. Perhaps directional constancy is always an abstraction from *location* constancies, which require representation of distance as well as direction.

[74] The olfactory characteristics of the home stream are not pheromones, since they do not come from an animal. Still, the same sensory capacities are in play.

[75] Peter B. Johnsen, 'Chemosensory Orientation Mechanisms of Fish', in David Duvall, Dietland Müller-Schwarze, and Robert M. Silverstein (eds.), *Chemical Signals in Vertebrates* (New York: Plenum, 1992). Johnsen's work builds on earlier work on sensitivity of odor perception in fish. A. D. Hasler, 'Odour Perception and Orientation in Fishes', *J. Fisheries Resch. Bd., Canada* 11 (1954), 107–129; A. D. Hasler and W. J. Wisby, 'Discrimination of Stream Odor by Fishes and its Relation to Parent Stream Behaviour', *American Naturalist* 85 (1951), 223–238. See also Braithwaite, 'Spatial Memory, Landmark Use and Orientation in Fish'. Navigation of comparable complexity, also based on odor, occurs in the homing pigeon: V. P. Bingman, 'Spatial Representations and Homing Pigeon Navigation', in ibid.

The sensory contribution to behavior is fully explained by appeal to registration of proximal stimulation on the animal's surfaces. There are no operations for forming representation as of a specific environmental source of information. No spatial relationships are represented. Only the type and intensity of the proximal stimulus are sensed. Spatial location is determined by repeated sampling techniques. For the salmon, the direction and ultimately the location of the original molting site are ascertained by following up serially on the intensity of relevant proximal stimulation on one or another side of the animal's body.

Salmon do not lack perception. Aspects of their visual systems are perceptual. Salmon use visual perception in finding and staying in the central channel of the home stream. But the olfactory sensing capacity that I have described is not perceptual. There is no systematic, structured capacity in the sensory system that separates registration of distributions of proximal stimulation from states that specify, and are as of, certain environmental attributes. A theory that takes the system to have a perceptual attributive as of direction can be too easily replaced by standard theory—which simply takes the system to engage in summing and averaging operations on registrations of surface stimulation. Information registration of proximal stimulation and representation as of environmental attributes are never distinguished or separated in the system. Standard non-representational theory suffices.

A related case suggests how certain perceptual sensory capacities may have evolved. Snakes rely on olfaction in trailing prey, or returning to a den. The forks in snake tongues are probably an adaptation for more efficient chemical sampling. The tongue tips in some snakes are separated by twice the width of the snake's head. This anatomical arrangement increases the concentration differential between chemical stimulations of the two tongue tips. It explains snakes' ability to maintain contact with the chemical trail without extensive zigzag movement.[76] This specialized operation is a refinement of the generalized sampling technique so far discussed. It is still probably not perception. Again, directional information appears to reside in the relative intensities of proximal stimuli on the ends of the snake's tongue. The snake also probably does not sum serially obtained information into some reusable structure governing navigation. The matter can be tested. If one deprived the animal of the sensory capacity after a run, its inability to make the run again would suggest lack of such a structure. Many animals navigate by homing, without spatial representation. I shall argue in Chapter 10 that even map-like navigational systems can in principle fail to be representational.

As sign of non-perceptual sensory registration, I have emphasized the way explanation of operation centers on registration of proximal stimulation and averaging of such registration across different bodily surfaces. Another feature of the examples is notable. All hinge on the intensity of a type of stimulation.

---

[76] Neil B. Ford, 'The Role of Pheromone Trails in the Sociobiology of Snakes', in Duvall, Müller-Schwarze, and Silverstein (eds.), *Chemical Signals in Vertebrates*.

Complex organisms can respond differentially to numerous types of stimulation. The responsiveness by animals with highly developed olfactory systems to chemical mixes, for example, can be exquisitely detailed. Still, the sensitivity is only to the intensity of a variety of parameters. The registration of these parameters is explicable entirely in terms of the proximal effect of the parameters on the sensors.[77]

A capacity to *localize* a distal source of stimulation *without serial sampling* is a reliable sign of perceptual objectification. Localization is a capacity to determine direction *and* distance. The salmon has a breathtaking capacity to localize the home stream. These localizations are not representational. The salmon localizes its molting site only by combining sensory and motor capacities to sample serial intensities of proximal stimulation. As far as is known, the salmon's olfactory system lacks any sensory state that determines both direction and distance of any object or property. The salmon stores a sequence of sensory registration types. Localization through the salmon's action is just a reliable effect of the system's serial sampling of intensities and serial responses to registrations of the types of proximal stimulation.

The most widely studied perceptual capacities in non-human animals are capacities for visual localization and associated capacities for spatial representation. They are among the most impressive products of perceptual objectification. The example of the sand scorpion shows that touch systems can localize distal disturbances. The various sonar systems of bats, dolphins, and whales perceptually localize by way of initiating signals and sensing their effects.

The barn owl has perceptual hearing that exhibits representational localization. Its ability to localize sound events, in the dark from a single sample, illustrates the difference with the salmon's serial sampling to localize the home molting site. The owl does not need head movement, or sampling through flight. Barn owls anticipate not only location but trajectory from a single hearing. When approaching prey in the dark, the rectangle that the owl's talons form is oriented in the direction of the trajectory defined by prey movement. As remarked earlier,

---

[77] An old view in philosophy and psychology holds that it is a necessary, but not sufficient, condition on being a perceptual representation that it have an organization that maps onto a part–whole structure. In traditional language, the perceptual system must represent *extensive magnitudes*, as distinguished from merely intensive magnitudes. See Kant, *Critique of Pure Reason*, B201–207. The part–whole structure, at least parts of it, must be represented simultaneously, either in perception or in memory. Distinguishing this case experimentally from a continuum of responses calibrated to the continuum of intensities is experimentally delicate, but empirical grounding for such a distinction is common. Representations with spatial or temporal structure are examples of representation of an extensive magnitude. Normal visual representation of color is mapped onto part–whole structure inasmuch as colors are represented as extended. But, in principle, I think there could be color constancy with insufficient retention of spatial extent to count as spatial representation. On the other hand, I think that there is some reason to think that representation of *temporal* part–whole structure may be necessary to any perceptual system. See Chapter 10, the section PERCEPTION AND ORIGINS OF SPATIAL REPRESENTATION.

the owl's location constancy rests on principles similar to those involved in binocular depth perception and localization in vision.[78]

Here I want to enter a short detour that develops the point just made about the objectivity of hearing evinced in location constancy. I believe that the point discredits some of what Strawson claims (and Evans accepts) regarding the spatial capacities of hearing. Strawson claims that it is obvious that 'where experience is supposed to be exclusively auditory in character, there would be [no] place for spatial concepts ...'. He seems to deny that audition can itself represent a spatial field analogous to that of the spatial field in vision. He denies that conceptual spatial representation could be derived from auditory perception in the way that it can be from visual perception. He writes:

A purely auditory concept of space, on the other hand, is an impossibility. The fact that, with the variegated types of sense-experience which we in fact have, we can, as we say, 'on the strength of hearing alone' assign directions and distances to sounds, and things that emit or cause them, counts against this not at all. For this fact is sufficiently explained by the existence of correlations between the variations of which sound is intrinsically capable and other non-auditory features of our sense-experience ... the *de facto* existence of such correlations is a necessary condition of our assigning distances and directions as we do on the strength of hearing alone. Whatever it is about the sounds that makes us say such things as 'It sounds as if it comes from somewhere on the left', this would not alone (i.e. if there were no visual, kinaesthetic, tactual phenomena) suffice to generate spatial concepts.[79]

This passage is difficult to interpret. However, as a matter of empirical fact, localization of sound in space is explained by psychological principles that are analogous to some that govern visual localization. The barn owl need not rely on non-auditory sensory capacities to localize sounds. Human hearing is similar.

In neither the vision case nor the hearing case is it obvious that essential reference must be made to sensory input from kinesthetic or tactile *sensory registration*, much less to what Strawson means by kinesthetic or touch *experience* (sensation consciously conceptualized). In both vision and hearing cases, the framework for representational-content individuation does commonly include practical activity. But specific capacities for spatial representation in both vision and hearing do not depend on efferent sensors from activity or from other crossmodal capacities. Convergence capacities in both vision and hearing do not.[80] I see no reason to think that localization by hearing must depend any more on such sensors in other sensory systems than localization through vision must. I see

---

[78] Klump, 'Sound Localization in Birds'. See also Erik I. Knudsen, 'Sound Localization in Birds', in Arthur N. Popper and Richard R. Fay (eds.), *Comparative Studies in Hearing in Vertebrates* (New York: Springer-Verlag, 1980).

[79] See Strawson, *Individuals*, chapter 2, pp. 56 ff. [66 ff.]. See also Evans, 'Things without the Mind', *passim*.

[80] Perception of distance through convergence commonly uses small head movements, presumably registered in proprioception, or other extra-retinal endogenous sources of information. I assume that this point applies to both vision and hearing. I think that such registration is not *constitutive* of distance perception through convergence.

no reason why spatial *concepts* cannot be derived from incorporating auditory perceptual representations into a system of propositional inference.[81]

I think that Strawson is mistaken to require as a constitutive condition on a concept of space that the individual represent continuants (bodies rather than events). I think that he underestimates the objectifying resources of hearing, and conceptualization of hearing. Of course, even in humans and barn owls, auditory representation of spatial location and spatial relations is less extensive and less acute than in most visual systems. Vision is the most virtuosic perceptual spatial capacity. Still, purely sensory localization and perceptual location constancy, hence objectification, occurs in hearing.

Localization is a very primitive capacity. Along with motion constancy, it is probably the most evolutionarily important type of perceptual objectification. A sensory capacity for localization in the distal environment through a single psychological state reliably indicates objectification, and perceptual constancy. The principles describing localization must be general. Positions in space lack characteristic sensory signals. So a single sensory state cannot correlate with position purely through responding to a single type of proximal stimulation. Localizing position through a single sensory state requires a capacity to process very different sensory inputs according to general principles. So the capacity must be capable of determining position given a wide variety of proximal stimulations. Hence a single-state sensory representational capacity for localization implies location constancy.

A second argument from sensory, single-state localization to perceptual constancy assumes a perceiver that can move. Although we can conceive of perceivers that cannot move, the capacity to move is so widespread that the argument seems worth articulating. To represent location, a mobile animal with a perceptual system must be able to operate from different egocentric perspectives in instantiating localization principles. The system must be able to convert from one perspective to another by systematic laws or operations. So particular locations must be representable from different egocentric origins, which will yield different proximal stimulations. So sensory localization in a single sensory state must operate under principles that determine location despite large variations in sensory information registration.

The distinction between mere sensory registration and perception does not divide sensory systems simply. A sensory perceptual system always has both perceptual capacities and non-perceptual capacities to register sensory information.

The distinction also does not correspond to a hierarchy of complexity among animals. Sometimes less complex animals have perceptual systems, and more complex animals rely primarily on non-perceptual sensory systems. Sensory

---

[81] Nor do I see why the essentially egocentric character of auditory perceptual spatial representation need prevent such representation from being conceptualized, or from being genuinely spatial. A space could be conceived as the system of spatial relations constant under transformations of egocentric spaces.

systems are not inherently simpler than perceptual systems; nor are the tasks they solve inherently less complex, as the salmon's olfactory system indicates.

Perceptual systems are special in being the most primitive capacities that exhibit objectification. Perceptual systems are also, I think, the most primitive systems that are representational and that have veridicality conditions in a sense that grounds explanation.

PERCEPTION, REPRESENTATION, PROPOSITIONAL KNOWLEDGE

I have tried to develop a conception of perception that applies to a psychological kind that lies at the constitutive, phylogenetic, and developmental origins of empirical objectivity and representation. Perception is a type of objective sensory representation by an individual. I want to remark briefly on some of this conception's philosophical implications.

I believe that one of the most pervasive and crippling mistakes in philosophy has been to fail to distinguish genuine perception from sensory registration of information.

Because Individual Representationalists recognized the need to find some objectifying capacities *in individuals' psychologies* in order to explain representational objectivity, and because they overlooked objectification in perception, they thought that they had to require that individuals represent conditions for objectivity.

Sense-data theorists took the most basic type of sensory awareness not to be about the physical world. So they took sensory experience to require supplement—usually through conceptual-descriptive resources—to make objectivity regarding the physical world possible. Phenomenologists looked for objectivity in a special sort of consciousness. Since objectivity is a functional, not a phenomenological notion, they did little to illuminate perceptual objectivity.

Second-family Individual Representationalists tended to distinguish sensory registration only from propositional attitudes. Again, they left out perception. Sometimes the omission derived from insisting that individuals have criteria. Sometimes it derived from misguided conceptions of conditions on singular representation. Sometimes it derived from dogmatic claims that language is the source of all representation.

Philosophers in the Deflationary Tradition produced programmatic, undifferentiated notions of representation because they failed to reflect seriously on perception.

A major irony in twentieth-century philosophy is that in a century largely dominated by empiricism, nearly all major philosophers neglected the central empirical psychological kind, *perception*.[82] Nearly all of them had wildly

---

[82] Quine's focus on proximal stimulation and his conviction that language is necessary for representation encouraged failure to reflect on perception. Sellars and Davidson deny that there is any representational capacity intermediate between mere sensitive discrimination and propositional representation. Strawson and Evans hold that no genuine grouping of particulars (a mark of perception) occurs apart from propositional thought.

mistaken views, driven by philosophical preoccupations other than perception itself, and nurtured by neglect of relevant science.

The threefold distinction between sensory discrimination (or functioning information registration), perception, and propositional thought—fivefold if one adds perception-based, non-propositional intermodal representaion and self-conscious or reflective thought—is foreign to most philosophical systems.

This criticism applies both to twentieth-century philosophy and to earlier philosophy. Kant is a major exception.[83] He distinguished sensations, intuitions, and concepts (predicates of judgment). As noted earlier, my conception of perception derives from his conception of empirical intuition.[84]

Descartes blurs the threefold distinction. He differs from the Deflationary Tradition, of course, in maintaining that among terrestrial beings, only human beings represent anything. But he is a source for the later tradition's holding that pain, perception of bodies as such, and thought about bodies as such differ primarily in "degree"—for him, degree of clarity or distinctness.

With Kant, I believe that these psychological types are subspecies of different fundamental kinds. Unlike Kant, I count only perception and thought, not information registration, as forms of representation. This difference may be partly terminological. There is, however, a substantive point to my divergence. Sensory information registration in itself bears no constitutive or explanatory relation to veridicality conditions, which I take to be constitutive of genuine representational states.[85]

Kant maintains that perception (what he termed empirical intuition) is a form of *objective* representation. He distinguishes sensory intuitions from concepts. Empirical intuition is approximately sense perception, with some qualifications not relevant to present issues. Kant explicated concepts as predicates of judgment. Judgments, at least as discussed in the first *Critique*, are clearly propositional. Few twentieth-century philosophers joined Kant on these points, even those otherwise influenced by him. Those who did join him, like Strawson and

---

[83] See Kant, *Critique of Pure Reason*, A320/B376–7.

[84] In my view, Kant erred mainly in not distinguishing ordinary conceptual thought from reflexive thinking (which he identified with thinking that involves a capacity for self-consciousness). He seems to have thought that the two were inseparable. They are certainly conceptually separable. There appear to be animals that engage in conceptual, propositional thought, but cannot represent their thinking as such.

[85] Kant probably did not regard veridicality conditions as a constitutive aspect of representation (*Vorstellung*). I think that he mixed different notions under that catch-all term. As indicated in the preceding note, a further difference with Kant is that I distinguish between having propositional attitudes and having capacities for reflection and self-consciousness. So my distinction is ultimately more reticulated whereas his is threefold.

As noted at the beginning of this chapter and in the section PERCEPTION AND THE INDIVIDUAL, I drop the requirement of consciousness from Kant's characterization. I think that this difference probably derives from difference in focus. Kant believed that many "representational" states are unconscious. Since he was primarily interested in explaining understanding and justification in scientific and other reflective cognitive and practical judgments, he focused on a psychological taxonomy that served his aims. My project here concerns origins—phylogenetic, developmental, constitutive—of mind. So I cast my terminological net more widely.

Evans, gave individual representationalist arguments for thinking that perception constitutively depends for representing physical reality on propositional thought.

The most obvious negative effect of not distinguishing between sensory registration and perception in twentieth-century philosophy, apart from Individual Representationalism itself, is a flattening of the complex terrain that constitutes representational mind. Especially in the second half of the twentieth century, philosophers fed on an impoverished diet of examples.

Representational aspects of mind either were assimilated to high-level capacities, which include scientific reasoning, self-consciousness, reflection, rule-following, linguistic expressions of thought, and the like; or were assimilated to dumbed-down systems that purported to provide either a reduction base for all mental phenomena or a class of phenomena that were dramatically contrasted with high-level mental capacities. The reduction base or contrast class (depending on the philosopher) included computers, simple measuring instruments like thermometers, and the sensory systems of simple organisms. Even now, accounts of representation ("intentionality") swing from approaches that insist that representation is the special achievement of reflective human beings or language users to approaches that maintain that representation is as common as causally based correlation that has a function. On such views, "representation" in furnaces, water pumps, thermometers, plants, amoebae, and worms is as representational as representation in science. The most important empirical representational kind—*perception*—is almost never discussed in a realistic and informed way.[86]

Recognizing that perception is a state with explanatorily non-trivial veridicality conditions that is formed through a primitive but distinctive type of objectification serves to limit both excesses.

Not distinguishing among perception, non-perceptual sensory systems, and propositional thought also affected accounts of meaning in both theories of mind and theories of language. Omitting perception as a source of objective representation encouraged use-based theories of meaning. Such theories tended to hold that meaning and reference depend entirely on intellectually high-level activities, like linguistic competence, propositional inference, intentional action, explicative understanding, or verification procedures.

These theories dominated mainstream philosophy for most of the last half-century. They underestimated ways in which representational states constitutively depend on relations to the environment. They neglected blind, subindividual capacities that make perception possible. Reference and meaning in language in its initial stages, and representation and representational content in belief, derive largely from perception. Perception contributes reference and representational content before propositional inference, intentional action, explicative understanding, or

---

[86] Psychology itself seems to me to have failed to highlight some of its primary explanatory kinds, *perception* and *representation*. Even many psychologists who contributed to the empirical basis for discrediting Individual Representationalism tend to conflate sensory registration with perceptual attribution—and intermodal representation with conceptual attribution.

verification procedures get started. The failure to isolate perception as a representational kind contributed to deficient theories of language and representational content.

Outside philosophy of mind and philosophy of language, the most significant negative effect of not distinguishing sensory registration, perception, and thought is a distorted epistemology. Theories of empirical knowledge and empirical warrant show this effect in a striking way. As illustration, I cite a line of thought that flows from Sellars's work.

Sellars mounted an effective attack on the "Myth of the Given".[87] 'The Given' was essentially a colorful term for sense data. Sellars drew broad conclusions from his attack. The main features of the Given were three. It was an immediate sensory presentation not a product of inference; it did not "presuppose" any other knowledge; and it provided an indefeasible warrant for belief, in particular, empirical belief about the physical environment. Sellars brought three points against the Given. He held in effect that all empirical warrant resides in inferential connections to propositional beliefs, that neither perception nor sense data in themselves provide warrant, and that all warrant for belief about the physical world is defeasible.

The third point is surely correct. It was the key element in Sellars's effective attack on the Given and on postulating sense data in an account of empirical knowledge. The first two points are, I think, mistaken.

Sellars maintained that the only possible epistemic warrant for perceptual belief lies in 'the space of reasons'. Reasons were understood to be propositional. So all epistemic warrant derives through propositional inferences from propositional attitudes. According to Sellars, insofar as perception is non-propositional, it plays no normative role in epistemic warrant or knowledge. As indicated in Chapter 5, Sellars claimed that perception is necessarily infused with rational propositional abilities expressed in language.

Sellars assimilates all sensory capacities to simple discriminative mechanisms. He often associates sensory systems with thermometers. He claims that such systems constitute mere causal enabling conditions for having warranted empirical belief, or knowledge. They lack genuine representational content. He maintains that the only role that they play in epistemology lies in their providing a subject matter for beliefs about their reliability. For example, a perceptual belief is justified only if it is accompanied by a further belief to the effect that in certain circumstances (identified in the belief), the believer's sensory cues are reliable signs of a certain environmental subject matter.[88] According to Sellars, sensory experiences in themselves play no further role in yielding epistemic warrant or justification.

Had Sellars distinguished sensory registration from perception, he could not have so easily dismissed non-propositional representation—perceptual

---

[87] Wilfrid Sellars, 'Empiricism and the Philosophy of Mind', in *Science, Perception and Reality.*
[88] Ibid. 164–170.

representation!—from epistemology. His failure to draw this distinction stemmed from his Individual Representationalism. He thought that representation depends on representation of, indeed knowledge of, conditions for representation.

Partly because Sellars combined his positive claim with a powerful critique of accounts of warrant that appealed to sense data, Sellars's views influenced subsequent theories of empirical knowledge. Philosophers influenced by Sellars tended to take one of two directions. Some held that nothing of direct epistemic relevance occurs in the causal chain between environmental objects and perceptual beliefs about them. They explicitly banished perception in itself from the epistemology of empirical knowledge. Such philosophers appealed purely to coherence considerations, not to perception, to try to explain warrant for perceptual belief. Others sought to save an epistemic role for perception by claiming that perception is itself propositional and constitutes propositional reasons for perceptual belief. They maintained that perception has to be propositional if perception is to play any role in epistemology; for reasons are propositional, and any such role must be within 'the space of reasons'.[89]

Both sorts of views are implausible in the extreme. One line holds that perception plays no role in epistemic warrant for perceptual belief. Such a view is wildly unattractive on its face. Inevitably it hyper-intellectualizes empirical warrant. Sellars's own account of empirical warrant that requires a belief about sensory experience and its reliability as a sign of the world is, I think, implausible in the extreme, because of its hyper-intellectualization. Such accounts make warrant depend purely on inferences to and from other beliefs. Individual perceptual beliefs in themselves have no warrant at all. They must be warranted through further beliefs, usually meta-beliefs about sensory experience and possible defeaters, to be worthy of belief.

The other line stemming from Sellars is less widespread. Claiming the perceptual must be propositional, for otherwise it could play no role in warranting belief, is also unattractive. The form of perception is not a matter that submits to stipulation or to other armchair pronouncements that derive from considering epistemic norms rather than perception itself. Whether perception has propositional form depends on what perception is. This variant on Sellars's view is further dubious on empirical grounds. There is no strong reason to believe that attribution of propositional capacities is needed in empirical explanations of the perceptual systems of bees, frogs, birds, or even humans. The issue is not advanced by echoing Sellars's claim that empirical *warrant* must occur within a 'space of reasons'.

---

[89] Philosophers who take the first line are Richard Rorty, *Philosophy and the Mirror of Nature* (Princeton: Princeton University Press, 1979); Lawrence Bonjour, *The Structure of Empirical Knowledge* (Cambridge, MA: Harvard University Press, 1985); Davidson, 'A Coherence Theory of Truth and Knowledge'. Quine was probably not influenced by Sellars, but he takes a similar line in *Word and Object*, chapters 1 and 2. See also Gilbert Harman, *Thought* (Princeton: Princeton University Press, 1973). A philosopher who takes the second line is McDowell, *Mind and World*. The issues sketched in this section are further discussed in my 'Perceptual Entitlement'.

Both neo-Sellarsian views rest on a false dilemma. They assume that either perception provides propositional reasons, or it contributes nothing to epistemic warrant for empirical belief. The dilemma is methodologically misguided. It sets a requirement on epistemic norms. Then it maintains that perception must meet this requirement or fail to be relevant to epistemic norms or evaluation. We then have the absurd situation of philosophers either maintaining that perception is epistemically irrelevant to *empirical* warrant or dictating that perception must be propositional, clearly an empirical issue that depends on the nature of perceptual capacities. The epistemic value of empirical belief depends on the contribution to empirical belief by perception. Norms apply to use of capacities. Perceptual capacities are obviously relevant to warrant for perceptual belief and knowledge. Sellars's method fails to ground empirical warrant in understanding of, or indeed any serious reflection on, perceptual capacity.

I accept Sellars's (Kant's) view that *reasons* that support knowledge must be propositional. Reason is fundamentally a faculty of apriori principles. Instances of reasons must be susceptible to being instances of principles. Principles and their instances are propositional.

I do not accept Sellars's assumption that reasons are the only source of epistemic warrant. Not all of epistemologically relevant belief formation falls within a 'space of reasons'. Animals, young children, and many adults lack *reasons* for their perceptual beliefs. But they are often warranted in having them—epistemically entitled to them. Warrant for perceptual belief consists partly in the individual's being in perceptual states that reliably figure in the formation of true beliefs. Such beliefs can instantiate perceptual knowledge. Such warrant for perceptual beliefs constitutes an entitlement but not a reason. Perception is not reason. Formation of belief from perception is not reasoning. Perception does not support a belief by being a reason for it. Epistemological warrants are not confined to reasons. Some warrants for an individual's empirical beliefs do not consist in the individual's having reasons or other principled support for the beliefs. Warrant, like representation, does not require the warranted individual's being able to explain or rationalize the warrant through contents that share structure with principles.

Norms for perceptual belief must be grounded in the relation of perceptual belief to perception and in the character of perception. Epistemic norms apply to the sorts of representational states that knowers in fact have. Epistemology cannot dictate to psychology. Nor should it exclude perception from its domain because perception does not meet an armchair conception of what form epistemic norms must take. One cannot carry on epistemology in the absence of understanding what perception is. The failure to isolate perception as a distinctive representational kind has seriously limited understanding of empirical knowledge.

A major reason why Sellars's approach seemed viable is that philosophy had not mapped territory between thermometers and reasoners. A richer understanding of perception opens possibilities for epistemic inquiry. Perception is a competence naturally associated with norms or standards for achieving veridicality, as argued in Chapter 8, the section REPRESENTATIONAL FUNCTION AND NATURAL NORMS. Epistemic warrant is a norm relevant to arriving at truth and knowledge.

The ramifications of distinguishing among non-perceptual sensory discrimination, perception, and propositional thought reach further. I hope to have suggested the philosophical importance of a clear conception of perception as a distinct representational kind.

10 *Origins of Some Representational Categories*

Time is rhythm: the inset rhythm of a warm humid night, brain ripple, breathing, the drum in my temple—these are our faithful timekeepers, and reason corrects the verish beat. . . . Maybe the only thing that hints at a sense of Time is rhythm; not the recurrent beats of the rhythm but the gap between two such beats, the gray gap between black beats: the Tender Interval. The regular throb itself merely brings back the miserable idea of measurement, but in between, something like true Time lurks. How can I extract it from its soft hollow?

Nabokov, *Ada, or Ardor*

I want now to discuss some relatively basic sorts of perceptual attribution: body, numerosity, spatial relations, temporal relations. I elaborate accounts of constitutive conditions for having each of these four types of representation. I also discuss the form and content of these types, and whether each type is constitutive to perceptual representation. These accounts further develop the notions <u>perception</u> and <u>representation</u>.

PERCEPTION AND BODY

I understand *bodies* to be relatively compact material entities. Since representation of, and as of, bodies loomed large in discussion of Strawson and Quine, I want to return to the matter, armed with our conception of perceptual representation.

In Chapters 6–7, I made some negative points about constitutive conditions for a capacity to represent bodies as such. I claimed that this capacity phylogenetically and developmentally precedes, and hence is constitutively independent of, language and thought.

I also held that to represent bodies as such, an individual need not be able to represent an allocentric map of space, or a seems/is distinction, or a criterion of reidentification. I argued that the representational content of perceptual states is fixed not by an individual's capacity to distinguish the kinds that are attributed from all other kinds, but by two other factors. One is a set of modular routines for filtering and processing proximal stimulations that provide likely cues to environmental kinds. The other is a set of causal interactions between individuals and those environmental kinds that enter into biological explanations of relevant individuals' biologically relevant functions, paradigmatically activities, and into the formation of perceptual systems.

Given anti-individualism regarding perception and given that macro-physical bodies are cited in biological explanations of eating, fleeing, mating, parenting, navigating, for many animals, it should unsurprising that many animals perceptually attribute the kind *body*.

Body Representation as Originating in Perception

Before discussing constitutive conditions for having perceptual attributives as of body, I want to reinforce the view that there *are* such perceptual attributives. This view is well grounded in perceptual psychology. But a developmental psychologist who has made important contributions to understanding human children's representation of, and as of, bodies has claimed that no such representation occurs in perceptual systems. Against this claim, I maintain that representation as of body originates in perception.[1]

Elizabeth Spelke claims that what she calls 'objects' (a term that appears to be at least approximately equivalent to 'bodies') are not *perceived*. She proposes: 'The apprehension of objects is a cognitive act, brought about by a mechanism that begins to operate at the point where perception ends.' She adds: 'The parsing of the world into things [bodies, events, and so on] may point to the essence of thought and to its essential distinction from perception.'[2]

Spelke argues against the view that 'object perception depends on a system of visual modules performing a hierarchy of computations on progressively more abstract, behaviorally appropriate representations in [or derived from] the optic array'. She champions the view that 'object perception may not depend on [is not produced by] a visual mechanism at all but on a mechanism that is more central'.[3] Preparatory for supporting the latter hypothesis, she writes:

---

[1] The claims of Elizabeth Spelke that I discuss are not Individual Representationalist claims. Spelke also does not hold that representation as of body occurs only in *propositional* thought. Her notion of thought is more liberal than mine. Her claims do, however, echo the old idea that representation as of body is too high level to be perceptual. I will argue that the claims rest on mistaken conceptions of perception that have no sound scientific basis.

As noted, Spelke has made important contributions to understanding representation, including body representation, by young children. I have referred to some of this work in earlier chapters and will cite more in later parts of this chapter. Her experimental work is not undermined by failure of the claims that I criticize here. But I think that those claims constitute serious theoretical mistakes about fundamental representational kinds.

[2] Elizabeth Spelke, 'Where Perceiving Ends and Thinking Begins: The Apprehension of Objects in Infancy', in A. Yonas (ed.), *Perceptual Development in Infancy* The Minnesota Symposia on Child Psychology, 20 (Hillsdale, NJ: Lawrence Erlbaum, 1988). The quotes are from pp. 199 and 229. A large excerpt of the article is reprinted in R. Schwartz (ed.), *Perception* (London: Blackwell, 2004). Spelke's article contains criticism of sensori-motor, gestaltist, and Gibsonian invariantist views on perception—criticism that remains cogent. I shall not discuss these parts of the article.

[3] Spelke, 'Where Perceiving Ends and Thinking Begins', 215. Bracketed expressions are mine.

If modality-specific modules organize the world into objects...objects might be perceived in different ways when they were seen, heard, and felt. Mechanisms of thought, in contrast, do not center on a single modality but operate on the world as it is perceived, regardless of the sensory source of one's perception. If a single, relatively central system organizes the world into objects, objects should be apprehended under the same conditions, barring sensory limitations, whether surfaces were encountered by looking, listening, or touching.[4]

My primary objection to the line of argument previewed by this quotation will be that Spelke's conclusion is not constrained by her evidence. One cannot show that object representation occurs *only* intermodally by showing that object representation occurs intermodally. If, contrary to her conclusion, objects are *perceived* as objects in the different modalities, it is antecedently empirically likely that there are intermodal or crossmodal ways of coordinating the different modalities for perceiving objects. It is also antecedently likely that the different perceptual modalities would respond to commonly perceived attributes of objects in similar ways *at a certain level of abstraction*. For example, both intermodal and perceptual (say, visual and haptic) systems would form representations of objects by connecting those representations with key features of object boundaries represented in similar ways in visual and haptic modalities. Vision and touch each would isolate objects by determining that objects are integral wholes bounded so as to be spatially distinct from one another. Differences in ways the modalities generate object perception would derive from the different sorts of proximal-stimulation registration that the different modalities receive. But at a certain intermodal level of abstraction, the principles would be common. It is antecedently likely that *if* objects (bodies) are perceived as such in different perceptual modalities, 'a single, relatively central [intermodal] system [also] organizes the world into objects' and objects will be 'apprehended under [many of] the same conditions...whether surfaces were encountered by looking...or touching'.[5]

Spelke's evidence does not support her conclusion that object representation does not occur in the individual perceptual modalities. Her evidence tells only against the antecedently implausible hypothesis that there are no principles (at any level of abstraction) common to the different perceptual modalities in representing objects. It does not tell against the hypothesis that objects are represented perceptually, and further represented intermodally, in ways that center on generic aspects of attributes common to the different perceptual modalities.[6]

---

[4] Ibid.

[5] Ibid. Bracketed inserts are mine.

[6] In fact, Spelke's formulations sometimes conflate the issue of whether representation as of objects occurs in an intermodal system with the issue of whether representation as of objects occurs *only* in an intermodal system and *not also* in individual modal perceptual systems, such as the visual and touch systems. Compare, or example, ibid. 215 ('object perception may not depend on a visual mechanism at all but on a mechanism that is more central') with pp. 218–219 ('These findings provide evidence that infants

As evidence for the view that representation as of objects (bodies) occurs only in an intermodal system, Spelke cites experiments that show that infants transfer habituation to the boundaries of objects between visual and haptic perceptual systems.[7] It is well known that habituation transfers relatively freely across perceptual modalities. In fact, crossmodal transfer occurs even with respect to those types of representation of properties that Spelke assumes *are* formed within individual perceptual modalities. For example, as we shall see, Spelke thinks that whereas visual perception does not form perceptions as of objects (bodies), it does form perception as of surfaces and their orientations in three-dimensional space. But crossmodal transfers of representation of surface slant occur between vision and touch.[8] There are levels of abstraction at which the different modalities can be seen as operating under similar geometric principles for identifying surface slant. Since crossmodal transfers occur even for representational states that indisputably are formed *within* perceptual modalities, Spelke's argument from habituation transfers between modalities cannot support the view that object representation is non-perceptual and purely amodal.[9] Her evidence does not separate her hypothesis from the hypothesis—widely held in perceptual psychology—that objects are represented as objects in individual perceptual modalities.[10]

---

apprehend the unity and boundaries of objects in the haptic modality as they do in the visual modality, by detecting common and independent motions of surfaces. Such evidence supports the hypothesis that a common, relatively central mechanism organizes the surfaces that infants see or feel into objects.'). Supporting the hypothesis that a common, relatively central mechanism organizes surfaces that infants see or feel into objects does nothing by itself to support the hypothesis that representation as of objects occurs *only* in a system and *not also* in perceptual systems. See also p. 216.

As is illustrated in the passage just quoted, pp. 218–219, Spelke sometimes writes of infants' apprehension of objects *in* individual perceptual modalities. I believe that she must mean that intermodal representation of objects supplements modal perceptual representation of surfaces (on which the intermodal representation depends), so that the intermodal representation operates *through* perceptual modalities.

[7] Spelke, 'Where Perceiving Ends and Thinking Begins', 215–219.

[8] M. O. Ernst, M. S. Banks, and H. H. Bülthoff, 'Touch Can Change Visual Slant Perception', *Nature Neuroscience* 3 (2000), 69–73.

[9] The habituation-transfer experiments are clearly intended to support the hypothesis that representation of objects is non-perceptual. See Spelke, 'Where Perceiving Ends and Thinking Begins', 215. But, in discussing the experiments, Spelke does not explain how they are supposed to show that perception as of objects begins only in an intermodal system. (See note 6.) She never argues squarely that the evidence is not fully compatible with the view that each modality produces representation as of objects. Yet her view that representation of objects is *not perceptual* is announced at the beginning and end of her article: ibid. 198–199, 226–227, 229–230.

[10] Distinguishing the hypothesis that there is a common amodal *mechanism* (and system of intermodal representations) from the hypothesis that there are merely common principles at certain levels of abstraction and crossmodal mechanisms, such as habituation and mutual effects on representations among the modal systems, is non-trivial. And I do not see that Spelke's habituation and co-development evidence strongly supports the former view over the latter. I think that there is empirical evidence, which I will not discuss here, that does support the view that there are pre-propositional, distinctively intermodal representations over and above the effect of crossmodal influence within the different perceptual modalities. So I simply grant Spelke's hypothesis that there is a common, pre-propositional amodal mechanism for forming amodal representations. On

Similarly, Spelke provides interesting evidence that, at about the same time (4 months of age), infants' vision and touch each develops a reliance on gestalt relationships, such as alignment of surfaces and edges among superimposed objects, in determining whether there are two objects or one. Again, this evidence does nothing to show that representation as of objects occurs *only* post-perceptually. Given perception as of objects in the different modalities, one could just as well argue that significant stages of development in the representation of objects will often coincide in the different modalities—and in coordination among the modalities.

Spelke claims that the hypothesis that object representation occurs only in an intermodal system is 'simpler' than the hypothesis that object representation occurs in each of haptic and visual modalities [as well].[11] This claim would carry no weight in vision science. Her view needs to show that neither the visual system nor the touch system by itself completes the processing involved in representing objects.

There is considerable empirical evidence against Spelke's view that object (body) representation is not perceptual. I shall cite two bodies of evidence. One derives from scientific work on individual perceptual modalities in vision science and the psychology of touch. The other derives from scientific work on crossmodal relations. I begin with crossmodal relations.

Crossmodal influence among the visual, haptic, and auditory modalities is among the most intensely studied topics in perceptual psychology. Let me mention one type of influence that is relevant to our topic. If visual perception is given stimulation from one sort of three-dimensional shape and haptic perception is (artificially) given stimulation from another sort of shape, where instances of the shapes are perceived as located in the same place, each modality frequently adapts its perceptual representation in proportion to its relative reliability in perceiving the relevant sort of property, given the relevant sort of cue information. So a compromise shape perception occurs in each modality under common, specifiable conditions. Apparently, all types of volume-shape perception that are used in body perception are subject to such crossmodal modification. Crossmodal influence *within* the modalities occurs on representation of shape properties sufficient for body representation—at least in cases of cue conflict.[12]

---

the non-triviality of the issue, see J. F. Norman, H. F. Norman, A. M. Clayton, J. Lianekhammy, and G. Zielke, 'The Visual and Haptic Perception of Natural Object Shape', *Perception and Psychophysics* 66 (2004), 342–351. It is worth noting that, in the developmental literature, the term 'amodal' is sometimes applied to *properties* represented in more than one modality. This usage is not in play here. I am discussing *representation* of properties (attributes).

[11] Spelke, 'Where Perceiving Ends and Thinking Begins', 203–215, 219. In 'Principles of Object Perception', 46.

[12] If five sounds are heard at a time roughly coincident with the visual system's being given four flashes, then the individual visually perceives there being five flashes. It is thought that, since hearing is better at temporal organization than vision, the visual system gives way in the direction of hearing, even producing illusions. Similar crossmodal influence—sometimes resulting in illusions in one modality, sometimes resulting in mutual, statistically based compromise in each modality's

These results support the view, nearly universally held in perceptual science, that formation operations yield representation as of body in each of several perceptual modalities (pre-eminently vision and touch). Perceptions as of body and volume shape, as well as nearly any other type of perceptual attributive, in each modality is influenced and modified, under certain conditions, by the relevant cues available in other modalities—especially in cases of cue conflict. Cue conflict is not just resolved in an intermodal compromise extracted after the specific modal representations are formed. It affects representations *within* specific perceptual modalities. Evidence regarding relations between the different modalities counts against the view that volume-shape representation and representation as of objects are non-perceptual.

The other, more basic type of evidence against the view that representation as of objects (bodies) is not perceptual derives from work on individual perceptual modalities. Along with localization, determining three-dimensional volume shape and identifying objects by their geometrical characteristics are commonly regarded as *the* primary representational tasks for mammalian visual systems. Research on formation principles governing the sorts of closed three-dimensional shapes that form the central basis for object (body) perception is a significant topic in research on the visual system.[13] Moreover, object (body) perception is determinable on the basis of visual cues alone. Formation of body perception from perception of certain three-dimensional shapes is an operation squarely attributed in scientific theory to visual systems.[14] Similar remarks apply to

perceptual representations—occurs between haptic and auditory modalities. For a sampling of the literature on crossmodal influence, see L. Shams, Y. Kamitani, and S. Shimojo, 'What You See is What You Hear', *Nature* 408 (2000), 788; J. M. Hillis, M. O. Ernst, M. S. Banks, and M. S. Landy, 'Combining Sensory Information: Mandatory Fusion within, but not between, Senses', *Science* 298 (2002), 1627–1630; M. O. Ernst and M. S. Banks, 'Humans Integrate Visual and Haptic Information in a Statistically Optimal Fashion', *Nature* 415 (2002), 429–433; M. O. Ernst and H. H. Bülthoff, 'Merging the Senses into a Robust Percept', *Trends in Cognitive Sciences* 8 (2004), 162–169; J.-P. Bresciani, M. O. Ernst, K. Drewing, G. Bouyer, V. Maury, and A. Kheddar, 'Feeling What You Hear: Auditory Signals Can Modulate Tactile Taps Perception', *Experimental Brain Research* 162 (2005), 172–180; J.-P. Bresciani and M.O. Ernst, 'Signal Reliability Modulates Auditory–Tactile Integration for Event Counting', *NeuroReport* 18 (2007), 1157–1161; H. B. Helbig and M. O. Ernst, 'Optimal Integration of Shape Information from Vision and Touch', *Experimental Brain Research* 179 (2007), 595–606.

[13] See, for example, Z. Pizlo and A. K. Stevenson, 'Shape Constancy from Novel Views', *Perception and Psychophysics* 61 (1999), 1299–1307; James T. Todd, 'The Visual Perception of 3D Shape', *Trends in Cognitive Sciences* 8 (2004), 115–121.

[14] The following is a small sample. In some cases, the physical basis for object determination has been localized to areas of the brain known to be specialized to vision. N. K. Logothetis, J. Pauls, H. H. Bülthoff, and T. Poggio, 'View-Dependent Object Recognition by Monkeys', *Current Biology* 4 (1994), 401–414; D. Kersten, 'Perceptual Categories for Spatial Layout', *Royal Society of London: Philosophical Transactions: Biological Sciences* 352 (1997), 1155–1163; J. L. Mundy, O. Faugeras, T. Kanade, C. d'Souza, and M. Sabin, 'Object Recognition Based on Geometry: Progress over Three Decades', *Philosophical Transactions: Mathematical, Physical and Engineering Sciences* 356 (1998), 1213–1231; Z. Kourtzi and N. Kanwisher, 'Representation of Perceived Object Shape by the Human Lateral Occipital Complex', *Science* 293 (2001), 1506–1509; K. Tsunoda, Y. Yamane, M. Nishizaki, and M. Tanifuji, 'Complex Objects are Represented in Macaque Inferotemporal Cortex by the

research on object perception in the touch and auditory systems.[15] Barring better arguments for a non-perceptual status for object (body) representation than Spelke provides, there appears to be overwhelming evidence that object (body) perception originates in specific perceptual modalities. Either innately or through learning, these modal perceptual capacities are coordinated and influenced, under certain conditions, crossmodally.

Even granted common intermodal principles, at some level of abstraction, for object representation, the formation operations and representational contents of perceptual states as of body in different perceptual modalities are different, even where the representations in each perceptual modality specify the same physical properties. Each modality operates on registration of different types of stimulation and forms perceptual attributives according to principles that are specific to cues deriving from the relevant types of stimulation. So their perceptual attributives as of body differ. There are further differences. For example, within the haptic system, object and shape identification is better from the back of an object, whereas, within the visual system, object and shape identification is better from the front. There are perspectival biases in haptic volume-shape identification that are specific to that modality.[16]

A second type of consideration that Spelke presents to support the hypothesis that representation as of objects begins only post-perceptually concerns the nature of key attributes of objects. This line of argument has two subdivisions. First, Spelke claims that some of the key attributes attributed in object representation are not perceivable. Second, she cites the fact that at very primitive representational levels, objects are represented at times when the objects are

Combination of Feature Columns', *Nature Neuroscience* 4 (2001), 832–838; N. Sigala and N. K. Logothetis, 'Visual Categorization Shapes Feature Selectivity in the Primate Temporal Cortex', *Nature* 415 (2002), 318–320; D. H. Foster and S. J. Gilson, 'Recognizing Novel Three-Dimensional Objects by Summing Signals from Parts and Views', *Proceedings: Biological Sciences* 269 (2002), 1939–1947; Z. Kourtzi, M. Erb, W. Grodd, and H. H. Bülthoff, 'Representation of the Perceived 3-D Object Shape in the Human Lateral Occipital Complex', *Cerebral Cortex* 9 (2003), 911–920; P. J. Kellman, 'Interpolation Processes in the Visual Perception of Objects', *Neural Networks* 16 (2003), 915–923; D. Kersten, P. Mamassian, and A. Yuille, 'Object Perception as Bayesian Inference', *Annual Review of Psychology* 55 (2004), 271–304; J. Berzhanskaya, S. Grossberg, and E. Mingolla, 'Laminar Cortical Dynamics of Visual Form and Motion Interactions during Coherent Object Motion Perception', *Spatial Vision* 20 (2007), 237–295.

[15] R. L. Klatzky and S. J. Lederman, 'Identifying Objects from a Haptic Glance', *Perception and Psychophysics* 57 (1995), 1111–1123; S. J. Lederman and R. L. Klatzky, 'Relative Availability of Surface and Object Properties during Early Haptic Processing', *Journal of Experimental Psychology: Human Perception and Performance* 23 (1997), 1680–1707; R. L. Klatzky and S. J. Lederman, 'Object Recognition by Touch', in J. Rieser, D. Ashmead, F. Ebner, and A. Corn (eds.), *Blindness and Brain Plasticity in Navigation and Object Perception* (New York: Erlbaum, 2008); U. Firzlaff, M. Schuchmann, J. E. Grunwald, G. Schuller, and L. Wiegrebe, 'Object-Oriented Echo Perception and Cortical Representation in Echolocating Bats', *PLoS Biology* 5 (2007), online; L. M. Herman, A. A. Pack, and M. Hoffmann-Kuhnt, 'Seeing through Sound: Dolphins (*Tursiops truncatus*) Perceive the Spatial Structure of Objects through Echolocation', *Journal of Comparative Psychology* 112 (1998), 292–305.

[16] F. Newell, M. O. Ernst, B. S. Tjan, and H. H. Bülthoff, 'Viewpoint Dependence in Visual and Haptic Object Recognition', *Psychological Science* 12 (2001), 37–42.

not perceivable. Regarding the first subdivision, Spelke cites her own important experimental work that shows that infants represent objects as cohesive, bounded, substantial (or solid), and spatiotemporally continuous. Regarding the second subdivision, she cites well-known research that shows that objects are tracked when they are fully occluded.

I begin with the first subdivision. I discuss it in some detail because it raises important issues about the role of generic attributions in perception. Spelke claims that the properties *cohesion, boundedness, substantiality* (*solidity*), and *spatiotemporal continuity* are *not perceivable*. She makes this claim as if it were self-evident. She writes: 'Each of these properties is abstract: It cannot be seen or smelled or touched. These properties can be known, however, because each constrains how objects can be arranged and how they can move.'[17]

This claim rests on confusion. Since every property and kind is an abstract repeatable, *in a sense* no property is perceivable. Only particulars, which are instances or bearers of properties (or relations, or kinds), that can enter into causal relations with sensory receptors at particular times and places can be perceived in that sense. The issue is whether the relevant properties can be perceptually indicated and perceptually attributed to particulars that instantiate or bear those properties. Can perceptual systems generate perceptual states that are perceptions of particulars *as* cohesive, bounded, solid, and spatio-temporally continuous? Can perception, prior to thought, group particulars according to these attributes? One cannot blithely urge negative answers to these questions as obvious. Spelke's claim that the properties of cohesion (and so on) are abstract and imperceptible cannot be given any weight.

It is plausible that particulars *can* be perceived as cohesive, bounded, solid, and spatio-temporally continuous. Perceptual psychology explains perceptual attribution of these very properties, attributions generated within perceptual systems. There is nothing about the properties that makes it impossible for perceptual attributives to indicate and attribute them. In this sense, all these properties are perceivable.

Spelke characterizes and discusses these four properties only in the context of how they reveal themselves in motion. A capacity to perceive bodies in motion is, of course, ubiquitous (or nearly ubiquitous) among animals capable of perceiving bodies. The capacity is obviously deeply important for the evolution and survival of many species.

I argue later in the section, however, that a capacity to perceive bodies in motion is not *constitutively* necessary for perception as of body. More obviously, all four properties can be perceptually attributed, in perceptual states formed within specific perceptual modalities, in cases in which bodies are at rest relative to the perceiver. One can perceive a particular as cohesive (as an integrated unscattered whole) and as bounded (as having a perimeter and as spatially distinct

---

[17] Spelke, 'Where Perceiving Ends and Thinking Begins', 226.

from other entities) when the perceived particular (body) is at rest. One can feel a body as solid when it does not move. One can even see a body as solid without watching it resist penetration by moving objects. And one can track a body as spatio-temporally continuous even though it is at rest. So, to perceive objects as having these properties, it is not necessary, on given occasions, that they be perceived in motion.

I shall discuss representation of bodies at rest as well as in motion. The exclusive emphasis on motion tends to suggest that these properties can be attributed only through "predicting" how an object will behave over time. Such prediction suggests, to many, that a conceptual capacity, not a perceptual capacity, is employed in the "prediction".[18]

There are several mistakes in such reasoning. One is to regard perception as a snapshot ability whose exercise can be entirely understood in terms of what can happen in a moment. In the first place, perception of motion and change is a fundamental area of vision research. There is no basis in scientific practice for confining even the representation of motion to intermodal systems. In the second place, the input that yields any given perceptual state—whether as of an object in motion or at rest—is never momentary. Individual perceptions are formed on the basis of visual stimulation over short periods of time, including across saccades.[19] Perception as of motion can be generated in a single perceptual state. In the third place, invoking "prediction" hyperintellectualizes the representational capacities. The representation of bodies in motion occurs in numerous lower animals that no one would be inclined to say are capable of prediction. Perceptual tracking and perceptual anticipation are the appropriate designations.

The most basic mistake in the reasoning sketched two paragraphs back is to fail to realize that the content of, and the laws governing, all perceptual capacities cannot be understood *fully* in terms of how an individual responds to any given stimulus at any given time. For example, the capacity to perceptually represent a surface as being at a specific orientation and slant is associated with capacities to represent the same surface at different slants. So being able to perceptually attribute one slant is constitutively associated with perceptual ability to attribute others. Moreover, the nature of the perceptual constancies requires that capacities for perceptually attributing any given attribute are integrated with capacities for perceptually attributing the same attribute under significantly different proximal stimulation. The capacity to have any given perceptual attributive in a perceptual

---

[18] In fairness, Spelke does not explicitly make this argument. She does discuss the properties as constraints on motion in the same paragraph in which she claims that the properties are not perceivable. And she introduces notions of the infants' "analyzing" motions and "predicting" future states of objects in the next paragraph. See ibid. 226–227. I think that the argument should be warned against, whether or not Spelke intends it.

[19] See, for example, David Melcher and M. Concetta Morronel, 'Spatiotopic Temporal Integration of Visual Motion across Saccadic Eye Movements', *Nature Neuroscience* 6 (2003), 877–881; and Maggie Shiffrar, 'Movement and Event Perception', in E. Bruce Goldstein (ed.), *Blackwell Handbook of Perception* (Oxford, Blackwell, 2001), chapter 8.

state, produced under the laws of formation from a given type of proximal-stimulation registration, must be linked in the perceiver's psychology to capacities to have other perceptual attributives as of the same attribute, produced under the laws of formation from *different* types of proximal-stimulation registration. In sum, having *systematically related* capacities to represent both different attributes and the same attributes differently is constitutively necessary to having any given capacity for perceptually attributing any given attribute.

What 'systematic relations' are involved in capacities to attribute cohesiveness, boundedness, and spatio-temporal continuity?[20] The question calls for detailed empirical answers. Although accounts of body perception are central in vision science, the science has not yet provided complete answers. I will, however, make some remarks on the "perceivability" of key properties involved in perception as of bodies.

Cohesiveness and boundedness are geometrical properties. Cohesion is spatial connection of all points in, or parts of, a shape or object. Boundedness is the having of a perimeter inside which all points or parts of the shape or object fall. Points or parts outside the perimeter are not in the shape or object. Perceptual systems have constancies for visible surfaces in three dimensions, and for three-dimensional volume shapes, that hinge on perception as of cohesiveness and boundedness.

Spelke proposes specific versions of principles for cohesion and boundedness that intermodal systems can be expected to capitalize upon. Visual systems operate under something like these principles as well. Her *cohesion principle* is that two (visible) surface points lie on the same object only if the points are linked by a path of (visible) surface points. Her *boundedness principle* is that two (visible) surface points lie on distinct objects only if no path of connected (visible) surface points links them.[21]

Such principles apply to perception as of surfaces in three-dimensional space. *Very* roughly speaking, visual systems that represent surfaces as cohesive and bounded form representations as of bodies—allowing (*a*) for conditions in isolating such shapes from a background, (*b*) for various types of defeater conditions, (*c*) for additional tracking principles to be discussed. Many visual systems produce perceptions as of bodies under such conditions even when the instances of the relevant shapes are at rest and when stimulation occurs over very short

---

[20] I omit discussion of the property *solidity* in what follows. Instances and bearers of solidity can clearly be perceived as solid, both haptically and visually. I believe that Spelke is right to emphasize that a capacity to perceive particulars as solid is an *empirically* central concomitant of perception as of body. I argue later in the section that representation as of solidity is not *constitutively necessary* to object (body) perception.

[21] Spelke, 'Principles of Object Perception', 49. Actual principles are probably more nuanced. Spelke formulates her principles in terms of representation of surface points. I believe that visual principles governing cohesiveness and boundaries of surfaces are more likely to describe operations that involve representation as of surface areas, or as of certain types of edges of surfaces, rather than surface points.

Spelke takes her boundedness principle to entail solidity. Although I have no large quarrel with any of Spelke's principles as empirical hypotheses about visual systems (and perhaps intermodal counterparts), I believe that a weaker principle of boundedness is *constitutive of* object perception.

periods of time. The reason is that the types of entities with such shapes that occur in the environments in which the visual systems were formed, and that interacted with animal needs and activities, tend to be bodies.

A further fact about bodies is that they are spatio-temporally continuous: they tend to maintain cohesion and boundedness over time. To produce perceptual states as of bodies, a perceptual system (or intermodal system serving perceptual systems) must be capable of *tracking* them over time. Later in the section, I discuss grounds for taking this tracking requirement to be constitutive. I simply assume it here. A transtemporal extension of the cohesion principle is that if visible parts of an object are continuous over time—whether at rest or moving along a continuous path—and if they maintain visible cohesiveness, then all visible parts of an object remain on connected paths over time.[22] A transtemporal extension of the boundedness principle is that objects tend to maintain their visible boundaries over time.

I believe that tracking bodies over time constitutively requires a capacity to represent a body as cohesive and bounded beyond stimulation intervals involved in forming perceptual states (even assuming, as I have above, that the intervals are not momentary). So I believe that perception as of bodies requires systematic relations to *transtemporal* utilizations of perception. Thus the 'systematic relations' between any given perceptual state as of body and other perceptual states include those governed by principles that describe and explain perceptual tracking. Such tracking capacities nearly always apply to bodies both in motion and at rest. Such principles can be expected to govern perceptual memory and perceptual anticipation. Tracking bodies is, of course, informed by the basic ways bodies "behave" over time. Bodies do not commonly shrink to a point, or suddenly clone, or scatter, or blend into other entities. They do not commonly disappear, unless occluded. They move on continuous paths. Tracking principles are commonly associated with capacities to anticipate these continuities, given perception—and perceptual memory—as of bodies. These anticipations of continuities over time are not to be thought of as conceptual or post-perceptual. They are not matters of prediction by the individual. They occur at relatively low levels of representation in perceptual systems—even levels that involve anticipation of continuities over saccades in very early visual processing.[23] Because a capacity for perceptually tracking bodies over time is a constitutive aspect of a capacity to form perceptions as of bodies, any given body perception tends to be systematically related to psychological states that are not perceptions—states of perceptual memory and perceptual anticipation.

---

[22] This formulation derives from one by Spelke, but differs in ways motivated by the first paragraph of note 21.

[23] See, for example, M. Wexler and R. M. Held, 'Anticipating the Three-Dimensional Consequences of Eye Movements', *Proceedings of the National Academy of Sciences of the United States of America* 102 (2005), 1246–1251.

It would be a mistake to think that this point even suggests that the attribute *body* is not perceivable (in the sense of being attributable by states formed in perceptual systems). It would be a mistake to think that the point entails that transtemporal cohesiveness or boundedness, or the motion of bodies over intervals beyond those involved in forming particular perceptual states, is not perceivable. It would be a mistake to think that this point shows that representation as of body is purely intermodal. All the relevant principles for tracking can—and do—govern relations among *visual* perceptions. It is just that visual tracking commonly involves relations among present visual perception, visual perceptual memory, and visual perceptual anticipation.

These remarks apply to Spelke's second subdivision. Spelke places great emphasis on the fact that objects are represented at times when the objects are not perceivable—particularly cases in which they are fully occluded. She correctly notes that when objects are fully occluded they are no longer perceived. Children and animals do not stop representing objects (bodies) when they are no longer perceived. They have definite anticipations as to where and when moving objects will reappear from behind occluders. And they have definite anticipations about where resting objects will be when occluders are removed.[24] These anticipations are naturally accommodated in a given perceptual modality. Perceptually tracking objects generally depends on capacities to relate perceptions to perceptual anticipations and perceptual memories. Tracking objects when they are fully behind occluders is just a special case of the point. A given perceptual modality, say vision, normally operates in conjunction with visual memory and visual anticipation. Empirically, such conjunction can be expected to have internalized basic physical principles governing object continuity and motion in representational tracking of bodies. Such principles key on maintenance of cohesion and boundedness, and on basic transtemporal patterns of body inertia and motion. There is no ground here to claim that representation as of objects (bodies) occurs only in non-perceptual intermodal systems.

Let us reflect on some general points about body perception. Certainly, there are aspects of body perception that are distinctive. A capacity to track bodies over time is constitutive to perception as of bodies. Perceptual memory and perceptual anticipation usually play roles in tracking bodies over time. Perception of bodies involves perception of entities that have backsides that cannot be perceived at any given time at which the bodies are perceived. The perception in a given modality involves a kind of amodal completion (a filling-in of a shape not fully seen). Perception of, and as of, bodies depends on formation operations that are more complex than those involved in perception of, and as of, surfaces. It is empirically

---

[24] Spelke, 'Where Perceiving Ends and Thinking Begins', 220–227. See also R. Baillargeon, 'Object Permanence in 3.5 and 4/5-Month-Old Infants', *Developmental Psychology* 23 (1987), 655–664; Hauser, 'Expectations about Object Motion and Destination'; Pepperberg and Funk, 'Object Permanence in Four Species of Psittacine Birds'; Regolin, Vallortigara, and Zanforlin, 'Detour Behavior in the Domestic Chick'; Regolin and Vallortigara, 'Perception of Partly Occluded Objects by Young Chicks'.

plausible that such principles begin with perception as of surfaces and form perceptions as of bodies through further operations backed by tracking capacities. One sees bodies by seeing surfaces as surfaces of bodies, under certain conditions. Perceptually attributing the kind *body* guides singular perceptual applications to bodies, when the applications bear appropriate causal relations to bodies. The fact that one does not simultaneously see the bodies' backsides is no more mysterious than the fact that one sees surfaces as being in depth relations even though one does not see the space behind the nearer surface.

Although I believe that I have undermined the grounds that Spelke gives for taking representation of objects (bodies) to be non-perceptual, I want to comment on her picture of the domain of perception. She writes:

Human perceptual systems appear to analyze arrays of physical energy so as to bring knowledge of a continuous layout of surfaces in a state of continuous change. We perceive the layout and its motions, deformations, and ruptures. This continuous layout contains no spatially bounded 'things' and no temporally bounded 'events': Perceptual systems do not package the world into units. The organization of the perceived world into units may be a central task of human systems of thought... Perceptual systems bring knowledge of an unbroken surface layout in an unbroken process of change.[25]

The talk of perception's being of 'continuous layout of surfaces', 'unbroken surface layout', and of perception's not 'packaging the world into units' bears no recognizable relation to the actual practice of vision science. A central part of vision theory is to explain perceptual representation as of the three-dimensional volume shapes and perceptual identification as of objects (bodies) through perceiving such shapes.

Spelke cites a remark by David Marr as congenial to her position. Marr suggested that the representation of surface layout in his 2½D Sketch marks 'the end, perhaps, of pure perception'.[26] Marr did not explain what he meant by 'pure perception'. It is not clear that what he meant was what Spelke means: that any representation of objects or volume shapes occurs only in an intermodal, post-perceptual system. In any case, Marr's 2½D Sketch has not, in subsequent vision theory, retained the position of a significant *cut* in visual processing.

There is certainly no basis in the research for holding that the layout of surfaces marks a unitary stage after which perceptual processing ends. One can get a feel for the role that depth information plays in visual perception as of objects by considering a half basketball attached to a wall. Removal of the wall so that the half basketball is suspended in space will yield a different perceptual attribution. Attached to the wall, the half basketball is perceived as half a sphere. Suspended in space, the half basketball is perceived (from the same angle) as spherical. The 2½D layout of the basketball's surface remains the same; but

---

[25] Spelke, 'Where Perceiving Ends and Thinking Begins', 229.
[26] Marr, *Vision*, 268; Spelke, 'Where Perceiving Ends and Thinking Begins', 230.

depth relations among surfaces affect perceptual attribution of volume shape, including perceptual attribution of unseen shape parts. The visual system's formation of the full-sphere perception is based not only on the surface orientation of the basketball (half or full) but on the depth relations between it and other surfaces in the scene. Depth relations in the scene that make room for a full sphere tend to prompt perception as of a full sphere. (The example was suggested by Johannes Burge.) The science tries to discover detailed principles for such formation of body representation in the visual perceptual system. Perception of and as of bodies and volume shapes is clearly within the purview of research into the visual, haptic, and auditory modalities. At its most primitive, representation as of body is perceptual representation.

Singular Applications in Perception of Bodies

To perceive something as a body, an individual must have *perceptual* capacities that are appropriately tuned to the kind *body*. What does appropriate attunement amount to? Merely being systematically caused by bodies to go into certain sensory states is not enough. The sensory states must be perceptual. Moreover, the fact that in appropriate conditions, sensory states, whether perceptual or not, enable an individual to eat, flee, mate with, parent, and navigate with respect to bodies is not enough. Something in the perceptual system must be psychologically specific to bodies and must in effect differentiate them from other environmentally relevant, discriminable entities. This element of specificity must be perceptual. The psychological specificity to bodies need not discriminate bodies from all other possible entities. It must be specific in comparison to other discriminable environmental entities that are also explanatorily relevant to basic animal functions.

A moth might find a mate using olfaction and the homing technique exemplified by salmon. That would not suffice to represent anything as a body. A spider might find a mate by responding to retinal stimulation or even a perception of a shape instance, supplemented by tactile sensing of frequencies stemming from web vibrations characteristic of conspecifics. Such an array of perception and sensings might suffice to enable the spider to interact successfully with its mate's body. It would not suffice to represent anything as a body.

Perceptual representation as of body cannot occur in isolation from other psychological capacities. What associated psychological capacities, especially perceptual capacities, are constitutively necessary for an individual to have if the individual is to perceptually represent something as a body? In what ways must perception be used to represent something as a body? What other attributes must an individual be capable of perceptually attributing if it is to perceptually represent something as a body?

Successful perceptual representation is always necessarily of particulars. Referents of a perception can only be particulars involved in causing it. Since perceptually indistinguishable particulars occur, and because perceptual attribu-tions commonly are veridical of more than one particular in the universe, perceptual reference is not fully determined by perceptual attributives. The occurrent token singular perceptual representational contents make an essential contribution to reference by being caused by the referents. They are thus context-dependent. I want here to discuss perceptual reference to particular bodies. Then in the next subsection I turn to perceptual attribution of the kind *body* to bodies—perception as of bodies.

Numerous studies of human visual perception show that attention, short-term memory, and individuation center on objects, particularly bodies, not locations. Priming effects associated with a briefly presented feature of a moving object remain attached to the object, not the location where the feature was present.[27] The phenomenon occurs in both human adults and 6-month-old human infants.[28]

Although a good bit of perceptual reference is subliminal, singular reference in perception that is most efficiently usable depends on attention.[29] Adult humans can attend to three to four objects at a time, bodies or not, at least outside the focal area of the visual field. So roughly three to four visual individual indexicals for bodies are available at any one time in the occurrent visual field. Randomly moving bodies can be tracked through occlusion using these indexes as long as motion is roughly continuous.[30] Parallel phenomena occur in pre-linguistic infants.[31]

[27] D. Kahneman, A. Treisman, and B. J. Gibbs, 'The Reviewing of Object Files: Object-Specific Integration of Information', *Cognitive Psychology* 24 (1992), 175–219.

[28] D. C. Richardson and N. Kirkham, 'Multi-Modal Events and Moving Locations: Eye Movements of Adults and 6-Month-Olds Reveal Dynamic Spatial Indexing', *Journal of Experimental Psychology: General* 133 (2004), 46–62.

[29] S. He, P. Cavanagh, and J. Intriligator, 'Attentional Resolution', *Trends in Cognitive Sciences* 1 (1997), 115–121; S. Ullman, 'Visual Routines', *Cognition* 18 (1984), 97–159; Kahneman, Treisman, and Gibbs, 'The Reviewing of Object Files'; S. Yantis, 'Objects, Attention, and Perceptual Experience', in R. Wright (ed.), *Visual Attention* (Oxford: Oxford University Press, 1998); Z. W. Pylyshyn, 'Situating Vision in the World', *Trends in Cognitive Science* 4 (2000), 197–207; R. A. Rensink, 'The Dynamic Representation of Scenes', *Visual Cognition* 7 (2000), 17–42; Z. W. Pylyshyn, *Seeing and Visualizing* (Cambridge, MA: MIT Press, 2003).
Demonstrative indexes and object files are set up for other entities besides bodies. See Richardson and Kirkham, 'Multi-Modal Events and Moving Locations'.

[30] The phenomenon is called 'multiple-object tracking'. In addition to the work by Pylyshyn cited in note 29, see Z. W. Pylyshyn, 'Visual Indexes, Preconceptual Objects, and Situated Vision', *Cognition* 80 (2001), 127–158; Z. W. Pylyshyn and R. W. Storm, 'Tracking Multiple Independent Targets: Evidence for a Parallel Tracking Mechanism', *Spatial Vision* 3 (1998), 179–197; B. J. Scholl, Z. W. Pylyshyn, and S. Franconeri, 'When are Spatiotemporal and Featural Properties Encoded as a Result of Attentional Allocation?', *Investigative Opthamology and Visual Science* 40 (1999), 4195; B. J. Scholl and Z. W. Pylyshyn, 'Tracking Multiple Items through Occlusion: Clues to Visual Objecthood', *Cognitive Psychology* 38 (1999), 259–290.

[31] E. W. Cheries, L. Feigenson, B. J. Scholl, and S. Carey, 'Cues to Object Persistence in Infancy: Tracking Objects through Occlusion vs. Implosion', abstract, *Journal of Vision* 5 (2005), 352. See Chapter 7, note 87.

There is evidence of a limit (of three to four bodies) on tracking behind barriers by non-human primates. And there is less fully developed evidence that domestic pigs can track similar small numbers of bodies behind barriers.[32]

'Attention' in the multiple-object-tracking experiments must be construed broadly. Attention does not require foveal focus. The attended-to object need not be at the focus of the visual field. Attention can be active, or it can be "grabbed" by sudden appearances of objects or other salient aspects of a scene. Perhaps among lower animals exogenous control of attention dominates over direction of attention.

A similar phenomenon regarding small numbers of perceptual referents emerges in change-detection experiments. An adult human is shown a small array of objects for less than a second. After a short delay, the individual is shown a second array, either identical to the first array or differing in one attribute of one of the objects. For up to three or four objects, changes are noticed for any of a variety of attributes. Above that limit, performance is poor.[33]

For example, a subject is shown an array of differently shaped, colored, and oriented bodies for a fraction of a second. After a couple of seconds of delay, the subject is shown, also for a fraction of a second, the same array with the one difference that an irregularly shaped body has been rotated by 90 degrees. For up to three or four bodies, the change in orientation—or any comparable single change in shape, size, color—is detected. If the number of bodies in the array is increased to larger than four, performance disintegrates.

Similar change detection shows up in pre-linguistic human children. The capacity is subject to limits similar to those that govern adult performance. Infants 4–6 months old can reliably detect such changes for only one perceptual object. There is, however, evidence that infant working memory does not develop to the capacity of adult working memory until the age of 10–12 months. By then infants succeed in the relevant change detection experiments with up to three to four objects, and not higher—thus replicating the performance of human adults.[34]

---

[32] M. D. Hauser, S. Carey, and L. B. Hauser, 'Spontaneous Number Representation in Semi-Free-Ranging Rhesus Monkeys', *Proceedings of the Royal Society*, London 267 (2000), 829–833; M. D. Hauser and S. Carey, 'Spontaneous Representations of Small Numbers of Objects by Rhesus Macaques: Examinations of Content and Format', *Cognitive Psychology* 47 (2003), 367–401; W. Bull and C. Uller, 'Spontaneous Small Number Discrimination in Semi-Free Ranging Domestic Pigs (*Sus Scrofa*)', abstract (2006), for paper presented at the XV Biennial Conference on Infant Studies. As noted, a capacity to track particulars behind barriers has been found in birds. See Regolin, Vallortigara, and Zanforlin, 'Detour Behavior in the Domestic Chick'; Pollok, Prior, and Guntrukun, 'Development of Object Permanence in Food-Storing Magpies (*Pica pica*)'. A similar capacity seems to occur in jumping spiders. See note 54 and the subsection SPATIAL REPRESENTATION IN NAVIGATION BY JUMPING SPIDERS AND OTHER ARTHROPODS below. Whether these beings are capable of multiple-object tracking is, as far as I know, unknown.

[33] See E. K. Vogel, G. F. Woodman, and S. J. Luck, 'Storage of Features, Conjunctions, and Objects in Visual Working Memory', *Journal of Experimental Psychology: Human Perception and Performance* 27 (2001), 92–114.

[34] S. Ross-Sheehy, L. Oakes, and S. J. Luck, 'The Development of Visual Short-Term Memory Capacity in Infants', *Child Development* 74 (2003), 1807–1822.

Singular applications of perceptual attributives occurs wherever there is genuine perception as of particulars, whether the perception is attentive or not. *Attention-based* singular applications of perceptual representational types play several special roles.[35] Where such applications are at the focal center of the visual field, they yield higher perceptual resolution. They also simplify behavior. Each application of a singular, attention-based element defines a context for generation of information available for the animal's behavior. Perceptual representations that are not bound to such singular indexes are subject to less rich, less accurate information processing. They play a more peripheral role in guiding behavior.

Object indexes set up object files, initially in short-term (working) memory. Tracking, together with the addition of new representations or the deletion of earlier ones, attach to these files. Attention can reactivate an established file for tracking an object from an earlier representation. Such files are necessary for bridging stimulus discontinuities produced by occlusion, saccades, and shifts of attention. In many species, a few of these short-term files are retained in longer-term memory.

In the psychological literature, some authors have taken the indexes in tracking multiple moving objects to represent 'visual objects', or two-dimensional 'visual patterns' that are 'reliably associated' with physical objects, or 'proximal counterparts of real physical objects', or 'proximal features that are precursors in detection of real physical objects'.[36] The *representata* are taken not to be physical bodies, or any other environmental entities.

I believe that this way of thinking is confused and deeply mistaken about what is being studied. The experiments apply to visual systems that can represent three-dimensionally shaped bodies in three-dimensional space. The representational content of the perceptions is explained, under perceptual anti-individualism and in scientific practice, by reference to the perceptual system's

---

[35] I develop this notion of a demonstrative-like context-bound singular *application* in various works, most fully in: 'Belief *De Re*' and 'Postscript to "Belief *De Re*"'; 'Disjunctivism and Perceptual Psychology'; and 'Five Theses on *De Re* States and Attitudes'. The attention-based indexicals discussed in the psychological literature are, properly construed, a subset of these applications. All attributives in vision (all grouping or categorizing elements) accompany singular context-bound applications. A small subset of these are recruited for object tracking, subitizing, and other attention-based referential aspects of perception, visual or otherwise.

[36] See J. M. Wolfe and S. C. Bennett, 'Preattentive Object Files: Shapeless Bundles of Basic Features', *Vision Research* 37 (1997), 25–43; Pylyshyn, 'Situating Vision in the World'; 'Visual Indexes, Preconceptual Objects, and Situated Vision'; Rensink, 'The Dynamic Representation of Scenes'. Much of the multiple-object-tracking research concerns moving figures on a screen. See notes 38–39. In *Seeing and Visualizing*, Pylyshyn writes inconsistently, or at best unclearly, on the matter. Sometimes he claims that the objects of indexical-like representations are individual distal 'objects in the world' (pp. 208, 211, 219n., 226n.). Other times he states that the relevant notion of object is relative to the visual system (p. 227n.), or is ambiguous as to whether the object is distal or proximal (pp. 173, 204, 215), or is an element in the visual field (p. 210). I believe that his claim that the indexes need not be accompanied by any encoding of a property, which I criticize in note 40 below, may be a residue of the earlier articles, in which the initial entities allegedly "picked out" by the indexes are not counted as distal.

evolutionary relations to bodies and other environmental entities, not merely to proximal counterparts of bodies. In view of the centrality of bodies in human activity, and in view of the fact that the principles of discrimination are associated—both in individual cases and in the development of the visual system—with constancies regarding basic geometrical and dynamical attributes of bodies, perceptual states that are specifically causally associated with bodies tend to represent bodies.

There are further specific scientific reasons to take individuals not always to be representing special (non-physical or at any rate non-bodily) visual objects. The tracking of objects on screens follows laws independently established for body tracking.[37] Tracking depends on the entity's maintaining shape cohesiveness. Further, tracking moving entities through occlusion follows standard laws determining image shrinking and image expansion, where such shrinking and expansion cue occlusion of objects.[38] It is not plausible that there are separate laws for visual patterns, 2-D surfaces, bodies, and figures-on-screens. And it is not plausible that the psychological laws governing tracking concern special non-spatial objects, given that the shrinking and expansion principles are clearly the product of causal interaction with a world in which bodies occlude one another. Tracking in the 2-D cases is determined by psychological laws that at least overlap, and are probably derivative from, laws that determine body perception.

General Elements in Perception of Bodies: Conditions for Body Attribution

I turn from singular perceptual context-dependent applications to attribution of the kind *body*. Singular context-dependent references in perception and perception-based memory are guided by general perceptual attributives. Such guidance is necessary whether context-dependent singular reference in perception is attention-based or not. One cannot perceive a particular without perceiving it by way

---

[37] It has been maintained that young children are inclined to reach for and pick up entities that are indexed—even entities on computer screens—until 18 months old. See J. S. Deloache, S. L. Pierroutsakos, D. H. Uttal, K. S. Rosengren, and A. Gottlieb, 'Grasping the Nature of Pictures', *Psychological Science* 9 (1998), 205–210. This particular claim has been brought into doubt: A. Yonas, C. E. Granrud, M. H. Chov, and A. J. Alexander, 'Picture Perception in Infants: Do 9-Month-Olds Attempt to Grasp Objects Depicted in Photographs?', *Infancy* 8 (2005), 147–166. So it may be that when infants are seeing figures on computer screens, the infants are representing two-dimensional surfaces as such. But the principles that govern tracking these objects certainly overlap those governing tracking three-dimensional bodies, as the image-shrinking and image-expansion cues indicate.

[38] These latter points are made by Carey, *The Origin of Concepts*, chapter 3. See Erik W. Cheries, Karen Wynn, and Brian J. Scholl, 'Interrupting Infants' Persisting Object Representations: An Object-based Limit?', *Developmental Science* 9 (2006), F50–F58. Other psychologists who firmly take what seems to me the correct view that the indexes refer only to distal particulars, including bodies, are A. Leslie, F. Xu, P. Tremoulet, and B. Scholl, 'Indexing and the Object Concept: Developing "What" and "Where" Systems', *Trends in Cognitive Sciences* 2 (1998), 10–18; S. Carey and F. Xu, 'Infants' Knowledge of Objects: Beyond Object Files and Object Tracking', *Cognition* 80 (2001), 179–213.

of some general, repeatable grouping capacity to *attribute* properties, relations, kinds veridically.[39] The nature of these general capacities is our primary concern. What capacities must attend *attribution* of the kind *body*?

[39] In the articles cited in note 36 and in *Seeing and Visualizing*, Pylyshyn holds that the particular-tracking, context-bound, singular applications, which he calls employed indexes, are not accompanied by any representation that 'encodes' a property. In *Seeing and Visualizing*, see pp. 180–181, 200, 202, 208–214, 217–222. I believe that this doctrine is untenable. I will not discuss the difficulties in detail. But, since Pylyshyn is widely read among psychologists and philosophers, I lay out some basic points. Pylyshyn insists that the objects initially picked out by the visual system are not guided by "conceptual" representations—representations that occur in all-purpose, non-modular aspects of cognition. In this insistence, he is certainly right. (See his excellent article 'Is Vision Continuous with Cognition?'.) His account of vision associated with the indexes, however, never discusses or even recognizes attributive (or grouping, categorizational) general aspects of visual perception that is the product of modular processing—visual perception proper. In fact, he sometimes *identifies* representational encodings of properties with conceptual capacities—capacities that are not attributable to the visual system *per se* (*Seeing and Visualizing*, 216, fig., 219 n.).

Pylyshyn also holds that reference in perception does not occur *purely* through descriptions or attributives (pp. 245–247, 252–254), that reference in perception does not depend on sortals for familiar natural kinds (p. 215; see note 40 below), and that some contextual singular reference in perception does not succeed in locating the *representatum* or in associating ordinary properties with it (pp. 219–221). In all these points, he is correct. But in making them, he often writes as if he is vindicating his own doctrine. None of these points provides the slightest positive support for that doctrine. The doctrine at issue is that perceptual singular context-bound reference to distal particulars ('objects') sometimes occurs without *any* representational encoding of *any* property (as) of a particular, where an encoding enters into computations (p. 218).

Pylyshyn holds that the indexes are tied to their referents causally (p. 213), but that they are initially guided by no attributive that encodes any property. He tries to explain how indexes can refer without being accompanied by representational encodings of properties (or other attributes) by appealing to various supposed analogies (pp. 218–221). None of these analogies helps makes his view plausible. 'Interruptions' in computer programs affect the programs causally without matching a descriptor to the causing event (pp. 218–219). There is no evident need to regard the interruption as *referring* to anything. If interruptions are supposed to refer to distal particulars, it is just as unclear how they can do so as it is how indexes (or context-bound singular applications) can do so, in the absence of perceptually representing the object as being of a certain sort or as having certain properties. The other supposed analogies are no more helpful.

Pylyshyn (at least sometimes, see note 36) takes the indexes to refer to particulars in the distal environment. Such particulars need not be bodies, but I will take bodies as paradigmatic. This view is surely correct. But, insofar as an index refers to a distal particular, the reference must be through a perceptual ability. The particular is picked out only by perception. Such perception involves some general, repeatable ability that responds to an *environmental* pattern. Motion and object constancies are clearly present in the empirical experiments that deal with indexes. The relevant responses group, categorize, or attribute. Pylyshyn often writes as if the visual system perceptually picks out bare particulars. It is certainly striking (as we have seen and shall see again) that many familiar properties need not be perceptually tracked or represented when bodies are tracked. But one cannot perceive a particular in the environment *neat*. This is impossible on its face. One must segment it from the rest of environmental reality in terms of repeatable patterns—attributes. (Here I think Pylyshyn's failure in his earlier writings firmly to indicate that the *representata* of the indexes are distal objects, paradigmatically bodies, figures in his tendency to think of indexing as a representation as of bare particulars.) Sometimes Pylyshyn writes as if the category *objecthood* or *individuality* (pp. 215, 226–227) might be associated with the index. But these categories are too unspecific to stand alone. They cannot explain what environmental patterns the perceptual system uses (perceptually) to isolate specific objects (or individuals) from other elements in the perceived environment. Just saying that the index refers to its cause, or picks out an object because of a proximal onset of stimulation, as Pylyshyn often does, is also too unspecific. There are always many causes, and many causally relevant aspects of any given cause. To refer to a particular, the system must isolate it by perceiving and perceptually

The capacities constitutively relevant to having the perceptual capacity to attribute the kind *body* are conveniently divided into synchronic and diachronic types.

A traditional philosophical view is that to represent bodies, the individual must segment physical reality into relatively narrow kinds of objects—balls, trees, rocks, bees, and so on.[40] These are called *sortals*. The view is often presented as an apriori claim about conditions for representation of physical reality. This view does not accord with facts concerning child development or the perceptual capacities of various animals. Visual capacities for many individuals delimit kinds at a much more generic level of kind attribution.

Whether bodies have simple, regular, or common shapes is not initially important for visual segmentation. There is extensive and varied evidence that children as young as 2 months old visually represent bodies according to individuative principles that are very generic and that center on a few aspects of bodies.[41] The individuative abilities are probably innate, in the sense that they are the products of a maturation that is normal for the species and does not depend on the specifics of individual learning. Cohesive, bounded objects of any shape are perceptually segmented from a background, and treated differentially.

The capacity to perceptually discriminate a three-dimensional figure from a background or surround is a relatively primitive synchronic perceptual capacity. I think that this capacity is apriori constitutively necessary to visually representing bodies as such. An individual that lacked this capacity could not see anything as a body. The same capacity is apriori constitutively necessary to perception as of

---

attributing some aspect of it that distinguishes it from other elements in the environment. What *perceptual* response to what aspects of the cause explains the repeatable *perceptual* ability to single out particulars of the types that are in fact singled out? Psychology needs to (and does) explain what attributes of the distal causes the perceptual system perceptually responds to in picking out the particulars, the objects, that it picks out and tracks. (I explain this point in much greater depth in section II of 'Five Theses on *De Re* States and Attitudes'.) Pylyshyn never considers this psychological issue. He does note, without seeing its relevance to his doctrine, that there are very specific aspects of the environment that perceptual systems perceptually represent that allow for discrimination and tracking of objects.

A lot is known about how such perceptual attributions of properties, relations, and kinds are computationally formed and used to pick out and track particulars. For example, for visual indexes that track bodies, the objects must be seen as wholes (in the distal environment); and the objects cannot be seen to be shrinking or growing in certain ways. Properties like spatial boundedness, spatial integrity, and continuity in motion are properties whose *representation* guides indexes for bodies. Oddly, in one passage, Pylyshyn comes close to recognizing these points, but fails to apply them to his doctrine, becoming concerned with whether the attributives are conceptual (pp. 266–267). (In beings with concepts, such attributives are surely both perceptual and conceptual.) Perceptual representations as of other properties guide singular indexes that pick out and track other particulars besides bodies, for example, tunes and object-like patterns that are not perceived as objects.

It is not tenable empirically, or I think even conceptually, to hold that the indexes carry out demonstrative-like perceptual reference to distal particulars that is not guided by *any* general perceptual representational types at all. See 'Five Theses on *De Re* States and Attitudes', sections II and III.

[40] Wiggins, *Sameness and Substance*. We saw this sort of view in Strawson and Quine, as well.
[41] Spelke, Brelinger, Macomber, and Jacobson, 'Origins of Knowledge'.

body by touch and echolocation. In this case the 'ground' is simply the surrounding environment. The perceptual capacity for touch must be capable of discriminating some three-dimensional aspect of particular bodies from a wider field of possible objects of touch—separating them off spatially from a contrast field. The field is spatial and might include other bodies in the same environment. Similarly, for those echolocation systems that are capable of discriminating the spatial boundaries of bodies.

In the absence of cues from motion, perceptual systems that form perceptions as of bodies – including such systems in human infants – do so by determining features of volume shapes, largely from spatial characteristics of surfaces in three-dimensional space. As noted in the first section of this chapter, the key spatial characteristics of both surfaces and volume shapes that ground representation as of body are *cohesion* and *boundedness*.[42]

Bodies are seen or felt as having three-dimensional shape. In vision, figure–ground relations in stationary displays are perceived by infants, in cases where figure and ground are separated in depth. By contrast, infants do not perceive figure–ground relations in stationary, two-dimensional pictures in which figure and ground are differentiated only in color and texture. Where there are depth cues, the occluded background behind an object in stationary, three-dimensional scenes is seen as continuous, despite being occluded.[43]

Among the visual-depth cues in stationary displays is the overwhelming statistical tendency for bodies to have convex shapes. Region convexity in the non-representational two-dimensional retinal image is an informational basis for distinguishing figure from ground (ordinal depth relations) and for perception of metric depth relations.[44] Here we have a striking instance of perceptual anti-individualism. The natures of representational content and formational processes in perception depend on patterns in the environment with which individuals interacted in the formation of perceptual systems. Registration of two-dimensional convexities in retinal registration tend to give rise to perceptions as of edges of bodies, because bodies tend overwhelmingly to be convex. A transformation process that yields a representation as of figure–ground and as of metric depth relations follows the regularity that holds between edges of three-dimensional

---

[42] Actual principles are more nuanced. These are just approximate.

[43] Spelke, 'Principles of Object Perception'; N. Termine, T. Hrynick, R. Kestenbaum, H. Gleitman, and E. S. Spelke, 'Perceptual Completion of Surfaces in Infancy', *Journal of Experimental Psychology: Human Perception and Performance* 13 (1987), 524–532; Hofsten and Spelke, 'Object Perception and Object-Directed Reaching in Infancy'.

[44] The *intuitive* basis for this point is developed in great detail in Kanizsa, *Organization in Vision: Essays on Gestalt Perception*, for example chapter 5, 'The Role of Regularity in Perceptual Organization'. For a striking mathematical development of the point, which supports the statistical point and models laws determining perception formation, see J. Burge et al., 'Natural Scene Statistics Predict How the Figure-Ground Cue of Convexity Affects Human Depth Perception'. See the discussion of the methodology underlying this work in Chapter 3 above, notes 42–43, and in Chapter 8, the section PERCEPTUAL PSYCHOLOGY AND THE DISTINCTION BETWEEN SENSORY INFORMATION REGISTRATION AND PERCEPTION, subsection DEPTH FROM CONVEXITY OF IMAGE REGIONS.

bodies and a background behind the body, marked by the convexity of a region in the (possibly non-representational) image that registers such edges. The capacity to distinguish the figures of bodies from their spatial background or surround is constitutive to being able to represent anything as a body. Visual systems capitalize, for the natures of their representational states and their transformation processes, on patterns that occur in the physical environment. Here, the pattern is statistical rather than law-like.

Perception of shapes and objects as three-dimensional is present very early in the development of human infants and non-human animals.[45] Simply finding bounded wholes appears to be fundamental to segregating bodies that are at rest. But, early on, further properties are used to distinguish non-moving bodies with *shared boundaries* under certain conditions. For example, initially infants see a horse and a rider on the horse as a single body, because the outlines of the pair appear cohesive and bounded. By roughly 4 or 5 months, infants have used experience of separable superimposed objects to see the horse–rider tableau as two adjacent bodies. Although basic formation processes for segregating physical wholes may be innate, priming can help infants to solve boundary problems by distinguishing bodies with shared boundaries, on the basis of prior perception of bodies with the relevant shapes or properties.[46]

So learned gestalt mechanisms operate in certain cases of figure–ground organization. But the basic, initial work of segregating objects from a background as discrete units in space seems to be carried out through innate geometrically centered processes responding to stimuli independently of learned recognitional abilities.

Most of these synchronic operations, such as amodal completion, grouping, configuration, and depth perception, occur at pre-attentive levels of processing. This fact indicates that body segmentation is a process in early vision that occurs independently of attention.[47] These capacities are in evidence in human children by 2 months old.

Capacities—visual, tactile, or sonar—to differentiate a body from its background seem clearly to be *constitutively* necessary for perceiving something as a body. I believe that *synchronic* versions of this capacity are nearly ubiquitous

[45] C. E. Granrud, 'Binocular Vision and Spatial Perception in 4- and 5-Month-Old Infants', *Journal of Experimental Psychology: Human Perceptual Performance* 12 (1986), 36–49; A. Yonas, M. E. Arterberry, and C. E. Granrud, 'Four-Month-Old Infants' Sensitivity to Binocular and Kinetic Information for Three-Dimensional-Object Shape', *Child Development* 58 (1987), 910–917; J. D. Kralik and M. D. Hauser, 'A Nonhuman Primate's Perception of Object Relations: Experiments on Cottontop Tamarins, *Saguinus Oedipus*', *Animal Behavior* 63 (2002), 419–435. See also the works cited in notes 41 and 43 of this chapter.

[46] Mary A. Peterson, 'Object Recognition Processes Can and Do Operate before Figure–Ground Organization', *Current Directions in Psychological Science* 3 (1994), 105–111; A. Needham and R. Baillargeon, 'Object Segregation in 8-Month-Old Infants', *Cognition* 62 (1997), 121–149; A. Needham and R. Baillargeon, 'Effects of Prior Experience on 4.5-Month-Old Infants' Object Segregation', *Infant Behavior and Development* 21 (1998), 1–24.

[47] Peterson, 'Object Perception'.

among animals capable of perceiving something as a body. I believe, however, that it is not constitutively necessary that there be a synchronic capacity. If an animal could only segment *moving* bodies from a surround, it could still represent something as a body. I also believe that a capacity to segment bodies in motion is not constitutively necessary for perceiving as of body. If an animal could only segment bodies at rest, it could still represent something as a body. Since motion is so crucial to life, there may be no actual animals that have body representation but that cannot apply it to bodies in motion.

I think that *certain* diachronic capacities—other than a capacity to detect bodies in motion—*are* constitutively necessary to having a capacity to perceive as of a body. The ability to track a particular, to represent it as the same over time, is constitutively necessary for perception of something as a body. One basis for this requirement is that events and bodies are both in the individual's environment and figure in animals' basic activities. To have a perceptual representation as of a body, an individual must have a perceptual capacity that differs from a capacity to represent something as an event. Tracking bodies over time is the central capacity for effecting the differentiation.

If an individual could never track an entity beyond the moment of distinguishing it from a background or ground, the individual's perception could not be as of a body. It would be as of something like the occurrence of a shape instance, or perhaps an event with that shape. Of course, other entities besides bodies are tracked. One can track the course of an explosion. One can track the dissipation or blowing-away of sand, or the disappearance of poured water. Tracking particulars over time is not sufficient for perception as of a body. The tracking must be linked to certain perceptual anticipations—particularly those regarding maintenance of integrity of boundaries. A capacity to track particulars over time is, however, necessary.

In actual perceptual systems that have the perceptual attributive <u>body</u>, the whole body is normally first segmented from a surround by perceiving its three-dimensional wholeness. The whole body is then tracked through time. If there are momentary objects, interactions with them play no role in establishing the content of perceptions as of body. I believe that the requirement of diachronic tracking is apriori constitutive of perceptual representation as of body.[48]

One must be careful here. Certain salient *forms* of diachronic perceptual body tracking are not apriori constitutively necessary for all species.

A common assumption, even among sophisticated psychologists, is that a capacity to track a body *in motion* or a body *behind occlusions* (whether or not the body is in motion) is constitutively necessary for representing something as a body. In fact, a capacity to represent "object permanence" is sometimes simply identified with an ability to track behind occlusions. I believe that these assumptions are mistaken.

---

[48] I believe that diachronic tracking capacities are also necessary for distinguishing bodies from shape instances.

A capacity to perceive a body, such as a small landmark, as the same body need not depend on tracking it, or any other body, behind occlusions, in motion, or even out of sight. I think that a capacity to perceptually track a body as a three-dimensionally bounded and cohesive volume shape while it remains in view (one could move to it and away from it) suffices. Imagine tracking a body that provides shelter, for example. As long as the relevant three-dimensional constancies are in play, an individual *could* represent the shelter as a body. No capacity to track in motion or behind occlusions need be in play.

Although not strictly constitutively necessary for perception as of body, tracking in motion and tracking behind occlusions are such central types of body reidentification that I want to say a little more about them.

Tracking bodies in motion is widespread among animals with visual perception. Tracking bodies behind occlusions is also relatively widespread. These are not sophisticated capacities. Numerous animals have them. They are certainly not the special preserve of human perceivers. Possibly spiders and certainly baby chicks, birds, dogs, pigs, chimps have them. Although not constitutively necessary, both these abilities are sufficient (given the other geometrical capacities mentioned earlier) to perceive particulars as bodies.

The key to both types of body reidentification lies in use of information that correlates with spatio-temporal continuity. Tracking of bodies in motion in many animals and in 2-month-old human infants is governed by something like applications to motion of the transtemporal cohesion and boundedness principles mentioned in the previous subsection.

Perceptual motion constancy is well established in young human infants. They distinguish between the perceived body's moving and the perceiver's moving. Bodies can be perceived as in motion despite a wide range of perceptual stimulations (for example, stimulations from the moving body or stimulations from partial occluders). Motion of a body is perceived even when the observer also moves. Such abilities predate the individual's self-locomotion. They are not learned as a result of distinguishing motion due to the observer's activity—'reversible motion' in the Kant–Helmholtz theory—from motion that is not under the observer's power.[49] These abilities seem to be innate not only in the perceptual systems of human infants, but in those of many animals.

Tracking bodies behind occlusions has been studied extensively, especially but not exclusively in human infants. In numerous ways it has been shown that such perception is as of a physical whole—not a series of retinal arrays, and not a gradually disappearing and then (as the object reappears) gradually growing shape. For example, 6-month-olds are allowed to watch a whole disc move

---

[49] P. J. Kellman, H. Gleitman, and E. S. Spelke, 'Object and Observer Motion in the Perception of Objects by Infants', *Journal of Experimental Psychology* 13 (1987), 586–593. The theory that motion constancy depends on learning—in particular learning to contrast self-locomotion from object motion—can be found in Helmholtz, *Treatise on Physiological Optics*; and in Piaget, *The Construction of Reality in the Child*. The approach is suggested in Kant, *Critique of Pure Reason*, the Second Analogy, though it is doubtful that Kant intended a developmental theory.

behind a screen from a fully visible position. The disc is fully visible or fully hidden only briefly, and is otherwise held in partly occluded positions. Dishabituation studies show that infants perceive the object as passing, whole, behind the occlusion, not becoming, at any time, a truncated disc.[50] Disappearance behind occluders must follow laws determining image-edge deletion mentioned in Chapter 7.[51]

The tracking abilities, both in infants and in adults, are emphatically tied to bodies that maintain their cohesion. If infants are first shown that a shape that is shape identical with a physical whole has been the result of pouring, infants do not anticipate continuity of movement, and do not track the number of objects, behind occlusions. If a complex object is shown to be assembled into the shape of a solid body, the assembled object is not tracked through disappearance behind occlusions.

Similarly, if in multiple-object-tracking experiments, objects disappear and reappear from behind occlusions in the way ordinary bodies do—so that images of the bodies change by deletion or accretion along a fixed contour—adults track them successfully. If the image shrinks to a point and then reappears by growing, tracking does not operate nearly as well. Visual perceptual systems track whole bodies that maintain integrity of their boundaries. Visual systems are not geared to follow fluid stuffs, assemblages, and oddities of disappearance.[52]

As noted, non-human animals can track bodies when they are out of sight. Chicks respond to whole bodies in a way that they do not respond to parts and properties. Within a few hours of interaction with other con-specifics, a young chick can recognize familiar con-specific individuals and distinguish them from unfamiliar ones. Chicks perceive the completed, approximate shapes of partly hidden objects as such (rather than as the shape that would result from truncating the object at the occlusion).[53] They perceptually anticipate the existence and location of fully hidden solid bodies. As with infants, motion prior to occlusion provides the dominant basis for singling out physical wholes. Detour behavior, in

---

[50] L. G. Craton and A. Yonas, 'The Role of Motion in Infant Perception of Occlusion', in J. T. Enns (ed.), *The Development of Attention: Research and Theory* (New York: Elsevier/North Holland, 1990); S. Carey and E. Spelke, 'Science and Core Knowledge', *Philosophy of Science* 63 (1996), 515–533.

[51] Kellman and Spelke, 'Perception of Partly Occluded Objects in Infancy'; Spelke, 'Principles of Object Perception'; Spelke, Kestenbaum, Simons, and Wein, 'Spatio-Temporal Continuity, Smoothness of Motion and Object Identity in Infancy'; Aguiar and Baillargeon, '2.5-Month-Old Infants' Reasoning about When Objects Should and Should Not Be Occluded', and 'Development in Young Infants' Reasoning about Occluded Objects'.

[52] Huntley-Fenner, Carey, and Salimando, 'Objects are Individuals but Stuff Doesn't Count'; Fei Xu, 'From Lot's Wife to a Pillar of Salt: Evidence that *Physical Object* is a Sortal Concept', *Mind and Language* 12 (1997), 365–392; Yantis, 'Objects, Attention, and Perceptual Experience'; Scholl and Pylyshyn, 'Tracking Multiple Items through Occlusion'; W.-C. Chiang and K. Wynn, 'Infants' Representation and Tracking of Multiple Objects', *Cognition* 77 (2000), 169–195.

[53] Giorgio Vallortigara, 'The Cognitive Chicken: Visual and Spatial Cognition in the Nonmammalian Brain', in E. A. Wasserman and T. R. Zentall (eds.), *Comparative Cognition: Experimental Explorations of Animal Intelligence* (Oxford: Oxford University Press, 2006).

which a chick pursues a goal object after losing a view of it, yields further evidence of object representation and object permanence in young chicks. Even jumping spiders evince similar abilities. Complex principles governing tracking objects behind occlusions apply to dogs, parrots, magpies, monkeys, apes.[54]

In diachronic tracking of bodies, "good" shapes or "natural" sorts are *not* the properties used in tracking, as I remarked in discussing Quine. Spheres, rectangles, and common object shapes seem to have no priority over irregularly shaped bodies, for many visual systems. Before substantial learning occurs, the visual system of human infants and many non-human animals are relatively impervious to changes in shape, color, ordinary kind (duck to sphere) in tracking bodies (whether moving or not), if continuity of cohesion and boundedness is maintained.[55]

Infants are surprised when, after watching an object pass behind an occlusion, they are shown a split object, or two objects. Suppose an infant watches the square face of a cube that moves back and forth behind an occlusion in such a way that its two sides (perhaps a third of the width of the square) alternately become visible on the two sides of the occlusion. Suppose that the center remains hidden. The infant is surprised when the occluder is removed to reveal two bodies with the faces of rectangles one-third of the width of the square, as opposed to one body with a square face. Given the motion of the partly hidden body, the infant perceives it as one connected body, rather than two bodies.

By contrast, suppose that the infant is shown a box, which is then occluded. The infant shows no surprise when a differently shaped object has replaced the box when the occlusion is removed. Similarly, infants show no surprise when a round sphere goes behind an occluder, but a duck or cube emerges on the other side, as long as speed and direction are more or less constant. Under partial

---

[54] Regolin and Vallortigara, 'Perception of Partly Occluded Objects by Young Chicks'; Regolin, Vallortigara, and Zanforlin, 'Detour Behavior in the Domestic Chick'; R. S. Wilcox and R. R. Jackson, 'Cognitive Abilities of Araneophagic Jumping Spiders', in Balda, Pepperberg, and Kamil (eds.), *Animal Cognition in Nature*; S. Gagnon and F. Y. Dore, 'Cross-Sectional Study of Object Permanence in Domestic Puppies (*Cani Familiaris*)', *Journal of Comparative Psychology* 108 (1994), 220–232; I. Pepperberg, 'Development of Piagetian Object Permanence in a Grey Parrot (*Psittacus Erithacus*)', *Journal of Comparative Psychology*, 111 (1997), 63–95; Pepperberg, *The Alex Studies*, chapter 10; Pollok, Prior, and Guntrukun, 'Development of Object Permanence in Food-Storing Magpies (*Pica pica*)'; J. J. Neiworth, E. Steinmark, B. M. Basile, R. Wonders, F. Steely, and C. Dehart, 'A Test of Object Permanence in a New-World Monkey Species, Cotton Top Tamarins (*Saguinus oedipus*)', *Animal Cognition* 6 (2003), 27–37.

[55] For a general review, see K. Nakayama, Z. J. He, and S. Shimojo, 'Visual Surface Representation: A Critical Link between Lower-Level and Higher-Level Vision', in S. M. Kosslyn and D. Osherson (eds.), *Visual Cognition: An Invitation to Cognitive Science*, ii (Cambridge, MA: MIT Press, 1995); Hofsten and Spelke, 'Object Perception and Object-Directed Reaching in Infancy'; Baillargeon, Spelke, and Wasserman, 'Object Permanence in Five-Month-Old Infants'; F. Xu and S. Carey, 'Infants' Metaphysics: The Case of Numerical Identity', *Cognitive Psychology* 30 (1996), 111–153; F. Xu, S. Carey, and J. Welch, 'Infants' Ability to Use Object Kind Information for Object Individuation', *Cognition* 70 (1999), 137–166; G. A. Van de Walle, S. Carey, and M. Prevor, 'Bases for Object Individuation in Infancy: Evidence from Manual Search', *Journal of Cognition and Development* 1 (2000), 249–280; F. Xu and S. Carey, 'The Emergence of Kind Concepts: A Rejoinder to Needham and Baillargeon', *Cognition* 74 (2000), pp. 285–301.

occlusion and in other cases where the parts of an object are revealed serially, infants do not anticipate the "simplest" shape or some sortal kind, as adults would. Although, in certain cases, featural information can affect tracking of objects in motion by young infants, such information is secondary to continuity of *any* figural wholeness. What is central to perception of bodies under occlusion in early infancy is the wholeness of the object and the continuity of its motion, not specific shapes, colors, or kinds. Similar principles apply to the visual systems of other animals.[56]

Human adults show similar results in studies of apparent motion, even though the adults have sortal concepts firmly in place. Adults are flashed images of two kinds of objects in different places at very short intervals. If the trajectory and time are right, a single object is seen as moving between the different places, even though no object occurs in the intervening trajectory, and even though a single object undergoing such changes would have to change kinds (which the adult knows to be impossible). The same phenomenon emerges in multiple-object tracking. Adults are shown ten to twelve simple (say, circular) objects. Four are highlighted momentarily. The subjects are asked to keep track of the four once all the objects are set in random motion. Subjects can track three to four (but no more) such objects for ten seconds, even if they move momentarily behind obstacles or disappear, as long as they remain on simple continuous trajectories. Subjects do not notice changes in shape and color during the tracking.[57]

These studies suggest that the laws of visual tracking in infants, who lack ordinary sortals for body individuation, are present in adult visual systems. Such laws determine visual perception in situations where the visual system is forced to represent moving bodies under extreme time or attentional constraints. In all these cases, the visual system tracks continuous motion of cohesive, bounded bodies—regardless of discontinuities in shape, color, or kind.

As children develop, beginning toward the end of the first year, they begin to use sortal-kind representations that carry further constraints on individuation of bodies. Their systems allow a smaller range of properties to change while a given object is tracked. But, as noted, even adult systems rely on the permissive whole-body representation in special situations.

Principles governing attribution of *body* are ongoing topics of investigation. Our discussion gives some indication, however, of how liberal the constitutive

[56] Spelke, 'Principles of Object Perception'; Spelke, Kestenbaum, Simons, and Wein, 'Spatio-Temporal Continuity, Smoothness of Motion and Object Identity in Infancy'; G. Van de Walle and E. S. Spelke, 'Spatiotemporal Integration and Object Perception in Infancy', *Child Development* 67 (1996), 2621–2640; M. E. Arterberry, 'Development of Spatiotemporal Integration in Infancy', *Infant Behavior and Development* 16 (1993), 343–363; M. E. Arterbery, L. G. Craton, and A. Yonas, 'Infants' Sensitivity to Motion-Carried Information for Depth and Object Properties', in C. E. Granrud (ed.), *Visual Perception and Cognition in Infancy* (Hillsdale, NJ: Erlbaum, 1993).

[57] Nakayama, He, and Shimojo, 'Visual Surface Representation'; J. A. Burkell and Z. W. Pylyshyn, 'Searching through Subsets: A Test of the Visual Indexing Hypothesis', *Spatial Vision* 11 (1997), 225–258; Scholl and Pylyshyn, 'Tracking Multiple Items through Occlusion'.

conditions on body representation are. Much less is required than traditional accounts supposed.

Psychology is a useful guide. But psychology is not concerned with constitutive conditions. Where psychologists make remarks that are relevant to the issue, even *they* tend to presume overly restrictive conditions on representation as of bodies. For example, as noted, tracking motion and tracking behind obstacles are often assumed to be necessary, as opposed to *de facto* central and virtually ubiquitous.

I conjecture that, as a constitutive matter, to represent something as a body, the individual's perceptual system must segment a three-dimensional whole from a surround by either synchronic or diachronic means. Its doing so is governed by principles for identifying cohesiveness and boundedness of three-dimensional volume shapes. And it must be able to track the wholes over time, either in motion or at rest. Tracking depends on attribution of maintenance of cohesiveness and boundedness of volume shapes. The attribution of maintenance of a cohesiveness and boundedness is usually evinced by anticipation of boundary maintenance, and by surprise if a three-dimensional entity scatters or dissipates. Capacities for segmentation and tracking must involve exercise of perceptual constancies.[58] Bearing causal relations to bodies in exercise of basic individual functions figured constitutively in the development and constitutive determination of the perceptual capacities. For example, representation as of body might be connected to acts such as predation, mating, navigating, or eating, that interact with bodies, where sensory capacities play a role in guiding the interaction.

Thus, given the constitutive background conditions regarding perceptual constancies and functional individual–environment relations with bodies, the capacity to differentiate a body from its surround by way of a bounded, cohesive volume shape, together with the capacity to attribute cohesive boundedness of volume shape over time seem to me the necessary and sufficient constitutive capacities for having the perceptual attributive body.

These capacities enable the perceiver to perceive bodies as instances of a kind, and as grounds for perceptual attributions of properties such as color, texture, specific shape, and as *loci* of change of color, size, shape, position, and so on.

---

[58] I have focused on visual tracking. At appropriate levels of abstraction, principles governing tracking in amodal and haptic systems are comparable. See this chapter, the section BODY REPRESENTATION AS ORIGINATING IN PERCEPTION, and E. S. Spelke, W. S. Born, and F. Chu, 'Perception of Moving, Sounding Objects by Four-Month-Old Infants', *Perception* 12 (1983), 719–732; P. Starkey, E. S. Spelke, and R. Gelman, 'Detection of Intermodal Numerical Correspondences by Human Infants', *Science* 222 (1983), 179–181; A. Streri, E. Spelke, and E. Rameix, 'Modality-Specific and Amodal Aspects of Object Perception in Infancy: The Case of Active Touch', *Cognition* 47 (1993), 251–279; A. Streri, 'Cross-Modal Recognition of Shape from Hand to Eyes in Human Newborns', *Somatosensory Motor Research* 20 (2003), 13–18; A. Streri, E. Gentaz, E. Spelke, and G. Van de Walle, 'Infants' Haptic Perception of Object Unity in Rotating Displays', *Quarterly Journal of Experimental Psychology: A Human Experimental Psychology* 57 (2004), 523–538; G. Bod-Bovy and E. Gentaz, 'The Haptic Reproduction of Orientations in Three-Dimensional Space', *Experimental Brain Research* 172 (2006), 283–300.

Perception of Body and Attribution of Solidity
and Generic Shape

Let us ask about a further constraint. Is anticipation of solidity and representation as of solidity a constitutive condition on perceptual representation as of body? An anticipation of solidity or impenetrability involves some disposition to be surprised if two bodies interpenetrate one another, occupying some or all of the same position, perhaps in their trajectories of movement, without resistance or damage. Are such anticipations constitutively necessary for perceiving as of body?[59]

Such anticipations are certainly widespread, perhaps ubiquitous, among perceivers with body representations. Two-month-olds exhibit anticipation of solidity at about the same time that they exhibit tracking by spatio-temporal continuity of shape. They are surprised when one object appears visually to have passed through another.[60]

Our question is not settled by the fact that solidity or resistance anticipation is widespread, perhaps even ubiquitous, among perceivers that attribute the kind *body*. Our question concerns necessary minimal constitutive conditions for having a capacity to attribute the kind *body* in perception.

It is often argued that solidity or impenetrability anticipation *is* constitutively necessary. It is argued that such anticipation is necessary to distinguish material, relatively rigid bodies from three-dimensional pac-man shapes, holograms, liquids, sand piles, and other penetrables.[61]

I am not convinced by such arguments. Holograms and penetrable pac-man shapes moving on a screen are clearly outliers in the environments in which perceptual systems evolved. They are not among the typical causal agents interacting with individuals' perceptual systems in fulfillment of individual biological functions. They do not figure in molding perceptual content. Basic perceptual representational content is not explainable in terms of patterns of relations to them. So the representational content of perceptual states is not explained by a capacity to distinguish anything from these environmental outliers. To have body representation, perceivers must distinguish bodies only from other types of

---

[59] Treating an object as solid could reside in dispositions to expect resistance to touch, but it could also reside in dispositions to be surprised by penetration, or by one body's passing through another without resistance or damage. Hofsten and Spelke, 'Object Perception and Object-Directed Reaching in Infancy'; Baillargeon, Spelke, and Wasserman, 'Object Permanence in Five-Month-Old Infants'.

[60] Baillargeon, 'Object Permanence in 3.5 and 4/5-Month-Old Infants'; S. Hespos and R. Baillargeon, 'Reasoning about Containment Events in Very Young Infants', *Cognition* 78 (2001), 207–245; Spelke, Breilinger, Macomber, and Jacobsen, 'Origins of Knowledge'.

[61] The degree of rigidity required for being a body is, I think, disputable. I am inclined to count soap bubbles bodies, even though they are capable of sharing space with other bodies—and thus are not solid or rigid. Similarly, I am inclined to count drops or pools (bodies) of water as special cases, as long as they maintain cohesiveness and boundedness for long enough to be tracked. Both the language and perceptual dispositions certainly treat these as at best special cases. Many tracking dispositions depend on anticipating relative rigidity, and tracking disintegrates in response to scatter or other dissolution and to evidence that a stuff is fluid. Nothing that I say in the text depends on taking a position on whether these are cases of bodies or not.

entities that are significant causal agents in the formation of the perceptual system through figuring in fulfillment of individuals' basic needs and activities. These outliers are not *relevant representational alternatives*. Perceivers need not distinguish bodies from such fluke-ish alternatives in order to have the perceptual attributive body. Representation of them as bodies are simply perceptual illusions.

The principle underlying this point is what I shall call the Principle of Relevant Representational Alternatives:

> (RRA) For an individual to perceptually indicate and attribute an attribute (kind, property, relation), the individual, or something in the individual's psychology, must be capable of distinguishing instances of that attribute from *relevant representational alternatives*. That is, the individual or psychology must be able to distinguish instances of that attribute from instances of other attributes that the individual can discriminate and that also ground explanations (in fact, these are biological explanations) of the individual's needs and activities in its normal environment. The *normal environment* is the environment in relation to which the representational states are individuated.[62]

The individual or system need not be able to distinguish instances of the kind from all possible entities, and need not be able to think principles or represent laws for distinguishing them.

The principle indicates a necessary condition. In effect, I conjectured in Chapter 9 that given that (RRA) is met, having perceptual constancies with respect to an attribute suffices to have a capacity to represent the attribute perceptually. I also hold that perceptual constancies are necessary for having perception in general. Necessary and sufficient conditions for perceptually representing specific attributes vary with the attribute. In this section, we are considering specific constitutive conditions on perceptually representing bodies as such.

Holograms can be mistakenly perceived as bodies. Suppose the relevant holograms are visually indiscernible in given cases from bodies. The mistaken attribution of *body* will usually be accompanied by a mistaken attribution of solidity. But the mistaken attribution of *body* need not be mistaken just because an *attribution* of solidity fails. The misattribution of body derives from the fact that the three-dimensional entities that partly explain the formation of the perceptual attribution and its representational content, through its role in individual functions with respect to bodies, are *bodies*—not holograms. Bodies are the sorts of things capable of mating, giving nourishment, being predators, providing landmarks or obstacles, providing shelter, and so on.

Pac-man figures and holograms are outliers, *ir*relevant representational alternatives. Where they cause perceptions as of body, the perceptions are mistaken,

---

[62] It should be clear that this principle is an expression of anti-individualism regarding perception. The term 'relevant alternative' has its original home in epistemology, where its meaning is related but different. See Fred Dretske, 'The Pragmatic Dimension of Knowledge', *Philosophical Studies* 40 (1981), 363–378.

in the absence of background knowledge or appropriate discrimination of these entities from bodies.

Liquids and piles of loose stuff like sand that lie in body-like shapes are *not* outliers in most animals' normal environments. They *are* relevant representational alternatives. An individual or psychological system must in some way operate differently with respect to them from the way it operates with respect to bodies, if it is to represent anything as a body.

Perhaps anticipations of solidity are a primary basis for having body representations, as distinguished from representations of masses. Attribution of solidity suffices (in the context of the other capacities we have been discussing) to provide a psychological difference between body representation and stuff representation. Representing a trackable three-dimensional whole as solid certainly is sufficient for representing the whole as a body, assuming that it is accompanied by expectation of the entity's maintaining the integrity of its boundaries. Humans and animals that perceive entities as bodies always, or almost always, perceive them as solid.[63] They often stop perceiving a particular as a body, if the particular is perceived as not being solid. (But see notes 61 and 63.)

It does not follow that attributing solidity is partly constitutive of attributing the generic kind *body*. I think that attributing solidity overdetermines attribution of body. Representing a particular as solid is not *constitutively necessary* to representing a particular as a body.

Attribution of solidity constitutively requires a capacity to track three-dimensional wholes over at least short temporal intervals, anticipating that integrity of boundaries will be maintained. This dependence is not symmetric. Tracking three-dimensional wholes while anticipating maintenance of their boundaries does not constitutively require anticipating solidity. So the issue is whether the addition of attribution of solidity to the dynamic geometrical attributional capacities is constitutively necessary to enable attribution of body to be psychologically distinct from attribution of relevant representational alternatives.

As a matter of physics, bodies that count as macro-solid can pass through one another. Visual systems do not, of course, hold open this possibility, anticipating physics. But human adults that learn that bodies are not solid in the sense that they have assumed from childhood do not have to give up their body concept, or

---

[63] It seems to me that this point applies not just to visual systems but to touch systems and sonar echolocation systems. In touch systems, solidity is usually a primary means of perceiving something as a body. But not all touch systems require contact *with the entity perceived*. A contact sense could track a body at a distance by tracking its three-dimensional outline. See Chapter 9, notes 51 and 52. Then touch perception could perceive something as a body independently of whether it represented the body as solid. The example is, of course, fictional. As far as I can see, touch systems *that depend on contact* with the entity perceived cannot represent bodies without representing them as solid. Even in cases of contact with the touched object, a capacity to perceptually track a bounded whole is, I think, the primary constitutive supplemental capacity in having the perceptual attributive body. Similarly, for sonar echolocation perceptual systems capable of determining a body's boundaries. I emphasize, however, that visual perception does not *have* to be supplemented by touch, if it is to represent entities as bodies, or as solid.

the primitive perceptual attributive on which it rests. The association of solidity with body is not constitutive, but a deeply grounded empirical association at the macro-level. The association is coded in animal and human perceptual development. As noted, attributions of solidity emerge as early as attributions of body do.

A capacity to distinguish bodies from a surround as having cohesive, bounded volume shape and a capacity to track them over time by tracking such generic shape constitutively suffice to represent as of body. These perceptual capacities are exercised in a system that functions to help individuals cope with an environment in which solid bodies are important to individuals' basic needs and activities, and constitutively entered causally into forming the capacities.

These shape-attribution and tracking capacities psychologically distinguish bodies from masses or stuffs. Many entities that have the shapes and the transtemporal continuities of bodies are not relevant representational alternatives. In perceivers' environments, the three-dimensional entities that tend to maintain cohesiveness and boundedness over time are overwhelmingly bodies. Bodies figured in the formation of perceptual capacities to represent bodies as bodies. Although those bodies were (at least mostly) in fact solid, encoding this fact is not constitutively necessary to representing as of body. The background of sensory–actional interaction with bodies, together with discriminative capacities to perceptually distinguish bodies from relevant representational alternatives in the normal environment, suffice for perceptual attribution of *body*.

Here again we see a specific application of perceptual anti-individualism. Given that bodies ground explanations in the causal background conditions for forming perceptual states, the capacities to attribute geometrical attributes and anticipate their continuation suffice to distinguish perceptual attribution of *body* from relevant alternative attributions.[64]

---

[64] Points similar to those just made regarding the requirement of solidity apply to the more refined position that representation of something as a body requires an 'intuitive mechanics' and a representation of conditions under which bodies exert *force* on one another. See Peacocke, 'Intuitive Mechanics, Psychological Reality, and the Idea of a Material Object'. (See above, Chapter 6, note 74.) Peacocke holds, p. 170, that perception as of a material object requires a *conception* of the magnitude of force. Peacocke's neo-Kantian position derives, I think, from some remarks of Evans. Even if one dropped the requirement of a *concept* of force, and reduced the requirement to some perceptual representation as of force, together with a know-how capacity to apply this representation to some mechanical interactions among bodies, I believe that the requirement would not be well grounded. Peacocke's argument for his requirement amounts to the claim (p. 171) that without it 'it seems impossible to answer the question of what makes it the case that it is the given property [*material object*] rather than some other, that the thinker is mentally representing.' (I prefer to discuss representation as of *body* rather than *material object*. Although I think all and only relevant bodies are material objects, I think that the perceptual representation body is more common than the perceptual representation material.) I came to my view before reading Peacocke's article. But I believe that I have answered the question that Peacocke thinks cannot be answered: The role of bodies in individual biological functions and the presence of perceptual constancies and tracking abilities regarding maintenance of boundaries—either in motion or at rest—suffice to distinguish bodies from other relevant representational alternatives in animal perceivers' normal environments. I believe that there are probably actual animals that perceive entities as bodies but that lack the capacity to represent force or other mechanical properties: none of their behavior needs explanation by attributing to them a representation as of force. Peacocke adds, without calling attention to it, the

Anti-individualist explanation motivates these spare constitutive conditions on having body representations. Tracking behind barriers, tracking in motion, and anticipations of solidity are common, perhaps almost ubiquitous, associations with body representations. They are not constitutive. The constitutive conditions are simple, but specific to bodies among relevant representational alternatives.

I motivated the tracking requirement on perception as of body by noting that the individual or system must be able to discriminate bodies from masses, events, and specific shapes. Bodies, masses, events, and specific shapes are each discriminable. All are explanatorily relevant to individuals' needs and basic activities in normal environments. Hence, masses, events, and specific shapes are relevant representational alternatives to bodies. Expectations of maintaining boundaries distinguish bodies from masses. Dispositions and capacities to track bodies distinguish bodies from events. Tracking also yields a psychological differentiation between the *specific* three-dimensional shape of a body (say, cubic) and the body. A body can be perceived as the same while its specific shape is perceived as changing.

Perceptual tracking constitutively relies on a body to maintain a *generic* three-dimensional integrity of its boundaries. Bodies remain wholes, whatever their specific shapes and whatever deformations the cohesive, bounded shape undergoes. Such cohesive boundedness is, of course, a shape type. I call this type, by which infants and non-human animals perceptually identify bodies, '*generic shape*'. Generic shapes are explanatorily relevant to relevant individuals' basic needs and activities. The relevant representational alternative principle (RRA) requires that the individual or individual's psychology distinguish bodies from generic shapes if the individual is to be able to perceive something as a body. How does a perceptual system mark a distinction between generic shape and body?

Anticipations of solidity can suffice to mark a distinction. Solidity is a property of bodies and not of shape instances. The individual or the individual's perceptual system can differentiate bodies from generic shape instances by associating the former with anticipations of solidity. As mentioned in Chapter 6, such anticipations can occur within the visual modality, as well as within touch perception and intermodal representation.[65]

---

further requirement that, to represent material objects, an individual must be sensitive to the role of force *in motion* (p. 172). I think that there may not be any individuals that perceive entities as bodies but do not track bodies in motion. But I think that even tracking bodies in motion is not a *constitutive* requirement on perception as of bodies, much less on representing bodies as agents of force (whether in motion or not).

It should be noticed that my answer to the question does not invoke a crude "co-variation" form of representation. I appeal to the notions of perception and representation developed in Chapter 9, and to the environment–individual relations that ground perceptual anti-individualism. Despite the lack of persuasive argument for a constitutive requirement of representation as of force or a requirement of an 'intuitive mechanics', Peacocke's article is a fine one. It makes several valuable points about perceptual representation.

[65] Baillargeon, Spelke, and Wasserman, 'Object Permanence in 5-Month-Old Infants'.

I propose, however, that anticipations of solidity are not *constitutively neces-sary* for having body representations. I think that the anticipation of holding a generic shape over time—of maintaining cohesiveness and boundedness—is the key source of differentiation between body and generic shape. Perception as of a coherent whole—of generic shape—is possible for a cloud of sand or moving water. Representation as of body is distinguished partly by being associated with anticipations of *holding* generic shape at least for short periods of time.

Generic three-dimensional volume shape, a topological property, figures in biological explanation of animal need and activity mainly in being a primary attribute through which bodies are identified. Such shape can help identify entities *other than bodies*. In such cases, perceptual systems and tracking systems attribute generic shape momentarily, but do not attribute body—or attribute body and then in tracking memory *cancel* the attribution.

A further constitutive basis for differentiation in perceptual systems between a perceptual attributive for generic shape and a perceptual attributive for body lies in the function that the attributive body has in the representational and practical economy of the perceiver. A perceptual body representation functions to unify representations of various sorts—shape, color, motion representations. A variety of attributives are bound together through their association with the body repre-sentation.[66] The same point cannot be made about color, motion, shape—even generic shape. It is a constitutive aspect of the ability to discriminate bodies—and only a contingent aspect of the ability to discriminate generic shape—that the perceived entity be trackable over at least short stretches of time, be the source of intermodal object files, and so on. Similarly, the perceptual attributive body is constitutively connected to individual causal/practical functions in ways that the generic-shape representation is not. I believe that the environmental basis for this primacy of body attributions over these property attributions lies in the causal centrality of bodies in the basic pursuits of animals.[67]

Perceptual psychology takes perceptions to be individuated in a way that accords with environmental facts, as described by other sciences. Mating, pre-dating, navigating depend for many animals on continuity of bodies through time. They also depend on the reproductive, nutritional, landmarking powers of bodies that endure through time. The diachronic kind *body* (at rest or in motion) is a biologically important kind that, for many individuals, perception functions to track. Shape instances play no such role.

---

[66] See Treisman, 'Feature Binding, Attention, and Object Perception'. Treisman argued that, under the circumstances that she studied subjects, binding requires attention. She assumed that attention requires consciousness. Some philosophers have relied on this assumption in giving consciousness a constitutive role in perception. It is clear that a great deal of unconscious perception is *by the individual*. It is now clear that attention and binding do *not* require consciousness. See Chapter 9, the section PERCEPTION AS THE INDIVIDUAL'S. See also Kentridge, Heywood, and Weiskrantz, 'Attention without Awareness in Blindsight'. I believe that, insofar as binding is a prevalent aspect of vision, it does not require attention in all circumstances. I will not go into the matter here.

[67] A further source of distinction is that bodies, with their material constitutions, are causal factors in the way that instantiations of shape are not. I will not develop this point.

Is representation as of bodies constitutively necessary for perception, or more generally for representation itself? I think not. Although a wide variety of perceivers represent bodies as such, I see no reason why body representation is constitutively necessary for perception or representation. Perceptual constancies can be exercised on many attributes—locations of sounds, for example—independently of attributing the kind *body*. It seems to me likely that some actual animals perceptually attribute other attributes, but lack the need or capacity to indicate or attribute the kind *body*.

The centrality of body representations lies in their contributions to higher levels of objectivity. They provide a stable framework by reference to which context-free spatial *systematization* can be developed. Even if representation of bodies is not constitutively necessary for perception, representation, or objectivity, it is a central element in *our* conceptual scheme, as Strawson emphasized. For recognizing the origins of our scheme, it is important to recognize how primitive and widespread a representational category body is.

PERCEPTION AND ORIGINS OF MATHEMATICAL CAPACITIES

Quine maintained that a necessary condition on representing bodies is a capacity to individuate them. He held that individuating them requires being able to use linguistic plurals and quantified sentences regarding identity and difference that are formally equivalent with counting. Such requirements are hyperintellectualized. There is an individuative capacity in the perceptual ability to attribute the kind body. When an individual perceives a body as a body, the perception marks off one body from a surround. The linguistic or even propositional counterpart is not required.

Almost any individual that can perceive something as a body can perceive more than one body, each as such, in a given scene. The individual perceives more than one integrated, three-dimensional, relatively rigid whole, spatially separated in space from one another. No capacity to count is required. Perceptually distinguishing one body from two consists in there being a perceptual difference between perceiving one body as a body, and perceiving two bodies each as a body.

Infants and various animals do associate primitive mathematical abilities with perceptual representation as of bodies, as well as other kinds. I think that these abilities are not constitutive prerequisites for objective representation, or even for perception as of bodies. However, the usefulness of such abilities makes it unsurprising that they are widespread.

Experiments have shown that, with certain severe limitations, animals and infants are *sensitive* to mathematical attributes—number, magnitude, proportion. These mathematical attributes are distinct from spatial arrangements, physical size, temporal duration, aggregate mass, aggregate energy, image arrangements of particulars, and so on. I will center on what perceptual, *representational*, capacities are associated with these sensitivities.

There appear to be two basic mathematical capacities in pre-linguistic individuals. I discuss these in turn.

Estimating Numerosity and Ratios of Aggregates

One of these capacities is analogous to estimating the numerical size of groups. In the psychological literature it is common to call this ability a sensitivity to *numerosity*. (Sometimes any primitive mathematical ability is said to concern numerosity.) 'Numerosity' is a hedge term meant to apply to number-like properties—especially approximate magnitudes of groups that are estimated in an analog way. The relevant properties are perceived as properties of perceivable entities. Numbers are not purely properties of perceivable entities. They number numbers, for example. Genuine numbers have a second-order character.[68]

In the psychological literature, there are differences over exactly what mathematical attribute numerosity is. Few theorists take the mathematical capacities that show up in perceptual discrimination of mathematical features of groups to be the same capacities that mature human beings exercise when they estimate the number of members in groups, or discriminate groups through counting. On the other hand, I believe that there is no clear and plausible account in the psychological literature of exactly what the representational content of the primitive capacity to estimate group size is. There is a corresponding unclarity about exactly what such representational content represents—about exactly what numerosity is.

The relevant perceptual capacity is an ability to estimate the approximate magnitude of aggregates or groups of particulars, and to discriminate (as smaller or larger) different aggregates whose size membership is no finer-grained, or smaller, than certain definite ratios.[69] Non-human animals and humans, including pre-linguistic infants, exhibit the capacity.

For example, aggregates of 24 particulars are systematically distinguished from aggregates of 12. Aggregates of 16/8, 12/6, and 8/4 are distinguishable. The capacity is an estimative or approximating capacity. There are severe, stable

---

[68] Frege established that numbers are essentially associated with what they count only relative to a way of sorting the counted entities. See Frege, *The Foundations of Arithmetic*, for example, sections 21–25. Accounting for the ontology and logical form of thought about the application of numbers in counting or other types of enumeration requires that the thought connect number concepts with attributions, and numbers with attributes (or, in more austere accounts, sets). It is this general idea that I have in mind when I call numbers 'second order'.

[69] I use 'aggregate' for a group of concrete particulars (entities in time with causal powers) that is individuated in terms of its members. Aggregates differ from sets in that they are concrete. There is no null or empty aggregate, and aggregates of aggregates are simply aggregates that consist of the union of members of the aggregated aggregates. Thus a singleton aggregate does not differ from its member. Members of aggregates are any concrete particulars. For a detailed development, see my 'A Theory of Aggregates', *Nous* 11 (May 1977), 97–117.

limits on what ratios are distinguishable by given individuals. I first describe the capacity as it occurs in non-human animals, human infants, and human adults. Then I discuss some of its general features.

The capacity to estimate numerosity of aggregates consistently shows instances of both the *distance effect* and the *magnitude effect*. The distance effect is the systematic dependence of error rate on quantitative separation. It is easier to discriminate aggregates, and fewer errors occur, if the difference between the aggregate number of members is greater. Aggregates of 12 are easier to discriminate from aggregates of 3 than from aggregates of 6 or 9. The magnitude effect is the systematic dependence of error rate on numerical size, for equal distances. More errors are made as quantities become larger, for equal quantitative differences between them. It is easier to discriminate aggregates with fewer members, given a fixed difference between the numbers of members. For example, aggregates of 4 are easier to discriminate from aggregates of 6 than aggregates of 10 are from aggregates of 12.

Both of these effects are signs that the capacity to distinguish aggregate quantities falls under Weber's Law. Weber's Law is that the size of a just discriminable difference is a constant ratio of the stimulus value. Or differently couched: the discriminability of two magnitudes is a strict function of their ratio. Weber's Law determines an enormous range of animal capacities.[70]

Non-human animals show powerful capacities to discriminate aggregate membership in certain ratios. Pigeons, crows, rats, monkeys, and apes can discriminate aggregates that differ in such ratios of their members as 6/4 and 5/4, but not 12/11 or 9/8. Such ratio discriminations can be made even with relatively large numbers of particulars involved. The ratios are commonly more fine-grained, or smaller, than those discriminable by very young human infants. Discriminations operate on aggregates of tones (in series), acts, bodies, figures, and so on. Experiments have controlled for various potential confounds, such as aggregate size and aggregate energy.[71]

---

[70] J. R. Platt and D. M. Johnson, 'Localization of Position within a Homogeneous Behavior Chain: Effects of Error Contingencies', *Learning and Motivation* 2 (1971), 396–414.

[71] G. Woodruff and D. Premack, 'Primitive Mathematical Concepts in the Chimpanzee: Proportionality and Numerosity', *Nature* 293 (1981), 568–570; W. H. Meck and R. M. Church, 'A Mode Control Model of Counting and Timing Processes', *Journal of Experimental Psychology: Animal Behavior Processes* 9 (1983), 320–334; A. Klein and P. Starkey, 'The Origins and Development of Numerical Cognition: A Comparative Analysis', in *Cognitive Processes in Mathematics* (Oxford: Clarendon Press, 1987); H. Davis and R. Perusse, 'Numerical Competence in Animals: Definitional Issues, Current Evidence and a New Research Agenda', *Behavioral and Brain Sciences* 11 (1988), 561–615; R. M. Church and H. A. Broadbent, 'Alternative Representations of Time, Number, and Rate', *Cognition* 37 (1990), 55–81; Gallistel, *The Organization of Learning*, chapter 10, especially 342–343; S. Dehaene, *The Number Sense* (New York: Oxford University Press, 1997), chapter 1; S. Dehaene, 'Precis of *The Number Sense*', *Mind and Language* 16 (2001), 16–36; E. Brannon, C. Wusthoff, C. R. Gallistel, and J. Gibbon, 'Numerical Subtraction in the Pigeon', *Psychological Science* 12 (2001), 238–243; M. D. Hauser, F. Tsao, P. Garcia, and E. S. Spelke, 'Evolutionary Foundations of Number: Spontaneous Representation of Numerical Magnitudes by Cotton-Top Tamarins', *Proceedings of the Royal Society, London* B270 (2003), 1441–1446; H. S. Terrace, L. K. Son, and E. M. Brannon, 'Serial Expertise of Rhesus Macaques', *Psychological Science*

At 6–7 months of age, human infants can discriminate between aggregates according to the number of their members, but only in the ratio 2/1. Discrimination can involve fairly large aggregates of objects (16/8). The experiments varied such parameters as position and aggregate size, both between tests and within tests. For example, different tests varied the size of the particulars in the aggregates being tested from test to test. And in given tests, small-sized particulars in the larger-membership aggregate were compared with large-sized particulars in the smaller-membership aggregate. The experiments also controlled for average brightness, distal contour length, and display density. The discriminated ratios depend on the number of members in the aggregated group. Successful discriminations were limited to cases where the ratio of difference between the aggregates of objects is relatively large, and (in most cases) where the size of at least one of the aggregates was larger than three members. I shall explain this point shortly.

Infants 6–7 months old discriminate the ratio 2/1 (in aggregate sizes of 16/8, 4/2, 8/4, 6/3, 32/16). They cannot discriminate the ratio 3/2 (in aggregates of 24/16, 12/8, or even 6/4). That is, they discriminate an aggregate of 12 from an aggregate of 6, but not an aggregate of 12 from an aggregate of 8. They exhibit surprise or increase attention when there is a change (say, after a screen is interposed and then lifted) from an aggregate of 12 to an aggregate of 6, but not if there is a change of an aggregate of 12 to an aggregate of 8.

By 9 months, infants discriminate aggregates in 3/2 ratios (for example, aggregates of 6/4 or 12/8 members), but not aggregates in smaller or finer-grained ratios—for example, aggregates of 8/6.[72]

Experiments again controlled for total filled area, array size and density, item size, brightness, and distal contour length. Again, the phenomenon emerges for aggregates of tones, acts, bodies, dots, and so on.

There is some evidence of limited number-like computational transformations in infants, beyond simply comparing aggregate membership in certain ratios. Some sensitivity to order of magnitude and to some analog of very simple

14 (2003), 66–73; J. I. Flombaum, J. Junge, and M. D. Hauser, 'Rhesus Monkeys (*Macaca mulatta*) Spontaneously Compute Large Number Addition Operations', *Cognition* 97 (2005), 315–325; J. F. Cantlon and E. M. Brannon, 'Shared System for Ordering Small and Large Numbers in Monkeys and Humans', *Psychological Science* 17 (2006), 401–406; J. F. Cantlon and E. M. Brannon, 'How Much Does Number Matter to the Monkey?' *Journal of Experimental Psychology: Animal Behavior Processes* 33 (2007), 32–41.

[72] P. Starkey and R. Cooper, 'Perception of Numbers by Human Infants', *Science* 210 (1980), 1033–1034; F. Xu and E. S. Spelke, 'Large Number Discrimination in 6-Month-Old Infants', *Cognition* 74 (2000), 1–11; J. S. Lipton and E. S. Spelke, 'Origins of Number Sense: Large Number Discrimination in Human Infants', *Psychological Science* 15 (2003), 396–401; J. S. Lipton and E. Spelke, 'Discrimination of Large and Small Numerosities by Human Infants', *Infancy* 5 (2004), 271–290; J. Wood and E. Spelke, 'Infants' Enumeration of Actions: Numerical Discrimination and its Signature Limits', *Developmental Science* 8 (2005), 1173–1181; F. Xu, E. S. Spelke, and S. Goddard, 'Number Sense in Human Infants', *Developmental Science* 8 (2005), 88–101.

addition and subtraction, involving discriminable ratios, has been demonstrated.[73]

Human adults evince the same capacity under circumstances in which they cannot count large aggregates and have to estimate. Adults have been tested on larger aggregates than children. They were given such tasks as indicating which aggregate is larger. Reaction times and error rates were predictable from ratios—showing distance and magnitude effects. Human adults show an approximate ratio limit of eight to seven.[74]

The predictions remain in intermodal cases. For example, if an individual is given an aggregate of tones to compare with an aggregate of dots, the limits on discriminating ratios and the distance and magnitude effects emerge. Similar intermodal discrimination has been found in human infants and non-human animals.

Again, analogs of simple arithmetical operations on the estimates were made by humans older than infants. For example, individuals, including children at stages in which mathematical competence is not advanced (5-year-olds), are asked to add or subtract successively presented aggregates and compare the result (larger or smaller) with a third aggregate. Aggregate size ranged from 9 to 63, and presentations were too swift to allow counting.

Addition was as accurate as simple two-way comparison, and subtraction only slightly less so. Intermodal tasks were performed with a facility comparable to that of intramodal comparison. The distance and magnitude effects emerge very clearly.

Several psychologists have maintained that adult arithmetical capacities are built on these primitive estimative capacities that human beings share with animals.[75]

What are the form and meaning (representational content) of these representational capacities? There is reason to construe them as broadly mathematical. As noted, experiments have specifically controlled for distinguishing between these relatively "pure" mathematical capacities and capacities to discriminate magnitudes or amounts of other parameters—such as size, distance, density of filling a space, temporal duration, length, shape, weight, spatial area of distribution, volume, mass, energy (of actions), and so on. What the discriminations seem to

[73] E. M. Brannon, 'The Development of Ordinal Numerical Knowledge in Infancy', *Cognition* 83 (2002), 223–240; K. McCrink and K. Wynn, 'Large-Number Addition and Subtraction by 9-Month-Old Infants', *Psychological Science* 15 (2004), 776–781.

[74] H. Barth, N. Kanwisher, and E. Spelke, 'The Construction of Large Number Representations in Adults', *Cognition* 86 (2003), 201–221; P. Pica, C. Lemer, V. Izard, and S. Dehaene, 'Exact and Approximate Arithmetic in an Amazonian Indigene Group', *Science* 306 (2004), 499–503.

[75] Dehaene, *The Number Sense*; J. Whalen, C. R. Gallistel, and R. Gelman, 'Nonverbal Counting in Humans: The Psychophysics of Number Representation', *Psychological Science* 10 (1999), 130–137; H. Barth, K. La Mont, J. Lipton, S. Dehaene, N. Kanwisher, and E. Spelke, 'Non-Symbolic Arithmetic in Adults and Young Children', *Cognition* 98 (2006), 199–222. See also D. Burr and J. Ross, 'A Visual Sense for Number', *Current Biology* 18 (2008), 1–4.

co-vary with and track is number of members of given aggregates, and ratios of numbers of the members of different aggregates.

It is often claimed that these capacities not only track but *"represent"* the cardinal numbers of set memberships. Let us alter this claim to a claim about aggregates rather than sets. Aggregates are limited to concrete perceptible groups, and are not subject to the powerful iterative and abstractive operations that sets are. Such an alteration still captures a common view among psychologists.

I believe that this view trades on the overly broad conception of representation that I have discussed from Chapter 8 onward. On the broad conception, representation just *is* co-variance or tracking, assuming that the capacity has a function. I will discuss the nature of the relevant representation in light of the distinctively psychological conception of representation that I have been elaborating.

Computational transformations require, as input, segmentation of aggregates into members, presumably through perceptual attributions. Some computational transformations do not require perceptual input. Computational transformations that achieve balance or that initiate angular turning of the body need not involve perceptual input, or involve representation, in a distinctively psychological sense, at all. Or to take another example: an animal could forage in one direction rather than another because the aggregate intensity of an olfactory registration on one side of its body is greater than that on the other. The computational transformation that yields its finally turning in one direction rather than the other could result from systematic comparison of the results of explorations resulting from turnings in the two directions. So there might be a computational transformation that compares the average smell intensity resulting from foraging in one direction with the average smell intensity resulting from foraging in the other. Although some computational transformation involving a magnitude would be involved, no perceptual state or other representational state need figure in the computational transformation. The principle governing the transformations could make reference purely to bodily impressions, not to representational states with veridicality conditions. In the next sections, concerning spatial and temporal representation, I further discuss such non-representational computational transformations, governed by principles that make reference to magnitudes.

I assume, however, that the estimative ability under discussion *does* take as input perceptual attributions that determine membership in an aggregate of particulars. I assume that the estimative ability is representational. For example, in estimating ratios of aggregates of bodies, an individual's psychology begins with perceptual attribution of the kind *body*. Then a magnitude is computed with respect to this kind-attribute as the relevant parameter for estimation. Finally, the magnitude is attributed to the perceived aggregate.

The relevant estimative capacity has a *second-order* character. Estimation of aggregate membership quantity, and of ratios between aggregates, depends on a prior attribution of a first-order kind that determines membership in an aggregate. The quantity attribution varies with the kind attribution, since the aggregate (*one* aggregate) is always identical with the totality of its members (usually *many*). By contrast, the physical weight of the cumulated members and the weight of the aggregate are always the same, since weight is a first-order cumulative property. (I assume that the aggregate is identical with its cumulated members.)

The numerosity of the aggregate is determinable only by distinguishing the kind-attribute (say, *body*) that determines members of the aggregate from the kind-attribute *aggregate*, which applies to the same thing as all the members. There is one aggregate; there are numerous aggregate members. The difference between one and numerous resides not in the thing itself (the aggregate *is* its members), but only relative to the kind-attributive. That is the way in which attribution of cardinal numbers works in counting.[76] One counts members of a set or aggregate relative to some guiding lower-order kind attributive that determines membership in a set or aggregate. The representational form of numerosity estimates is analogous.

So I assume that relevant computational principles concern *mathematical* magnitudes and that, in view of their involving perceptual states, the relevant computational transformations yield *representational* states. Moreover, the relevant magnitude seems to concern the magnitude of aggregates, in the sense that number and ratios of relevant aggregate membership co-vary with the input and output, respectively, of the computations. Finally, as we have seen, there is some evidence that the capacity involves competence with analogs of simple arithmetical operations—addition and subtraction. I believe that these four considerations support the view that some type of mathematical representation is at issue. These considerations have been taken to support the view that the relevant individuals represent cardinal number.

On the other hand, there are aspects of the representational capacity that do not accord with the idea that it represents the cardinal number of aggregate membership. In the first place, the representational capacity seems to be analog or continuous rather than discrete. The representational capacity can co-vary only in ways that are *roughly proportional* to the cardinal numbers of aggregates. The applicability of Weber's Law and the distance and magnitude effects suggest that the form of representation is analog rather than digital. Of course, the integers could be represented by analog representations—by spatial lengths or temporal durations of symbols, for example. But further considerations militate against this possibility.

The capacity seems to be essentially and entirely estimative or approximative. We who can use arithmetic to represent cardinal numbers of aggregates do engage in estimation. But it is one thing to engage in estimation while having a

---

[76] This is Frege's point again. See note 68. There is one aggregate and a large magnitude of bodies. There is one deck of cards, a large numerosity of cards, a smaller numerosity of suits. The aggregate that consists of the deck is the same physical entity as the cards, and these are collectively the same physical entity as the suits. Similarly there is one aggregate of shoes in the closet, a larger numerosity of pairs of shoes, and a larger numerosity yet of shoes. Numerosity magnitudes have the same second-order representational character that cardinal numbers of aggregates or sets do.

background arithmetical capacity, and another thing to engage in estimation with no capacity to count aggregate membership at all. The relevant estimative capacity appears not to be associated (except in relatively developed human beings) with a capacity to count.

Similarly, although comparisons of aggregate magnitudes that yield representation of ratios suggest a capacity for determining numerical equivalence or non-equivalence through one–one matching between the members of different aggregates, there is no evidence, to my knowledge, of actual one–one matching in the comparisons. So it appears that the analog form of representation may never be used digitally.

This point can be deepened. Early accounts of the estimative capacity postulated an accumulator model to account for the computational transformations underlying estimation of aggregate magnitude and ratios between aggregates. Suppose that the nervous system has some form of a pulse generator that generates pulses at a constant rate. Suppose that there is a gate that allows energy from the pulses to pass into an accumulator mechanism, in such a way that the accumulator somehow registers how much energy has been let through. Suppose that a unit of energy passes through the gate for each particular in the aggregate, as determined by some attributive; and this cumulative energy is tracked, regardless of other attributes that the particular might have. Suppose that during estimation, the gate is opened for a constant amount of time for each pulse passing through. The energy accumulated at any given time is a constant function of the cardinal number (natural number) of the particulars in the aggregate. It might be, and in fact has been, concluded that the total amount of energy could serve as analog representation of the natural number.[77]

One could imagine a bucket filling with water, where the hose lets so much water through per time unit, and where there are markers on the bucket at different levels that correspond to the amount of water that enters the bucket per time unit. The result (the water level) could be regarded as producing an approximating, analog "representation" of natural number unit marked by the marker closest to the actual water level.

This model could be regarded as instantiating a counting procedure using representations in analog form. Successive levels of accumulation correspond to successive numerals. The accumulated levels are in 1–1 correspondence with particular members in an aggregate, and the final state of accumulation corresponds to the number of particulars in the aggregate.[78]

This correspondence between accumulation and counting would not suffice— even if the correspondence was functional for an organism—to make the

---

[77] Meck and Church, 'A Mode Control Model of Counting and Timing Processes'; R. M. Church and W. H. Meck, 'The Numerical Attribute of Stimuli', in H. L. Roitblatt, T. G. Bever, and H. S. Terrace (eds.), *Animal Cognition* (Hillsdale, NJ: Erlbaum, 1984).

[78] C. R. Gallistel and R. Gelman, 'Preverbal and Verbal Counting and Computation', *Cognition* 44 (1992), 43–74. See Gallistel, *The Organization of Learning*, 338–343.

accumulator mechanism a genuinely representational operation, in my sense of 'representation'.

In neither the bucket example nor the nervous-system example, as so far described, is there the slightest need to invoke veridicality conditions to help explain the mechanism or capacity. The model models sensitivity to number, or number discrimination, or number registration. It is not a representational operation. We are, however, taking the model to be embedded in a perceptual representational system. The accumulator model does suggest an analog of counting, but there is no digital usage underlying the analog usage. So, even considered as serving perception, the accumulator model does not provide sufficient ground to regard the system as representing cardinal numbers, which are discrete magnitudes.

Although the accumulator model suggests an analog of counting, it does not correctly model the relevant estimative capacity. That estimative capacity is even further from counting and representation of natural numbers than the accumulator model is. That model predicts that estimating the magnitude of aggregates with more members takes more time than estimating the magnitude of aggregates with fewer members. This prediction is not borne out. Estimation of larger aggregate magnitudes does not take longer than estimation of simultaneously presented smaller aggregate magnitudes. Similarly, for ratio comparisons.[79]

Other models besides the accumulator model postulate different computational transformations underlying estimation of numerosity. For example, Dehaene and Changeux hypothesize that for each perceptually represented entity in an aggregate (for example, for each body in an aggregate or for each tone in an aggregate), there is a normalizing operation that assigns a constant number of neurons for each particular representation. For each body, *regardless of size*, a given number of neurons is assigned by the estimative capacity to each perceptual body representation, even if more neurons enter into the initial perception of larger bodies than of smaller bodies. The normalization washes out differences in size to fix on bodies *per se*. Then the estimate of the magnitude of the aggregate derives from registering the total number of (normalized) neurons engaged (or energy corresponding to the total number of neurons engaged), and dividing the total by the number of neurons in a single normalization.[80]

Let me give another example of a model that unlike the accumulator model is not defeated by evidence, as far as I know. This model, proposed by Church and Broadbent, represents average density or duration (spatial or temporal) of particulars in an aggregate, represents the total extent (spatial or temporal) of the

[79] J. Intriligator and P. Cavanagh, 'The Spatial Resolution of Attention', *Cognitive Psychology* 43 (2001), 171–216; J. N. Wood and E. Spelke, 'Chronometric Studies of Numerical Cognition in Five-Month-Old Infants', *Cognition* 97 (2005), 23–39.

[80] S. Dehaene and J. P. Changeux, 'Development of Elementary Numerical Abilities: A Neuronal Model', *Journal of Cognitive Neuroscience* 5 (1993), 390–407; Dehaene, *The Number Sense*, 31–34.

aggregate, and then divides the latter by the former to yield an estimate of magnitude of aggregate membership.[81]

What is striking about both these models is that they are not iterative or recursive. There is no apparent use for the operation of adding one. The representation of larger aggregate membership magnitudes is not formed through an ordinal sequence that corresponds to the sequence of natural numbers. There is no analog of counting. And individual aggregate magnitudes intermediate between the basic unit and the magnitude of the whole aggregate do not come into play. The model fixes on a single ratio between the basic unit and something (say, the total spatial or temporal magnitude covered by an aggregate) that is not a pure mathematical magnitude at all.[82]

I have highlighted two facts about the capacity for estimating numerosity. One is that the capacity is an analog form of representation that is never used digitally. The other is that the capacity appears not to have an iterative form. I think that these facts, indeed the first taken alone, show that the capacity for estimating numerosity cannot represent the natural cardinal numbers, the positive integers, *as such*. It cannot attribute positive integers in numbering aggregate membership. Further, I think that in the absence of any attribution of cardinal natural numbers *as such* to aggregates, the capacity cannot have them as *representata*. For if no representation in the capacity represents the positive integers as such, no representation distinguishes the positive integers, as a distinctive mathematical structure.

The fact that the capacity is sensitive to, correlates with, certain aspects of the natural number structure and the fact that the natural numbers can be approximately mapped onto the representational structure exhibited by the capacity do not show that the capacity represents the natural numbers as such, or even takes natural numbers as *representata* at all. The veridicality conditions of the

---

[81] Church and Broadbent, 'Alternative Representations of Time, Number, and Rate'.

[82] Susan Carey, *The Origin of Concepts*, 137–147 and 293–295, makes this point against other psychologists, in particular Dehaene and Gallistel. She gives further empirical reasons. Her view that *natural* numbers are not represented by the system for estimating numerosity is, however, associated with the terminologically misleading claim that analog numerosity representations represent the cardinal number of sets (for example, pp. 151, 291–292.) Given that the relevant representations do not, on her own account, represent any specific numbers (natural numbers, integers, rationals, reals), it is implausible that they represent number at all. To say that they represent 'approximate cardinal values' (p. 296) does not seem good theoretical practice. Virtually all perceptual representation is approximate. 'Approximate' modifies the form or accuracy of representation, not the objects of representation. Carey certainly seems correct to say that numerosity representations are 'number relevant' and that they approximately track the cardinal number of sets. She notes some of the oddity of counting numerosity representations as representations of number, but then passes off the issue as a merely terminological matter (p. 296). But getting the terminology right seems to me part of understanding exactly what the capacity is and what is represented by it. I will make some suggestions toward solving the problem toward the end of this section. I emphasize that this terminological/theoretical drawback does not affect the main thrust of her empirical account. Her firm distinction between the two systems in chapters 4 and 8, and her conjectural account of the development of genuine arithmetical cognition in her chapters 8 and 9 both seem to me illuminating. On the latter, see note 106 below.

representational content of the capacity do not seem to be explainable in terms of key structural aspects of that structure.

If the system does not represent the natural numbers, it is hard to see how it could represent any of the other numbers. Representation of the rationals and reals would constitute representation of the natural numbers plus further numbers. Of course, the capacity may help ground the later development of a capacity to apply numerical systems to aggregates and relatively continuous magnitudes in the physical world. But at this stage the capacity does not seem to be numerical.

A third fact may count against taking estimation of numerosity to represent number. The psycho-physical facts that apply to estimation of numerosity also apply to estimation of aggregate physical size of groups and to aggregate temporal duration of events.[83] This result suggests that the format or formats for representing spatial, temporal, and aggregate-membership magnitudes may be unified or very closely related. It is not plausible that representation of temporal and spatial magnitudes is numerical at this stage.

Some psychologists distinguish between what is explicitly represented and what is implicitly represented. In this case, the analog symbols themselves might be said to be part of explicit representation. Thus what those symbols represent would be explicitly represented. The operations of division and quasi-1–1 mapping involved in ratio comparison might be said to be represented implicitly. The idea would be that explicit representation is analog, but the digital aspects of numerical structures are represented implicitly.

This way of thinking is confused in ways discussed in Chapter 9, the section PERCEPTION AS OBJECTIFICATION. The operations in perception are laws of formation of representational states, or of transformation among representational states. Except in sophisticated individuals, the laws or operations are not represented at all. The operations are genuinely mathematical, and they involve genuine representational states with mathematical representational contents. But the operations themselves are not represented. The content involved in specifying the operations is not the content of any representational state in the relevant system.[84]

I believe that psychologists have held that the capacity represents numbers for want of a salient alternative. The capacity concerns *some* mathematical entities or structures. It bears on aggregate size in the way natural numbers bear on the cardinalities of sets or aggregates. Natural numbers can be correlated with some of the capacity's discriminative powers. So natural numbers are taken to be *representata*.

The trouble is that the natural numbers can be correlated with quite a lot of mathematical structures. It does not follow that the structures constitute the natural number structure. In this case, the lack of any division of analog

---

[83] L. Feigenson, 'The Equality of Quantity', *Trends in Cognitive Science* 11 (2007), 185–187.

[84] I believe that one should reserve 'implicit representation' for unconscious representation or for capacities that can be realized in definite states or occurrences. Most uses of the phrase tend to fudge distinctions or cover confusion.

representations into subunits that correspond to the sequence of natural numbers, and the lack of any representation of digital operations on the representations, make it untenable, I think, to hold that the capacity for estimating numerosity represents the natural numbers, or other numbers, or operations on them, even "implicitly".

If the capacity for estimating numerosity does not represent numbers (as such or by having them as *representata*), what *does* the capacity represent?

I believe that some help may be available from ancient Greek ways of thinking about mathematics. Aristotle construed mathematics as being about quantity—either discrete quantity or continuous quantity.[85] An alternative terminology derives from Euclid. It was taken up in the early modern period. This terminology divides pure magnitudes into discrete and continuous subspecies.[86] A pure magnitude is a magnitude not specific to any further type of magnitude—such as spatial extent or size, temporal duration, weight, and so forth. Eudoxus, as presented by Euclid, developed a theory of ratios that does not appeal to numbers *per se*—though, of course, ratios can be expressed, in modern mathematics, in terms of numbers.[87] Simple operations of addition, subtraction, multiplication, division, and magnitude comparison were explained as applicable to such magnitudes. As with numerosities, the entities postulated by Eudoxus' theory are applicable only to concrete particulars whose counting or measuring are basic to practical life.

I believe that it would be fruitful to use Eudoxus' theory to understand representational contents of the perceptually based capacity to estimate numerosity. Such contents represent pure magnitudes as such. The magnitudes can fall into ratios, but they are represented in a way that is not specific as between continuous magnitudes and discrete magnitudes. At any rate, they do not represent discrete pure magnitudes—the numbers.

Of course, the base units of representation for the computational transformations—particular bodies, dots, tones, acts—are discrete. But the transformations do not keep track of this discreteness. The capacity estimates magnitudes of aggregates with respect to membership. The members are not counted. They are discriminated in ratios that fall roughly into the patterns of ratios between integers. This remark about ratios between integers is a meta-theoretic remark about the approximate discriminative capacities of the individuals. It does not correspond to the form or content of the capacity's representation.

Similarly, simple mathematical operations on magnitudes do not engage in the abstractions involved in representing the natural numbers. They are operations on concrete analog representations of magnitudes that, *as a matter of fact*, tend to

---

[85]　Aristotle, *Categories* vi 4^{b}20 ff.

[86]　Euclid, *Elements*, book 5.

[87]　Ibid., book 5, def. 5. See Howard Stein, 'Eudoxus and Dedekind: On the Ancient Greek Theory of Ratios and its Relation to Modern Mathematics', *Synthese* 84 (1990), 163–211; Daniel Sutherland, 'Kant on Arithmetic, Algebra, and the Theory of Proportions', *Journal of the History of Philosophy* 44 (2006), 533–558.

yield approximate ratios of integers. The operations are quantitative transformations among analog representations. The representational content of the analog
representations is not specific as between discrete and continuous magnitudes.
The fact that the representational contents can be approximately mapped onto the
positive intergers is a psychological meta-theoretical fact about the contents.
Taking this fact as a straightforward indication that natural numbers are represented (albeit in analog form) underrates the differences between estimation of
numerosity and estimations with the representations of the natural numbers, or
any other cardinal numbers. I conjecture that the early Greeks articulated and
formalized basic animal and childhood capacities when they theorized about
magnitudes and ratios in a way that is unspecific as to whether the magnitudes
are numbers or continuous quantities.

Mathematical Tracking of Indexed Particulars

I mentioned two pre-linguistic, mathematical capacities in animals and young
children. The second capacity involves sensitivity to the *exact* cardinal number of
particulars in *very small* aggregates. It is a capacity quickly to determine and to
track the number of such particulars.[88]

This capacity differs from estimation of numerosity in several ways. But two
are most salient. It is not an estimative capacity. And it is applicable only to small
numbers of *representata*. Like estimation of numerosity, this capacity can be
found in adult human psychologies, as well as those of human infants and non-
human animals.

Infants respond differentially to the exact cardinality of a small group of
entities (distinguishing one from two, and less reliably two from three). As
applied to body, this ability is associated with tracking capacities discussed in
the section PERCEPTION AND BODY.

The infant is allowed to watch one or two objects placed behind a screen. The
screen is removed after as long as ten seconds to show one object or two. Infants
exhibit longer looking times, relative to a baseline—thus showing a novelty
reaction—when the number of objects shown differs from the number that the
infant saw placed behind the screen. These abilities are accompanied by analogs
of addition and subtraction. At 5 months of age infants can anticipate correctly
the outcomes of 1+1 and 2−1, even when the test is set up so that they cannot be
tracking the same bodies through occlusion. The infants are not surprised when,
after the screen is removed, the color, shape, or kind of the bodies has changed.
They are surprised when the number has changed. Given certain experimental
controls, there is reason to believe that the child sometimes tracks number of

---

[88] The capacity, which is closely associated with multiple-object tracking (discussed above, the
section PERCEPTION AND BODY), seems to have been first clearly described by W. S. Jevons, 'The Power
of Numerical Discrimination', *Nature* 3 (1871), 263–272.

particulars rather than continuous parameters—such as aggregate size. The capacity applies not only to bodies but to syllables, tones, and sequences of physical acts.

These results are very robust—frequently replicated in a wide variety of contexts.[89] Various non-human animals show similar abilities.[90]

A significant feature of these experiments is a definite aggregate membership limit. For 5-month-olds, the limit is 2 particulars. 10-month-olds show a limit at 3. That is, they perform similarly to the 5-month-olds with 2 vs 1. But they also perform well on 3 vs 2 and 3 vs 1 particulars. Non-human primates can discriminate, and track in memory, exact aggregate membership sizes of small groups of particulars, in the range of 3 or 4. Birds (pigeons, jackdaws, ravens, parrots) evince similar abilities with apparent limits in the 3–7 range.

The aggregate membership size limit is so striking that it bears elaboration. A child (or monkey) might be shown an experimenter placing two pieces of food in one container and three in another. The child (or monkey) is then allowed to move toward the containers. The experiment focuses on which container, which food source, the subject moves toward and retrieves food from. Monkeys show a size limit at 4. They go for the larger number at 2 vs 1, 3 vs 2, and 4 vs 3. But they are at chance at 5 vs 3, 5 vs 2, 8 vs 4, and 8 vs 3. As noted, 10-month-olds show a size limit at 3. They go for the larger number of food units at 2 vs 1, 3 vs 2, and 3 vs 1. But they are at chance at 4 vs 3, 4 vs 2, and even 4 vs 1.[91] The general point is that when one aggregate exceeds the membership-size limit, performance disintegrates.

Various controls, particularly making use of search situations, indicate that infants and monkeys at least sometimes respond to *number*, and not to aggregate

[89] E. Loosbroek and A. W. Smitsman, 'Visual Perception of Numerosity in Infancy', *Developmental Psychology* 26 (1990), 916–922; Wynn, 'Addition and Subtraction by Human Infants'; K. Wynn, 'Children's Acquisition of the Number Words and the Counting System', *Cognitive Psychology* 24 (1992), 220–251; K. Wynn, 'Infants' Individuation and Enumeration of Physical Actions', *Psychological Science* 7 (1996), 164–169; R. Bijeljac-Babic, J. Bertoncini, and J. Mehler, 'How Do 4-Day-Old Infants Categorize Multisyllabic Utterances?', *Developmental Psychology* 29 (1993), 711–721; E. Koechlin, S. Dehaene, and J. Mehler, 'Numerical Transformations in Five-Month-Old Infants', *Mathematical Cognition* 3 (1998), 89–104; L. Feigenson, S. Carey, and M. Hauser, 'The Representations Underlying Infants' Choice of More: Object-Files versus Analog Magnitudes', *Psychological Science* 13 (2002), 150–156; L. Feigenson and S. Carey, 'On the Limits of Infants' Quantification of Small Object Arrays', *Cognition* 97 (2005), 295–313; Wood and Spelke, 'Chronometric Studies of Numerical Cognition in Five-Month-Old Infants'.

[90] Klein and Starkey, 'The Origins and Development of Numerical Cognition'; M. D. Hauser, P. MacNeilage, and M. Ware, 'Numerical Representation in Primates', *Proceedings of the National Academy of Sciences USA* 93 (1996), 1514–1517; E. M. Brannon and H. S. Terrace, 'Ordering of the Numerosities 1 to 9 by Monkeys', *Science* 282 (1998), 746–749; Bull and Uller, 'Spontaneous Small Number Discrimination in Semi-Free Ranging Domestic Pigs (*Sus Scrofa*)'.

[91] Hauser, Carey, and Hauser, 'Spontaneous Number Representation in Semi-Free-Ranging Rhesus Monkeys'; D. Barner, J. Wood, M. Hauser, and S. Carey, 'Evidence for a Non-Linguistic Distinction between Singular and Plural Sets in Rhesus Monkeys', *Cognition* 107 (2008), 603–622; Feigenson, Carey, and Hauser, 'The Representations Underlying Infants' Choice of More'; Feigenson and Carey, 'On the Limits of Infants' Quantification of Small Object Arrays'.

food amount (though this is what the subjects are geared to maximize), or total amount of time taken in placing food in the containers, or the like. For example, when 12-month-olds are shown one, two, or three objects placed in a container, they search for exactly the number seen to be put in the container. At higher numbers, they do not.[92]

Human adults show similar abilities to discriminate exact numbers of particulars under time pressure. Adults can enumerate as many as three or four bodies or dots in a glance. This activity is called '*subitizing*'.[93] Reaction time takes six-hundredths of a second longer per object between two and four, but two to three times as much longer per object above four objects. This result may perhaps be explained in terms of the individuals' having available three to four short-term object indexes (see the account of multiple-object tracking in the section PERCEP-TION AND BODY). These indexes can be assigned in an attentive glance. The quick enumeration of up to four objects is apparently carried out by an automatic sensitivity to the number of activated indexes.[94] Above that limit, counting or estimation must take over.

Subitizing in adults may be an aspect of the same system of perceptual tracking that occurs in infants, primates, other mammals, and birds. At any rate, infants, adults, and primates have fast systems sensitive to the exact number of membership of small aggregates of particulars—abstracting from other quantitative properties, such as item or cumulative size.

What is the form of these abilities to determine and track the numbers of items in small aggregates? The ability appears best accounted for in terms of tracking individuals and their differences, or some other simple, bounded matching

---

[92] Van de Walle, Carey, and Prevor, 'Bases for Object Individuation in Infancy'; Feigenson, Carey, and Hauser, 'The Representations Underlying Infants' Choice of More'; Feigenson and Carey, 'On the Limits of Infants' Quantification of Small Object Arrays'. It is currently a complex empirical issue to determine under what conditions individuals primarily attend to number of members of small aggregates and under what conditions they aggregate amounts or magnitudes of other attributes—such as aggregate or cumulative size—of the members. But it appears that individuals can track either. Which attribute is tracked (number of particulars or some cumulative magnitude of a property) depends on context.

[93] The term originates with E. L. Kaufman, M. W. Lord, T. W. Reese, and J. Volkman, 'The Discrimination of Visual Number', *American Journal of Psychology* 62 (1949), 498–525. The term strictly applies to the ability to discriminate exact aggregate membership size of small numbers of items at much faster rates than ordinary counting. Even in subitizing, reaction times, in both humans and other animals, increase with increases in the number of items (from 1 to 2 to 3, and so on). This fact has led some to hold that subitizing is a different phenomenon from the phenomenon involved in multiple-object tracking, and may be connected with estimations of numerosity of aggregates. Sounds, sights, objects, events are subitized in lower mammals as well as in humans and primates. I use the term in its original meaning.

[94] S. Ullman, 'Visual Routines'; L. Trick and Z. W. Pylyshyn, 'What Enumeration Studies Tell Us about Spatial Attention: Evidence for Limited Capacity Pre-Attentive Processing', *Journal of Experimental Psychology: Human Perception and Performance* 19 (1993), 331–351; L. M. Trick and Z. W. Pylyshyn, 'Why are Small and Large Numbers Enumerated Differently? A Limited Capacity Pre-Attentive Stage in Vision', *Psychological Review* 101 (1994), 80–112. Even in subitzing, in humans and other animals, reaction times increase with increases in the number of items, suggesting some serial element in the capacity.

process. There need be no representational content that refers to the numbers, like the contents 1, 2, or 3. There need be no use of conjunction or negation in the perceptual representation (as in: <u>that is a body and this is a body and this is not that</u>), which in this case would produce a representational content that is logically equivalent to a count of two bodies. The tracking of two bodies can be through a perception or perceptual memory that contains two representational contents as of different particular bodies separated in space.[95] The representational content has two singular context-dependent elements, guided by perceptual attributives. Such contents are available for acts, tones, and other entities besides bodies.

These perceptual abilities are commonly linked to intermodal representational contents—contents that are not specific to any one perceptual modality, like vision. The tracking of multiple particulars is not specific to vision or visual memory. In fact, simple arithmetical matching can operate on combinations of seen and heard (or seen and felt) items. When the abilities are trained for one sensory modality, they transfer spontaneously to another modality and to a combination of modalities.[96] Both within a perceptual modality and intermodally, it appears that singular, context-dependent files for tracking particulars are set up in individuals' psychologies. The size limit on tracking particulars is associated with a limit on the number of singular reference files available at any one time.

The files can be singular place-holders. They need not be attached to specific particulars. In habituation, an individual is not necessarily shown the same object twice. The individual's psychology still sets up an expectation involving a model that has ready files for a specific number of particulars. For example, if an individual is repeatedly shown two bodies (but different bodies each time), the individual's habituation might contain an anticipation with a representational content containing two object files for bodies, each of which has the semantics of a place-holder rather than a singular content with a definite referent: that$_1$body, that$_2$body. As particular bodies are shown, the standing place-holder content could temporarily take on reference to particular bodies.[97]

---

[95] For more on the relation between the experiments on adults and infants in the areas of subitizing, multiple-object tracking, tracking through occlusion, and so on, see Leslie, Xu, Tremoulet, and Scholl, 'Indexing and the Object Concept'; Carey and Xu, 'Infants' Knowledge of Objects'; S. Carey, 'Cognitive Foundations of Arithmetic: Evolution and Ontogenesis', *Mind and Language* 16 (2001), 37–55.

[96] Church and Meck, 'The Numerical Attribute of Stimuli'; Starkey, Spelke, and Gelman, 'Detection of Intermodal Numerical Correspondences by Human Infants'.

[97] Of course, I do not rule out the possibility that these capacities are best explained in terms of representation of some second-order equivalence operation on attributives. At some point in human development, a propositional representation with such a form emerges. However, since these mathematical capacities occur in numerous animals, almost surely including animals that lack propositional attitudes, the representational capacities in them are extremely low level, and very likely entirely first order. The issues are empirical. My discussion is meant to highlight the simplicity of the representational contents at the lowest levels at which the mathematical capacities show themselves.

Mathematical operations, like addition or subtraction, seem not to be represented in these perceptual and intermodal capacities. There is evidence that individuals' representational states are transformed in accord with mathematical operations, and are explained in terms of such operations. But there is no evidence that individuals represent the operations. The operations are like the laws or operations for transforming representational contents that I have discussed in other contexts. The effect of such operations is gotten through the anticipatory production or deletion of singular context-dependent object files.

Such production and deletion have arithmetical implications. In fact, the operations involved in the use of these object files in tracking the number of members in small aggregates seem close to counting. But the differences are as impressive as the similarities.

There is, of course, a low upper bound on the number of indexes available for perceptual tracking. There is no evidence that the process meets any of the formal conditions on counting—that exactly one second-order representation be assigned to each entity relative to an attributive (determining aggregate membership), that the order of assignment of second-order representations is the same on each occasion of counting, and that the final representation assigned be applied to the aggregate, rather than to the particular member counted.[98] Human children commonly do not realize that a sequence of numerals that they have learned to recite determines the cardinality of an aggregate of entities until they are 3½ years old.[99] Ordinary, untrained non-human primates may never attain to counting in this sense.

Moreover, whereas infant and animal perceivers distinguish a specific number of particulars, and represent those particulars, they do not (in utilizing this capacity) represent any number *per se*. Even more importantly, they do not seem to *represent* computational operations. There is no clear evidence or explanatory need to claim that infant and animal perceivers *represent* subtraction, addition, or division (or even analogs of these operations). No representational content, conscious or unconscious, specifies these operations. Perceptual or intermodal representational systems carry out computational analogs of subtraction, addition, division. These mathematical operations figure in the transformation processes that operate on perceptual representations and perceptual anticipations. But they are not represented.

This point is, I think, poorly recognized, even among sophisticated psychologists—partly because of the widespread use of deflated notions of representation. I think it of immense importance for understanding the explanatory kinds that figure in primitive representational systems. So I will dwell on it yet again.

The perceptual system goes through transformations—operations on perceptual and other sensory states. Principles specifying these transformations

---

[98] R. Gelman and C. R. Gallistel, *The Child's Understanding of Number* (Cambridge, MA: Harvard University Press, 1978).

[99] Wynn, 'Children's Acquisition of the Number Words and the Counting System'.

represent mathematical operations. But neither the perceptual system nor the animal itself specifies or represents these operations. There is no more basis for attributing representation of these operations than there is for attributing to the visual system a representation of the second derivative of the local distribution of light intensity registered on the retina. The system certainly computes this second derivative, in the sense that it produces perceptual representations from the initial registrations of light intensity in accord with, and explainable by, that mathematical principle (embedded in a principle stated by the psychologist). One can expect to find psychological and perhaps physical changes that are partly explained in terms of the relevant mathematics. But the perceptual system does not take as *representata* any of the mathematical structures or operations. And the system lacks relevant mathematical attributives corresponding to such structures or operations.

The mathematical computational principle indicates a transition law or law-like pattern that can be partly explained by citing such mathematical operations. The perceptual system does not have a state with representational content needed to specify the mathematical operations involved in the computational transformation. It does not *represent* such operations (or the laws or principles)—take them as *representata*—even "implicitly". To take the system (or individual) to represent such matters is to give in to, without evidential basis, the individual representationalist syndrome of taking individuals (or, more weakly, their subsystems) to represent conditions that make representation possible. The laws of a representational system are explained in terms of principles with specific mathematical content. But those principles are not the representational content of any state or transition. Nor does the representational system represent the laws, regularities, or operations that are specified by those mathematicized principles, and that in effect have mathematical properties.

The infant's surprise at there being one object when the screen is lifted after two objects had been placed behind the screen rests on perceptual representation of a particular object. A perceptual representation that comprised two singular representational contents indexed for different objects would not have yielded the surprise reaction. There is no perceptual representation of the numbers 1 or 2, or of addition.

The reasons for taking these positions are a combination of the empirical and the conceptual. Once a clear, non-deflated conception of representation is in place, it is evident, I think, that there is not the slightest empirical evidence to support taking *representation* of mathematical *operations* in these limited "number-tracking" capacities. Only use of overly broad conceptions of representation, together with confused invocation of implicitness, support doing so. The ground for not taking specific *numbers* to be represented is a straightforward inference to best explanation. The basic capacity seems to be a first-order one that need not mention higher-order entities like the numbers or even membership magnitudes.

In this latter respect, the system for individuating particulars and forming anticipations linked to the demonstrative-marked files for these particulars so as to determine exact number of aggregates is different from the system of estimating numerosity. Whereas estimating numerosity involves a second-order representation of aggregate magnitude relative to an attribute that determines membership, the present system is entirely first order in its mode of representation. The representation is of individual particulars and their kinds. Not only are no mathematical operations (addition, subtraction, division) represented. No mathematical entities are represented at all.

Beyond the lack of empirical ground to do so, there is a further reason, mentioned in Chapter 9, the section PERCEPTION AS OBJECTIFICATION, for not taking individuals' psychologies—in these small-number cases—to represent mathematical operations, even "implicitly". Any mathematical operation (subtraction, averaging, differentiation) can be represented in multiple ways. Individuals' perception and perceptual memory can be explained in terms of principles that make reference to simple mathematical operations. But no particular way of representing those operations is privileged in explaining perception or perceptual memory. Many equivalent mathematical representations of an operation will do for the statement of the principles that govern the psychological transformations. Empirical explanatory practice indicates that mathematical operations such as subtraction can be specified in nearly any mathematically equivalent way, modulo considerations of simplicity in best explanations. Explanatory practice certainly does not support the view that such operations are represented in exactly one way, or that the perceiver has a representational perspective on them. Reference to mathematical operations simply figures in the explanations of the transformations within perceptual systems.

Transformations of perceptual representations proceed in accord with patterns explained in mathematical terms.

I believe that the distinction between what is represented, in my stricter sense of 'represented', and what is needed to explain the law-like transformations in a perceptual system is fundamental to understanding perception and other relatively primitive representational capacities. Most of the writers in animal psychology and developmental psychology that I have cited blur the distinction.[100]

Blurring the distinction between computational transformations governed by principles and representation in the psychology of the individual is very common in even the most brilliant and methodologically sophisticated work. The blurring is, I think, a consequence of use of the term 'representation' in a deflationary way.[101] The problem is not that the claims are false on their own terms. It is that

---

[100] Similarly, the term 'knowledge' is attributed freely to lower animals, a usage that I think is misleading. It is also attributed freely in the child-developmental literature to infants, where I think more careful exposition of the percept/concept distinction(s) is very much needed.

[101] See Gallistel, *The Organization of Learning*, chapter 2 (for example, pp. 37–38) and p. 574. See also Carey, *The Origin of Concepts*, 4, 8. Gallistel is fully aware of what he is doing. He explicitly expounds the deflationary conception of representation, discussed in Chapter 8 above. Carey employs a more nuanced but less clearly explicated notion of representation. But neither isolates the kind *representation* (where 'representation' is used in my way). I regard *representation* as the central

such deflated ways of conceiving representation obscure deep differences among explanatorily relevant psychological kinds. Those ways of thinking produce excitement and controversy, but miss, I think, some of what is deeply interesting and *different* about central psychological kinds.[102]

The Two Mathematical Capacities

Both primitive mathematical systems that I have described are exercised in perceptual systems. Both also operate intermodally. And both can be taken up into conceptualized systems involving propositional attitudes. I will continue to concentrate on the systems in their perceptual form, since their exercises within intermodal and conceptual systems seem to be grounded in perceptual exercises.

Both systems take as starting points perceptions of particulars. Both systems produce representations and transformations that signal mathematical capacities. Both probably figure in the later learning, in human beings, of arithmetic, pure and applied.

The psychological limits on the two systems are quite different. The discriminative sensitivity of the system for estimating numerosity is constrained by the ratio of membership size between aggregates. The capacity for keeping track of the indexing of particulars is limited by the number of individuals in an aggregate, always a very small number.

Sensitivity to the exact number of index files for particulars is part of tracking not only particulars but also their attributes. The capacity to estimate numerosity does not keep track of the particular perceptual references in determining ratios of aggregate membership magnitudes. As a result, in the latter system, there is no memory of details of the attributes of the particulars whose aggregate-membership magnitude is estimated. In the former system, the index-file system, attributes of the particulars are maintained in memory. Consequently, in studies of that system, the cumulative magnitude of some property (such as size) is often confounded with the number of particulars—since the individual tracks both. In investigating the index-file tracking system, only careful experimentation succeeds in separating operations that determine the number of particulars from

---

generic kind that is distinctive of psychology. Numerous further examples of the deflationary use of 'representation' could be adduced. Significantly, usage in *perceptual psychology*, especially the psycho-physics of vision, is better—though by no means consistent—at keeping structured sensory information and genuine perceptual representation distinct.

[102] See Gallistel, *The Organization of Learning*, 332. Gallistel sees the relevant representations and computations as merely inaccessible to the animal, but nevertheless fully, if only "implicitly", represented. I think that this way of thinking is of a piece with thinking of a hose and bucket (perhaps a functioning hose and bucket) as implicitly representing differentiation or integration. I believe that the substantial empirical insights of Gallistel's work, and those of many others who write in similar ways, can be reinterpreted and preserved while introducing the notion of representation in a stricter, more psychologically distinctive sense. What tends to be lost by being content with the deflationary sense is an understanding of fundamental psychological kinds.

operations that determine the cumulative magnitude of some attribute. Often, of course, it is the latter that matters more—for example, in foraging.[103]

The mathematical operations in the capacity for estimating numerosity operate on representational contents that refer to pure magnitudes—though I believe that the specific nature of the magnitude, even whether it is discrete or continuous, is not determined by the representational contents. The psychological transformations in the capacity for tracking small numbers of particulars operate on singular index files that refer to concrete particulars—not on any representations of magnitude or number.

The two systems seem unable to operate at the same time in the same context. When one system is operating, the other system seems to be "turned off ". In most tasks, the capacity for tracking particulars in small aggregates normally overrides the capacity for estimating numerosity, when a small number of particulars can be picked out and tracked. As we have seen, children and apes fail to compare magnitudes of aggregate membership when one of the aggregate's membership size is larger than the number limit on the capacity, even when the ratio is well within the limit on minimal ratio magnitude. For example, infants choose 3 desired particulars over 1 desired particular, but are at chance in choosing 4 desired particulars over 1. 4/1 is a ratio well within the limit on the infant's estimation of numerosity, but 4 is above the limit for indexical tracking of particulars. Only in some special circumstances do infants seem able to rely on the system for estimating numerosity when aggregates with small membership sizes are in play.[104] Empirical work on what triggers one system rather than another is ongoing.

Neither of the two mathematical capacities constitutes a capacity for elementary arithmetic. Human children learn to count, in a fairly complex developmental process, between the ages of 2 and 4. They master a symbolic list in a definite order. Then they learn to correlate the list 1–1 with other entities. Finally, they learn that the last symbol in the list that is actually correlated with an entity is the cardinal number of the counted aggregate.[105]

Genuinely arithmetical capacities seem to be decidedly propositional and conceptual. They emerge, at least in performance, only after the advent of language. Although it is possible that they are fully formed but not yet operative in pre-linguistic stages of human development, I know of no evidence that clearly supports such a view. Non-human animals can with laborious training develop some approximation to counting up to very low limits (so far, roughly 9). But, so far, no recursive capacity beyond the trained limit has been demonstrated. It is

---

[103] This point is illustrated and developed in Carey, *The Origin of Concepts*, chapter 4. See also E. Margolis and S. Laurence, 'How to Learn the Natural Numbers: Inductive Inference and the Acquisition of Number Concepts', *Cognition* 106 (2008), 924–939.

[104] E. M. Brannon, D. Lutz, and S. Cordes, 'The Development of Area Discrimination and its Implications for Numerical Abilities in Infancy', *Developmental Science* 9 (2006), F59–F64.

[105] K. Wynn, 'Children's Understanding of Counting', *Cognition* 36 (1990), 155–193; Wynn, 'Children's Acquisition of the Number Words and the Counting System'.

thus doubtful whether they understand the symbols as representing natural numbers. The symbols seem to be triggers to some ordered correlation process. At most, all that has been shown is a capacity to count up to a definite number. It is possible that genuine recursive arithmetical capacities emerge only in human development. I conjecture that recursive arithmetical competence is a conceptual, post-perceptual phenomenon.[106] For this reason, investigating genuine arithmetical capacities appears to lie beyond the scope of our discussion of *perceptual* categories.

Neither of the two mathematical capacities featured in this section is constitutively necessary for objective perceptual representation. Both capacities are, however, widespread in animals with perceptual systems. In humans, non-human primates, and no doubt other animals, perceptual representations come to be incorporated into a conceptual system, a system of propositional thought and propositional inference.

There is some reason to believe that even some adult humans lack the ability to engage in genuine counting, or to represent numerical operations like addition.[107] But both these humans and various primates have propositional attitudes. Arithmetical capabilities do not seem constitutively, or psychologically, necessary for either perception or propositional *thought*.

Still, mathematical uses of perceptual representations, and intermodal representations mediating among perceptual systems, are a significant, primitive element in enabling animal representation to mark out basic aspects of the physical environment. They constitute an important base for the development of higher levels of objectivity.

PERCEPTION AND ORIGINS OF SPATIAL REPRESENTATION

I turn to some foundational issues about spatial sensitivities and spatial representation. The forms of spatial sensitivity among organisms are extremely varied.

---

[106] T. Matsuzawa, 'Use of Numbers by a Chimpanzee', *Nature* 315 (1985), 57–59; D. Biro and T. Matsuzawa, 'Use of Numerical Symbols by the Chimpanzee (*Pan Troglodytes*): Cardinals, Ordinals, and the Introduction of Zero', *Animal Cognition* 4 (2001), 193–199; M. Hauser, N. Chomsky, and W. T. Fitch, 'The Faculty of Language: What is it, Who has it, and How did it Evolve?', *Science* 298 (2002), 1569–1579. My conjecture is partly indebted to this latter article and to Carey, *The Origins of Concepts*, chapter 8. Carey provides an illuminating account of the way genuine arithmetical skills develop. This issue remains controversial and under intense empirical investigation.

[107] Certain Amazonian Indians, the Piraha and Munduruku, seem to lack the linguistic resources to count. They have shown no other signs of counting. There is evidence that they have the other two mathematical systems that we have been discussing. See P. Gordon, 'Numerical Cognition without Words: Evidence from Amazonia', *Science* 306 (2004), 496–499; D. L. Everett, 'Cultural Constraints on Grammar and Cognition in Piraha: Another Look at the Design Features of Human Language', *Current Anthropology* 46 (2005), 621–646; P. Pica, C. Lerner, V. Izard, and S. Dehaene, 'Exact and Approximate Arithmetic in an Amazonian Indigene Group', *Science* 306 (2004), 499–503; R. Gelman and C. R. Gallistel, 'Language and the Origin of Numerical Concepts', *Science* 306 (2004), 441–443.

Bacteria have magnetic sensitivities that orient them with respect to polar north. Amoebae have light–dark sensitivities that lead them to liquid areas likely to serve their chemical needs. Crickets use sound to locate mates. Birds are sensitive to magnetic, olfactory, and visual input that guides migrations.

Many of these sensitivities are non-perceptual and non-representational. They work off relatively simple methods like the homing or beaconing method. Such methods can be explained as momentary or serial responses to proximal stimulation on one or another side of the body.

Bacterial capacities to navigate space and the spatial perceptual constancies of a mammal's visual system are of fundamentally different kinds. There is nothing distinctively representational about a bacterium's sensory capacities. Usage even in psychology, however, often blurs the distinction.

Commonalities are cheap. Bacteria and mammals both have sensory systems adapted to space. There are systematic mathematical mappings between their sensory states and spatial attributes or spatial particulars relative to contexts. There is nothing wrong with introducing a term, even a term spelled 'representation', for this commonality. But such usage is frequently associated with failure, even in psychology, to notice large explanatorily relevant differences between the organisms' states. I have in mind especially differences between sensory states that have veridicality conditions—states that ground non-trivial appeal to veridicality conditions in explanation—and sensory states that can trivially be assigned veridicality conditions, but that are easily explained without reference to them. I believe that this distinction corresponds to a difference between an organism's having a capacity for objectification and an organism's lacking any such capacity. Broad, indiscriminate use of 'representation' tends to obscure differences in explanation that signal origins of objectivity.[108]

Indiscriminate use of the term 'representation' is prevalent in psychology. Whereas such use in philosophy is usually *intended* to be deflationary, such use in psychology is usually intended to "inflate" psychology beyond restrictive behaviorist paradigms, in order to highlight a level of explanation distinct from behaviorist explanation. Nevertheless, the effect of using the term in such broad ways is to deflate distinctions between distinctively psychological phenomena and phenomena that are shared with the simplest animals, with unicellular organisms, with plants, and even (on some purely information-theoretic uses of 'representation') with non-living, non-artifactual physical systems. More importantly, the effect of broad uses is to distract attention from some of the most fundamental kinds that are distinctive to psychology and that psychology is in the process of discovering laws (or law-like patterns) for. These are the kinds

---

[108] The reader may want to review discussion of representation and the term 'representation' in Chapter 8, the section DEFLATIONARY CONCEPTIONS OF REPRESENTATION; BIOLOGICAL FUNCTION AND REPRESENTATIONAL FUNCTION, and this chapter, the subsection MATHEMATICAL TRACKING OF INDEXED PARTICULARS, in the section PERCEPTION AND ORIGINS OF MATHEMATICAL CAPACITIES.

representation, understood in the narrower way that I am elaborating, and *perception*.

I will discuss one psychologist's use of the term. But the discussion applies to field-wide tendencies. Gallistel's use of 'representation' is typical among psychologists, except that it is especially well explained:

A representation is a correspondence between the formal structure of the *represented system* and the formal structure of the *representing system* that enables one to predict results in the represented system on the basis of operations conducted within the representing system ... [109]

The brain is said to represent an aspect of the environment when there is a functioning isomorphism between some aspect of the environment and a brain process that adapts the animal's behavior to it. [110]

There is nothing in Gallistel's further account that *requires* or *motivates* the idea that an organism must have a brain, or even be an animal, if it is to engage in representation. His account is self-consciously non-anatomical. The overall account's explication of representation as a functioning isomorphism applies to simple organisms that lack central nervous systems.

On this conception, bacteria "represent" magnetic forces and spatial directions, as well as light and dark, day and night. Here representation talk is obviously and immediately dispensable in favor of information registration, or other correspondences that are functional. There is no distinctive role for veridicality conditions in the explanation. There is nothing that counts as the beginning of the sort of representation that represents particulars as having attributes and that involves objectification beyond sensory registration. There are no perceptual constancies.

Well-established scientific usage already covers what the definition covers: functioning information carrying, information registration, functional sensory encoding through statistical correlations, or other systematic correspondences that are functional. Using 'representation' to be equivalent with 'information'— or 'structured information correlation' plus an invocation of biological function—produces needless terminological duplication.

More importantly, such usage distracts from the large differences in psychological kind that I have been emphasizing. I think it well to distinguish the two kinds, to distinguish use of the two terms, and to reserve 'representation' for the psychological kind that lies at the origin of perspective, perception, objectivity—a distinctively psychological kind. [111]

---

[109] Gallistel, *The Organization of Learning*, 582. Gallistel calls this conception 'the mathematical conception' of representation. As applied to organisms, Gallistel adds a further condition on representation—that the representing system function or be adapted to yield the mathematical correspondence. The next quotation in the text illustrates this addition. This is precisely the conception that I discussed at length in Chapter 8.

[110] Ibid. 15; see also pp. 582–583.

[111] As I will indicate in the section ASSOCIATION, COMPUTATION, REPRESENTATION below, I think that information registration is a psychological kind. But it is equally a biological kind. Representation is a

In one passage that concerns not extremely simple organisms, but a very simple navigational system, Gallistel may indicate awareness of the oddity of applying any ordinary notion of representation at these very low levels. He writes of an ant that uses a more complex navigational system than a simple beaconing system (which I shall discuss shortly):

We know that it is not following a beacon—a substance (for example, a volatile chemical) or a disturbance (for example, light or sound) that spreads out more or less radially from its source. Beacons can be used to home on their source if the direction from which they emanate may be determined by some sensory process. Beacon homing requires no representational capacity beyond the nominal; the animal need only distinguish the emanations from the source it seeks from emanations from other sources.[112]

I take it that a 'nominal' representational capacity still fits Gallistel's definition of a 'representational' capacity: a capacity for a functioning isomorphism.[113] Gallistel's remark may be a concession to a common response that representation is not appropriately attributed to the sensory capacities of bacteria, or to sensory aspects of simple homing systems.

Natural associations of the term 'representation' should not be allowed to color understanding of such systems. Objectification, perception, veridicality conditions, and perspective on a subject matter play no role in the explanations. These simple sensory systems are just capacities to discriminate and average intensities of sensory stimulation.

Counting such a system *representational* distorts the notion traditionally used in philosophy and psychology. More importantly, it is misleadingly different from the notion of representation that applies to a distinctive psychological kind in various parts of cognitive or perceptual psychology, *as psychology is now being pursued*. I believe that applying or defining (however explicitly) the term 'representation' in the broad way that I have been discussing invites misunderstanding of or obliviousness to the basic distinction between genuine representation and sensory information registration, or other similar sensory correspondences. The definition applies to a wide variety of organisms, including extremely simple ones. But the term 'representation' retains its association with a

---

kind distinctive of psychology in an old and familiar sense. The reader should reconsult the discussion of information registration (functional, encoding, grounded in systematic statistical correlation) in Chapter 8, the section DEFLATIONARY CONCEPTIONS OF REPRESENTATION; BIOLOGICAL FUNCTION AND REPRESENTATIONAL FUNCTION. Sensory information registration involves a causal grounding of the statistical correlations.

[112] Gallistel, *The Organization of Learning*, 59.

[113] Beaconing is a relatively simple navigational capacity, certainly simpler than the path integration system that Gallistel goes on to discuss. Perhaps 'nominal' just means minimal. The simplicity should not be overstated. Actual directional beaconing systems usually require internal comparisons between levels of intensity on different parts of the organism's body. Sometimes these comparisons are quantitatively complex. I am less interested, however, in degrees of complexity than in differences in kind that bear on objectification. Below, I argue that neither beaconing nor path integration is, in itself, a representational capacity in my sense of 'representational'.

more specific range of capacities, which neither science nor common sense attribute to very simple organisms.

Let me return to *my* use of 'representation'.

Spatial representation is probably the most impressive and widespread type of primitive perceptual representation. It occurs in visual systems throughout the animal kingdom from arthropods to primates. (See Chapter 9, notes 59–62.) It is, of course, constitutively necessary for attributing the kind *body*. It is probably more widespread than attribution of the kind *body* in animal vision. A lot is known about the early development of spatial perception and spatial constancies, especially in monkeys, apes, and humans.[114]

Although spatial representation is almost omnipresent in perception, I believe that it is not constitutively necessary to either perception or representation. There could in principle be primitive perceptual representational systems that lack spatial representation. Let me begin with the denial, and then return to the 'strictly speaking'.

An animal could have a visual system capable only of attributing lightnesses or colors. The system could exercise primitive lightness and color constancy that distinguishes reflectance from illumination, and thus from registration of surface stimulation by light. Such a system might be incapable of representing three-dimensional shapes, or tracking locations of achromatic lightnesses, or locations of colors. It need not be capable of any constancies regarding three-dimensional space. The animal perceives lightness or color, but lacks any capacity to attribute any spatial relations, including spatial relations between an occurrence of lightness or color and the animal itself. If it perceives two colors at once, it cannot retain or use anything about the spatial relations between the colors. No spatial constancies are in its repertoire.

A representational content of the state would be something like that$_1$ red!. Red perceptually attributes the property *red* to an occurrence or instance. The exclamation point marks the committal nature of perception. That$_1$ marks an *occurrent singular application* of a perceptual context-dependent singular element, guided by the attributive. The function of the singular application is to single out a particular red occurrence. The attribution could be mistaken. What is perceptually singled out could be a green occurrence. Or the application could fail to single out anything. There could be no environmentally relevant cause that is perceived. The singular application reference to a particular occurrence is

---

[114] Stereopsis is developed by about 10 weeks in human infants. Other types of spatial representation, binocular and monocular, are available earlier. Acuity and proficiency with various depth cues develop through the first year of human life. See C. E. Granrud, A. Yonas, and L. Pettersen, 'A Comparison of Monocular and Binocular Depth Perception in 5- and 7-Month-Old Infants', *Journal of Experimental Child Psychology* 38 (1984), 19–32; E. Birch and B. Petrig, 'FPL and VEP Measures of Fusion, Stereopsis, and Stereo Acuity in Normal Infants', *Vision Research* 36 (1996), 1321–1327; C. O'Dell and R. G. Boothe, 'The Development of Stereoacuity in Infant Rhesus Monkeys', *Vision Research* 37 (1997), 2675–2684; A. M. Brown and J. A. Miracle, 'Early Binocular Vision in Human Infants: Limitations on the Generality of the Superposition Hypothesis', *Vision Research* 43 (2003), 1563–1574.

determined by causal relations to the occurrence, together with the constancy capacities in the visual system. Perhaps the animal closes its shell in response to instances of some colors, or some achromatic spectrums of lightness, and opens its shell in response to others.

Such a system would have met conditions for perceptual representation, but would have been incapable of spatial representation. Lightness must in fact be extended at least two-dimensionally. But the system could be incapable of representing or retaining anything about the extension, much less capable of representing three-dimensional attributes.[115] It is one thing to represent occurrence of an attribute in space and another thing to be able to represent spatial relations. Even representing a two-dimensional plane as such requires a capacity to represent simple relations of distance or direction on the plane, and relations between different parts of the plane. I think it clearly possible to represent the incidence of lightness or color, without being able to represent, use, or retain the sort of systematic relations constitutively involved in spatial representation. Whether there are any such visual systems in nature I do not know.[116] But any such visual systems would be representational and perceptual. I see no *constitutive necessity* that perception, or representation more generally, involve spatial representation.[117]

---

[115] Lightness constancy in humans and other animals actually uses depth perception. See Gilchrist, 'Perceived Lightness Depends on Perceived Spatial Arrangement'; Zemach and Rudd, 'Effects of Surround Articulation on Lightness Depend on the Spatial Arrangement of the Articulated Region'. But lightness constancy is possible without 3-D information. It can operate purely on luminance ratios at luminance contours—that is, on information in the retinal arrays caused by light arrays (together with their spectral properties), where the information is not processed for representation of depth relations. See Wallach, 'Brightness Constancy and the Nature of Achromatic Colors', and M. E. Rudd and I. K. Zemach, 'Quantitative Properties of Achromatic Color Induction: An Edge Integration Analysis', *Vision Research* 44 (2004), 971–981. Of course, such a system would be less flexible, more approximate, and more subject to error than actual human visual systems. Lightness constancy is, however possible in simple displays *with no spatial (depth) cues*, not only for an imaginary animal but in human beings. It also appears likely that, although two-dimensional spatial information is utilized in lightness constancy, this information is not perceptual. The processing of spatial information can be explained purely in terms of the two-dimensional array of retinal sensory registrations—in effect, in terms of the functioning spatial arrangements of the neural firings in the retina. The processing of this information that yields simple lightness constancy depends on no spatial constancy, even one involving two-dimensional arrangements in physical space. Some of the processing is retinal; some occurs in the V1 array of the brain. But, apparently, no spatial *constancy* need figure in the transformations involved in primitive forms of lightness constancy. Lightness constancy can occur as a primitive constancy, one that depends on no other perceptual constancy. Again, in actual human visual systems, lightness constancy and the three-dimensional spatial constancies are inter-mixed. See Rudd and Zemach, 'Quantitative Properties of Achromatic Color Induction'; I am indebted in this footnote to Iris Zemach, by correspondence.

[116] Since, as mentioned in note 115, an element in actual lightness constancy capacities can in principle operate independently of spatial representation, it seems likely that such operations evolved, somewhere, independently of spatial constancy operations, and then got amalgamated with them as a result of selection for fitness advantages. Perhaps animals with pure, non-spatial lightness constancy capacities evolved and then died out. I conjecture that there are, or have been, cases of perception systems with lightness constancy but no spatial constancies. The constitutive point—that perception does not require spatial representation—seems clear.

[117] I draw a different conclusion regarding temporal representation, in the next subsection.

I said that 'strictly speaking' spatial representation is not constitutively necessary to perception or to representation. A perceptual system of the sort just
described would meet only the barest minimum condition on objectification. It
could not track the primary attributes of the macro-physical environment. Any
objective perceptual representation of such attributes must utilize spatial representation. Although spatial representation is not necessary to perceptual representation, it is necessary to any representation capable of forming a basis for
higher levels of objectivity. Lightness and color representation *in themselves* are
empirical dead ends. Evolutionarily, they are very specialized capacities. Among
visual perceptual systems, spatial representation is nearly ubiquitous, and probably equally prevalent among other types of perceptual systems. Visual representation of lightness or color alone would be an exceptionally limited capacity
for coping with the world.

A further issue regarding spatial representation that I want to discuss is its
relation to navigational capacities. I will discuss whether each of various capacities is representational in itself. I hope to sharpen issues about what spatial
representation is, and what role it plays in origins of objectivity.

Spatial sensitivity among lower animals has been most intensely studied in its
role in navigation. Many types of animals exhibit impressive navigational capacities. I shall discuss some empirical background for understanding the relations
among navigation, non-representational information registration, and perceptual
representation—as I have been explicating these latter two notions.

Beaconing

Navigation by *beaconing* or homing is movement toward a target in response to
stimulation that derives from the target location. For example, an individual can
respond to a magnetic field, a chemical, a sound, or a light source by simple
attraction. Organisms can navigate toward or away from a source of the stimulation, but I count only movement toward the source as beaconing. Beaconing
enables simple organisms, such as paramecia, to move in directions beneficial to
them. Stimulation above a given threshold of intensity occasions movement in
any direction that maintains intensity of stimulation above the threshold.

A somewhat more complex beaconing system responds to a weighted average
of signal intensities on different sides of the body in establishing direction of
movement. Salmon exhibit a highly developed form of this response. They find
their home streams by responding to a sequence of chemical traces. In effect, they
use a chained sequence of beaconings. The capacity utilizes a sophisticated
sampling technique. It uses weighted averages of the intensity of registrations
of relevant odor plumes on different sides of the body. In beaconing navigation,
spatial sensitivity is a by-product of sensitivity to proximal simulation whose
directional properties, particular distributions on the body's sensors, enable the
individual to reach a location—the source of the stimulation.

Path Integration

Certain systems of navigation by organisms more complex than paramecia evince internal transformations on sensory stimulation that carry quantitative information that functions to enable the individual to cope with the metric properties of direction and distance. A widely studied example of such a system is *path integration*, sometimes called *dead reckoning*. Path integration is a computational transformation that yields an informational vector, constituted by a distance and a direction, from information that correlates with speed, direction, and time.

From its nest, a desert ant walks a convoluted 600-meter route around a featureless desert until it finds a dead fly. After finding the fly, it returns with its booty in a nearly straight line to the nest. A straight line from find to nest is about 133 meters. The ant's homeward journey is 141 meters.[118] A system in the ant tracks and updates distance and direction information during its outward walk. The system instantiates computation of a vector, called the *global vector*. The vector is in effect the sum of component distances and directions during the outward journey. It constitutes a registration of information that correlates with straight-line direction and distance (to within approximately 6 percent) from the location where the fly was found to the nest.

This desert ant does not use beacons or landmarks in the main part of its journey. It lacks a general map of the space that it traversed. These facts are known through displacement experiments. If during the outward-bound journey the ant is displaced, it does not head toward the nest. It heads in a direction of the global vector from the point from which it was displaced. It does not use beacons, landmarks, or a map to adjust to displacement.

Dogs can be blindfolded, deprived of auditory information, and led from a bait by a detour route. They return to the site of the bait (with the bait and its smell removed) by almost the most direct route possible.[119] A wide range of other animals perform similar feats.

The global vector commonly accumulates failures of correlation with the needed route. Presumably evolved to compensate for such failures, a second search system takes over when the ant completes walking its global vector. On its completion, if the ant is not exactly at its nest, it begins to move in ever-widening loops. Each loop ends with a return to the center of the search, the end point of the global vector. This second system also involves path integration—instantiation of computation of a vector that allows the ant to return to the center.

---

[118] R. Wehner and S. Wehner, 'Insect Navigation: Use of Maps or Ariadne's Thread?', *Ethology, Ecology, and Evolution* 2 (1990), 27–48. See also the older classic source of this work: S. Wehner and M. V. Srinivasan, 'Searching Behavior of Desert Ants, Genus *Cataglyphis (Formicidae, Hymenoptera)*', *Journal of Comparative Physiology A* 142 (1981), 335–338, and reflection on this older work in Gallistel, *The Organization of Learning*, 59 ff.

[119] Jennifer S. Cattet and Ariane S. Etienne, 'Blindfolded Dogs Relocate a Target by Path Integration', *Animal Behavior* 68 (2004), 203–212.

Path integration requires a determination within the traveler of both direction and distance. In some animals, these components seem to instantiate separate computations, and then instantiate an integration of the separate computations. In other cases, a simultaneous computation of both components seems to be instantiated. In either case, there must be a running registration and summation of information that correlates with direction and distance.

In the absence of landmarks or beacons, there are various sources for these running records. Visual, vestibular, and proprioceptive sensory systems are among the primary sources.

In determining *direction*, in the absence of beacons or landmarks, mammals rely primarily on vestibular information regarding rotation and on proprioceptive information that correlates with head direction, given a starting-point direction. Spiders rely on proprioceptive information regarding rotation from strain receptors in the legs. Bees and ants rely primarily on visual information that correlates with the direction of the sun, particularly patterns of polarized light. Birds use registration of information deriving from the sun or stars and from magnetic forces emanating from the earth.[120] In most animals, information from different sensory systems that functions to correlate with direction is pooled and averaged intermodally. These resources instantiate a running computation of directional information.

In determining *distance*, in the absence of beacons or landmarks, mammals rely primarily on visual cues and on non-vestibular proprioception, which can operate in the absence of vision. Spiders and crabs depend on proprioceptive motion cues, such as summing energy from leg movements in walking. Ants rely on stress receptors in the joints and probably gravity receptors in hair-plates. For bees, distance information derives from registration of retinal optic flow.[121]

The computation of a distance/direction vector is equivalent to trigonometrical computations, although there is little evidence regarding the nature of the computational transformations in the various animals. In fact, the question of the *exact* mathematical form of the computational transformation probably does not admit of an answer, since the mathematics lies in the principle that describes the law or operation that instantiates formation of the vector. The principle is the

---

[120] Ariane S. Etienne and Kathryn J. Jeffery, 'Path Integration in Mammals', *Hippocampus* 14 (2004), 180–192; Berthold, 'Spatiotemporal Aspects of Avian Long-Distance Migration'; K. Cheng, 'Arthropod Navigation: Ants, Bees, Crabs, Spiders Finding their Way', in Wasserman and Zentall (eds.), *Comparative Cognition*; S. Zill and E. A. Seyfarth, 'Exoskeletal Sensors for Walking', *Scientific American* 275 (1996), 70–74; K. von Frisch, *The Dance Language and Orientation of Bees* (1947; London: Oxford University Press, 1967).

[121] Etienne and Jeffery, 'Path Integration in Mammals'; Cheng, 'Arthropod Navigation'; Sandra Wohlgemuth, Bernhard Ronacher, and Rüdiger Wehner, 'Ant Odometry in the Third Dimension', *Nature* 411 (2001), 795–798; G. Grah, R. Wehner, and B. Ronacher, 'Desert Ants do not Acquire and Use a Three-Dimensional Global Vector', *Frontiers in Zoology* 4 (2007), online. The latter two articles demonstrate that ants compensate for slope, but do not store the 3-dimensional slope information, in registering information that correlates with and functions to enable the animal to cope with distance. The experiments rule out registrations of step cumulation, visual flow, energy expenditure, and time as bases for the relevant ant's odometer.

scientist's description of the law. Although physiological conditions instantiate the law, there is no *representation* of the law or operation in the animal. Many equivalent mathematical accounts are equally good in explaining the transformation of informational states in the animal. The animal's sequence of states instantiates a computational law, but does not represent the law.

Beaconing and path integration are two types of navigation in animals. Use of landmarks is a third. Use of landmarks is functionally like beaconing, except that the landmarks are used not as goals but as signs along a route that facilitate finding goals. Local vectors are set to or from landmarks on a route. These local vectors usually supplement and correct global vectors set by path integration. For example, the information from landmarks provides checks on the global vector. The checks correct or limit failures of correlation with space that accumulate in the global vector.[122]

When information from different modalities (vision, olfaction, proprioception from self-motion) conflicts, a course is set by a weighted average among the modalities—and as between landmark registration and path integration. The modality that is more reliable with respect to a given task tends to carry greater weight. Frequently, vision outweighs olfaction, which outweighs proprioception that registers self-motion. In some cases, a dominant modality may be discounted. For example, if a visual cue is wildly at odds with other cues, the visual cue might receive no weight. Such discounting in favor of contextually more reliable modalities is adaptive. The total absence of weight from a visual cue, for example, might normally derive from motion by a landmark. It is known that in rats the weight given to a visual cue from a landmark depends heavily on whether there is a stable sensory relation with respect to the cue.[123]

Information from landmarks typically guides finding a goal. Often finding a goal, for example a nest hole for an ant or bug, requires more precise positioning than the global path-integration vector can provide. Landmarks or beacons commonly figure in ending the second phase of a path-integration search, the one involving widening loops after the global vector has been traversed. Often information deriving from landmarks is registered at the beginning of an outbound journey, to be used on the return.[124]

[122] Cheng, 'Arthropod Navigation'; M. Knaden and R. Wehner, 'Ant Navigation: Resetting the Path Integrator', *Journal of Experimental Biology* 209 (2006), 26–31; Ken Cheng and Marcia L. Spetch, 'Mechanisms of Landmark Use in Mammals and Birds', in Healy (ed.), *Spatial Representation in Animals*, 1–17.

[123] J. J. Knierim, H. S. Kudrimoti, and B. L. McNaughton, 'Place Cells, Head Direction Cells, and the Learning of Landmark Stability', *Journal of Neuroscience* 15 (1995), 1648–1659; H. Maaswinkel and I. Q. Whishaw, 'Homing with Locale, Taxon, and Dead Reckoning Strategies by Foraging Rats: Sensory Hierarchy in Spatial Navigation', *Behavioral Brain Research* 99 (1999), 143–152.

[124] Etienne and Jeffery, 'Path Integration in Mammals'; M. Collett and T. S. Collett, 'How do Insects Use Path Integration in their Navigation?', *Biological Cybernetics* 83 (2000), 245–259; M. Hironaka, L. Fillipi, S. Nomakuchi, H. Horiguchi, and T. Hariyama, 'Hierarchical Use of Chemical Marking and Path Integration in the Homing Trip of a Subsocial Shield Bug', *Animal Behavior* 73 (2007), 739–745.

I have described the input of these spatial tasks as information registration. Computational transformations from this input depends on information carried by the input states. Not all sensory information registration is perceptual. And not all computational transformations among sensory states involve representational states, in the non-deflationary sense of 'representation'. Some registration of information that correlates with spatial relations is not, and is not involved in, spatial representation, perceptual attributions of spatial relations, or perception as of entities in space. The various spatial skills involved in path integration provide an interesting basis for sharpening these distinctions and yielding insight into the application of the notions of information, computation, perception, and representation. I barely scratch the surface of these issues.

I have already indicated in Chapter 8 that navigation by *beaconing* is in many animals pre-perceptual. The movements of a moth toward a light source, of a protozoa along a magnetic field, and of a salmon following an olfactory trail, involve no spatial representation. They yield navigational prowess without spatial representation. Success in these spatial tasks consists in directional response to information registration of surface stimulation.

A similar point applies to *path integration*. Path integration in itself requires no spatial *representation*. It computes and utilizes information that *correlates* with spatial properties. The capacities evolved and *function* to enable an animal to find its way in space. But the informational states need not represent spatial properties or relations as such. Veridicality conditions play no non-trivial role in explanations of the natures or formations of the states.

There is no question that path integration can acquire spatial representational content. It does so in animals that use perception, involving spatial constancies, in determining elements of distance or direction that are used in path integration. Where location is determined by binocular disparity or convergence or motion parallax, and representation of location is incorporated into path integration, states in the path-integration system represent spatial relations. Birds and mammals use visual perception to localize entities, at least in some aspects of their uses of path integration—for example, in identifying landmarks.[125] Their path-integration systems form states that represent spatial relations.

What I maintain is just that path integration *in itself* does not represent spatial attributes. There can be, and seemingly *are*, path-integration systems that do not represent any specific spatial or, more narrowly, metric properties or relations as such. Some systems of path integration register information that correlates with distance and direction, and function to do so—but do not *represent* distances or directions as such.

In the next subsection I make a parallel point about path integration *supplemented with landmark use*. But I begin with the simpler case of pure path integration. Let me sketch some ways in which lower animals' path-integration

---

[125] Cheng and Spetch, 'Mechanisms of Landmark Use in Mammals and Birds'.

systems register information that correlates with direction and distance, and function to enable the animal to navigate direction and distance.

First, some cases of registering information that correlates with *distance*. Bees' visual systems register information that correlates with distance in flight by measuring the flow of contrasting stimulations across the retina.[126] Summing this retinal flow correlates well with distance in flight. The system surely evolved to enable the bee to navigate distances to useful positions—a hive or food source, for example. The function of the system is to enable the bee to navigate distances. So the retinal optic flow fulfills conditions for registering information that correlates with distance.

Registering information is not having representational content. We can judge the information in the bee that correlates with distance as accurate or inaccurate. We can correlate the bee's states systematically with distance. We can safely claim that the states function to correlate with distance in enabling the bee to navigate. But the bee's navigational states are formed by summing retinal flow. Nothing in the explanation of the bee's states need appeal to representational content, with veridicality conditions.

As far as it has been described so far, the bee's visual system does not represent anything as being at a given distance. It does not represent anything. It registers only cumulation of the flow of proximal stimulations across the retina. So the sensory input into the path-integration system that correlates with distance does not represent distance, or anything at a distance. The state registers cumulative amount of the stimulus.

The system is *in effect* an odometer. It evolved to guide navigation as an odometer might. But there is a significant *psychological* difference between a visual system that can represent the distance of a given entity, and a system that sums flow of proximal stimulations across the retina. The difference is that between representational systems, in a full-blown sense, and information-processing systems that are representational only in a deflationary or stretched sense.

Registering retinal flow involves no perceptual constancies. Of course, information that correlates with a given distance can derive from many types of retinal stimulation as long as they all produce the same summation of retinal flow. But this is no perceptual constancy. No explanatory insight is gained by invoking representational states with veridicality conditions.

---

[126] H. E. Esch and J. E. Burns, 'Distance Estimation by Foraging Honeybees', *Journal of Experimental Biology* 199 (1996), 155–162; M. V. Srinivasan, and S. W. Zhang, 'Visual Control of Honeybee Flight', in M. Lehrer (ed.), *Orientation and Communication in Arthropods* (Basle: Birkhauser Verlag, 1997); M. V. Srinivasan, S. W. Zhang, and N. J. Bidwell, 'Visually Mediated Odometry in Honeybees', *Journal of Experimental Biology* 200 (1997), 2513–2522; J. Tautz, S. W. Zhang, J. Spaethe, A. Brockmann, A. Si, and M. Srinivasan, 'Honeybee Odometry: Performance in Varying Natural Terrain', *PLoS Biology* 2 (2004), 915–923; M. Dacke and M. V. Srinivasan, 'Honeybee Navigation: Distance Estimation in the Third Dimension', *Journal of Experimental Biology* 210 (2007), 845–853.

Information that correlates with distance in other arthropod path-integration systems is registered through variants on a "step-counting" mechanism (or cumulation-of-step-energy mechanism).[127] In effect, the proprioceptive system sums energy, or some other magnitude reliably correlated with number of steps, from the departure from home to the finding of food, or from the finding of food back to home. The cumulated information deriving from the number of steps is modified by directional information in the computational transformation that results in instantiation of a vector. I shall discuss directional information shortly. The system of step "counting" works by summing the distinctive stress in the legs from taking a step, or summing efferent impulses that lead to taking a step. The system records the cumulation of repetitive stresses or efferent impulses. Again, the input of the distance component into the path-integration system at no point represents distance or any entity at a given distance. The internal state simply registers cumulation of distinctive types of stress in the leg joints, or efferent impulses to the legs. There is no measure of the distance of any given step. Nothing in the system represents distance, as opposed to simply *correlating functionally with* distance.

The system is like an odometer system in a car that goes into a different state corresponding to each tick produced by a full revolution of a wheel, without any capacity to measure the size of the wheels. If *we* know the circumference of the wheels, we can correlate a state that sums the ticks with distance. But the workings of the system can be explained purely as a cumulative response to information regarding revolutions. The information registered by the odometer does function to enable the individual to traverse distances of use to it. The system evolved because of its connection to distance. But its correlation with distance is entirely external to the state itself. In arthropods' step-recording system, no state represents distance (or, incidentally, number) of steps. Nothing in the explanation of the state needs to take it as representing, as having veridicality conditions, at all.

Let us turn to sources of *directional* information in path-integration systems. Some systems for registering information that correlates with direction in path integration are no more complex than those that occur in simple beaconing systems. Such systems simply register average intensity of relevant stimuli on one or another side of the body. For example, certain sensory systems for registering magnetic fields in the earth enable an animal to orient to north, or to

---

[127] L. Chittka, N. M. Williams, H. Rasmussen, and J. D. Thomson, 'Navigation without Vision: Bumblebee Navigation in Complete Darkness', *Royal Society Proceedings: Biological Sciences* 266 (1999), 45–50; John E. Layne, W. Jon P. Barnes, and Lindsay M. J. Duncan, 'Mechanisms of Homing in the Fiddler Crab *Uca Rapax*: 2 Information Sources and Frame of Reference for a Path Integration System', *Journal of Experimental Biology* 206 (2003), 4425–4442. Since crabs can run at different speeds, the actual theory is more complex than the one cartooned in the text. The theory includes postulation of feedback from efferent impulses that lead to steps. I believe that many vestibular systems that provide information that correlates with angular momentum, for example in ants, are no more perceptual than visual-flow or step-cumulation systems.

some relation with respect to north. But the sensory system responds to the effects of magnetic fields. No entity in space need be perceived, or otherwise represented, as being in a certain direction. The animal's internal states simply record a succession of stimulation patterns, and the animal's motor system responds in a functionally beneficial way.[128]

More complex systems register information that correlates with direction by registering intensities of light rays from the sun sensed on different parts of the body. Or they register patterns of stimulation from polarized light emanating from the sun.[129] In path-integration systems, visually registering directional information is much more complex than sensory systems that work on simple principles of beaconing. To register directional information for path integration, stimulation from sun rays or polarized light must be calibrated with respect to phases of the circadian cycle. Since the sun moves during the day, it produces different patterns of polarized light depending on its position. Further, as with use of distance information in path integration, there must be a system for keeping a running cumulative record of successive stimulations to contribute to instantiating computation of a vector.

The computational complexity and efficiency of such systems are impressive. Still, explanations of the formation of the states need not appeal to veridicality conditions regarding direction. The directional aspect of these path-integration systems can be explained in terms of registration of patterns of proximal stimulation, a running cumulative record of the results, and an updating of the motor commands ready to turn the body, when the homeward bound journey is triggered to begin. The internal states correlate with direction and evolved to do so. But they are simply running registrations of proximal stimulation—a cumulative record of generation and release of energy associated with torque.

It might be thought that since the navigational system integrates distance and directional information intermodally, there is some reason to conceive of these path-integration systems as genuinely representational. I believe that this thought would be mistaken.

Let us suppose that the sensory input into both components of the direction/ distance vector is non-perceptual. Suppose that distance information derives from retinal optic flow, and that directional information derives from a running

---

[128] M. M. Walker, 'Magnetic Orientation and Magnetic Sense in Arthropods', in Lehrer (ed.), *Orientation and Communication in Arthropods*; Shaun D. Cane, Larry C. Boles, John H. Wang, and Kenneth J. Lohmann, 'Magnetic Orientation and Navigation in Marine Turtles, Lobsters, and Molluscs: Concepts and Conundrums', *Integrative and Comparative Biology* 45 (2005), 539–546. In the latter article, it is stated that the sensory *and* motor systems that respond to magnetic fields are served by *six* neurons in the brain of a mollusc. I know of no evidence, however, that the mollusc is capable of path integration. It does orient its navigation in response to magnetic fields. Magnetic fields seem to play a role in path-integration systems of some arthropods and many birds. See, for example, Berthold, 'Spatiotemporal Aspects of Avian Long-Distance Migration'.

[129] Tobias Merkle, Martin Rost, and Wolfgang Alt, 'Ego-Centric Path Integration Models and their Application to Desert Ants', *Journal of Theoretical Biology* 240 (2006), 385–399; Cheng, 'Arthropod Navigation', 191.

summation of tension and release of tension in the joints. Neither of these sources of information specifically concerns spatial relations (in the environment) as such. Retinal optic flow is registration of change in proximal stimulation across the retina. Cumulation in stresses in joints *correlates* with changes in direction of walking, but carries information that correlates equally with summation of twists of the body, producing ultimately a certain final twist of the body. There is no objectification of a specific environmental subject matter as distinct from matters concerned with bodily surfaces and bodily dispositions. The connection to objective distal reality is purely functioning correlation.

The intermodal state that results from the computational transformation that begins with two non-perceptual informational states is the result of integrating the two states into a single state, and repeatedly updating the resulting state as new information comes in. Since the information being integrated does not represent spatial attributes, it is hard to see how the combination of the information mathematically into a vector makes the information any more specific to spatial attributes (distance/direction). The vector correlates with distance and direction, and the computational transformation functions to enable individuals to navigate distance and direction. But the vector is just as relevant to the following command as it is to spatial attributes: 'after producing such and such motor movements (in fact resulting in a reversal of body heading), move the legs without producing certain types of stresses (in fact resulting in no turning) so as to produce such and such amount of retinal optic flow; then stop.'

Explanation of formation of the vector and navigation according to the vector can remain strictly in terms of summing and updating proximal stimulation, and combining it so as to produce states that cause movement of specific parts of the body. One can note that the system functions to provide information that correlates with spatial structure and enables animals to cope with space. But there is no gain in the explanation *of the individual's states* in claiming that they represent space. No specific part of space, nothing in space, is ever represented. There is no non-trivial role for assigning states with accuracy conditions or for carrying out explanations that make non-trivial reference to states with such conditions. As so far described, the individual and its system do not represent location or spatial relation to destination.

A condition on representation of a subject matter is that there be *de re* representation of particulars in the subject matter.[130] The individual must have a capacity to connect its abilities representationally with *particular instances* of the attributes attributed. Having *de re* capacities is, I think, a condition on a system of states' having representational directedness to a subject matter. Such abilities are constitutive elements in genuinely representing a subject matter, as

---

[130] This claim is part of a general thesis about the constitutive association of representational states with *de re* representational states. *De re* states apply representational content in immediate, singular ways to a subject matter. See my 'Belief *De Re*'; 'Postscript to "Belief *De Re*"'; 'Five Theses on *De Re* States and Attitudes'.

distinguished from merely correlating with a subject matter in a systematic way, and capitalizing on such correlations to cope with the environment. The path-integrating individual that lacks perception lacks a capacity to engage in *de re* representation of particulars in spatial locations and spatial relations. No particular place, or anything in space, is ever represented. The hypothetical individual just discussed is like a wind-up toy that updates potentials for motor commands in response to various twists of its joints or rubbings of its surface. The wind-up toy might be placed in, or fitted to, an environment that enables it to return to its starting point by integrating the twists with the rubbings. The toy would represent nothing spatial, indeed nothing at all.

The fact that path-integration information systems have evolved to cope with space is part of the marvel of nature. But such systems form no states that objectify spatial attributes. Relevant animals lack states specific to particulars in space. They represent no specific spatial positions or relations. Explaining the animal's states need not invoke states with veridicality conditions. Attributing representation is picturesque but not explanatory.

Landmark Use

Perhaps a role for spatial representation is more inviting in the case of *landmark use* in path integration. Many animals use visual perception in identifying landmarks, and in forming spatial representations of relations among landmarks or between landmarks and positions. In such cases, landmark use involves *representing* entities as being in spatial relations. When *such* landmark use is added to path integration, I believe that it provides the path-integration system with spatial representational content.

I shall argue, however, that landmark use in path integration does not *entail* presence of spatial representation, in our non-deflated sense. There is no essential appeal to veridicality conditions in explaining the individual's states.

In many arthropods on the move, landmark use depends on matching retinal arrays, together with averaging techniques.[131] Thus, turns in response to information from landmarks result from motor commands' responding to retinal stimulation that is associated with homing, or with correction of the global vector.

---

[131] Thomas S. Collett and Jochen Zeil, 'Places and Landmarks: An Arthropod Perspective', in Healy (ed.), *Spatial Representation in Animals*; S. P. D. Judd and T. S. Collett, 'Multiple Stored Views and Landmark Guidance in Ants', *Nature* 392 (1998), 710–714; Thomas S. Collett and Matthew Collett, 'Memory Use in Insect Visual Navigation', *Nature Reviews Neuroscience* 3 (2002), 242–252. The technique is often called 'image matching'. Here the images are surely non-representational. It is not known whether the animal has a conscious two-dimensional phenomenal image deriving from retinal stimulation. What is known is that the retinal stimulation yields registration that has the geometrical properties of a two-dimensional array. Sometimes such arrays can be mapped onto arrays of neuron firings. See the exposition of the term 'image' in Chapter 8, the section PERCEPTUAL PSYCHOLOGY AND THE DISTINCTION BETWEEN SENSORY INFORMATION REGISTRATION AND PERCEPTION.

No entity is perceived. No appeal to representation of spatial relations improves explanation of the visual processing.

In such cases, the non-perceptual sensory landmark information does not provide the animal with a representation of, or as of, its location, its spatial relation to the landmark, or attributes of the landmark. The visual information that correlates with landmarks is a factor in a chain of causes of movement. It may correct a global vector. It may enable the animal to turn in response to proximal stimulation (stimulation that in fact derives from the landmark). The registration of proximal stimulation may be sufficiently similar to a stored template registration to enable the animal to move to where it receives stimulation that matches the template.

Thus, in some types of navigation, simple animals use landmarks, but do not *represent* them. They simply record information that causally derives from landmarks, and that functions in determining movements within a route. No state with representational content and veridicality conditions plays any non-trivial role in explanations of the animal's landmark use. No perceptual constancies are in play. The science centers on motor commands that derive from registrations of proximal stimulation. The fact that the relevant states function to enable the animal to cope with space, and operate according to trigonometrical principles, is to be distinguished from the animal's engaging in spatial representation.

These reflections are meant to distinguish psychological kinds and types of psychological explanation.

All animals with perceptual capacities also have non-perceptual capacities for sensory registration. As I have emphasized, non-perceptual sensory capacities are commonly integrated intermodally. Perceptual and non-perceptual capacities can also be integrated intermodally.

All or nearly all the arthropods whose non-perceptual spatial sensory systems I have been discussing have perceptual systems. As indicated earlier, bees have visual perceptual systems. Bees' visual systems have distance constancy, location constancy, size constancy, and color constancy. They just do not use such constancies in their primary activities in path integration and large-scale landmark use. They do not rely on *perceptual* capacities when they are flying fast in route.[132] Much of the product of the bee's visual system is non-perceptual. The system operates, to a large extent, on cumulation of retinal flow and on retinal pattern matching.[133]

---

[132] Lehrer, 'Shape Perception in the Honeybee'; Lehrer, 'Spatial Vision in the Honeybee'; Horridge, Zhang, and Lehrer, 'Bees Can Combine Range and Visual Angle to Estimate Absolute Size'; Lehrer et al., 'Motion Cues Provide the Bee's Visual World with a Third Dimension'. Because apian eyes are close together, bees seem not to rely on binocular techniques to determine distance. Distance is determined mainly by motion parallax—which capitalizes on difference in changes of retinal effects from near and far objects—and by differences produced in retinal angular size by familiar types of objects as they occur nearer or farther away.

[133] The reader may wish to consult again the exposition of the distinction between perceptual capacities as objectifying capacities and the more liberal conception of perception as 'form

I shall return to the issue of the mix of representational and non-representational systems in these lower animals. For now, my purpose is to distinguish explanatorily relevant kinds. Discussion is idealized to serve this purpose.

Map Use

Since the 1980s, intense empirical controversy has raged over whether spatial information in various animals is stored in map-like ways. A *map-like system* is an allocentric system of information that correlates with a systematic grid of metric spatial relations on a given terrain, and that functions to enable an animal to navigate the terrain. An allocentric system lacks an egocentric origin. The systems of path integration that I have been discussing are not *in themselves* map-like. They are 'route-based'. They correspond to a path in space, but not a grid of spatial relations. The distinction is common in the scientific literature.

Path integration together with a series of stored landmark retinal images do not in themselves constitute a map. Recall that 'image' does not imply representation in perception or perceptual memory. (See Chapter 8, the section PERCEPTUAL PSYCHOLOGY AND THE DISTINCTION BETWEEN SENSORY INFORMATION REGISTRATION AND PERCEPTION.) The stored images can be retained as a sequence. Or they could just trigger navigation from one landmark to the next along the route. In either case, no information that correlates with a grid of metric relations need be stored. Path integration works on updating information that could discard past spatial information and never sum it into a map. The landmark images could serve to trigger movement until the next image is received. The landmark images could modify or be modified by a vector.[134]

Map-like *behavior* is following a direct route to a target from anywhere in the mapped terrain. Map-like behavior can be taken to support the hypothesis that individuals store allocentric, metric maps of a familiar terrain. Displacement during a journey followed by travel by direct route to the target can be used to evince a map-like system.

Unfortunately, the issue is complicated by the fact that if an individual can register landmark information from a displaced position, its system might use beaconing or averaging of stored landmark retinal images to produce a direct route to the target. Such map-like landmark use would be consistent with purely route-based navigation. It would be consistent with lacking any capacity that correlates mathematically with a map.

---

extraction'. Here the geometrical forms are not representational. See Chapter 9, the section PERCEPTION AS OBJECTIFICATION AS OPPOSED TO PERCEPTION AS EXTRACTION OF FORM.

[134] With respect to bees, the modern proposal of navigation by metric map traces to J. L. Gould, 'The Locale Map of Honey Bees: Do Insects have Cognitive Maps?', *Science* 232 (1986), 861–863. See Gallistel, *The Organization of Learning*; C. R. Gallistel, 'Insect Navigation: Brains as Symbol-Processing Organs', in *Invitation to Cognitive Science*, iv (Cambridge, MA: MIT Press, 1996).

In fact, much of the evidence that first seemed to support storage of metric maps in insects fell prey to just this problem. When displaced bees managed to chart a course to the target, they had access to landmarks. Lacking landmarks, they could not pass the test. They could not arrive at the target after they were displaced. They seemed not to rely on a stored map together with, say, cues from the sun, to set a course.[135]

More recently, some evidence of new map-like behavior that appears to be landmark-free has emerged. Capacities to engage in such behavior without landmarks seem to have been masked by experimental set-ups.[136]

Even in the face of evidence of map-like behavior that does not use landmarks, it can be unobvious whether the behavior is correctly explained by reference to a metric map—together with compass readings from some large-scale source, such as the sun or stars, available anywhere on the terrain. It remains in dispute whether the evidence regarding bees can be accommodated by a theory that attributes a capacity to connect learned route-based vectors in ways that stop short of a metric map.[137]

Humans certainly use allocentric maps. It is more widely accepted that non-human mammals use maps than that bees do.[138] The issues remain experimentally and theoretically complex. The issue over maps in bees is interesting, I think, because it suggests a philosophical question about the relation between principles that explain navigational capacities in terms of computational transformations that are merely mathematically equivalent to allocentrically anchored metric maps and principles that explain such capacities by reference to spatial *representation* that takes the form of allocentrically anchored metric maps.

Perhaps all animals that store and are guided by maps in navigation use *perceptual* representation that attributes spatial properties and relations. But for the sake of argument, suppose that certain arthropods do not. That is, suppose that all sensory input into beaconing, path integration, and landmark use is non-

---

[135] F. C. Dyer, 'Bees Acquire Route-Based Memories but not Cognitive Maps in a Familiar Landscape', *Animal Behaviour* 41 (1991), 239–246; F. C. Dyer, 'Spatial Memory and Navigation by Honeybees on the Scale of the Foraging Range', *Journal of Experimental Biology* 199 (1996), 147–154; Dyer, 'Spatial Cognition'; Rüdiger Wehner, 'Navigation in Context: Grand Theories and Basic Mechanisms', *Journal of Avian Biology* 29 (1998), 370–386. Wehner opposes attributing metric maps to a variety of animals including bees.

[136] R. Menzel, R. Brandt, A. Gumbert, B. Komishke, and J. Kunze, 'Two Spatial Memories for Honeybee Navigation', *Proceedings of the Royal Society of London, Series B, Biological Sciences* 267 (2000), 961–968; Menzel et al., 'Honey Bees Navigate According to a Map-Like Spatial Memory'. A good overview can be found in Cheng, 'Arthropod Navigation', 201–204.

[137] Cheng, 'Arthropod Navigation'; T. S. Collett and J. Baron, 'Learnt Sensori-Motor Mappings in Honeybees: Interpolation and its Possible Relevance to Navigation', *Journal of Comparative Physiology A* 177 (1995), 287–298; Ken Cheng, 'Shepards' Universal Law Supported by Honeybees in Spatial Generalization', *Psychological Science* 11 (2000), 403–408.

[138] Ariane S. Etienne, 'Mammalian Navigation, Neuronal Models, and Biorobotics', *Connection Science* 10 (1998), 271–289; C. R. Gallistel and A. E. Cramer, 'Computations on Metric Maps in Mammals: Getting Oriented and Choosing a Multi-Destination Route', *Journal of Experimental Biology* 199 (1996), 211–217. There is also evidence that humans have masked vestiges of path-integration systems that they can rely on in the absence of instruments.

perceptual. Suppose that direction is determined by simple responses to time-relative responses to distributions of registrations of polarized light. Suppose that distance is determined by retinal flow. Suppose that landmark use derives from averaging registrations of two-dimensional retinal registration of proximal stimulation (retinal patterns). Suppose that no perceptual model of the world is ever formed in the navigation. No perceptual constancies are employed.

I believe that an animal that lacks perceptual states cannot have states with motor actional representational content. I will not argue this belief here. I stipulate that the hypothetical animal that I will discuss lacks both sensory and motor-representational content: Suppose that the animal's motor movements can be fully explained in terms of responses to proximal stimulations together with body-mechanical responses (however computational) to those stimulations.

The key supposition is that a hypothetical animal's navigational capacities are not correctly explained in terms of route-based vectors. They must be explained through computational principles that are mathematically equivalent to an allocentrically anchored metric map. But the computational transformation does not otherwise involve any perceptual or actional states with representational content. Thus all the animal's map-like behavior is correctly explained in terms of a map-like mathematics whose sensory input is purely *non-perceptual*. Although this supposition may not correspond to any actual case, it is not so far from empirical actuality that it could be considered impossible.

My question is whether an animal that lacked any perceptual or actional states with representational content could nevertheless have a map that *represents* space.

What is involved in supposing that an animal's capacities are explained in terms of computational transformations that are mathematically equivalent to an allocentric map of some part of physical space—despite *lacking* any sensory or motor states that have spatial representational content? Of course, the animal's states register spatial information, just as the sensory systems do. Positions on the map correlate with positions in physical space. They function, through evolution, to facilitate navigation. But these points do not in themselves explain wherein the animal's states, including the mathematical structure governing transformations among the states, attribute relations in space.

I have supposed that sensory states and transactions can be explained as registrations of proximal stimulation and computational transformations among such registrations—without invoking principles that specify such registrations as states that attribute attributes in physical space. Analogous resources apply in explanations of motor states. The animal's movements can be fully explained in terms of its responses to proximal stimulations—without non-trivial invocation of veridicality conditions. The mere functional relevance of stored structures to metrical relations in physical space does not invest those structures with representational content regarding space, any more than the functional relevance of the sensory registrations to physical space provides them with spatial representational content. Would such a metric map be a specifically *spatial* map in any stronger sense than that it has a structure that corresponds mathematically to spatial structure, and functions to help the animal negotiate space? Of course, the internal structure corresponds in a more complex way to space than do the structures of beaconing and path-integration devices. This fact might tempt one into insisting that the structure involves spatial representation. On such a view, a representational spatial structure would be explanatorily and perhaps phylogen-etically prior to representation of entities *in* space.

I think that one should resist the temptation. Geometrical structures can have specifically representational content as of physical space only in association with *de re* representational applications to particular places or to particular entities as being in spatial relations.[139] Given that sensory and motor processing can be explained without non-trivial invocation of states with veridicality conditions, there is no *applicational* role for veridicality conditions in understanding the use of the map-like structure in the animal's psychology. There appears to be no explanatorily relevant use for the map-like structures that grounds explanation in terms of veridicality conditions. The appropriate explanations of the map-like structure are causal-correlational and functional, not representational in my sense. To be representational, the capacities must be associated with some sort of objectification. Nothing in the hypothetical animal's capacities indicates that the mathematical structure that functions in causing movements, and that *corre-lates* with spatial structure, is representationally applied to physical space by any psychological state of the animal. For there is no psychological process in the animal that distinguishes between the use of the map-like structure in responding to proximal stimulation and a use that systematically distinguishes proximal information from distal information that is specific to positions in space. Of course, the positions in space are functionally crucial for the animal. But the animal's *psychology* does nothing to target positions of space, or to map *them*. The animal's psychology consists of responses to arrays of sensory stimulation that are functionally well correlated with the environment.

I think that no representation of objective spatial relations can occur apart from some objectifying capacity *in the animal* that makes the relevant psycho-logical states specifically relevant to spatial relations. There is no apparent objectifying capacity in the supposed animal. At any rate, the psychological kinds in the hypothetical animal are deeply different from kinds involved in having a map-like representational structure applied through perceptual capaci-ties.

The hypothetical animal's capacities have geometrical structure. But it is well known that *pure* geometries need not be interpreted as applying to physical space. Each geometry is mathematically equivalent to an algebraic structure. Pure geometries do not in themselves concern physical space.[140] To have that status,

---

[139]　See my 'Five Theses on *De Re* States and Attitudes'.

[140]　That is the lesson of Einstein's demonstration that *which* among various geometries, Euclidean and Non-Euclidean, applies to physical space is an empirical issue.

they must be applied. Application must occur through objectifying psychological capacities that ground non-trivial invocation of veridicality conditions. Fundamentally, I think, application requires perceptual constancies.

Thus, even if, say, a structure that corresponds to or realizes a full Euclidean geometry is embedded in the psychology of an animal, it does not follow that the structure represents physical space. There is no question that the hypothesized geometrical structure in the animal registers information that correlates with physical space, given the animal's actual interaction with the terrain. What I doubt is that it represents physical space. The structure is not best explained by taking it to have veridicality conditions in application to physical space, or as representing space or spatial relations as such.

It is no accident that geometrical structures in sensory-motor memory correlate with the structure of physical space. They evolved to help animals navigate space. They enable an animal's psychology to connect retinal image arrays, motor impulses, path-integration vectors, and so on—in a way that functions to make navigation possible. The network of relations among these psychological elements realizes a mathematical structure. Its transformations are explained by mathematical principles. The realized structure is *mathematically equivalent* to the structure described by a geometry that is representationally applied to, or genuinely purports to describe, relations in physical space. But no representational relation between our hypothetical animal's psychology and physical space enables the geometrical structure in the animal's states to describe or represent physical space. The animal lacks any perceptual or actional mode of representation of any particular place or relation in physical space. The animal lacks perceptual constancies regarding attributes of entities in space. The geometrical structure lacks specifically physical–spatial representational content. To have such content it must be integrated with perceptual representational applications to physical space—or to entities in physical space as having spatial attributes. Application must, I believe, be through perception or actional states.[141]

The geometrical structure in the hypothetical animal's psychology, on this view, does not describe or represent anything. It is a mathematically structured network of sensori-motor states whose structure is mathematically equivalent to a pure geometry that *could be* representationally applied to physical space. But nothing *in the animal's psychology* applies it in this way.

---

[141] These views derive from work on *de re* representation and its constitutive role in representation and in the possibility of representational content. See my 'Belief *De Re*'; 'Postscript to "Belief *De Re*"'; and 'Five Theses on *De Re* States and Attitudes'.

A remark on knowledge. Psychology of spatial representation requires perception. To have spatial representation, one must have perception. Knowledge of the mathematical structure, once the spatial representations are in place, need not depend for its justification on perception. Whether any part of a structure of *physical* space (for example, some very abstract spatial representational core common to the different geometries) could be known without warranting the knowledge through perception is a matter I leave open.

The psychological realization of a quantitative map-like geometrical structure could be phylogenetically prior to perception. The psychological structure would inform animal capacity to process proximal registration and yield motor commands, a capacity that evolved to connect the animal to physical space. The psychological structure is not tied down (*de re*) to any spatial entities *represented as spatial*. The animal does not represent where it is.

Whether or not there are actual animals like the hypothetical one, mathematical structure instantiated by computational transformations among sensory-motor states can, constitutively, become representational through and only through sensory-motor states' being supplemented by further psychological capacities. It gains representational content through structuring *de re* representational perceptual and representational actional applications to spatial particulars.

The example illustrates how evolution can encode an environmental structure into the pre-representational capacities of an animal. In this case, a mathematical structure that mirrors a metric spatial structure is encoded into pre-representational sensory-motor capacities. Such encoding constitutes a pattern of pre-representational causal relations between environment and psychological capacity that help determine the representational content of a psychological state—once relevant objectifying capacities are also present. The example illustrates the causal, pre-representational relations between environment and individual cited by anti-individualism. These patterns of relations to specific spatial aspects of the environment figure in determining the representational natures of perceptual, actional, and intermodal psychological states.

Spatial Representation in Navigation by Jumping Spiders and Other Arthropods

I have been arguing that certain types of spatial capacities in lower animals are not *in themselves* representational. I have indicated, however, that many of these same animals do have spatial perceptual representation. I want to discuss a case in which an arthropod relies on spatial capacities that are clearly representational—in both perceptual and actional representation. Once representational perceptual capacities are integrated with the computational non-representational systems that function in an animal's coping with space, I believe that at least some forms of information registration come to *represent* space.[142] Then intermodal memory systems and actional systems tend to become representational. Spatial representation spreads into the heart of the animal's spatial navigational capacities.

The intermodal quantitative systems for route-based or map-like navigational systems stand ready to be infused with representational content. They need

---

[142] I am imagining that some sources of input into the intermodal (say, map-like) system might remain non-representational, even if the intermodal system and *other* sources of input are representational.

nothing more than input from *de re* representational (referential and attributional) connection with particulars in space, or with particular places and spatial relations, to become representational. *De re* representational connection requires a subindividual capacity for objectification, a capacity to distinguish systematically between surface registration of information, on one hand, and particulars and attributes in a wider reality, on the other.

The jumping spider, genus *Portia*, exemplifies infusion, through perception, of spatial representational content into a navigational system. *Portia* is a genus consisting of about twenty species of jumping spiders primarily from the tropics. Portia preys on other spiders. It exhibits remarkable flexibility in its hunting behavior, and astonishing facility in learning efficient strategies. For example, it tests the characteristic web vibrations that other spiders (capable of hundreds of types of vibration) sense in responding to a mate; it learns to produce that form of vibration; and it captures the victim, with its guard down, in the victim's web.

Portia's vision is more acute than that of all other arthropods, and even of some birds. Portia has eight eyes, six of which are low-resolution eyes that serve primarily as peripheral motion detectors. The two primary eyes provide acute telescopic vision with a very narrow visual field. The spider achieves a larger range of relatively acute vision through scanning movements, pendular and rotary.

Portia has all the primary spatial visual–perceptual constancies and perhaps a modest form of color vision. The visual system can identify several specific animal shape types at thirty body lengths. More general motion, size, shape, and prey determination occurs at greater distances. In stalking prey, Portia crawls closer to the prey and makes accurate jumps onto the victim from several body lengths away. The distance constancy suggested by this sort of performance probably derives mainly from motion parallax—made possible by scanning movements.[143]

There is substantial evidence that Portia can set and hold in memory a detailed route. Following the route often involves extensive detour behavior. Portia commonly forages in a jungle tangle of branches and vines. In such an environment, detours are often necessary. Observations, both in the wild and in experimentally controlled situations, indicate numerous variations on the following pattern.

Portia fixes on a prey by vision. Then through a lengthy advance scanning process, including rejecting alternative, non-viable routes, the spider determines a route, usually the best one. For example, some vine lines that the spider scans will be broken or will otherwise not lead to the prey. After scanning, Portia does

---

[143]   R. Schwab and R. Jackson, ' . . . Deceived with Ornament', *British Journal of Opthamology* 90 (2006), 261; Duane P. Harland and Robert R. Jackson, '*Portia* Perceptions: The *Umwelt* of an Araneophagic Jumping Spider', in Rederick R. Prete (ed.), *Complex Worlds from Simpler Nervous Systems* (Cambridge, MA: MIT Press, 2004); Robert Jackson and Daiqin Li, 'One-Encounter Search Image Formation by Araneophagic Jumping Spiders', *Animal Cognition* 7 (2004), 247–254.

not follow them. Through vision the spider selects among routes that do and do not lead to the prey. The selected route commonly takes the spider out of view of the prey for as long as an hour, often in the opposite direction from the prey, in order to circumvent obstacles on the ground or in trees. The route may require climbing the back of a vine before re-emerging at a jumping platform suitable for surprising the victim. Following the route commonly involves fixing various intermediate 'landmark' subgoals. Eventually, Portia leaps on its prey—sometimes from above, sometimes by swinging in on a self-made dragline, sometimes by attacking across the web after vibration-testing—and disables it with a poisonous bite.

Route selection requires use of size, shape, distance, direction, and location constancies. There is no question that in establishing a route, the spider relies on spatial perceptual representation. Early research on route-following attributed to the spider a complete planning of the route. A route is surely sketched in advance. But route-following has come to be seen as involving repeated route- or landmark-checking, and some trial and error. It is not clear whether the spider has and remembers a map of a spatial grid, including locations off route. It appears at least to form a provisional sketch of a route from scanning, filling in, and checking details as it goes. And it shows a fallible but relatively reliable capacity to distinguish viable routes from impossible routes, where following the viable routes commonly requires extensive movement by the spider while it is out of visual contact with the prey.[144]

The spider has spatial representation of routes and subroutes. The spider's use of size and shape constancy in spotting prey involves spatial representation. The spider's use of distance, direction, and location constancies in scanning routes and in using landmarks in subroutes involves spatial representation. The spider's visual system engages in objectification—distinguishing surface registrations, and mathematical manipulations of them, from states *specific* to environmental particulars and attributes. Use of objective representation in navigation makes the memories of routes representational of, and as of, spatial positions and relations.

Portia may completely lack map-like capacities. The spider's spatial memory may be entirely route-based. It is the particular type and use of spatial capacities—not the mathematical complexity of them—that determines whether they are representational.

Portia's is a thoroughly studied case in which representational capacities infuse navigational capacities. The cases of other small arthropods are more

---

[144] R. R. Jackson and S. D. Pollard, 'Predatory Behavior of Jumping Spiders', *Annual Review of Entymology* 41 (1996), 287–308; M. S. Tarsitano and R. R. Jackson, 'Araneophagic Jumping Spiders Discriminate between Routes that do and do not Lead to Prey', *Animal Behavior* 53 (1997), 257–266; Wilcox and Jackson, 'Cognitive Abilities of Araneophagic Jumping Spiders'; Michael S. Tarsitano and Richard Andrew, 'Scanning and Route Selection in the Jumping Spider', *Animal Behavior* 58 (1999), 255–265; Michael Tarsitano, 'Route Selection by a Jumping Spider (*Portia Labiata*) during the Locomotory Phase of a Detour', *Animal Behavior* 72 (2006), 1437–1442.

equivocal. Sometimes, whether there is a role for genuine representation in navigation is empirically unclear.

I have intimated that insofar as bees use visual *perception*, as distinguished from retinal optic flow and retinal-image template matching, in determining distance and direction, or in fixing on landmarks, such spatial *representation* can infuse what would otherwise be non-perceptual route-based, or even map-like, sensory-motor systems. Of course, the optic-flow odometer and the joint-stress registrations of directional information do not become representational just by occurring in the same psychological system as a capacity for visual spatial perception. But retained spatial information seems to me to be representational if at least one of its sources of informational input is representational. If the bee can connect a visual perception that uses spatial constancies with some position on the route, or some node in the map-like grid, then the route or map information involves non-perceptual, memory-based representation of space.

Recent work on bees suggests that the enormous versatility and variety of sources of inputs into their navigational systems makes it very probable that their navigational, intermodally sourced memory systems have representational content.[145]

For their sensory input into navigational systems, ants and various types of bugs use information from joint stresses and joint movement together with olfactory cues for navigation. It is unclear to me whether such systems involve spatial representation. Even if they do not, the systems can be *as* efficient as representational spatial systems. What they may lack is subindividual capacities for objectification necessary to instantiate representational kinds.

In the preceding subsections on navigation, I have described differences in psychological kinds that ground different psychological explanations. The contrast between merely informational states computationally processed and representational states also computationally processed is very prominent in the psychological states underlying systems in arthropods for coping with space. I have focused on arthropods because theorizing about them vividly illustrates the distinction in psychological kinds.

Both types of states occur in most arthropods. Various beaconing systems and bare-bones path integration *cum* landmark systems simply register and compute spatial information. On the other hand, the visual systems and some aspects of the actional systems of several arthropods are clearly representational. There are surely interactions among these different types of psychological states and capacities. Bees' use of landmarks is retina-based in large-scale movements. But bees can see three-dimensional shapes, and it would be surprising if the retina-based landmark use were isolated in the bee's psychology from the capacity for visual perception. Similarly, insofar as bees have metric map-like

---

[145] See R. Menzel and M. Giurfa, 'Dimensions of Cognition in an Insect, The Honeybee', *Behavioral and Cognitive Neuro-Science Reviews* 5 (2006), 24–40. This article does not specifically address the point at issue. But it tends to support, I think, the conjecture in the text.

capacities, those capacities are almost surely informed with representational content through the bees' use of visual perception, at least in small-scale, slow-moving enterprises.

Issues about how and wherein representational capacities can provide representational content to capacities that are in themselves merely information-processing systems seem to me to invite further psychological and philosophical exploration.

PERCEPTION AND ORIGINS OF TEMPORAL REPRESENTATION

In the section PERCEPTION AND BODY, I argued that the constitutively necessary conditions on perceptual *representation of bodies as such* are substantially less stringent than many philosophers and even many psychologists have supposed. Two of the conditions that I think *are* constitutively necessary for representing bodies have implications for frameworks of representation. Segmenting a three-dimensional whole from a background implies having a framework of spatial representation (though not an allocentric one, or a comprehensive one). Tracking such a whole over time implies having a framework of temporal representation.

I did not argue that a capacity to represent something as a body is necessary for perception, or objective representation. I think it possible for an individual to have perceptual constancies regarding sounds, shapes, or colors, but lack any perceptual attribute that specifies *body*. While such representations are wide-spread among perceivers and fundamental to our own perceptual–conceptual schemes, they are not constitutively necessary for perception or objectivity.

I also maintained that spatial representation is not constitutively necessary for perception, representation, or objectivity. Perceptual representation of color and lightness seem in principle possible without any perceptual representation of spatial attributes.

I want to reflect here on whether temporal representation is necessary for objective empirical representation. First, I sketch some empirical background regarding primitive temporal sensitivities and temporal representation.

Temporal sensitivity takes three main forms in the animal kingdom. One is a sense for temporal order. Many animals can discriminate and retain an order of stimulations that corresponds to an order of events. For example, an organism might be able to discriminate and respond to an order in which certain stimulations occur, without being able to discriminate and respond to when they occur, or to what time intervals separate the occurrences.[146]

---

[146] Rats learn the order in which different sources provide food, without learning what time of day the sources do so. J. A. R. Carr and D. M. Wilkie, 'Rats Use an Ordinal Timer in a Daily Time–Place Learning Task', *Journal of Experimental Psychology: Animal Behavior Processes* 23 (1997), 232–247.

A second, more specific temporal sensitivity is a sense for *phases within cycles*. This sense is grounded in self-sustaining oscillators embedded in the physical structures of the animal, such as muscle tissue. It is obvious that an ability to anticipate events at certain times within cycles is of considerable value in coping with the environment. Such oscillators mark time and affect behavior in relative independence of daily input from the environment. Cyclic temporal sensitivity enables organisms to anticipate events without depending on input from them.

Circadian oscillators tuned to daily cycles operate independently of daily input from dark–light–dark changes. The oscillators came to be what they are through evolutionary selection that connects physical structures in the animal with the day–night cycles in the environment. Changes from dark to light surely played a causal role in innate presence of the oscillators. In individual animals, the oscillators operate independently of further input.

Well, almost independently. Oscillations tend to be or go out of phase. Since physical systems are imperfect and because the twenty-four-hour cycle is, in different locations, subject to different relations to dark–light changes, oscillations do not perfectly mirror the twenty-four-hour cycle. What prevents systems from going further and further out of phase is the fact that the cycle is repeatedly tuned through sensitivity to contextual input, such as changes of light at sunrise or sundown. It is as if a clock is reset. This periodic fixing is called *entrainment*.

Although circadian oscillators are very common, there are other sorts of cycles marked in animal temporal phase systems. There are systems for longer cycles— like lunar cycles or seasonal cycles. There are also short cycles, ultraradian cycles of a few minutes or hours. These sensitivities to different cycles are analogous to the way the minute and second hands of a watch measure different periods from the hour hand. Most animals have multiple oscillators tuned to different cycles.

The simpler animals tend not to be able to learn cyclic events that do not accord with the cycles to which their oscillators are tuned. For example, bees learn very quickly if events occur regularly at a certain time of day. They can even track numerous event types if each event type is associated with a time in the twenty-four-hour cycle. But, if an event type occurs every fifteen hours, for example, they cannot learn to anticipate its occurrence.

The third primary form of temporal sensitivity is a sensitivity to *intervals*. These are usually relatively short-term sensitivities, commonly ranging from a few seconds to several minutes. This sort of sensitivity is grounded in decay or accumulator systems embedded in the physical structure of the animal. This sensitivity marks durations, not cycles or particular temporal stages within a cycle.

Again, the value of such a sensitivity in coping with the environment is obvious. Birds need to be able to record how long flowers take to regenerate sugar. Regeneration is not associated with any particular time of day. To cope, an animal must balance waiting for a satisfying regeneration against the risk of a competitor's pre-empting the meal. Similarly, young hares return to a spot to be fed by the mother at a certain interval after sundown each day. The time of day varies with the time of year, and does not depend on the ambient light, since it also varies. The hares learn to mark the relevant interval. Often learning occurs in a single trial.

A sense for temporal phases seems to be present in all arthropods and vertebrates—hence roughly throughout the macro-sized parts of the animal kingdom. A sense for temporal intervals seems ubiquitous in vertebrates, but has not been demonstrated in insects, to my knowledge.[147]

It seems clear that none of these temporal sensitivities *must* be associated with perceptual representation, as distinguished from non-perceptual sensory registration. The sensitivities can be part of non-perceptual sensory systems. The sensitivity to temporal phases can be a product purely of basic rhythms in the organism's body.[148] Entrainment can be effected through sensitivity to proximal stimulation from light and dark, without relying on perception.

Similarly, a sense for temporal interval can rest on nothing more than appropriate accumulator or decay mechanisms triggered by any proximal stimulation that is reliably linked to the relevant cycle. Perceptual temporal reference is not guaranteed by temporal sensitivity. There is something fundamentally primitive, pre-perceptual, about the basic temporal sensitivities, especially the senses for temporal order and temporal phase. These sensory capacities occur in many organisms that seem to lack perception altogether.

These capacities vividly exemplify the primal antecedents of perceptual representation postulated by anti-individualism. The rhythms of the environment are encoded in an organism's physical rhythms. The correspondence between its rhythms and those of the environment enable the animal to anticipate and cope with the environment. The rhythms are stamped into the animal's life so that the animal is approximately in tune with objective reality. The basic causal molding is, however, pre-perceptual and pre-representational. The patterns help type-individuate perceptual representational content once a capacity for perceptual representation is developed. Objective intunement precedes objective representation.

Under what conditions does a temporal sensitivity, one that registers temporal information, have perceptual representational content? Under what conditions are times and temporal relations genuinely represented in an individual's

---

[147] I use several sources here: D. S. Farner, 'Annual Rhythms', *Annual Review of Physiology* 47 (1985), 65–82; R. Kolterman, 'Periodicity in the Activity and Learning Performance of the Honey Bee', in L. B. Browne (ed.), *The Experimental Analysis of Insect Behavior* (Berlin: Springer, 1974); Gallistel, 'Animal Cognition'; Gallistel, *The Organization of Learning*, chapters 7–9; Russell M. Church, 'Behavioristic Cognitive, Biological, and Quantitative Explanations of Timing', in Wasserman and Zentall (eds.), *Comparative Cognition*.

[148] René Descartes, *Discourse on Method* (1637), in *The Philosophical Writings of Descartes*, volume i, ed. and trans. J. Cottingham, R. Stoothoff, and D. Murdoch (Cambridge: Cambridge University Press, 1984), 141: 'it is nature which acts in [the beasts] according to the disposition of their organs. In the same way, a clock, consisting only of wheels and springs, can count the hours and measure time more accurately than we can with all our wisdom.'

perceptual system, as opposed to merely ingrained in the individual's sensory capacities?

Like representations of numerosity, perceptual representations of time are parasitic on perception as of other kinds of things. Representation as of temporal relations is not second-order in the way that mature representation as of number is. But, like mathematical representation, temporal representation gets its original *representational* role derivatively, through its association with perception of other things. Temporal sensitivities obtain their representational role through association with (*de re*) perceptual singular application to particulars. *De re* temporal application in perception is application to times in tense indexes or timings of perceptual (hence *de re*) singular applications to other particulars.

Temporal sensitivity and temporal information registration become temporal representation through providing a framework for the exercise of perceptual objectification. I believe that, at least in actual animal life, the functioning of temporal sensitivity in perception (and hence representational agency) is necessary and sufficient for temporal representation. A functioning psychological coordination of perception of *other matters* with temporal sensitivity is both necessary and sufficient for temporal representation in perception.

I will explain this thesis by first elaborating the sufficiency claim, then elaborating the necessity claim, and finally outlining the resulting picture of the relation between temporal registration and temporal representation.

First, sufficiency. Suppose that an animal tracks a moving particular. The tracking relies on sensitivity to temporal order. The particular is represented as the same through the motion. The coordination of later perceptions with earlier perceptions in representing the particular depends on sensitivity to temporal order. Then temporal sensitivity is incorporated into perceptual representation of movement. One represents the particular's being in one position as temporally after its being in an earlier position. A present perception is coordinated with a (recently) past perception in perceptual memory, where the memory marks its perceptual representation as indicating an earlier time. Or a single diachronic perception contains a representation of temporally ordered change. Such perceptions are further coordinated with actional representations guided by perceptual memory. The representations are temporally indexed or tensed, and coordination of the temporal representations figures in the nature of the perceptual tracking and the perceptually guided agency. Incorporation of sensitivity to temporal order in perception of change or movement is probably the simplest sort of temporal representation in perception. Similar points apply to sensitivity to temporal intervals.

Suppose that an animal is sensitive to some temporal cycle. Suppose that this sensitivity figures in the individual's use of perception in returning to a food source. Then the representational states involve tensing and representation of times and temporal relations.

Sugar water is perceived at the feeding station by a bee. The perception is associated with a given phase in the circadian cycle. There is an allocentric mapping of the cycle in the bee's memory, with mapping anchored on a day–night changeover. The perceptual and actional systems of the bee are egocentrically tensed. Present perceptions are present-tensed; some temporal order is retained in perceptual memory, which guides actional representation. The present tensed perception of the sugar water is mapped onto the allocentric cyclic temporal system running in the bee's memory, including action-guiding perceptual memory. The bee is then in a position to return to the same place at the same time the next day.

A role for temporal-order sensitivity, temporal-phase sensitivity, or temporal-interval sensitivity *in perception or representational agency* suffices to make the sensitivity representational of, and as of, temporal order, *loci* within phases, or intervals. The temporal sensitivity becomes representational through perceptual application to particulars in time and perceptual attribution of temporal relations among them.

I turn to the necessity claim. In actual animal life, in the absence of some capacity for perceptual application to particulars as being in temporal relations, I think that the temporal sensitivities would be mere information registration. If, for example, sensitivity to temporal cycle is not integrated with perception of entities in time, the sensitivity would be non-representational information registration, not representation of temporal relations.

This point seems to me fairly evident. A temporal sequence of sensory registrations that functionally corresponds to a temporal sequence of causes does not suffice for temporal representation, despite the biological functional significance of the correspondence between cause and effect. Merely having a bodily rhythm that pulsates in a regular way and that causes temporally adapted behavior does not suffice to *represent* time or temporal relations. Similarly, sensory-motor sensitivity to temporal intervals does not suffice to represent anything.

In themselves neither path integration nor body clocks constitute forms of representation, except in the deflationary sense of information registration. Such capacities sometimes pre-date perception. In both cases, perception appropriates a prior informational structure.

Without some such application in perception, temporal sensitivity would not be representational. It would only register and yield responses that depend functionally on temporal order, phases, or intervals. There would be no distinctive appeal to perspective or veridicality conditions in explanations of the encoding or the motor movement. And there would be nothing to distinguish mere functional incorporation of nature's temporal orders, rhythms, and intervals in the animal's physiology and psychology from representation of those temporal relations. At the constitutive and phylogenetic origins of temporal representation lie the harnessing of antecedent temporal sensitivities to perceptual constancies.

The idea here is similar to that which grounded the account of perceptual objectification. Unless there is a systematic distinction in the animal's psychology between the effect of nature on the animal and the way things are independently of the animal's inner impressions in a wider environment, there is no representation. In perception, this distinction is the product of the perceptual constancies. The objectification of temporal sensitivities, in representation of temporal relations, cannot be carried out, in primitive animals, by itself. Temporal objectification is a product of incorporation of temporal sensitivities into a system of perceptual objectification. The incorporation is not sequential, but structural and constitutive. Temporal representation is a by-product of temporal organization of (*de re*) singular perceptual applications to environmental particulars in perception. Temporal representation, originally, is a product of the temporal ordering and timing of perceived particulars, including changes or events.

Crudely, representation in general requires some sort of *de re* application of attributives to particulars in a subject matter. Temporal subject matter cannot be perceived or thought about *neat*. It must be represented through the timing or temporal ordering of particulars in time.[149] I believe that these claims identify constitutive necessities regarding temporal representation.

In actual animal life, the functioning of temporal sensitivity in perception (also representational agency) is necessary and sufficient for temporal representation. The qualification 'in actual animal life' is important. As intimated in the Introduction, I think that the dependence of temporal representation on *de re perceptual* applications to particulars in time is not constitutively necessary for every possible temporal representation.

All animals, including humans, first employ temporal representation in perception. I believe that, psychologically speaking, no animal, including no human, could represent (refer to, indicate, or attribute) temporal relations unless it first represented them in perception. But I do not think that these points are paralleled by apriori constitutive points about conditions for temporal representation. I think that there is no good apriori argument that temporal representation must be grounded in, or explained in terms of, *perceptual* capacities.[150]

---

[149] I do not intend to rule out a pure representation of the passage of time or of temporal intervals, abstracted from representation of particular events. I am not sure that there are clear cases of such representation. What I do deny is that any such representation is possible in a being that could not time or order *other matters*. One can certainly *think* about the structure of time in the abstract. But temporal representation is fundamentally and constitutively timing of entities in time. It is constitutively indexing of thought or perception as of other things.

[150] A view like the one that I reject here is often attributed to Kant in opposition to Descartes. I believe that Kant maintains the view primarily about cognition: no *cognition* of time without cognizing it as an aspect of perceptual capacities (sensibility). (See Chapter 6, the section KANT.) From his transcendental point of view, time is a form for perception. So, from that point of view, representation of time, though it can be purely apriori, is inseparable from the form of perception. See *Critique of Pure Reason*, the Transcendental Aesthetic. Descartes seems to think of temporal representation as not necessarily associated with perceptual capacities. He thinks of time (along with substance and number) as a universal idea that applies in all domains. He seems to think that time is knowable through pure thought, without reliance on any perceptual or 'sensible' capacities. See *Principles of Philosophy* I, 48; and *Rules for the Direction of the Mind* in *The Philosophical Writings of Descartes*, ed. and trans. J. Cottingham, R. Stoothof, and D. Murdoch (Cambridge, Cambridge University Press, 1984), i. 45. I think that Descartes is closer to the truth on the question

I think that there is nothing incoherent in representing temporal relations in pure thought, where the temporal representation is not constitutively explained by reference to perceptual capacities. The constitutively necessary *de re* capacities that must connect a temporal framework to the timing and temporal ordering of particulars could be exercised in pure thought, without any *constitutive* reliance on perception. One could track the order of, perhaps even intervals between, pure self-conscious thoughts: I am now thinking that time is abstract, and earlier I was thinking about number. One could follow the order of such *cogito* thoughts, without the application of temporal representation bearing any essential representational or epistemic relation to temporal order in *perception* or *perceptual* thought.

In actual animal life, however, perception is psychologically necessary for temporal representation. In actual animal life, temporal representation in perception precedes temporal representation in pure thought. Psychologically speaking, without being grounded in specific perceptual attribution of temporal relations through *perceptual de re* singular applications to particulars in time, temporal representation cannot get started.

The thesis that I have been elaborating yields a striking picture of the phylogenesis of temporal representation. The abstract structure of temporal order, whether that of short linear sequences or of cycles, occurs in aboriginal preperceptual aspects of sensory-motor systems. Here the picture of temporal structure is similar to the mathematical structure of path integration. There too a quantitative structure was in place before, or at least independently of, any representation of a subject matter. The computational structure of both spatial and temporal sensitivities ante-dates, or at least is independent of, perceptual representation.

For example, with phase sensitivity, there is a non-representational correspondence already in place between structures in primitive organisms and environmental temporal structures. Such structures help mediate between sensory intake and motor impulse, even in extremely simple, non-representational organisms. Perceptual representation of other matters coopts this antecedent quantitative informational framework. So an aboriginal self-sustaining rhythm in the physical

---

of the epistemic relation of time to perception. Kant's view tracks how temporal representation actually arises in phylogenetic and developmental history—although these matters are not his main concern. See also *Critique of Pure Reason*, B1. As a psychological matter, I doubt that we could have intellectual apprehension of time (through apprehension of order in pure thought), unless we had first gained that apprehension through perception. But I think it *epistemically* possible to be *warranted* in beliefs about time from reflection on one's own non-perceptual thinking. The warrants need not be grounded in empirical experience. I believe that similar points apply to number. In actual individual and species development, numerical capacities become representational through perception. No animal could learn to apply numerical representation except through first applying it in perception. Similarly, for other mathematical representation. But mathematical representation has no constitutive or epistemically necessary connection to sense perception. Mathematical belief can be warranted through pure intellection. In this note I am, of course, skating swiftly over complex issues regarding representation and knowledge of time, number, and self.

structures of very primitive organisms provides temporal sensitivity. In the order of phylogenetic development, this sensitivity is involved in temporal representation when and only when the rhythm is enlisted in perceptual representation of other matters.[151]

Temporal representational tracking of *cycles* seems naturally to be allocentrically indexed. No part of the cycle is egocentrically privileged. Any time in the changeover between day and night is a viable origin for a temporal framework that represents the day–night cycle. The temporal representation of order and intervals is commonly egocentrically indexed.

To make *use* of the allocentric representation of the cycles, the animal's actional system marks when a time in the cycle, or when the beginning or end of an interval, is *present*. Since use is necessary to representational content, an allocentric temporal framework must be coordinated with an egocentric one.

In animal phylogeny and development, temporal representation, like spatial representation, must be associated with perceptual representation and actional representation. All perceptual and actional representations are constitutively egocentrically indexed. All perceiving and all plans for action are necessarily from the egocentric perspective of the perceiver or agent. Allocentric spatial representations in the psychologies of animals coordinate with and serve representation in egocentric frameworks. So, although allocentric temporal frameworks derive from very primitive, pre-perceptual sensitivities to cycles, such frameworks must (in actual animal life) be harnessed to egocentric ones to be representational at all.

This interaction between egocentric and allocentric temporal representation is probably more primitive than any such analog in spatial representation. Recall that allocentric map-like spatial representation is probably abstracted from earlier, egocentrically indexed route-based representation. It is a disputed question whether, strictly speaking, arthropods have allocentrically anchored spatial maps. Allocentric temporal frameworks clearly show up in a variety of arthropods, as well as in more complex animals. The antecedent quantitative, information-bearing, cycle-sensitive structures are preperceptual. They are innate, not abstracted from perception, or even from antecedent sensitivities to temporal intervals. Cyclic, pre-perceptual bodily rhythms are already in place when they are coopted by the perceptual and actional representational systems. They probably need not be abstracted from egocentric temporal representation in the way that map-like allocentric spatial frameworks seem to be learned and abstracted from egocentric spatial representation.

---

[151] There is evidence that in rats numerical-like computational transformations make some use of the temporal phase oscillators. It is natural, I think, to suppose that the oscillators are selected because of their connection to temporal sequences in the environment and that the numerical use of these oscillators grew out of the original temporal function. The numerical and temporal series are, however, specialized and distinguishable from one another in their application and use. See Meck and Church, 'A Mode Control Model of Counting and Timing Processes'.

The hypothetical animal in the subsection MAP USE did not abstract the map-like informational structure from perception. It seems empirically possible that map use could sometimes be like path integration and sensitivity to temporal phases of cycles in not being abstracted from perceptual experience—being in place prior to perception. I conjecture that this possibility is unlikely to be a normal actual occurrence. However, all these matters are open to empirical investigation. The variety in psychological nature never ceases to surprise and charm.

These points about probable origins of allocentric representation of temporal cycles are compatible with the points made earlier about the *constitutive dependence* of allocentric temporal *representation* on uses in perception and action that involve egocentric temporal representation. In the order of constitutive explanation of *representation*, egocentric temporal representation is prior to allocentric temporal representation. The quantitative computational structure of pre-representational, pre-perceptual temporal sensitivity to phases in cycles *becomes* representational (usually allocentrically indexed) when it is allied with perception.

Is the representation of a temporal framework constitutively necessary to perception? This is not a question about ubiquity or about psychological necessity. I have no doubt that, as a matter of fact, the perceptual capacities of all animals are exercised in temporal representational frameworks, at least those indexing temporal order. The question is whether there is a constitutive connection between perception and temporal representation.

I have maintained that there is such a connection between perception as of *bodies* and both temporal and spatial representation. This claim does not answer our question. For the representation as of bodies, though widespread among animals, is not constitutively necessary for perception.

I think that the answer to the question is, however, affirmative. There *is* a constitutive relation between having perceptual capacities and having a capacity for temporal representation. I believe that the relation can be known apriori.

I believe that perceptual states constitutively depend for their representational content on being involved in some use by an animal. Perception must have a use in individual functioning if it is to have its meaning or representational content. Perhaps the use need not be agential. It could be any functional response to the perception, active or not. It might be the formation of an emotion; or it might be a passive, behavioral *schreck* reaction. The only requirement is that the use be functionally caused by, guided by, perception. Insofar as the use is functionally caused by, or guided by, or "motivated" by perception, the use must be representational. It must have a representational content. The use's being representational follows, I think, from its being a use *of* perception. The actional or other behavioral representational content pertains to its being a response to the perception that makes use of *it*. The representationality of the perception engenders representationality in the responsive state, act, or occurrence.

Here is an argument, making use of the foregoing ideas, for thinking that all perception is constitutively associated with temporal representation. I number steps for convenience.

(1) A capacity for perception must be associated with a capacity for guiding representational use of perception.

(2) Use cannot always be simultaneous with perception, but must sometimes follow it in time: use cannot both be guided by perception and always co-occur with it instantaneously. The transition from perception to use plays itself out over at least short time intervals. Even in cases where perception effects what we are inclined to call 'immediate' release of simple inflexible instinctual behavior, there is necessarily at least a brief time lag between the occurrence of the perception and impetus to a use.

(3) For perception to guide use, past perception must be coordinated through memory with present or anticipated representational use.

(4) This coordination requires sensitivity to temporal order. It requires a functioning representational capacity that connects present use determination with a previous perceptual state. The coordination requires some sensitivity, at least to temporal order, in the perception–response systems of the animal.[152]

(5) As argued earlier, the systematic coordination of temporal sensitivity, including sensitivity to temporal order, with perceptual representation suffices for representation of time or temporal relations. The intermodal system that mediates perception, perceptual memory, and use determination *represents* temporal relations if the coordination employs temporal sensitivities in representational enterprises. What it *is* for a temporal sensitivity to be representational is for it to be appropriated systematically in perceptual enterprises—more generally, representational enterprises.

(6) Therefore, a capacity for perception must be associated with a capacity for temporal representation. There must be some past–present representation of temporal order, in the relation between perception and perceptual memory (possibly also in the perceptual system itself) and the relation between perception, perceptual memory, and use representation.

The anticipatory representation of action, or in non-active states, is guided by past perceptual representation stored in memory and functionally/indexically marked as past. This harnessing of temporal sensitivity suffices for representational, context-dependent markings of temporal-order relations.[153] So the sensi-

---

[152] I doubt that the relevant temporal sensitivity must be to cycles, much less intervals. Minimal sensitivity is, I think, to temporal order.

[153] See Jeannerod, *The Cognitive Neuroscience of Action.*

tivity to temporal order involved in mediating perception and use must tag perception and use representations (pre-eminently actional representations) with temporal indexes—context-dependent time markers—that are temporally ordered in the context of a given use.

The argument locates temporal representation in relations among perception, perceptual memory, and use. A second argument locates temporal representation in a perceptual capacity.

Any capacity to perceive change must systematically employ temporal sensitivity to temporal order. But (as in step (5) of the previous argument), any capacity for perceptual representation that is systematically coordinated with sensitivity to temporal order engages in temporal representation—representation of time and temporal relations. So any perceptual capacity to represent change must index perceptions that track change in such a way as to represent the situation after the change as occurring after the situation before the change.

The first argument, from the dependency of perception on use, is, I think, an apriori argument that identifies a constitutively necessary link between perception and temporal representation. The epistemic status of this second argument may be somewhat different. Kant believed that it is contingent, and only empirically knowable, that the world contains change.[154] I take no position on this issue. It does seem to me that it is necessary and apriori that any world that contains perceptions contains change. Actual perceptions require a sensory state's being caused by something. In fact, a world that contains an individual with perceptual *capacities* must contain change. According to perceptual anti-individualism, which in its broadest forms I believe to be necessarily and apriori true, in order for an individual to have a perceptual capacity there must be, or have been, causal interactions between instances of the system containing that capacity and the subject matter of the perceptual capacity. Causal interactions are changes. So it is, I think, apriori that any world in which there is a being with perceptual capacities must be a world in which there is change.

The second of our arguments requires more than that there be change, however. It requires a perceptual system to *track* change. I doubt that it is apriori that being a perceiver or perceptual system constitutively involves a capacity to perceive change. Perhaps there could be a perceiver capable only of awakening and having a perception of color or shape. If one color or shape is perceptually represented, the perceiver goes back to sleep. If another color or shape is represented, the perceiver opens its mouth and receives nutrients flowing by, and goes back to sleep. Perhaps such an individual or system could have perception but lack a capacity to perceptually track change. If all the foregoing is correct, the second argument is not an apriori constitutive argument about any possible perceiver. It does apply apriori to any perceiver that *can* track change. Obviously, the argument applies broadly. Perceiving change, even perceiving

---

[154] Kant, *Critique of Pure Reason*, B3.

motion, is among the most basic of perceptual capacities—fundamental to the fitness of most or all actual animals with perception.

In any case, in accord with the first argument, it is apriori that temporal representation is present in any psychological system that includes perception. Thus temporal representation, unlike spatial representation, is constitutively associated with perception. However, both are fundamental to the representational capacities of most or all perceivers.

ASSOCIATION, COMPUTATION, REPRESENTATION

Neither philosophy nor psychology should be satisfied with an exhaustive contrast between associative connections and representational states. There are at least three types of theoretical postulation of psychological states. Associative postulations should be distinguished from postulations of non-associative psychological structures that transform informational states according to quantitative principles. Both of these should be distinguished from postulation of representational states.

The states appealed to by theorists of insect navigation are not associationist, dispositional states. Postulating states that fit behaviorist strictures offers no hope of explaining path integration. Relations of strength and weakness of association, and states that have relatively straightforward relations to types of behavior, cannot explain navigation, beyond the simplest beaconing behavior. Appeals to quantitative information processing have been empirically successful. Making that point is near the core of a lot of 'representation' talk in psychology. I think that the main motive for such talk is to contrast quantitative information-processing models with behaviorist models of explanation.[155]

Empirical theory credibly attributes quantitative structure and computational transformations to the psychologies of lower animals. The quantitative structure informs sensory-motor states. It is embedded in transformations of registrations of spatial information.

An animal that navigates by path integration moves because its psychological system operates according to laws that involve computational transformations of quantitative information. The system undergoes systematic transformations correctly explained as instantiating quantitative principles. The system evolved as an adaptive upshot of interaction with a spatially structured environment.

The system can still operate without a representational perspective. It can lack states subject to explanations that invoke the specific veridicality conditions of genuine representational states. It can lack the representational content of a geometry applied to physical space. It can lack the content of mathematical

---

[155] A further motive is the relative clarity of information-theoretic, deflationary conceptions of representation. See Claude E. Shannon's classic paper 'A Mathematical Theory of Communication', *Bell System Technical Journal* 27 (1948), 379–423, 623–656; Masud Mansuripur, *Introduction to Information Theory* (New York: Prentice Hall, 1987).

vectors that represent—have non-trivial veridicality conditions regarding—routes in physical space. The states do not attribute, indicate, specify, or refer to anything. They do not in themselves represent spatial structures or spatial routes, in the sense of 'represent' that has a secure place in perceptual psychology.

No objectification occurs in such sensory-motor systems. Nothing in the sensory system distinguishes proximal stimulations from the entities and attributes in the environment. Nothing in the motor system distinguishes motor commands from objectives or goals in the physical world, or even from bodily movement that is the object of the command. Nothing in the intermodal processing that mediates between sensory and motor systems distinguishes specific structures in physical space from sensory-motor conditions in the animal.

Spatial representation does not reside purely in an internal sensory-motor structure that transforms psychological states governed by mathematical principles, and that functions to capitalize on systematic correspondences to positions in physical space in enabling an animal to navigate. Spatial representation resides in a system that systematically distinguishes sensory-motor registrations from states relevant to spatial relations among specific elements in the spatial environment. The system must ground explanations that make non-trivial reference to states with veridicality conditions.

Lumping together representational states with mathematically computed information-carrying states does not match well with distinctions that are fundamental to what is probably the most advanced part of the science of psychology—perceptual psychology. In explanations of perception, the invocation of representational states is associated with a form of explanation that makes non-trivial reference to veridicality conditions, and functions to distinguish, systematically, information registration from genuine representation. In perceptual psychology, invoking veridicality conditions is not easily and uncontroversially eliminable. I believe that such invocation is *ineliminable*. In theories of path integration, 'representation' talk can easily be eliminated (and often is) in favor of talk of functioning information or functioning correlation.

The fundamental thing about representation—its setting of specific, explanatorily relevant veridicality conditions and constituting a specific mode by which *representata* are referred to, indicated, and attributed—plays no non-trivial explanatory role in many highly quantitative, computational explanations. Some of the forms of explanation discussed in preceding subsections are examples. Lumping together representation with functional information-carrying, or functional information-registration, blurs a significant distinction between psychological kinds, and a corresponding distinction between types of psychological explanation. The distinction is clear in contrasts between explanations by appeals to perceptual constancies in perceptual psychology and the generalized explanations of the role of the senses in path integration or route-finding by landmark use that I have been discussing. The former types of explanation attribute a form of objectification. The latter do not.

There is an important distinction between postulating informational states processed according to mathematical principles and postulating "associationist" states.[156] But drawing the contrast by not sharply distinguishing between information-theoretic explanations (however computational) and genuine representational explanations (also commonly computational) blurs perhaps the most fundamental distinction among psychological kinds. The distinction is between genuine perspectival, attributional representation of a subject matter, on one hand, and highly structured, non-representational sensory and actional states that functionally correlate with elements in a subject matter, on the other. This distinction is first marked in perception. The distinction lies at a constitutive, as well as phylogenetic, origins of objectivity.

---

[156] Associationist notions may have some role to play in explaining very low-level processes. But see C. R. Gallistel and J. Gibbon, 'Time, Rate, and Conditioning', *Psychological Review* 107 (2000), 289–344; C. R. Gallistel and J. Gibbon, 'Computational versus Associative Models of Simple Conditioning', *Current Directions in Psychological Science* 10 (2001), 146–150; C. R. Gallistel, 'Conditioning from an Information Processing Perspective', *Behavioural Processes* 61 (2003), 1–13; C. R. Gallistel, 'Deconstructing the Law of Effect', *Games and Economic Behavior* R52/2 (2005), 410–423.

11   *Glimpses Forward*

> *The mind, that Ocean where each kind*
> *Does straight its own resemblance find;*
> *Yet it creates, transcending these,*
> *Far other Worlds, and other Seas . . .*
> Andrew Marvell, 'The Garden'

I conclude by outlining three philosophical issues suggested by the discussion of perceptual objectivity. The three issues are (*a*) determining the epistemic status of general principles governing constitutive conditions on objective empirical representation, (*b*) explicating relations between perception and propositional thought, and (*c*) mapping levels and types of objectivity.

THE EPISTEMIC STATUS OF CONSTITUTIVE PRINCIPLES GOVERNING PERCEPTION

I have held that some claims about constitutive conditions on perception are apriori. A *constitutive condition* is one that is central to determining a nature. Something's *nature* is the type that constitutes what it is to be that thing. For example, a constitutive condition on a sensory state is that, in central cases, instances of the state be caused by something in a way that figures in the state's function. If something were never the effect of causation, or if its causes did not figure in some function, it could not be a sensory state.

There is a kind of necessity in constitutive conditions and natures. A constitutive condition for attributes, including natures, helps determine those natures by metaphysical necessity. And the nature of any entity is metaphysically necessary for that entity. The entity could not be that entity if it did not have that nature.

The necessity that constitutive conditions and natures signal is special. It is not just any metaphysical necessity. The nature of a sensory state is not just any necessary attribute of the sensory state. A sensory state is necessarily a kind of state that when added to another kind of state makes two kinds of states. But being a kind of state that when added to another kind of state makes two kinds of states is not an aspect of the nature of a sensory state. It is also not a constitutive condition on a sensory state. Constitutive conditions on being a particular or an attribute, including a nature, are not just any necessary conditions. Constitutive conditions ground *constitutive explanations*—explanations of what it is to be that particular or attribute. They are the central conditions referred to in correct explanations of natures. For example, constitutive conditions on being a perception as of something's being round ground explanations of *what it is to be* a perception as of something's being round.[1]

Natures are *among* constitutive conditions for an entity's being of that nature. So some constitutive conditions are identical with or are aspects of natures. But not all constitutive conditions are aspects of the nature whose constitutive explanation they help ground. Constitutive conditions for a nature help ground explanations of what it is to be that nature. But natures, basic kinds, can ground explanations that some of their constitutive conditions do not enter into.

For example, being a visual perception with a certain perspectival mode of presentation as of something's being round is the nature of a psychological state. Reference to that kind of perception enters into empirical psychological explanations. The kind is embedded in psychological law-like patterns. It is governed by law-like principles. A constitutive explanation of what it is to be that kind of perception might appeal to constitutive conditions, such as being causally associated with past patterns of causal interactions between three-dimensionally shaped physical entities and sensory states. Those patterns of causal interaction are among the constitutive conditions for being a perception of that kind. But they are not part of, elements in, the state's nature. They are mentioned in explanations of the state's nature. But they are not mentioned when one mentions that kind of perceptual state—for example, in empirical psychological explanations. Psychological explanations that appeal to that kind of the perceptual state *assume* those constitutive conditions. But the explanations are not about constitutive conditions that make psychological natures what they are. The nature of psychological state and the constitutive conditions for it are not in general to be identified.

Constitutive explanations are explanations of what it is to be such and such, or what it is to be a particular. Such explanations clarify what it is to be an attribute or particular. Such explanations used to be called *real definitions*. But not all such explanations are definitional. And many traditional conceptions of definition are misleading or mistaken. So I have avoided counting constitutive explanations definitions.[2]

Constitutive explanations are not ordinary empirical explanations in psychology. Constitutive explanations focus on *what* not on *how*. Explanations in psychology explain *how* perceptual states arise, and how they give rise to other

---

[1] I emphasize again that explanation, a human activity, is not essential to most conditions on natures. The conditions are what they are independently of any actual explanation. Rather, good constitutive explanations are what they are because of the central role constitutive conditions play in making natures what they are. The conditions ground the explanations.

[2] I discuss these issues in my *Foundations of Mind*, especially the Introduction and Chapters 10–12.

things. Constitutive explanations explain the most general conditions under which psychological kinds can be *what* they are.

I have said that some representations of constitutive conditions are apriori. Saying that some such representations are apriori is shorthand for saying that some claims about constitutive conditions can be warranted apriori. For a claim or belief to be warranted apriori is for the warrant not to depend for its force on sense perception, or other sensory material, or on perceptual belief. The force of the warrant normally rests instead on understanding or reason. The explanation of the warranting support does not appeal even partly to sense perception, sensory material, or perceptual belief. It appeals to understanding or reason.

Warranted beliefs in pure mathematics and pure logic are commonly, and I think correctly, regarded as apriori. The beliefs are warranted even though the warrant does not draw on sense experience.

Of course, it may be psychologically or causally necessary to have had sensory input, perhaps even perception, to come to have logical or mathematical beliefs. But this is not a point about warrant. It is a psychological or causal point. It surely applies to many apriori beliefs.

The question is: Once one has had enough experience to be able to have the relevant belief, does epistemic support or warrant for the belief have to appeal to sense perception, or to other sensory input, or to perceptual belief? If not, and if the belief is warranted, then the belief is warranted apriori. Mathematicians and logicians often do not seem to need to appeal to sense perception, or other sensory input, or perceptual belief, in order to be warranted in their beliefs. They seem to rely purely on understanding, reason, argument. They often do not seem to need to rest their beliefs on empirical considerations. Philosophical claims about certain structural aspects of the world can appear to be similar.

Claims of apriority are commonly misunderstood. Misunderstanding is a primary source of resistance. To say that a belief is apriori is not to say that it is innate, obvious, rationally certain, indubitable, infallible, imposed on the world, or immune to revision (even empirical revision). To say that a belief is apriori is not to say that it is easy to recognize that it is true, or that it is uncontroversial—much less that it is easy to recognize that it is apriori.

Arriving at apriori warranted beliefs can be difficult. Showing that they are apriori and explaining their apriority can be even more difficult. Many claims of apriority have been mistaken—either because the putatively apriori belief was not warranted at all, or because its warrant was empirical. Many explanations of apriority have been confused, unsatisfying, or embedded in preposterous philosophical systems.

A great deal of philosophy is made up of empirical reflection. Such reflection systematizes or generalizes from empirical beliefs—some scientific, some truistic. Many claims in philosophy that purport to be apriori are either empirical or untrue. Many derive from long assimilated, very general, or very obvious empirical beliefs. Throughout this work I have criticized numerous claims of conditions on objective representations that were assumed to be apriori. Still, I believe that some philosophical theses are apriori warranted.

The claim that some beliefs about constitutive conditions are apriori is controversial. Some philosophers even contest the claim that pure mathematics and pure logic are warranted apriori. I will not discuss these matters here. I just want to flag them and advocate their interest.

Let me collect some examples of beliefs that I have held to be apriori warranted.

In Chapter 8 I claimed that it is apriori that sense-perceptual states have the representational function of being veridical. It should be remembered always that this claim is an idealization. As noted in the preceding chapter, perceptual representational contents when successful, are commonly only veridical within some range. So *approximate* veridicality is what is often at issue. Still, veridicality is at the center of the natures and laws or law-like transformations that are central to perception and the subject matter of perceptual psychology. Insofar as perceptual states have a representational function, perception is a teleological notion. And being inaccurate or non-veridical is a kind of failure or shortcoming for perception. Nothing could count as a perceptual state if it would not undergo a kind of failure if it were not approximately accurate. These are matters that we can know by reflection, without support from empirical considerations.

A corollary of this claim is that it is apriori that sense-perceptual states have veridicality conditions. Having veridicality conditions or accuracy conditions is an aspect of what it is to *be* a perceptual state. That is, perceptual kinds constitutively, and by nature, include veridicality conditions. The perceptions are veridical or accurate when these conditions are fulfilled. Such representational conditions are representational contents.

In Chapter 8 I claimed that it is apriori that where there are representational functions, there are standards, or norms, for representational success. The baseline standard for perception is the standard *veridicality*, or approximate veridicality. What it takes for a *particular* perceptual system to yield veridical perception is, of course, determined only empirically. But the connection between having the representational function of being veridical and there being standards for being veridical is apriori. It seems apriori that this representational function is associated with subordinate standards—such as a standard for representing as well as possible, given the sensory input and given the limitations of a perceptual system.

In Chapter 9 I claimed that it is apriori that the representational contents of perceptual states are structured and that they have both singular and general (attributive) elements. This claim derives from more detailed reflection on the representational function of perception.

The foregoing considerations center on the representational aspects of sense perception. Other considerations center on the sensory aspect. I think it apriori that for a perceptual state to be a (successful) perception of a particular, the particular must be in a causal relation to the state.

Further considerations center on the connection between perception and capacities of individuals. I think it apriori that any sensory capacity, including perception, has a function of serving individual function or use. It follows that it is apriori constitutive of perception that it be a capacity of individuals.

I claimed that it is apriori that perception is from an egocentric perspective. I argued, with less certainty, that it is apriori that perception employ temporal representational.

I think that it is apriori that perceptual anti-individualism is true of perceptual states. I think that it is plausibly apriori that if there are perceptual states, some of them must represent physical entities. I do not take a position here on whether it is apriori that there *are* perceptual states. I think it *empirically* known that there are perceptual states. Whether there is a further, apriori warrant to believe that in fact perceptual states represent physical particulars as having physical attributes seems to me a more complex and difficult question.

Empirical reflection on perception forms much of the basis for taking perception to be real and to be an actual objective form of representation. I have *assumed*, contrary to scepticism, the existence of a physical environment. I have taken it as empirically obvious that there are individuals with sensory systems. There is also empirical reason to believe that there is a sensory form of representation that meets conditions for being perception and that represents particulars in the physical environment as having specific physical attributes. A question is whether there is another way, an apriori way, of warranting the objectivity of perception (its representing a mind-independent environment as having specific attributes that are mind-independent). A closely related question— roughly speaking, a version of the question of philosophical scepticism—is whether there is an apriori way of warranting the claim that there is perception in this sense, and that we have it. Answering this latter question affirmatively in a way that confronts scepticism requires showing that the affirmative answer does not beg, against the sceptic, a reasonable question.

I am optimistic that there is a way of warranting affirmative apriori answers to these questions. But a full account of the *epistemic bases* of the claim that perception is objective and of the claim that we have perception, construed as objective, is extremely complex and difficult. These issues are beyond the scope of this book.

I have maintained that some claims about constitutive conditions on more specific types of perception are apriori. For example, I held that it is apriori that to perceive a body as such, an individual must be able to discriminate a three-dimensional figure from its surround. I held that it is apriori that to perceive a body as such, an individual must be able to track bodies over time.

All these claims and conjectures about the epistemic status of beliefs about constitutive conditions on perception are problematic. I advance them as plausible and worthy of reflection. In some cases I gave arguments that suggest the apriority of constitutive conditions. But explaining in depth the different types of apriori warrant is a task for other occasions.

I want to highlight the fact that inasmuch as these collected claims are warranted, their warrant does not seem to lie in their explanation of empirical evidence. They can be suggested by reflection on empirical research. They can guide empirical research. But they do not seem to stand or fall with a body of empirical evidence.

These appearances could, of course, be illusory. Philosophy is no shining beacon of reliability in this domain. Even if they are not illusory, the relation between existence claims—claims that there are perceptual systems—and certain modal claims about the boundaries of kinds—certain claims that perception has a certain nature—are delicate. The separation of the empirical and apriori aspects of any warranted belief is a difficult matter.

Most of what I have said, both critical and constructive, is independent of the precise epistemic status of the claims. I believe that I have provided a way of thinking about perception and objectivity that will be valuable, regardless of how the various components of this way of thinking are warranted—assuming that they *are* warranted.

THE UPPER BORDER OF THE PERCEPTUAL: PERCEPTION AND PROPOSITIONAL ATTITUDES

My account of the origins of empirical objectivity has centered on perception. Perception has also been at the center of my criticism of Individual Representationalism.

I framed the discussion so as not to rely in any fundamental way on my views regarding the relation between perception and propositional thought. As a terminological point, I conceive of thought as propositional and concepts as elements in propositional structures.[3] I believe that perceptions are not propositional states. They do not constitutively involve capacities to engage in propositional inference, and their representational contents do not have propositional structure.

Even if perceptions were propositional states, they would not constitutively depend on the sorts of states required by second-family Individual Representationalists. None of the specific capacities demanded by Individual Representationalists is among the minimal constitutive conditions on objective perceptual representation.[4] Perception does not require quantification, self-tracking through

---

[3] There are, of course, various forms of intermodal processing of representational states—including perhaps forms of individual activity—that are not propositional forms. I do not count these non-propositional forms *thoughts*, and I do not count their components *concepts*. This matter is terminological. If one wanted to broaden these terms, then using 'propositional' to modify 'thought' would not be a mere reminder, as it is when I use the latter term. It would be a substantive qualification.

[4] Some developmental psychologists claim that a perceptual causal category emerges relatively early in the development of children—by age 6 months. See A. M. Leslie, 'The Perception of Causality in Infants', *Perception* 11 (1982), 173–186. I believe that various conceptual issues need sorting out in order to adjudicate such claims. I believe, however, that having attributives for causation

allocentric space, a capacity to represent a seems/is distinction, a capacity to use language, or a capacity for meta-representation. No argument has established that perception requires such things. Empirical science, not to mention common sense, shows that it does not require them.

So the criticism of Individual Representationalism and the development of an alternative do not rest on distinguishing perception from conception. Individual Representationalism's failure can be certified even as the validity and nature of this distinction are left open.

I think that there *is* a structural difference between perception and propositional attitudes. Perceptual systems are very widespread among animals. A much more limited range of animals, including humans, have propositional attitudes—including *propositional* perceptual *beliefs.*[5] There is evidence that apes have them. Probably several other non-human animals have them. There is, however, strong empirical ground to believe that the abilities of many of the animals that have perceptual systems can be fully explained without appeal to states with propositional structure. Explanations of perceptual systems do not attribute propositional contents or propositional states to perceivers or perceptual systems, in any non-trivial way.[6]

---

is not constitutively necessary for representing bodies or events as such, much less a constitutively necessary condition for perceptual or conceptual representation. I have chosen not to pursue these issues in this work.

[5] I assume that all beliefs are constitutively propositional. Especially outside professional philosophy, usage of terms like 'thought' and 'belief' is so varied, however, that I emphasize the qualifier ('*propositional*' beliefs and '*propositional*' thought), even though for me it is redundant. See note 3.

[6] A huge literature discusses notions of non-conceptual content. I will not cite even a representative sampling. Work by Goodman (and authors reflecting on Goodman), work by Dretske, and work by Peacocke seem to me to be broadly in the right direction. Goodman said little specifically about perception, but his discussions of other types of representation are clearly relevant to understanding it. See Nelson Goodman, *Languages of Art* (Indianapolis: Bobbs-Merrill Inc., 1968). An improvement on Goodman's work is John Haugeland, 'Analog and Analog', *Philosophical Topics* 12 (1981), 213–226. As a sample of other relevant work, see Fred Dretske, 'The Role of the Percept in Visual Cognition', *Minnesota Studies in the Philosophy of Science* 11 (1978), 107–127; *Knowledge and the Flow of Information* (Cambridge, MA: MIT Press, 1981); Christopher Peacocke, *A Study of Concepts* (Cambridge, MA: MIT Press, 1992), especially chapter 3; and 'Does Perception have a Nonconceptual Content?', *The Journal of Philosophy* 98 (2001), 239–264. I do not endorse either the specific conceptions of non-conceptual content or the arguments for there being non-conceptual content that are presented by Dretske and Peacocke. I think that although many of these arguments are effective against particular versions of the view that perception is conceptual (propositional), I believe that most of them, in particular most of Peacocke's, beg the question against certain possible types of conceptualist views. I regard some aspects of Dretske's and Peacocke's positive views on this matter, however, as broadly congenial. None of this work isolates context-bound singular elements (perceptual singular applications) in perceptual content. Peacocke, except in the last piece cited, and Dretske (see Chapter 8, note 20, above) hold that perceptual representation involving non-conceptual content requires propositional attitudes in the perceiver's psychology. Both authors rely on Evans in holding this view. Evans's conception of non-conceptual content is, though relatively undeveloped, untenable—as I argued in Chapter 6, the section EVANS ON CONSTRAINTS ON OBJECTIVE REFERENCE IN PERCEPTION. Even in the last piece cited, Peacocke seems not to recognize, in perceptual representational content, singular applications to perceived entities. He seems to assume that singular representation *of perceived entities* occurs only in thought (and perception is confined to general

Understanding the distinction between perception and propositional thought is difficult. It deserves a project in itself. Here I just sketch some points about the distinction and discuss how Individual Representationalism looks in light of it.

Let me review some basics about perception. The representational content of perception is a veridicality condition, that when (and only when) met by a appropriately sensed subject matter is veridical. The representational content of a perception includes singular and attributive elements. A perceptual state functions to apply to particulars in a singular context-dependent way. Perception is always as of particulars. So the veridicality condition of a perception must contain singular representational elements. Perception always categorizes or groups particulars that it represents. A perceptual state functions to indicate properties, relations, or kinds, and to attribute them to particulars. So the veridicality condition must also contain general attributive elements.[7] These attributive elements are inevitably from a perspective. They are one of many possible ways of perceptually attributing whatever property, relation, or kind is attributed.

So veridical perceptual representation both singles out particulars and groups them as instances of repeatable attributes. A perceptual ability constitutively involves both singular representational applicational abilities and general attributive abilities. Every perceptual attributive accompanies and guides a contextual singular perceptual application. I think that it is the fact that attributive abilities are never exercised separately from singular applications in perception that helps mark the non-conceptual, non-propositional status of perception.

The problem of explaining how objective reference emerges in *thought* is not that of explaining how conceptual abilities (much less linguistic abilities) make possible a breakthrough to objectivity or to singular reference. Objectivity and singular reference are constitutively present in autonomous perception. The problem is to explain what it is to separate attribution from its role in aiding singular reference, to arrive at propositional predication. A capacity for such separation is a central aspect of achieving the specific context independence and generality that are embodied in pure attribution, propositional thought, and rational inference.

"ways" of perceiving, anchored egocentrically); perception is accorded no singular demonstrative representation of objects perceived. I believe that this unargued (and I think deeply mistaken) assumption undermines some of the arguments he gives that perceptual content is not conceptual. I agree, of course, that perceptual representational content is not *in fact* conceptual (propositional). Peacocke does cite the fact that animals that apparently lack concepts have perceptual representational content. I believe that this fact grounds one reason to maintain that perception is non-conceptual.

My view that perceptual representation does not have the form of propositional content rests largely on reflection on the commitments and requirements of explanation in perceptual psychology. Propositional structures are not attributed in mainstream explanations. Nor do there seem to be any distinctively propositional capacities in perception that such structures are needed to explain. This complex topic invites more exploration.

[7] In the terminology of my 'Five Theses on *De Re* States and Attitudes', the generality is semantical, syntactic, and ability general.

I approach an explanation of this point by starting further back. Both perceptual and propositional representational contents have singular elements and attributive elements. But the elements in perception are organized non-propositionally. Let us suppose that they are organized in ways that are structurally isomorphic with a topological or geometrical structure. Think of a map. A map does not have a sentence-like structure. It is a singular noun-like representation that functions to correspond to a piece of geography. In vision, the elements in perception have something like the form of a map or sketch from an egocentric perspective.[8] There are levels of abstraction for the attributives. A perception as of a particular shade of red can also be a perception as of red.

I take concepts to be certain elements in *propositional* representational contents.[9] Although perceptions are normally imputable to individuals (perceivers), as are propositional attitudes, the transformations among perceptions are never, or almost never, attributable to individuals. By contrast, propositional inferences are normally acts by individuals.

I think that there are logical operations that occur in propositional thought that do not occur in perceptual representation. For example, although there may be a kind of perception of absence, such perceptions do not apply propositional negation. Similarly for the other true logical constants. I do not want to develop these issues here. The point that I want to develop concerns predication and attribution.

The perceptual representational content of every perceptual attributive is linked to a perceptual context-dependent singular element, a perceptual application of a demonstrative analog. Wherever perception groups, its grouping guides, accompanies, and helps single out a purported instance of the grouping. Perceptual attribution is never separated from contextual singular representation that purports to refer to and single out particulars. Every perceptual occurrence of a perceptual attributive accompanies, guides, and aids purported contextual singling-out of a particular. Every occurrence of the perceptual attributive green or square or body modifies and guides a context-dependent singular element. The attributives are primary guides of reference to a contextual instance, or a bearer, or group of particulars that are *relata*. In the terminology of Chapter 2, the section REPRESENTATION-AS AND REPRESENTATIONAL CONTENT, every perceptual attributive is part of a (purported) *primary way of referring* contextually to a particular.

---

[8] Of course, the "map" in perception is *not* perceived or looked at. It is *not* an object of perceptual representation. It is the form of perceptual representation, the form of perceiving.

[9] More specifically, concepts are constant, freely repeatable elements in propositional representational contents. See my 'Five Theses on *De Re* States and Attitudes'. The most salient type of freely repeatable element is the conceptual attributive. This is the analog in thought content of linguistic predicates. Other types of concepts are functional notions (like the successor of), individual constants, logical constants, and constant demonstrative elements, like I or this (as distinguished from their event-like applications in a context). Elements in propositional contents that are not concepts are occurrence-based, or context-bound, applications.

Although perceptual memory can abstract from or lose track of perceived particulars, *use* of perceptual memory must always employ remembered attributives to guide purported reference to particular instances. The remembered attributives form templates for guiding singular application. They do not, I think, enter into believed or asserted propositions.

In thought, by contrast, we commonly make occurrent use of attributives that do not guide a contextual singular application in singling out a referent. Not all occurrences of conceptual attributives accompany and guide contextual singular applications. Not all occurrences help single out a purported particular, or are part of a primary way (or indeed any way) of contextually referring to a particular. For example, the following occurrences of attributives in thought do not guide purported context-bound reference to a particular: cats and are animals in cats are animals; plants and are green in some plants are green; is a number in 3 is a number.[10] Even in demonstrative-marked singular thoughts, there are attributional elements that do not serve to guide contextual reference to particulars: is a thief, in that man is a thief. Attributives in propositional structures have uses other than the use of guiding a context-bound referential application to a particular.

Call an occurrence of attribution that does not play a role in guiding contextual singular application in singling out a referent '*pure attribution*'. Pure attribution is not part of a (purported) *primary way of referring* contextually to a particular.[11] I believe that to have propositional attitudes, one must be able to use attributives both in guiding contextual singular application *and* in pure attribution. Attributives that mark a capacity to engage in pure attribution are *conceptual attributives*, or *predicates*.[12] Conceptual attributives, or predicates, are by nature elements in propositional structure. To have conceptual attributives, one must be able to use attributives other than in modifying and guiding context-dependent singular representation as of a particular. An ability to engage in pure attribution is constitutively necessary to having propositional and conceptual ability.[13]

Not all concepts are attributives. The context-independent individual concept 3 is not. Logical-connective concepts and quantifier concepts are not. But I think that having any concept requires having conceptual attributives, and having conceptual attributives constitutively requires having an ability to engage in pure attribution. Concepts, in fact attributive concepts (predicates in thought content), are constitutively necessary elements in every propositional

---

[10] Among the concepts in these representational contents, 3 and the quantifiers are not attributives.

[11] Recall from Chapter 2 that I am bracketing plural reference. A broader statement of the points made in this section would contrast the role of *pure* attribution with an attributive role in *guiding* context-bound reference to particulars in *plural* as well as singular reference.

[12] Conceptual attributives are, of course, not prohibited from also marking an ability to guide context-dependent (paradigmatically singular) application to particulars. Thus the conceptual attributive body can be used in pure attribution or in guiding context-dependent reference to particulars.

[13] Pure attribution is graphically signaled by the copula.

representational content. Since a capacity for pure attribution is a constitutive condition on having conceptual attributives, a capacity for pure attribution is a constitutive condition on having states, acts, events, or capacities with propositional representational contents.

Thus one must be able to find, in an individual's propositional attitudes, a distinction between the occurrence of F in this F and the occurrence of F in this G is F. This is a functional distinction between attribution in the service of guiding a singular contextual application in (purportedly) picking out a particular, and attribution that does not occur in that role, pure attribution. Examples of the latter type of attribution are quantified attributions (Fs and Gs in All Fs are Gs), attributions to particulars that are *independently* contextually singled out (is F in this G is F), and attributions that guide non-contextual reference (F in the one and only F is a G).

Perception, unsupplemented by propositional thought, cannot engage in representation that is functionally independent of a role (either an attributive role or a singular applicational role) in contextually referring to particulars. Perception is essentially, at every point, context-bound singling-out of particulars. Its attributions function in presenting particulars.

Of course, this functional distinction between pure attribution and attributive guidance in context-dependent singular reference need not be reflected upon or represented as such. It is enough that it be present in, and explanatory of, an individual's psychological states, acts, events.

With propositional attitudes, there is the beginning of a freeing of occurrent representation from presentation of particulars.[14] Pure attribution marks a subtle kind of freedom from the here and now. This freeing of attribution, in pure attribution, from a role in context-bound singling-out of particulars is a step beyond the primitive objectivity involved in perception. Perception separates a perspective on the physical environment from the immediate effects of the environment on the individual's surfaces. Pure attribution, including conceptual attributives, marks a capacity to separate attribution, a constitutive element in any representational perspective, from its role in guiding contextual singling-out of particulars that have a causal impact on the individual and the individual's perspective.

A further sort of freedom from the here and now shows itself in propositional inferential abilities. These are abilities to draw inferences that hinge on the logical, propositional forms of the propositional representational contents of propositional attitudes. For empirical attribution of propositional attitudes to

---

[14] I do not, of course, claim that the freeing is a developmental step in any individual. It is possible that all individuals capable of propositional attitudes have them from the first moments in which they engage in representation. The freeing is a stage in a conceptually distinguishable, abstract order of degrees and types of objectivity. Individuals who have propositional attitudes have capabilities that are in one respect more objective and more removed from the here and now than individuals who have only perceptions.

·

individuals to be justified, there must be some explanatory point to explaining inferences that hinge on propositional structure.

Such inferential abilities are illustrated by abilities to think in ways that are explainable as according with inference rules like

> This F is not G;
> This F is identical with that H;
> so   That H is not G.

Suppose that that H is used in a memory of an earlier perceived object. The object has been tracked and is now singled out by the content this F. It is important to the point of the example that use of the attributive G in the inference does not depend on being tied to any particular instance of being G.[15]

Another example of propositional inferential ability is the ability to think in ways explainable as according with the following inference rule from the propositional calculus:

> Either that F (perceptually remembered) is G or that (same) F is H;
> That F is not G;
> so   That F is H.

(For concreteness suppose that that F refers to a desired object, and G and H attribute locations.) Here not, and either-or are logical constants whose applicability is independent of any particular presentation of a particular. Some non-human animals and pre-linguistic children can, I think, engage in such inference patterns.

Logical connectives depend for their being propositional on their connecting propositional representational contents. Propositional form constitutively depends on a capacity for predication—conceptual attribution. So logical connectives cannot precede the separation of pure attribution from attribution that guides context-bound singular reference. The capacity to make the separation is, I believe, constitutively necessary to having propositional capacities at all. It is necessary to distinguishing conceptual attribution from perceptual attribution.

The generality that is achieved in an ability to use attributives independently of singling out particulars—the generality involved in conceptual abilities—does not in itself involve quantification (every, some). Quantification constitutes a

---

[15] I use negation in the example. It is an interesting question whether, in inferences involving perceptual belief, the separation of pure attribution from singular reference can be sharply illustrated without using negation, and without relying on schematic or quantificational generalization in the inferences. As indicated in the text, I believe that the separation of pure attribution can be explained by distinguishing attribution's role in primary and secondary ways of carrying out referential representation. (See Chapter 2, the section REPRESENTATION-AS AND REPRESENTATIONAL CONTENT.) Even in cases where a propositional content is engaged in context-bound reference, there is a difference between the role of the attributive that guides the reference and the role of the attributive that attributively applies to a particular *that has been singled out independently of that attribution.* Inasmuch as occurrences of attributives in secondary ways of referring are not essential for context-dependent reference (in the way that guiding attributives in primary ways of referring are), they count as pure attributions. Whether negation or generalization has a role in explaining this distinction is an issue for another occasion.

yet higher level of objectivity, beyond the independence from context-bound reference to particulars involved in pure attribution and propositional inference.

There may be animals that have propositional attitudes but lack propositional attitudes that contain quantifiers in their propositional contents. At any rate, I suppose this to be a conceptual possibility. All the thought by such individuals would be about perceived, or perceptually remembered, or perceptually anticipated, or perceptually imagined particulars. None of it would be in the form of quantified generalizations in propositional form.

Non-quantificational thought, in being propositional, nonetheless comprises ways of thinking—in pure attribution and in propositional inference—that themselves have roles or uses other than guiding the context-dependent presentation of particulars. Such thought involves a type of generality and a step toward greater objectivity that is not quantificational.[16]

This minimal freedom from the here and now, this minimal generality that resides in pure attribution (pure conceptual attribution) and propositional inference, constitutes a higher level of objectivity than that involved in perception itself. Propositional thought takes a constitutive step beyond the constitutive origin of objectivity in perception.

PROPOSITIONAL ATTITUDES, INDIVIDUAL REPRESENTATIONALISM, AND CONCEPTUALIZATION OF PERCEPTION

What should we say about reapplying second-family Individual Representationalism to the minimal sorts of objectivity present in having propositional attitudes—those sorts of objectivity that reside in pure attribution and propositional inference? Does having propositional abilities require having the sorts of abilities demanded by Strawson, Quine, and Davidson?

None of the arguments or claims offered by such philosophers provides any more support for Individual Representationalism with respect to propositional perceptual belief than they provide for the position with respect to perception. No reason has been given to think that having propositional attitudes requires mastery of the particular concepts, the belief in general principles, the ability to represent criteria, or the linguistic abilities demanded by second-family versions of Individual Representationalism.

---

[16] Various types of generality are relevant here. Quantificational generalization is a particular type. For discussion of the distinction between schematic and quantificational generalization, see my 'Logic and Analyticity', section VI. Other relevant notions of generality are discussed in my 'Five Theses on *De Re* States and Attitudes'. Perceptual memory may involve a non-propositional type of schematic generalization—a capacity to leave open a place for singular reference without actually engaging in it. But I think that propositional inferences that hinge on schematic generalization are probably a step beyond the most primitive propositional inferential capacities. I think that the most primitive capacities contain neither inferential schemas nor quantifiers. They produce inferences that hinge on propositional connectives and/or specific identities.

As in the case of perception, there are empirical explanations that attribute propositional attitudes to higher animals and young children. They do not attribute any of the supplemental capabilities that individual representationalists demanded. No conceptual incoherence ensues. Anti-individualism again provides a context within which these empirical studies and the rejection of Individual Representationalism can be "made intelligible".

Perceptual belief makes use of the singular and attributive elements in perception. In perceptual belief, pure attribution is separated from, and supplements, attributive guidance of contextual purported reference to particulars. Attributives figure in pure attribution in addition to figuring in singling out particulars. Perceptual belief takes over singular applicational elements and attributive elements from perception and gives them uses in a propositional framework.

Of course, perceptions can be incorrectly conceptualized. The perceptual system may present a perception as of a small, square figure. But the individual might form a mistaken perceptual belief as of a large, round figure. The mistake might derive from the individual's strongly expecting a figure different from the one that is actually perceived. In the normal course of things, however, perceptual belief makes use of perception without substantial distortion. Then attributive elements in perceptual content are correctly conceptualized.[17]

Correct conceptualization of a perceptual attributive involves taking over the perceptual attributive's range of applicability and making use of its (perceptual) mode of presentation. A perceptual attributive as of roundness is correctly conceptualized as a conceptual attributive as of roundness. Insofar as the concept is a perceptual concept, the conceptual ability must make use of the perceptual attributive as of roundness in its (the concept's) application to round things. The conceptualization is conceptual, not *purely* perceptual. What it is for an attributive concept to be a conceptualization is partly that it has uses, in the individual's psychology, beyond the use (essential to perceptual attributives) of modifying singular applications to particulars. It has pure-attributional uses. These uses are necessarily also associated with abilities, on the part of the individual, to engage in propositional inference. Engaging in inference entails having inferential capacities marked by logical constants (such as not, either-or, if-then, is identical to).

Conceptualization of perceptual attributives entails a capacity for pure attribution and a capacity for propositional inference. The latter capacity makes use of logical form, including pure attribution and logical constants. A constitutive condition on conceptualization is having these capacities. Of course, conceptualizations of perceptual attributives may take on richer content through propositional use and through association with other propositional attitudes.[18]

---

[17] The discussion of conceptualization that follows elaborates discussion in my 'Perceptual Entitlement', sections IV and VIII–IX.

[18] The philosophical tradition represented by Quine and Davidson vastly overplays holistic elements in conceptual capacities. I do think that it is constitutive of concepts that they figure in propositional inference. I think that there is little or no conceptual structure "in" most concepts. Moreover, in most cases there are only few (if any) *specific* inferences among concepts that an individual *must* be disposed to make

In themselves, perceptual systems have a limited array of types of perceptual attributives. Visual systems have attributives for shape, spatial relations, color, motion, texture, perhaps danger, food, conspecifics, and so on. Call such attributives *perceptually basic*. Visual systems lack attributives for many of the kinds that we come to think about. Perceptual beliefs containing only conceptualizations of perceptually basic attributives are *basic perceptual beliefs*. Many beliefs that are naturally and correctly counted perceptual beliefs use conceptual attributives that go beyond the range of concepts that conceptualize perceptually basic attributives.

Thus, we have perceptual beliefs as of baseball bats, CD-players, hybrid autos, skin cancer, poor neighborhoods, self-conscious facial expressions, and so on. Perceptual systems *per se* appear to have no attributives that apply to these types as such. Since perceptual beliefs involving these attributives do not strictly take over the modes of presentation of perceptions, or even preserve the application ranges of perceptual attributives, they are not conceptualizations of perceptual attributives. They do depend for their empirical application on perceptual attributives. Attributives for baseball bats depend for their application on the size, shape, color that baseball bats in fact have. They also depend on background belief regarding other properties that help determine the types that the beliefs are about. The background beliefs might concern functions, uses, or constitutions. Perceptual beliefs with representational contents that do not simply conceptualize perceptually basic attributives are 'perceptual' in a broader sense than are perceptual beliefs that contain only conceptualizations of perceptual attributives. In any particular application, however, the broader type of perceptual beliefs ultimately relies on conceptualizations of basic perceptual attributives.

The singular elements in perceptual beliefs also make use of the singular elements in perception. The singular elements in perceptual beliefs are associated with concepts and with the inferential propositional framework associated with concept use. Thus the occurrent singular elements in perception—what I call singular, context-bound *perceptual applications*—are also connected to occurrent singular elements in a propositional content—what I call singular, context-bound *applications in thought*. Both are singular demonstrative-like applications, individuated in terms of occurrent uses. The latter can take over the referents of the counterpart perceptual applications. They can inherit the perceptual tracking of particulars and the memories or memory files associated with perceptions of particulars. The applications in thought must be embedded in a network of abilities to engage in pure attribution and propositional inference. Commonly, they are also associated with connections between basic perceptual beliefs (beliefs about color, shape, motion, body, and so on) and a broader range of empirical belief.

The singular abilities may also connect with abilities to generalize quantificationally. Thus, from singular applications in propositional contexts, an individual

(or even capable of making) in order to have a given conceptual ability. I discuss this issue briefly in 'Five Theses on *De Re* States and Attitudes', section IV.

may be able to engage in quantificational inference—existential generalization or universal instantiation. I believe that this type of generalization, unlike the type implicit in propositional inference and the type implicit in pure attribution, is not strictly constitutively necessary for having propositional attitudes. Capacities for pure attribution and for propositional inference are constitutive of the most basic empirical propositional abilities—most basic in the order of psychological and constitutive origins. Quantificational ability is nonetheless a relatively primitive ability that enlarges on these origins of empirical propositional ability. It constitutes a further psychological and constitutive step beyond the origins of empirical objectivity in perception.

ORIGINS, LEVELS, AND TYPES OF OBJECTIVITY

Minimal perceptual objectivity is not a construct out of references to sense data. It does not depend on supplementary abilities to represent general preconditions of objectivity. Perceptual representation of physical particulars as having specific physical properties does not constitutively require rationality, language, self-consciousness, or any ability to *represent* conditions of objectivity. Objectivity is present in and partly constitutive of the most basic type of empirical representation, perception.

Anti-individualism and empirical science show that objective empirical representation is grounded in non-representational relations to a wider environment, and in our animal natures as perceivers. The objectivity of perceptual states is formed partly through patterns of non-representational causal relations to a mind-independent environment, and partly by subindividual objectifying operations in sensory systems that distill the environmental from the sensory effects of proximal stimulation. Both of these sources of objectivity are blind. The patterns of causal relations are part of blind nature impacting the lives of simple organisms and of the blind primitive agency of organisms on nature. The objectification is not an exercise of individual agency. The developmental, phylogenetic, psychological, and constitutive sources of objectivity in perception lie below the level of individual representation, control, awareness, or responsibility.

Thus, primitive objectivity does not depend on individuals' producing it. Individuals do not construct objective perception from subjective representation or consciousness. They do not render it possible through linguistic abilities, abilities to apply criteria, belief in principles, or abilities to generalize quantificationally. Perceptual representation is constitutively independent of these abilities. It precedes them. It starts with an openness to the physical environment as it is. Perceptual state kinds and perceptual representational content are, from the outset, objective. They are constitutively what they are through causal non-representational relations, as well as representational relations, to a mind-independent environment. Perceptual representation gets its relations to a mind-independent environment through patterns of causal interaction with it. What is distinctive about perceptual capacities is a systematic, structured subindividual, non-agential screening of effects of proximal stimulation for relevance to specific environmental entities.

This screening begins the slow growth toward science and reflection. It is the first step in representational distancing from the here and now. To return to Thomas Nagel's words: 'A view or form of thought is more objective than another if it relies less on the specifics of the individual's makeup and position in the world . . . '.[19] A constant theme in a flowering tracery of objectification is the separation of representation from the proximal, the local, the idiosyncratic, the subjective.

What is remarkable to me about origins of empirical objectivity is not that objectivity is constitutively present at the beginning of empirical representation. That is an important point. It is insisted upon by Wittgenstein and Davidson, and with qualifications by Strawson and Quine. But that point is not special to the late twentieth century. Aristotle made it.

What is remarkable is how primitive the origins are. Perception is the root objectivity and, I believe, the developmental and phylogenetic origin of genuine representation. Perception is shared by humanity with many arthropods, reptiles, birds, and fish, and probably with all other mammals. Perception is constitutively independent of capacities for propositional thought. I have tried to elicit a sense of the primitiveness of the developmental, phylogenetic, and constitutive origins of empirical objectivity.

I have criticized traditions in philosophy that portray human individuals as originating objectivity. *Non*-human animals are not the makers of objectivity either. Although primitive agency pre-dates perceptual representation and objectivity, agency does not produce objectivity. Rather, animal agency gains a primitive type of objectivity when non-representational relations to the environment and pre-representational psychological structures yield perception.[20] The origins of empirical objectivity lie in perceptual organization blindly fashioned by pre-representational, subindividual forces.

Therein, nature outdid itself. Of course, nature did not go supernatural. Rather, genuine representation as marked by objectification emerges as a by-product, or subcomponent, of evolution, in the operation of sense organs of relatively simple animals. Psychological kinds and explanations, specifically perceptual kinds and explanations, appear not to be reducible to biological kinds and explanations.

---

[19] Nagel, *The View from Nowhere*, 5.

[20] There may still be a literal sense in which the objectivity involved in primitive perception in the simplest perceivers—for example, bees—is nevertheless blind. There is no known connection between perceptual objectivity and consciousness. Some animals that perceptually, hence objectively, represent may not be conscious. This is a further reason to resist sense-data theorists' claim that objectivity is built from elements of subjective consciousness. A more basic reason is that the building methods postulated by first-family Individual Representationalism are not available to primitive perceivers.

Representational veridicality and objectivity *per se* are not driving forces of evolution. They are not selected for *per se*. Representational function is not biological function. Nature nonetheless evolved sensory systems that are representational and primitively objective. Representational function and objectivity in representation are closely enough related to evolutionary success that evolution can aid understanding of the emergence of structures that serve veridicality and objectivity, as well as fitness.

Perception is constitutively a type of *objective sensory representation by the individual*. Representation is constitutively associated with veridicality conditions. A distinctive type of objective representation occurs in the sensory systems of individuals that appear not to have any propositional abilities, much less those required by Individual Representationalism. The objectivity is that involved in representing a physical (mind-independent or constitutively non-perspectival) reality as having specific physical attributes.

I have also argued that perception marks the lower border of representation. Perception lies not only at the root of empirical objectivity. It is, I think, where states with veridicality conditions first clearly emerge. The epistemic ground for this claim lies in the apparent fact that explanation does not need to invoke representation and veridicality conditions in explaining pre-perceptual sensory systems. I believe that perception constitutes, phylogenetically, the first important kind that is *representational* in a specific, interesting, psychologically distinctive, and probably irreducible sense. Representational mind begins at the lower border of perception. It begins with primitive objectivity.

A large theme in second-family Individual Representationalism is the representation of bodies as such. There is no question that bodies loom large in our perception and thought about the empirical world. I believe that representation of bodies as such is near the phylogenetic roots of perceptual representation. A representational system can be objective without representing bodies as such. There are almost surely animal perceptual systems that represent events or instances of other attributes in the physical environment without representing bodies. Nevertheless, bodies are the key causal factors in the basic pursuits of many animals. Many animals eat, are eaten by, mate with, and navigate around bodies. It should be expected that perceptual representation of bodies as such is widespread among animals with perceptual systems. Such representation is not one of the distinctive achievements of humankind.

It hardly need be added that perceptual representation as of bodies does not constitutively require representation of mind-independence or of a seems/is distinction. Human children have perceptions as of bodies before they have any representation of mind-independence as such. Few if any non-human animals represent mind or mind-independence—ever. Bodies *are* mind-independent, of course. We come to understand this point once we acquire the concepts needed to raise the issue. Perceiving and conceiving bodies as such does not require a capacity to understand the point. Children's representations are realist in this very basic sense: they represent a mind-independent reality without engaging in or presupposing any reference to mind.

Children and non-human animals are realists not because they represent bodies as mind-independent, but because they cannot help but ignore idealism. We as philosophers should emulate the children.

I have barely gestured at the remarkable variety and complexity of the growth that representation and empirical objectivity undergo beyond their phylogenetic and constitutive origins in perception. The gestures serve only to suggest some of the ways in which humankind freed itself from the proximal, the impacts on sensory surfaces, the local, the here and now. In this variety and complexity lie the real contributions of human beings in the development of objectivity, empirical or otherwise.

Perception, the constitutive origin of empirical objectivity, is shared by a huge sector of the animal world. The fact that objectivity, representation in a rich distinctively psychological sense, and normative standards for representation appear at such elementary levels of animal life provides, I think, a new perspective on representation, sensing, perception, action, and norms grounded in them. This perspective is interesting to me partly insofar as it sheds light on development of further types of objectivity. Mapping these stages and types is a worthwhile philosophical enterprise—one large enough to require the efforts of many talented individuals.

Growth from the roots of objectivity is many sorted. There is the dramatic extension present in propositional organization—in the generality implicit in pure attribution and in propositional inference. There is the further extension of this generality in quantificational generalization. Objectivity takes a major branching turn in capacities to take principles as their representational contents, and to represent laws that structure reality. An equally impressive branch is representation of the objective as such, including representation of a distinction between the objective and the local, the proximal, the egocentric, the subjective. On this branch lies self-representation, at various levels of sophistication.

Of course, in this development, the local, the contextual, the particular, and the subjective take on their own values. By separating the non-objective from the objective, one can appreciate values and nuances of each.

Moreover, empirical objective representation is always necessarily anchored in both egocentric frameworks and demonstrative-like context-dependent representation—the kind of perspective-dependent and context-dependent representation constitutive of perception.

Still, furthering the growth of objectivity from its roots in context-dependent perception, and in context-driven action that is motivated by representation of a goal, is one of the most impressive achievements of human kind. In the practical domain, there is the subordination of self-interest to morality. There is the rule of law and the egalitarianism of democracy. There is the rejection of differences of race, color, religion, gender, sexual orientation as irrelevant to principles governing rights and opportunities. There is the building of institutions, art, and communicative systems that transcend and outlive the individuals and individual perspectives that make them go. In the theoretical domain there are the abstractions and generalities of mathematics, the systematizations of natural science, and the retrospectives of history. There are even the reflections of philosophy, on the scattered occasions when they make progress. Mathematics, natural science, history, law, morality, philosophy—theoretical and practical—have repeatedly shown perspectives that had seemed final and absolute to be infected with egocentricity or provincialism. I hope that the present account contributes to this tradition.

Philosophy in this century would do well to elaborate a more realistic perspective on representation of the physical environment. From such a perspective, we will be better placed to understand what is really special about human representational capacities.

Bibliography

Adelson, E. H., 'Lightness Perception and Lightness Illusions', in M. Gazzaniga (ed.), *The New Cognitive Neurosciences* (2nd edn., Cambridge, MA: MIT Press, 2000).

Adler, J., 'Chemotaxis in Bacteria', in M. J. Carlile (ed.), *Primitive Sensory and Communication Systems* (London: Academic Press, 1975).

Aguiar, A., and Baillargeon, R., '2.5-Month-Old Infants' Reasoning about When Objects Should and Should Not Be Occluded', *Cognitive Psychology* 39 (1999), 116–157.

Aguiar, A., and Baillargeon, R., 'Development in Young Infants' Reasoning about Occluded Objects', *Cognitive Psychology* 45 (2002), 267–336.

Aristotle, *Categories*.

Arterberry, M. E., 'Development of Spatiotemporal Integration in Infancy', *Infant Behavior and Development* 16 (1993), 343–363.

Arterberry, M. E., Craton, L. G., and Yonas, A., 'Infants' Sensitivity to Motion-Carried Information for Depth and Object Properties', in C. E. Granrud (ed.), *Visual Perception and Cognition in Infancy* (Hillsdale, NJ: Erlbaum, 1993).

Austin, J. L., *Sense and Sensibilia* (Oxford: Clarendon Press, 1962).

Ayer, A. J., *The Foundations of Empirical Knowledge* (1940; London: MacMillan & Co. Ltd, 1962).

Ayer, A. J., 'Phenomenalism' (1947–1948), in *Philosophical Essays* (London: MacMillan & Co. Ltd, 1954).

Baillargeon, R., 'Object Permanence in 3.5 and 4/5-Month-Old Infants', *Developmental Psychology* 23 (1987), 655–664.

Baillargeon, R., and DeVos, J., 'Object Permanence in Young Infants: Further Evidence', *Child Development* 62 (1991), 1227–1246.

Baillargeon, R., Spelke, Elizabeth S., and Wasserman, S., 'Object Permanence in Five-Month-Old Infants', *Cognition* 20 (1985), 191–208.

Barner, D., Wood, J., Hauser, M., and Carey, S., 'Evidence for a Non-Linguistic Distinction between Singular and Plural Sets in Rhesus Monkeys', *Cognition* 107 (2008), 603–622.

Barth, H., Kanwisher, N., and Spelke, E., 'The Construction of Large Number Representations in Adults', *Cognition* 86 (2003), 201–221.

Barth, H., La Mont, K., Lipton, J., Dehaene, S., Kanwisher, N., and Spelke, E., 'Non-Symbolic Arithmetic in Adults and Young Children', *Cognition* 98 (2006), 199–222.

Berkeley, George, *A New Theory of Vision and Other Select Philosophical Writings* (1732; New York: E. P. Dutton & Co., 1919).

Bermudez, J. L., Marcel, A., and Eilan, N. (eds.), *The Body and the Self* (Cambridge, MA: MIT Press, 1995).

Berthold, P., 'Spatiotemporal Aspects of Avian Long-Distance Migration', in S. Healy (ed.), *Spatial Representation in Animals* (Oxford: Oxford University Press, 1998).

Berzhanskaya, J., Grossberg, S., and Mingolla, E., 'Laminar Cortical Dynamics of Visual Form and Motion Interactions during Coherent Object Motion Perception', *Spatial Vision* 20 (2007), 237–295.

Bijeljac-Babic, R., Bertoncini, J., and Mehler, J., 'How Do 4-Day-Old Infants Categorize Multisyllabic Utterances?', *Developmental Psychology* 29 (1993), 711–721.

Bingman, V. P., 'Spatial Representations and Homing Pigeon Navigation', in S. Healy (ed.), *Spatial Representation in Animals* (Oxford: Oxford University Press, 1998).

Birch, E., and Petrig, B., 'FPL and VEP Measures of Fusion, Stereopsis, and Stereo Acuity in Normal Infants', *Vision Research* 36 (1996), 1321–1327.

Biro, D., and Matsuzawa, T., 'Use of Numerical Symbols by the Chimpanzee (*Pan Troglodytes*): Cardinals, Ordinals, and the Introduction of Zero', *Animal Cognition* 4 (2001), 193–199.

Bischof, N., 'Optic-Vestibular Orientation to the Vertical', in H. H. Kornhuber (ed.), *Handbook of Sensory Physiology*, vol. VI/2, *Vestibular System Part 2: Psychophysics, Applied Aspects and General Interpretation*s (Berlin: Springer-Verlag, 1974).

Block, Ned, 'On a Confusion about a Function of Consciousness', *Behavioral and Brain Sciences* 18 (1995), 227–247.

Block, Ned, 'Two Neural Correlates of Consciousness', *Trends in Cognitive Sciences* 9 (2005), 46–52.

Block, Ned, 'Consciousness, Accessibility, and the Mesh between Psychology and Neuroscience', *Behavioral and Brain Sciences* 30 (2007), 481–499.

Bloom, P., 'Syntactic Distinctions', *Child Language* 17 (1990), 343–355.

Bod-Bovy, G., and Gentaz, E., 'The Haptic Reproduction of Orientations in Three-Dimensional Space', *Experimental Brain Research* 172 (2006), 283–300.

Bonjour, Lawrence, *The Structure of Empirical Knowledge* (Cambridge, MA: Harvard University Press, 1985).

Boring, Edwin G., *A History of Experimental Psychology* (1929; New York: Appleton-Century-Crofts, Inc., 1950).

Bower, T. G. R., 'The Object in the World of the Infant', *Scientific American* 225/4 (1971), 30–38.

Brainard, D. H., Brunt, W. A., and Speigle, J. M., 'Color Constancy in the Nearly Natural Image. 1. Asymmetric Matches', *Journal of the Optical Society of America* A/14 (1997), 2091–2110.

Braithwaite, V. A., 'Spatial Memory, Landmark Use and Orientation in Fish', in S. Healy (ed.), *Spatial Representation in Animals* (Oxford: Oxford University Press, 1998).

Brandom, Robert, *Making It Explicit* (Cambridge, MA: Harvard University Press, 1994).

Brannon, E. M., 'The Development of Ordinal Numerical Knowledge in Infancy', *Cognition* 83 (2002), 223–240.

Brannon, E. M., and Terrace, H. S., 'Ordering of the Numerosities 1 to 9 by Monkeys', *Science* 282 (1998), 746–749.

Brannon, E., Wusthoff, C., Gallistel, C. R., and Gibbon, J., 'Numerical Subtraction in the Pigeon', *Psychological Science* 12 (2001), 238–243.

Brannon, E. M., Lutz, D., and Cordes, S., 'The Development of Area Discrimination and its Implications for Numerical Abilities in Infancy', *Developmental Science* 9 (2006), F59–F64.

Bresciani, J.-P., and Ernst, M. O., 'Signal Reliability Modulates Auditory–Tactile Integration for Event Counting', *NeuroReport* 18 (2007), 1157–1161.

Bresciani, J.-P., Ernst, M. O., Drewing, K., Bouyer, G., Maury, V., and Kheddar, A., 'Feeling What You Hear: Auditory Signals Can Modulate Tactile Taps Perception', *Experimental Brain Research* 162 (2005), 172–180.

Broad, C. D., *Scientific Thought* (London: Routledge & Kegan Paul Ltd, 1923).

Broad, C. D., *The Mind and its Place in Nature* (London: Routledge & Kegan Paul Ltd, 1925).

Brown, A. M., and Miracle, J. A., 'Early Binocular Vision in Human Infants: Limitations on the Generality of the Superposition Hypothesis', *Vision Research* 43 (2003), 1563–1574.

Brownell, P. H., 'Prey Detection by the Sand Scorpion', *Scientific American* 251 (1984), 86–97.

Bruce, Vicki, and Green, Patrick, *Visual Perception: Physiology, Psychology, and Ecology* (1985; 4th edn., Hillsdale, NJ: Lawrence Erlbaum, 2004).

Bruner, J., Goodnow, J., and Austin, G., *A Study of Thinking* (New York: John Wiley, 1956).

Brunswik, Egon, *Perception and the Representative Design of Psychological Experiments* (1947; Berkeley and Los Angeles: University of California Press, 1956).

Brunswik, E., and Kamiya, J., 'Ecological Cue-Validity of "Proximity" and of other Gestalt Factors', *American Journal of Psychology* 66 (1953), 20–32.

Böhler, K., *Handbuch der Psychologie* I, 1 (Jena, 1922).

Bull, W., and Uller, C., 'Spontaneous Small Number Discrimination in Semi-Free Ranging Domestic Pigs (*Sus Scrofa*)', abstract (2006), for paper presented at the XV Biennial Conference on Infant Studies.

Buller, David J. (ed.), *Function, Selection, and Design* (Albany, NY: SUNY Press, Series in Philosophy and Biology, 1999).

Burge, J., Fowlkes, C. C., and Banks, M. S., 'Natural Scene Statistics Predict How the Figure-Ground Cue of Convexity Affects Human Depth Perception', forthcoming.

Burge, Tyler, 'Belief *De Re*', *The Journal of Philosophy* 74 (1977), 338–362; reprinted in *Foundations of Mind: Philosophical Essays, Volume 2* (Oxford: Clarendon Press, 2007).

Burge, Tyler, 'A Theory of Aggregates', *Nous* 11 (May 1977), 97–117.

Burge, Tyler, 'Individualism and the Mental', *Midwest Studies in Philosophy* 4 (1979), 73–121; reprinted in *Foundations of Mind: Philosophical Essays, Volume 2* (Oxford: Clarendon Press, 2007).

Burge, Tyler, 'Sinning Against Frege', *Philosophical Review* 88 (1979), 398–432; reprinted in *Truth, Thought, Reason: Essays on Gottlob Frege* (Oxford: Clarendon Press, 2005).

Burge, Tyler, 'Other Bodies', in A. Woodfield (ed.), *Thought and Object* (London: Oxford University Press, 1982); reprinted in *Foundations of Mind: Philosophical Essays, Volume 2* (Oxford: Clarendon Press, 2007).

Burge, Tyler, 'Cartesian Error and the Objectivity of Perception', in J. McDowell and P. Pettit (eds.), *Subject, Thought, and Context* (New York: Oxford University Press, 1986); reprinted in *Foundations of Mind: Philosophical Essays, Volume 2* (Oxford: Clarendon Press, 2007).

Burge, Tyler, 'Individualism and Psychology', *The Philosophical Review* 95 (1986), 3–45; reprinted in *Foundations of Mind: Philosophical Essays, Volume 2* (Oxford: Clarendon Press, 2007).

Burge, Tyler, 'Intellectual Norms and Foundations of Mind', *The Journal of Philosophy* 83 (1986), 697–720; reprinted in *Foundations of Mind: Philosophical Essays, Volume 2* (Oxford: Clarendon Press, 2007).

Burge, Tyler, 'Individuation and Causation in Psychology', *Pacific Philosophical Quarterly* 70 (1989), 303–322; reprinted in *Foundations of Mind: Philosophical Essays, Volume 2* (Oxford: Clarendon Press, 2007).

Burge, Tyler, 'Wherein is Language Social?', in A. George (ed.), *Reflections on Chomsky* (London, Basil Blackwell, 1989); reprinted in *Foundations of Mind: Philosophical Essays, Volume 2* (Oxford: Clarendon Press, 2007).

Burge, Tyler, 'Philosophy of Language and Mind: 1950–1990', *The Philosophical Review* 101 (1992), 3–51; an expanded version of the part of the article that is on philosophy of mind is reprinted as 'Philosophy of Mind: 1950–2000' in *Foundations of Mind: Philosophical Essays, Volume 2* (Oxford: Clarendon Press, 2007).

Burge, Tyler, 'Mind–Body Causation and Explanatory Practice', in J. Heil and A. Mele (eds.), *Mental Causation* (Oxford: Oxford University Press, 1993); reprinted in *Foundations of Mind: Philosophical Essays, Volume 2* (Oxford: Clarendon Press, 2007).

Burge, Tyler, 'Intentional Properties and Causation', in C. MacDonald and G. MacDonald (eds.), *Philosophy of Psychology: Debates on Psychological Explanation* (Oxford: Blackwell, 1995); reprinted in *Foundations of Mind: Philosophical Essays, Volume 2* (Oxford: Clarendon Press, 2007).

Burge, Tyler, 'Comprehension and Interpretation', in Lewis Hahn (ed.), *The Philosophy of Donald Davidson* (Chicago: Open Court Publishers, 1999).

Burge, Tyler, 'Concepts, Conceptions, Reflective Understanding: Reply to Peacocke', in M. Hahn and B. Ramberg (eds.), *Reflections and Replies: Essays on the Philosophy of Tyler Burge* (Cambridge, MA: MIT Press, 2003).

Burge, Tyler, 'Logic and Analyticity', *Grazer Philosophische Studien* 66 (2003), 199–249.

Burge, Tyler, 'Memory and Persons', *The Philosophical Review* 112 (2003), 289–337.

Burge, Tyler, 'Perception', *International Journal of Psychoanalysis* 84 (2003), 157–167.

Burge, Tyler, 'Perceptual Entitlement', *Philosophy and Phenomenological Research* 67 (2003), 503–548.

Burge, Tyler, 'Social Anti-Individualism, Objective Reference', *Philosophy and Phenomenological Research* 67 (2003), 682–690; reprinted in *Foundations of Mind: Philosophical Essays, Volume 2* (Oxford: Clarendon Press, 2007).

Burge, Tyler, 'Some Reflections on Scepticism: Reply to Stroud', in M. Hahn and B. Ramberg (eds.), *Reflections and Replies: Essays on the Philosophy of Tyler Burge* (Cambridge, MA: MIT Press, 2003).

Burge, Tyler, 'Disjunctivism and Perceptual Psychology', *Philosophical Topics* 33 (2005), 1–78.

Burge, Tyler, *Truth, Thought, Reason: Essays on Gottlob Frege: Philosophical Essays, Volume 1* (Oxford: Oxford University Press, 2005).

Burge, Tyler, 'Abstract: "Perceptual Objectivity"', in G. Apel (ed.), *Kreativität*, XX Deutsche Kongress für Philosophie (September 26–30, 2005) (Hamburg: Felix Meiner Verlag, 2006).

Burge, Tyler, 'Postscript: "Mind–Body Causation and Explanatory Practice"', in *Foundations of Mind: Philosophical Essays, Volume 2* (Oxford: Clarendon Press, 2007).

Burge, Tyler, *Foundations of Mind: Philosophical Essays, Volume 2* (Oxford: Clarendon Press, 2007).

Burge, Tyler, 'Postscript to "Belief *De Re*"', in *Foundations of Mind: Philosophical Essays, Volume 2* (Oxford: Clarendon Press, 2007).

Burge, Tyler, 'Postscript to "Individualism and the Mental"', in *Foundations of Mind: Philosophical Essays, Volume 2* (Oxford: Clarendon Press, 2007).

Burge, Tyler, 'Predication and Truth: Review of Donald Davidson, *Truth and Predication*', *The Journal of Philosophy* 104 (2007), 580–608.

Burge, Tyler, 'Psychology Supports Independence of Phenomenal Consciousness', *Behavioral and Brain Sciences* 30 (2007), 500–501.

Burge, Tyler, 'Reflections on Two Kinds of Consciousness', in *Foundations of Mind: Philosophical Essays, Volume 2* (Oxford: Clarendon Press, 2007).

Burge, Tyler, 'Five Theses on *De Re* States and Attitudes', in J. Almog and P. Leonardi (eds.), *The Philosophy of David Kaplan* (Oxford: Oxford University Press, 2009).

Burge, Tyler, 'Perceptual Objectivity', *The Philosophical Review* 118 (2009), 285–324.

Burge, Tyler, 'Primitive Agency and Natural Norms', *Philosophy and Phenomenological Research* 74 (2009), 251–278.

Burkell, J. A., and Pylyshyn, Z. W., 'Searching through Subsets: A Test of the Visual Indexing Hypothesis', *Spatial Vision* 11 (1997), 225–258.

Burr, D., and Ross, J., 'A Visual Sense for Number', *Current Biology* 18 (2008), 1–4.

Byrne, Richard, *The Thinking Ape* (Oxford: Oxford University Press, 1995).

Campan, R., 'Tactic Components in Orientation', in M. Lehrer (ed.), *Orientation and Communication in Arthropods* (Basel: Birkhauser Verlag, 1997).

Campbell, John, *Past, Space, and Self* (Cambridge, MA: MIT Press, 1995).

Campbell, John, *Reference and Consciousness* (Oxford: Clarendon Press, 2002).

Campbell, John, 'Demonstrative Reference, the Relational View of Experience, and the Proximality Principle', in R. Jeshion (ed.), *Essays on Singular Reference* (Oxford: Oxford University Press, forthcoming).

Cane, Shaun D., Boles, Larry C., Wang, John H., and Lohmann, Kenneth J., 'Magnetic Orientation and Navigation in Marine Turtles, Lobsters, and Molluscs: Concepts and Conundrums', *Integrative and Comparative Biology* 45 (2005), 539–546.

Cantlon, J. F., and Brannon, E. M., 'Shared System for Ordering Small and Large Numbers in Monkeys and Humans', *Psychological Science* 17 (2006), 401–406.

Cantlon, J. F., and Brannon, E. M., 'How Much Does Number Matter to the Monkey?', *Journal of Experimental Psychology: Animal Behavior Processes* 33 (2007), 32–41.

Carey, Susan, 'Speaking of Objects, as Such', in G. Harman (ed.), *Conceptions of the Mind: Essays in Honor of George A. Miller* (Hillsdale, NJ: Erlbaum, 1993).

Carey, Susan, 'Does Learning a Language Require the Child to Reconceptualize the World?', *Lingua* 92 (1994), 143–167.

Carey, Susan, 'Cognitive Foundations of Arithmetic: Evolution and Ontogenesis', *Mind and Language* 16 (2001), 37–55.

Carey, Susan, *The Origin of Concepts* (Oxford: Oxford University Press, 2009).

Carey, S., and Spelke, E., 'Science and Core Knowledge', *Philosophy of Science* 63 (1996), 515–533.

Carey, S., and Xu, F., 'Infants Knowledge of Objects: Beyond Object Files and Object Tracking', *Cognition* 80 (2001), 179–213.

Carlile, M. J., 'Taxes and Tropisms: Diversity, Biological Significance and Evolution', in M. J. Carlile (ed.), *Primitive Sensory and Communication Systems* (London: Academic Press, 1975).

Carnap, Rudolf, *The Logical Construction of the World: PseudoProblems in Philosophy* (1928), trans. Rolf A. George (Berkeley and Los Angeles: University of California Press, 1969).

Carnap, Rudolf, *Meaning and Necessity* (1947; Chicago: Chicago University Press, 1956; reprinted 1967).

Carr, J. A. R., and Wilkie, D. M., 'Rats Use an Ordinal Timer in a Daily Time–Place Learning Task', *Journal of Experimental Psychology: Animal Behavior Processes* 23 (1997), 232–247.

Carrasco, M., 'Covert Attention Increases Contrast Sensitivity: Psychophysical, Neurophysiological, and Neuroimaging Studies', in S. Martinex-Conde, S. L. Macknik, L. Martinez, J.-M. Alonso, and P. U. Tse (eds.), *Progress in Brain Research* vol. 154: *Visual Perception, Part 1* (Amsterdam: Elsevier, 2006).

Carrasco, M., Ling, S., and Read, S., 'Attention Alters Appearance', *Nature Neuroscience* 7 (2004), 308–313.

Carthy, J. D., *An Introduction to the Behaviour of Invertebrates* (London: George Allen & Unwin Ltd, 1958).

Cassirer, Ernst, *The Philosophy of Symbolic Forms*, iii. *The Phenomenology of Knowledge*, trans. Ralph Manheim (1929; New Haven: Yale University Press, 1957).

Cassirer, Ernst, 'The Concept of Group and the Theory of Perception', *Philosophy and Phenomenological Research* 5 (1944), 1–35.

Cassirer, H. W., *Kant's First Critique* (London: George Allen & Unwin Ltd, 1954).

Cattet, Jennifer S., and Etienne, Ariane S., 'Blindfolded Dogs Relocate a Target by Path Integration', *Animal Behavior* 68 (2004), 203–212.

Cheng, Ken, 'Shepards Universal Law Supported by Honeybees in Spatial Generalization', *Psychological Science* 11 (2000), 403–408.

Cheng, Ken, 'Arthropod Navigation: Ants, Bees, Crabs, Spiders Finding their Way', in Edward A. Wasserman and Thomas R. Zentall (eds.), *Comparative Cognition* (Oxford: Oxford University Press, 2006).

Cheng, Ken, and Spetch, Marcia L., 'Mechanisms of Landmark Use in Mammals and Birds', in S. Healy (ed.), *Spatial Representation in Animals* (Oxford: Oxford University Press, 1998), 1–17.

Cheries, E. W., Feigenson, L., Scholl, B. J., and Carey, S., 'Cues to Object Persistence in Infancy: Tracking Objects through Occlusion vs. Implosion', abstract, *Journal of Vision* 5 (2005), 352.

Cheries, Erik W., Wynn, Karen, and Scholl, Brian J., 'Interrupting Infants Persisting Object Representations: An Object-based Limit?', *Developmental Science* 9 (2006), F50–F58.

Chiang, W.-C., and Wynn, K., 'Infants Representation and Tracking of Multiple Objects', *Cognition* 77 (2000), 169–195.

Chittka, L., Williams, N. M., Rasmussen, H., and Thomson, J. D., 'Navigation without Vision: Bumblebee Navigation in Complete Darkness', *Royal Society Proceedings: Biological Sciences* 266 (1999), 45–50.

Chomsky, Noam, *Syntactic Structures* (The Hague: Mouton, 1957).

Chomsky, Noam, *Aspects of Syntax* (Cambridge, MA: MIT Press, 1965).

Chomsky, Noam, 'Quine's Empirical Assumptions', in Donald Davidson and Jaakko Hintikka (eds.), *Words and Objections* (Dordrecht: D. Reidel, 1969).

Church, Alonzo, 'The Need for Abstract Entities in Semantic Analysis', in *Proceedings of the American Academy of Arts and Sciences* 80 (1951), 100–112.

Church, Alonzo, *Introduction to Mathematical Logic* (Princeton: Princeton University Press, 1956).

Church, Russell M., 'Behavioristic Cognitive, Biological, and Quantitative Explanations of Timing', in E. A. Wasserman and T. R. Zentall (eds.), *Comparative Cognition: Experimental Explorations of Animal Intelligence* (Oxford: Oxford University Press, 2006).

Church, R. M., and Broadbent, H. A., 'Alternative Representations of Time, Number, and Rate', *Cognition* 37 (1990), 55–81.

Church, R. M., and Meck, W. H., 'The Numerical Attribute of Stimuli', in H. L. Roitblatt, T. G. Bever, and H. S. Terrace (eds.), *Animal Cognition* (Hillsdale, NJ: Erlbaum, 1984).

Clayton, N. S., Griffiths, D. P., Emery, N. J., and Dickinson, A., 'Elements of Episodic-Like Memory in Animals', in A. Baddeley, J. P. Aggleton, and M. A. Conway (eds.), *Episodic Memory: New Directions in Research* (Oxford: Oxford University Press, 2002).

Collett, M., and Collett, T. S., 'How do Insects Use Path Integration in their Navigation?' *Biological Cybernetics* 83 (2000), 245–259.

Collett, T. S., 'Peering: A Locust Behavior for Obtaining Motion Parallax Information', *Journal of Experimental Biology* 76 (1978), 237–241.

Collett, T. S., and Baron, J., 'Learnt Sensori-Motor Mappings in Honeybees: Interpolation and its Possible Relevance to Navigation', *Journal of Comparative Physiology A* 177 (1995), 287–298.

Collett, Thomas S., and Collett, Matthew, 'Memory Use in Insect Visual Navigation', *Nature Reviews Neuroscience* 3 (2002), 242–252.

Collett, Thomas S., and Zeil, Jochen, 'Places and Landmarks: An Arthropod Perspective', in S. Healy (ed.), *Spatial Representation in Animals* (Oxford: Oxford University Press, 1998).

Craton, L. G., and Yonas, A., 'The Role of Motion in Infant Perception of Occlusion', in J. T. Enns (ed.), *The Development of Attention: Research and Theory* (New York: Elsevier/North Holland, 1990).

Cummings, Robert, 'Functional Analysis', *The Journal of Philosophy* 72 (1975), 741–765.

Dacke, M., and Srinivasan, M. V., 'Honeybee Navigation: Distance Estimation in the Third Dimension', *Journal of Experimental Biology* 210 (2007), 845–853.

Danckert, James, and Rossetti, Yves, 'Blindsight in Action: What Can the Different Sub-Types of Blindsight Tell Us about the Control of Visually Guided Actions?', *Neuroscience & Biobehavioral Reviews* 29 (2005), 1035–1046.

Davidson, Donald, 'Agency' (1971), in *Essays on Actions and Events* (2nd edn., Oxford: Clarendon Press, 2001).

Davidson, Donald, 'Psychology as Philosophy' (1974), in *Essays on Actions and Events* (2nd edn., Oxford: Clarendon Press, 2001).

Davidson, Donald, 'Thought and Talk' (1975), in *Inquiries into Truth and Interpretation* (Oxford: Clarendon Press, 1984).

Davidson, Donald, 'Rational Animals' (1982), in *Subjective, Intersubjective, Objective* (Oxford: Clarendon Press, 2001).

Davidson, Donald, *Inquiries into Truth and Interpretation* (Oxford: Clarendon Press, 1984).

Davidson, Donald, 'The Very Idea of a Conceptual Scheme', in *Inquiries into Truth and Interpretation* (Oxford: Clarendon Press, 1984).

Davidson, Donald, 'A Coherence Theory of Truth and Knowledge', in E. LePore (ed.), *Truth and Interpretation* (Oxford: Blackwell, 1986); reprinted in *Subjective, Intersubjective, Objective* (Oxford: Clarendon Press, 2001).

Davidson, Donald, 'Epistemology Externalized' (1990), in *Subjective, Intersubjective, Objective* (Oxford: Clarendon Press, 2001).

Davidson, Donald, 'Three Varieties of Knowledge' (1991), in *Subjective, Intersubjective, Objective* (Oxford: Clarendon Press, 2001).

Davidson, Donald, 'The Second Person' (1992), in *Subjective, Intersubjective, Objective* (Oxford: Clarendon Press, 2001).

Davidson, Donald, 'The Problem of Objectivity' (1995), in *Problems of Rationality* (Oxford: Clarendon Press, 2004).

Davidson, Donald, 'The Emergence of Thought' (1997), in *Subjective, Intersubjective, Objective* (Oxford: Clarendon Press, 2001).

Davidson, Donald, *Essays on Actions and Events* (2nd edn., Oxford: Clarendon Press, 2001).

Davidson, Donald, *Subjective, Intersubjective, Objective* (Oxford: Clarendon Press, 2001).

Davidson, Donald, 'What Thought Requires' (2001), in *Problems of Rationality* (Oxford: Clarendon Press, 2004).

Davidson, Donald, *Problems of Rationality* (Oxford: Clarendon Press, 2004).

Davis, H., and Perusse, R., 'Numerical Competence in Animals: Definitional Issues, Current Evidence and a New Research Agenda', *Behavioral and Brain Sciences* 11 (1988), 561–615.

Dehaene, S., *The Number Sense* (New York: Oxford University Press, 1997).

Dehaene, S., 'Precis of *The Number Sense*', *Mind and Language* 16 (2001), 16–36.

Dehaene, S., and Changeux, J. P., 'Development of Elementary Numerical Abilities: A Neuronal Model', *Journal of Cognitive Neuroscience* 5 (1993), 390–407.

Dehaene, Stanislas, Naccache, Lionel, Le Clec'H, Guryan, Koechlin, Etienne, Mueller, Michael, Behaene-Lambertz, Ghislaine, Moortele, Pierre-François van de, and Le Bihan, Denis, 'Imaging Unconscious Semantic Priming', *Nature* 395 (1998), 597–600.

Deloache, J. S., Pierroutsakos, S. L., Uttal, D. H., Rosengren, K. S., and Gottlieb, A., 'Grasping the Nature of Pictures', *Psychological Science* 9 (1998), 205–210.

Dennett, Daniel C., 'Intentional Systems', *The Journal of Philosophy* 68 (1971), 87–106.

Dennett, Daniel C., *The Intentional Stance* (Cambridge, MA: MIT Press, 1989).

Descartes, René, *The Dioptrics in Philosophical Writings: Descartes* (1637), ed. E. Anscombe and P. T. Geach (Indianapolis: Bobbs Merrill, 1971).

Descartes, René, *Discourse on Method* (1637), in *The Philosophical Writings of Descartes*, volume i, ed. and trans. J. Cottingham, R. Stoothof, and D. Murdoch (Cambridge: Cambridge University Press, 1984).

Descartes, René, *Meditations on First Philosophy* (1641), in *The Philosophical Writings of Descartes*, volume ii, ed. and trans. J. Cottingham, R. Stoothoff, and D. Murdoch (Cambridge: Cambridge University Press, 1985).

Descartes, René, *The Philosophical Writings of Descartes*, ed. and trans. J. Cottingham, R. Stoothof, and D. Murdoch (2 vols.; Cambridge: Cambridge University Press, 1984, 1985).

Donnellan, Keith, 'Reference and Definite Descriptions', *The Philosophical Review* 75 (1966), 281–304.

Donnellan, Keith, 'Proper Names and Identifying Descriptions', *Synthese* 21 (1970), 335–358.

Dretske, Fred, *Seeing and Knowing* (Chicago: University of Chicago Press, 1969).

Dretske, Fred, 'The Role of the Percept in Visual Cognition', *Minnesota Studies in the Philosophy of Science* 11 (1978), 107–127.

Dretske, Fred, *Knowledge and the Flow of Information* (Cambridge, MA: MIT Press, 1981).

Dretske, Fred, 'The Pragmatic Dimension of Knowledge', *Philosophical Studies* 40 (1981), 363–378.

Dretske, Fred, 'Misrepresentation', in R. J. Bogdan (ed.), *Belief, Form, Content, and Function* (Oxford: Oxford University Press, 1986).

Dretske, Fred, *Explaining Behavior* (Cambridge, MA: MIT Press, 1988).

Dretske, Fred, *Naturalizing the Mind* (Cambridge, MA: MIT Press, 1995).

Dummett, Michael, *The Interpretation of Frege's Philosophy* (Cambridge, MA: Harvard University Press, 1981).

Dyer, F. C., 'Bees Acquire Route-Based Memories but not Cognitive Maps in a Familiar Landscape', *Animal Behaviour* 41 (1991), 239–246.

Dyer, F. C., 'Spatial Memory and Navigation by Honeybees on the Scale of the Foraging Range', *Journal of Experimental Biology* 199 (1996), 147–154.

Dyer, Fred C., 'Spatial Cognition: Lessons from Central-Place Foraging Insects', in R. P. Balda, I. M. Pepperberg, and A. C. Kamil (eds.), *Animal Cognition in Nature* (San Diego: Academic Press, 1998).

Ernst, M. O., and Banks, M. S., 'Humans Integrate Visual and Haptic Information in a Statistically Optimal Fashion', *Nature* 415 (2002), 429–433.

Ernst, M. O., and Bülthoff, H. H., 'Merging the Senses into a Robust Percept', *Trends in Cognitive Sciences* 8 (2004), 162–169.

Ernst, M. O., Banks, M. S., and Bülthoff, H. H., 'Touch Can Change Visual Slant Perception', *Nature Neuroscience* 3 (2000), 69–73.

Esch, H. E., and Burns, J. E., 'Distance Estimation by Foraging Honeybees', *Journal of Experimental Biology* 199 (1996), 155–162.

Etienne, Ariane S., 'Mammalian Navigation, Neuronal Models, and Biorobotics', *Connection Science* 10 (1998), 271–289.

Etienne, Ariane S., and Jeffery, Kathryn J., 'Path Integration in Mammals', *Hippocampus* 14 (2004), 180–192.

Euclid, *Elements of Geometry*.

Evans, Gareth, 'A Causal Theory of Names' (1973), in *Collected Papers* (Oxford: Clarendon Press, 1985).

Evans, Gareth, 'Identity and Predication' (1975), in *Collected Papers* (Oxford: Clarendon Press, 1985).

Evans, Gareth, 'Things without the Mind: A Commentary upon Chapter Two of Strawson's *Individuals*' (1980), in *Collected Papers* (Oxford: Clarendon Press, 1985).

Evans, Gareth, *The Varieties of Reference* (Oxford: Clarendon Press, 1982).

Evans, Gareth, *Collected Papers* (Oxford: Clarendon Press, 1985).

Everett, D. L., 'Cultural Constraints on Grammar and Cognition in Piraha: Another Look at the Design Features of Human Language', *Current Anthropology* 46 (2005), 621–646.

Farah, Martha J., 'Visual Perception and Visual Analysis after Brain Damage: A Tutorial Overview', in C. Umilta and M. Moscovitch (eds.), *Attention and Performance XV: Conscious and Nonconscious Information Processing* (Cambridge, MA: MIT Press, 1995), 37–75; reprinted in N. Block, O. Flanagan, and G. Güzeldere (eds.), *The Nature of Consciousness* (Cambridge, MA: MIT Press, 1998).

Farner, D. S., 'Annual Rhythms', *Annual Review of Physiology* 47 (1985), 65–82.

Feigenson, L., 'The Equality of Quantity', *Trends in Cognitive Science* 11 (2007), 185–187.

Feigenson, L., and Carey, S., 'On the Limits of Infants' Quantification of Small Object Arrays', *Cognition* 97 (2005), 295–313.

Feigenson, L., Carey, S., and Hauser, M., 'The Representations Underlying Infants' Choice of More: Object-Files versus Analog Magnitudes', *Psychological Science* 13 (2002), 150–156.

Finger, Thomas E., Silver, Wayne L., and Restrepo, Diego (eds.), *The Neurobiology of Taste and Smell* (2nd edn., New York: John Wiley & Sons, 2000).

Firzlaff, U., Schuchmann, M., Grunwald, J. E., Schuller, G., and Wiegrebe, L., 'Object-Oriented Echo Perception and Cortical Representation in Echolocating Bats', *PLoS Biology* 5 (2007), online.

Flombaum, J. I., Junge, J., and Hauser, M. D., 'Rhesus Monkeys (*Macaca mulatta*) Spontaneously Compute Large Number Addition Operations', *Cognition* 97 (2005), 315–325.

Fodor, Jerry A., *The Language of Thought* (1975; Cambridge, MA: Harvard University Press, 1979).

Fodor, Jerry A., *The Modularity of Mind* (Cambridge, MA: MIT Press, 1983).

Fodor, Jerry A., 'Semantics, Wisconsin Style', in *A Theory of Content and Other Essays* (Cambridge, MA: MIT Press, 1990).

Fodor, Jerry A., *A Theory of Content and Other Essays* (Cambridge, MA: MIT Press, 1990).

Fodor, Jerry A., *Concepts* (Oxford: Clarendon Press, 1998).

Foelix, Rainer F., *Biology of Spiders* (Oxford: Oxford University Press, 1996).

Foley, Richard, 'Quine and Naturalized Epistemology', *Midwest Studies in Philosophy* 19 (1994).

Foran, Sean, 'Animal Movement', manuscript; extracted from his dissertation 'Animal Movement' (UCLA, 1998).

Ford, Neil B., 'The Role of Pheromone Trails in the Sociobiology of Snakes', in David Duvall, Dietland Müller-Schwarze, and Robert M. Silverstein (eds.), *Chemical Signals in Vertebrates* (New York: Plenum, 1992).

Foster, D. H., and Gilson, S. J., 'Recognizing Novel Three-Dimensional Objects by Summing Signals from Parts and Views', *Proceedings: Biological Sciences* 269 (2002), 1939–1947.

Fowlkes, C. C., Martin, D. R., and Malik, J., 'Local Figure-Ground Cues are Valid for Natural Images', *Journal of Vision* 7 (2007), 1–9.

Fraenkel, Gottfried, 'Beiträge zur Geotaxis and Phototaxis von Littorina', *Zeitschrift für wissenschaftliche Biologie*, 5 (1927), 585–597; translated in C. R. Gallistel, *The Organization of Action: A New Synthesis* (Hillsdale, NJ: Lawrence Erlbaum Associates, 1980).

Fraenkel, Gottfried S., and Gunn, Donald L., *The Orientation of Animals* (Oxford: Clarendon Press, 1940).

Frankfurt, Harry G., 'The Problem of Action' (1978), in *The Importance of What We Care About* (Cambridge: Cambridge University Press, 1988).

Frege, Gottlob, *Begriffsschrift* (1879), in *From Frege to Güdel*, ed. Jean van Heijenoort (Cambridge, MA: Harvard University Press, 1981).

Frege, Gottlob, *The Foundations of Arithmetic* (1884), trans. J. L. Austin (1950; Evanston, IL: Northwestern University Press, 1968).

Frege, Gottlob, 'On Sense and Reference' (1892), in *Translations from the Philosophical Writings of Gottlob Frege*, ed. P. Geach and M. Black (1952; Oxford: Blackwell, 1966).

Frege, Gottlob, 'The Thought' (1918–1919), in *Collected Papers*, ed. Brian McGuinness (Oxford, Basil Blackwell, 1984).

Frege, Gottlob, *Translations from the Philosophical Writings of Gottlob Frege*, ed. P. Geach and M. Black (1952; Oxford: Blackwell, 1966).

French, J. W. V., 'Individual Differences in *Paramecium*', *Journal of Comparative Psychology* 30 (1940), 451–456.

Friedman, Michael, *A Parting of the Ways* (Chicago: Open Court, 2000).

Frisch, K. von, *The Dance Language and Orientation of Bees* (1947; London: Oxford University Press, 1967).

Gagnon, S., and Dore, F. Y., 'Cross-Sectional Study of Object Permanence in Domestic Puppies (*Cani Familiaris*)', *Journal of Comparative Psychology* 108 (1994), 220–232.

Gallistel, C. R., 'Animal Cognition: The Representation of Space, Time and Number', *Annual Review of Psychology* 40 (1989), 155–189.

Gallistel, Charles R., *The Organization of Learning* (Cambridge, MA: MIT Press, 1990).

Gallistel, C. R., 'Insect Navigation: Brains as Symbol-Processing Organs', in *Invitation to Cognitive Science*, iv (Cambridge, MA: MIT Press, 1996).

Gallistel, C. R., 'Conditioning from an Information Processing Perspective', *Behavioural Processes* 61 (2003), 1–13.

Gallistel, C. R., 'Deconstructing the Law of Effect', *Games and Economic Behavior* R52/2 (2005), 410–423.

Gallistel, C. R., and Cramer, A. E., 'Computations on Metric Maps in Mammals: Getting Oriented and Choosing a Multi-Destination Route', *Journal of Experimental Biology* 199 (1996), 211–217.

Gallistel, C. R., and Gelman, R., 'Preverbal and Verbal Counting and Computation', *Cognition* 44 (1992), 43–74.

Gallistel, C. R., and Gibbon, J., 'Time, Rate, and Conditioning', *Psychological Review* 107 (2000), 289–344.

Gallistel, C. R., and Gibbon, J., 'Computational versus Associative Models of Simple Conditioning', *Current Directions in Psychological Science* 10 (2001), 146–150.

Geisler, W. S., 'Visual Perception and the Statistical Properties of Natural Scenes', *Annual Review of Psychology* 59 (2008), 10.1–10.26.

Geisler, W. S., Perry, J. S., Super, B. J., and Gallogly, D. P., 'Edge Co-Occurrence in Natural Images Predicts Contour Grouping Performance', *Vision Research* 41 (2001), 711–724.

Gelman, R., and Gallistel, C. R., *The Child's Understanding of Number* (Cambridge, MA: Harvard University Press, 1978).

Gelman, R., and Gallistel, C. R., 'Language and the Origin of Numerical Concepts', *Science* 306 (2004), 441–443.

Gemma, A., Calvert, C. S., and Stein, B. E. (eds.), *The Handbook of Multisensory Processes* (Cambridge, MA: MIT Press, 2004).

Gibson, J. J., *The Ecological Approach to Visual Perception* (Boston: Houghton Mifflin, 1979).

Gilchrist, A. L., 'Perceived Lightness Depends on Perceived Spatial Arrangement', *Science* 195 (1977), 185–187.

Gilchrist, A. L., 'Lightness Contrast and Failures of Constancy: A Common Explanation', *Perception and Psychophysics* 43 (1988), 415–424.

Gilchrist, Alan L., and Annan, Vidal, Jr., 'Articulation Effects in Lightness: Historical Background and Theoretical Implications', *Perception* 31 (2002), 141–150.

Gilchrist, A., Kossyfidis, C., Bonato, F., Agostini, T., Cataliotti, J., Li, X., Spehar, B., Annan, V., and Economou, E., 'An Anchoring Theory of Lightness Perception', www-psych.rutgers.edu/~alan/theory3.

Godfrey-Smith, Peter, 'Misinformation', *Canadian Journal of Philosophy* 19 (1989), 533–550.

Godfrey-Smith, Peter, 'Indication and Adaptation', *Synthese* 92 (1992), 283–312.

Godfrey-Smith, Peter, 'Functions: Consensus without Unity', *American Philosophical Quarterly* 74 (1993), 196–208.

Godfrey-Smith, Peter, *Complexity and the Function of Mind in Nature* (Cambridge: Cambridge University Press, 1996).

Goodale, M. A., and Milner, A. D., *The Visual Brain in Action* (Oxford: Oxford University Press, 1995).

Goodman, Nelson, *The Structure of Appearance* (Cambridge, MA: Harvard University Press, 1951).

Goodman, Nelson, *Languages of Art* (Indianapolis: Bobbs-Merrill, 1968).

Gopnik, A., and Astington, J. W., 'Children's Understanding of Representational Change, and its Relation to the Understanding of False Belief and the Appearance–Reality Distinction', *Child Development* 59 (1988), 26–37.

Gordon, P., 'Numerical Cognition without Words: Evidence from Amazonia', *Science* 306 (2004), 496–499.

Gould, J. L., 'The Locale Map of Honey Bees: Do Insects have Cognitive Maps?' *Science* 232 (1986), 861–863.

Grah, G., Wehner, R., and Ronacher, B., 'Desert Ants do not Acquire and Use a Three-Dimensional Global Vector', *Frontiers in Zoology* 4 (2007), online.

Granrud, C. E., 'Binocular Vision and Spatial Perception in 4- and 5-Month-Old Infants', *Journal of Experimental Psychology: Human Perceptual Performance* 12 (1986), 36–49.

Granrud, C. E., Yonas, A., and Pettersen, L., 'A Comparison of Monocular and Binocular Depth Perception in 5- and 7-Month-Old Infants', *Journal of Experimental Child Psychology* 38 (1984), 19–32.

Grice, Paul, *Studies in the Ways of Words* (Cambridge, MA: Harvard University Press, 1989).

Griffiths, Paul E., 'Functional Analysis and Proper Functions', *British Journal of the Philosophy of Science* 44 (1993), 409–422.

Hahn, M., and Ramberg, B. (eds.) *Reflections and Replies: Essays on the Philosophy of Tyler Burge* (Cambridge, MA: MIT Press, 2003).

Harland, Duane P., and Jackson, Robert R., '*Portia* Perceptions: The *Umwelt* of an Araneophagic Jumping Spider', in Rederick R. Prete (ed.), *Complex Worlds from Simpler Nervous Systems* (Cambridge, MA: MIT Press, 2004).

Harman, Gilbert, *Thought* (Princeton: Princeton University Press, 1973).

Hasler, A. D., 'Odour Perception and Orientation in Fishes', *J. Fisheries Resch. Bd., Canada* 11 (1954), 107–129.

Hasler, A. D., and Wisby, W. J., 'Discrimination of Stream Odor by Fishes and its Relation to Parent Stream Behaviour', *American Naturalist* 85 (1951), 223–238.

Haugeland, John, 'Analog and Analog', *Philosophical Topics* 12 (1981), 213–226.

Hauser, M. D., 'Expectations about Object Motion and Destination: Experiments with a Non-Human Primate', *Developmental Science* 1 (1998), 31–38.

Hauser, Marc D., *Wild Minds* (New York: Henry Holt, 2000).

Hauser, M. D., and Carey, S., 'Spontaneous Representations of Small Numbers of Objects by Rhesus Macaques: Examinations of Content and Format', *Cognitive Psychology* 47 (2003), 367–401.

Hauser, M. D., MacNeilage, P., and Ware, M., 'Numerical Representation in Primates', *Proceedings of the National Academy of Sciences USA* 93 (1996), 1514–1517.

Hauser, M. D., Carey, S., and Hauser, L. B., 'Spontaneous Number Representation in Semi-Free-Ranging Rhesus Monkeys', *Proceedings of the Royal Society*, London 267 (2000), 829–833.

Hauser, M., Chomsky, N., and Fitch, W. T., 'The Faculty of Language: What is it, Who has it, and How did it Evolve?', *Science* 298 (2002), 1569–1579.

Hauser, M. D., Tsao, F., Garcia, P., and Spelke, E. S., 'Evolutionary Foundations of Number: Spontaneous Representation of Numerical Magnitudes by Cotton-Top Tamarins', *Proceedings of the Royal Society, London* B270 (2003), 1441–1446.

He, S., Cavanagh, P., and Intriligator, J., 'Attentional Resolution', *Trends in Cognitive Sciences* 1 (1997), 115–121.

Healy, Sue, Hodgeson, Zoe, and Braithwaite, Victoria, 'Do Animals Use Maps?', in K. J. Jeffery (ed.), *The Neurobiology of Spatial Behaviour* (Oxford: Oxford University Press, 2003).

Heijenoort, Jean van (ed.), *From Frege to Güdel* (Cambridge, MA: Harvard University Press, 1981).

Heffner, Rickye S., and Heffner, Henry E., 'Evolution of Sound Localization in Mammals', in Douglas B. Webster, Richard R. Fay, and Arthur N. Popper (eds.), *The Evolutionary Biology of Hearing* (New York: Springer-Verlag, 1992).

Heidegger, Martin, *Being and Time* (1927), trans. John Macquarrie and Edward Robinson (New York: Harper & Row, Publishers, 1962).

Helbig, H. B., and Ernst, M. O., 'Optimal Integration of Shape Information from Vision and Touch', *Experimental Brain Research* 179 (2007), 595–606.

Helmholtz, H. von, *Treatise on Physiological Optics* (originally in German, 3 vols., 1857, 1860, 1867), trans. J. Southall (New York: Dover, 1962).

Hempel, Carl, 'Empiricist Criteria of Cognitive Significance: Problems and Changes' (1950), reprinted in *Aspects of Scientific Explanation* (New York: Free Press, 1965).

Hensel, Herbert, *Thermal Sensations and Thermoreceptors in Man* (Springfield, IL: Charles C. Thomas, 1982).

Hering, E., *Outlines of a Theory of the Light Sense* (1878), trans. L. M. Hurvich and D. Jameson (1920; Cambridge, MA: Harvard University Press, 1964).

Herman, L. M., Pack, A. A., and Hoffmann-Kuhnt, M., 'Seeing through Sound: Dolphins (*Tursiops truncatus*) Perceive the Spatial Structure of Objects through Echolocation', *Journal of Comparative Psychology* 112 (1998), 292–305.

Hespos, S., and Baillargeon, R., 'Reasoning about Containment Events in Very Young Infants', *Cognition* 78 (2001), 207–245.

Hillis, J. M., and Banks, M. S., 'Are Corresponding Points Fixed?', *Vision Research* 41 (2001), 2457–2473.

Hillis, J. M., Ernst, M. O., Banks, M. S., and Landy, M. S., 'Combining Sensory Information: Mandatory Fusion within, but not between, Senses', *Science* 298 (2002), 1627–1630.

Hironaka, M., Fillipi, L., Nomakuchi, S., Horiguchi, H., and Hariyama, T., 'Hierarchical Use of Chemical Marking and Path Integration in the Homing Trip of a Subsocial Shield Bug', *Animal Behavior* 73 (2007), 739–745.

Hofsten, C. von, 'The Role of Convergence in Visual Space Perception', *Vision Research* 16 (1976), 193–198.

Hofsten, Claes von, and Spelke, Elizabeth S., 'Object Perception and Object-Directed Reaching in Infancy', *Journal of Experimental Psychology: General* 114 (1985), 198–212.

Hölldobler, Bert, and Wilson, E. O., *The Journey of the Ants* (Cambridge, MA: Harvard University Press, 1995).

Hopfield, J. J., 'Olfactory Computation and Object Perception', *Proceedings of the National Academy of Science* 88 (1991), 6462–6466.

Hopfield, J. J., 'Pattern Recognition Computation Using Action Potential Timing for Stimulus Representation', *Nature* 376 (1995), 33–36.

Horridge, G. A., Zhang, S. W., and Lehrer, M., 'Bees Can Combine Range and Visual Angle to Estimate Absolute Size', *Philosophical Transactions of the Royal Society London* B337 (1992), 49–57.

Houten, Judith van, 'Chemoreception in Microorganisms', in Thomas E. Finger, Wayne L. Silver, and Diego Restrepo (eds.), *The Neurobiology of Taste and Smell* (2nd edn., New York: John Wiley & Sons, 2000).

Huntley-Fenner, G., Carey, S., and Salimando, A., 'Objects are Individuals but Stuff Doesn't Count: Perceived Rigidity and Cohesiveness Influence in Infants' Representation of Small Numbers of Discrete Entities', *Cognition* 85 (2002), 203–221.

Husserl, Edmund, *Ideas—General Introduction to Pure Phenomenology* (1913), trans. W. R. Boyce Gibson (London: George Allen & Unwin Ltd, 1952).

Husserl, Edmund, *Experience and Judgment* (1938), trans. James S. Churchill and Karl Ameriks (Evanston, IL: Northwestern University Press, 1973).

Ingle, D., 'Selective Visual Attention in Frogs', *Science* 188 (1975), 1033–1035.

Ingle, D., 'Shape Recognition in Vertebrates', in R. Held, H. Liebowitz, and H. Teuber (eds.), *Handbook of Sensory Physiology*, viii (Berlin: Springer Verlag, 1978).

Ingle, David, 'Perceptual Constancies in Lower Vertebrates', in Vincent Walsh and Janusz Kulikowski (eds.), *Perceptual Constancy* (Cambridge: Cambridge University Press, 1998).

Intriligator, J., and Cavanagh, P., 'The Spatial Resolution of Attention', *Cognitive Psychology* 43 (2001), 171–216.

Jackson, Robert, and Li, Daiqin, 'One-Encounter Search Image Formation by Araneophagic Jumping Spiders', *Animal Cognition* 7 (2004), 247–254.

Jackson, R. R., and Pollard, S. D., 'Predatory Behavior of Jumping Spiders', *Annual Review of Entymology* 41 (1996), 287–308.

James, William, *The Principles of Psychology* (New York: Henry Holt and Company, 1890).

James, William, 'Percept and Concept: The Import of Concepts', in *Some Problems of Philosophy* (New York: Longman's, Green, and Co., 1911).

Jeannerod, Marc, *The Cognitive Neuroscience of Action* (Oxford: Blackwell, 1997).

Jennings, H. S., *Behavior of the Lower Organisms* (1906; Bloomington: Indiana University Press, 1962).

Jevons, W. S., 'The Power of Numerical Discrimination', *Nature* 3 (1871), 263–272.

Johnsen, Peter B., 'Chemosensory Orientation Mechanisms of Fish', in David Duvall, Dietland Müller-Schwarze, and Robert M. Silverstein (eds.), *Chemical Signals in Vertebrates* (New York: Plenum, 1992).

Johnston, Robert E., 'Chemical Communication and Pheromones: The Types of Chemical Signals and the Role of the Vomeronasal System', in Thomas E. Finger, Wayne L. Silver, and Diego Restrepo (eds.), *The Neurobiology of Taste and Smell* (2nd edn., New York: John Wiley & Sons, 2000).

Judd, S. P. D., and Collett, T. S., 'Multiple Stored Views and Landmark Guidance in Ants', *Nature* 392 (1998), 710–714.

Kahneman, D., Treisman, A., and Gibbs, B. J., 'The Reviewing of Object Files: Object-Specific Integration of Information', *Cognitive Psychology* 24 (1992), 175–219.

Kanizsa, Gaetano, *Organization in Vision: Essays in Gestalt Perception* (New York: Praeger, 1979).

Kanizsa, G., and Gerbino, W., 'Convexity and Symmetry in Figure-Ground Organization', in M. Henle (ed.), *Vision and Artifact* (New York: Springer, 1976).

Katz, David, *The World of Touch* (1924), ed. and trans. Lester E. Krueger (Hillsdale, NJ: Lawrence Erlbaum, 1989).

Kaufman, E. L., Lord, M. W., Reese, T. W., and Volkman, J., 'The Discrimination of Visual Number', *American Journal of Psychology* 62 (1949), 498–525.

Kellman, P. J., 'Kinematic Foundations of Infant Visual Perception', in C. E. Granrud (ed.), *Carnegie-Mellon Symposia on Cognition*, vol. 23, *Visual Perception and Cognition in Infancy* (Hillsdale, NJ: Erlbaum, 1993).

Kellman, P. J., 'Interpolation Processes in the Visual Perception of Objects', *Neural Networks* 16 (2003), 915–923.

Kellman, P., and Spelke, E. S., 'Perception of Partly Occluded Objects in Infancy', *Cognitive Psychology* 15 (1983), 483–524.

Kellman, P. J., Gleitman, H., and Spelke, E. S., 'Object and Observer Motion in the Perception of Objects by Infants', *Journal of Experimental Psychology* 13 (1987), 586–593.

Kenshalo, Dan R., Sr, 'Phylogenetic Development of Feeling', in Edward C. Carterette and Morton P. Friedman (eds.), *Handbook of Perception* (New York: Academic Press, 1978).

Kentridge, R. W., Heywood, C. A., and Weiskrantz, L., 'Attention without Awareness in Blindsight', *Proceedings: Biological Sciences* 266/1430 (1999), 1805–1811.

Kentridge, R. W., Heywood, C. A., and Weiskrantz, L., 'Spatial Attention Speeds Discrimination without Awareness in Blindsight', *Neuropsychologia* 42 (2004), 831–835.

Kersten, D., 'Perceptual Categories for Spatial Layout', *Royal Society of London: Philosophical Transactions: Biological Sciences* 352 (1997), 1155–1163.

Kersten, D., Mamassian, P., and Yuille, A., 'Object Perception as Bayesian Inference', *Annual Review of Psychology* 55 (2004), 271–304.

Klatzky, R. L., and Lederman, S. J., 'Identifying Objects from a Haptic Glance', *Perception and Psychophysics* 57 (1995), 1111–1123.

Klatzky, R. L., and Lederman, S. J., 'Object Recognition by Touch', in J. Rieser, D. Ashmead, F. Ebner, and A. Corn (eds.), *Blindness and Brain Plasticity in Navigation and Object Perception* (New York: Erlbaum, 2008).

Klatzky, R. L., Lederman, S. J., and Metzger, V. A., 'Identifying Objects by Touch: An Expert System', *Perception and Psychophysics* 37 (1985), 299–302.

Klein, A., and Starkey, P., 'The Origins and Development of Numerical Cognition: A Comparative Analysis', in *Cognitive Processes in Mathematics* (Oxford: Clarendon Press, 1987).

Klump, Georg M., 'Sound Localization in Birds', in Robert J. Dooling, Richard R. Fay, and Arthur N. Popper (eds.), *Comparative Hearing: Birds and Reptiles* (New York: Springer-Verlag, 2000).

Knaden, M., and Wehner, R., 'Ant Navigation: Resetting the Path Integrator', *Journal of Experimental Biology* 209 (2006), 26–31.

Knierim, J. J., Kudrimoti, H. S., and McNaughton, B. L., 'Place Cells, Head Direction Cells, and the Learning of Landmark Stability', *Journal of Neuroscience* 15 (1995), 1648–1659.

Knill, David C., 'Surface Orientation from Texture: Ideal Observers, Generic Observers, and the Information Content of Texture Cues', *Vision Research* 38 (1998), 1655–1682.

Knill, David C., 'Discrimination of Planar Surface Slant from Texture: Human and Ideal Observers Compared', *Vision Research* 38 (1998), 1683–1711.

Knudsen, Erik I., 'Sound Localization in Birds', in Arthur N. Popper and Richard R. Fay (eds.), *Comparative Studies in Hearing in Vertebrates* (New York: Springer-Verlag, 1980).

Koechlin, E., Dehaene, S., and Mehler, J., 'Numerical Transformations in Five-Month-Old Infants', *Mathematical Cognition* 3 (1998), 89–104.

Koechlin, Etienne, Naccache, Lionel, Block, Eliza, and Dehaene, Stanislas, 'Primed Numbers: Exploring the Modularity of Numerical Representations with Masked and Unmasked Semantic Priming', *Journal of Experimental Psychology: Human Perception and Performance* 25 (1999), 1882–1905.

Koffka, K., *Principles of Gestalt Psychology* (1935; New York: Harcourt, Brace & World, 1963).

Köhler, Wolfgang, 'Optische Untersuchungen am Schimpansen und am Haushuhn', *Berliner Abhandlungen* phys.-math. Kl. Nr 3 (1915).

Köhler, Wolfgang, 'Die Farben der Sehdinge beim Schimpansen und beim Haushuhn', *Zeitschrift für Psychologie* 77 (1917), 248–255.

Köhler, Wolfgang, *Gestalt Psychology* (New York: Horace Liveright, 1929).

Kolterman, R., 'Periodicity in the Activity and Learning Performance of the Honey Bee', in L. B. Browne (ed.), *The Experimental Analysis of Insect Behavior* (Berlin: Springer, 1974).

Kourtzi, Z., and Kanwisher, N., 'Representation of Perceived Object Shape by the Human Lateral Occipital Complex', *Science* 293 (2001), 1506–1509.

Kourtzi, Z., Erb, M., Grodd, W., and Bülthoff, H. H., 'Representation of the Perceived 3-D Object Shape in the Human Lateral Occipital Complex', *Cerebral Cortex* 9 (2003), 911–920.

Kraft, J. M., and Brainard, D. H., 'Mechanisms of Color Constancy under Nearly Natural Viewing', *Proceedings of the National Academy of Sciences of the United States of America* 96 (1999), 307–312.

Kral, Karl, 'Behavioral–Analytical Studies of the Role of Head Movements in Depth Perception in Insects, Birds and Mammals', *Behavioral Processes* 64 (2003), 1–12.

Kralik, J. D., and Hauser, M. D., 'A Nonhuman Primate's Perception of Object Relations: Experiments on Cottontop Tamarins, *Saguinus Oedipus*', *Animal Behavior* 63 (2002), 419–435.

Kripke, Saul, *Naming and Necessity* (Cambridge, MA: Harvard University Press, 1972).

Kripke, Saul, 'A Puzzle about Belief', in A. Margalit (ed.), *Meaning and Use* (Dordrecht: D. Reidel Publishing Company, 1979).

Kripke, Saul, *Wittgenstein on Rules and Private Language* (Cambridge, MA: Harvard University Press, 1982).

Land, E. H., and McCann, J. J., 'Lightness and Retinex Theory', *American Journal of Optical Society of America* 61 (1971), 1–11.

Land, Michael F., 'Visual Tracking and Pursuit: Humans and Arthropods Compared', *Journal of Insect Physiology* 38 (1992), 939–951.

Land, M. F., and Nilsson, D.-E., *Animal Eyes* (Oxford: Oxford University Press, 2002).

Layne, John E., Barnes, W. Jon P., and Duncan, Lindsay M. J., 'Mechanisms of Homing in the Fiddler Crab *Uca Rapax*: 2 Information Sources and Frame of Reference for a Path Integration System', *Journal of Experimental Biology* 206 (2003), 4425–4442.

Lederman, S. J., and Klatzky, R. L., 'Relative Availability of Surface and Object Properties during Early Haptic Processing', *Journal of Experimental Psychology: Human Perception and Performance* 23 (1997), 1680–1707.

Lehrer, M., 'Spatial Vision in the Honeybee: The Use of Different Cues in Different Tasks', *Vision Research* 34 (1994), 2363–2385.

Lehrer, Miriam, 'Shape Perception in the Honeybee: Symmetry as a Global Framework', *International Journal of Plant Sciences* 160 (1999), S51–S65.

Lehrer, M., Srinivasan, M. V., Zhang, S. W., and Horridge, G. A., 'Motion Cues Provide the Bee's Visual World with a Third Dimension', *Nature* 332 (1988), 356–357.

Leonardi, Paolo, and Santambrogio, Marco (eds.), *On Quine* (Cambridge: Cambridge University Press, 1995).

Leslie, A. M., 'The Perception of Causality in Infants', *Perception* 11 (1982), 173–186.

Leslie, A., Xu, F., Tremoulet, P., and Scholl, B., 'Indexing and the Object Concept: Developing "What" and "Where" Systems', *Trends in Cognitive Sciences* 2 (1998), 10–18.

Lewis, C. I., *Mind and the World Order* (New York: Charles Scribner's Sons, 1929).

Lewis, C. I., *An Analysis of Knowledge and Valuation* (1946; La Salle, IL: Open Court Publishing Company, 1950).

Lewis, David, 'Psycho-Physical and Theoretical Identification', *Australasian Journal of Philosophy* 50 (1972), 249–258.

Lewis, David, 'Radical Interpretation', *Synthese* 27 (1974), 332–334.

Lewis, David, 'Veridical Hallucination and Prosthetic Vision', *Australasian Journal of Philosophy* 58 (1980), 239–249.

Li, F. F., VanRullen, R., Koch, C., and Perona, P., 'Rapid Natural Scene Categorization in the near Absence of Attention', *Proceedings of the National Academy of Sciences of the United States of America* 99 (2002), 9596–9601.

Lipton, J. S., and Spelke, E. S., 'Origins of Number Sense: Large Number Discrimination in Human Infants', *Psychological Science* 15 (2003), 396–401.

Lipton, J. S., and Spelke, E. S., 'Discrimination of Large and Small Numerosities by Human Infants', *Infancy* 5 (2004), 271–290.

Logothetis, N. K., Pauls, J., Bülthoff, H. H., and Poggio, T., 'View-Dependent Object Recognition by Monkeys', *Current Biology* 4 (1994), 401–414.

Logvinenko, A. D., and Maloney, L. T., 'The Proximity Structure of Asymmetric Surface Colors and the Impossibility of Asymmetric Lightness Matching', *Perception and Psychophysics* 68 (2006), 76–83.

Loosbroek, E., and Smitsman, A. W., 'Visual Perception of Numerosity in Infancy', *Developmental Psychology* 26 (1990), 916–922.

Lorenz, Konrad, 'A Consideration of Methods of Identification of Species-Specific Instinctive Behaviour Patterns in Birds' (1932), in *Studies in Animal and Human Behaviour*, i, trans. R. Martin (Cambridge, MA: Harvard University Press, 1970).

Lorenz, Konrad, 'The Establishment of the Instinct Concept' (1937), in *Studies in Animal and Human Behaviour*, i, trans. R. Martin (Cambridge, MA: Harvard University Press, 1970).

Lorenz, Konrad, *The Foundations of Ethology* (1978), trans. K. Z. Lorenz and R. W. Kickert (New York: Springer-Verlag, 1981).

Luck, Steven J., Vogel, Edward K., and Shapiro, Kimron L., 'Word Meanings Can Be Accessed but not Reported during the Attentional Blink', *Nature* 393 (1996), 616–618.

Maaswinkel, H., and Whishaw, I. Q., 'Homing with Locale, Taxon, and Dead Reckoning Strategies by Foraging Rats: Sensory Hierarchy in Spatial Navigation', *Behavioral Brain Research* 99 (1999), 143–152.

McCrink, K., and Wynn, K., 'Large-Number Addition and Subtraction by 9-Month-Old Infants', *Psychological Science* 15 (2004), 776–781.

McDowell, John, 'The Content of Perceptual Experience', *Philosophical Quarterly* 44 (1994), 190–205.

McDowell, John, *Mind and World* (Cambridge, MA: Harvard University Press, 1994).

Mansuripur, Masud, *Introduction to Information Theory* (New York: Prentice Hall, 1987).

Margolis, E., and Laurence, S., 'How to Learn the Natural Numbers: Inductive Inference and the Acquisition of Number Concepts', *Cognition* 106 (2008), 924–939.

Marois, René, Yi, Do-Joon, and Chun, Marvin M., 'The Neural Fate of Consciously Perceived and Missed Events in the Attentional Blink', *Neuron* 41 (2004), 465–472.

Marr, David, *Vision* (San Francisco: W. H. Freeman and Company, 1982).

Matsuzawa, T., 'Use of Numbers by a Chimpanzee', *Nature* 315 (1985), 57–59.

Mazokhin-Porshnyakov, Georgii A., 'Recognition of Colored Objects by Insects', in C. G. Bernhard (ed.), *The Functional Organization of the Compound Eye* (Oxford: Pergamon Press, 1966).

Mazokhin-Porshnyakov, Georgii A., *Insect Vision*, trans. R. and L. Masironi (New York: Plenum, 1969).

Meck, W. H., and Church, R. M., 'A Mode Control Model of Counting and Timing Processes', *Journal of Experimental Psychology: Animal Behavior Processes* 9 (1983), 320–334.

Melcher, David, and Morronel, M. Concetta, 'Spatiotopic Temporal Integration of Visual Motion across Saccadic Eye Movements', *Nature Neuroscience* 6 (2003), 877–881.

Meltzoff, A. N., and Borton, R. W., 'Intermodal Matching by Human Neonates', *Nature* 282 (1979), 403–404.

Meltzoff, A. N., and Moore, M. K., 'Imitation of Facial and Manual Gestures by Human Neonates', *Science* 198 (1977), 75–78.

Menzel, Charles, 'Progress in the Study of Chimpanzee Recall and Episodic Memory', in Herbert S. Terrace and Janet Metcalfe (eds.), *The Missing Link in Cognition: Origins of Self-Reflective Consciousness* (Oxford: Oxford University Press, 2005).

Menzel, Randolf, 'Spectral Sensitivity and Color Vision in Invertebrates', in H. Autrum (ed.), *Comparative Physiology and Evolution of Vision in Invertebrates: Invertebrate Receptors* (Berlin: Springer Verlag, 1979).

Menzel, R., and Giurfa, M., 'Dimensions of Cognition in an Insect, The Honeybee', *Behavioral and Cognitive Neuro-Science Reviews* 5 (2006), 24–40.

Menzel, R., Brandt, R. Gumbert, A., Komishke, B., and Kunze, J., 'Two Spatial Memories for Honeybee Navigation', *Proceedings of the Royal Society of London, Series B, Biological Sciences* 267 (2000), 961–968.

Menzel, R., Greggers, U., Smith, A., Berger, S., Brandt, R., Brunke, S., et al., 'Honey Bees Navigate According to a Map-Like Spatial Memory', *Proceedings of the National Academy of Sciences* 102 (2005), 3040–3045.

Merkle, Tobias, Rost, Martin, and Alt, Wolfgang, 'Ego-Centric Path Integration Models and their Application to Desert Ants', *Journal of Theoretical Biology* 240 (2006), 385–399.

Merleau-Ponty, Maurice, *Phenomenology of Perception* (1945), trans. Colin Smith (London: Routledge & Kegan Paul, 1966).

Merleau-Ponty, Maurice, 'The Primacy of Perception and Its Philosophical Consequences' (1947), in *The Primacy of Perception and Other Essays*, ed. James M. Edie (Evanston, IL: Northwestern University Press, 1971).

Merleau-Ponty, Maurice, 'Phenomenology and the Sciences of Man' (1961), in *The Primacy of Perception and Other Essays*, ed. James M. Edie (Evanston, IL: Northwestern University Press, 1971).

Miller, George, 'The Magic Number 7 Plus or Minus Two: Some Limits on our Capacity for Processing Information', *Psychological Review* 63 (1956), 81–97.

Miller, George A., and Buckhout, Robert, *Psychology: The Science of Mental Life* (2nd edn., New York, Harper & Row, 1973).

Miller, G., Galanter, E., and Pribram, K., *Plans and the Structure of Behavior* (New York: Holt, Rinehart & Winston, 1960).

Millikan, Ruth Garrett, *Language, Thought, and Other Biological Categories* (Cambridge, MA: MIT Press, 1984).

Millikan, Ruth Garrett, 'Biosemantics', *The Journal of Philosophy* 86 (1989), 281–297; reprinted in *White Queen Psychology and Other Essays for Alice* (Cambridge, MA: MIT Press, 1993).

Millikan, Ruth Garrett, 'Compare and Contrast Dretske, Fodor, and Millikan on Teleosemantics', *Philosophical Topics* 18 (1990), 151–161; reprinted in *White Queen Psychology and Other Essays for Alice* (Cambridge, MA: MIT Press, 1993).

Millikan, Ruth Garrett, 'Truth Rules, Hoverflies, and the Kripke–Wittgenstein Paradox', *The Philosophical Review* 99 (1990), 323–353; reprinted in *White Queen Psychology and Other Essays for Alice* (Cambridge, MA: MIT Press, 1993).

Millikan, Ruth Garrett, 'What is Behavior? A Philosophical Essay on Ethology and Individualism in Psychology', in *White Queen Psychology and Other Essays for Alice* (Cambridge, MA: MIT Press, 1993).

Mitchell, P., *Introduction to Theory of Mind: Children, Autism and Apes* (London: Arnold, 1997).

Möhl, Bernhard, 'Sense Organs and the Control of Flight', in Graham J. Goldsworthy and Colin H. Wheeler (eds.), *Insect Flight* (Boca Raton, FL: CRC Press, Inc., 1989).

Moore, G. E., 'Some Judgments of Perception' (1918–1919), in *Philosophical Studies* (London: Kegan, Paul, Trench, Trubner & Co. Ltd, 1922).

Moore, G. E., 'The Status of Sense-Data' (1913–1914), in *Philosophical Studies* (London: Kegan, Paul, Trench, Trubner & Co. Ltd, 1922).

Morris, James P., Pelphrey, Kevin A., and McCarthy, Gregory, 'Face Processing without Awareness in the Right Fusiform Gyrus', *Neuropsychologia* 45 (2007), 3087–3091.

Mundy, J. L., Faugeras, O., Kanade, T., d'Souza, C., and Sabin, M., 'Object Recognition Based on Geometry: Progress over Three Decades', *Philosophical Transactions: Mathematical, Physical and Engineering Sciences* 356 (1998), 1213–1231.

Myowa-Yamakoshi, M., Tomonaga, M., Tanaka, M., and Matsuzawa, T., 'Imitation in Neonatal Chimpanzees *(Pan troglodytes)*', *Developmental Science* 7 (2004), 437–442.

Nagel, Thomas, 'What Is It Like to Be a Bat?', *The Philosophical Review* 83 (1974), 435–450.

Nagel, Thomas, *The View from Nowhere* (Oxford: Oxford University Press, 1986).

Nakayama, K., He, Z. J., and Shimojo, S., 'Visual Surface Representation: A Critical Link between Lower-Level and Higher-Level Vision', in S. M. Kosslyn and D. Osherson (eds.), *Visual Cognition: An Invitation to Cognitive Science*, ii (Cambridge, MA: MIT Press, 1995).

Needham, A., and Baillargeon, R., 'Object Segregation in 8-Month-Old Infants', *Cognition* 62 (1997), 121–149.

Needham, A., and Baillargeon, R., 'Effects of Prior Experience on 4.5-Month-Old Infants' Object Segregation', *Infant Behavior and Development* 21 (1998), 1–24.

Neiworth, J. J., Steinmark, E., Basile, B. M., Wonders, R., Steely, F., and Dehart, C., 'A Test of Object Permanence in a New-World Monkey Species, Cotton Top Tamarins *(Saguinus oedipus)*', *Animal Cognition* 6 (2003), 27–37.

Neumeyer, Christa, 'Comparative Aspects of Color Constancy', in V. Walsh and J. Kulikowski (eds.), *Perceptual Constancy* (Cambridge: Cambridge University Press, 1998).

Newell, A., Shaw, J. C., and Simon, H. A., 'Elements of a Theory of Human Problem Solving', *Psychological Review* 65 (1958), 151–166.

Newell, F., Ernst, M. O., Tjan, B. S., and Bülthoff, H. H., 'Viewpoint Dependence in Visual and Haptic Object Recognition', *Psychological Science* 12 (2001), 37–42.

Norman, J. F., Norman, H. F., Clayton, A. M., Lianekhammy, J., and Zielke, G., 'The Visual and Haptic Perception of Natural Object Shape', *Perception and Psychophysics* 66 (2004), 342–351.

O'Dell, C., and Boothe, R. G., 'The Development of Stereoacuity in Infant Rhesus Monkeys', *Vision Research* 37 (1997), 2675–2684.

O'Shaughnessy, Brian, *The Will* (2 vols.; Cambridge: Cambridge University Press, 1980).

Oucet, E. S. B., and Thinus-Blanc, C., 'Landmark Use and the Cognitive Map in the Rat', in S. Healy (ed.), *Spatial Representation in Animals* (Oxford: Oxford University Press, 1998).

Palmer, Stephen E., *Vision Science* (Cambridge, MA: MIT Press, 2002).

Papineau, David, *Reality and Representation* (Oxford: Blackwell, 1987).

Peacocke, Christopher, 'Demonstrative Thought and Psychological Explanation', *Synthese* 49 (1981), 187–217.

Peacocke, Christopher, *Sense and Content* (Oxford: Oxford University Press, 1983).

Peacocke, Christopher, 'When is a Grammar Psychologically Real?', in A. George (ed.), *Reflections on Chomsky* (Oxford: Basil Blackwell, 1989).

Peacocke, Christopher, *A Study of Concepts* (Cambridge, MA: MIT Press, 1992).

Peacocke, Christopher, 'Intuitive Mechanics, Psychological Reality and the Idea of a Material Object', in N. Eilan, R. McCarthy, and B. Brewer (eds.), *Spatial Representation* (Oxford: Basil Blackwell, 1993).

Peacocke, Christopher, 'Does Perception have a Nonconceptual Content?', *The Journal of Philosophy* 98 (2001), 239–264.

Peacocke, Christopher, 'Implicit Conceptions, Understanding, and Rationality', in M. Hahn and B. Ramberg (eds.), *Reflections and Replies: Essays on the Philosophy of Tyler Burge* (Cambridge, MA: MIT Press, 2003).

Pepperberg, I., 'Development of Piagetian Object Permanence in a Grey Parrot (*Psittacus Erithacus*)', *Journal of Comparative Psychology*, 111 (1997), 63–95.

Pepperberg, Irene Maxine, *The Alex Studies* (Cambridge, MA: Harvard University Press, 2002).

Pepperberg, I. M., and Funk, F. A., 'Object Permanence in Four Species of Psittacine Birds', *Animal Learning and Behavior* 14 (1990), 322–330.

Peterson, Mary A., 'Object Recognition Processes Can and Do Operate before Figure–Ground Organization', *Current Directions in Psychological Science* 3 (1994), 105–111.

Peterson, Mary A., 'Object Perception', in E. Bruce Goldstein (ed.), *Blackwell Handbook of Perception* (Oxford: Blackwell, 2001).

Piaget, Jean, *The Construction of Reality in the Child* (New York: Basic Books, 1954).

Pica, P., Lemer, C., Izard, V., and Dehaene, S., 'Exact and Approximate Arithmetic in an Amazonian Indigene Group', *Science* 306 (2004), 499–503.

Pinker, Steven, 'So How *Does* the Mind Work?', *Mind and Language* 20 (2005).

Pizlo, Z., and Stevenson, A. K., 'Shape Constancy from Novel Views', *Perception and Psychophysics* 61 (1999), 1299–1307.

Platt, J. R., and Johnson, D. M., 'Localization of Position within a Homogeneous Behavior Chain: Effects of Error Contingencies', *Learning and Motivation* 2 (1971), 396–414.

Pollok, B., Prior, H., and Guntrukun, O., 'Development of Object Permanence in Food-Storing Magpies (*Pica pica*)', *Journal of Comparative Psychology* 114 (2000), 148–157.

Popper, Arthur N., 'Behavioral Measures of Odontocete Hearing', in René-Guy Busnel and James F. Fish (eds.), *Animal Sonar Systems* (New York: Plenum Press, 1980).

Popper, A. N., and Fay, R. R., *Hearing in Bats* (New York: Springer-Verlag, 1995).

Povanelli, Daniel, *Folk Physics for Chimps* (Oxford: Oxford University Press, 2000).

Price, H. H., *Perception* (London: Methuen Co. Ltd, 1932).

Price, H. H., 'Review of *The Foundations of Empirical Knowledge*', *Mind* NS 50 (1941), 280–293.

Prinz, W., and Hommel, B. (eds.), *Common Mechanisms in Perception and Action* (Oxford: Oxford University Press, 2002).

Putnam, Hilary, 'Is Semantics Possible?' (1970), in *Philosophical Papers*, ii (Cambridge: Cambridge University Press, 1975).

Putnam, Hilary, 'The Meaning of "Meaning"', in K. Gunderson (ed.), *Language, Mind and Knowledge*, Minnesota Studies in the Philosophy of Science VII (Minneapolis: University of Minnesota Press, 1975); reprinted in *Philosophical Papers*, ii (Cambridge: Cambridge University Press, 1975).

Putnam, Hilary, *Reason, Truth, and History* (Cambridge: Cambridge University Press, 1981).

Putnam, Hilary, 'Models and Reality', in *Philosophical Papers*, iii (Cambridge: Cambridge University Press, 1983).

Putnam, Hilary, 'Sense, Nonsense, and the Senses: An Inquiry into the Powers of the Human Mind', *The Journal of Philosophy* 91 (1994), 445–517.

Pylyshyn, Zenon, 'Is Vision Continuous with Cognition? The Case for Cognitive Impenetrability of Visual Perception', *Behavioral and Brain Sciences* 22 (1999), 341–365.

Pylyshyn, Z. W., 'Situating Vision in the World', *Trends in Cognitive Science* 4 (2000), 197–207.

Pylyshyn, Z. W. 'Visual Indexes, Preconceptual Objects, and Situated Vision', *Cognition* 80 (2001), 127–158.

Pylyshyn, Z. W. *Seeing and Visualizing* (Cambridge, MA: MIT Press, 2003).

Pylyshyn, Z. W., and Storm, R. W., 'Tracking Multiple Independent Targets: Evidence for a Parallel Tracking Mechanism', *Spatial Vision* 3 (1998), 179–197.

Quine, W. V., 'On What There Is' (1948), in *From a Logical Point of View* (New York: Harper and Row, 1953).

Quine, W. V., 'Identity, Ostension, and Hypostasis' (1950), in *From a Logical Point of View* (New York: Harper and Row, 1963).

Quine, W. V., 'Two Dogmas of Empiricism' (1951), in *From a Logical Point of View* (New York: Harper and Row, 1953); reprinted in *Quintessence: Basic Readings from the Philosophy of W. V. Quine*, ed. Roger F. Gibson (Cambridge, MA: Harvard University Press, 2004).

Quine, W. V., 'The Scope and Language of Science' (1957), in *The Ways of Paradox* (New York: Random House, 1966).

Quine, W. V., 'Speaking of Objects' (1958), in *Ontological Relativity and Other Essays* (New York: Columbia University Press, 1969); reprinted in *Quintessence: Basic Readings from the Philosophy of W. V. Quine*, ed. Roger F. Gibson (Cambridge, MA: Harvard University Press, 2004).

Quine, W. V., *Word and Object* (Cambridge, MA: MIT Press, 1960).

Quine, W. V., 'Ontological Relativity' (1968), in *Ontological Relativity and Other Essays* (New York: Columbia University Press, 1969).

Quine, W. V., 'Epistemology Naturalized', in *Ontological Relativity and Other Essays* (New York: Columbia University Press, 1969).

Quine, W. V., 'Existence and Quantification', in *Ontological Relativity and Other Essays* (New York: Columbia University Press, 1969).

Quine, W. V., 'Natural Kinds', in *Ontological Relativity and Other Essays* (New York: Columbia University Press, 1969).

Quine, W. V., *Ontological Relativity and Other Essays* (New York: Columbia University Press, 1969).

Quine, W. V., 'Propositional Objects', in *Ontological Relativity and Other Essays* (New York: Columbia University Press, 1969).

Quine, W. V., *Philosophy of Logic* (Englewood Cliffs, NJ: Prentice Hall, 1970).

Quine, W. V., *The Roots of Reference* (La Salle, IL: Open Court, 1973).

Quine, W. V., 'On the Individuation of Attributes' (1975), in *Theories and Things* (Cambridge, MA: Harvard University Press, 1981).

Quine, W. V., *Theories and Things* (Cambridge, MA: Harvard University Press, 1981).

Quine, W. V., 'Things and their Place in Theories', in *Theories and Things* (Cambridge, MA: Harvard University Press, 1981).

Quine, W. V., *Pursuit of Truth* (Cambridge, MA: Harvard University Press, 1990).

Rawson, Nancy E., 'Human Olfaction', in Thomas E. Finger, Wayne L. Silver, and Diego Restrepo (eds.), *The Neurobiology of Taste and Smell* (2nd edn., New York: John Wiley & Sons, 2000).

Regolin, L., and Vallortigara, G., 'Perception of Partly Occluded Objects by Young Chicks', *Perception and Psychophysics* 57 (1995), 971–976.

Regolin, L., Vallortigara, G., and Zanforlin, M., 'Detour Behavior in the Domestic Chick: Searching for a Disappearing Prey or a Disappearing Social Partner', *Animal Behavior* 50 (1995), 203–211.

Rensink, R. A., 'The Dynamic Representation of Scenes', *Visual Cognition* 7 (2000), 17–42.

Richardson, D. C., and Kirkham, N., 'Multi-Modal Events and Moving Locations: Eye Movements of Adults and 6-Month-Olds Reveal Dynamic Spatial Indexing', *Journal of Experimental Psychology: General* 133 (2004), 46–62.

Rock, Irving, *The Logic of Perception* (Cambridge, MA: MIT Press, 1983).

Rorty, Richard, *Philosophy and the Mirror of Nature* (Princeton: Princeton University Press, 1979).

Ross, Helen E., and Plug, Cornelis, 'The History of Size Constancy and Size Illusions', in Vincent Walsh and Janusz Kulilowski (eds.), *Perceptual Constancy* (Cambridge: Cambridge University Press, 1998).

Ross-Sheehy, S., Oakes, L., and Luck, S. J., 'The Development of Visual Short-Term Memory Capacity in Infants', *Child Development* 74 (2003), 1807–1822.

Rozemond, Marleen, 'Evans on *De Re* Thought', *Philosophia* (1994), 275–298.

Rudd, M. E., and Zemach, I. K., 'Quantitative Properties of Achromatic Color Induction: An Edge Integration Analysis', *Vision Research* 44 (2004), 971–981.

Rudd, M. E., and Zemach, I. K., 'Contrast Polarity and Edge Integration in Achromatic Color Perception', *Journal of the Optical Society of America* A/24 (2007), 2134–2156.

Russell, Bertrand, 'On Denoting', *Mind* 14 (1905), 479–493.

Russell, Bertrand, *The Problems of Philosophy* (1912; Oxford: Oxford University Press, 1982).

Russell, Bertrand, 'The Nature of Acquaintance' (1914), in *Logic and Knowledge*, ed. Robert Charles Marsh (London: Unwin Hyman, 1989).

Russell, Bertrand, *Our Knowledge of the External World* (London: George Allen & Unwin Ltd., 1914).

Schacter, Daniel L., McAndrews, Mary Pat, and Moscovitch, Morris, 'Access to Consciousness: Dissociations between Implicit and Explicit Knowledge in Neuropsychological Syndromes', in L. Weiskrantz (ed.), *Thought without Language* (Oxford: Clarendon Press, 1989).

Schnitzler, H.-U., and Henson, O. W., Jr., 'Performance of Airborne Animal Sonar Systems I. Microchiroptera', in René-Guy Busnel and James F. Fish (eds.), *Animal Sonar Systems* (New York: Plenum Press, 1980).

Scholl, B. J., and Pylyshyn, Z. W., 'Tracking Multiple Items through Occlusion: Clues to Visual Objecthood', *Cognitive Psychology* 38 (1999), 259–290.

Scholl, B. J., Pylyshyn, Z. W., and Franconeri, S., 'When are Spatiotemporal and Featural Properties Encoded as a Result of Attentional Allocation?', *Investigative Opthamology and Visual Science* 40 (1999), 4195.

Schwab, R., and Jackson, R., '. . . Deceived with Ornament', *British Journal of Opthamology* 90 (2006), 261.

Schwartz, Bennett L., 'Do Nonhuman Primates Have Episodic Memory?', in Herbert S. Terrace and Janet Metcalfe (eds.), *The Missing Link in Cognition: Origins of Self-Reflective Consciousness* (Oxford: Oxford University Press, 2005).

Schwartz, R. (ed.), *Perception* (London: Blackwell, 2004).

Searle, John, 'Proper Names', *Mind* 67 (1958), 166–173.

Sellars, Wilfrid, 'Empiricism and the Philosophy of Mind' (1956), in *Science, Perception and Reality* (London: Routlege & Kegan Paul, 1963).

Sellars, Wilfrid, 'Phenomenalism', in *Science, Perception and Reality* (London: Routlege & Kegan Paul, 1963).

Shams, L., Kamitani, Y., and Shimojo, S., 'What You See is What You Hear', *Nature* 408 (2000), 788.

Shannon, Claude E., 'A Mathematical Theory of Communication', *Bell System Technical Journal* 27 (1948), 379–423, 623–656.

Shepard, Roger N., 'Ecological Constraints on Internal Representation: Resonant Kinematics of Perceiving, Imagining, Thinking, and Dreaming', *Psychological Review* 91 (1984), 417–447.

Shepard, Roger N., 'Perceptual–Cognitive Universals as Reflections of the World', *Behavioral and Brain Sciences* 24 (2001), 581–601.

Shiffrar, Maggie, 'Movement and Event Perception', in E. Bruce Goldstein (ed.), *Blackwell Handbook of Perception* (Oxford: Blackwell, 2001).

Sigala, N., and Logothetis, N. K., 'Visual Categorization Shapes Feature Selectivity in the Primate Temporal Cortex', *Nature* 415 (2002), 318–320.

Simmons, J. A., 'Directional Hearing and Sound Localization in Echolocating Animals', in W. A. Yost and G. Gourevitch (eds.), *Directional Hearing* (New York: Springer-Verlag, 1987).

Simoncelli, E. P., and Olshausen, B. A., 'Natural Image Statistics and Neural Representation', *Annual Review of Neuroscience* 24 (2001), 1193–1216.

Smith, A. D., *Perception* (Cambridge, MA: Harvard University Press, 2002).

Soja, N., Carey, S., and Spelke, E., 'Ontological Categories Guide Young Children's Inductions of Word Meaning', *Cognition* 38 (1991), 179–211.

Spelke, Elizabeth, 'Where Perceiving Ends and Thinking Begins: The Apprehension of Objects in Infancy', in A. Yonas (ed.), *Perceptual Development in Infancy* The Minnesota Symposia on Child Psychology, 20 (Hillsdale, NJ: Lawrence Erlbaum, 1988).

Spelke, Elizabeth, 'Principles of Object Perception', *Cognitive Science* 14 (1990), 29–56.

Spelke, E. S., 'Initial Knowledge: Six Suggestions', *Cognition* 50 (1994), 431–445.

Spelke, E. S., Born, W. S., and Chu, F., 'Perception of Moving, Sounding Objects by Four-Month-Old Infants', *Perception* 12 (1983), 719–732.

Spelke, E. S., Brelinger, K. Macomber, J., and Jacobson, K., 'Origins of Knowledge', *Psychological Review* 99 (1992), 605–632.

Spelke, E. S., Vishton, P., and Von Hofsten, C., 'Object Perception, Object-Directed Action, and Physical Knowledge in Infancy', in M. S. Gazzaniga (ed.), *The Cognitive Neurosciences* (Cambridge, MA: MIT Press, 1995).

Spelke, E. S., Kestenbaum, R., Simons, D. J., and Wein, D., 'Spatio-Temporal Continuity, Smoothness of Motion and Object Identity in Infancy', *British Journal of Developmental Psychology* 13 (1995), 113–142.

Sperling, G., 'The Information Available in Brief Visual Presentations', *Psychological Monographs* 24 (1960).

Srinivasan, M. V., and Zhang, S. W., 'Visual Control of Honeybee Flight', in M. Lehrer (ed.), *Orientation and Communication in Arthropods* (Basel: Birkhauser Verlag, 1997).

Srinivasan, M. V., Zhang, S. W., and Bidwell, N. J., 'Visually Mediated Odometry in Honeybees', *Journal of Experimental Biology* 200 (1997), 2513–2522.

Stalnaker, Robert, 'On What is in the Head', in J. E. Tomberlin (ed.), *Philosophical Perspectives, 3: Philosophy of Mind and Action Theory* (Atascadero, CA: Ridgeview, 1989), 187–216.

Starkey, P., and Cooper, R., 'Perception of Numbers by Human Infants', *Science* 210 (1980), 1033–1034.

Starkey, P., Spelke, E. S., and Gelman, R., 'Detection of Intermodal Numerical Correspondences by Human Infants', *Science* 222 (1983), 179–181.

Stein, Howard, 'Eudoxus and Dedekind: On the Ancient Greek Theory of Ratios and its Relation to Modern Mathematics', *Synthese* 84 (1990), 163–211.

Stimson Wilcox, R., and Jackson, Robert R., 'Cognitive Abilities of Araneophagic Jumping Spiders', in R. P. Balda, I. M. Pepperberg, and A. C. Kamil (eds.), *Animal Cognition in Nature* (San Diego: Academic Press, 1998).

Stopfer, M., Jayaraman, V., and Laurent, G., 'Intensity versus Identity Coding in an Olfactory System', *Neuron* 39 (2003), 991–1004.

Strawson, Galen, *Mental Reality* (Cambridge, MA: MIT Press, 1994).

Strawson, P. F., 'Particular and General' (1953–1954), in *Logico-Linguistic Papers* (London: Methuen and Co. Ltd, 1971).

Strawson, P. F., 'Singular Terms, Ontology and Identity', *Mind* 65 (1956), 433–454.

Strawson, P. F., *Individuals* (1959; Garden City, NY: Anchor Books, 1963; reprinted London: Routledge, 2002).

Strawson, P. F., 'Singular Terms and Predication', *The Journal of Philosophy* 58 (1961), 393–412.

Strawson, P. F., *The Bounds of Sense: An Essay on Kant's Critique of Pure Reason* (1966; London: Routlege, 1989).

Strawson, P. F., 'The Asymmetry of Subjects and Predicates' (1970), in *Logico-Linguistic Papers; Subject and Predicate in Logic and Grammar* (London: Methuen and Co., 1974).

Strawson, P. F., 'Entity and Identity' (1976), in *Entity and Identity and Other Essays* (Oxford: Clarendon Press, 1997).

Strawson, P. F., 'Reference and its Roots', in *The Philosophy of W. V. Quine* (La Salle, IL: Open Court Publishing Company, 1986); reprinted in *Entity and Identity and Other Essays* (Oxford: Clarendon Press, 1997).

Strawson, P. F., 'My Philosophy', in *The Philosophy of P. F. Strawson*, ed. P. K. Sen and R. R. Verma (New Delhi: Indian Council of Philosophical Research, 1995).

Streri, A., 'Cross-Modal Recognition of Shape from Hand to Eyes in Human Newborns', *Somatosensory Motor Research* 20 (2003), 13–18.

Streri, A., Spelke, E., and Rameix, E., 'Modality-Specific and Amodal Aspects of Object Perception in Infancy: The Case of Active Touch', *Cognition* 47 (1993), 251–279.

Streri, A., Gentaz, E., Spelke, E., and Van de Walle, G., 'Infants' Haptic Perception of Object Unity in Rotating Displays', *Quarterly Journal of Experimental Psychology: A Human Experimental Psychology* 57 (2004), 523–538.

Sutherland, Daniel, 'Kant on Arithmetic, Algebra, and the Theory of Proportions', *Journal of the History of Philosophy* 44 (2006), 533–558.

Tarsitano, Michael, 'Route Selection by a Jumping Spider (*Portia Labiata*) during the Locomotory Phase of a Detour', *Animal Behavior* 72 (2006), 1437–1442.

Tarsitano, Michael S., and Andrew, Richard, 'Scanning and Route Selection in the Jumping Spider', *Animal Behavior* 58 (1999), 255–265.

Tarsitano, M. S., and Jackson, R. R., 'Araneophagic Jumping Spiders Discriminate between Routes that do and do not Lead to Prey', *Animal Behavior* 53 (1997), 257–266.

Tautz, J., Zhang, S. W., Spaethe, J., Brockmann, A., Si, A., and Srinivasan, M., 'Honeybee Odometry: Performance in Varying Natural Terrain', *PLoS Biology* 2 (2004), 915–923.

Taylor-Clarke, M., Jacobsen, P., and Haggard, P., 'Keeping the World a Constant Size', *Nature Neuroscience* 7 (2004), 219–220.

Termine, N., Hrynick, T., Kestenbaum, R., Gleitman, H., and Spelke, E. S., 'Perceptual Completion of Surfaces in Infancy', *Journal of Experimental Psychology: Human Perception and Performance* 13 (1987), 524–532.

Terrace, H. S., Son, L. K., and Brannon, E. M., 'Serial Expertise of Rhesus Macaques', *Psychological Science* 14 (2003), 66–73.

Thorpe, W. H., *Learning and Instinct in Animals* (London: Methuen, 1963).

Thouless, R. H., 'Phenomenal Regression to the "Real" Object', *British Journal of Psychology* 21 (1931), 339–359.

Tinbergen, N., *The Study of Instinct* (1951; New York: Oxford University Press, 1969, with new introduction).

Todd, James T., 'The Visual Perception of 3D Shape', *Trends in Cognitive Sciences* 8 (2004), 115–121.

Tomasello, Michael, and Call, Josep, *Primate Cognition* (Oxford: Oxford University Press, 1997).

Treisman, Anne, 'Feature Binding, Attention, and Object Perception', in G. W. Humphreys, J. Duncan, and A. Treisman (eds.), *Attention, Space, and Action* (Oxford: Oxford University Press, 1999).

Trick, L., and Pylyshyn, Z. W., 'What Enumeration Studies Tell Us about Spatial Attention: Evidence for Limited Capacity Pre-Attentive Processing', *Journal of Experimental Psychology: Human Perception and Performance* 19 (1993), 331–351.

Trick, L. M., and Pylyshyn, Z. W., 'Why are Small and Large Numbers Enumerated Differently? A Limited Capacity Pre-Attentive Stage in Vision', *Psychological Review* 101 (1994), 80–112.

Tsunoda, K., Yamane, Y., Nishizaki, M., and Tanifuji, M., 'Complex Objects are Represented in Macaque Inferotemporal Cortex by the Combination of Feature Columns', *Nature Neuroscience* 4 (2001), 832–838.

Uexküll, J. Van, 'Über Reflexe bei den Seeigeln', *Zoologische Biologie* 34 (1897), 298–318.

Ullman, S., 'Visual Routines', *Cognition* 18 (1984), 97–159.

Ullman, Shimon, *High-Level Vision: Object Recognition and Visual Cognition* (Cambridge, MA: MIT Press, 1996).

Vallortigara, Giorgio, 'The Cognitive Chicken: Visual and Spatial Cognition in the Nonmammalian Brain', in E. A. Wasserman and T. R. Zentall (eds.), *Comparative Cognition: Experimental Explorations of Animal Intelligence* (Oxford: Oxford University Press, 2006).

Van de Walle, G. A., and Spelke, E. S., 'Spatiotemporal Integration and Object Perception in Infancy', *Child Development* 67 (1996), 2621–2640.

Van de Walle, G. A., Carey, S., and Prevor, M., 'Bases for Object Individuation in Infancy: Evidence from Manual Search', *Journal of Cognition and Development* 1 (2000), 249–280.

Verfaellie, M., Milberg, W. P., McGlinchey-Berroth, R., Grande, L., and D'Esposito, M., 'Comparison of Cross-Field Matching and Forced Choice Identification in Hemispatial Neglect', *Neuropsychology* 9 (1995), 427–434.

Vickers, N. J., 'Mechanisms of Animal Navigation in Odor Plumes', *Biological Bulletin* 198 (2000), 203–212.

Vogel, E. K., Woodman, G. F., and Luck, S. J., 'Storage of Features, Conjunctions, and Objects in Visual Working Memory', *Journal of Experimental Psychology: Human Perception and Performance* 27 (2001), 92–114.

Volpe, Bruce T., Ledoux, Joseph E., and Gazzaniga, Michael S., 'Visual Processing of Visual Stimuli in an "Extinguished" Field', *Nature* 282 (1979), 722–724.

Walker, M. M., 'Magnetic Orientation and Magnetic Sense in Arthropods', in M. Lehrer (ed.), *Orientation and Communication in Arthropods* (Basel: Birkhauser Verlag, 1997).

Wallach, Hans, 'Brightness Constancy and the Nature of Achromatic Colors', *Journal of Experimental Psychology* 38 (1948), 310–324.

Wehner, R., 'Spatial Vision in Arthropods', in H. Autrum (ed.), *Comparative Physiology and Evolution of Vision in Invertebrates: Invertebrate Visual Centers and Behavior* (Berlin: Springer Verlag, 1981).

Wehner, Rüdiger, 'Navigation in Context: Grand Theories and Basic Mechanisms', *Journal of Avian Biology* 29 (1998), 370–386.

Wehner, R., and Wehner, S., 'Insect Navigation: Use of Maps or Ariadne's Thread?', *Ethology, Ecology, and Evolution* 2 (1990), 27–48.

Wehner, S., and Srinivasan, M. V., 'Searching Behavior of Desert Ants, Genus *Cataglyphis (Formicidae, Hymenoptera)*', *Journal of Comparative Physiology A* 142 (1981), 335–338.

Weiskrantz, L., *Blindsight* (New York: Oxford University Press, 1986).

Weissburg, M. J., 'Chemo- and Methanosensory Orientation by Crustaceans in Laminar and Turbulent Flows: From Odor trails to Vortex Streets', in M. Lehrer (ed.), *Orientation and Communication in Arthropods* (Basel: Birkhauser Verlag, 1997).

Wellman, H. M., and Woolley, J. D., 'From Simple Desires to Ordinary Beliefs: The Early Development of Everyday Psychology', *Cognition* 35 (1990), 245–275.

Wexler, M., and Held, R. M., 'Anticipating the Three-Dimensional Consequences of Eye Movements', *Proceedings of the National Academy of Sciences of the United States of America* 102 (2005), 1246–1251.

Whalen, J., Gallistel, C. R., and Gelman, R., 'Nonverbal Counting in Humans: The Psychophysics of Number Representation', *Psychological Science* 10 (1999), 130–137.

Wiggins, David, *Sameness and Substance* (Oxford: Blackwell, 1980); updated version, *Sameness and Substance Renewed* (Cambridge: Cambridge University Press, 2001).

Wilcox, R. S., and Jackson, R. R., 'Cognitive Abilities of Araneophagic Jumping Spiders', in Russell P. Balda, Irene M. Pepperberg, and Alan C. Kamil (eds.), *Animal Cognition in Nature* (San Diego: Academic Press, 1998).

Wilson, R. I., and Mainen, Z. F., 'Early Events in Olfactory Processing', *Annual Review of Neuroscience* 29 (2006), 163–201.

Wiltschko, W., and Wiltschko, R., 'Magnetic Orientation and Celestial Cues in Migratory Orientation', in P. Berthold (ed.), *Orientation in Birds* (Basel: Birkhauser Verlag, 1991).

Wiltschko, Wolfgang, and Wiltschko, Roswitha, 'The Navigation System of Birds and its Development', in Russell P. Balda, Irene M. Pepperberg, and Alan C. Kamil (eds.), *Animal Cognition in Nature* (San Diego: Academic Press, 1998).

Wimmer, H., and Hartl, M., 'Against the Cartesian View on Mind: Young Children's Difficulty with Own False Beliefs', *British Journal of Developmental Psychology* 9 (1991), 125–138.

Wimmer, H., Hogrefe, G.-J., and Perner, J., 'Children's Understanding of Informational Access as a Source of Knowledge', *Child Development* 59 (1988), 386–396.

Wittgenstein, Ludwig, *Tractatus Logico-Philosophicus* (1921; London: Routledge & Kegan Paul, 1961).

Wittgenstein, Ludwig, *Philosophical Investigations* (1953; New York: MacMillan Publishing Co., 1968).

Wittgenstein, Ludwig, *On Certainty* (London: Blackwell, 1969).

Wohlgemuth, Sandra, Ronacher, Bernhard, and Wehner, Rüdiger, 'Ant Odometry in the Third Dimension', *Nature* 411 (2001), 795–798.

Wolfe, J. M., and Bennett, S. C., 'Preattentive Object Files: Shapeless Bundles of Basic Features', *Vision Research* 37 (1997), 25–43.

Wood, J. N., and Spelke, E., 'Chronometric Studies of Numerical Cognition in Five-Month-Old Infants', *Cognition* 97 (2005), 23–39.

Wood, J., and Spelke, E., 'Infants' Enumeration of Actions: Numerical Discrimination and its Signature Limits', *Developmental Science* 8 (2005), 1173–1181.

Woodruff, G., and Premack, D., 'Primitive Mathematical Concepts in the Chimpanzee: Proportionality and Numerosity', *Nature* 293 (1981), 568–570.

Wright, Larry, 'Functions', *The Philosophical Review* 82 (1973), 139–168.

Wundt, Wilhelm, *Outlines of Psychology*, trans. C. H. Judd (Leipzig: Englemann, 1907).

Wynn, K., 'Children's Understanding of Counting', *Cognition* 36 (1990), 155–193.

Wynn, Karen, 'Addition and Subtraction by Human Infants', *Nature* 358 (1992), 749–750.

Wynn, K., 'Children's Acquisition of the Number Words and the Counting System', *Cognitive Psychology* 24 (1992), 220–251.

Wynn, K., 'Infants' Individuation and Enumeration of Physical Actions', *Psychological Science* 7 (1996), 164–169.

Xu, Fei, 'From Lot's Wife to a Pillar of Salt: Evidence that *Physical Object* is a Sortal Concept', *Mind and Language* 12 (1997), 365–392.

Xu, F., and Carey, S., 'Infants' Metaphysics: The Case of Numerical Identity', *Cognitive Psychology* 30 (1996), 111–153.

Xu, F., and Carey, S., 'The Emergence of Kind Concepts: A Rejoinder to Needham and Baillargeon', *Cognition* 74 (2000), pp. 285–301.

Xu, F., and Spelke, E. S., 'Large Number Discrimination in 6-Month-Old Infants', *Cognition* 74 (2000), 1–11.

Xu, F., Carey, S., and Welch, J., 'Infants' Ability to Use Object Kind Information for Object Individuation', *Cognition* 70 (1999), 137–166.

Xu, F., Spelke, E. S., and Goddard, S., 'Number Sense in Human Infants', *Developmental Science* 8 (2005), 88–101.

Yantis, S., 'Objects, Attention, and Perceptual Experience', in R. Wright (ed.), *Visual Attention* (Oxford: Oxford University Press, 1998).

Yonas, A., Arterbery, M. E., and Granrud, C. E., 'Four-Month-Old Infants' Sensitivity to Binocular and Kinetic Information for Three-Dimensional-Object Shape', *Child Development* 58 (1987), 910–917.

Yonas, A., Granrud, C. E., Chov, M. H., and Alexander, A. J., 'Picture Perception in Infants: Do 9-Month-Olds Attempt to Grasp Objects Depicted in Photographs?', *Infancy* 8 (2005), 147–166.

Yost, William A., 'Auditory Localization and Scene Perception', in E. Bruce Goldstein (ed.), *Blackwell Handbook of Perception* (Oxford: Blackwell, 2001).

Zemach, I. K., and Rudd, M. E., 'Effects of Surround Articulation on Lightness Depend on the Spatial Arrangement of the Articulated Region', *Journal of the Optical Society of America* A/24 (2007), 1830–1841.

Zill, S., and Seyfarth, E. A., 'Exoskeletal Sensors for Walking', *Scientific American* 275 (1996), 70–74.

Author Index

Adelson, E. H. 351n
Adler, J. 329n
Agostini, T. 351n
Aguiar, A. 247n, 461n
Alexander, A. J. 454n
Alt, W. 505n
Annan, V. 351, 408n
Aristotle 289, 482, 548
Arterberry, M. E. 458n, 463n
Astington, J. W. 268n
Austin, G. 140n
Austin, J. L. 117n, 137n, 138n
Ayer, A. J. 16, 111, 120, 126, 137n,
   138n, 234

Baillargeon, R. 228n, 247n, 248n, 252n,
   253n, 263n, 264n, 448n, 458n, 461n,
   462n, 465n, 469n
Banks, M. S. 349n, 361n, 440n, 442n
Barner, D. 484n
Barnes, W. J. P. 504n
Baron, J. 510n
Barth, H. 475n
Basile, B. M. 462n
Behaene-Lambertz, G. 375n
Bennett, S. C. 453n
Berger, S. 206n
Berkeley, G. 16, 111–112, 118, 120,
   121n, 154, 347n
Berthold, P. 420n, 500n, 505n
Bertoncini, J. 484n
Berzhanskaya, J. 443n
Bianchi, A. xix, 206n
Bidwell, N. J. 503n
Bijeljac-Babic, R. 484n
Bingman, V. P. 425n
Birch, E. 496n

Biro, D. 492n
Bischof, N. 414n
Block, N. xviii, 188n, 190n,
   375n, 376n
Block, E. 375n
Bloom, P. 249n
Bod-Bovy, G. 464n
Boles, L. C. 505n
Bonato, F. 351n
Bonjour, L. 434n
Boothe, R. G. 496n
Boring, E. G. 115n
Born, W. S. 464n
Borton, R. W. 248n
Bouyer, G. 442n
Bower, T. G. R. 228n
Brainard, D. H. 351n
Braithwaite, V. A. 202n, 420n, 425n
Brandom, R. 210n
Brandt, R. 206n, 510n
Brannon, E. M. 473n, 474n, 475n,
   484n, 491n
Bratman, M. xix, 370n
Brelinger, K. 256n, 263n
Bresciani, J.-P. 441n, 442n
Broad, C. D. 15n, 16, 21, 125–126, 234
Broadbent, H. A. 473n, 479, 480n
Brockmann, A. 503n
Brown, A. M. 496n
Brownell, P. H. 209n, 414n, 421n
Bruce, V. 93n, 100n
Brueckner, T. xix, 173n
Bruner, J. 140n
Brunke, S. 206n
Brunswik, E. 359–360, 367, 408n
Brunt, W. A. 351n
Buckhout, R. 113n

Bühler, K. 408n
Bull, W. 452n, 484n
Bülthoff, H. H. 440n, 442n, 443n
Burge, T. xviii–xix, 15n, 22n, 33n, 50n,
   51n, 62n, 63n, 66n, 70n, 72n, 73n, 75n,
   79n, 80n, 82n, 84n, 99n, 140n, 141, 145n,
   146n, 148n, 174n, 176n, 180n, 188n,
   190n, 212n, 224n, 231n, 251n, 256n,
   270n, 272n, 273n, 278n, 280n, 309n,
   311n, 312n, 316n, 359n, 362n, 364n,
   381n, 385n, 391n, 394n, 401n, 404n,
   409n, 411n, 434n, 472n, 506n, 512n,
   513n, 533n, 539n, 540n, 544n, 545n
Burge, J. xviii–xix, 361n, 450, 457n
Burkell, J. A. 463n
Burns, J. E. 503n
Burr, D. 475n
Byrne, R. 279n

Call, J. 268n, 279n
Campan, R. 329n
Campbell, J. 188n, 209n, 259n, 364n
Cane, S. D. 505n
Cantlon, J. F. 474n
Carey, S. xviii, 170n, 235n, 236n, 248n,
   249n, 252n, 347n, 451n, 452n, 454n,
   461n, 462n, 480n, 484n, 485n, 486n,
   489n, 491n, 492n
Carlile, M. J. 329n
Carnap, R. 16, 111, 116, 118,
   120–123, 126, 130–131, 135–136,
   138n, 264, 285
Carr, J. A. R. 518n
Carrasco, M. 365n
Carthy, J. D. 306n
Cassirer, E. 18, 133–136, 264, 409n
Cassirer, H. W. 154n, 155n
Cataliotti, J. 351n
Cattet, J. S. 499n
Cavanagh, P. 451n, 479n
Changeux, J. P. 479
Cheng, K. 500n, 501n, 502n, 510n
Cheries, E. W. 451n, 454n
Chiang, W.-C. 461n
Chittka, L. 504n
Chomsky, N. xviii, 82n, 90n, 141n,
   213n, 492n
Chov, M. H. 454n

Chu, F. 464n
Chun, M. M. 376n
Church, A. 138n
Church, R. M. 473n, 478n, 479, 480n,
   486n, 520n, 525n
Clayton, A. M. 441n
Clayton, N. S. 252n, 259n
Collett, M. 501n, 507n
Collett, T. S. 209n, 419n, 501n,
   507n, 510n
Cooper, R. 474n
Cordes, S. 491n
Cramer, A. E. 510n
Craton, L. G. 461n, 463n
Cummings, R. 320n

D'Esposito, M. 375n
d'Souza, C. 442n
Dacke, M. 503n
Danckert, J. 374n
Davidson, D. 18, 20–21, 28, 33, 105–106,
   129, 134, 140n, 148, 150–151, 153,
   210–211, 213n, 217, 224n, 225n, 232n,
   264–282, 285–286, 322, 327n, 329n,
   370n, 430n, 434n, 544–545, 548
Davis, H. 473n
Dehaene, S. 375n, 473n, 475n, 479, 480n,
   484n, 492n
Dehart, C. 462n
Deloache, J. S. 454n
Dennett, D. C. 293n
Descartes, R. 17, 73n, 74n, 80n, 132n
   347n, 431, 520n, 523n
DeVos, J. 263n, 264n
Dickinson, A. 252n, 259n
Donnellan, K. 141, 145–146, 148–149,
   173n, 196n, 239
Dore, F. Y. 462n
Dretske, F. 184n, 296n, 299, 300n,
   304–307, 316n, 322, 466n, 538n
Drewing, K. 442n
Dummett, M. 18, 148, 210n
Duncan, L. M. J. 167n, 504n
Dyer, F. C. 202n, 510n

Economou, E. 351n
Emery, N. J. 252n, 259n
Erb, M. 443n

Ernst, M. O. 440n, 442n, 443n
Esch, H. E. 503n
Etienne, A. S. 499n, 500n, 501n, 510n
Euclid 482
Evans, G. xix, 18, 28, 103, 106, 147n, 153–154, 160, 176, 181–209, 216–223, 230, 234, 254–255, 263, 268, 275, 287, 304n, 369n, 382n, 428, 430n, 432, 468n, 538n
Everett, D. L. 492n

Farah, M. J. 375n
Farner, D. S. 520n
Faugeras, O. 442n
Faulkner, W. 291
Fay, R. R. 415n
Feigenson, L. 451n, 481n, 484n, 485n
Fillipi, L. 501n
Firzlaff, U. 443n
Fitch, W. T. 492n
Flombaum, J. I. 474n
Fodor, J. A. xviii, 39n, 95n, 101n, 249n, 282n, 296n, 300n, 307, 322
Foelix, R. F. 419n
Foley, R. 224n
Foran, S. 337n
Ford, N. B. 426n
Foster, D. H. 443n
Fowlkes, C. C. 360n, 361n
Fraenkel, G. S. 328n, 329n, 330n, 422n
Frankfurt, H. G. 335n
Frege, G. 18, 115–118, 121–122, 132–135, 138, 140, 145n, 146n, 151–152, 235, 385n, 472n
French, J. W. V. 306n
Friedman, M. 121n
Frisch, K. v. 500n
Funk, F. A. 209n, 263n, 264n, 420n, 448n

Gagnon, S. 462n
Galanter, E. 140n
Gallistel, C. R. xviii, 206n, 209n, 263n, 264n, 296n, 305n, 330n, 414n, 473n, 475n, 478n, 480n, 487n, 489n, 490n, 492n, 494–495, 499n, 509n, 510n, 520n, 531n
Gallogly, D. P. 360n
Garcia, P. 473n

Gazzaniga, M. S. 375n
Geisler, W. W. 99n, 360n
Gelman, R. 464n, 475n, 478n, 486n, 487n, 492n
Gentaz, E. 464n
Gerbino, W. 360n
Gibbon, J. 473n, 531n
Gibbs, B. J. 451n
Gibson, J. L. 91n, 101n, 130n, 438n
Gilchrist, A. L. 351n, 408n, 497n
Gilson, S. J. 443n
Giurfa, M. 517n
Gleitman, H. 457n, 460n
Goddard, S. 474n
Godfrey-Smith, P. 300n, 316n, 320n
Goodale, M. A. 188n, 337n
Goodman, N. 111, 122n, 538n
Goodnow, J. 140n
Gopnik, A. 268n
Gordon, P. 492n
Gottlieb, A. 454n
Gould, J. L. 509n
Grah, G. 500n
Graham, P. xviii
Grande, L. 375n
Granrud, C. E. 454n, 458n, 496n
Green, P. 92n, 100n
Greggers, U. 206n
Grice, P. 298
Griffiths, D. P. 252n, 259n
Griffiths, P. E. 320n
Grodd, W. 443n
Grossberg, S. 443n
Grunwald, J. E. 443n
Gumbert, A. 510n
Gunn, D. L. 328n, 329n, 330n, 422n
Guntrukun, O. 420n, 452n, 462n

Haggard, P. 414n
Hariyama, T. 501n
Harland, D. P. 515n
Harman, G. 434n
Hartl, M. 268n
Hasler, A. D. 425n
Haugeland, J. 538n
Hauser, M. 209n, 263n, 264n, 279n, 420n, 448n, 452n, 458n, 473n, 474n, 484n, 492n
He, S. 451n

He, Z. J. 462n, 463n
Healy, S. 202n
Heffner, H. E. 318n, 422n
Heffner, R. S. 318n, 422n
Heidegger, M. 131–133
Helbig, H. B. 442n
Held, R. M. 447n
Helmholtz, H.v. 91n, 92–93, 408n, 460
Hempel, C. 140
Hensel, H. 416n
Henson, O. W. 420n
Hering, E. 408n
Herman, L. M. 443n
Hespos, S. 465n
Heywood, C. A. 374n, 470n
Hillis, J. M. 349n, 442n
Hironaka, M. 501n
Hodgeson, Z. 202n
Hoffmann-Kuhnt, M. 443n
Hofsten, C.v. 99n, 253n, 274n, 346n,
    457n, 462n, 465n
Hogrefe, G.-J. 268n
Hölldobler, B. 423n
Hopfield, J. J. 415n
Horiguchi, H. 501n
Horridge, G. A. 419n, 508n
Houten, J. v. 329n, 330n, 331n, 403n
Hrynick, T. 457n
Huntley-Fenner, G. 170n, 235n, 461n
Husserl, E. 16, 121n, 130–133

Ingle, D. 323n, 337n, 420n
Intriligator, J. 451n, 479n
Izard, V. 475n, 492n

Jackson, R. R. 209n, 419n, 462n,
    515n, 516n
Jacobsen, P. 414n, 465n
Jacobson, K. 263n, 456n
James, H. 1
James, W. 8, 16, 112–113, 116, 214n
Jayaraman, V. 415n
Jeannerod, M. 324n, 527n
Jeffery, K. J. 500n, 501n
Jennings, H. S. 306n, 318n, 329n, 330n,
    336n, 373n, 422n
Jevons, W. S. 483n
Johnsen, P. B. 425n

Johnson, D. M. 473n
Johnston, R. E. 423n
Judd, S. P. D. 507n
Junge, J. 474n

Kahneman, D. 451n
Kamitani, Y. 442n
Kamiya, J. 359n
Kanade, T. 442n
Kanizsa, G. 360n, 417–418, 457n
Kanwisher, N. 442n, 475n, 476n
Katz, D. 408n, 414n
Kaufman, E. L. 485n
Kellman, P. J. 98n, 247n, 443n,
    460n, 461n
Kenshalo, D. R. 318n, 422n
Kentridge, R. W. 374n, 470n
Kersten, D. 442n, 443n
Kestenbaum, R. 247n, 457n, 461n, 463n
Kheddar, A. 442n
Kirkham, N. 451n
Klatsky, R. L. 414n, 443n
Klein, A. 473n, 484n
Klump, G. M. 420n, 428n
Knaden, M. 501n
Knierim, J. J. 501n
Knill, D. C. 355n, 359n
Knudsen, E. I. 428n
Koch, C. 372n
Koechlin, E. 375n, 484n
Koffka, K. 114n, 408n
Köhler, W. 114, 408n
Kolterman, R. 520n
Komishke, B. 510n
Kossyfidis, C. 351n
Kourtzi, Z. 342n, 343n
Kraft, J. M. 351n
Kral, K. 419n, 458n
Kralik, J. D. 458n
Kripke, S. 18, 128–129, 141, 145–146,
    148–149, 173n, 180, 196n, 239,
    282n, 301n
Kudrimoti, H. S. 501n
Kunze, J. 510n

LaMont, K. 475n
Land, E. H. 351n
Land, M. F. 263n, 422n

Landy, M. S. 442n
Lappe, C. 1
Laurence, S. 491n
Laurent, G. 415n
Lawlor, K. xix
Lawrence, G. xix
Layne, J. E. 504n
Le Clec'H, G. 375n
Le Bihan, D. 375n
Lederman, S. J. 414n, 443n
Ledoux, J. E. 375n
Lehrer, M. 419n, 508n
Lemer, C. 475n
Leslie, A. M. 454n, 486n, 537n
Lewis, C. I. 16, 111, 120, 126–127
Lewis, D. 282n, 382n
Li, D. 515n
Li, F. F. 372n
Li, X. 351n
Lianekhammy, J. 441n
Ling, S. 365n
Lipton, J. S. 474n, 475n
Logothetis, N. K. 442n, 443n
Logvinenko, A. D. 351n
Lohmann, K. J. 505n
Loosbroek, E. 484n
Lord, M. W. 485n
Lorenz, K. 336n
Luck, S. J. 375n, 452n
Lutz, D. 491n

Maaswinkel, H. 501n
MacNeilage, P. 484n
Macomber, J. 263n, 456n, 465n
Mainen, Z. F. 415n
Malik, J. 360n
Maloney, L. T. 351n
Mamassian, P. 443n
Mansuripur, M. 529n
Margolis, E. 491n
Marois, R. 376n
Marr, D. xvii–xviii, 93, 99n, 348n, 449
Martin, D. R. 360n
Marvel, A. 532
Matsuzawa, T. 248n, 492n
Maury, V. 442n
Mazokhin-Porshnyakov, G. A. 419n
McAndrews, M. P. 375n

McCann, J. J. 351n
McCarthy, G. 375n
McCrink, K. 475n
McDowell, J. 149n, 183n, 184n, 189n,
    195n, 208n, 369n, 434n
McGinn, C. xix
McGlinchey-Berroth, R. 375n
McNaughton, B. L. 501n
Meck, W. H. 473n, 478n, 486n, 525n
Mehler, J. 484n
Melcher, D. 445n
Meltzoff, A. N. 447n, 448n
Menzel, C. 252n
Menzel, R. 206n, 419n, 510n, 517n
Merkle, T. 505n
Merleau-Ponty, M. 16, 132–133
Metzger, V. A. 414n
Milberg, W. P. 375n
Miller, G. A. 113n, 140n
Millikan, R. G. 294n, 300, 301n,
    302n, 331n
Milner, A. D. 188n, 337n
Mingolla, E. 443n
Miracle, J. A. 498n
Mitchell, P. 268n
Möhl, B. 318n
Moore, G. E. 8, 16, 21, 123–124, 126n, 127n
Moore, M. K. 247n
Moortele, P.-F. v.d. 375n
Morris, J. P. 375n
Morronel, M. C. 445n
Moscovitch, M. 375n
Mueller, M. 375n
Mundy, J. L. 442n
Myowa-Yamakoshi, M. 248n

Nabokov, V. 437
Naccache, L. 375n
Nagel, T. 50, 51n, 190n, 548
Nakayama, K. 462n, 463n
Needham, A. 458n, 462n
Neiworth, J. J. 462n
Neumeyer, C. 419n, 420n
Newell, A. 141n
Newell, F. 443n
Nilsson, D.-E. 422n
Nishizaki, M. 442n
Nomakuchi, S. 501n

Norman, H. F. 441n
Norman, J. F. 441n

O'Dell, C. 496n
O'Shaughnessy, B. 327n
Oakes, L. 452n
Olshausen, B. A. 360n
Oucet, E. S. B. 420n

Pack, A. A. 443n
Palmer, S. E. 91n, 92n, 100n, 274n, 348n, 351n, 355n, 417n
Papineau, D. 301n
Pauls, J. 442n
Peacocke, C. xviii, 184n, 187n, 200n, 209n, 296n, 382n, 404n, 406n, 468n, 469n, 538n, 539n
Pelphrey, K. A. 375n
Pepperberg, I. M. 209n, 263n, 264n, 420n, 448n, 462n
Perner, J. 268n
Perona, P. 372n
Perry, J. S. 360n
Perusse, R. 473n
Peterson, M. A. 263n, 458n
Petrig, B. 496n
Pettersen, L. 496n
Piaget, J. 8, 113–114, 154, 253n, 264, 460n
Pica, P. 475n, 492n
Pierroutsakos, S. L. 454n
Pinker, S. 309n
Pizlo, Z. 442n
Platt, J. R. 473n
Plug, C. 408n
Poggio, T. 442n
Pollok, B. 420n, 452n, 462n
Popper, A. N. 415n, 420n
Povanelli, D. 268n, 279n
Premack, D. 473n
Prevor, M. 462n, 485n
Pribram, K. 141n
Price, H. H. 16, 125–126, 234
Prior, H. 420n, 452n, 462n
Putnam, H. 64n, 65n, 77n, 79n, 82n, 141, 146, 148, 282n
Pylyshyn, Z. W. 101n, 343n, 451n, 453n, 455n, 456n, 461n, 463n, 485n

Quine, W. V. 8, 18, 20n, 21, 28, 69n, 105n, 112n, 113, 116, 128, 129n, 133–135, 137n, 138, 140, 142, 148, 150–151, 153, 164n, 165, 210–266, 272, 275–276, 282–283, 286, 296n, 319, 322, 370n, 382n, 430n, 434n, 437, 456n, 462, 471, 544, 545n, 548

Radalescu, A. xix, 186n
Rameix, E. 464n
Rasmussen, H. 504n
Rawson, N. E. 423n
Read, S. 365n
Reese, T. W. 485n
Regolin, L. 209n, 263n, 264n, 420n, 448n, 452n, 466n
Rensink, R. A. 451n, 453n
Richardson, D. C. 451n
Rock, I. 351n
Ronacher, B. 500n
Rorty, R. 434n
Rosengren, K. S. 454n
Ross, J. 475n
Ross, H. E. 408n
Ross-Sheehy, S. 452n
Rossetti, Y. 374n
Rost, M. 505n
Rozemond, M. 193n
Rudd, M. E. 351n, 497n
Russell, B. 8, 15–16, 18, 21, 43n, 105n, 111, 115–116, 118–126, 131, 138n, 144–146, 192, 234, 264, 284

Sabin, M. 442n
Salimando, A. 170n, 231n, 461n
Schacter, D. L. 375n
Schnitzler, H.-U. 420n
Scholl, B. J. 451n, 454n, 461n, 463n, 486n
Schubert, F. 1
Schuchmann, M. 443n
Schuller, G. 443n
Schwab, R. 515n
Schwartz, B. L. 252n
Searle, J. 141, 146
Sellars, W. 18, 21, 137n, 138–139, 140n, 151n, 430n, 433–435
Seyfarth, E. A. 500n
Shakespeare, W. 109

Shams, L. 442n
Shannon, C. E. 529n
Shapiro, K. L. 375n
Shaw, J. C. 141n
Shepard, R. N. 98n, 99n, 100n
Shiffrar, M. 445n
Shimojo, S. 442n, 462n, 463n
Si, A. 503n
Sigala, N. 443n
Simmons, J. A. 415n
Simon, H. A. 141n
Simoncelli, E. P. 360n
Simons, D. J. 247n, 461n, 463n
Smith, A. 206n
Smith, A. D. 409n
Smitsman, A. W. 484n
Soja, N. 235n, 249n
Son, L. K. 473n
Spaethe, J. 503n
Spehar, B. 351n
Speigle, J. M. 351n
Spelke, E. S. 98n, 99n, 170n, 228n, 235n,
   247n, 248n, 249n, 252n, 253n, 263n,
   264n, 438–454, 456n, 457n, 460n, 461n,
   462n, 463n, 464n, 465n, 469n, 473n,
   474n, 475n, 479n, 484n
Sperling, G. 141n
Spetch, M. L. 501n, 502n
Srinivasan, M. V. 419n, 499n, 503n
Stalnaker, R. 65n
Starkey, P. 464n, 473n, 474n, 484n, 486n
Steely, F. 462n
Steinberg, I. xix
Stein, H. 482n
Steinmark, E. 462n
Stevenson, A. K. 442n
Stimson Wilcox, R. 209n, 419n
Stopfer, M. 415n
Storm, R. W. 451n
Strawson, G. 70n
Strawson, P. F. xix, 8, 18, 20n, 21, 28, 106,
   133, 134n, 135, 137n, 138, 140n, 141,
   142n, 144–146, 149–151, 153–183, 186,
   187n, 191–192, 194, 197–198, 201,
   205–206, 208–210, 217, 227, 231,
   234, 236n, 239–240, 251, 254, 255n,
   263–266, 268, 275, 281–283, 285–287,
   382n, 428–431, 437, 456, 471, 544, 548

Streri, A. 464n
Super, B. J. 360n
Sutherland, D. 482n

Tanaka, M. 248n
Tanifuji, M. 442n
Tarsitano, M. S. 516n
Tautz, J. 503n
Taylor-Clarke, M. 414n
Termine, N. 457n
Terrace, H. S. 473n, 484n
Thinus-Blanc, C. 420n
Thompson, J. D. 504n
Thomson, J. J. 338n
Thorpe, W. H. 306n, 307n, 373n
Thouless, R. H. 408n
Tinbergen, N. 318n, 330n, 335n, 422n
Tjan, B. S. 443n
Todd, J. T. 442n
Tomasello, M. 268n, 279n
Tomonaga, M. 248
Treisman, A. 167n, 451n, 470n
Tremoulet, P. 454n, 486n
Trick, L. M. 485n
Tsao, F. 473n
Tsunoda, K. 442n

Uexküll, J. V. 373n
Uller, C. 452n, 484n
Ullman, S. 343n, 451n, 485n
Uttal, D. H. 454n

Vallortigara, G. 209n, 263n, 264n, 420,
   448n, 452n, 461n, 462n
Van de Walle, G. 462n, 463n,
   464n, 485n
VanRullen, R. 372n
Verfaellie, M. 375n
Vickers, N. J. 424n
Vishton, P. 99n
Vogel, E. K. 375n, 452n
Volkman, J. 485n
Volpe, B. T. 375n

Walker, M. M. 505n
Wallach, H. 351n, 497n
Wang, J. H. 505n
Ware, M. 484n

Wasserman, S. 228n, 248n, 252n, 253n, 462n, 465n, 469n
Wehner, R. 209n, 419n, 499n, 500n, 501n, 510n
Wehner, S. 499n
Wein, D. 247n, 461n, 463n
Weiskrantz, L. 374n, 470n
Weissburg, M. J. 408n
Welch, J. 462n
Wellman, H. M. 268n
Wexler, M. 447n
Whalen, J. 475n
Whishaw, I. Q. 501n
Whitman, C. O. 291
Wiegrebe, L. 443n
Wiggins, D. 209n, 456n
Wilcox, R. S. 209n, 419n, 462n, 516n
Wilkie, D. M. 518n
Williams, N. M. 504n
Wilson, E. O. 423n
Wilson, R. I. 415n
Wiltschko, R. 263n, 420n
Wiltschko, W. 263n, 420n
Wimmer, H. 268n
Wisby, W. J. 425n
Wittgenstein, L. 18, 20–21, 118, 123n, 127–129, 137n, 138, 140–141, 146–147, 151, 180, 208, 210, 213, 282n, 508
Wohlgemuth, S. 500n

Wolfe, J. M. 453n
Wonders, R. 462n
Wood, J. 474n, 479n, 484n
Woodman, G. F. 452n
Woodruff, G. 473n
Woolley, J. D. 268n
Wright, L. 320n
Wundt, W. 8, 112–114, 116, 264
Wusthoff, C. 473n
Wynn, K. 247n, 454n, 461n, 475n, 484n, 487n, 491n

Xu, F. 454n, 461n, 462n, 474n, 486n

Yamane, Y. 442n
Yantis, S. 451n, 461n
Yi, D.-J. 376n
Yonas, A. 454n, 458n, 461n, 463n, 496n
Yost, W. A. 415n
Yuille, A. 443n

Zanforlin, M. 209, 263n, 264n, 420n, 448n, 452n, 462n
Zeil, J. 507n
Zemach, I. K. 351n, 497n
Zhang, S. W. 419n, 503n, 508n
Zielke, G. 441n
Zill, S. 500n

Subject Index

I conceive the index as a fine-grained research tool. Thus there are often more page citations per entry than in most indexes. Italicized numerical entries indicate elementary or basic explications, or fundamental substantive discussions, usually for technical terms. So readers who wish to use the index as a glossary or as a way of looking up *basic* points can focus on the italicized entries.

ability general representational content *242*, 266, 379–380, *394*, 539, 543; *see also* concept; context-bound representational content; kind, attributional
ability particularity, *see* context-bound representational content
abnormality 98, 299, 346, 348, 350, 364, 377, 387
aboutness 43–44; *see also* indication; intentionality; reference; representational content; representational relation
absence, perception of 540
abstract entities 32, 42, 46, 64, 117, 221, 260, 324, 379
abstraction 37–39, 53–54, 96, 166, 170–171, 205, 207, 364, 417, 425, 439, 525–526
abstraction, levels of in representation 41, 55, 104, 381, 440, 443–444, 464–465, 540
access to consciousness or reflection 94–97, 112, 119–120, 126–127, 131–133, 155, 179, 188–190, 207, 346, 369, 375–376, 403, 490
accuracy (correctness) ix, 5–6, *9*, *12*, 27, 30, 38–39, *46*, *49*, 52, 54, 59, 74, *80*, 82, 88–90, *91–92*, *99*, 156, 175–176, 184–187, 226, 241, 286, 298, *300–304*, 308–311, *313*, 317–318, 339, 342, 345, 350, 355, 357–358, 361, 365, 379–381, 395, 397, 400–401, *403*, 410–411, 480, 503, 506, 535; *see also* objectivity, as veridicality
action, *see* agency
action attributive 324
actional representation, or actional state *74–75*, 81, 101, 206, 248, 258, 280, 309, 337, *339–341*, 378, 424, 468, *511–514*, 517, 521–522, 525–527
actional system 101, 258, 280, 323, 337, 340, 343, 424, 514, 517, 522, 525; *see also* anticipatory representation
addition 247, 475, 477, 482–484, 487–489, 492
agency (action) 39, 75, 199, 201, 287–288, 311–313, 315, 326–341, 368–370, 372–376, 378, 427, 525–527, 547–548, 550; *see also* intention; orientation; self-locomotion; whole-organism coordination
agency, group 331–333
agency, objective 337–341, 548; *see also* agency, representational
agency, and perception 40, *70*, 102, 152, 262, 310, 315, *320–321*, 326–327, 337–341, 370–373, 376, 521–523, 536, 548; *see also* goal, as *representatum*; guidance, of action by perception

agency, primitive (pre-representational) 292, 315, 321–322, 324–341, *331–334*, 370, 376–377, 547; *see also* control, in agency and perception; whole-organism, coordination

agency, psychological 337–341

aggregate *472–491*

algorithm 93, 95, 97, 346

allocentric index or framework 182, *201–208*, 286, 437, 509–511, 518, 521–522, 525–526, 538

allocentric index or framework, spatial 182, 187, 201–208, 286, 437, 509–511, 518, 525, 538

allocentric index or framework, temporal 206, 521–522, 525–526

amodal completion *417–418*, *448*, 458

amoeba 3, 28, 268, 295, 303–306, 315, 317, 319, 325, 328, 330, 334, 336, 338, 372, 423, 432, 497

amphibian 104, 220

analog 305, 472, 477–484, 538

analytic philosophy, *see* mainstream philosophy

analytic/synthetic distinction 265

anatomy 319, 334

angular momentum 504

angular turning 476

animal psychology xiii–xiv, 22, 325, *367*, 371, 489–490; *see also* ethology

animism 134, 136

ant 495, 499–501

anticipation of stimulation 224, 246, 346

anticipatory representation 183, 243, 246–248, 252, 258, 267, 378, 417, 427, 445, 447–448, 459, 461, 463–470, 486–488, 519–520, 527; *see also* actional representation, or actional state

anti-individualism (general) *10–11*, *25–26*, 61–108, *61–67*, *75–82*, 127–128, 141–143, *149–150*, 208, 359–361, 386, 390, 409, 469, 514, 520, 545, 547; *see also* two-dimensionalism

anti-individualism, perceptual *25–26*, *71*, 82–108, *82*, *87*, *98–101*, 203, 208–210, 212, 260–261, 273, 276, 284, 310, 319, 322, 358–361, 386, 390, 407, 409, 438, 453, 466, 468–469, 520, 528, 536, 547

ape 7, 23, 114, 209, 252, 264, 268, 279, 281, 462, 473, 491, 496, 538

appearance 14–19, 21–24, 56, 103, 106, 111, 285, 403, 409

appearance/reality distinction (seems/is distinction) 11, 19, 28, 105, 151, 158, 162, 208, 277–278, 281, 285–286, 437, 538, 549; *see also* Individual Representationalism, second family; looks; perspective; subjective representation

application, actional 262, 514

application, attributional (or functional) 31–32, 35, 106, 128–129, 142, 145, 167, 180–181, 192, 197, 209, 218–220, 231, 245, 265–266, 281–282, 293, 323, 338, 381, 525, 546

application, singular *83–84*, 167, 197, 201, 512–513, 521–524, *538–546*; *see also* memory, singular elements

   in thought 42, 72, 201, 538–546

   in perception 45, 72, 83, 231, *362*, 364, *381–386*, *390–394*, 399, 412, 449–455, 496, 513, 522–524, *538–546*

in memory (perceptual or propositional) 412, 541
apprehension 15–16, 21, 105, 111–112, 121–124, 243–246
approximate veridicality 53, 87–88, 94, 98, 310, 345, 380, 480, 535
apriori claims (some made, some rejected) 5, 69–70, 74, 101, 190, 203, 207, 273, 279,
     310–313, 338–339, 360, 369, 376–377, 380–381, 406, 415, 456, 523, 528–529,
     532–537; *see also* arm-chair argument or claim, reflection, apriori
apriority 5, *18, 59,* 435; *see also* rationalism; reason; reflection, apriori
arm-chair argument or claim *59,* 98, 189–190, 206–207, 209, 265, 269, 283, 434–435
arthropod 206, 209, 375, *397,* 419, 496, 504–505, 507–508, 510, 514–528, 520,
     525, 548
artifact 47, 293–294, 304, 308–309, 317, 321–323, 339
assent 213, 215–233, 239
association (as an empiricist explanatory kind) 68, 116, 130, 215, 223, 306–307, 529–531
associative learning, *see* learning, associative
atomism (about representation) 114, 139
attention 15, 102, 287, 322, *337*–338, 365, *372, 374,* 451–454, 458, 463, *470*
attention, direction of (as a psychological act) 337–338, 372
attribute (noun) 35, *37, 41, 44–45,* 49, 53–54, *55–56,* 68, *73, 76, 78–79, 84,* 98, 101, 188,
     212, 231, 235, 242, 245, *256,* 260, 269–270, 274, 281, 283, 295, *308, 365–366,* 381,
     385–387, 391–392, *398*–399, *408–409, 412*–413, 425, 438, 444–448, 452, 465–483,
     485, 489–491, 497, *532–533*; *see also* functional attribute; kind; nature; property;
     relation; universal
attribution 3, 7, 9, 13, 17, *24–25, 30–36,* 41, 44–45, 52, 54, 68, *76,* 84, 87, 93, 100–101,
     104, 131, 152, 168, *170,* 178, 183, 188–189, 196, 204, 212–213, 215, 217, 231, 235,
     240, *242,* 251–252, 260, 262, 266, *295–296, 305, 308,* 323, 325, 344, *364–366,*
     368–369, *379–381, 383*–384, 386–394, *386–391,* 401, 412, *432,* 437–438, 444–445,
     449–451, 454–472, 476–477, 480, 496, 510–512, 515, 522–524, 530–531, *539–547,*
     550; *see also* categorization; conceptual attributive; general elements in perception;
     grouping; guidance, of singular application by attribution; indication; perceptual
     attributive; reference; semantic determination; specification
attribution, pure 539, *541*–547, 550; *see also* inference (propositional), propositional
     structure (propositional form)
attributional psychological kind, *see* kind, attributional
attributive, action, *see* action attributive
attributive, conceptual, *see* conceptual attributive
attributive, functional, *see* functional attributive
attributive, perceptual, *see* perceptual attributive
attributive guidance, *see* guidance, of singular application by attribution
autonomy of objective representation 128, 151–152

backsides, of bodies 98, 243–244, 246, 448–449
bacterium 9, 46–47, 269, 295, 300, 315, 325, 329, 331, 493–495
balance 421, 476
barn owl 427–429
bat 415, 420, 427
beaconing (homing) 258, 415, 420, 423–426, 450, 493, *495, 498–507,* 509–510, 512, 517,
     519, 537; *see also* path integration

bee xiii, 102, 188, 190, 202, 305, 331, 375–376, 419, 434, 500, 503, 508, 510, 517–522, 548

behavior xiii, 81, 83, 127–128, 189, 212, 217, 219–220, 276, 282, 302, 305, 329–339, *331–334*, 377, 409, 424–426, 509–511, 526–527, 529; *see also* agency; agency, primitive; function, individual; *schreck* reactions

behaviorism xiv, 8, 21, 76, 113–116, *140–143*, 149, 227–229, 265, 296, 305–308, 493, 529; *see also* functionalism

belief xv, 3–4, 19–20, 24–28, *38–45*, 47, 49, 59, *62*, *67*–68, 71, *73–75*, 81, 101–102, 107, 118, 127, 151–152, 163, 176, 192, 207, 225, 239, 265–283, 285, 293, 301, 303, 305, *309*, *312–315*, 327, 339, 343, 378, 390, 403, 416, 421, 432–435, 524, 534–538

belief, concept of 266–268, 283, 298, 309

belief, empirical xvii, 72, 127, 145, 205, 264–266, 278, 433, 435, 546

belief, perceptual 3, 7, 16–18, 20, 23, *25*–26, 56, 121, 127, 144, 151–*152*, 161–162, 173, 178–179, 183–184, 191–202, 225, 235, 271, 275, 277–283, 312, 315, 364, 433–435, 534, *538*, *543–546*; *see also* perceptual belief, basic

beliefs, general 265, 544, 547

biasing principle, *see* formation principle

binding 167, 470

binocular disparity *see* disparity, binocular

biological fitness, *see* fitness, biological

biological function, *see* function, biological

biological kind 85, 261, 302, 438, 470, 494, 548

biological notions, reduction to 63, 291, 293–326

biological sciences or explanations xiii, 28, 211, 213, 215, 233, 256, 261–262, 273, 275–276, 292, 299–300, 326–327, 347, 407, 438, 466, 470; *see also* ethology; evolution; zoology

biologically basic activities or needs 24, 101, 197–198, 212–213, 215, 246, 256, 261–262, 273, 275–276, 292, 299–300, 326–327, 347, 407, 438, 466, 470; *see also* agency; function, biological; function, individual

bird xiii, 7, 24, 47, 102, 169, 189, 209, 252, 264, 330, 336–337, 351, 420, 434, 460, 484–485, 493, 500, 502, 504, 515, 519, 548

blindness, Kant's notion of 154–156

blindsight 188–189, 374–375

body, as *representatum* 3, 15–16, 19–20, 23, 25–26, 47–48, 52, 89, 101, 120, 123–127, 150–151, 157–181, 195–201, 212–223, 227–229, 232–286, 322–326, 387, 394, *407*, 429, 431, 437–471, *463–464*, 476–479, 483–486, 496, 518, 526, *536*, 538, 541, 549–550; *see also* boundedness; boundedness principle; cohesion; generic shape; perceptual constancy, object constancy; object permanence; occlusion; spatial representation; solidity; surfaces, perception of; temporal representation; tracking

body, at rest 444–447, 458–459, 464, 468, 470

body, in motion 71, 235, 250, 260–263, 444–445, 447, 456, 459–460, 463–*464*, 468–470

body identification or individuation 57, 154–199, 209, 236, 282, *463–464*; *see also* criteria for identification or individuation

body image 414, 422

body reidentification 148, 154–199, 209, *249*, *258*, *262*, 282, *459–460*; *see also* criteria for reidentification

boundedness 253, 444, 446–449, 456–458, 460, 462–465, 467–470

boundedness principle *446*–447, 460
bracketing, Husserlian 131
brain *xiii–xiv*, 93, 95, 188–190, 309, 362–363, *369*, 375, 442, 494, 497, 505;
    see also biological sciences; neural explanation
Brunswik's method 359–360; *see also* natural scene statistics
bug 324, 501, 517

Cartesian dualism 297
categorization xvii, 24, 26, 31, 55, 70, 83, 88, 104, 130–132, 149, 152–156, 249, 276,
    304, 318, 375, 379, 381, *453*, 455, 492, 537, *539*; *see also* grouping (perceptual);
    attribution
causal picture of reference 143, 147–150
causal power 125, 380, 444, 472
causal relations to environment (constitutive) xvi, 11, 24–25, 40, 59, 61–73, 76–81,
    85–87, 87–94, *99*–100, *106*, 141–142, 147, 149–150, 197, 212, 245, 256–258,
    261, 265, 269, 271–273, 283–295, 291, 321–322, 361, 363–364, *365*–366, *370*,
    385–394, 407, 411, 413, 454, 456, 464–468, 470, 514, *520*, 528, 533, 547;
    see also anti-individualism; explanation in terms of veridicality; sensory state,
    capacity, or system; perceptual system
causation xvii, 157
causation and assent 219, 225, 229–233
causation and singular linguistic reference 143, 147–150
causation and singular reference in memory 193
causation as *representatum* 15, 19, 113, 209, 240, 537–538
causation in information registration 9, 186, 294, 298–301, 303, 325, 337, 342, 374,
    376–378, 398, 421, 432, 495, 512, 514, 519–520, 522, 532
causation in perceptual reference 5–6, 15, 19, 53–54, 83–84, 87–94, 119–120, 175,
    183–186, 256, 260, 270–276, 308, 316–318, 322–325, *342*–354, 364, 372–373,
    376–378, 380–383, *384*, 389, *392*, 407, 418, 434, 437–438, 444, 450–451, 455–456,
    497, 535, 542; *see also* property, noninstantiated
cause, as representational content 155
cause, normal 94
central behavioral capacity 331–335, 369
cephalopod 420
certainty, 15, 18, 22, 118, 123
characteristic 74–*75*, 125–126, 135, 156, 162, 203, 235, 344, 379, 442, 457;
    see also property
chemical senses 415, 423–424; *see also* taste; olfaction
chemical stimulations 329–330, 372, 415, 423–427, 495, 498
chicken 114, 169, 209, 264, 420, 460–462
circadian oscillator 519
clam 315
clarity xv, 431, 529
cnidaria 46–47
cognition 31, 34, 97, 116, 139, 197, 248, 455
cognition (Kant's *Erkenntnis*) *155*–156, 367, 523
cohesion 444, 446–448, 454, 456–458, 460–465, 468–470

cognitive psychology (as distinct from perceptual and developmental psychology) 82, 115, 495

cohesion principle *446–447*

color 48, 52, 55, 86–87

color constancy *see* perceptual constancy, color constancy

color vision 15, 24, 88, 94, 166–167, 249, 253, 261, 280, 323, 345, 369, 387–388, 390, 407, 417, 427, 452, 457, 462–464, 470, 483, 497–498, 515, 518, 528, 546

committal representational states 35, 40, *74*–75, 81, 83, 127, 131, 378, 496; *see also* actional representation, or actional state; anticipatory representation; belief; imagination; memory, perceptual; perception, as the individual's

common sense 6–8, 12, 22, 26–27, 40, 46–48, 52, 63, 65, 67, 71, 74, 88, 124–125, 131–132, 137, 162, 226, 269–270, 272, 280, 283, 294–298, 311, 414, 496, 538

Compensatory Individual Representationalism, *see* Individual Representationalism

computability 95, 97, 346, 348, 356

computational theory or principle 39, 92–97, 104, 297, *346*–349, 356, 477, 488, 511

computational transformation (or operation or process) *95*–97, 104, 346, 349, 352, 412, 414, 421, 423–425, 438, 455–456, 474, 476–479, 482, 487–490, 499–502, 504–506, 510–511, 514, 517, 524–531; *see also* non-representational processing; perceptual processing; psychological processing

communication 18, 34, 69–70, 82, 129, 138, 147, 157, 216, 223–227, 233, 269–270, 275, 282; *see also* linguistic meaning

concept xv–xvi, 5, *32*, 35–*36*, 38–44, 63, 68–71, 75–79, *104*, 106, 139, 154–156, 161–181, 183–198, *192*, *207*, 217, 266–270, 275–281, 367, 428–429, *431*, 467–468, 489, 539, *540*–*541*, 544–545; *see also* application, attributional; application, singular; attribution, pure; conceptual attributive; functional concept; individual concept; logical operation or operator; logical connective

concept, meta-representational, *see* meta-representation

concept, natural kind, *see* natural kind concept

concept, of body, *see* body, as *representatum*

concept, perceptual 170, 279, 456, 518, *545*–*546*

concept, spatial 199–208, 428–429

conceptual attributive 79, *540*–542, 545–546; *see also* application, attributional; application, singular; attribution, pure; functional attributive; logical operator or operation; perceptual attributive; sortal concept (or sortal predicate)

conceptual question 5, 57

conceptual scheme, mature adult 157–162, 177, 180, 203, 471

conceptualization of constitutive conditions 17, 161–162, 169–171, 178–180, 198–200, 203, 247, 403, 405; *see also* criteria

conceptualization of perceptions or sensations *25*, 193, 278, 416, 428–429, 490, *544*–*547*

concrete particular *54*–56, 167, 187, 212, 253, 260, *380*–381, 412, 472, 476, 482, 491; *see also* causal relations to environment (constitutive); causation in information registration; causation in perceptual reference; perceptual reference; property, non-instantiated; temporal representation

concreteness, *see* concrete particular

condition, *see* constitutive condition

configuration 384, 417, 458

confirmation procedure (verification procedure) 114, 123, 142, 150, 154, 178, 271, 432–433; *see also* Verificationism

consciousness xiii, *4*, 12, 14–15, 47, *93*, 112, *121*, 132, 154–155, 161, 188, 190, 249, 287, *305*, 347, 362, 364, 368–369, 372, *374–376*, *396*, 404, 406, 430–431, 470, 547–548; *see also* access to consciousness or reflection; apprehension; consciousness, phenomenal; experience; perception, conscious; perception, unconscious; phenomenlogy; qualitative feature; self-consciousness; sensation; unconscious psychological state

consciousness, phenomenal *121*, 144, 188, 190, 251, 254, 260, 362, 374–376, 402, 409, 412, 507; *see also* phenomenology; qualitative feature; sensation

constancy, *see* perceptual constancy

constitutive condition *xv*, 3–4, *5–6*, 12–14, 17, 19–20, 25, 30, 37, 53, 54, *57–59*, 61, *65*, 70, 72, 75, 79–80, 105, 107, 153, 156–157, 160, 171–172, 178–179, 199, 208, 242–243, 246–247, *254–255*, 257, 276–277, 281, 283–286, Part III *passim*, *378–379*, *400*, *437–439*, *526–529*, *532–533*, 534–538, *542*, 545; *see also* anti-individualism; constitutive question; environment, normal; nature; necessity

constitutive dependence 11, 56, 61, *63–64*, 86, 111, 142, 152, 203, 256, 432, 526, 543

constitutive determination 72, 327, 346, 464

constitutive explanation (or account or explication) 6, 23, 52, 63, *65–69*, 71, 81, *85–86*, 141, *403*, 524, 526, *533–534*; *see also* anti-individualism

constitutive non-representational relation (to the environment) 11, *45*, *62*, 71, 105, 283, 346, *520*, 547–548; *see also* causal relation to environment (constitutive)

constitutive necessity 6, 29, 62, 64, 66, 69–70, 72, 106, 166, 207, 248, 262, 281, 283, 287, 402, 444, 446, 450, 456–460, 465–471, 492, 497–498, 518, 523–524, 526, 528, 538, 541, 543, 547; *see also* nature

constitutive origin 6, 544, 547–548, 550

constitutive question *xv–xvi*, *5*, 57–59, 98

constitutively non-perspectival, *see* objectivity, as being constitutively non-perspectival

construction (of objectivity or reality) 105, 111–116, 119–123, 127, 130, 132–135, 138–139, 187, 409

context-bound representational content 83, 231, 364, *379*, *381*, *385–386*, 390, 393–394, *453*, 455, 538, 540–544, 546; *see also* application, singular; singular elements in perception

control, in agency and perception 334–335, 452, 527

convergence 102, *122*, 274–275, 319, 323–324, *347–350*, 351–356, 411, 415, 420, 428, 502; *see also* disparity, binocular; vergence angle; version angle

convergence, angle of, *see* vergence angle

convexity of image regions 359–363, 411, 457–458

corporations 369

correctness, *see* accuracy

coughing 332–333

counting 178, 286, 471–472, 475, 477–480, 482, 485–487, 491–492

crab 500, 504

cricket 493

criteria 16, 127–129, 134, 139, 145, 149, *150–151*, 154, 166–170, 178, 180–181, 196–197, 209, 265–268, 282–283, 286, 407, 413, 430, 544, 547

criteria for identity or individuation 144, 150–151, 157–181, 187, 191–199, 236,
    241–288; *see also* resemblance
criteria for reidentification 106, 148, 154, 163–181, 187, 209, 241–288, 437;
    see also tracking
crossmodal influence 101–102, 243, 248, 428, 439–442; *see also* habituation, crossmodal
crow 473
cue conflict 441–442
cyclopean eye 348, 350

danger, as attributive 280, 300, 324–325, 546; *see also* edible, as attributive
Dasein, Heideggerian 131
data, *see* evidence
de re capacities 506, 524
de re representation 72, *506*–507, 512, 514–515, 521–524; *see also* application, singular;
    context-bound representational content; individual concept; perceptual reference
dead reckoning, *see* path integration
deer 332
definition xv–xvi, 14, 59, 63, 140, 163, 186, 201, 215, 230, 306, 335, 360, 408, 417, 494–495
definition, real (or scientific definition) xvi, *533*
definition, scientific, *see* definition, real
deflationary notions of representation 27, 207, 292–307, *293*, *299*, 362, 396, 405, 421,
    430–431, 489–490, 493–495, 502–503, 522, 529; *see also* functioning correlation;
    information registration; reduction of the representational to the non-representational
Deflationary Tradition *293*–294, 298–299, 304, 330–331; *see also* behaviorism;
    naturalism; reduction of the representational to the non-representational
deflations, Quinean 224, 227, 229, 253, 259
depth (and distance), as *representatum* 94, 102, 347, 359–361, 363, 377, 411, 428,
    449–450, 457, 496–497, 536; *see also* perceptual constancy, depth constancy;
    perceptual constancy, distance constancy
depth constancy, *see* perceptual constancy, depth constancy
depth perception 94, 102, *347*, 359–366, *360*, 411, 428, 449–450, 457–458, 496–497;
    see also convergence; convexity of image regions; disparity, binocular; distance
    perception; echolocation; parallax estimation
Descriptivism 22, *141–143*, 148–149
determination, *see* constitutive determination; semantic determination
development, psychological 57, 72, 112–114, 135, 152–154, 162, 167, 170–171,
    211–215, 228–229, 232, 235, 239, 247, 250, 255, 263, 265, 268, 272, 280–281,
    440–441, 454, 456, 458, 464, 468, 480–481, 486, 491–492, 496, 525, 537;
    see also feature placing; pre-individuative (or proto-objective) stage
developmental origin xi, 16, 430–431; *see also* phylogenetic origin
developmental psychology xiii–xiv, xviii, 26, 107, 113–115, 228, 245, 268, 284, 438, 489,
    537; *see also* psychological development
digital 305, 477–482
direction constancy, *see* perceptual constancy, direction constancy
discrimination, epistemic 192–193, 198, 236, 250
discrimination, sensory or perceptual *9–10*, 24, 34, 56, *94*, 99, 101, 172, 179, 198,
    202–213, *215*, 231–232, *256*–257, 260–265, 268–269, *273*–277, *286*, *291*, 293–294,

300, *303*–304, 307, *315*–*318*, 320, *324*–*325*, 327, 337, *341*–366, 368, *370*–*372*, *376*–*379*, 395, *407*, 410, 416, 422, 430–436, *450*, 454–457, 466–470, 472–475, 479–485, 490, *495*, 518, 536; *see also* causation in information registration; causation in perceptual reference; non-representational processing; perceptual processing; perceptual reference; sensory registration; seeing; sensation; visual differentiation
discriminatory knowledge, *see* knowledge, discriminative
disjunction problem 212, 269–276, 319–325, *321*, 370
disjunctivism *362*–*364*, 369, *392*–*393*, 409; *see also* naive realism
disparity, binocular 361, 415, 420, 502
dissociation 375
distal condition 89–93, *94*, 142, 216, 229, 232–234, 257, 265, 269–271, 276–277, 301–302, 319, 323, 344–354, 363–364, 371, 377, 384–390, 393–395, 399–401, 429, 454–456, 506, 512; *see also* causal relations to the environment (constitutive); causation in perceptual reference; environmental patterns (laws, regularities)
distal stimulation 216, 232, 257, 269, 345–348, 350, 352, 377, 416, 427
distance constancy, *see* perceptual constancy, distance constancy
distance effect 473
distance perception 3, 41, 54, 88, 91, 102, 204, *212*, *274*, 281, *287*, 308, 319, 323–324, 347–350, 353–354, 356, *360*–361, 363, 365–366, 380, 388, 399, 409–411, 414, 419, 421, *425*, 427–429, 467, 497, 499–508, 511, 515–517; *see also* convergence; depth perception; disparity, binocular; echolocation; parallax estimation; perceptual constancy, distance constancy; touch, perception from a distance
distinctness 166, 168–169, 176–178, 181, 194, 431; *see also* criteria for identity or individuation
dividing reference, *see* reference, dividing
dog 241, 252, 258–259, 328, 460, 462, 499
dolphin 415, 420, 427
domain specificity 101–102
dragonfly 318, 422
duplication argument, Strawson's 144

early vision, *see* vision, early
earthworm 273, 275, 317, 422–423; *see also* flatworm
eating 94, 189–190, 212, 272, 292, 319–320, 325–328, 330–334, 350, 373, 438, 450, 464, 549; *see also* predating
echolocation 414–415, 443, 456–457, 467
edible, as attributive 258, 323–324
eel 335
effective procedure 95; *see also* computability, computational transformation
egocentric index or framework *187*, *199*, 286–288, *287*–*288*, 341, 349, *401*, 522, 536, 539–541, 550; *see also* allocentric index or framework
egocentric index or framework, spatial 201–207, 286, 401, 429, 509, 525
egocentric index or framework, temporal 287, 401, 522, 525–526
eliminationism 150
emotion 52, 280, *321*, 346, *526*
empirical, Quine's notion 223–227
empirical explanation in psychology 70–71, 74, 87–97, 98–108, 112, 152, 189, 270, 310, 318–319, 322, 342–366, 395–396, 400, 403–404, 413, 424, 428, 441–450, 489,

529–531, 533; *see also* explanation in terms of veridicality; formation principle; perceptual psychology

empirical knowledge 6, 11, 22, 433–436; *see also* scepticism

empirical representation xiv–xvii, *3–8*, 11–29, 52–54, 57–59, *passim*; *see also* perception, as representation

empirical science xv, 6, 26–27, 59, 82, 162, 169–170, 183–184, 190, 205–207, 234–235, 237, 247, 249, 263–264, 272, 279, 284, 296–297, 532–537, 538, 545, 547

empirical warrant *3*, 5–6, 59, 72, 433–446

empiricism 8, 15–18, 111–132, 242–248, 265, 430; *see also* rationalism

encapsulation 101–102

encoding 303, 305, 311, 315–317, 325, 342–346, 351–352, 356, 361, 395, 398, *400*, 422, 424, 494–495, 514, 520, 522; *see also* sensory registration; information registration

endogenously driven behavior 336–337

entitlement, *see* epistemic entitlement

entity *56*; *see also* subject matter

entrainment 519–520

environment, normal 66, 98–99, 256, 286, 300, 301, 364, 377, 386–387, *466*

environmental conditions, *see* distal conditions; distal stimulation; causal relations to the environment (constitutive)

environmental patterns (laws, regularities) 16, 19, 23, 49–51, 67, 70, 81–82, 92, *99–100*, 115, *197*, 261–262, 272–273, 285, 292, *346*, 356, *359–361*, 367, 455, *457–458*; *see also* causal relations to the environment (constitutive); distal condition; constitutive condition

epistemic entitlement 312, 435

epistemic warrant (epistemic basis) *3–5*, 18, 51, 59, 72, 115, 155, 176, 225, *312–315*, 362, 386, *433–436*, 513, 524, 534–537; *see also* apriority; empirical warrant; empirical knowledge; epistemic entitlement; scepticism

error 86, 92, *94*, 118, 121, 125, 127, *143*, 157, 226–228, 229, 269–270, 275, 281, *299*, *301*, 303, 307–308, *346*, 392, 401, 412, 473, 475; *see also* accuracy; truth

error, immunity to 125, 228, 391; *see also* fallibility

error theories 88

essence 17, 46, 57, 63–64, 131, 297; *see also* nature

estimating numerosity 472–483, 485, 489–491

ethology xiii–xiv, 6, 11, 26, 107, 189, 213, 268, 279–280, 284, 319, 321–322, 326–327

Euglena 318, 329, 422

eukaryote 329–330

events, as *representata* 55, 84, 157, 164–171, 173, 198, 243, 246, 262, 286–287, 323, 380, 407, 427, 429, 438, 459, 469, 481, 485, 519, 523, 538, 549; *see also* body, as *representatum*

evidence 224–227, *225*, 367; *see also* experience; perceptual object; perceptual reference; observation; sense data

evolution 6, 10–11, *69–71*, 197, 256–257, 268, *301–303*, 310, 317, *321*, 340, 350, 360, 372, 377, *407*, 413, 416, 424, 429, 444, 454, 511, *514*, 519, *548–549*; *see also* causal relations to environment (constitutive); function, biological; function, representational; phylogenetic origin

experience (sense experience) 15–16, 48, 86–87, 111–136, 145, 155–156, 158–163, 177–178, 182–183, 187–188, 228, 239–240, 243–246, 251, 285, 306, 362, 364, 412,

428, 430, 433–434, 458, 524, 526, 534; *see also* empirical representation; perception, as sensory objectification

experience, Kant's notion of 155–156

explanation, in terms of veridicality 12, *84*, *88–89*, 233, *292–308*, *316–319*, 319–326, 342–366, *347*, 368, *379–397*, 410–411, 416, 421, 424–425, 430–432, 476, 479–480, *493–495*, 502–508, 511–513, 522, *529–531*, *549*; *see also* undetermination problem

explanatory primitiveness *58*, 63; *see also* fundamental explanatory kind

explication 27, 30, *63–64*, 81, 85–86, 163, 166, 408

extensive magnitude 427

extinction neglect syndrome 375

extraction of form 416–419, 508–509

eye cup 417, 422

factive 62

fallibility 23, 47, 83–84, *94*, 118, 245, *345–346*, 349, 353, 358, 364, 381, 385, 388, 401, 516, 534

feature 55

feature placing 139, *163–171*, 176–177, 186, 227, 231, 234–235, 251

fictional representation 378

file, demonstrative 412, 451, *453*, 470, *486–488*, 490–491, 546

fish xiii, 7, 24, 102, 189, 328, 331, 335–336, 372, 415, 420, 423, 425, 548

fitness, biological 302–303, 308, 310, 315, 317, 320, 338–340, 376, 497, 528–529

flatworm 307, 422

flourishing 326, 340

foraging 476, 491, 515

form, extraction of, *see* extraction of form

formality, *see* syntactical states

formation law or law-like pattern 99–100, 246–248, 285–286, 364–365, 383–*386*, 384–416, 457; *see also* anti-individualism; perceptual constancy

formation operation, *see* perceptual processing

formation principle *92–102*, 169, 245–248, 256, 272, *342–347*, 348–366, *361–366*, 383–416, 442–443; *see also* explanation in terms of veridicality

formation process, *see* perceptual processing

formation transformation, *see* perceptual processing

frog 41–42, 45, 69, 71, 322, 420, 434

fundamental ground of difference *194*–195

fundamental idea *194*–196, 198–200

function (general) 9, 16, 31, 142, 261, 276, *320*, 338, *341*, 377, 410, 430, 532; *see also* good; norm (general); teleology

function, artifactual 68, 292–293, 308–309, 431, 490

function, as flourishing, *see* flourishing

function, biological 24, 27, 65–66, 75, 156, 212–213, 262, 268–269, 291–341, *299*, *301–302*, *320*, 374–377, 385, 395, 398, 407, 411, 424, 438, 468, 494, 522, 549; *see also* fitness, biological; norm, biological

function, individual (or whole animal) xvii, 24, 70, 94, 190, 213, 272, 320–326, *320*, *326*, 330–341, *370–371*, 407–408, 413, 450, 464–468, 478, 499–500, 526; *see also* agency; agency, and perception; agency, primitive; eating; mating; navigation; norm, natural; parenting; perception, as the individual's; predating

function, mathematical, *see* mathematical function

function, representational 31–32, 37–45, 62, 68, 74–75, 81–83, 94, 121, 134, 145, 167, 185–186, 207, 261, 281, 291, 303–319, *303*, *308–310*, *339*, 345–366, 376–385, 403, 406, *411*, 470, 496, 526–527, 530, 535–536, 539–542, 549; *see also* committal representational states; norm, representational

functional attribute (perceptual or conceptual) 34, 101, 244, 323–324

functional attributive 260, 323; *see also* danger, as attributive; edible, as attributive

functional concept 34, 280

functional representation 244, 280

functionalism *76*, 81–82, 85, 282

functioning correlation (a type of contribution to biological functioning) xi–xii, 9, 27–28, 91, 294, 303–308, *317*, 325, 342, 398–400, 421–424, 431, 476, *494*–495, 497, 500–514, 521–523, 525, 530–531

general condition, representing a *16*, 19–20, 23–26, 103, 106, 111, 128, 134–136, 147–148, 151–153, 178, 210, 237–238, 242, 247, 255, 258, 265–266, 269, 295, *403*–404, *547*; *see also* criteria; Individual Representationalism, second-family

general elements in perception *83–84*, *380*, 454–464; *see also* guidance of singular application by attribution; perceptual attributive; singular elements in perception

generality 11, 16, *24*, 113, 139, *170*, *185–186*, 194–199, 207, 237, 241–244, *247–252*, *258*, *265–266*, 295, 405, 534, *543–547*, 550; *see also* beliefs, general; quantification

ability generality, *see* ability general representational content

predicational (pure attributional) generality 539

quantificational generality 236, 238, *242*, 250–*251*, 266, 282, 286, 543–544, 546–547, 550

schematic generality 221, 242, *251*, 255–256, 405, 543–544

semantical generality 380

syntactic generality 380

Generality Constraint 187, *196*, 206–207

generic shape 176, 468–470, *469*; *see also* perceptual constancy, shape constancy; tracking

geometrical attribute 125, 259, 381, 442, 446, 454, 468, 517

geometrical constancy, *see* perceptual constancy, geometrical constancy

geometrical principle 204–205, 347–349, 440

geometrical structure 509, 512–514, 529–530, 540

geometry, pure 513

gestalt forms or principles 114, 359, 441

Gestalt psychology 114–115, 408, 416, 438

global vector *499*, 501, 507–508

goal, as *representatum* 47, 74, 291, 320, 315, 328, *337–341*, 370–371, 462, 501, 516, 530, 550

God (and God) 33, 47

good *311*, *338*, 341, 415

gopher 318, 322

governing (by principles or by laws) 23, *93–95*, 97, 102, 113–114, 170–171, 197–199, 202, 204, 238, 245–247, 254, 256, 258, 295, 323, 349, 353, 382, 385–386, 389–391, 393–395, 448, 452, 454, 460, 462–464, 476, 489, 511, 530, 532–533, 550

grammar 33–34, 43–44, 90, 147, 217
group, *see* aggregate
group action, *see* agency, group
grouping (perceptual) xvii, 22, 26, *32–33*, 39, 55, 76–79, *83–84*, 104, 122, 188, 198, 213, 220–221, 228, 231, 234–235, 253, 267, 284, 304–305, 323, 359, 368, *379–381*, 430, 444, 453, 455, 458, 539–540
grouse 335, 337
guidance, of action by perception 101, 189, 199, 206, 315, 324, 334–340, 370, 372, 374–375, 453, 464, 501, 503, 510, 521–522, 526–527, 539; *see also* control
guidance, of singular application by attribution 24, 35, 83, 168, 174–176, 178, 183, 194, 196–197, 204, 240, 449, *454–456*, 477, 486, 496, 510, 521, 540–545
guidance and norms 313–315, 340

habituation (and dishabituation) *306*–307, 410, 418, 440, 461, 486
habituation, crossmodal 440
hallucination, *see* referential illusion, veridical hallucination
haptic system, *see* touch system
hearing 98, 275, 318, 399, 414, 420, 422, 427–429, 441
heat 63, 112–113, 268, 303–304, 315, 328–330, 332, 416, 421, 425
heat sensors 273, 416
history 7, 30, 114, 136, 197, 256, 321, 327, 407, 413, 524, 551
holism 18, 20, 150–151, 279–281; *see also* confirmation procedure
holism, about perception 152, 281
hologram 44, 175–176
homing, navigational systems, *see* beaconing
homing pigeon 425
homogeneity, of surface textures 358
homunculus 367, 403
human xi–xiii, xvi, 7–8, 11, 20, 23, 26, 47, 72, 67, 90, 93–95, 102–103, 107, 114–115, 121, 133–136, 139, *152*, 155, 167, 170–171, 179, 188–190, 196, 206, 211, 235, 248–249, 253, 264, 270, 274–276, 284, 295, 305, 314, 319, 323, *343*, 347, 351, 354, 359–361, 364, 367, 369–370, 406, 413–415, *420–421*, 428–429, 431–434, 438, 449, 451–452, 454, 457–458, *460*–462, 467–468, 472–475, 478, 483–487, 490–492, *492*, 496–497, 510, 523, 533, 538, 543, *548–551*
hydra 336, 423
hyper-intellectualization 13, *27*, 97, *107*, *116–117*, 152, 161, 176, 196, 201, 205, 210, 257, 263, 276, 278, *283*, 285–286, *314*, 434, 471

idea (in British empiricism) *111*, 116
idea, fundamental, *see* fundamental idea
idealism 21–22, 46–47, *52*, 87, 133, 154–155, 550; *see also* phenomenalism
identity, *see* criteria for identity or individuation
identifying reference (in Strawson) 144, 157, 163–168, 173–181, *175*, 240
illumination 94, 274, *345*, *351*, 351–354, 386, 410–412, 496
illumination edge 352–354
illusion, *see* hallucination; misperception; reference failure

image, two-dimensional *91*, 246, 342, *344–345*, 355–356, 358, 453–454, 457, 497, 507, 521; *see also* retinal image

image matching (template matching, pattern matching) 419, *507–509*, 517

images 117, 135, 274, 279, 353–363, *356*, 411, 413–414, 417, 422, 454, 457–458, 461, 463, 471, *507–509*, 513; *see also* body image; retinal image

imagination *74–75*, 83, *378*, 544

implicit representation, *see* representation, implicit

indeterminacy theses (Quine's) 211, 225

index, (anchor, origin) for frameworks *199–201*, 203–205, 215, 217, 287, 349, 455, 490–491, 509, 525, 528, 550; *see also* application; allocentric index or framework; egocentric index or framework

indicant 14, 43, 79; *see also* indication

indication 27, *31–37*, 40, *42–45*, 53–59, 62, 68, 74, 76–79, *76–77*, 81, 83–86, 106, 129, 147, 163, 167, 176, 195, 197, 204–205, 207, 217, 235, 292–293, 349, 361–362, 365, *379–381*, 385, 395, 401, 405, 412, 444, 466, 471, 521, 523, 530, 539; *see also* attribution; representational content; semantic determination; specification

individual, *see* function, individual; subsystem of individual; agency; perception, as the individual's

individual-subsystem distinction 24, 189–190, *320*, *372–376*; *see also* modularity; function, individual (or whole animal); perception, as the individual's; subsystem of individual; whole organism attributability; whole organism coordination

individual concept 33, 35, 541

Individual Representationalism *12–23*, *25–26*, 103–108, Part II *passim*, *283–288*, 294–295, 304, 322, 401, 403–404, 432, 434, 537–539, 544–545, 548–549; *see also* objectification, Individual Representationalist

Individual Representationalism, first-family 12–23, *12–16*, 103, 105, 107, 111–136, 548

Individual Representationalism, second-family *12–14*, *16–24*, 103, 105–107, 111, 117, 128, 133, 137–288, *153*, *254*, *282*; *see also* criteria; general condition, representing a; generality

individualism *25*; *see also* anti-individualism

individuation 16–17, 19, 25, 35, *37–41*, *45–46*, 58, *73–75*, *83–84*, *86–87*, *94–96*, *99–100*, 150–151, 168, 172–173, 176–179, 181, 198, 200, 215–218, 226, 227–288, 296, 308–310, 319, 342, 359, 361–365, 370, *379–380*, *384–386*, *389–396*, *407*, 413, 428, 451, 466, 470–472, 488, 520, 546; *see also* constitutive determination; criteria; marking; sortal concept (or sortal predicate); sortal kind or universal

indubitability 534

infallibility 15, 23, *112*, 118–120, 124–126, 144, 228, 243, 245–246, 392, 534; *see also* fallibility

infant 7, 112–113, 170, 214, 228, 234, 248–254, 261, 263–264, 343, 439–441, 444–445, 451–463, 469, 471–492, 496, 537; *see also* human

inference (propositional) 25, 42, 45, 88, 95, 104, 130, 169–170, 174, 179, 189, 191, 198, 266, 278–283, *278–280*, *283*, *298*, 309, *313–314*, 339, 377–378, 381, *405–407*, 429, 432–434, 492, *537–547*, 550; *see also* non-representational processing; norm, for inference; perceptual processing; propositional attitude; propositional structure (propositional form); psychological processing

inference pattern 138

inference rule 95, 405, 543

information 9, *27*, *90–93*, 96, 102, 274, 296–300, 303–308, 315–326, 336–366, 367–430, 433, 457, 460, 490, *494–496*, 498–514, 518–529, *529–531*; *see also* functioning correlation; representational content

information carrying 90, 184, 294, 298–300, *304*, 307, 315–317, *316*, 356, 360, 400, 494, 499, 506, 530

information processing, *see* non-representational processing; perceptual processing; psychological processing

information registration xii, 12, *27–28*, 96, 285–286, 316–*317*, 341, 365, 368, 372, 392, 400, 426, 429, 431, *494–495*, 498, 502, 506, 514, 521–522, *529–531*; *see also* encoding; explanation in terms of veridicality; functioning correlation; image; representational content; sensory registration; retinal stimulation

information-theoretic notion or explanation 296–297, 299, 318, 337, 342, 411, 493, 529, 531

informational state 363, 369, 501–502, 506, 517, 529–530

informational state on Evans's definition *184–191*

innateness 268, 307, 359, 422, 443, 456, 458, 460, 519, 525, 534

insect, *see* arthropod

instances (instantiations of attributes), as *representata* 24, 26, *32–33*, 38–*39*, *44*, *55*, 58–59, 63, 68, 70–73, 83–84, 95, 157, 164–170, 196–197, 212, *234*, 242–243, 246, 260–261, 263, 266, 269, *281–282*, 298, *307*, 346, 362–365, 376, 379, *380–396*, 412, 441, *444*, 446, 450, 459, 464, 466, 469–470, 496–497, 506, 539–541, 543, 549; *see also* causation in perceptual reference; concrete particular; property, noninstantiated

instinct 197, 228, 279, 291, *330*, *335–337*, 527

intellectualism 18, 115–118, 130, 132, 135, 245; *see also* hyper-intellectualization

intelligibility 7, 13, 21–24, *57*, 76, 103, 111, 142, 150–153, 158, 160, 206, 208, 254, 258, 264, 270, 282, 545

intensity, of surface stimulation 399, 415, *422–427*, 476, 495, 498, 504

intensive magnitude 427

intention 27–28, 38–39, 43, 47, 52, *74–75*, *81*, 304, *309*, 313, 315, *327*, *330*, 332–334, 341, 432

intentionality *4*, 28, 34, *43–44*, 184, 277, 409, 432; *see also* representation

interference 93, 95, 299, 346, 364, 383, 385–386; *see also* noise

intermodal coordination 101–102, 243, 248, 320, 326, 330–335, 338, 341, 373, 439–40, 441, 443, 521, 525, 527; *see also* crossmodal influence; habituation, crossmodal

intermodal representation or system 40, *243–244*, *247–249*, 258, 378, 413, 432, *439–449*, 470, 475, *486–487*, 490–492, 500, 505–508, 514, 517, 527, 530; *see also* actional representation, or actional state; actional system; agency, and perception; propositional attitude

interpretation (of data in perception) 367

interpretation (of language), *see* linguistic interpretation

intersubjective agreement 223

intersubjectivity 117, 223; *see also* objectivity, as intersubjectivity

intrinsic constitution 66–67

introduction of particulars in propositions 171

introspection 15–16, 41, 73, 112, 114, 132–133, 135

jackdaw 484
justification *3*, 115, 119–120, 126–127, 129, 155–156, 225, 276, 431–*435*;
    see also epistemic entitlement; reason

Kanizsa triangle 417–418
kind (kind representation and kind as *representatum*) 24, 33–35, *43–44*, 49, *55–59*,
    62–66, 68–69, *73*, 76–79, 83–87, 90, *98*, 143–148, 161–171, 194–209, 212,
    217–276, 281–283, 367–436, 437–450, 456–464, 465, 471–483; *see also* constitutive
    condition; constitutive determination; kind, explanatory; nature; norm, natural;
    psychological kind
kind, attributional (attributives specifically of kinds) 43–45, 49, 71–73, *76–79*, 161–171,
    178, 235, 253, *386–396*; *see also* anti-individualism, perceptual; causal relations
    to environment, constitutive; explanation in terms of veridicality; perceptual
    psychology; sortal concept (or sortal predicate); sortal kind or universal; specification
kind, explanatory xi–xiii, *xv–xvi*, 3, 9, 12, *27–28*, *55–59*, *62–63*, 84–87, *98–101*, 147, 225,
    256, 291–366, *310–315*, *319*, *341*, *367*, 379–436, *389*, *432*, 437–531, *487*, 533,
    548–549; *see also* empirical explanation in psychology; explanation in terms of
    veridicality; psychological kind
kind, fundamental explanatory xv, 56–57, 62–63, 99, 194, 431
kind, natural, *see* natural kind
kinesis 328–329
knowing which 144, 160, 172–173, 176, 179, 191–193, 200; *see also* Russell's Principle
knowledge xvi, 4–6, 15, 17–18, 22, 62, 115–124, 131, 144, 160, 169, 172–181, 191–199,
    285, 312, 412, 417, *430–435*, 489, 513, 524
knowledge, discriminatory 192–193; *see also* Russell's Principle

landmark 202, 206, 262, 324, 419, 460, 466, 470, 499–502, *501*, 507–511, *507–508*,
    516–517, 530
language xvi–xvii, 7–9, 11, 18–19, *23*, 28, 47, 56, 95–96, 102, 116, 118, 127–130,
    133–136, 137–149, *148*, 151, 165, 183–184, 191–193, 211–288, 295, 430, 432–433,
    437, 491, 538; *see also* linguistic community; philosophy of language
language learning 145, 165, 213–264, 432, 491
language of thought 39, 95–*96*, 282, 385, 406
law 15–19, *49–50*, 59, 67, 70, 83, *87*, 92, 94–100, 116–118, 122, 170, 246, 256, 285, 299,
    307, 310, *345–347*, 353–359, 361, 363–365, 383–386, 388–396, *389*, *401–407*, 429,
    445–446, 454, 457, 461–466, 481, *487–489*, 493, 500–501, 529, 533, 535, *550*;
    see also formation law or law-like pattern; objectivity, as law or representation of
    law; psychological kind
law (as a discipline) 7, 550–551
law-like pattern or principle 16, 23, 27, *49–50*, 58, 67, 70, 82, 88–89, 92, 95–97, 99–100,
    118, 246, 248, 272, 285, 292, 298–299, 307, *346*–347, 353–358, 361, 365, 383, 386,
    389, 393–395, 399, 403, 458, 489, 493, 533, 535; *see also* formation law or law-like
    pattern; governing (by laws or by principles); psychological kind
learning *304–307*, 344, 410, 422, 443, 456, 458, 460, 462, 467, 487, 490–491, 510, 515,
    518–520, 524–525, 534; *see also* language learning; maturation
learning, associative 116, 215, 223, 305–307, 529–531
learning, conditioned 215, 223, 277, 279
learning, habituation *306–*307, 410, 418, 440, 461, 486

learning, trial and error 306–307, 516
light xi, 27–28, 59, 70, 89–94, *94*, 98–101, 112, 175–176, 190, 212, 225, 268–269,
    271, 274, 295, 303–305, *315–319*, 322–325, 328–330, *342–346*, 351–354, 356–366,
    372–377, *383–384*, 387–388, 411, 417–418, 422, 425, 488, 493–498, 500–502, 505,
    519–520; *see also* information registration; perceptual constancy, color constancy;
    perceptual constancy, lightness constancy; vision; visual psychology
light frequency 89
lightness *351*–354, 359, 365–366, 411, 496–498
lightness constancy, *see* perceptual constancy, lightness (brightness) constancy
linguistic community 145–146, 157, 226, 270–271, 282
linguistic interpretation 211–288, *271–272, 278–279, 282*; *see also* translation
linguistic reference, *see* reference, linguistic
linguistic representation 32–37, 40, 42–46, 138, 141–149, 430
local vector 501; *see also* global vector
localization 102, 113, 150, 155, 198, 200, 286, 298, 414, 420, 421–422, *427–429*, 442, 502;
    see also perceptual constancy, location constancy
location constancy, *see* perceptual constancy, location constancy
locust 102, 419
logic xvii, 50, 71–72, 115, 118, 130, 238, 240, 534
logical connective 39, 239, 541–545
logical construction 116, 121–122, 135, 138
logical form 116, 145, 151, 166, 185, 215, 278, 286, 405, 472, 542–543, 545
logical operator or operation 5, 32, 34, 39, 118–20, 151, 540–545; *see also* operator,
    for tense or place
Logical Positivism 123, 140–143
logical system 95, 406; *see also* inference (propositional); inference, norms for
look-alikes 144, 149, 260; *see also* application, singular; context-bound representational
    content; duplication argument, Strawson's
looks 41, 388, 391–392, 412
luminance contour *351*–359, 418, 497

magnetic field sensors 285, 300, 330, 420, 425, 498, 502, 504–505
magnitude 381, 468, 471–483, 485, 488–491, 504; *see also* extensive magnitude;
    intensive magnitude
magnitude, pure and continuous 481–483
magnitude, pure and discrete 482–483
magnitude effect 473, 475
magnitudes, as providing structure of perceptual content 104, 381; *see also* perceptual
    representational content
magpie 462
mainstream philosophy 17–18, 107, *115*–117, 129–131, 135, 137–138, 140, 148, 150, 432
mammal xiii, 24, 27, 47, 55–56, 102, 169, 189, 259, 263, 318–319, 330, 337, 343, 351,
    353, 372, 374, 420–421, 442, 485, 493, 500, 510, 548
map-like behavior *509*–511
map-like psychological structure (representational or not) 446, *509*–517; *see also*
    geometrical structure
map-like representational system *509*–517, *514, 517*, 525; *see also* landmark; path
    integration; sketch

marking 13–14, 23, 37–39, 42, 45, 74, 89, 121, 168, 197, 227, 230, 287, 320, 349,
    364–365, 376–380, 382, 396, 400–401, 408–413, *408–410*, 417, 430, 469, 519–520,
    525, 527, 539, 541
Marr's three levels of explanation 93
Marr's ½-D Sketch 449
masses (or mass) 20, 55, 164, 167, 171, 212, 228, 236, 360, 471, 475; *see also* body,
    as *representatum*
mass-like representation 151, 163–165, 170, 221, 228, *234–237*, 240, *249–250*, 467–469,
    468; *see also* body, as *representatum*
materialism 46; *see also* Cartesian dualism, functionalism
mathematical entity 46, 52, 71, 471–483; *see also* magnitude; number, as *representatum*;
    numerosity
mathematical function 72, 120, 473, 478, 540
mathematical operation 346, 400, 404–405, 482, 487, 491
mathematical representation 17, 72, 79, 97, 136, *404*, 471–531, *488–489*, *500*
mathematics xv, 4, 7, 50, 71–72, 115, 117–118, 129, 135, 235, 280, 482, 511, 534–535, 551
mathematics, knowledge of or warrant for 4, 115, 524, 534; *see also* apriority
mathematics, pure or applied 71–72, 280, 512, 534–535; *see also* geometrical structure;
    geometry, pure
mating 94, 189, 212, 261–262, 272, 292, 308, 310, 319–320, 324, 326–328, 331, 334–335,
    339, 370, 373, 424, 438, 450, 464, 466, 470, 515, 549; *see also* eating; navigation;
    parenting; predating
maturation (biological or psychological) 20, 247, *305–6*, *331*, 456; *see also* behavior;
    development, psychological
meaning, linguistic xvi, *37*, 44, 77, 79, 81–82, 96, 115, 127, 135, 138, 140–143, 145–*146*,
    150, 166, 178, 181, 211, 215–216, 218, 220, 226–227, 229–234, 265, 282, 432;
    see also natural meaning; perceptual representational content; propositional
    representational content; representational content; stimulus meaning; translation
memory 62–63, 83–84, 122, 144, 204, 243, 246, 258, 415–416, 427, 470, 484, 490,
    514–517, 522, 527, 546; *see also* actional representation or actional state; anticipatory
    representation; intermodal representation or system; imagination
memory, episodic long-term 252, *258–259*
memory, long-term 252–253, 258–259, 262, 453, 515–517, 522
memory, perceptual 83–84, 187, 193, 202, 246–248, 258–259, 270, 378, 447–448, 454,
    486, 489, 509, 521, 527–528, 541, 544; *see also* intermodal representation or system
memory, sensory-motor 513
memory, short-term 378, 451–453, 521
memory, singular elements in 83–84, 258, 382, 454, 490, 544, 546; *see also* application,
    singular, in memory; files, demonstrative
memory, working 452–453
mental state 11, 14, *25*, 46, 49, *61–73*, 74–87, *105–106*, 127, 142–143, 148–150, 158–159,
    271, 280, *292*; *see also* anti-individualism; kind, psychological
meta-representation (meta-perspective) 156–160, 183, 266–270, 278–280, 314, 538;
    see also belief, concept of; mind independence, as represented; objectivity,
    conception of; self-consciousness; self-representation; truth, concept of
metric property 204, 361, 411, 457, 499, 502, 509–511, 514, 517
mouse 336, 422

mind xi–xiv, *xiii*, xvi, *3–4*, 9–10, 12, 27, 46–54, 67, 87, 112, 119, 125–126, 131, 133, 154, 157–159, 296, 347, 367, *396*, 431, 549; *see also* consciousness; mental state; philosophy of mind; representation
mind, representational xi–xiii, xviii, 3–4, 9–10, 12, 66, *432*, *549*; *see also* perceptual psychology
mind independence xiii, 3, 12, 15, 24, 46–49, 51–54, 59, 61, 112–113, 120, 125, 128, 143, 148, 150, 152, 155–157, 163, 397–399, 403, 408, 536, 547, 549–550; *see also* idealism; objectivity, as mind-independence; objectivity, as being constitutively non-perspectival
mind independence, as represented 20, 157, 163, 165, 172, 177–178, 286, *402*, *549–550*
mind–body problem 67, 73, 297, 317; *see also* materialism; Cartesian dualism
misperception 91, 142, 149, 353, 355, 384; *see also* hallucination; referential illusion; veridical hallucination
modal claim 13, 64, 72, 199, 202, 537
modal concepts 280
modality, sensory or perceptual 99, 243, 248–*249*, *377–378*, 439–443, 448–449, 486, *501*; *see also* crossmodal influence; hearing; intermodal representation or system; olfaction; proprioception; taste; touch; vision
mode of presentation (way of representing), *see* representational content
modularity *24*, 83, *101*, 104, 189, 249, 257, 292, 368–369, 398, 401, 437, 455; *see also* psychological processing
mollusc xi, xiii, 305, 315, 318, 325, 336, 422, 505
mongoose 422
monkey 252, 264, 462, 473, 484, 496; *see also* ape
moth 336, 422, 450, 502
motion, as *representatum* 3, 24, *54–55*, 96, *98*, 100–101, 199, 202, 204, 228–229, 235, 250–253, 258–263, 280, 287, 323–324, 374–375, *410*, 414, 417, 419, 429, 439–440, *444–449*, 451, 453–456, 457–465, *457*, *459–460*, 468–470, 500–502, 508, 515, 521, 528–529, 546; *see also* bodies at rest; bodies in motion; perceptual constancy, motion constancy; orientation; tracking
motion constancy, *see* perceptual constancy, motion constancy
motion parallax 508, 515
multiple object tracking 451–453, 461–463, 483–486

naive realism 148, 362, 392
natural kind xvi, 76–77, 82, 141, 146–149, 280, *323*, 455
natural kind term (or concept or other representation) 77–78, 82, 141, 146–149, 280; *see also* kind, natural
natural meaning *298–299*
natural norm, *see* norm, natural
natural number, *see* number, natural
natural scene statistics 359–366, *360–361*; *see also* Brunswik's methodology; convexity of image regions; depth perception
natural science 4, 50, 89, 115, 133, 137, *211–213*, 273, 280, *286–287*, 305–308, *384*, 551
natural similarity class 270, 322; *see also* disjunction problem; natural kind
naturalism 232, 296, 308, 311, 322
nature xi, *xv*–xvii, 3–6, 11, *16*, 18, *22*, *25*–26, 37, 42, 46, 48–49, 52, *57–59*, *61–67*, 69–71, *74–76*, *79–82*, *84–87*, 88, 93, *95–100*, 102, 104–106, 119, 123–127, 130–133,

142–143, 149, 152, 167, 180–181, 187, 189, 208, 213, 226, 257, 259, 260, 262, 265, 279, 283, 285, *292*, *297*, 310, *312*, 315, 323, 324–327, 331, 339, *344*, 349, 358–359, 366, *368*, 370, 377, 391, 393, 406, 413, 424, 435, 443, 445, 455, 457–458, 476, 496–500, 502, 514, 521, 526, *532–537*, 541, 547; *see also* anti-individualism, constitutive dependence; constitutive determination; constitutive necessity; constitutive question; essence; norm, natural

navigation 94, 189, 202, 204, 206, 212, 261–262, 272, 292, 320, 324, 326, 334, 339, 370, 373, 398, 419–420, 424, 426, 438, 450, 464, 470, 492–518, *502–503*, *508*, *514*, *529–531*, 549; *see also* beaconing; landmark; map-like representational system; path integration; route-based system; spatial representation

necessity 47, *59*, 207, 497, 521–522, 526, *532*; *see also* constitutive necessity; modal claim; nature; possibility

negation, as logical operator 32, 218–219, 236–238, 250, 255, 286, 486, 540, 543

neo-Kantianism 28, 105, 121, 134, 150, 154–210, *156*, *208–210*, 282, 468

nest 206, 320, 335, 422, 499, 501

neural explanation *xiii–xiv*, 97–100, 297, *309*; *see also* psychology

neural state or occurrence xiii, 67, 76, 85, 97–99, 232, 309, 318, 410, 497; *see also* brain

noema 131

noise 93, 346, 364, 385–386, 408, 410

non-instantiated property, *see* property, non-instantiated

non-representational processing (or operation or transformation), including sensory processing 27, 85, 97, 190, 303, 305, 325, 331–334, 369, *371–374*, 378, 398–399, 410, 415, 418, 421–430, *424*, 479, 494–495, *498–514*, 517–518, *529–531*, 548; *see also* sensory registration

non-representational relation (to the environment), *see* constitutive non-representational relation (to the environment)

norm (general) 50, *311*–315, 338–340; *see also* guidance and norms; standard

norm, biological 291, *312–315*, 338–341

norm, epistemic 4, 280, *312–314*, 341, 433–436

norm, for belief 280, *312–313*, 435

norm, for inference 280, *313–314*, 405

norm, for perception *312–315*, 341, 405, 434–436, 535, 550

norm, for rationality 280, 291, 341

norm, moral 313–314, 339–340, 550–551

norm, natural 280, 308–315, *311–314*, 338–339

norm, practical (or instrumental) 280, *313–315*, 338–341, 550

norm, prescriptive or guiding *314–315*; *see also* norm, reflexive (but natural)

norm, reflexive (but natural) *313–315*, 340–341

norm, representational 4, 142–143, *312–315*, 338–341, 436, 535, 550

normal environment, *see* environment, normal

notion, *see* concept

number, as *representatum* 32, 46, 54, 235, 239, 383–384, 471–492, *472*, 521, 523–524; *see also* magnitude, discrete; mathematical representation; numerosity

number, natural 476–492

numerosity 437, *472–483*, *480–483*, 485, 489–491; *see also* aggregate; estimating numerosity; magnitude; set

numerosity, its second-order character 476

object constancy, *see* perceptual constancy, object constancy

object permanence *459*, 462; *see also* body, at rest; body, in motion; occlusion; tracking

objectification, Individual Representationalist 56–7, Part II *passim*, 136, 207–208, 214, 227–229, 232–234

objectification, intermodal 413–414

objectification, perceptual 10, 20–21, *23*, 25, *56–57*, 207–208, *256–258*, 285, 317, 321, 338, 354, 371, *396–416*, 416–436, 437–531, *523*, *530*, *547–548*; *see also* formation law or law-like pattern; perceptual constancy; perceptual processing; resources, psychological

objective particular (Strawson) 158–159

objective representation xi, *xiii*, 4–5, *7–8*, *10–11*, *13*, 14–22, *24–28*, *49–54*, 56–59, 61, 101, 103, 106–108, 111–136, 139–140, 143, 147–148, 150–153, 154–210, *208–210*, 211–288, *283–288*, 291–366, *398–416*, *432*, 437–531, *526–528*, *549–550*; *see also* accuracy; truth; veridicality

objective representation, priority of, *see* priority of objective representation

objective subject matter *46–49*, 52, 57, 105–106, 138, 277, 285

objectivity, as being constitutively non-perspectival 24, *47–48*, *52*, 54, 59, 61, 397–398

objectivity, as impersonality *50–51*, 206

objectivity, as inter-subjectivity *50*–51, 117, 122, 137–138, 223

objectivity, as law or representation of law *49–50*, 118, 122–123, 136, 285

objectivity, as mind-independence xiii, 3, 12, 15, 20, 24, *46–49*, 51–52, 59, 61, 113, 120, 128, 150, 155–157, 172, 177–178, 286, 398–399, *403*, *408*, 536, 547, *549–550*

objectivity, as veridicality 46, 49–*53*, *59*, *397*, *passim*

objectivity, concept (conception) of 156–162, *156–157*, 169, 172, 178, 182–183, 195, 203, 205–208, 255, 266–283; *see also* truth, concept of

objectivity, conceptions of 46–54

objectivity, horizontal 51

objectivity, in action, *see* agency, objective

objectivity, procedural 50

objectivity, vertical 51–52

observation, 69, 177, 223, 225–226, 228, 238, 240–242, 251–252, 259, 262, 378; *see also* evidence; experience; modality, sensory or perceptual

observation sentence (Quinean) *215*–216, 223, 226–228, 230–231, 237, 251–252

observation statement 23

obviousness 534

occlusion 94, *247*, *262*, 360–361, 417, 444, 447–*448*, 451, 453–454, 457, 459–463, *462–463*, 483, 486

occurrence-based representational content, *see* context-bound representational content

octopus 420

olfaction 251, 254, 258–259, 408, *415*–416, *419–430*, *425*, 444, 450, 476, 493, 498, 501–502

one-word sentence 216, 220, 226–232, 264; *see also* propositional structure (propositional form)

ontogeny, *see* development, psychological

operation, logical, *see* logical operation

operation, mathematical, *see* mathematical operation

operation, in a psychology, *see* non-representational processing; perceptual processing; psychological processing;

operator, for tense or place 166, 171, 231
orca 331
orientation (in animal movement) *328*–330, 335, 423–425, 504–505; *see also* taxes

pac-man 465–466
pain xiii, 4, 14, 52, 113, 188, 332, 372, 374, 402, *416*, *421–422*, 431
parallax estimation 420, 502
paramecium xiii, 273–274, 306, 315, 318, 328–331, 333–336, 372, 411, 422–423, 425, 498–499
parenting 212, 262, 320, 326–327, 368, 438, 450; *see also* eating; navigation; predating
parrot 462, 484
particular 3, 5–6, 13–16, 18, 24–26, 30, 33, 39, 44–45, 50–51, 53, *54–55*, 67–68, 71, *83*, 88, 90, 93, 105, *111*, 113–114, 120–121, 135, 139, 143–145, 151, 157–181, 184–208, 212–213, 223, 228, *230–231*, 234–242, 250–254, *256*–263, 270, 274–277, 281, *284*, 286, 295, *308*, 319, 342, 344, 365–372, 376, 379–396, *379–381*, 399–403, *399–400*, 408, *411*–413, 430, *444*–446, 450–457, 459–460, 467, 471–496, *506*–507, 512–516, *521*–524, 532–536, 539–547, 550; *see also* attribute; concrete particular; instances (instantiations of attributes)
particular, basic (in Strawson) 158, 164–165, 167–181, *169*, 251
particular, concrete, *see* concrete particular
path integration (dead reckoning) 495, *499*–510, 512–513, 517, 522, 524, 526, 529–530; *see also* landmark; global vector; route-based system
patience *xii*, 30
perceivability 446
percept 106, 349, 489
perception, as objective representation *see* objectification, perceptual
perception, as representation 379–396
perception, as sensory 376–379
perception, as sensory objectification 396–416; *see also* objectification, perceptual
perception, as the individual's 93, 104, 285–286, 337–341, 362–363, *369–376*, 540
perception, conscious *xiii*, 41, 52, 90, 93, 121, 188, 190, 285, 362–364, 368–269, *373–376*, 385–386, 393, 402, 412, 507, *548*
perception, depth, *see* depth perception
perception, unconscious 90, 93, 188, 285, 287, 363–364, 368–369, *374–376*
perceptual anticipation, *see* anticipatory perception
perceptual application, *see* application, singular, in perception
perceptual attributive *36*, 38, *44*, 69, 76, 79, 104–106, *174*, 176, 198, 207, 217, 323–324, 364, *380–383*, 412, 426, 438, 442–446, *450–454*, 459, 464, 466–470, 486, 518, *539–540*, 545–546
perceptual attributive, basic 546
perceptual belief, *see* belief, perceptual
perceptual belief, basic 546
perceptual constancy *114*, 188–189, 233, 258, 260, 270, *274–275*, 281–283, 285, 287, 321, 323–324, *349*–366, 375, 385–430, *388*, *397*, *408–413*, 437–470, *466*, 492–529, 530
    color constancy 274, 354, 375, *387*, *410*–412, 419–420, 427, 496–497, 508
    depth constancy 411, 497; *see also* depth perception

direction constancy 424–425, 502

distance constancy 274, 323, 347–350, 354, 388, 409–411, 414, 419–420, 497, 502, 508, 515

geometrical constancy 350, 355, 363, 410, 414

independent constancy 354

lightness constancy (brightness constancy) 114, *351*–354, 357, 411, 497–498; *see also* illumination; illumination edge

location constancy (distance plus direction constancy) 274, 323, 347–350, 374–375, 414, 420–421, 425, 428–429, 454, 460, 471, 496–497, 508, 515–516; *see also* convergence; disparity, binocular; echolocation; localization; parallax estimation

motion constancy 374–375, 410, 419–420, 429, 454–455, 459–460

object constancy 387, 420, 438–450, 454, 460, 468, 518; *see also* object permanence; occlusion; tracking

shape constancy 375, 409, 419–421, 454, 460, 496–497, 508, 515–516

size constancy 374, 387–388, 409, 419–420, 454–455, 460, 496–497, 508, 515–516

slant constancy 355–359, 411

texture constancy 414, 421

vertical constancy 413

perceptual constancy, primitive 354, 357

perceptual illusion, *see* misperception

perceptual memory, *see* memory, perceptual

perceptual modality, *see* modality, sensory or perceptual

perceptual object (object(s) of perception) *15*, *86*, 90, *94*, *119–120*, *124–125*, 226, 275, 285, *324*, 383, 385–*392*, 398, 409, 421, 452; *see also* perceptual attributive; perceptual reference

perceptual processing (or operation or transformation) *23*, 71, 82, 85–86, *87–100*, 101–102, 104, 167, 187, 197–*198*, 204, 207, 212, 232, 246, 249, 256, 263, 275, 285–286, 298–299, 304, 310–311, 314, 318–319, 342–366, *342–347*, 348–368, *361–366*, *368*, *369*, *371*, 375–376, 378, 383–416, *398–411*, 417–419, 425–430, *425*, *429*, 437, 442–443, 447–450, 453, 455–458, *457–458*, 476–479, 481, 487, 489, 494, 497, 507–508, 515, 525, *535*, 540, 547; *see also* formation law or law-like pattern; non-representational processing (or operation or transformation); perception, conscious; perception, unconscious

perceptual psychology xiii–xiv, xvi–xvii, 9–11, 26–28, 40, 62, *87–101*, 103–104, 107, 115, 121, 189, 211–212, 216, 225, 232, 261, 272–275, 284, 292, *296*, *298*, 301–303, *307*, 310–311, *317–327*, *342–366*, *365–366*, 369, 379, 383–421, *383–384*, 438–450, 470, 490, 495, 530, 535, 539; *see also* anti-individualism; explanation in terms of veridicality; formation principle

perceptual reference xvi, 9, *30*, *36*, 62, 77, *83–88*, *93*, 118–121, 124–128, 130–132, *144*, *148–149*, 151–152, 154–156, 160–163, 166–167, 169–171, 174–176, 178–179, 184–210, 212–217, 225–226, 231–236, 240, 243–250, 253–264, 267, 270–276, 277–290, 321, 324, *362–364*, *376*, 380–396, *380–385*, *392*, 399–415, *401*, 450–456, *450–454*, 486–490, 491, *496*, 514–515, 520, 523, 529–530, 539–544, 545–546; *see also* application, singular; application, singular, in perception; causation in perceptual reference; memory, perceptual; perceptual constancy; reference, linguistic; representation failure; seeing; singular elements in perception perceptual representational content 36, *39–46*, 70–71, 76, *82–101*, *104–105*, *120–121*, *130*–131, 148, 166–167, 170, 187, 213, 215, 233, 245–246, 256, 262, 285, *292*, 299, *307*, *310–312*, 317–322, 326–327, 339–341, 342–347, 350, 355–356, 358, 360–366, *362*, 370–373, 377–378, *379–396*, *397*, 400, 403–413, *411*, 428, 432–433, 437–531, *496*, *503*, *506*, 535, *537–544*, *545–546*, 547; *see also* application, singular, in perception; norm, representational; perceptual constancy; perceptual attributive; propositional structure (propositional form); topological perceptual organization

perceptual representational content, as non-propositional 538

perceptual system xv, xviii, 10, *12*, *23*–24, 41, 52, 69–71, 76, 81–82, *87–105*, 107, 167, 170, 189–190, 197–199, 204, 207–208, 212, 231, 249, 251, 254, *256–259*, 261, 264, 270–283, *285–287*, 299, 307, *309–325*, *327*, 342–436, *369–376*, *378*, *395–396*, *397*, *400*, *408*, *430*, 437–531, 535, *538*, *545–546*, 549; *see also* actional system; causal relations to environment, constitutive; function, representational; imagination; individual-subsystem distinction; intermodal representation or system; memory, perceptual; norm, representational; perception, as the individual's; visual system

peripheral response (reflex or system) 305–306, 331–334, 377, 515

perspective 9, 16, *21*, 24, 27, 36, *37*–38, 41, 47–52, *73*–74, 84, 98, 111, 121, 124, 132, 199–201, 205, 207, 212, 225, 270, *274*, 281, *285–287*, 337, 358, 362, 366, *371–373*, 376, *379*, 383, *385–392*, 394–*395*, 401–403, *408*, *411*, 413, 429, 443, 489, *494*–495, 522, 525, 529, 531, 533, 536, 539–540, 542, 551; *see also* looks; objectivity, as being constitutively non-perspectival; representational content (or states), as perspectival

phenomenalism 111, 113, *119–120*, 124–126, 131, 137, 154, 253

phenomenology, the discipline 17, 116, *130*–133, 135–136, 138–139, *430*

phenomenology, the phenomenon 15, 18–19, 23, 48, 76–77, 86, 100, 111–112, 114, 119, 125, 127, 355, 375–376, 409; *see also* appearance; experience

pheromone *422–423*

philosophy *xi–xviii*, *6–10*, 12, *15–18*, 19–22, 24, *26–28*, 30, 44, *65*, 71, 107, 111–112, *115–118*, 121, 123, 126–127, 129, 132, 137–138, 140, 143, 148, 150, 173, 284, *296–298*, 304, 308–309, 313, 327, 427, *430*–436, 493, 495, 529, 534, 537, *548*, *551*; *see* also mainstream philosophy

philosophy of language xvi–xvii, 138, 148, 433

philosophy of mind xvi, 140–141, 432–433

philosophy of perception 392

phlogiston 35–36, 42–44, *68*–72, 307

photosynthesis 333–334

phototaxis 303, 329

phylogenetic origin xi, *xiii*, xv, *4–6*, *11–12*, 70, 217, *326–327*, *367*, *397*, *402*–403, 420, 430–431, 437, 512, 514, 522, 524–525, 531, *547–550*

physiological (including sensory) psychology xiii, xviii, 11, 26, 374, 421

pig 452, 460

pigeon 104, 425, 473, 484

plurals *32*, 228, *236*, 238, 240, 250, 286, 471, 541; *see also* quantification

polarized light 500, 505, 511

Portia, *see* spider

Positivism, *see* Logical Positivism

possibility 64, 111, 159–161; *see also* conceptual question; intelligibility; modal claim

poverty of stimulus argument 90–91; *see also* undetermination problem praying mantis 419

predating (prey, predator) 213, 261–262, 272, 280, 301–302, 320, 322, 327–328, 332, 336, 340, 373, 414–415, 426–427, 460, 464, 466, 470, 515–516; *see also* navigation

predicate 19, *32–33*, 145–147, 166, 168, 171, 180–181, 186, 194, 196, 216–220, 223, 235–240, 250, 278, 283, 368, 431, 539–543; *see also* attribution, pure; conceptual attributive; perceptual attributive; pre-individuative (or proto-objective) stage; sortal concept (or sortal predicate); sortal kind or universal

pre-individuative (or proto-objective) stage *19–20*, 113, 134, 139, 151–152, 154, 163–171, 186, 213, *215–216*, 227–244, 251–252, *254*, 259, 264; *see also* feature placing; informational state; one-word sentence; sense of externality

primate 169, 452, 484–485, 487, 492, 496

principle 11, *17*, 19–20, 23–26, 58, 62, 91–92, 106, 113, 115, 120, 134, 142, 151–153, 163, 169–171, 176–210, 219, 238, 242–288, 310, 323, 340, 345–366, 388–389, 393–416, *400*, *403–404*, 420, 428–429, 435, 439–440, 442–450, 454, 456–457, 460–464, 466, 476–477, 487–489, 500, 505, 508, 510–511, *513*, *529–530*, 532–537, 544, 547, *550*; *see also* criteria for identity or individuation; explanation in terms of veridicality; formation principle; governing (by principles or by laws); law-like pattern or principle

principle of charity 69

principle, representing a 14, *17*, 256, 406

priority of objective representation xi, *264–265*, 397–403, *402–403*, *548*; *see also* subjective representation

processing, *see* non-representational processing; perceptual processing; psychological processing

prokaryote 329

pronoun 50, 236–240, 249–250

proper name xvi, 141, *145–147*, 173, 180

property 7, 13, 15, 23–26, *32–34*, 40–42, 44–45, *48–54*, 54–57, *55*, 65–68, 71, 73–74, 76, 79, 83, *84–85*, *87–90*, 92–94, 101, 106, 113–114, 118–120, 122, 149, 153, 163–165, 169, *172*, 181–210, 212, 217, 219, *233*, 238, 249, 253–254, 256–260, 268, 271, 292, 298–301, *307*–308, 316, 323, 343, 352, 354, 362, 369, *380*, 385, 388, *390–392*, 407–408, 411, 427, 440–450, *444*, 453, *455–456*, 458, 461–464, *466*, 468–470, 472, 477, 485, 488, 490, 496–499, 502, 507, 510, 539, 546–547; *see also* instances, as *representata*; kind; relation, as *representatum*

property, noninstantiated 307, 392

proportion, *see* ratio

propositional attitude 11, 34, *36*, 40, 74, 85, *101*, *104*, 107, 116–117, 127, 130–131, 135, 139, 151–152, 154, 156, *169*–210, *170*, *191*, *217*, 247–248, 258, 263–268, 274–283, *280*, *298*, 304–305, 312–313, 341, 342, 351, 377, 405, 417, 430–435, 438, 471, 486, 490–492, *537–547*, 548–550; *see also* attribution, pure; belief; belief, perceptual; concept; intention; predication

propositional function (Russellian) 126

propositional inference, *see* inference (propositional)

propositional representational content 39–40, *67*, 73–74, 101, 105, 123, 126, 138, 145, 151, 164, 168–210, *174*, 217, 280–283, 405–406, *434*, *537–547*; *see also* perceptual representational content

propositional structure (propositional form) *36*, *61*, *104*–105, 116–117, 119, 170, *280*,
     381, *434*, 486, *537–547*, 550; *see also* logical form
propositional truth, *see* truth
proprioception 89–90, 98, 152, 247–248, 272, 318, 335, 343–344, 350, 372, 383, 399,
     413–*414*, 422, 428, 500–501, 504; *see also* body image
prosopagnosia 375
protozoa 306, 318, 410, 502
proximal stimulation 17, 44–45, 71, *76*, *88–94*, 96, 98–101, 113–114, 207, 215–218,
     223–234, 257, 265, 268–276, 285–286, 303, 310–311, 317–319, 323–325, 328–331,
     335–337, *342–349*, 350–366, *364*, *371*, *374*, *376–378*, *383–404*, *407–408*, 409–416,
     418–419, 421–429, 430, 437, 439, 441, 443, 446–447, 450, 455, 460, 493, *495–496*,
     498–512, 518–520, 530, *547–548*; *see also* distal stimulation; formation law or
     law-like pattern; non-representational processing; retinal image; retinal stimulation
Proximality Principle 364, 386
proximity of similars, Gestalt rule of 359
psychological development, *see* development, psychological
psychological explanation, *see* psychology
psychological kind 3, 6–7, *9–10*, *12*, 27–28, 35, *37–46*, 55, 58, *62–68*, 69, 76, 80–82,
     84–87, 95–96, *98–101*, 261–262, 278, 291–366, *291–293*, 367–436, 437–531,
     489–490, *494–496*, *530–531*, 537–551, *548–549*; *see also* anti-individualism;
     causal relations to environment, constitutive; disjunction problem; kind, attributional;
     marking; representational content
psychological processing (or operation or transformation)—general 189, 197–198,
     258–259, 280, 310, 325, 374, 378, 429, 441, 474, 476–483, 487, 510–514, 525, 537;
     see also non-representational processing; perceptual processing
psychology (as a discipline) xiii–xiv, xviii, 6, *8–9*, 12, 15, 27, *58*, *62–63*, 67, 74, 81, *98*,
     112–114, 116, 140, 184, 211–212, 224–225, 276, 284, *291–292*, 294–296, 303,
     308–310, 322, 367, *369*, 379, 384, *396–397*, 427, 432, *435*, 464, *489–495*, *529–531*,
     533; *see also* behaviorism; animal psychology; cognitive psychology; developmental
     psychology; empirical explanation in psychology; Gestalt psychology; neural
     explanation; perceptual psychology; physiological (including sensory) psychology;
     visual psychology

qualitative feature (or phenomenal characteristic) 14, 48, 67, 76, 87, 121, 144–145, 150,
     379, 442; *see also* representationalism; sense data; sensation
quantification 19, 39, 105, 119–120, 145, *151*, 166, 175, 185–186, 214, 217, 219,
     236–249, *238–239*, *241–242*, *247–249*, 250–255, 266, 282, 286, 471, 537, *541–547*,
     550; *see also* generality, quantificational; generality, schematic; pronoun
quantity, continuous, *see* magnitude, continuous
quantity, discrete, *see* magnitude, discrete

rat 45, 189, 473, 501, 525
ratio, as *discriminatum* 471–483, 490–491
rational certainty, *see* certainty, rational
rationalism 17–18, 115, 154
raven 284
real definition, *see* definition, real

reason 18, 72, 298, *434–435*, 534; *see also* norm, for inference; norm, for rationality; space of reasons

reduction in science 58, *63*, 81, 235, *298*

reduction, of the representational to the non-representational xiv, 9, *27–28*, *63*, 76, 79–81, *85*, 140, 207, 268, 291–315, *296–299*, 303, *308–309*, 316, 322, 339, 432, *548–549*; *see also* representation, deflationary conceptions of

reference xiii, *xvi–xviii*, 14–17, 24, *31–37*, 39, *42–45*, 53, 58–59, 62, 67–68, 71, 77–79, *83–86*, *89*, *93*, 104, 106, 124–128, 130–132, 135, 139, 141, 143–152, *143–149*, 154–210, *169*, 211–290, 292, 296, 310–311, 315, 322–325, 362–364, 380–396, 399–415, *401*, 432, 450–456, *450–454*, 486–490, 491, *496*, 514–515, 520, 523, 529–530, *539–544*, 545–546; *see also* application, singular; context-bound representational content; identifying reference; indication; individual concept; perceptual reference; reference, linguistic; representational content; representation failure; singular elements in perception; singular term; specification

reference, causal picture of 143, 147–150

reference, context-dependent 185, 231, 240, *363–264*, *381*, 454, 486–487, 496, 527, 539, 540–544, 550; *see also* application, singular; context-bound representational content; perceptual reference; reference, non-descriptive elements in

reference, dividing 235, 237, 479

reference identifying (in Strawson), *see* identifying reference

reference, linguistic xvi–xvii, *31–33*, *36*, 42–46, 77–79, 128, 138, *141–149*, 150–151, 212–213, 235–283

reference, non-descriptive elements in 145, 149

reference, plural 32, 228, 236, 250, 541; *see also* plurals

reference as, in the primary sense 34–35

reference as, in the secondary sense *35*, 537–544

reference failure, *see* representation failure

referent xvi, *14*, *33–34*, *43*, 77–79, 83, 121, 133, *141–147*, 149, 151, 172–173, 180, 212, 215, 324, *380–385*, *450–451*, 452, 455, 485, 541, 546; *see also* indicant; perceptual object

referential illusion (in perception) 42–46, 362–364, 382–294; *see also* hallucination; veridical hallucination

reflectance 48, 345, *352–354*, 357, 496; *see also* color; illumination; light; perceptual constancy, color constancy; perceptual constancy, lightness constancy

reflectance edge 352–354, 357

reflection xii, 4, 6, 11, 13, 16, 18, 22, 25, 35, *59*, 83, 91, 100, 107, 120, 123, 136, 137, 143, 147–148, 171, 178–179, 229, 272, 279, 284, 288, 310, 322, 326–328, 396, *431–432*, 435, 499, 508, 524, 534–537, 539, 548, 551; *see also* apriority; armchair argument or claim; empirical knowledge; explication

reflection, apriori 524, 535

reflection, empirical 6, *534*, 536

reflection, phenomenological 130–131, *133*, 135–136

reflection, transcendental 130–131, 154–156, 523

reflex (classic reflex arc) 267, 306, 333–334

reidentification 19, 151, 154, 163–166, *170–171*, 177–178, *179*, 187, 241–263, *258–259*, *262*, 282, 287, 460; *see also* criteria for reidentification; tracking

relation, as *representatum* xv, 7, 15, 19, 24, 32–34, 40, 44–45, 49, 51, 54–56, *54–55*,
    66–67, 73, *79*, 83–84, 86, 90–91, 93, 98, 101, 125, 152, 160–161, 172, 182, 190–191,
    199–200, 202–207, 209, 231, 239, 249, 272, 279–281, 286–*287*, 360–363, 380, 391,
    404, *411*, 420, 429, 437, *444*, 449–450, 454–457, *466*, *497*, 502, *506–530*, 539,
    546; *see also* geometrical structure; map-like representational structure; spatial
    representation; temporal representation
relevant representational alternative 469
representation 30–46, *passim*; *see also* attribution; indication; meta-representation;
    reference
representation, analog, *see* analog
representation, degree of 244, 294–295, 431
representation, deflationary conceptions of 27, 141, 207, 216, 227, 229, 253, 259,
    292–307, 316, 362, 396, 405, 421 430–431, 487–496, 503, 522, 529; *see also*
    deflations, Quinean; Deflationary Tradition; sensory registration
representation, empirical, *see* empirical representation
representation, explicit 406–407, *481*
representation, implicit 95–97, 107, 168–170, 179, *197–198*, 257, 283, 312, *403–407*,
    481–482, *488–490*; *see also* unconscious psychological state
representation, objective, *see* objective representation
representation, subjective, *see* subjective representation
"representation", the term xii, 4–5, *9–10*, 28, 30–31, 34, 39, *293–296*, 300, *304*, 319, 368,
    479, *489–490*, *493–496*, 502
representation as *34–42*, *45*; *see also* representational content; semantic determination;
    specification
representation as of *42–46*, *69*, *77*, 91–92, 167, 378, 395–396, 426, 455; *see also*
    representation failure; representational content; semantic determination; specification
representation as such 15, 25, *36–37*, *40*–41, 52, *78–80*, 84, *101*
representation failure (including reference failure) 37, *42–46*, 68, *73–75*, 81–82, 98, 302,
    309–310, 365, 379, 383, 390, 395, 411, 535; *see also* function, representational;
    hallucination; misperception; phlogiston; referential illusion; veridical hallucination
representational alternative 466–469
representational alternative principle 466, 469
representational content 14, 17, 24, *30*, *32*, *34–46*, 47–56, 64, *67–82*, 82–101, 104–105,
    117, 124, 127–130, 134, 138, *140–143*, 149, *151*–152, 166–167, 169–171, 184–187,
    190–210, 211–217, 225, 227, 255–256, 262, 266–272, 275–285, *292*, 296, *307*,
    310–312, 314–315, 317–322, 326–327, 339–341, 342–347, 350, 355–356, 358,
    360–366, *362*, 370–373, 377–378, *379–396*, *397*, 400, 403–413, *411*, 428, 432–433,
    435, 437–531, *506*, *513–514*, *537–544*, *545–546*, 550; *see also* attribution; indication;
    meaning, linguistic; marking; perceptual constancy; perceptual representational
    content; perspective; propositional representational content; reference; specification
representational content (or states), as perspectival 24, 27, 38, 45, 47, *51–52*
representational mind xi–xii, xviii, 12, 66, 432, 549
representational relation *31–32*, 35, 51, 62, 68–69, 72, 76, *80–81*, 125, *166*, 217, 261;
    see also indication; non-representational relation; reference
representationalism (as distinguished from Individual Representationalism) 14
representing a general condition, *see* general condition, representing a
representing a principle, *see* principle, representing a

representatum 14, *34*, *42–45*, 68, 71, 76–77, *79*, 82, *84*, 89, 92, 124, 146, 148, 211–212, 217, 220, 275, 321–322, 325–326, *344*, 349–350, 352, 370–371, 378, 389, 392, 397, 399, 403, 405, *408*, *411–413*, 453, 455, 480–483, 488, 530; *see also* perceptual object; referent; indicant

reptile xiii, 22, 303–304, 420, 548

resemblance (vs. identity) 259–263

resources, psychological 3, *7*, *13*, 16–17, *21*, 25–26, 28, *56–57*, 105, 112–113, 139–143, 146, 151, 163–166, 195–196, 247, 278, 343, 403–406, 429–430, 492; *see also* psychological kind

retinal flow 503, 508, 521

retinal image 274, 353–354, 357–358, 361, 363, 457, 509, 513, 517

retinal stimulation 44, 71, 89, 342–434, 357, 387, 419, 450, 503, 507

reversible motion 460

revisability 18, 534

revision, immunity to 534; *see also* revisability

robot 331, 369

route-based system 509–517, 525

Russell's Principle 176, *191–193*, 196, 199, 208, 255

saccade 333, 372, 445, 447, 453

salmon 398, 425–427, 430, 450, 498, 502

scepticism xiv, 21, 57, 72–73, 88, 120, 123, 128–129, 144, 150, 243, 536

sceptical solution 128–129

schreck reactions 332, 377, 526

science *xi–xviii*, 8, 10–*12*, 22, *26–27*, *44*, 58–59, 63, 65, *71*, 82, 107, 114, 117, 122–123, 131–133, 138–140, 142, 150, 156, 162, 206, 225, 232, 234, 236–242, 245, 260, 264, 269–270, 272, 284, 291, 293–294, 296–298, 307–308, 310–311, 331, 362, 364, *395*–396, 401, 430–431, 496, 538, 547–548; *see also* animal psychology; biological sciences or explanations; cognitive psychology; developmental psychology; empirical explanation in psychology; empirical science; ethology mathematics; natural science; neural explanation; perceptual psychology; physiological (including sensory) psychology; psychology; visual psychology; zoology

scorpion 399, 414, 420, 427

sea urchin 373

secondary quality 48, 86–87

second-order concept, *see* meta-representation

seeing 33, *62*, *88–89*, 117, 139, 195, 226, 244, 251, 304–305, *311*, 318, *363–364*, *370*, 383–*384*, 389–390, 394, 449

seeing, non-epistemic (in Dretske) 304–305

seems/is distinction, *see* appearance/reality distinction

self 154, 162–163, 278, 524; *see also* egocentric index or framework

self-consciousness 19, 155, 157–158, 161, 183, 208, 287–288, 431–432, 524, 547; *see also* egocentric index or framework; self-tracking

self-locomotion 330, 422, 460, 501

self-representation 160, 162–163, 182–183, 200–208, 270, 278, 288, 550; *see also* egocentric index or framework

self-tracking 19, 28, 160, 182–183, 202, 208–209, 287, 537

semantic determination *76–77*, 141, 143, 146–147, 149, 491; *see also* specification
sensation 7, 11–12, 14–19, 52, 112–113, 119, 122, 125–126, 129, 132, 139, 243, 276–277, *367–368*, *374*, 407, 428, 431; *see also* pain
sensation/perception distinction 11, *367–368*, Part III *passim*
sense data *14–16*, 19, 21, 23, 53, 103, 105, *111–112*, 116, *118–132*, *137–138*, 139–140, 144–145, 149, 167, 186, 234, 243, 245, 264, 284–285, 323–324, *367–368*, 379, *392*, *430*, *433–434*, 547–548
sense of externality 112–113, 228
sensory discrimination, *see* discrimination, sensory or perceptual
sensory fatigue 305–306
sensory imagination, *see* imagination
sensory modality, *see* modality, sensory or perceptual
sensory-motor memory, *see* memory, sensory-motor
sensory registration *xi*, 9, 12, *27–28*, 70, 76, *89–97*, 99, 190, 233, *245–246*, 285–286, 300, 302–303, 310–314, *315–318*, 325, 329, 335–338, 341–366, *341–347*, *364*, 367–436, *368*, *372–379*, *397–400*, *402*, *408–411*, *421–430*, 439, 443, 446, 457–458, 476, 478, 488, *494–495*, 496–531, *530*; *see also* encoding; formation law or law-like pattern; functioning correlation; image; non-representational processing; perceptual processing; proximal stimulation; sensation
sensory state, capacity or system—general xi, *xiii*, xviii, 3–4, 12, 15, 18, 70, *88–93*, 102, 104, 116–128, 130, 134, 136, 182, 186, 190, 236, 243–246, 257, 273–274, 284, 300–307, *300–304*, *315*, 320–321, *325*, 342–366, 367–436, *372*, *376–378*, *395–396*, *410*, 437–531, *532–536*, 547, *549*; *see also* anticipatory sensory representation; causal relations to environment, constitutive; discrimination, sensory or perceptual; experience; imagination; intermodal representation or system; perceptual memory; perceptual system; sensory registration
sensory state, capacity, or system—non-representational xi, xiii, 4, 70, 88–93, 186, 207, 211, 215, 223–229, 255, 259, 263–265, 269–270, 274, 285, *291–294*, 300–307, *300–304*, *315*–318, 320–321, *325*, *328–330*, 336, 340–341, 341–366, *341–347*, 367–436, *368*, *372–374*, *395–396*, *398*, *401–403*, *407–411*, *413*, *423–430*, 437–531, *493–497*, *521*, *529–531*, 547, 549–550; *see also* functioning correlation; information registration; non-representational processing; perceptual system
set 54, *472*, 476, 479–481; *see also* aggregate
shape constancy, *see* perceptual constancy, shape constancy
shape, generic, *see* generic shape
shape, specific, *see* specific shape
shelter 101, 280, 324, 460, 466
shrimp 336
singular elements in perception 83–84, *167*, 184–187, 258, 380–381, 383, 393, 496, 538, 540, 546; *see also* application, singular, in perception; context-bound representational content; perceptual attributive; perceptual reference
singular place-holder 486
singular term 36, 192, 207, 237–240, *239*
size constancy, *see* perceptual constancy, size constancy
sketch 516, 540
slant, *see* surface slant
slant constancy, *see* perceptual constancy, slant constancy
smell, *see* olfaction

snake 336, 372, 422, 426
sneezing 332–333, 377
social correction 128–129
solidity 243, 248, 444, 446, 465–470
solipsism 162–163
sortal concept (or sortal predicate) 19, 175, 178–181, 195, 235–238, 249–250, 253, 255, 435–436, 463
sortal kind or universal 19, 149, *178*, 180–181, 195, 235, 238, 250, 253, 443; *see also* sortal concept (or sortal predicate)
sound 83, 101, 177, 182, 225, 243, 304, 318, 320, 330, 332, 414–415, 420, 425, 427–428, 441, 471, 485, 493, 495, 498, 518; *see also* echolocation; hearing
sound frequency 304, 405
space, comprehensive spatial network 19, 28, 150, 154, 157, 160, 177, 182, 208, 278, 286, 518; *see also* allocentric index or framework; self-tracking
space of reasons 433–435
spatial representation 183, 199–208, 262, 286, 354, 355–361, 420, 426–429, 492–518, 525–526, 529–530; *see also* allocentric index or framework, spatial; egocentric index or framework, spatial; map-like representation; navigation; temporal representation; tracking
spatiotemporal continuity 444, 460, 465; *see also* criteria for reidentification; tracking
specific shape 253, 463–464, 469; *see also* generic shape; perceptual constancy, shape constancy
specification 3, 24–26, 30, *36–37*, 45, 49, 52–54, 56, 58–59, 62, 71, 74, *76–86*, 87–93, 100, 103, 156, 161–162, 169–170, 172, 178, 188, 190–191, 203, 209, 212, 217, 234, 248, 256, 270–271, 277, 282–283, 295, 311, 323, 342, *344*, 383, 396, *398–411*, 421, 425–426, 443, *450*, 456, 466, 469, 481, 487–488, 502, 506–507, 512–514, 516, 529–530, 536, 547–549; *see also* semantic determination
spider xiii, 102, 188, 327, 335–336, 340, 375–376, 414, 419, 430, 450, 452, 460, 462, 500, 514–517
standard 19, 86, 309, *311–313*, 326, *338–341*, *435–436*, 535, 550
starling 336
stashing 262
steel balls 193
stereopsis 496
stereotype 78–79
stimulus meaning *216*, 218–232
stress reactions, *see schreck* reactions
stuffs, *see* masses
subindividual, *see* subsystem of an individual
subitizing 453, *485–486*
subject matter *11*, 13, 15–16, 20, 23–24, *27*, *31–32*, *34*–35, 38, *43–44*, *46–54*, 57–62, *67–72*, *86*, 105–106, 125, 138, 150, *191*, 208, 251, *275*, 277–278, 285, *292*, 313, 372, *379*, *397*, *402–403*, 404, 408, *411*, 495, 506–507, *523–524*, 528, *531*, 535, 539; *see also* anti-individualism; attribute; causal relations to environment, constitutive; explanation in terms of veridicality; indicant; instances, as *representata*; kind; nature; objective representation; objective subject matter; objectivity, as veridicality; particular; perceptual object; property; referent; relation, as *representatum*
subjective representation xi, 26, 105, 112, 120, 152, 422, 547; *see also* objectivity, conceptions of; pain; priority of objective representation

subjectivism 122
subjectivity 20, 50, 286; *see also* sense data; subjective representation
substance, concept of 154, 523
subsystem of an individual 24, 93, *104*, 108, *189–190*, 197, 199, 208, 255–257, 276,
    282, 284–285, 320, 324, 326, 328, 331–334, 339, *368–369*, *372–376*, 401–403,
    412, 432, 488, 515, 517, *547–548*; *see also* function, individual (or whole animal);
    individual-subsystem distinction; modularity; perceptual system; processing,
    non-perceptual; processing, perceptual; sensory state, capacity, or system; whole
    organism coordination
subtraction 475, 477, 482–483, 487, 489
surface slant *355–357*, 366, *383–384*, 411, 440, 445; *see also* perceptual constancy;
    slant constancy; surface texture
surface texture 3, 24, 44–45, 54, 84, 94, 101, 253, 349, *355–359*, 407, 411, *414*, 417, 421,
    457, 464, 546; *see also* perceptual constancy; slant constancy
surfaces, perception of 124–125, 226, 281, 345, 352–354, 357, 359–362, 363, 411–412,
    418, 439–450, *448–449*, 454, 457
syntactical states (in perception) 93, *95–97*, 99; *see also* language of thought

tacit knowledge 198, 406
tactile perception, *see* touch, perceptual
tapeworm 422
taste 243, 415–416, 421; *see also* olfaction
taxes 328–331, 423; *see also* kinesis; phototaxis
teleology *75*, 81–83, 143, 293, 297, *299*, *309–310*, 320, 339, 341, 535
temporal index 287, 527; *see also* allocentric index or framework; egocentric index or
    framework; index, (anchor, origin) for frameworks
temporal intervals, sensitivity to 165, 287, 518, *519–525*, *527*
temporal order, sensitivity to 287, 518, 520–524, 526–528
temporal phases, sensitivity to 519–520, 522, 525–526
temporal representation 112, 177, 187, 206, 281, 287, 372, 476, 497, *518–529*, 536, 551;
    see also allocentric index or framework, temporal; egocentric index or framework,
    temporal; temporal index
temporal stages (slices), of environmental entities 212–213, 215, 324; *see also*
    pre-individuative (or proto-objective) stage
texture, *see* surface texture
texture constancy, *see* perceptual constancy, texture constancy
theory of descriptions, Russell's 43, 116, 119, 131
thought, as propositional 538; *see also* intermodal representation or system; propositional
    attitude; propositional representational content
thrush 335, 337
tick xiii, 328, 335–336, 372, 374
topological perceptual organization 381, 540
topological property (or magnitude) 253–254, 381, 470
touch xviii, 40, 98, 101, 172, 179, 243, 247–248, 267, *275*, 343–344, 377–378, *399–400*,
    414, 417–418, *420–421*, 427–428, *439–444*, 450, 456–458, *465–469*; *see also*
    proprioception
touch, perception from a distance 399, 414, 467

tracking (representational and non-representational) 19, 28, 166, *169–171*, 198–202, *198–199*, 208, *235*, 238, 241, 243–244, *246–247*, 250, *252–254*, *257–264*, 274, *286–287*, 323, 361, *388*, 390–391, *409–412*, *444–456*, *459–470*, 476, 478, 480, 483–491, 493, 496–499, 518–519, 521, 524–525, 528, 536, 541, 543, 546; *see also* criteria for reidentification; functioning correlation; information registration; multiple object tracking; occlusion; perceptual constancy; self-tracking
tracking non-moving bodies (in view or out of view) 166, 262–263, *444–445*, *460*
transformation, computational, *see* computational transformation (or operation or process)
transformation, psychological, *see* non-representational processing; perceptual processing; psychological processing
translation 213–216, 218, 220, 224, 228, 232–233
transtemporal utilizations of perception, *see* tracking
triangulation 204–205, 270–275, 319, 370, 413–414, 420; *see also* convergence; disparity, binocular; objectification, perceptual
trope, *see* instance (instantiation of attributes)
tropism 328
truth 4, 19, 38–39, *49*, 51, 62, 226, 228–232, 276, 278, 281–282, 286, *301*, *309*, *313–314*, *339*, 436; *see also* accuracy; objectivity, as veridicality
truth, concept of 266–267, 270, 276, 278–283, 303
truth condition 38, 166, 186, *191*–192, 228–232, 266, 278–282, 301
truth of *71*, 172–173, 237, 239
two-dimensionalism 79
type-individuation, *see* individuation, marking

unconscious psychological state 23–24, 92–95, 97, 188–189, 197, 263, 313, 374–375, 396, 401, 404, 406, 412, 431, 470, 481; *see also* consciousness, phenomenal; modularity; perception, as the individual's; unconscious perception
underdetermination problem (and underdetermination) *90–92*, *344–345*, 351, 353, 358, 364, 384, 392, 397
uninstantiated property, *see* property, noninstantiated
universal 118, 163, 165–170, 173, 175, 178, 181, 186, 194, 213, 215
use-based theories of meaning 432

V1 497
Venus Fly Trap 331
vergence angle 348, 350
veridical hallucination 381–383
veridicality *39* and *passim*; *see also* accuracy, truth
veridicality condition 9–10, 12, *27–28*, *38–39*, 48, 62, *74–75*, *80*, 83, *84–86*, *88–89*, 207, 233, 257, *292*, *303*, 307–310, *316–318*, 325, *342*, 347, 354, 362–366, 368, *379–416*, *379–384*, 402, *410–411*, 421–435, 437–531, *478–480*, *493–495*, *502–505*, *508*, *522*, *529–530*, 535, *539*, 549; *see also* accuracy; application, singular; attribution; concept; context-bound representational content; explanation in terms of veridicality; perception, as representation; perceptual attributive; perceptual representational content; predicate; propositional representational content; representational content; singular elements in perception, truth condition

veridicality of 51; *see also* true of

verification procedure, *see* confirmation procedure

Verificationism 22, *140*, 142, 150, 178, 210; *see also* Logical Positivism

version angle 348, 350

vestibular system xi, 413–414, 504; *see also* perceptual constancy, vertical constancy

vertical constancy, *see* perceptual constancy, vertical constancy

vision xii, xviii, 27, *36*, *40–42*, 45, 70–71, 73, 83–84, *87–104*, 117, 122–124, 142, 167,
    188–190, 204, 212, 224, 227, 229, 231–232, 235, 243–254, 269–272, 274, 280, 286,
    298, 304–305, *309–310*, 318–319, 322–324, 335–336, 342–366, *342–347*, *369–370*,
    375, 381–384, 390, *399*, 401, 409–411, 413–414, *417–420*, 422, 426–429, *438–450*,
    451–464, 465–470, 486, 488, 493, 496–498, *500*–503, 505–508, 515–518, 533, *540*,
    546; *see also* hearing; olfaction; proprioception; seeing; taste; touch

vision, early 98, 263, 285–286, 369, 375, 447, 458

vision, high-level 343

visual differentiation 305

visual psychology xiii–xiv, xvii–xviii, 8, 41, *87–104*, 189, 232, 272, 298, *307–311*,
    317–319, 342–366, *342–347*, *370*, 383–384, 411, *441–450*, *490*; *see also* Brunswik's
    methodology; explanation in terms of veridicality; formation principles; natural scene
    statistics

visual psychology, primary problem *89–92*, 99–100, *342–344*; *see also* underdetermination
    problem

visual system xii, 41, *87–104*, 167, 189, 212, 249, 253, 259, 263, 274–275, 319, 323–324,
    342–366, *369–377*, *382–384*, 401, 409–411, 413–414, *418–420*, 422, 426, *438–450*,
    453–458, 461–464, 467–470, 488, 493, 496–498, *500–503*, 508, 515–518, 546;
    see also formation laws or law-like patterns; perceptual processing; perceptual
    constancy; perceptual representational content

warrant, *see* epistemic warrant

water buffalo 331

Weber's Law 473, 477

whale 420, 427

whole organism, attributability 103, 189–190, 272–274, 292, 320–321, 326, 328,
    330–333, 337, 370–374; *see also* function, individual (or whole animal); perception,
    as the individual's

whole organism, coordination 328, *330–335*, 370–374; *see also* peripheral response
    (reflex or system)

yeast 422

zoology xiii, 6, 213, 272, 319–323, 325–327; *see also* animal psychology; ethology